W9-AAQ-523

Praise for

THE BOOK OF MISO

"A CONTEMPORARY CLASSIC."
East West Journal

"Crammed full of historical information, traditional and Western recipes, explicit instructions for homemade miso in Japanese life."
Library Journal

"Numerous excellent illustrations . . . Useful as a guide for food technologists, home economists, dieticians, and others interested in fermented soybean products."
Food Technology

"WONDERFULLY ENTERTAINING AND COMPREHENSIVE."
Mother Earth News

"THE DEFINITIVE SOURCE ON THE SUBJECT."
Alternatives

Also by William Shurtleff & Akiko Aoyagi
available now from Ballantine Books:

THE BOOK OF TOFU

THE BOOK OF
MISO

Revised and Updated

Savory, High-Protein Seasoning

William Shurtleff & Akiko Aoyagi

Illustrated by Akiko Aoyagi

BALLANTINE BOOKS • NEW YORK

Copyright © 1976 by William Shurtleff and Akiko Aoyagi

All rights reserved under International and Pan-American Copyright Conventions. Published in the United States by Ballantine Books, a division of Random House, Inc., New York, and simultaneously in Canada by Random House of Canada, Limited, Toronto, Canada.

Library of Congress Catalog Card Number: 76-19599

ISBN 0-345-29107-7

This edition published by arrangement with
Autumn Press, Inc.

All information on the history of miso and other soyfoods not found in the original Autumn Press edition of *The Book of Miso* is excerpted with permission from the forthcoming *Soyfoods History* by Shurtleff & Aoyagi.

Manufactured in the United States of America

First Ballantine Books Edition: April 1981

Cover illustration by Hal Just

For all the world's children
whose lives are filled with hunger . . .
and can't understand why.

And for all beings
who are dedicated to doing something about it.

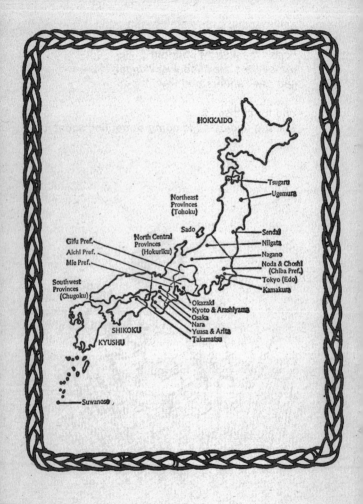

HOKKAIDO

Tsugaru
Ugemura

Northeast
Provinces
(Tohoku)

Sado

Sendai
Niigata
Nagano
Noda & Choshi
(Chiba Pref.)
Tokyo (Edo)
Kamakura

Gifu Pref.

North Central
Provinces
(Hokuriku)

Aichi Pref.

Mie Pref.

Southwest
Provinces
(Chugoku)

Okazaki
Kyoto & Arashiyama
Osaka
Nara
Yuasa & Arita
Takamatsu

SHIKOKU

KYUSHU

Suwanose

Contents

What Is Miso? ix

Preface xiii

Acknowledgments xix

PART I

Miso: Savory, High-Protein Seasoning

1. Soybeans, Protein, and the World Food Crisis 3
2. Miso as a Food 23
3. The Miracle of Fermentation 43
4. The Varieties of Miso 47

PART II

Cooking With Miso

5. Getting Started 89
   Favorite Miso Recipes 120
6. Recipes from East and West 123
   Miso Toppings, 124; Miso in Dips & Hors D'oeuvres, 163; Miso in Spreads & Sandwiches, 177; Miso Dressings with Salads, 186; Miso in Soups & Stews, 226; Miso in Sauces, 270; Miso with Grains, Beans & Tofu, 287; Miso in Baked Dishes, 326; Miso Sautéed & Simmered with Vegetables, 335; Miso in Grilled Dishes, 354; Miso in Deep-fried Dishes, 361; Miso & Eggs, 372; Miso in Desserts, 377; Miso Pickles 385; Koji Cookery, 400

PART III
The Preparation of Miso

7. Making Miso at Home and in Communities   407

8. Japanese Farmhouse Miso   457

9. Traditional and Modern Miso Production   481

Appendix A: A History of Chiang, Soy Nuggets, Miso, Tamari, and Shoyu   487

Appendix B: Other East Asian Misos: Chiang, Jang, Taucho, and Tausi   531

Appendix C: The Microbiology and Chemistry of Miso Fermentation   548

Appendix D: People and Institutions Connected with Miso   565

Appendix E: Miso Additives   580

Appendix F: Miso with Seafoods, Chicken, and Meat   582

Appendix G: Measures, Weights, and Equivalents   586

Appendix H: So You Want to Study Miso in Japan?   588

Bibliography   591

Glossary   599

Index   605

What Is Miso?

Miso (pronounced MEE-so, and also known as "fermented soybean paste") is a savory, high-protein seasoning made from soybeans, grain (usually rice or barley), salt, water, and *Aspergillus oryzae* culture. Miso has no equivalent in the West—which may be one reason it has caught on here so quickly. Its range of flavors and colors, textures and aromas is as varied as that of the world's fine cheeses and wines. Miso's texture resembles that of a soft peanut butter. Its many warm colors range from deep chocolate browns, reddish browns, and russets, through ambers, clarets, and

cinnamon reds, on up to creamy beiges and sunlight yellows for some sweeter, more modern varieties. To the sensitive palate, no two of the many miso varieties taste the same. The darker, more traditional types have flavors and aromas that are deep, rich, and hearty, almost meaty at times, making them ideal for the preparation of savory meatless dishes; the lighter, more modern misos are subtly sweet and delicately refreshing. The wonderfully fragrant aroma of traditional miso has been compared with that of freshly ground coffee.

Miso is one of East Asia's most important soyfoods. In Japan, over 70 percent of the population starts each day with a health-giving, nutritious, and warming cup of miso soup instead of coffee. Its alkalizing effect wakes up the body and mind, providing it with a steady supply of high-quality energy that lasts all morning. Miso can be used as an all-purpose seasoning in many of the same ways as salt, yet because it contains only 5.5 to 13 percent sodium chloride (versus 99% in table salt) it can serve as the key seasoning in moderate- or low-salt diets that are still rich in flavor. But miso is much more than just a seasoning. Highly nutritious, it is such a concentrated source of protein, vitamin B-12, and other essential nutrients, that the Japanese consider it to be a basic staple and full-fledged "food," although typically only several tablespoons are used per person each day. Moreover, like yogurt, miso is a living, cultured food containing lactic acid–forming bacteria (such as *Pediococcus halophilus* and *Lactobacillus delbruekii*) plus other health-giving microorganisms and digestion-aiding enzymes. Traditional misos can be stored for months without refrigeration. And in 1980, a month's supply of natural miso for a person in North America using it twice daily (1½ tablespoons a day) cost as little as $2.55.

Miso is prized by cooks for its almost unlimited versatility. It can be used like bouillon or a rich meat stock in soups, meatless gravies, or stews; like soy sauce or *shoyu,* Worcestershire sauce, or ketchup in sauces, dips, and dressings; as an unmatched thickener in barbecue sauces; like cheese in casseroles and spreads; like chutney or relish as a topping for grains, fresh vegetable slices, or open-faced sandwiches; as a gravy base with sautéed or steamed foods; or even like vinegar as a pickling medium. Used in many of these ways for centuries in Japanese kitchens, it has set its distinctive mark of fine flavor on the entire panorama of Japanese cuisine and added zest and variety to a diet that has long consisted primarily of grains, land-and-sea vegetables, and tofu.

There are six main types of miso among which are found more than 28 distinctly different varieties. The three basic types are rice, barley and soybean miso, the first two made from soybeans, salt and the respective grain, the last made from soy beans and salt alone. Two "special" types, finger-lickin' and sweet-simmered miso, contain bits of chopped vegetables, nuts and/or seasonings and are delectably sweet and chunky. Finally, there are a number of "modern" misos developed since 1945, including dehydrated and low-salt/high-protein varieties.

The progenitor of present-day miso originated in China some 2,500 years ago. Called *chiang* (pronounced jang), it was brought to Japan during the 7th century by Buddhist priests. During the following centuries, Japanese craftsmen transformed *chiang* into miso and shoyu (all-purpose Japanese soy sauce), two unique and distinctive foods which are now quite different from their Chinese counterparts. Indeed the word "miso" was first coined in Japan and its many varieties were created and developed there. *Chiang* or Chinese-style miso continues to be widely used throughout its mother country and at least five varieties are now available in the West, as are a number of types of *jang* or Korean-style miso.

First introduced to America on a small scale in the early 1960s, miso is now becoming better known and appreciated. High-quality varieties are available throughout the United States at reasonable prices in most natural- and health-food stores, co-op markets, Japanese and Chinese grocery stores, and a growing number of supermarkets. Some stores carry as many as 15 different varieties sold in both bulk and pre-packaged 1- to 2-pound quantities. Several types of American-made miso are now being marketed, and many people—especially those in communities—have taken to preparing their own at home.

We feel that miso has come to the West to stay, and that in the near future it will come to be considered an essential element in America's evolving cuisine, a basic seasoning to be found in kitchens throughout the country. It can—and should—play an increasingly important role in the cookery and nutrition of people around the world.

Preface

I RECEIVED MY first introduction to fine miso while working as a cook at California's Tassajara Zen Mountain Center. It was there that I first participated in the preparation of miso—we made a 50-gallon vatful once each year—and learned its many uses as a seasoning. But it was only while living in Japan and working together with Akiko on *The Book of Tofu* that we both really discovered the enormous wealth and variety contained in the world of miso and began to recognize the great value this savory soyfood has to offer the world. This learning experience was an adventure, and not the least of its many pleasures was shopping for the different varieties of miso needed to prepare our recipes.

Throughout Japan, thousands of small shops specialize in the sale of miso (and miso pickles), and a sampling of forty to fifty varieties will generally be available. Each is displayed in a 5-gallon cedar keg ringed with broad hoops of braided bamboo and marked in bold black characters with the miso's name, price, and province of origin. The hues and shades create a festival of autumn-maple colors, and the total atmosphere has all the warmth and rustic beauty of a Florentine cheese shop or a small wine cellar in the French countryside.

We enjoyed learning the names of Japan's traditional favorites and their distinguished makers, and slowly developed the ability to judge quality and character. Using miso as a seasoning in our daily cookery, we found it made many of our Western-style dishes even more delicious. Its versatility seemed almost unlimited and its deep, rich flavors served to enrich and add variety to our meatless diet. In fine restaurants, we enjoyed a wide variety of different dishes featuring miso and found that it had long been important in the two main schools of Japanese haute cuisine: Zen Temple Cookery and Tea Ceremony Cuisine. I soon came to understand that, for many Japanese, miso is the very epitome of the satisfying flavors and aromas of home cooking; the mere mention of mother's or grandma's miso soup can evoke all the warm feelings that come to most Westerners at the thought of a loaf of home-baked bread, piping hot from the oven.

As our interest deepened, we began to visit, learn from, and eventually become friends with a number of

Miso in crocks

the more than 2,400 master craftsmen who make Japan's miso. Working in shops which are usually located adjacent to their homes, many of these men honored the traditional spirit of fine craftsmanship in a way that transformed daily work into an art and spiritual practice. We were drawn to their handsomely crafted tools, their high-roofed shops with massive arching rafters, and their huge cedar vats—often more than 150 years old—that stand taller than a man. In the morning air, billows of steam would rise from the great iron caldron and large cedar steamer in which half a ton of soybeans and rice were being cooked. When freshly harvested *koji* (rice or barley covered with a cottony mycelium of fragrant white mold) was removed from its granite-hewn incubation room, it would fill the entire shop with an incomparable lingering aroma, rich and subtly sweet, like that of freshly roasted chestnuts or coffee.

I was eventually given the opportunity to do an informal apprenticeship with Mr. Kiyoshi Tsujita, an exemplary miso master living quite near our home. A strong traditionalist and purist at heart, he made the most delicious miso—and the *only* brown-rice miso—that we had ever tasted. Studying with him and watching him at work, I began to appreciate the mysteries of the fermentation process, the complexities of its chemistry and microbiology, and the harmony of its interaction with the great movements of the four seasons. He stressed that the essence of his art could not be transmitted in words, for it was linked to one's local climate and the soil in which soybeans, rice, and barley grow; embodied in the strains of microorganisms which for generations had permeated the air, wood, and rock walls of a shop; half hidden in the muscles and bones, feeling and intuition of each craftsman. It was a total understanding, rooted in a particular place and in a man who becomes imbued with it like one who, unbeknownst to himself, becomes wet by walking through a mist. As in the ancient wine châteaux throughout Europe, it reflected a tradition and culture that took centuries to mature.

Nevertheless, he wanted to help both Akiko and me to understand his craft and convey its fundamentals to people in the West. He therefore encouraged us to begin making our own miso and helped us get started. Under his tutelage, we prepared many small batches and, for more than a year, patiently endured the suspense of waiting, wondering how they would turn out. When we seemed pleased with the results, he teased us with the Japanese proverb saying that, naturally, every person likes his own homemade miso best!

Over a period of some four years, Akiko and I had

the opportunity to visit miso shops throughout Japan
and study the preparation of most of the main traditional varieties. Though ordinarily quite protective of
their traditional secrets, the shops' masters were pleased
to see our sincere interest in their work and, without
exception, spared no time or effort in showing us
everything we wanted to see, answering all our questions, and in some cases, later carrying on a detailed
correspondence.

Early in the spring of 1973, we made our first contact with country-style miso, a tradition started hundreds of years ago by Buddhist priests in their temples
and rural peasants in their farmhouses, and which still
accounts for an estimated 17 percent of all Japanese
miso production. At the Banyan Ashram, a community
of young people living a simple life of meditation and
farming on tiny Suwanose Island, we learned how to
make barley koji (mold barley) in the ancient way by
"catching" natural wild mold spores floating in the air.
Invited one sunny April morning to join in the work,
we used a large wooden mortar and heavy pestles to
mash koji and cooked soybeans together. In an atmosphere of down-home merriment, everyone lent rhythm
to the pounding by clapping, stomping, and chanting.
The women packed the mashed ingredients into tall
earthenware crocks, which were then ceremoniously
sealed. We were urged to return for the grand opening
when the fermentation had finished, but warned not
to be late, since even fifty gallons of homemade barley
miso wouldn't last long in a large community of hungry, hard-working men and women.

As our book began to take form, we traveled to
Taiwan and Korea to visit local miso makers at their
work, study new varieties of Chinese- and Korean-style
miso in sprawling outdoor marketplaces, and sample
miso cuisine at restaurants representing the full gamut
of provincial cooking styles.

In the fall of 1974, we traveled deep into the mountains of the northeast provinces to visit one of Japan's
"long-life" villages, where many people live past the
age of ninety and most families still prepare their own
miso using an ancient method. Upon arrival we were

invited to join our host family in a light meal featuring farmhouse-style *Dengaku;* fresh homemade tofu was pierced with bamboo skewers, coated on both sides with homemade miso, and grilled around a bed of live coals in the open-hearth fireplace. We were deeply touched to discover that both the miso and tofu had been made entirely from soybeans grown in the village fields, and the mere fragrance of that sizzling *Dengaku* made our 600-mile trip well worthwhile. As we studied the miso-making process, we could not help but notice how vigorous and healthy the villagers seemed, and how this simple life close to nature had made each person the master of many useful arts. Here we first came to realize how miso could make a major contribution to the life of self-sufficiency.

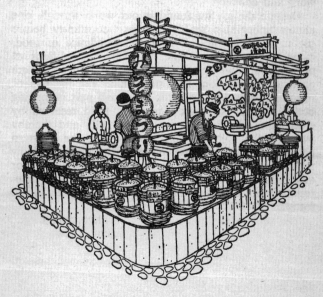

While Akiko worked with miso in day-to-day cookery, I spent considerable time studying Western and Japanese literature on miso fermentation and visiting Japan's most modern research institutes and factories. I discovered that during the past few decades a revolution has taken place in miso manufacturing as the use of large-scale, automatic machinery, quick fermentation in heated rooms, and high-speed polyethylene packaging have made it possible to mass-produce miso at low cost and distribute it throughout the nation and even the world. The uniqueness and character of traditional provincial varieties are gradually being lost and the new factories have become a threat to the very existence of Japan's many small shops and their high-quality natural products.

Continuing our daily experimentation with miso cookery, we eventually prepared more than 600 recipes, from which we chose our favorites for use in this book. In the mornings and evenings we practiced meditation; our days were given over to writing and research, artwork and cookery.

Despite the joy we found in our work, though, one almost unbearable reality has been constantly before us: in a world blessed with an abundance of food, indeed more than enough for everyone, millions of people are now faced with perpetual hunger, severe protein malnutrition, and starvation. Yet the use of miso allows each of us to do our small part in making better use of the earth's precious food reserves by enjoying soy and grain proteins directly and thereby avoiding the colossal waste inherent in the Western pattern of feeding these proteins to livestock. How fortunate, we feel, that miso offers us its fine flavor and remarkable nutritional value together with a time-tested promise to help make the world a better home for all.

Tokyo, Japan
June 1976

Acknowledgments

ALL BEINGS, past and present, have shared in the creation of this book, yet to some we wish to express special thanks: Mr. Kiyoshi Tsujita, mentor and friend, who taught us the art of traditional miso making and supplied us with the finest brown-rice miso we have ever tasted; Mr. Wataru Kawamura, Japan's "miso sensei," who introduced us to the romance of miso history and its place in the heart of the people; Messrs. Hideo Ebine, Masahiro Nakano, Kazuo Shibasaki, Clifford W. Hesseltine, and Ms. Hwa L. Wang, miso scholars from East and West, who have pioneered the way in scientific exploration of the mysteries of miso fermentation; Messrs. Kiyoshi Kaneko and Choichi Kato, directors of Japan's two Hatcho miso companies; Messrs. Shigeru Honda and Keinosuke Ishino, owners of Kyoto's two famous sweet white miso shops; Messrs. Kojiro Ikeda and Yanosuke Kanemitsu, makers of fine barley miso; Messrs. Soichi Nishida, Nobushi Takeyama, and William Higa, makers respectively of red, sweet red, and mellow white miso; Messrs. Shigeo Sasaki, Kenichiro Sasaki, and Hiroshi Haga, of the Sendai Miso Co.; Mr. Yojuro Watanabe, production manager at Japan's largest miso factory; Messrs. Yasu Niimi and Akira Chiba, makers of fine koji starter; Messrs. Denei Fujimori and Zenichi Matsushita of the Japanese National Miso Association; Mr. Kinichiro Shibata, producer of commercial miso pickles; Mmes. Saiyo Miura and Kazuko Shinya, who taught us how to make farmhouse *tama-miso* in remote Ugemura village; the members of Banyan Ashram, who taught us the preparation of sweet-potato miso using wild mold spores; Mr. Akiyoshi Kazama who kept us well informed on the world of international miso trade; Mr. Masahiro Miyashita of Kikkoman International, who provided us with extensive information about shoyu; Bob Gerner and Gordon Bennett who gave us support and advice; Messrs. Junsei Yamazaki, Noboru Muramoto, Wally Gorell, Thom Leonard, and Blake Rankin, who have helped to get the word out; and makers of *chiang* and *jang* throughout Taiwan and Korea who gave generously of their time and experience.

Finally, we would like to give particular thanks to: Herman and Cornellia Aihara, Michio and Aveline Kushi, and Pierre Gaevert, who were instrumental in preparing the way; Frances Moore Lappé, Lester R. Brown, E. F. Schumacher, and Stephen Gaskin, whose teachings have inspired our work; Ty Smith and Paul Discoe, whose initial encouragement gave birth to this book; Bobbie and Lawton, Fumio and Kinjiro, for their love and generosity; Beverly, for her inspired design; and Nahum Stiskin, our friend and publisher, whose vision and ceaseless striving for excellence have won our deepest admiration.

PART I

Miso:
Savory, High-Protein Seasoning

1

Soybeans, Protein and the World Food Crisis

DURING THE past decade, the population/food crisis has suddenly emerged as the most serious problem facing mankind. We are now experiencing the greatest famine in history and the situation is clearly getting worse. Experts estimate that starvation and malnutrition-caused diseases are now taking the lives of between 15 and 20 million people each year (45,000 to 60,000 *daily*), and more than half of the victims are children under five. According to the United Nations Food and Agricultural Organization (FAO), an additional 400 to 500 million children (more than twice the population of the United States) living in the 60 poorest countries suffer from such severe chronic malnutrition that their growth and mental capacity are permanently retarded. And more than one-quarter of the earth's present four billion inhabitants confront inescapable hunger during some part of each year. At this turning point in history, we have, for the first time, rounded the bend on three dangerous exponential curves—population, resource-andenergy consumption, and pollution—and are heading almost vertically upward at a dizzying pace. These cold statistics add up to immense human suffering, which is quickly becoming the dominant reality of daily life for poor people throughout the world.

In the least developed nations, where population generally doubles every 20 to 25 years and most of the good land is already intensively cultivated, food supplies cannot possibly keep up with demand. As the gap between the poor and rich nations widens, and the latter use increasingly large quantities of already scarce corn, soy, wheat, and oats to fatten their livestock, the price of these basic foods is pushed out of reach of the destitute and hungry. What once were local short-term famines now threaten to engulf entire nations, leading to social and political chaos. Already millions find themselves trapped in unimaginable squalor. And poverty, illiteracy, and malnutrition, transferred from generation to generation in an accelerating downward spiral, continually degrades the quality of individual lives and must soon have grave consequences for all people everywhere.

We in the affluent West have been fortunate. We have forgotten how it *feels* to be always hungry, for hunger has remained a news item from faraway countries. Most of us have been spared—perhaps unfortunately—the terrible and unforgettable experience of witnessing firsthand a death by starvation. And slowly many of us have allowed ourselves to become numbed —even apathetic—to the painful reality of what is happening all around us in the world. Often quite unconsciously, many have already given up the situation as hopeless, and this attitude has emerged as one of the primary forces allowing the problem to grow worse. Some feel there is not enough room in the lifeboat to save the drowning, not realizing that the earth presently produces more than enough food for everyone. Others believe it is already too late and that there is nothing they could do to make a difference, forgetting that the way they eat—which only they can change—may be one of the basic causes of worldwide food shortages. Still others argue pessimistically that to help in any way would only stimulate snowballing population growth which would ultimately make the problem even worse and simply delay the day of reckoning; they fail to understand that the easiest—if not the only—way to lower birth rates is to ensure adequate food supplies and improve living standards.

Discarding false or unexamined myths and assumptions can lead from a sense of hopelessness and helplessness to a genuine, realistic commitment to change. The present food/population crisis, if neglected, will not somehow work itself out or gradually go away. It will only get worse and worse. In our small and increasingly interdependent global village, the burden of suffering will eventually be visited upon everyone. Will we continue to live as a privileged and wealthy minority, consuming vastly more than our share of precious food (and energy) resources, until we are a tiny island in a sea of hunger, compelling the deprived, in desperation, to force us to stop? Or will we start now to really care and, thus, to work for change? These are life-and-death matters on which the balance of this century will turn.

Soybeans: Protein Source of the Future

Experts studying the world food crisis are quick to emphasize that the key nutrient in shortest supply is protein. World hunger is primarily protein hunger and most starvation—especially among children—is caused not by a lack of calories but of this relatively costly and scarce nutritional component. Thus it is often said that the food crisis is more specifically a protein crisis, and that if the protein gap could be filled, the most difficult part of the problem would be solved. While these experts agree that the situation admits of no easy solution, they also are virtually unanimous in their opinion that soybeans will be a key protein source for the future. Why? Because soybeans can produce more usable protein per acre of land than any other known crop—33 percent more on the average (360 percent more under ideal conditions) than second-place rice and 20 *times* as much as if the land were used to raise beef cattle or grow their fodder. This fact becomes increasingly important as farmland grows more and more scarce.

Soybeans have served as the protein backbone of the East Asian diet for over 2,000 years and today—used in the form of tofu, miso, shoyu, soymilk, tempeh, fresh green soybeans, and a host of other delicious foods—they are an integral part of the diet of more than one billion people. Containing 34 to 36 percent high-quality protein—more than any other plant or animal food—plus all of the eight essential amino acids, they are rightfully known throughout the

Orient as "the meat of the fields." From the body's point of view, the amount of usable protein contained in ½ cup dry soybeans (1 cup cooked) is no different from that contained in 5 ounces of steak. And low-cost, low-calorie soybean foods contain no cholesterol and almost none of the saturated fats so abundant in most animal-derived products.

Americans are often surprised to learn that their country is the world's largest soybean producer, accounting for about 67 percent of the planet's total yearly output. In 1975, over 600,000 U.S. soybean farmers planted a total of 54 million acres and sold their crop for $7.5 billion. Soybeans are one of our largest and most important farm crops, second only to corn (and ahead of wheat) in total dollar value, and third in total acreage. Exporting about half of the domestic crop, America is the largest international supplier, providing 70 percent of the total trade. These beans are our biggest farm export, worth over $5 *billion* in 1975.

Institutionalized Protein Waste

But what happens to all these soybeans and the 18 *million* tons of protein they contain? Virtually all of the non-exported crop is sent to huge factories where the soy oil—which contains no protein—is extracted with hexane solvent. Then, approximately 95 percent of the protein-rich meal left over is fed directly to livestock. The soybeans exported to Russia, Europe, Poland, Iran, and other countries now building up their livestock herds follow the same route. Only in East Asia are large quantities of soybeans transformed into high-protein foods. If all of this U.S. soy protein were used directly, it could fulfill about 25 percent of the yearly protein requirements of every person on the planet.

The system responsible for this immense waste is the feedlot, which was designed after World War II in an era of huge farm surpluses as a way of transforming excess grains and soy into more "profitable" meat. Although we now live in an era of famine with reserves at a precariously low level, an astonishing 50 percent of all U.S. farmland is still used to grow crops that end up being fed to animals. In addition to soybeans, we feed livestock a full 78 percent of our cereal grains including about 90 percent of our corn, oats, and barley, and 24 percent of our wheat, all of which could, of course, serve as foods for human beings. As a result, the average American now consumes the equivalent of 2,000 pounds of grain and soybeans annually, 200 pounds of which is used directly, while the remaining 90 percent is consumed in the form of meat, poultry, dairy products, and eggs. But the average person in developing countries consumes only 400 pounds per year, virtually all of which is used directly in meatless diets. Thus, the birth of one typical American baby has *five* times the adverse effect on precious world food reserves (not to mention water, fertilizer, energy, and land resources) as the birth of a child in Asia, Africa, or Latin America.

And as other countries become affluent, they quickly follow the American pattern. Resource geographer Georg Borgstrom estimates that the developed world, with 28 percent of the world's population, consumes some two-thirds of world grain production and three-fourths of the world's fish catch (much of which is purchased from protein-starved Latin America and used to feed cats and dogs as well as livestock). In fact, the rich use practically as much cereal grains to feed animals as the poorer half of mankind eats directly as food. The 6 percent of the world's population who live in the United States eat 30 percent of the world's meat and drink half its milk. Our beef consumption has jumped from 50 pounds per capita in 1950 to 124 pounds in 1975, and our total intake of beef, pork, and poultry averages 11 ounces daily (254 pounds a year). Moreover, we consume $25 billion worth of alcoholic beverages (made largely from grains) at an annual cost of $120 per person. Thus, while population still accounts for the major part of rising food demand, it is often said that a ravenous new rival, affluence, has emerged to further increase food shortages.

As a result, livestock and pets in wealthy countries are in direct competition for basic foods with hungry people throughout the rest of the world. On the international grain markets, U.S. livestock farmers, supported by the growing demand for meat, can always outbid representatives from poor grain-eating countries. Thus, basic foods go to cows and pigs, chickens and turkeys, instead of to the people who need them most. America's 90 million dogs and cats alone consume an annual $1.5 billion worth of pet food containing enough protein to feed 4 million human beings. In his authoritative *Nutrition and our Overpopulated Planet,* Sohan Monocha concludes that "animals in developed countries eat a better, more nutritionally balanced diet than two-thirds of the human population in poorer countries." Until quite recently, though, cattle were grazed on land unfit for farming or fed vegetable refuse (such as cornstalks) that could not be eaten by people; at present only 30 percent are still raised in this way. Every effort (legal, political, and personal) should be made to return to this system as soon as possible, and consumers who feel they need beef should insist on the grass-fed variety.

Food Energy

Food is a form of energy, and in a sense, the fundamental energy crisis is getting human beings enough food calories and protein. All food is ultimately derived from plants, which do the primary work of energy transformation that makes other life forms possible. Without plants we would have sunlight, water, air, and earth—but no food. As energy flows through a food chain, about 80 to 90 percent is degraded to useless heat at each step of the chain as explained by the second law of thermodynamics and illustrated in figure 1. The shorter the food chain between plants and man, the less the energy lost as heat and the greater the food calories available. Most people in the world—and especially those living in areas which have long been densely populated—eat low on the food chain, avoiding meat and eating plants

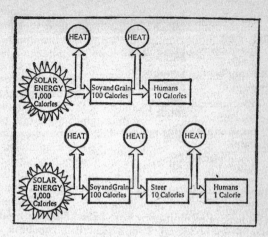

Fig. 1. Energy Flow Through Food Chains

directly. About 70 percent of the world's protein presently comes from plants and only 30 percent from animal-derived products, yet in affluent countries, these figures are often reversed. In developing countries, cereal grains alone generally provide 65 to 70 percent of the protein intake and 70 to 80 percent of the calories. This traditional grain-centered diet will support about seven times the population as its meat-centered counterpart.

The process of running grains and soybeans through animals and then eating the animals is so inefficient, uneconomical, and energy-expensive as to be virtually inexcusable. Clearly, the earth cannot support this level of waste. On the average, it takes about 7 pounds of grain- or soy protein to make 1 pound of livestock protein, but in the case of the feedlot steer, the least efficient converter, it takes a full 15 pounds. In other words, 93 percent of the protein fed to a steer is lost to human consumption, being used instead to support the animal's metabolism or build inedible parts of its body. The "return on investment" for other livestock products is shown in figure 2.

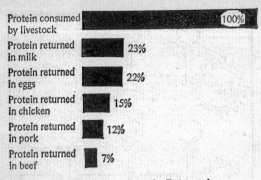

Fig. 2. Protein Consumed vs. Protein Returned

In her incisive million-copy best-seller, *Diet for a Small Planet,* Frances Moore Lappé describes the basic situation vividly: "To imagine what this means in practical everyday terms, simply set yourself at a restaurant in front of an 8-ounce steak and then imagine the room filled with 40 to 50 people with empty bowls in front of them. For the 'feed cost' of your steak, each of their bowls could be filled with a full cup of cereal grains."

Soy Protein for a Hungry Planet

Experts studying the world food crisis generally agree that one of the easiest and quickest ways that we in affluent countries can do something concrete to help is to greatly reduce our consumption of livestock products—especially meat. Each person that cuts his or her consumption of grain-fed beef by only one pound frees 15 pounds of grains and soybeans to be used directly as food. And a reduction in American meat consumption of only 10 percent would free 12 million tons of these basic foods per year, enough to meet the annual grain requirements of about 60 million people in less developed countries.

The key to making the transition toward a balanced meatless diet while still maintaining an adequate intake of high-quality protein lies in the use of soyfoods served together with the very grains that are now fed to livestock. Cereal grains have been the staff of life in virtually every traditional society, and the god of food has usually been more specifically the god of grain, as with the Roman deity Ceres, from whom we derive the word "cereal." Throughout most of East Asia, rice has long been the primary food. It was wheat in Europe, corn in North and South America, sorghum in Africa and parts of Asia, barley in Tibet, oats in Scotland, millet in northern China and Japan, rye in Mediterranean countries, and buckwheat in Russia. To this day, wheat and rice remain the primary foods for two-thirds of the human population, followed in importance by corn, sorghum, and barley in that order. Cereal grains and soy are the most democratic of foods, for nature produces them in such abundance that there is enough to go around at prices everyone can afford. And because soyfoods—such as miso—contain an abundance of the very amino amino acids lacking in grains, their use as a regular part of a grain-based diet can raise the quality of the protein combination to the same level as that found in most meats, while boosting the total available protein by as much as 40 percent (see p. 26). For these reasons, it is particularly important that people in protein-scarce developing countries learn to use soy.

Relying more on plant protein and less on meat can do wonders for your food budget, health, weight, conscience, and ecological environment, which is perhaps why an estimated 10 million Americans have now turned to meatless diets and why the number is rapidly increasing. Since plant foods have no cholesterol and very little saturated fats or harmful environmental contaminants (DDT, etc.), your intake of these substances will be greatly reduced, as will your susceptibility to heart disease and cancer (see pp. 40, 41). In a world plagued by malnutrition and starvation, 67 percent of all Americans report that they are trying to lose weight, and a recent Public Health Survey shows that 25 to 45 percent of all U.S. adults are more than 20 percent overweight (i.e., "obese"); vegetarians, on the other hand, are found to be 20 pounds below the national average. Animals will be grateful to you for not eating them and hungry people everywhere will thank you for taking no more than your share.

While their American counterparts have sold their beans to be used for oil and fodder, farmers throughout East Asia have long used homegrown soybeans as a basic daily protein source. Recently, however, a Tennessee-based new-age community called *The Farm* has taken the historic step of cultivating soybeans for use primarily as a food staple in the vegetarian diet of its 1,100 members. The 200 acres they planted yielded 65 tons, most of which was made into soymilk at their soy dairy or tempeh in their incubators; some of the crop, however, was shared with people in famine-stricken areas around the world in an attempt not only to help but also to educate them in the many wonders of soy. Thanks to *The Farm*'s ongoing efforts to teach other Americans about soybeans, small communities across the country are starting to grow them for home consumption.

South American nations have recently turned to soy farming on a massive scale. In 1974, Brazil (with extensive financial and technical aid from Japan) passed China to become the world's second largest producer, and Argentina is actively following Brazil's lead. In Mexico, soy imports jumped from 2 million bushels in 1971 to 30 million in 1975. Until recently most of the beans have been used for fodder or exported, but in 1975, representatives from numerous Latin American countries met in Mexico with experts from around the world to discuss ways of using soy proteins directly to help feed local populations. The first conference of its kind, this historic event will undoubtedly have important implications for people in all developing countries.

Soybeans and Agriculture

Food production can be increased either by expanding farm acreage or by increasing per-acre yields. Virtually all advances during the past quarter century have come in the latter area, largely through the use of genetically engineered hybrid seeds and fossil fuels in the form of mechanization, irrigation, chemical fertilizers, pesticides, and herbicides. The result has been a 60 percent increase in U.S. farm output since 1950. However in developed countries, the intensive use of agrichemicals is now considered to have reached a point of diminishing returns. This represents a basic change in the nature of the food problem and, as agricultural economist Lester R. Brown says, "points to the urgency of a radical shift in the traditional approach to its solution—the need to concentrate much more effort than in the past on slowing the growth in world *demand* for food." With all the major resources used to produce food—water, fertilizer, energy, and land—now scarce, and the worldwide demand from burgeoning populations of people and livestock unceasing, it is believed that food prices will continue to skyrocket.

A related question that many farmers in developed countries now raise is no longer "How much food can we produce?" but "What are the environmental consequences of doing so?" Large corporations, determined to apply the principles of industry to agriculture, have been grossly negligent of the health of our soil. Believing they have emancipated themselves from dependence upon nature, agribusiness technologists have come to view soil simply as a mixture of nitrogen, phosphorous, and potassium rather than as a living, fragile substance replete with microorganisms, humus, and organic matter. Corporate executives involved in large-scale farming seem not to take the time to understand the needs of the land and its natural cycles. A growing number of farmers, however, prompted by soaring energy costs (the price of nitrogen fertilizer alone more than quadrupled between 1971 and 1980) and a solid intuition that we can't remain insensitive to the quality of our soil without eventually suffering the consequences, are taking new interest in traditional organic techniques.

Chemical fertilizers, now applied at the average level of 150 pounds per acre, were virtually unused before 1940. Up until that time, farmers practiced

crop rotation, planting legumes—such as soybeans—
every three years to regenerate soil nutrients and
help control monoculture insect populations. Rhizobia
bacteria living in the legumes' root nodules capture
atmospheric nitrogen and "fix" it in the soil; this nitrogen (the main component in protein) serves as a
source of free natural fertilizer that nourishes the plant
and future crops. When chemical fertilizers (anhy-
drous ammonia or amonium nitrate) are applied to
the soil, plants utilize only about 50 percent of their
nitrogen, the rest being lost to seepage and runoff
which often pollute local waterways. Yet the nitrogen
fixed by bacteria is used completely and there is no
resulting pollution. Soybeans can fix about 100 pounds
of nitrogen per acre, the chemical equivalent of which
would cost about $30. The American Indians appar-
ently recognized the soil enriching value of legumes,
for they generally planted beans in alternate rows with
corn. The corn, which has a hearty appetite for nitrogen, sucks up the excess nitrogen as fast as the legumes can produce it, thereby signalling the latter to
produce much more total nitrogen than if there were
no intercropping. Some farmers and gardeners now
use soy to yield a triple bonus: first, free fertilizer; second, high-protein beans; and finally, humus-forming
organic matter when the plants are turned under in
the fall as green manure. Most important, organic
gardeners using natural fertilizers (manure and com-
post) find they can obtain soybean yields of 50 bushels or more per acre, almost twice the national
average, accompanied by substantial savings from not
using chemicals. And soybeans have such a hardy
resistance to disease and insects, that avoiding the use
of toxic pesticides often makes little or no difference
in crop yields, while not using herbicides helps keep
the root bacteria alive and vital.

Throughout the world, there is a movement away
from the energy-expensive, environmentally damag-
ing agricultural methods now popular in industrial
countries. The fact that it often costs *ten times* as
much to grow an acre of "green revolution" rice as an
acre of the traditional crop is bringing this lesson home

to poor farmers everywhere. Soybeans thrive in virtually any climate from tropical Brazil to Japan's snowy Hokkaido, and they are as well suited for use in small vegetable gardens as on huge farms. Due to their unique ability to nourish both the soil and human beings, they are bound to play a key role in the planet's emerging agriculture.

Soyfoods: Modern and Traditional

We in the West must learn to use soybeans directly as foods. And with soy oil now facing severe competition from low-cost Malaysian and African palm oil, with growing popular resistance to the wasteful and expensive feedlot system, and with the expanding need for low-cost protein foods in developing countries, the time is ripe for the influential American Soybean Association, the food industry, and concerned individuals to begin to take a serious interest in developing these foods.

Advanced Western technology is already being used to manufacture a number of new fabricated soy products: protein concentrates, isolates, spun fibers, and textured vegetable proteins (TVP). The latter are now widely used as meat extenders or, in combination with numerous artificial coloring and flavoring agents, as simulated meats: sausages, bacon bits, chicken, and the like. Although these products still utilize less than 2 percent of all United States soy protein, their domestic consumption is expected to increase 10-fold from 500 million pounds in 1972 to 5 billion pounds by 1985. Yet the technology and cost required to produce such products places them out of reach of the poor in developing countries who need them most, while their synthetic qualities generally limit their appeal to the growing number of Westerners interested in natural foods.

In both the developed and developing nations, there is a growing interest in methods of production employing decentralized, small-scale technology and simple, honest craftsmanship. Mass production and heavily centralized technology have created work that is mechanical and monotonous, overcrowded cities to the point of breakdown, caused severe industrial pollution, and led in many cases to massive unemployment. Most of East Asia's soyfoods are still produced in small shops which use little energy and require a minimum of capital investment to start. Traditional miso-making is a fine example of such a craft, providing truly enjoyable work that nourishes and enlivens; a beautiful mode of self-expression, self-discipline, and self-sufficiency. Compatible with the basic needs and aspirations of human beings, it is well suited to be a model of craftsmanship for future generations.

Deeper Causes of World Hunger

We have seen how soybeans offer great promise as a key protein source for the future on our small planet, and how each of us, by moving away from meat-centered diets that support the highly wasteful feedlot system, can take a significant first step toward alleviating world food shortages. Yet we must understand that this is only a first step. As Frances Moore Lappé says in *Diet for a Small Planet* (Ballantine Books, 1975, revised edition), the notion of "meatless, guiltless" can be a seductively simple escape preventing further involvement. For even if the practice of feeding basic foods to animals were abandoned altogether, there would be no automatic guarantee that the vast amounts of grains and soybeans thereby released for direct consumption would actually become available to the poor at prices they could afford. Thus, if we are really serious about bringing an end to hunger and starvation on our planet, we must make an even deeper commitment to understand the larger forces that cause hunger and to do something, each in our own way, to stop them. What *are* these forces causing hunger and what *can* we do?

Population: At the present population growth rate of 1.64 percent, the population of the planet will double every 43 years. Many of the poorer nations, with growth rates of 3 percent, double every 23 years and therefore (theoretically) increase a staggering nineteenfold every century. During the 1970s, the rate of increase began to slow, perhaps for the first time in history—a promising sign. Yet each morning 178,000 new faces appear at the breakfast table and each year there are 64 million more passengers on Spaceship Earth. Roughly 85 to 90 percent of all new babies are born in the have-not countries, and the fastest-growing populations are the ones that are the most miserable. In 1789, the English clergyman-economist Thomas Malthus accurately foresaw our predicament: "The power of population is so superior to the power of earth to provide subsistence" that man will succumb to "gigantic inevitable famine." In his excellent book *The Twenty-ninth Day* (W.W. Norton, 1978), Lester Brown, president of the World-watch Institute, shows how population growth is putting increased stresses on the earth's four major biological systems that support all life: croplands, oceanic fisheries, grasslands, and forests. In each area, as demand exceeds sustainable yield, populations begin to undercut their own well-being and threaten their future survival. In economic terms, they consume principal as well as interest. Brown urges governments to make a multipronged attack on the population problem by making family-planning services universally available, liberating women from traditional roles, meeting basic social needs such as health care, nutrition, and illiteracy that are usually associated with reduced fertility, educating people about the consequences of rapid population growth, and reshaping national economic and social policies to encourage small families. Brown points out that governments such as China and Singapore which have moved on all these fronts at once have been extremely successful in slowing population growth. And, of course, each of us can make a vital contribution to population control by limiting our own family size to two children or less.

Many citizens in the affluent nations tend to think of the population problem as being confined primarily to developing countries where the increase in human numbers is the highest. Yet in terms of resource consumption and pollution, the problem is actually *more* severe in the industrial nations with slower population growth. That 25 percent of the passengers on Spaceship Earth traveling in the first-class and tourist compartments consumes 80 percent of the yearly supply of food, energy, and mineral resources, while contributing 75 percent of the pollution. The remaining 75 percent of the passengers traveling in the hold without adequate food, water, or shelter are beginning to get upset. It should be clear, then, that as a precondition to helping the third-class passengers, those traveling in the luxurious quarters should take all possible measures to bring their own population growth to zero while sharply limiting their consumption and waste.

While virtually all experts agree that every effort must be made on every level by almost every country to reach zero population growth as soon as possible, not all agree that population growth is a primary cause of hunger. In their brilliant and pioneering *Food First* (Ballantine Books, 1979), Frances Moore Lappé and Joseph Collins make a strong case that both hunger and population growth, rather than being causes, are symptoms of the same deeper disease—the insecurity and poverty of the majority resulting from the control over national productive resources by a small and wealthy power elite. High birth rates are seen as symptomatic of the failures of a social system, reflecting people's need to have many children in an attempt to provide laborers to increase their meager family income, to provide old-age food security, and to compensate for the high infant death rate, the result of inadequate nutrition and health care. Thus parents are in a tragic double bind—acting quite rationally in having large families yet knowing full well they may not be able to feed them—often have no interest in birth-control programs. As Lappé and Collins point out: "To attack high birth rates without attacking the causes of poverty that make large families the only survival option is not only fruitless, it is a tragic diversion our planet simply cannot afford."

Affluence: We have seen above how people (including the upper classes in less developed countries), as they become more affluent, tend to increase their consumption of foods derived from animals. In 1979, to produce these products, roughly 35 percent of the world's grain harvest (including 79 percent of the U.S. grain harvest) was fed to livestock, grain that could have been used as human food. Thus while population growth accounts for about two-thirds of the annual growth in world food demand, this affluent pattern of feeding livestock grain and soy via the feedlot system accounts for the remaining one-third.

Narrow Focus on Increasing Productivity: The standard analysis that hunger is a result of food scarcity has inevitably led to programs to increase food production, generally through technological modernization. Yet when new argricultural technology enters a system based on severe economic and power disparities, it selectively benefits the rich and powerful, who have the money, land, intelligence, credit worthiness, and political influence to take fullest advantage of the new opportunities. In the end, the rich get richer and the poor poorer. A major study by the International Labor Organization (confirmed in a similar study by the United Nations Institute for Social Development) documents that in seven South Asian countries comprising 70 percent of the rural population of the nonsocialist world there has been a rise in per capita grain production, while the food consumption of the rural poor is less than it was 10 to 20 years ago; more people are more hungry and poorer than ever before. In many cases the so-called Green Revolution, expected to abolish hunger, has actually made it worse. Farm mechanization has left large numbers of farm workers without jobs and the high cost of the "inputs" necessary to grow the special new hybrid seeds—inputs such as irrigation, chemical fertilizers and pesticides, farm machinery, and the seeds themselves—have caused small farmers to go bankrupt or forced them to sell their farms to the landed elite. Not only are the poor left without a source of income, the large landowners often move the land out of basic food production and start to grow export cash crops such as grapes for wine or even flowers, which greatly increase per-acre profits.

International Food Exploitation: Large agribusiness corporations from the industrialized countries have recently begun to buy up huge quantities of basic foods from the less developed countries to sell in supermarkets at home. They have turned the planet into a Global Farm to supply a Global Supermarket, where the poor must compete with affluent foreigners for food grown in their own countries. By 1976 over 50 percent of the winter and early-spring fruits and vegetables sold in U.S. supermarkets were grown in Latin America on land formerly used to feed local people. This system also puts U.S. farm workers out of work.

Land Monopolization and Misuse: In many less developed countries a small and wealthy percentage of the population owns most of the land. Based on a study of 83 developing countries, slightly more than 3 percent of all landowners controlled almost 80 percent of the farmland. The landed elite prevent land reform and redistribution by using their great political power. Yet where land redistribution has taken place, farmers who own their land are found to produce two to three times as much food per acre as tenant farmers and sharecroppers, who have no incentive to make long-term agricultural improvements on the land. All efforts must be made to give farmers control over their own land and to remove the obstacles that prevent them from growing the food they need.

Cash Crop System of Export Agriculture: The finest land in less developed countries is now widely used to grow export cash crops (coffee, sugar, cocoa, bananas, etc.) instead of growing food for the people. This system generally benefits the rich, while the poor go hungry. Clearly, agriculture must become, first and foremost, a way for people to produce the food they need and only secondly a source of foreign exchange.

An in-depth discussion of each of these problems and their complex interrelationships is given in *Food First*. Read this book! Called "one of the most stimulating books in years" by the *New York Times Book Review,* it has been highly praised by the emerging American hunger movement and by Third World leaders alike as offering a penetrating new perspective on the hunger crisis. While challenging the basic assumption that the main causes of hunger are too many people and not enough food, the authors show that hunger exists in the face of plenty and is caused primarily by social, economic, and political structures that block development and prevent people from democratically controlling the resources that would allow them to produce their own food. An important part of our work is to see that our own government stops its support of foreign elites and their partners, multinational corporations, that increasingly represent primary causes of the problem, then commits itself, as we each must commit ourselves, to putting an end to worldwide hunger and starvation at the same time that we put an end to the proliferation of nuclear weapons, nuclear power, and deadly environmental chemicals. Our work is cut out for us, and it will not be short or easy. But what joy in such a great and noble challenge.

Going Beyond Ourselves

An ancient Chinese proverb reminds us that "A time of crisis is a time of great opportunity." Outmoded life-styles and patterns of thought are beginning to crack under the strain of change so rapid it borders on discontinuity, and overlapping crises are forcing us to totally re-evaluate the very basis of our being. At the still point within us all a new vision of reality, richly detailed yet strikingly simple, is beginning to take form. In part it is the holistic and contemporary view of ecology, mother of all the sciences, that sees the perfect interconnectedness of all things, the jewelled matrix form-and-energy body of the world. In part it is the holy and ancient understanding of the spiritual paths that points to an underlying oneness in which the impossible union of opposites is made real. Our expanding vision must inevitably be a call to action, and it is abundantly clear that nothing less than selfless service and loving kindness—which accord with the truth of our oneness—are suited to the immense task we face. The child wasting in the forgotten village is our child; thus do we realize that we are all brothers and sisters. We must bring food. Watch in the years to come how selflessly soybeans offer themselves to help us feed a hungry world.

2

Miso as a Food

ALTHOUGH SOYBEANS are a treasure trove of high-quality protein and other nutrients, only a portion of these are available to the body when the whole beans are served in their baked, boiled, or roasted forms. However through the process of natural fermentation, soybeans undergo a total biochemical transformation in which virtually all of their complex protein, carbohydrate, and lipid (oil or fat) molecules are broken down into readily digestible amino acids, simple sugars, and fatty acids. Most important, the process of leisurely fermentation unfolds a panorama of delicious new flavors and aromas.

Rich in High-quality Protein

The 21 amino acids which constitute all protein are the building blocks of the body: in children and adolescents they are essential for providing new tissue for growth, while in adults they supply the material for routine body maintenance. Eight (or occasionally ten) of these amino acids are termed "essential" because if they are available from the food a person eats, the body can manufacture the others. Because soybeans—and miso—contain the eight essential amino acids, they are known as sources of "complete protein."

The protein value of a food depends on both the quantity and quality of the protein in that food: Miso is unusually high in both.

Protein *quantity* is a measure of the percentage by weight of the protein actually present in a food. The average of all miso varieties is about 12 to 13 percent, and certain types (such as Hatcho) containing a large

percentage of soybeans exceed 20 percent. These figures compare very favorably with common Western
protein sources such as chicken (21%), beef or cottage cheese (20%), hamburgers or eggs (13%), and
whole dairy milk (3%).

Protein *quality* is a measure of the percentage of
protein in a food that can actually be utilized by the
body. Usually expressed in terms of Net Protein Utilization (NPU), it depends primarily on the configuration of essential amino acids in the food and on
the food's digestibility. It is now becoming widely
recognized that there is no fundamental difference
between animal and vegetable protein: it is simply
a question of degree. All foods, animal and vegetable,
can be ranked on a simple scale which shows their
protein quality or NPU. Generally speaking, animal
foods have relatively high NPU ratings. Eggs, for example, with an NPU of 94, have the highest quality
protein of any known food. This means that of the
13 grams of protein present in 100 grams of eggs, 94
percent (12.2 grams) can actually be utilized by the
body. Other animal foods with high NPU ratings are
milk (82), fish (80), cottage cheese (75), cheeses
(70), beef and hamburger (67), and chicken (65).
But a number of plant foods are also high on the
scale. Rice, with an NPU of 70, contains the highest
quality protein of any basic plant food. Soybeans
(NPU=61) and barley (NPU=60) are also both
relatively high. Miso, however, has NPU ratings of

up to 72, *higher than any of its constituent ingredients!* This is largely because in the production of miso, rice (or barley) and soybeans are *combined.* Due to the fact that soy and grain proteins *complement* each other, the NPU of the resultant combination is higher than that of either of the individual foods, and the final product contains all of the eight essential (plus nine non-essential) amino acids in a configuration which is highly utilizable by the human body (fig. 3). Moreover, the process of fermentation renders each of the basic component foods more digestible and, therefore, increases their individual NPUs. Because red miso, the most common variety (made with rice and soybeans), contains 13.5 percent protein and has an NPU of 72, one hundred

Fig. 3. Amounts of Essential Amino Acids and Their Percentages of Minimum Daily Requirements in 100 Grams of Miso
(Source: *Japanese Scientific Research Council*)

Amino Acids	MDR (gm)	Red (Rice) Miso (gm)	MDR (%)	Barley Miso (gm)	Hatcho (Soybean) Miso (gm)
(Methionine-Cystine)	1.10	.29	26	.27	.45
Lysine	.80	.57	71	.65	1.36
Tryptophan	.25	.19	76	.16	.33
(Phenylalaline-Tyrosine)	1.10	1.09	99	1.23	2.10
Valine	.80	.80	100	.79	1.21
Methionine	.20	.20	100	.17	.25
Leucine	1.10	1.37	125	1.28	1.68
Isoleucine	.70	.92	131	.94	1.18
Threonine	.50	.71	142	.74	1.03
Phenylaline	.30	.57	190	.63	1.25
Protein	61.5	13.5	22	12.8	21.0

Note: Amino acids in shortest supply are listed first. Those in parentheses are important combinations of essential and semi-essential amino acids with common properties. Thus 100 grams (5½ tablespoons) of red miso (13.5% protein) contains .29 grams of the sulfur-containing amino acids (methionine-cystine), or 26 percent of the minimum adult daily requirement of 1.10 grams.

grams of this product can supply us with 9.7 grams of usable protein—more than from an equal weight of hamburger (13% protein; NPU=67).

Miso has long been a key source of protein in the Japanese diet. It presently accounts for up to 25 percent of the protein consumed in some inland rural areas and more than 8 percent for the population as a whole. The average Japanese enjoys about 16 pounds of miso each year, or about 19 grams (3½ teaspoonsful) per day.

A Powerful Protein Booster

We saw above how the combination of two foods whose proteins are complementary—such as soybeans and grains—can lead to an increase in NPU and therefore create extra usable protein at no extra cost. Yet miso *itself* is also ideal for use in combining proteins. Because it contains an abundance of precisely the amino acids lacking in other basic foods (especially wheat, corn, sesame, and even rice), the addition of as little as several teaspoons of miso to preparations containing these foods can result in large increases in usable protein. Thus miso is not only a good source of protein, but also a protein booster. Therein lies one of its basic advantages over salt as a daily seasoning.

Miso has long been considered an important nutritional complement to rice in East Asia's grain-based diet. Similarly, the use of miso with whole-wheat bread in the form of a spread, for example, or with noodles, pizza, bulgur, or other Western-style grain dishes, can increase the sum of the protein available by as much as 30 to 40 percent.

Aids Digestion and Assimilation

Miso is prized for its ability to aid in the digestion and assimilation of other foods. At least four digestive agents are contained in all non-pasteurized miso: natural digestive enzymes, lactic acid-forming bacteria (Lactobacilli), salt resistant yeasts, and the mold and other microorganisms present in koji. Only the very heartiest microorganisms are able to survive the rigors of several years' fermentation in the presence of salt. Thus they and their enzymes are well suited to continue their work in the large and small intestines where they break down or digest complex proteins, carbohydrates, and fats into simpler, more easily assimilable molecules. Because enzymes (catalysts promoting digestion) are destroyed at temperatures above 104°F, and lactic acid bacteria by several minutes of simmering, only unpasteurized miso which has not been overcooked can create within our bodies a living digestive culture. In Japan, commercially available digestive enzymes are often made from the same type of koji used to make miso.

Lactic acid bacteria are one of the basic factors which make both yogurt and miso excellent aids to digestion. Russian longevity experts have recently suggested that either the beneficial effects of the Lactobacilli organisms in aiding digestion or the effect of the lactic acid they produce in altering the pH in the intestines may be a basic cause for the association of yogurt with long life and good health. It is well known that the use of penicillin or other antibiotics kills the beneficial microflora that ordinarily live in the human digestive tract. A quick, easy, and healthful way to replenish them after use of antibiotics is by drinking a cup of miso soup.

The process of lengthy aging in cedar vats—in effect, "external" digestive systems—breaks down 80 to 90 percent of miso's basic nutrients into their simpler forms. When the human system tries to do the same job (in a much shorter time) it is not as successful: roasted soybeans are only 60 percent digestible and whole boiled soybeans 68 percent. By eating miso, the body's energy ordinarily needed to digest soybeans is freed to work on other foods. The fermentation process also serves to eliminate the factors in whole soybeans that may cause flatulence, and to inactivate trypsin inhibitors, substances found in all fresh and uncooked dried soybeans which prevent the full utilization of soy nutrients by the body.

Fig. 4. Composition of Nutrients in 100 Grams of Miso

Sources: Standard Tables of Food Composition (Japan), the Japanese National Miso Association Nutrient Tables, and Data Supplied by Miso Producers

Type of Miso	Food Energy (Calories)	Moisture (Percent)	Protein (Percent)	Fat (Percent)	Carbo-hydrates (incl. fiber) (Percent)	Fiber (Percent)	Ash (Percent)	Sodium Chloride (Percent)	Calcium (Mg)	Sodium (Mg)	Phosphorous (Mg)	Iron (Mg)	Vit. B1 (Thiamine) (Mg)	Vit. B2 (Riboflavin) (Mg)	Vit. B3 (Niacin) (Mg)
Red Miso	153	50	13.5	5.8	19.1	1.9	14.8	13.0	115	4600	190	4.0	0.03	0.10	1.5
Light-yellow Miso	155	49	13.5	4.6	19.6	1.8	12.8	12.5	90	4100	160	4.0	0.03	0.10	1.5
Mellow Red Miso	162	42	11.2	4.2	27.9	1.3	14.5	13.0	81	3200	135	3.5	0.04	0.10	1.5
Mellow Beige Miso	165	44	13.0	4.2	29.1	1.2	8.5	7.0	80	2500	133	3.5	0.04	0.10	1.5
Mellow White Miso	215	57	12.3	1.4	27.5	1.3	4.9	9.1	31	3200	138	1.3	0.03	0.10	1.5
Sweet Red Miso	168	46	12.7	4.0	31.7	1.4	8.1	6.0	75	2100	134	3.0	0.03	0.08	3.0
Sweet White Miso	178	47	11.1	1.9	35.9	1.0	7.5	5.5	70	2100	120	4.0	0.04	0.10	1.5
Barley Miso	154	48	12.8	5.0	21.0	1.9	14.9	13.0	116	4600	190	3.5	0.04	0.10	1.5
Mellow Barley Miso	160	46	11.1	5.0	29.8	1.3	14.6	10.0	86	3500	139	3.6	0.04	0.10	1.5

Hatcho Miso	224	40	21.0	10.2	12.0	1.8	16.8	10.6	154	4100	264	7.1	0.04	0.13	1.3
Soybean Miso	180	48	19.4	6.9	13.2	2.2	13.0	11.2	140	3800	240	6.5	0.04	0.12	1.2
Tamari Miso	160	61	16.3	5.7	11.4	1.6	11.7	9.8	138	3600	220	6.3	0.04	0.11	1.1
Kinzanji Miso	172	58	11.3	2.0	30.1	2.1	5.1	8.0	95	2800	131	3.5	0.04	0.10	1.5
Peanut Miso	432	17	16.1	27.6	37.1	1.3	4.8	7.0	80	3100	180	5.6	0.04	0.10	1.3
Akadashi Miso	169	44	16.0	4.1	31.9	1.4	10.8	8.0	75	2800	135	3.6	0.05	0.10	1.4
Dehydrated Miso	303	5	32.2	9.0	35.8	3.6	26.6	18.5	180	7500	320	8.0	0.05	0.15	2.0
Low-salt/ High-protein Miso	140	53	17.6	6.4	24.0	1.9	13.1	6.3	112	4600	180	4.0	0.03	0.11	1.6

Note: Values for each product vary widely depending on the maker; many of those listed are averages. The Standard Tables of Food Composition contain detailed data for red, light-yellow, sweet white, soybean, and dehydrated varieties. The Miso Association tables contain moisture, protein, fat, carbohydrate, and ash data for barley, mellow barley, mellow red and beige, and sweet red. Hatcho, peanut, and mellow white data were obtained from the makers. All other figures were derived by interpolation.

Adds Flavor to Low-Salt Diets

A growing number of Western doctors and nutritionists are coming to favor a relatively low-salt diet as one of the simplest ways of combatting high blood pressure, hypertension and, in some cases, obesity. Most people use salt to accentuate the flavors inherent in foods. But, because miso, which contains an average of only 12 percent salt, has its own rich flavor, it can actually impart all of the desired taste and aroma with the addition of considerably *less* salt than would ordinarily be used if the food were seasoned with salt alone.

In our ongoing study of American eating patterns, we have noticed repeatedly that Americans tend to be extremists. For example, they tend to consume either a high-salt diet or a salt-free or low-salt diet. Yet common sense and an abundance of scientific evidence shows that *moderation* in the use of salt (as of many other ingredients and nutrients) is the healthiest way. Mankind's traditional diet based on grains and vegetables, when prepared with little or no added salt is simply too bland to be enjoyed day after day. Equally important is the *quality* of the salt we use. Natural sea salt supplies us with an abundance of trace elements (micronutrients) so essential for good health and metabolic balance. Moreover, recent experiments suggest that the fermentation process actually changes the effect of salt on the human body: rats have been shown to be able to tolerate a considerably higher salt intake in the form of miso than in the form of table salt. The Japanese, who may have developed an intuitive understanding of these phenomena during their long contact with fermented soybean seasonings, now obtain less than 10 percent of their total salt intake from table salt; miso supplies 20 percent, shoyu 30 percent, and *tsukemono* (salt-pickled vegetables) 40 percent.

People on a very low salt diet might consume 1 tablespoon per day of red, barley, or Hatcho miso (the equivalent of ½ teaspoon salt): an average intake is 4 tablespoons (equivalent to 2 teaspoons salt). Low-salt/high-protein miso (p. 84) lends itself particularly well to salt-restricted diets.

Miso's salinity is four times that of sea water, but because the salt is mellowed by the presence of amino acids and natural oils, miso does not taste particularly salty. And if the salt is removed, what remains tastes remarkably sweet.

A Key to Low-fat Cookery

Miso contains an average of 5 percent natural oils —mostly unsaturated and completely free of cholesterol. These give miso its savory flavor and aroma. And because they are primarily soy oils, unrefined and unprocessed, they are rich in lecithin and linoleic acid which help disperse accumulations of cholesterol and other fatty acids in the circulatory system.

In the West, our total intake of fats (a high proportion of them saturated) is about three times that of Japan. The fact that the Japanese have fewer problems with heart disease, high blood pressure, arterio- and atherosclerosis, and overweight than people in any other part of the world has often been attributed to their low consumption of fats. One of the keys to this low-fat cookery lies in the use of miso (and shoyu) in place of salt. Since we in the West generally use salt as our basic seasoning, we tend to also use fairly large amounts of oil or butter—as in dressings, sauces, or sautéed dishes—to soften the salt's intrinsic sharpness. Yet miso's saltiness is mellowed by the natural (unsaturated) oils and amino acids already present in it, and by the slow process of fermentation. Thus miso can be used in place of salt to prepare a host of delicious Western-style dishes— ranging from miso French dressings to savory white sauces—each using less than one-half the amount of fats called for in standard recipes.

An Excellent Seasoning for Weight-watchers

A welcome addition to the diet of weight watchers, miso has one of the highest known ratios of protein to calories found in any natural food: a typical portion (1 tablespoon) contains a total of only 27 calories or as little as 11 calories per gram of protein. By comparison, brown rice contains 45, bread 34, and eggs 12 calories per gram of protein. Stated slightly differently, a 100-gram portion of red miso (containing 150 calories) will fulfill 30 percent of the daily male adult protein requirement while costing only 5 percent of the typical calorie allotment. And we saw above how using miso in place of salt can help to reduce fat intake; this is an additional aid in helping us watch our weight, since the reduction of only 1 tablespoon of oil from a dish means a decrease of some 153 calories.

While carbohydrates are a food's main source of "fattening" calories, those same calories also provide us with energy. As a result of the process of fermentation, miso's carbohydrates are largely in the form of simple, easily digestible sugars and contain relatively little fiber or cellulose. Thus miso can serve as a concentrated source of stamina.

A Vegetarian Source of Essential Vitamin B-12

B-12 is one of the vitamins most commonly deficient in the diets of those vegetarians who exclude dairy products as well as meat from their diet. Until as recently as 1977, many nutritionists believed that *only* foods of animal origin contained vitamin B-12, the most concentrated sources being beef liver, tuna, eggs, and Swiss cheese. Recent research, however, has shown that there are a number of excellent vegetarian sources of vitamin B-12 including fermented soyfoods (tempeh, natto, miso, and shoyu), sea vegetables, and some single-cell proteins. By far the best soyfood source is tempeh (see our *Book of Tempeh,* Harper & Row, 1979); a typical 100-gram (3½ ounce) serving of tempeh sold in the U.S. contains from 3.9 to 8.8 micrograms of vitamin B-12. Since the official U.S. recommended daily allowance (RDA) of B-12 for adults is 3 micrograms, one serving of tempeh can provide 130 to 294 percent of the RDA. A study in Japanese by Dr. Jusaku Takahashi (Studies on Sources of Vitamin B-12, *Eiyo to Shokuryo,* 8 (2): 25–27, 1955) showed that light-yellow miso contained 0.17 micrograms of vitamin B-12 per 100 grams, or 5.6 percent of the RDA. A typical serving of 1 tablespoon (18 g) of this miso would provide 0.5 percent of the RDA.

In each of the above foods, vitamin B-12 is produced by certain bacteria or molds. It is important to note that many nutritionists feel that the U.S. RDA for vitamin B-12 of 3 micrograms per day is much too high. The corresponding figure set by the prestigious United Nations Food and Agricultural Organization is 2 micrograms. An intake of 0.6 to 1.2 micrograms per day is generally considered sufficient for normal blood formation and good health but it will not replenish liver stores if they are depleted. We must also recall that, for centuries, Japanese Buddhist monks, who consume no foods of animal origin but obtain their vitamin B-12 from miso, natto, shoyu, and sea vegetables, have been renowned for their good health, vigor, and longevity.

Promotes Long Life and Good Health

Although the Japanese are well aware that miso is an excellent source of essential nutrients, they prize it even more for properties which are not easily defined or measured, but which are believed to promote good health and long life. After centuries of experimentation using intuitive and systematic methods based on a wholistic view of life, people have found that eating miso together with a diet low in animal foods is an effective way to improve one's physical constitution and internal environment.

In his delightful and remarkably comprehensive *We Japanese*, written in 1937, Mr. Atsuharu Sakai begins his chapter on miso by saying: "It is generally believed in Japan that miso (bean paste) is responsible in great measure for the generally sound physical health of the Japanese." In recent years, scientific studies have been conducted in order to isolate the causes of longevity in Japanese communities where many of the inhabitants live to be over one hundred. One finding that has received considerable publicity concerns the high correlation between long life and the regular consumption of miso—most of which is homemade and served in soups. When we visited a "long-life" village located deep in the mountains west of Tokyo and asked a number of the villagers what they felt were the secrets of health and long life, the most frequent responses were: hard work in the fields, clean mountain air, a diet of grains and vegetables—and plenty of miso soup. (It is interesting to note that the centenarians living in the Balkans and Eastern Europe give almost the same advice except that they recommend another fermented food: yogurt.)

Recent Western laboratory experiments offer scientific explanations for the fact that traditional Oriental cultures have shown such a strong resistance to disease. Of the 161 strains of aerobic bacteria isolated in miso, almost all have been found to be antagonistic to *Escherichia coli* and *Staphylococcus aureus*—two organisms responsible for food poisoning. And specific miso bacteria are thought, by analogy, to be useful as controllers of disease-causing agents. In 1972, Drs. H. L. Wang and C. W. Hesseltine of the Northern Regional Research Center of the U.S. Department of Agriculture (p. 572) demonstrated that the molds of tempeh, shoyu, and wine-fermented tofu (*doufu-ru*), each fermented soybean products, inhibited the growth of harmful bacterial cultures. The possibility that miso molds contain similar antibacterial substances is now being investigated.

Countless laboratory tests have checked for the

existence of mycotoxins and especially aflatoxins (toxins caused by harmful molds) in miso. None have been found.

The Perfect (Alkaline) Coffee Substitute

We consider a morning cup of miso soup to be the perfect coffee substitute. Coffee hits the nervous system with a jolt of acidic caffeine (often amplified in effect by white sugar) that snaps open droopy eyes and provides a quick shot of speedy energy, followed, unfortunately, by a depressing drop in energy. On the other hand, miso soup, as well as being a source of abundant nutrients, wakes up the nervous system gently yet effectively by alkalizing the bloodstream, then providing a steady flow of energy throughout the morning. We have many friends who have kicked the coffee habit with miso soup and discovered how great it feels to be *really* awake.

Throughout East Asia, miso's alkalizing and cleansing effects are considered to be extremely important in the development of an alkaline constitution, which is widely believed to promote resistance to disease. In standard East Asian nutritional sourcebooks, basic foods are categorized as either alkaline or acidic. This information is common knowledge throughout the culture since it is considered one of the basic principles of maintaining good health. Most of the foods which we moderns consider special treats (sweets, alcohol, meat) are listed as acidic; taken in excess, they are said to weaken the constitution. With the consumption of sugar and liquor climbing to dangerously high levels in many affluent nations, the use of alkaline miso could at least provide a counterbalance until better eating patterns are resumed; thereafter, it could be used to promote good health.

A well-known Japanese proverb states that a bowl of miso soup each day keeps the doctor away, and traditional folk wisdom abounds with sayings about the value of miso as a medicine used to cure colds, improve metabolism, clear the skin, and help develop resistance to parasitic diseases. Miso soup is often used quite specifically in the same way Westerners use Alka-Seltzer or Milk of Magnesia to settle an upset stomach, ameliorate a hangover, or get rid of acid indigestion.

May Prevent Radiation Sickness

In recent years, Japanese doctors and scientists have begun to consider the possibility that miso may also be an effective agent in preventing radiation sickness. Interest in this subject was stimulated by a book called *Physical Constitution and Food,* written in 1965 by Dr. Shinichiro Akizuki, director of the Saint Francis Hospital in Nagasaki. Born with a congenitally weak constitution, Dr. Akizuki has devoted his career to researching the use of food as preventive medicine, placing special emphasis on a holistic (rather than symptomatic) approach to healing, and on traditional natural foods native to Japan. Throughout his intensive experimentation and research—which included the study of Japanese folk medicine, "long-life" villages, and modern nutritional science—he continually applied the findings to his own life in an attempt to develop a strong physical constitution or *taishitsu.* This latter concept, which in Japanese means literally "the quality of the body" and has a somewhat deeper meaning than its English equivalent, soon became the key to his work. As miso soup and brown rice became the central foods in his diet, he experienced a steady rejuvenation accompanied by physical strength, vigor, and resistance to disease. Soon not only his family but also his entire hospital staff and patients were including miso soup and brown rice in their daily meals. A lengthy and detailed examination of the results led him to write:

> I feel that miso soup is the most essential part of a person's diet. . . . I have found that, with very few exceptions, families which make a practice of serving miso soup daily are almost never sick. . . . By enjoying miso soup each day, your constitution will gradually improve and you will develop resistance

to disease. I believe that miso belongs to the highest class of medicines, those which help prevent disease and strengthen the body through continued usage. . . . Some people speak of miso as a condiment, but miso brings out the flavor and nutritional value in all foods and helps the body to digest and assimilate whatever we eat. . . . I use and have deep respect for modern medicines such as antibiotics and modern surgical techniques, yet they must only be employed when absolutely necessary. Of prime importance is the development of a strong constitution through proper eating. The basic condition of a person's constitution determines whether or not he will be only mildly and temporarily affected by diseases, or be seriously and chronically affected.

In 1945, when the atomic bomb fell on Nagasaki, Dr. Akizuki's hospital—located only one mile from the epicenter of the blast—was left in ruins. Fortunately, he and his nurses and co-workers were not in the building and were uninjured. Throughout the following two years, though, Dr. Akizuki and his staff worked daily in prolonged close contact with fallout victims in areas of Nagasaki which were heavily damaged and highly radioactive. Nevertheless, neither he nor his associates suffered from the usual and expected effects of radiation. Dr. Akizuki was extremely interested in this phenomenon, which he hypothesized may well have been due to the fact that he and his staff had been drinking miso soup regularly. But he felt that only a thorough scientific study of the phenomenon could provide the full answer.

In 1972, a number of Japanese scientists, including Dr. Morishita Kenichiro (p. 565), doing agricultural research stimulated by Dr. Akizuki's writings discovered that miso contained dipicolinic acid (*zybicolin* in Japanese). Produced by miso and natto microorganisms, it is an alkaloid which chelates (grabs onto) heavy metals such as radioactive strontium and discharges them from the body. The discovery received front-page coverage in Japan's major newspapers.

In 1978, we received the following letter from a woman in America:

> My mother just underwent six weeks of radiation treatments for cancer. The doctors told me she would be very ill and uncomfortable from the aftereffects of the radiation. I gave her miso soup and other miso recipes and she experienced almost no aftereffects. The doctors couldn't believe it. When I told them about the miso they laughed it off—but I'm convinced.

We feel that phenomena such as this deserve careful study by doctors and in America, a country where some 25 percent of the population now dies of cancer.

Neutralizes the Effects of Smoking and Air Pollution

There is a traditional saying in Japan that smokers should drink miso soup, and some authorities contend that the amino acids contained in miso are effective in neutralizing the harmful influences of tobacco and in eliminating them from the bloodstream. In her book *Miso Cookery*, Tatsumi Hamako relates the following story:

> Since I was a little girl, my grandmother emphasized repeatedly that each morning's miso soup and pickles should be carefully and tastefully prepared, especially if they were to be served to someone who smokes. She said that miso is a solvent for nicotine and helped to carry it out of the body.
>
> One day she placed 2 or 3 drops of miso soup in the small, ½-inch-deep metal bowl of a clogged, long-stemmed Japanese pipe (*kiseru*). She held the metal bowl over a charcoal fire until we could hear the sound of the miso soup simmering. After about one minute, all of the liquid had evaporated and only the nicotine which had dissolved in the miso soup was left in the bowl. This condensed into a small pellet and suddenly jumped out. When we placed the pipe to our lips, we found that it now

drew freely and easily. But at other times, when we tried using water or *bancha* tea in place of miso soup to clear the congested pipe, the nicotine refused to dissolve. Even if we blew vigorously on the pipe, we could not clear it. I realized that what grandmother had been saying was true.

It is said to be common knowledge among Japanese traffic policemen that the consumption of miso soup each day ameliorates the effects on the body of auto exhaust pollutants. Even today, in many areas where the police department provides communal lunches, a conscientious effort is made to include miso soup.

So if you have to smoke or breathe polluted air, at least protect yourself by drinking miso soup too.

A Seasoning of Unlimited Versatility

Even if there were only one variety of miso, its uses would invite endless experimentation. Yet each of the many miso varieties has its own unique flavor and aroma, color and texture, and each can lend the crowning touch to a wide variety of your favorite Western-style and Oriental dishes. The more than 400 recipes in the following pages give only an inkling of the many possibilities.

In a vegetarian diet, often characterized by the simple, light flavors of grains, land and sea vegetables, and soyfoods, miso has long served to add depth of flavor and savory richness.

A Traditional Natural Food

Capable of being stored without refrigeration, even in semitropical climates, miso is a traditional, natural food. Many commercial varieties are still prepared in small-scale shops using traditional technologies and without chemical additives.

An Inexpensive Delicacy

Miso is a remarkably inexpensive food, even in the West where prices of the best imported varieties are of necessity higher than they are in Japan. The per capita cost of a month's supply of top-quality miso (1½ tablespoons per day) in San Francisco, Boston, or New York need not exceed a few dollars (fig. 13, p. 91). And if the miso is prepared at home using ingredients now readily available throughout the United States, it will cost only a fraction as much.

A Key to the Vegetarian Transition

Polls taken in 1980 show that there are ten million people in the United States who eat no meat, and that the number is rapidly increasing. Recently, doctors and nutritionists have joined the bandwagon. Their arguments:

1. **Physiology:** Man's digestive system, like that of the anthropoid apes, is fundamentally different from that of carnivores. The latter have very short bowels (3 times the body's length) for rapid expulsion of putrefying meat, stomachs with ten times as much hydrochloric acid as non-carnivores for processing saturated fats and cholesterol, and sharp elongated canines for tearing flesh. Man, however, has a long bowel (12 times the body's length) ideal for the slow digestion of plant foods; his dental structure is that of a strictly herbivorous animal with molars designed for grinding grains and nuts and his incisors for slicing vegetables and fruits.

2. **Heart Disease:** Over 54 percent of all deaths in the United States are caused by cardiovascular illnesses which are practically unknown in societies where meat consumption is low. About 40 percent of the fat in our diet comes from meat, and 40 percent of this is the saturated, cholesterol-producing type. A recent study of Seventh Day Adventist vegetarians showed that they had only 40 percent the incidence of heart disease as the general population, and those that

ate neither eggs nor dairy products had only 23 percent. Heart specialists estimate that if we were to reduce our saturated fat intake by 35 to 50 percent, our heart attack rate could be cut in half.

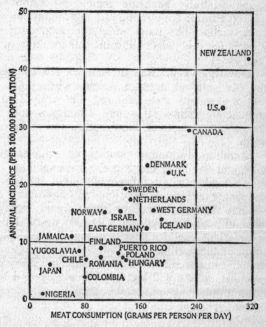

Fig. 5. Intestinal Cancer vs. Meat Consumption Among Females

(Source: Scientific American; Nov. 1975)

3. **Cancer:** The graph in figure 5, reprinted from the prestigious *Scientific American* magazine, shows the striking relationship between cancer of the large intestine and meat consumption among women in 23 countries; the writers explain that "an alternative explanation attributes cancer . . . to a low consumption of cereals. The two hypotheses are hard to distinguish from each other because high meat consumption and low cereal consumption tend to go together." Large

studies of Mormons (who characteristically eat little meat) show an incidence of cancer 50 percent below the norm.

4. **Longevity:** Repeated studies by anthropologists throughout the world show that vegetarians live longer and are generally healthier than meat eaters. The long-lived Hunzas are almost total vegetarians.

5. **Arthritis:** The most widely recommended dietary cures for this painful ailment call for strict avoidance of meat.

6. **Obesity:** Vegetarians in America are 20 pounds below the national average weight, while those following a standard meat-centered diet are 12 to 15 pounds above their ideal weight. Obesity is now considered a major cause of heart disease and many other illnesses.

7. **Stamina:** Numerous studies of athletes show that vegetarians have much more stamina than meat eaters, are able to perform endurance tests several times longer before exhaustion, and take less than one-fourth the time to recover from fatigue. A growing number of world record and Olympic medal holders are vegetarians. And for strength—look at the elephant, the bull, or the gorilla.

But . . . in the face of all this evidence, many people still ask, where will I get that meaty flavor I love?

From miso.

3

The Miracle of Fermentation

THE KEY TO the art of making fine miso lies in the process of fermentation, a process which, throughout its long and varied history around the world, has served three fundamental purposes: the improvement of a food's digestibility; the transformation of its flavor and aroma, color and texture; and its preservation without refrigeration. Watching the drama enlarged a thousandfold and presented in time-lapse color photography, one witnesses a near-miraculous world in which tiny spores burst into blossom like elegant and complex flowers, enzymes reach out inquisitively like long fingers melting solid particles at their touch, and populations of mold explode until they have totally enveloped the foods—or "substrates"—which support their life.

Just as Western craftsmen have fermented milk to form cheese and yogurt, or grapes to form wine, Eastern craftsmen have fermented soybeans and grains to form miso, shoyu, and tempeh. In each case, the *dramatis personae* are myriads of microorganisms which serve as the vital essence and force of the living fermentation process. These tiny creatures work best at their own unhurried pace, timed by the great rhythmic movements of the four seasons and the delicate biochemical changes occurring in their "household." Man serves his highest function by understanding the laws of change written into these life processes and providing the optimum conditions for their natural unfoldment. He thus becomes a partner with the Master Alchemist in creating a masterpiece of fine flavor.

All natural miso is prepared in basically the same

way, using a two-part fermentation process.* To prepare rice miso, for example, rice is soaked overnight,
drained, and then steamed. Cooled to body temperature, it is mixed with a small amount of "koji starter"
consisting of spores of the mold *Aspergillus oryzae*
(*Ass-per-JIL-us oh-RAI-zee*). Every craftsman prizes
and guards his favorite strains of this mold, since they
are essential to imparting a unique character to his
miso. Some strains have been in the custody of family-
run shops for generations: they permeate the tools,
the vats, the very air.

The inoculated rice is spread in shallow wooden
trays and incubated in a warm, humid room for about
45 hours. Here it becomes bound together by a bloom
of fragrant white mold. This mold-covered grain is
called *koji*. The function of the koji molds is to produce enzymes that will later break down proteins,
starches, and fats into more readily digestible amino
acids, simple sugars, and fatty acids.

The first fermentation complete, the koji is crumbled to break up the mat-like mycelium, thereby giving the koji an appearance similar to rice crispies that
have been dusted with flour. It is then combined with
cooked soybeans, a little of the soybean cooking
liquid, salt, and a small amount of mature miso from a
previous fermentation. This "seed miso" introduces
distinctive yeasts and bacteria from the shop's miso
lineage while making it possible to complete the next
step in a shorter time.

The ingredients are mashed together (traditionally
underfoot, like grapes for wine, in shallow wooden
tubs), then packed into 6-foot-deep cedar vats. Covered with a layer of sheeting and a wooden pressing
lid topped with heavy weights, they now begin their
second fermentation. While enzymatic digestion gets
underway, a small amount of liquid rises to the surface creating a sealed, airtight environment that prevents the entry of contaminating microorganisms.
Once the complex soy and grain nutrients have been

* For a more detailed discussion of the microbiology and
chemistry of miso fermentation, see Appendix C.

broken down into their simpler forms, yeasts and bacteria propagate. The bacteria, primarily lactic acid–formers such as *Pediococcus halophilus* and *Lactobacillus delbruekii,* transform simple sugars into various organic acids which impart a unique flavor to the miso and help prevent spoilage. The yeasts react with sugars to produce alcohols, contributing to the miso's aroma. Eventually, alcohols and acids react with one another to produce esters, which become the chief components of the miso bouquet. Time mellows the sharpness of the salt and harmonizes it with the other deepening flavors. Slowly the color of the mixture turns from its initial light tan or yellow to rich shades of brown.

The character of a miso is determined largely by the proportions of koji and salt to soybeans. Misos made from a mixture in which koji predominates tend to be sweet since the koji enzymes break down the abundant grain carbohydrates into simple sugars. The use of a relatively large proportion of salt slows down the fermentation process and the resulting lengthy aging yields a product having a dark color and deep, rich flavor. By contrast, a miso low in salt and rich in koji requires only a short fermentation and its sweet flavor is usually accompanied by a light color.

In large tile-roofed, almost window-less buildings that serve to insulate the miso from extremes of heat and cold, fermentation continues throughout the year with the greatest activity during the warm months and almost none at all during the dead of winter. When, after one to three summers, the miso has come to maturity, it contains an immense number of vital and very beneficial microorganisms and enzymes. These are present in the natural miso you serve, ready to continue their work of aiding digestion within the human body.

Miso Aging (from Miso Daigaku)

4

The Varieties of Miso

THE MOST COMMON classification divides the world of miso into three basic groups: *regular miso,* consisting of three types—rice, barley, and soybean—is used primarily in cooking and, in Japan, particularly in soups; *special miso,* consisting of two types—finger lickin' and sweet simmered miso—is used primarily as a topping for grain dishes, fresh vegetable slices and tofu, and is usually not cooked; and *modern miso* consisting of a group of products developed since the end of World War II. Each type is represented by a number of unique varieties (fig. 6), for every batch of miso differs according to the proportions of ingredients used, the cooking methods employed, and the duration and temperature of fermentation. Each craftsman, professional or amateur, produces miso which is an expression of his tradition, his mastery of the craft and, in the case of natural miso, the dominant and subtle climatic factors affecting the environment in which he lives. As is the case with the world's fine cheeses or wines, individual representatives of the same miso variety, each often bearing the name of its birthplace, differ according to their region and year of origin: a red (rice) miso made in Sendai, for example, is not the same as one made in Tokyo, while one shop's barley miso of 1980 "vintage" may be distinctly different from that made the year before using identical ingredients.

In recent years, the number of miso varieties has steadily increased. Many unknown several generations ago outside the immediate region in which they have traditionally been prepared are now available throughout the country and even in the West.

An Overview

Before we go on to a discussion of the classical varieties and their major subdivisions, it might be best to begin with an overview. The world of miso lends itself to just such a perspective since all varieties share six principal attributes: method of fermentation, flavor, color, texture, cost, and region of origin.

' **Natural vs. Quick Miso:** Natural miso, universally regarded as having the finest flavor, is prepared in the traditional way and has three basic characteristics: it is fermented slowly and leisurely (usually for six months to three years) at the natural temperature of its environment; it is made from only natural ingredients and contains no defatted soybean meal (an inexpensive substitute for whole soybeans) or chemical additives (except, in some cases, ethyl alcohol, p. 580); and it is never pasteurized. Most natural misos have a distinctive texture imparted by clearly visible chunks of whole soybeans and koji. About 97½ percent of Japan's miso is made with whole beans, 70 percent contains no chemical additives, 50 percent is not pasteurized, and 35 percent is fermented under natural conditions. Since some of the varieties which are not pasteurized *do* contain additives, only about 25 percent of Japan's total output is estimated to be *completely* natural. The three varieties most widely prepared in the traditional way (red, barley, and Hatcho) are called for in the majority of recipes in this book.

When measuring the age of natural miso, the Japanese (and Chinese) use an unusual system which has caused some confusion in the West. In the Orient, the age of miso—and of people—is calculated in the same way we reckon the age of race horses; regardless of the actual date of production or "birth," the miso becomes one year older on the first day of each new year. Thus New Year's, the most important holiday of the year in East Asia, is everyone's and everything's birthday. And miso started in the fall of one year and harvested 12 months later is called "two-year miso," since it has been in existence during two calendar years. "Three-year" barley and Hatcho miso are often actually aged for only 18 months.

Quick miso, a 20 to 30 percent less expensive modern product, is fermented for a short time (generally about three weeks but sometimes for as little as three days) in a temperature-controlled, heated environ-

GROUP	TYPE	VARIETY	FLAVOR	COLOR	FRAGRANCE AND AROMA	NATURAL AGING TIME	JAPANESE NAMES AND SUB-VARIETIES	PLACE OF PRODUCTION	PROTEIN %	CARBO-HY-DRATE %	SALT %	INGREDIENTS PER 10 LBS. SOYBEANS	
												DRIED KOJI (LBS.)	SALT (LBS.)
REGULAR MISO	Rice Miso	Red Miso (incl. Brown-rice Miso)	Deep rich saltiness	Reddish brown to russet	Deep fermented aroma	6 to 12 months	Aka-miso, Genmai Miso, Sendai, Sado, Echigo, Tsugaru	Tohoku, Niigata, Sado, Hokkaido, Hokuriku, Chugoku	13.5	19.1	13.0	8.5	4.4
		Light-yellow Miso	Mature rounded saltiness with subtle tartness	Bright light yellow	Light refreshing aroma	1 to 2 years	Shinshu Miso, Akita Miso	Nagano, Tokyo Area, Akita	13.5	19.6	12.5	7	4.1
		Mellow Red Miso	Deep semi-sweetness	Yellowish red	Rich fragrance	3 to 6 months	Amakuchi Aka-miso, Gozen Miso	Urban Centers	11.2	27.9	13.0	14	4.0
		Mellow Beige Miso	Light semi-sweetness	Yellow to tan	Light mild fragrance	5 to 20 days	Amakuchi Tanshoku Miso, Ajiro Miso, Mochigomé Miso	Nagano, Tokyo Area, Urban Centers	13.0	29.1	7.0	12	4.7
		Mellow White Miso	Rich, heady mellowness	Light beige	Subtly sweet, fermented fragrance	4 weeks	Shiro-koji Miso	Hawaii	12.3	27.5	9.1	15	3.4
		Sweet Red Miso	Rich, deep sweetness	Lustrous reddish brown	Savory and sweet	5 to 20 days	Edo Ama-miso	Tokyo	12.7	31.7	6.0	13	2.2
		Sweet White Miso	Light, rich dessert-like sweetness	Ivory to yellowish white	Light, sweet springtime fragrance	1 to 4 weeks	Shiro Miso, Saikyo Miso, Fuchu Miso, Sanuki Miso	Kyoto, Hiroshima, Takamatsu	11.1	35.9	5.5	20	2.4
	Barley Miso	Barley Miso	Deep rich saltiness	Dark reddish brown	Prominent barley aroma	1 to 3 years	Karakuchi Mugi Miso	Kyushu, Saitama	12.8	21.0	13.0	10	4.6
		Mellow Barley Miso	Deep, rich subtle sweetness	Yellowish brown to russet	Subtle barley fragrance	10 to 20 days	Amakuchi Mugi Miso	Kyushu, Chugoku, Shikoku	11.1	29.8	10.0	17	4.8
	Soybean Miso	Hatcho Miso	Mellow richness, subtly tart	Chocolate brown	Distinctive rich, deep aroma	18 to 36 months	Hatcho Miso, Waka-Hatcho, Sanshu Miso	Aichi, Okazaki	21	12	10.6	0	2.0
		Soybean Miso	Mellow saltiness	Dark reddish brown	Prominent soy aroma	1 year	Ichi-nen Namé Miso, Nagoya Miso	Aichi, Mie, Gifu	19.4	13.2	11.2	0	2.1
		Tamari Miso	Deep saltiness	Dark brown	Deep, heavy soy aroma	1 year	Tamari Miso	Aichi, Mie, Gifu	20	12.3	11.3	0	2.4
SPECIAL MISO	Finger-Lickin' Miso	Kinzanji Moromi Hishio Namémiso Natto Goto	Rich fermented sweetness	Golden brown to dark amber	Deep barley fragrance	20 to 60 days	Namémiso	All Japan	11	30	8	20	3
	Sweet Simmered Miso	Peanut Walnut Sesame Yuzu Kinomé Red-snapper Tekka	Sweet and varied	Varied	Varied		Nerimiso	All Japan, Homes, Restaurants	14	37	7	-	-
MODERN MISO	Modern Miso	Akadashi Miso	Rich, mellow sweetness	Dark reddish brown	Savory sweet		Akadashi Miso	Aichi, Kyoto	16	31.9	10	-	-
		Dehydrated Miso	Varied	Varied	Varied		Kanso Miso, Kona Miso	Tokyo	32.2	35.8	18.5	-	-
		Low-salt/High-protein Miso	Mild saltiness	Tan	Mild aroma		Gen-en Miso	Tokyo	17.6	14.0	6.3	-	-

Fig. 6. The Varieties of Miso

ment. The short fermentation does not allow it to develop the full mellowness of flavor and aroma, deep color, and long-lasting properties characteristic of natural miso. Hence, various chemicals and synthetics (bleaches, food colorings, sweeteners, vitamins, and monosodium glutamate) are occasionally added together with preservatives (ethyl alcohol or sorbic acid). Most quick miso is also pasteurized to prevent its microorganisms from producing carbon dioxide which would cause the plastic bags in which it is packaged to swell and sometimes explode. Pasteurization, like overcooking, causes a further decline in the miso's flavor and aroma, and, by killing the microorganisms which would otherwise aid digestion in the human body, lowers the miso's nutritional value. Most quick miso has a smooth texture since the soybeans and koji are ground together usually twice, once in the vats to shorten the fermentation time and again later during pasteurization. Prepared with a large proportion of koji and small amount of salt to further accelerate fermentation, quick miso is also usually quite sweet. First manufactured on a large scale during the 1960s, it is now mass-produced in modern factories, as described in Chapter 10.

Like quick miso, naturally fermented varieties are also now available in 1- to 2-pound polyethylene bags which allow for better distribution. To prevent swelling, most miso (except Hatcho) sealed in bags is pasteurized and/or contains ethyl alcohol or sorbic acid preservative. If packed in bulk kegs or cottage cheese-type containers, pasteurization and additives become unnecessary.

Salty vs. Sweet Miso: All misos can be grouped according to their salt content as shown in figure 7.

Varieties containing 10½ to 14 percent salt are generally low in carbohydrates (20% or less) and have a savory, rather salty flavor. At the other extreme, those containing less than 7 percent salt are generally rich in carbohydrates (30 percent or more) and enjoy a heady sweetness. Note that all misos are assumed to be salty unless specifically designated otherwise. When thinned in ½ cup water, 2 teaspoons of salty miso produce about the same strength broth as 3 to 4 teaspoons mellow or 5 to 6 teaspoons

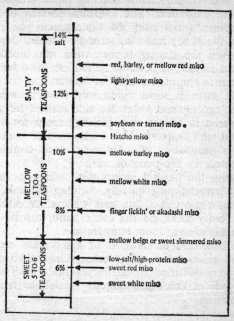

Fig. 7. The Percentage of Salt in Different Miso Varieties

sweet miso. (Mellow red miso, which contains 13 percent salt, falls outside its proper domain; due to its abundant carbohydrates, it actually has a flavor similar to that of mellow barley miso.)

Japan's sweetest misos are found in Kyoto, her ancient capital, and Tokyo, her present-day metropolitan center. As one moves from modern urban areas to more traditional farming and fishing districts, the preferred miso grows saltier and more of it is made at home. Consumption patterns demonstrate that urban office workers, young people, and the upper classes prefer the sweeter varieties, whereas farmers, laborers, and elderly adults prefer the saltier. As one might expect, the consumption of sweet miso has increased and that of salty miso has decreased since the end of

World War II, paralleling Japan's rapid urbanization and industrialization. The Western pattern of sugar consumption (now over 14 tablespoons per person daily in the U.S.) has also strongly affected Japanese tastes. And the shorter fermentation time needed by the sweet misos has been an added incentive for manufacturers to emphasize their production.

Sweet miso is most commonly used in toppings, spreads, sauces, and vegetable side dishes; salty miso is preferred in soups, as a pickling agent for vegetables, and with seafoods. One tablespoon of sweet miso and 1½ teaspoons of salty miso each contain approximately ¼ teaspoon of salt.

Because the natural sugars with which it abounds tend to ferment quite quickly, forming alcohols, sweet miso has a short shelf life and is therefore difficult to export. Salty miso, on the other hand, can be stored indefinitely even at room temperature.

The sweetness or saltiness of a miso has no hard-and-fast relationship to its color. Generally, though, saltier varieties tend to be darker since both salinity and depth of color are directly related to length of fermentation.

Red vs. White Miso: Like wines, all misos can be divided into reds (actually russets and warm chestnut browns) and whites (soft light-yellows and creamy beiges). Most red miso, like red wine, obtains its coloration from natural changes requiring lengthy aging, whereas white miso is generally prepared by quick, temperature-controlled fermentation. In general, rice miso tends to be lighter in color than barley miso, and barley miso tends to be lighter than soybean miso.

The great majority of Japan's white miso is made with rice koji and contains a large proportion of carbohydrates and relatively little salt; hence, most white miso is rather sweet. The soybeans used are carefully selected to exclude dark varieties, dehulled to give them an even lighter coloration, and then pressure cooked under water (rather than in steam) for a relatively short time; in some cases a small amount of bleach is added to the cooking and/or soaking water.

After cooking, all water is immediately expelled (with the loss of valuable nutrients), and the beans are cooled rapidly in a partial vacuum inside the pressure cooker to further minimize oxidation and browning. Yellow-riboflavin food coloring (vitamin B-2) is sometimes added before fermentation to give the bleached end-product a more natural-looking luster. Packed into vats and well sealed, the miso is fermented quickly in a warm environment. Very light-colored sweet varieties are often shipped to retailers before the end of fermentation; they come to maturity en route and on the shelves in order to minimize darkening and spoilage. Varieties sealed in bags may have bleach added just before packaging.

Most white miso is a very modern product. The ancient sweet white miso of Kyoto was not nearly as white as its present descendants, since it was prepared by natural fermentation without bleaches or pressure cooking, and contained less carbohydrates. Recently, the consumption of light-colored miso has grown rapidly with the increase in the number of large-scale miso factories which find it more profitable to produce, and under the influence of modern advertising which has worked to create the image that "white" (as in white rice, white bread, and white sugar) is beautiful. Like most sweet miso, and for the same reasons, white varieties have a short shelf life and are difficult to export.

NOTE: In Japan, the term "red miso" (*aka* miso), used in its usual narrow sense, refers only to salty red rice miso. However, in its broad sense it may refer to any miso with a reddish or dark brown color. The term "white miso" (*shiro* miso) usually refers only to Kyoto-style sweet white miso; "light-colored miso" (*tanshoku* miso) is generally used to refer to all yellowish or whitish varieties. Occasionally the term "black miso" is used to refer to the darker varieties of soybean miso.

Chunky and Koji vs. Smooth Miso: Chunky miso (*tsubu miso*) is any variety in which the shape of the soybeans (and usually of the koji grains) is still visible.

It is the oldest form of miso and comprised virtually all that made before 1945. During the mixing and mashing of ingredients before the fermentation of natural miso, almost all of the koji and at least half of the soybeans were left in their natural form. The koji gradually dissolved as the miso aged, but the beans generally retained their individual form, even after three years of fermentation, thereby lending the finished miso a distinctive, flavor-enhancing texture.

In koji miso, the form and texture of the koji grains are still visible. Prepared by mashing the cooked soybeans thoroughly before they are combined with the koji and salt, koji miso, with its distinctive texture, is usually quite young (12 to 18 months). It nevertheless retains a strong appeal among miso connoisseurs.

Smooth miso is that which has been blended or ground to a homogeneous purée. First prepared after 1945, it now comprises about 80 percent of all miso sold in Japan. It derives much of its appeal from the fact that the Japanese have traditionally ground their miso with a little water before adding it to soups; smooth miso saves modern cooks the time and trouble. In factories making quick miso, this smooth-textured product is an inevitable result of the production process since all of the ingredients are ground anyway, once to shorten the fermentation time and then again to reinforce the effects of pasteurization.

Expensive vs. Inexpensive Miso: In Japan, miso varieties sold in polyethylene bags through supermarkets and grocery stores are the least expensive. The same miso automatically rises in price when it is sold out of open-top kegs at traditional miso retail outlets. To avoid pasteurization and the use of preservatives, much natural miso is still sold in the latter way, but many varieties of even natural (unpasteurized) miso now contain ethyl alcohol preservative and can be found in natural food stores for relatively low prices packaged in polyethylene bags.

In general, rice miso is less expensive than barley miso, and barley miso is less expensive than soybean miso. The least expensive misos, often characterized by a soft texture due to the addition of extra water, are usually quick misos made by large-scale production methods. More expensive misos are frequently natural varieties made by small, tradition- and quality-oriented companies.

In 1980 miso prices in Japan ranged from about $0.43 per pound for quick light-yellow miso to about $1.13 per pound for Hatcho, sweet white, and other fine natural misos. The average price per pound of quick miso was $0.48 compared with $0.69 for natural varieties. At the same time in the United States, imported natural miso packaged in polyethylene bags sold at natural-food stores for the following average prices per pound: red miso $1.54, brown-rice miso $1.84, barley miso $1.70, Hatcho miso $2.04, and finger-lickin' miso (including natto miso) $2.05. For other U.S. miso prices, see page 91.

Miso from the Provinces: In Japan, the many varieties of miso are often grouped according to the provinces or regions in which they are produced. Like many of the world's wines and cheeses, the majority of Japan's traditional misos bear the name of their birthplace. A miso having a history deeply rooted in the provinces is often called *tochi* miso, or "miso of the land," and is especially prized.

If one travels the entire length of the Japanese archipelago from southwest to northeast—a distance of about 1,360 miles—one would find that as the climate changes from warm to cold, the preferred miso generally changes from sweet to salty and consumption tends to increase. In the southern third of Japan, barley miso is preferred; in the central third, soybean miso; and in the northern third, rice miso (fig. 8).

REGULAR MISO

Our overview complete, let us proceed to the three major groupings outlined at the start of this chapter. The first group, regular miso, constitutes about 90 to 95 percent of all commercial miso prepared in Japan. The three basic types—rice, barley, and soybean miso—are classified according to the basic raw material or substrate used for the koji. The production of rice miso predominates (81% of yearly output in this category), followed by barley (11%) and soybean (8%). Each type may be further divided on the basis of flavor into sweet, mellow, and salty, and then subdivided on the basis of color into red, light-yellow, and white varieties (fig. 6, p. 49).

The following three types and 12 varieties of miso are widely available throughout Japan. Within each variety are hundreds of subvarieties which differ according to the maker, process, ingredients, and locality of origin.

Rice Miso
(Komé Miso)

Prohibitively expensive as recently as 50 to 100 years ago, rice miso now accounts for 81 percent of the miso sold in Japan. In fact, today all miso is assumed to fall under this classification unless otherwise stated, just as all miso is assumed to be salty-tasting unless specifically called sweet; hence salty red rice miso is simply called "red miso." Very rich in glucose and other natural sugars, rice serves as the basis of the koji used in most of Japan's sweet, quick, and white misos. The finest salty rice misos have traditionally been produced in the cold provinces north of Tokyo noted for yielding high-quality rice.

The scarcity of rice miso in traditional Japan is thought to be due to the fact that rice—and especially the polished or milled rice from which most rice miso has always been made—was a food reserved for the aristocracy and samurai. Feudal peasants were required to send the rice they grew to their lords, leaving them with only barley, although in some areas, the farmers were allowed to collect broken rice kernels to prepare their miso. Thus, part of the present popularity of rice miso in Japan is an expression of the ancient tendency to regard rice and rice miso as foods of the upper classes.

Variety	Native Region	Soy-beans	Rice	Salt	Natural Fermentation
Red Miso (incl. Brown-rice miso)	Northeast provinces	10	8.5	4.4	1-3 years
Light-yellow	Shinshu	10	7.0	4.1	1-3 years
Mellow Red	Urban centers	10	14.0	4.0	4-7 weeks*
Mellow Beige	Urban centers	10	12.0	4.7	3-4 weeks*
Mellow White	Hawaii	10	15.0	3.4	4-6 weeks
Sweet Red	Tokyo (Edo)	10	13.0	2.2	2-5 weeks
Sweet White	Kyoto	10	20.0	2.4	1-4 weeks
					*Quick fermentation only

Red Miso *(Aka Miso):* Fermented naturally for one to three years or by temperature-controlled methods for three to four months, red miso has a rich-and-savory salty flavor with subtly sweet undertones. Deeply fragrant, its color ranges from lustrous russet to dark reddish brown; its texture from chunky-and-soft to smooth-and-firm. It takes its Japanese name (*Sendai miso*) from the city in the northeastern provinces which has served as the center of red miso production since ancient times.

Of all types of regular miso, whether rice, barley or soybean, red miso has the lowest proportion of carbohydrates (19.1%), the second highest proportion of protein (13.5%), and the highest proportion of salt (13%). Thus the natural product can be stored for several years at room temperature and, in most cases, the flavor will actually improve over time. A popular and versatile miso, it is well suited for use in all types of cookery. An estimated 75 percent of all the rice miso now sold commercially in Japan, and virtually all the rice miso prepared in farmhouses, is red (or light-yellow, as described below).

Well-known sub-varieties of red miso are listed in figure 9; their places of origin are shown on the map on page 58. Of particular historical interest is the de-

Fig. 8. Geographical Miso Preference

licious Sado miso, which was developed about 350 years ago on Sado Island in the Japan Sea far to the north of Tokyo. Centuries ago, a famous shipping route led from Osaka around the southern tip of Honshu to Sado Island, and then on to Japan's north-ernmost island, Hokkaido. Ships transported Sado miso to Hokkaido where it was too cold to make a local variety, and on the return voyage brought back high-quality Hokkaido soybeans, which were used in subsequent batches of Sado miso. Sado islanders now grow their own fine beans, and their miso is known for its subtly-sweet flavor and koji texture.

A sub-variety of rice miso that has recently won considerable favor in the West is brown-rice miso. It has a delectable natural flavor, deep and mellow, and a satisfying fragrance. This miso is endowed with real character, is loaded with nutrients found in the rice's bran layers, and is priced quite reasonably. Its fermentation time is 6 to 18 months. At present, a number of Japanese producers make brown-rice miso (see Appendix D); the product most widely sold in

America is made by Sendai Miso-Shoyu. Most red miso has always been made with white rice because: 1) the surface layers of brown rice are so nutritious that alien microorganisms as well as the koji mold spores tend to thrive and produce off-flavors; 2) preventing this phenomenon requires delicate temperature control during koji preparation; 3) the koji mycelium has difficulty penetrating the bran layers and therefore in breaking down the central portions of the rice kernels; 4) most modern Japanese prefer the flavor of white to brown rice. The rice used to make brown-rice koji is polished very slightly to aid penetration of the mycelium; about 2½ pounds of bran are removed from each 100 pounds of unpolished grain as compared with 10 pounds when making white rice. In some cases, the rice is also split before being steamed. The preparation of the koji is identical to that using white rice except that the temperature is kept within a narrower range of the ideal at each step in the process.

Light-Yellow Miso *(Shinshu Miso):* Shinshu refers to the ancient province north of Tokyo—now Nagano prefecture—where this popular variety was first developed. Originally resembling Sendai red in proportion of basic ingredients, color, and flavor, Shinshu contained slightly less salt and therefore enjoyed a subtle and highly prized tartness. Whereas Sendai miso was generally chunky, Shinshu was smooth, and some varieties were prepared with black soybeans. Traditional Shinshu, usually fermented for at least one year, is still made in farmhouses in its native locality but is no longer widely available on a commercial basis. Akita miso, its close relative, has a sweeter flavor and lighter color (see chart below).

Modern Shinshu, which we call light-yellow miso, is a quick miso the best examples of which have a mature and mellow salty flavor, and a subtle tart quality. Light and refreshing in aroma, its color ranges from light yellow to yellowish brown, and its firm texture is almost always smooth. Low in carbohydrates (19.6%) and quite high in both salt (12.5%) and protein (13.5%), it keeps for up to two months at room temperature, but for longer storage must be refrigerated. Prepared by temperature-controlled fermentation in only three to four weeks, light-yellow miso is Japan's least expensive variety. Some varieties may contain bleach and vitamin B-2 food coloring.

According to popular tradition, the original Shinshu miso was developed about 450 years ago by Takeda Shingen, a great and powerful samurai living in the Nagano area. This progenitor of modern Shinshu was prepared commercially in farmhouses as early as 1924 (using sodium sulfite bleach), but large-scale production and distribution did not start until after 1945. Most light-yellow miso is still produced in Nagano, although 95 percent of it is shipped throughout the rest of Japan and accounts for over 20 per-

Fig. 9. Famous Subvarieties of Salty Rice Miso

Japanese Name	Koji (% by wt. of soybeans)	Salt (% by wt. of miso)	Characteristics
Sendai	60	13.6	Chunky texture, soybeans cracked coarsely, deep-red color, long aging
Echigo Red miso	60–65[1] 80–120[2]	14.0 12.2	Chunky texture with white koji mosaic on fine-grained soybean base
Sado	60–65	15.4	Chunky or smooth texture, long aging
Tsugaru	50	14.6	Deep-red color, long aging
Shinshu Light-yellow miso	60–90	13.0	Radiant light-yellow color, smooth texture
Akita	80–100	12.3	Yellowish gold color midway between Shinshu and Sendai, relatively low salt content
	1) Niigata type	2) Joetsu type	

cent of all miso consumed in the nation. Especially popular in Tokyo and central Japan, it is used in all types of cooking. The most widely available miso presently produced in the United States falls under this category. Light-yellow miso may be substituted for red or barley miso in any of the recipes in this book.

Mellow Red Miso *(Amakuchi Akamiso):* A close relative of red miso, this variety is prepared with exactly the same amount of salt (13.0%) but a much larger percentage of koji and thus of carbohydrates (27.9% vs. 19.1%), resulting in a slightly sweeter flavor. The traditional representative of this category is Gozen miso, a specialty of the city of Tokushima on Shikoku Island. Fermented naturally for six to 12 months, it attains a deep reddish-brown color. Since World War II, a number of quick varieties have been developed, which are prepared with pressure-steamed ingredients and fermented without the use of additives in a temperature-controlled environment for three to six months.

Mellow Beige Miso *(Amakuchi Tanshoku Miso):* This broad category is a catch-all for the many quick, light-colored misos developed as imitations of modern Shinshu but forbidden by law to use the Shinshu name. *Amakuchi* means "moderately sweet" and *Tanshoku* means "light-colored," indicating that these products are midway in flavor between sweet and salty, and in color between red and white. By 1969 this miso (together with its close relatives mellow red miso and light-yellow Shinshu) accounted for a full 70 percent of all miso sold in Japan, but its popularity is now waning as traditional varieties return to favor.

Mellow beige miso was explicitly designed to use proportions of raw materials that would minimize both the fermentation time and the cost of ingredients, and thereby maximize profits. Thus, typical products are relatively rich in carbohydrates (29.1%), and low in salt (7.0%) and protein (13.0%). The light color is produced by pressure-boiling and short fermentation (3 to 4 weeks) in a temperature-controlled environment, often together with the use of bleach and food coloring.

The traditional representatives of this category are Aijiro miso and Kyushu miso, neither of which is now widely available. Aijiro, made only in Shizuoka prefecture, was first created about 350 years ago as an imitation of Kyoto's sweet white miso, but it is not quite as sweet.

A unique subvariety of mellow beige miso is Glutinous-Rice Miso *(mochigomé miso)*. Prepared with 3 parts soybeans and 7 parts glutinous rice, it has a thick smooth texture, light yellow color, and fairly sweet flavor. First developed during the 1970s, it is sold only by the Hinode Miso Co.

Mellow White Miso *(Shiro Koji Miso):* The rich natural flavor of this variety is nicely harmonized with a subtly sweet fermented fragrance, reminiscent of *amazaké*. Unlike its slightly sweeter relative, sweet white miso, this mellow miso is a completely natural product, fermented at the temperature of its environment and prepared without pasteurization, preservatives, or bleach. Made only in Honolulu, it is now widely available on the American mainland where it is reasonably priced ($1.29 per pound) and generally sold in white cottage cheese-type containers bearing the name "Shiro White Miso." It is not available in Japan.

Midway between red and sweet white miso in salt content, it is highly versatile and can be substituted for either in most recipes in this book; use twice as much mellow white as red miso or two-thirds as much as the sweet miso called for. A good approximation of sweet white miso's flavor can be obtained by mixing ½ teaspoon honey with 4 teaspoons mellow white miso. By using a pinch of salt instead of the honey you can approximate the flavor of light-yellow miso.

Sweet Red Miso *(Edo Miso* or *Edo Ama-miso):* Endowed with a rich, slightly savory aroma and a deep, mellow sweetness, Edo miso contains a large proportion of carbohydrates (32%) and is relatively low in salt (6%) and protein (12.7%). Ranging in color from light reddish brown to lustrous russet, its traditional texture was always chunky, but many contemporary products are smooth and soft. Because virtually all varieties, even though they now contain preservatives, begin to change flavor after two to four weeks unless refrigerated, Edo miso is difficult to export.

Edo, the ancient name of modern Tokyo, is also the title of an era which began in 1603. It is said that Ieyasu Tokugawa, Japan's ruling shogun at the time, developed Edo miso in order to combine the best features of Hatcho miso, his hometown favorite, and Kyoto's sweet white miso, very popular at the time among the upper classes. In the days before the Japanese had access to sugar, Edo miso was a widely used sweetening agent. Today it is most popular in soups, where it is often mixed with red miso. Mixed with *azuki* beans, it becomes the filling for *Kashiwa Mochi* (p. 384), a famous confection served each year on Boy's Day. It is also used in Dengaku (p. 355), Nuta (p. 224), Sweetened Tekka Miso (p. 144), and nabé dishes such as Doténabé (p. 350). In Western-style preparations, it is delicious in spreads, dips, and dressings.

Most of Japan's sweet red (Edo) miso is still produced and consumed in the Tokyo area. To this day, it is made by an ingenious method of natural temperature-controlled fermentation: the miso is packed into vats while the soybeans are still hot, and the vats are wrapped with heavy rice-straw mats to keep in the heat. Although fermented for as few as ten to 20 days in summer and four to five weeks in winter, this miso enjoys a deep reddish color thanks to a unique cooking method in which the beans are boiled for a long time, allowed to stand overnight in the cauldron, then reheated before going into the vat.

A fairly good approximation of Edo miso's flavor can be obtained by mixing 3 parts red miso with 1 part honey.

Sweet White Miso *(Shiro Miso, Kyoto Shiro Miso,* or *Saikyo Miso):* Also known as "Kyoto white miso" or simply "white miso," this variety is made by combining as much as 4 parts by weight of rice koji with only 2 parts soybeans and 1 part salt. Deliciously sweet, it is so smooth it can be spread like butter on pancakes or bread. Its light refreshing flavor goes well with fresh fruits and crisp vegetables, and lends a rich, mellow quality to desserts. Ranging in color from ivory to light yellow, its fragrance is reminiscent of springtime.

Highest of all misos in carbohydrates (36%) and lowest in salt (5.5%) and protein (11.1%), its abundance of natural sugars hastens the fermentation process so that the average *natural* aging period is only three weeks, becoming as short as one week during the summer and as long as one to two months during winter. Many makers now calculate the fermentation time to include the time in transit to food stores and sitting on the shelves. If allowed to stand unrefrigerated for more than one week in summer or one month in winter, it develops a slightly alcoholic or sour flavor and reddish color. Refrigerated, however, it will keep for two months or more. Difficult to export, many varieties—whether sold in open-top kegs or sealed polyethylene bags—have been pasteurized and contain preservatives plus small amounts of bleach; some contain 2 to 3 percent added sweeteners from refined grain sugars (*mizuamé*)

Costing 63 to 83 cents per pound, this is one of Japan's most expensive misos. It is used as a pickling agent for fish and vegetables, as a topping for the grilled tofu dish Dengaku, in a special New Year's soup, Ozoni (p. 246), in Japanese confections (mixed with *azuki* beans), and in a wide variety of *aemono* or salad dressings, sauces and spreads. Except in the Kyoto area, it is used rather infrequently in soups.

For centuries a famous product of Kyoto, it is a featured ingredient at many of the city's restaurants offering Zen Temple Cookery or Tea Ceremony Cuisine. Two large, well-known Kyoto companies, Honda and Ishino (p. 570), account for most of the nation's production. One delicious variety sold as "Hanabishi Shiro Miso" is now widely available in the United States. Produced by Nakamuraya & Co., it is pasteurized and contains preservatives and bleach. Well known sub-varieties of sweet white miso include Hiroshima's Fuchu Miso and Takamatsu's Sanuki Miso.

The commercial preparation of sweet white miso involves a rather complex process which is said to be a well guarded secret of its Kyoto manufacturers. Many Tokyo shops have tried to duplicate it but none have succeeded. Due to its short shelf life, this miso was traditionally prepared in shops only during the cold months (from October until March) without preservatives or bleaches. It is still made in farmhouses in Wakayama prefecture, especially during March and April. In modern factories, it is prepared in the general manner described previously for white miso except that, like sweet red (Edo) miso, it is packed into the fermentation vats while the mixture is still quite hot.

Since this miso can be prepared very quickly, it is an excellent variety to try making at home. A fairly good approximation of its flavor can be obtained by mixing 2 parts by volume of light-yellow miso, 1 part honey, and 1 part water.

Barley Miso (*Mugi Miso*)

Most barley miso is darker, saltier, and aged longer than rice miso. Generally sold in the traditional chunky or koji form, its distinctive texture is one of its preferred characteristics. Each barley grain has a clearly visible dark line—known in Japanese as its "loincloth"—running the length of the kernel: this line gives the miso a unique appearance. The koji is prepared from polished or pearled barley—either the regular (*O-mugi*) or "naked" (*Hadaka-*

mugi) varieties—which are higher in protein (11% vs. 7.5%) and lower in carbohydrates (67% vs. 73%) than polished rice. Therefore barley miso is generally not as sweet as its rice counterpart and takes a longer time to ferment.

At present, barley miso comprises only 11 percent of the miso sold in Japan. Nevertheless, since low-cost barley was once widely grown throughout the warmer parts of the country, and since the Chinese ideograph for the word *koji* is composed of characters meaning "barley" and "chrysanthemum," many miso scholars believe that barley miso was Japan's most popular variety from ancient times up until 50 to 100 years ago. Other authorities contend, however, that miso has always been made using the predominant grain of each region and that in most areas rice and rice miso have always been produced in greater quantities. In any event, although a large amount of farmhouse miso is still made with barley koji and many farmers believe that barley and barley miso are foods which promote long life and good health, barley miso has nevertheless gradually decreased in popularity during the past century.

Barley miso's decline has been most pronounced among urbanites and young people. Japanese miso makers, scholars, and cooks suggest a number of possible reasons for this phenomenon: 1) Barley, which even now sells for only 40 percent the cost of rice, has long been considered a poor man's grain. The miso made from it seems to have acquired low-class associations, and as people move upward socially and economically, they tend to use less and less of it, preferring rice miso instead; 2) Barley miso's heady flavor and earthy aroma, its high salt and low sugar content, no longer suit the more refined tastes and needs of urbanites; and its dark color is considered to be outdated; 3) Its chunky texture makes it inconvenient for use in creamy-smooth miso soups since it must be hand-ground and strained before use; 4) Koji-textured barley miso, made from regular barley rather than the softer "naked" barley, is said to leave a slight residue on the tongue from the firm "loin-cloth" line.

Yet, in parts of Japan where barley fields are still more common than rice paddies and the traditional culture has retained its vitality, barley miso continues to be produced and enjoyed in large quantities. In urban areas, mellow barley miso is swiftly taking the place of its saltier traditional counterpart; a typical Tokyo miso retail store offering 40 varieties of miso will generally have only one barley miso, and it will likely be mellow.

An estimated 80 percent of all Japan's barley miso is still prepared by natural fermentation, and most of the salty varieties are made only during the cold months, from November to April, when the new-crop barley is at its best flavor, the water is clear and delicious, and the air is cold and free of contaminating microorganisms.

The traditional home and present center of barley miso production is the southern third of the Japanese archipelago, and particularly the southernmost main island, Kyushu, where barley miso became popular in about 1600 and 75 percent of Japan's total output now originates. In the various provinces of Kyushu, the following percentages of all miso produced are barley miso: Kagoshima 100, Kumamoto 80, Nagasaki, Saga and Oita 70, and Fukuoka 50. Likewise in Yamaguchi and Hiroshima prefectures located at the southern end of Japan's main island in the Chugoku region, the proportion of miso which is barley miso is respectively 50 and 30 percent. Two of the traditional barley miso areas, Saitama prefecture located near Tokyo and Shikoku island, now produce only small amounts.

Variety	Native Region	Soy-beans	Barley	Salt	Fermentation
Barley Miso	Southern Japan	10	10	4.6	1–3 years
Mellow Barley Miso	Southern Japan	10	17	4.8	10–14 days

Barley Miso *(Karakuchi Mugi Miso):* Although the name of this particular variety is identical to that of the larger category described above, the "barley miso" called for in recipes always refers specifically to this product. Its relatively high salt content (13% or more) is mellowed by lengthy natural fermentation and harmonized by the barley's underlying subtle sweetness to give the miso a deep rich flavor. Many connoisseurs in fact contend that fine barley miso actually tastes *sweeter* than Sendai rice miso! Low in carbohydrates (21%) and high in protein (13%), it is fermented naturally for at least one full year, at the end of which time it has acquired its characteristic reddish-brown color, chunky texture, and prominent fragrance. When aged for three years, the color turns a deep chocolate brown, the texture becomes more homogeneous, and the flavor grows richer, subtler, and more elaborate. Although barley is generally less than one-half as expensive as rice, lengthy fermentation makes this miso more expensive than most varieties of rice miso: natural three-year barley miso *(sannen-miso)*, at more than $1 per pound, is one of Japan's most expensive varieties.

Most of the natural barley miso now exported to the United States is this salty product. It is strongly favored by the American macrobiotic community, which has been one of the main influences working to popularize the use of miso in the West. Barley miso is used in soups and a wide variety of other types of cookery.

Mellow Barley Miso *(Amakuchi Mugi Miso):* Although this variety has a pleasant sweetness, the koji from which it is prepared demands a fairly high minimum level of salt for proper fermentation. Hence it is impossible to make this miso as sweet as the sweet white or sweet red rice misos. Compared with the latter variety, mellow barley miso contains almost twice as much salt (10.0% vs. 6.0%), and a little less carbohydrates (30% vs. 32%) and protein (11.0% vs. 12.6%). The color ranges from light yellow for the quick varieties to reddish brown for those produced naturally. The texture is usually chunky. It has a distinctive flavor characteristic of both the koji and soybeans, and a light fermented aroma. Popular on the island of Kyushu—and especially in Nagasaki and Kumamoto—for over 350 years, it is known in some areas as "10-day miso" due to its short natural fermentation time of one to two weeks. At present, most mellow barley miso is prepared on a large scale using temperature-controlled fermentation, typically for 20 to 35 days in a warm room and then 15 to 20 days at room temperature, or in some cases for as few as four to six days. Although it generally contains preservatives and bleach (some varieties also contain 1% honey), this quick miso spoils rather quickly and changes color unless refrigerated. It is therefore difficult to export. Used mostly in cooked vegetable dishes and as a topping for Dengaku (p. 355), it is also combined with salty barley miso in the preparation of soups.

Soybean Miso
(*Mamé Miso*)

Soybean miso is fundamentally different from rice and barley miso in that it contains no grain; its koji is made exclusively from soybeans. Due to a consequent lack of carbohydrates and a moderately high salt content, soybean miso requires lengthy aging, most of which is still done in the slow, natural way.

Much of Japan's earliest farmhouse and commercial miso was probably of this type. In the clear, cold uplands of northern Japan, it is still prepared in the ancient way, with wild mold spores and cooked soybeans that are crushed and shaped into large balls (*miso-dama*). The balls are wrapped or tied with rice straw and hung outdoors under the eaves or indoors over an open-hearth fireplace or wood-burning kitchen stove. After a month or so when the balls are covered with mold, they are crushed, mixed with salt and water, and fermented in kegs or crocks (p. 476).

Commercial soybean miso was developed and is still most widely prepared and consumed in central Japan, in Aichi, Mie, and Gifu prefectures. It presently constitutes 8 percent of all miso sold in the nation as a whole. Since it is impossible to vary the ratio of grains in the basic ingredients, the different varieties have a relatively narrow range of flavors and aromas. All are fermented naturally for at least one year. The darker ones are occasionally called "black miso" (*kuro miso*), and all are frequently called Sanshu miso, the ancient name of central Japan.

Variety	Native Region	Soy-beans	Salt	Fermentation
Hatcho Miso	Okazaki near Nagoya	10	2.1	18–36 months
Soybean Miso	Central Japan	10	2.1	8–12 months
Tamari Miso	Central Japan	10	2.5	10–12 months

Hatcho Miso (*pronounced HOT-cho*): No other miso in Japan is endowed with such a lofty and aged tradition. For centuries, Japanese poets, connoisseurs, and statesmen have celebrated Hatcho's ineffable savory aroma, deep mellow sweetness, and uniquely astringent flavor, each faintly reminiscent of chocolate; these lend the miso a sense of what the Japanese call *shibui*, a term which in its broader aesthetic usage refers to subdued yet refined tastefulness which borders on subtle, almost severe beauty. Other "shibui" things include a Zen brush painting, a sparse haiku, a tart—almost puckery—autumn persimmon.

Dark cocoa brown, Hatcho has a slightly chunky texture that in most cases is so firm you can cut it with a knife. Higher in protein (21.0%) and lower in carbohydrates (12.0%) and water (40%) than any other miso, it nevertheless contains less salt than either red or barley miso (10.6% vs. 13%).

Although any maker of Hatcho-type miso is legally allowed to use the traditional name for his product, only two companies, Hayakawa and Ota (p. 567), both of which claim to have been founded over 600 years ago (p. 505), are generally recognized as Japan's originators and present manufacturers of the real thing. Both are located in the same block, or *cho,* on the banks of the Yahagi River in the town of Okazaki near the bustling city of Nagoya (see map, p. vi). Hat-cho, or "Eighth-street" miso, takes its name from this location. The Tokugawa family, which founded Japan's feudal shogunate in 1603 and moved its capital to Edo (now Tokyo), originally resided in this area. Very fond of their native miso, they imported it by boat to their new capital where, as it happens, it never became widely popular.

In making Hatcho miso, a unique species of mold, *Aspergillus hatcho* said to flourish in the Okazaki area, was traditionally used in place of the regular *Aspergillus oryzae.* The fermented soybean koji is mixed with salt and a relatively small amount of water (see p. 210), then packed into huge cedar vats, some of which are 150 to 200 years old. Their thick cedar staves bound together with wide and beautifully woven hoops of braided bamboo, typical vats are 6 feet deep and 7 feet in diameter, with a capacity of 4 to 5 tons (1,600 gallons). A heavy wooden pressing lid is placed on top of the miso, and at least 100 large rocks, equal in their total weight to the weight of the miso, are then piled on (see frontispiece). Even with this enormous pressure, however, the mixture contains so little moisture that virtually no liquid (*miso-damari*) rises to the surface!

Because all Hatcho miso must age through at least two full summers, the youngest batches, which start to ferment in the late spring, are about 16 months old; older batches, begun in early fall, have been aged for at least 24 months. Hatcho makers say that the miso begins to reach its best flavor only after 24 months and peaks at three *full* years, but miso this old is very uncommon at present. Yet due to the unusual Japanese way of measuring a miso's age, Hatcho which is actually only 18 to 24 months old is often sold as "three-year" miso.

Since all Hatcho is prepared by lengthy natural fermentation, it costs about 79 cents per pound, or roughly 40 percent more than most rice miso. The oldest batches, which have had a large proportion of their protein broken down into amino acids, are valued for their medicinal properties. Only about 1 to 2 percent of the miso produced each year in Japan is Hatcho, and about half of the total is employed in the production of akadashi miso (see below). Most often used in soups, Hatcho is usually mixed with 3 parts red, light-yellow, or sweet rice miso to soften its astringent qualities. It is also the key ingredient in Tekka Miso (p. 141), and small chunks of the well-aged product can be served as is, to be enjoyed as a rich and mellow hors d'œuvre. When used in place of red or barley miso—as called for in most of the recipes in this book—the quantity should be increased by 15 to 20 percent to impart the equivalent degree of saltiness.

In recent years a product called "Young Hatcho Miso" *(Waka-Hatcho)* has begun to be sold. Prepared by the traditional Hatcho companies, it differs from the true Hatcho in that it is aged through only one full summer (usually for a total of 12 to 14 months) and has a lighter weight on the vat's pressing lid. Slightly less mellow in flavor, lighter in color, softer in texture, and about 15 percent less expensive, it is often preferred to true Hatcho by students of macrobiotics who feel that the latter is too *yang* due to its lengthy aging in such a warm climate.

Hatcho is said to be the Emperor's favorite miso, and he takes it with him on overseas trips. Formerly certain fine producers of miso, shoyu, and other foods received the honor of being supplier to the Imperial Household, but recently a more democratic approach has been adopted. No company is allowed to be a special supplier to the Emperor, even if they offer their goods free, because the resulting publicity is considered to give them an unfair advantage over competitors. The Emperor must buy and pay for his beloved Hatcho miso just like everyone else.

Hatcho has been taken on all six Japanese expeditions to the South Pole, and is considered an essential food by many athletes and mountain climbers who use it as a condensed source of protein and energy. Regarded also as a key ingredient in Tea Ceremony Cuisine (*(kaiseki ryori)*, it is now widely available in the West and is the only miso sold in sealed bags that is not pasteurized and contains no alcohol.

Soybean Miso *(Mamé Miso or Ichi-nen Mamé Miso):* Also called "one-year" or "regular" soybean miso to distinguish it from other soybean misos, this variety is prepared like Hatcho except that the minimum aging requirement is one year rather than two and the usual *Aspergillus oryzae* mold is used to make the koji. Compared to Hatcho, its flavor is less rich; its color is redder; its texture is softer due to its higher water content (48% vs. 40%); and its price is about 30 percent lower. Much of this miso is used as a substitute for Hatcho in akadashi (see below). About 80 to 90 percent of the soybean miso made in Japan is of this type. The term "Nagoya Miso," the name of the most popular brand, is often used as a synonym for "soybean miso."

Tamari Miso: Prepared in miso and shoyu shops in central Japan since 1500, this is the miso-like residue that remains after producing tamari-shoyu, an early prototype of modern shoyu. (Tamari-shoyu is made from a pure soybean koji, while modern shoyu is made with a koji consisting of equal parts soybeans and roasted wheat.)

In making tamari miso, soybean koji prepared as for Hatcho or regular soybean miso is mixed with the usual amount of salt plus about five times as much water. The resulting mash, called *moromi,* has a consistency like that of applesauce; it is placed into a huge cedar vat in the center of which is stacked a series of inverted, bottomless wooden kegs which form a hollow cylinder. The base of the cylinder is joined to an inverted V-shaped trough that is permeated with small holes and connected at one end to a spigot at the bottom of one side of the keg. Liquid tamari from the moromi mash quickly collects in and fills the cylindrical core. Each day some of this tamari is ladled over the surface of the moromi to stimulate fermentation and, since the usual pressing lid is not used, to prevent the formation of mold. After 10 months or more of natural fermentation, the spigot is opened and the thick, richly-flavored tamari runs out. Traditionally it was the well-drained *moromi* remaining in the vat that was sold as tamari miso. At present, however, most of the moromi is ladled into cloth sacks and hydraulically pressed to extract its full content of liquid tamari; the pulpy dry residue is then discarded or used as cattle fodder. Hence, tamari miso is now quite rare, although not extinct.

Long regarded as a very high-class food, tamari miso has a subtle natural sweetness and a distinctive flavor similar to that of fine, natural Chinese soy sauce. However, because it contains no grain koji and is fermented for a relatively short period of time, it has rather little aroma. Generally used in miso soups, it is also popular as a relish-like topping or dip for fresh vegetable slices. For a description of the liquid tamari, see pages 462 and 510.

SPECIAL MISO

Special misos are different from their regular counterparts in four basic ways: 1) In addition to the usual miso ingredients (soybeans, koji, and salt), they contain chopped vegetables, nuts, seeds, seafoods, or natural seasonings and spices which impart a distinctive chunky texture; 2) They are generally quite sweet and, unless refrigerated, have a relatively short shelf life; 3) Generally served at the dining table for use as a topping or seasoning, they never appear in miso soups and are further cooked in only a few special dishes such as Dengaku (p. 355) and

Broiled Miso (p. 156); 4) They are usually sold in small quantities (200 grams) from 2-quart crocks rather than large kegs at prices slightly higher than even the most expensive regular misos. The two basic types are finger lickin' miso and sweet simmered miso.

Finger Lickin' Miso
(Namémiso)

Each variety of *namémiso*—a word derived from the verb *nameru* meaning "to lick"—is prepared by fermenting a small amount of finely-chopped salt-pickled vegetables and spicy seasonings (about 10%) with whole cooked soybeans (15%) and a large proportion (75%) of a unique whole-grain koji usually containing barley or wheat. The resulting consistency is similar to that of apple sauce but slightly chunkier, and the color is generally a warm light brown. The high proportion of grain carbohydrates which are broken down into sugars gives this miso its characteristic rich sweetness and heady, delectable aroma.

Now available in different parts of the United States, finger lickin' miso seems particularly well suited to Western tastes. In Japan, the different varieties are favorite toppings for crisp vegetable slices, hot rice or rice porridge, Ochazuké, regular or deep-fried tofu, crackers and canapés, rice balls and *mochi,* baked potatoes and other root vegetables, and even some *aemono* salads. Finger lickin' miso is also delicious in Western-style sauces and dressings, especially with sesame tahini and seasonings such as orange juice, garlic, onion, gingerroot, shoyu, and/or honey. The following varieties which retail for an average of $1.50 per pound in Japan, are listed in order of their availability and popularity there: refrigerated, each will keep for three to six months.

Kinzanji Miso: Kinzanji is made from a special koji containing *both* whole-grain barley and soybeans. (In most misos, it will be remembered, either grains or soybeans but never both are used in the koji.) The individual barley grains are abundant and clearly visible, and the soybeans, which have been roasted, cracked and dehulled, give the finished product a slightly nutty aroma and chunky texture. Most Kinzanji contains minced eggplant, gingerroot, white *uri* melon, *kombu* and burdock root; some varieties may contain *daikon* and cucumbers, plus green beefsteak leaves and seeds, *sansho* green pepper, and slivered red chilies *(togarashi)* used to enhance the fragrance. These vegetables and seasonings are added either at the start of or halfway through the natural six-month fermentation process. Traditional Kinzanji contained equal portions by weight of soybeans and barley, but many modern varieties contain four times as much barley as soybeans in order to give a sweeter product, and reduce the cost, time, and difficulty of preparation. For even greater sweetness some makers add rice koji to the original mixture, and *mizuamé* (barley- or millet jelly) at the end; the *mizuamé* also improves luster. Modern varieties may contain brown food coloring, and pasteurization or preservatives are often used to increase shelf life. Two types of Kinzanji are available, one quite sweet and the other rather mild.

Several theories are offered to account for this miso's origin. The first traces it to *Kinzanji*, the Temple of the Golden Mountain, one of China's five great Sung dynasty Zen centers. According to popular oral tradition, the Zen priest Kakushin brought a prototype back with him from China in 1255 A.D. and taught the method of its preparation to the people of Yuasa in Wakayama prefecture, where the same ancient technique is employed to this day. Yuasa has since become a famous center of shoyu production as well, and legend has it that shoyu's earliest progenitor was discovered as the dark, fragrant liquid left over at the bottom of the Kinzanji barrel! The Osaka-Wakayama area is the present center of Kinzanji production, yet manufacturers in Shizuoka prefecture to the north have developed ten new varieties plus a ready-made dried koji for use in preparing a home-made type.

A second theory suggests that some of the earliest

types of Chinese chiang (see Appendix A), containing pieces of fish or meat fermented with grains and soybeans, were actually prototypes of Kinzanji, and that all the devotedly vegetarian Japanese had to do was substitute vegetables and seasonings for the meat and fish. In fact, the earliest *hishio* (the progenitor of Japanese shoyu; see below) was probably very similar to Kinzanji. The basic method for preparing this Kinzanji is believed to have been transmitted not by a priest but by a book, the *Ch'i-min Yao-shu*, written in China about 535 A.D., which when translated and circulated widely in Japan had a profound influence on Japanese fermented food preparation and agricultural methods. This theory places the origin of Kinzanji 400 years after the time of Kakushin and fails to establish its famous link with the origin of shoyu. A third theory suggests that Kinzanji originated from the practice of soaking vegetables in *hishio* to make "vegetable hishio" (*kusa hishio*).

Four close relatives of Kinzanji are *Sakura Miso, Shiina Miso, Hamana Miso,* and *Bonito Miso. Sakura* —which means "cherry"—has a deep red color and is prepared from barley koji plus *mizuamé* and sugar; a modern miso with the same name is described on page 82. *Shiina*—which means "China," in honor of the fact that most finger lickin' miso originated there —and *Hamana* contain soybeans, wheat-(or barley-) and rice koji, plus diced eggplants, beefsteak seeds, and gingerroot. Some varieties contain *amazaké* (p. 400). Fermented for 20 days during the winter, they are prepared and sold mostly in Fukui prefecture. Bonito (*Katsuo*) Miso, a specialty of Tosa City on the island of Shikoku, substitutes chunks of raw bonito for the usual vegetables. It is occasionally used in soups.

Moromi Miso: Moromi is the mash from which shoyu is made. It consists of a koji made of soybeans, cracked roasted wheat, salt, and water. After a natural fermentation period of one year, it is ordinarily ladled into cloth sacks and pressed to yield the liquid shoyu.

The earliest moromi miso, developed during the 16th century in Kyushu and Shikoku by shoyu makers, was simply shoyu moromi (made with whole rather than cracked roasted wheat) taken from the fermentation vats either before or after the shoyu was filtered off. To develop their own version, all that miso makers had to do was reduce the amount of water used in the mash, add chopped, salt-pickled vegetables, and substitute miso starter (*Aspergillus oryzae* mold) for the shoyu starter to activate the fermentation. The resulting product, from which the liquid was never filtered or pressed, was dark brown and had a consistency like that of applesauce.

Today, most moromi miso contains chopped egg-plants, cucumbers, and gingerroot; Nagasaki's delicious Batten Moromi also contains short sections of *wakame* midrib *(kukiwakame)*. Two varieties of moromi, prepared by miso makers, are available; one is quite sweet and slightly pink, the other tan and mild. Retailing for about 80 cents per pound, both are most widely served on fresh cucumber slices.

Hishio: The word *hishio* (pronounced HEE-shee-oh) is the Japanese pronunciation of the Chinese character *chiang,* and the present-day product is thought to bear a close resemblance to this progenitor of all Japanese miso and shoyu (see Appendix A). Commercial hishio is generally prepared from drained, unpressed shoyu moromi to which are added salt-pickled vegetables (eggplant, white *uri* melon, and gingerroot); the mixture is then further fermented by natural methods for 20 to 60 days, usually during the months of March and April. Traditional farm-house hishio—still widely prepared in the Osaka, Chugoku, and Shikoku areas (see map inside cover) where it is also known as *namémono* or *o-namé*—is generally prepared by fermenting the vegetables to-gether with a barley koji from the beginning, and often contains soybeans which have been split and dehulled. Both commercial and farmhouse hishio, prized as gift items in Japan, are now available at only the best miso shops.

Namémiso: Closely related to the three varieties described above, namémiso is characterized by the presence of 3-inch-long strips of *kombu* together with diced pickled eggplants, gingerroot, and *uri* melons. Some varieties contain only wheat or barley koji and no soybeans.

Natto Miso: Prepared in the area of Nagasaki since the 1700s, natto miso contains a relatively large proportion of soybeans which gives it an appearance similar to the famous sticky fermented soybeans called *natto,* although there are no real *natto* in natto miso. Containing whole soybeans, barley koji, slivered kombu, gingerroot, and, in some modern varieties, *mizuamé* (a natural honeylike sweetener extracted from rice, millet, or barley), this miso is fermented at the natural temperature for about 30 days. One delicious and very popular variety, now widely available in the United States, is free of preservatives, artificial or refined sweeteners, and all other additives—proving that it can still be done. We would prefer to see this and all similar misos labeled as "Finger Lickin' Miso;" we feel the general term is more appealing and less confusing.

Goto Miso: A *to* is a Japanese unit of measure equal to 4¾ gallons, and the word *go* means "five." This miso is prepared by combining one *to* of each of the following five ingredients: cooked soybeans, rice koji, sake lees, salt, and sugar. The fermentation requires only ten days.

Relatives of finger lickin' miso: The numerous varieties of farmhouse miso enriched or extended with potatoes, sweet potatoes, *kobocha* or corn-(or with koji made from these foods), and the farmhouse miso in which vegetables are buried and pickled are closely related to finger lickin' miso (see p. 475).

Sweet Simmered Miso
(Nerimiso)

Sweet simmered miso is prepared by combining regular miso with a mixture of sweetening (sugar, honey, or *mizuamé*), a little water or sake, and nuts, seeds, minced vegetables, seafoods, or seasonings. The mixture is cooked in a skillet and stirred constantly until it attains the same degree of firmness as regular miso. The most widely available commercial variety is peanut miso, which is chock full of whole peanuts, roasted sesame seeds and, in special cases, raisins; the use of *mizuamé* imparts a thick taffy-like consistency and deep amber color, while the peanuts and sesame boost the protein level to over 16 percent. Commonly sold in 3½-ounce sealed polyethylene bags or rectangular containers, it is now also available commercially and at school cafeterias in tiny ¾-ounce packets which provide a single serving for only 5 cents and are used as a sandwich spread as well as a topping for rice, tofu, and fresh vegetable slices. Other readily available commercial varieties include walnut, sesame, *yuzu*, *kinomé,* and red snapper. Since these and numerous other varieties are also prepared non-commercially in homes and restaurants, a detailed discussion of sweet simmered miso is given in the recipe section (p. 125).

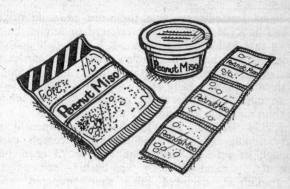

MODERN MISO

Three varieties of miso, all developed since 1945, fall under this classification. They are composed of traditional misos processed or mixed in unique ways. When two or more varieties of miso are combined, the resulting commercial product is designated as "mixed miso" (*chogo-* or *awasé miso*), the best known example of which is akadashi, described below. Modern miso represents about 5 percent of all miso consumed today in Japan.

Akadashi Miso: This dark reddish-brown and rather sweet miso is prepared by combining 1 part Hatcho miso with 2 parts of various other misos (mellow beige, sweet white, and/or one-year soybean). Many varieties also contain caramel syrup, *mizuamé*, refined sugar, monosodium glutamate, shoyu, and sorbic acid preservative. The mature misos and other ingredients are simply mixed, puréed or blended, pasteurized, and packaged; the process takes less than two days since no additional fermentation is required. Hatcho akadashi miso, the finest variety, is guaranteed to contain authentic Hatcho miso, whereas less expensive varieties often substitute regular soybean miso. *Sakura* (cherry) and *Kyozakura* are types of akadashi containing about two-thirds sweet white miso.

Some Japanese say that the word *akadashi* originated in Kyoto and initially referred to any soybean miso that had a strong aroma; it is said that geishas would grind the soybean miso finely in a *suribachi* (serrated earthenware mortar), then rub it through a sieve to make a tasty miso soup. In Kyoto, the soybean miso first came to be mixed with sweet white miso to make the forerunner of today's akadashi.

Richly fragrant and hearty-tasting, akadashi is very popular in most Japanese urban centers even though its price is fairly high (48 to 73 cents per pound). Its name—literally "red dashi"—comes from a traditional, deep-red miso soup prepared with Hatcho miso, often containing oysters, and highly prized for its wonderful flavor (see p. 244).

Dehydrated Miso (Freeze-dried or Spray-dried): Called *Kanso Miso* or *Kona Miso* in Japan, this variety, developed in 1959, has become quite popular since the late 1970s, especially as the main ingredient in instant miso soups (now available at natural-food stores and supermarkets throughout the U.S.), and also in the soup for instant Miso Ramen noodles. One popular natural instant miso soup, brand-named Miso Cup, contains a mixture of dehydrated onions, parsley, sea vegetables (wakame), and miso. In Japan, the most popular varieties contain slivered freeze-dried leeks, plus dried wakame and wheat gluten (or deep-fried tofu); many Japanese and supermarket products also contain chemical additives such as monosodium glutamate, sodium succinate, and isosinic acid. The mixture is sealed in tiny one- or two-serving packets (9 grams make an 8-ounce cup of instant miso soup) and five to ten packets are sold together in a foil package or box. At least three varieties are available to make red, white, or akadashi miso soup. The soup, prepared by simply mixing the contents of one packet with hot water, is ready in less than a minute at a very small cost per serving. Ideal for backpacking and camping, this miso also makes an excellent seasoning; we like to keep some in a shaker and sprinkle it on salads, sandwiches, brown rice, noodles, or crisp-fried tempeh, or to mash it with tofu for use as a spread or dip.

Of the 560,000 metric tons of miso made in Japan in 1979, no more than 2½ to 3½ percent end up dehydrated. Of the 10,000 to 15,000 tons of dehydrated product, an estimated 80 percent is freeze-dried and 20 percent is spray-dried. Yamajirushi is the largest maker of freeze-dried miso and Marukome and Nagatani-en are the biggest makers of spray-dried miso.

Initially, most of the dehydrated miso in Japan was made by spray-drying. Miso (containing 50 percent solids) is mixed with enough water to give a slurry containing only 10 percent solids; this is blown in a fine spray from an atomizer into the top of a 150-foot-tall tower filled with circulating hot air. The miso dries as it falls. The spray inlet temperature is 482°F (250°C) and the exit temperature is 167 to 176° F (75-80°C). In recent years, freeze-drying has come to be more widely used than spray-drying. Regular miso is spread to a depth of about 1 inch (2-3 cm) on large stainless-steel trays, which are slid into shelves in a large vacuum chamber. First the miso is quick-frozen at a very low temperature (-22°F or -30C°), then dried using a strong vacuum (0.5 to 0.8 mm of mercury or torr) at a relatively low drying temperature (104°F or 40°C) for 10 to 15 hours, to yield dehydrated miso containing only 4 to 5 percent moisture, but 32.2 percent protein, 18.5 percent salt, and 35.8 percent carbohydrates. Though slightly more expensive, freeze-drying gives a finished product with a noticeably better flavor and aroma (some of which are lost at the high temperatures used for spray-drying), a product that is slightly more nutritious and dissolves more readily in water. Freeze-drying is labor-intensive, has a long drying time, and uses expensive, complex equipment with a small capacity but low noise level. Spray-drying is easy to mechanize, has a short drying time, and uses simple, inexpensive equipment with a large capacity, but which is very noisy.

Low-salt and Salt-free Miso (*Gen-en Miso and Mu-en Miso*): Typical low-salt miso is made by pressure-steaming dehulled, defatted soybeans, hydrolizing them with enzymes, then mixing them with an equal weight of mature red or light-yellow miso and fermenting the mixture at 86°F to 95°F for three to five days. First developed in 1965, the resulting product contains only 6.3 percent sodium chloride together with 17.6 percent protein and 53 percent moisture. Since its low salt content requires that the fresh miso be stored at below 50°F, it is usually freeze-dried and sold in 7-ounce bottles for about $1.70. Generally used as a health food, the dehydrated form contains 14 percent sodium chloride, 26.4 percent protein, and 6 percent moisture.

Some varieties, typically containing 5 percent salt and prepared like light-yellow miso using an 80-day fermentation, contain 3 to 3.5 percent alcohol as a preservative and are sold pasteurized in cans. Other methods of making low-salt miso include substituting ethyl alcohol for part of the salt (2–5 percent), adding *Saccharomyces rouxii* yeasts to generate natural alcohol as in wine, or reducing the moisture content to 40 percent.

Salt-free miso, which typically contains 3.5 percent alcohol, has a very noticeable alcohol flavor and aroma that we find unappetizing, except when it is masked by seasonings as for use in dressings (see recipe, p. 190) or sauces. A canned salt-free red miso contains 53.7 percent moisture, 13.9 percent protein, 6.7 percent fats, and 24.2 percent carbohydrates including the 3.5 percent ethanol (ethyl alcohol), and has 189 calories per 100 grams.

Total production of both these types of miso is still very limited, but the appeal is growing since the Japanese per capita salt consumption is the highest in the world, 30 grams per capita in northern Japan and 18 grams in the rest of Japan, as compared with 11 grams in the United States. It is now well known that excess salt consumption can cause high blood pressure (hypertension). These products may eventually even find a market in the West.

New American Misos: American miso makers in homes, communities, and commercial shops have had good results making new types of miso using peanuts, garbanzo beans (chick peas), black soybeans, azuki beans, common beans (*Phaseolus vulgaris,* including pinto, navy, kidney, great northern, etc.), *natto* (fermented soybeans), okara (soy pulp), green lentils, or green peas as the protein source in place of regular soybeans. They have also made koji from corn (dent or flint), millet, wheat, or buckwheat. Try your own combinations or see page 429.

The Proteus company is developing a product called *Promiso,* a mixture of 50 percent Hatcho miso and 50 percent spirulina (a type of microalgae); a prototype contains 24.2 percent protein and a remarkable 20 micrograms of vitamin B-12 per 100 grams of the mixture, with only 7.6 percent salt.

A product resembling miso, produced in America by Loma Linda Foods and widely used by Seventh Day Adventists, is called *Savorex.* Made from extract of brewer's yeast, vegetable flavoring, and salt, it imparts a rich and meaty flavor. In 1980 it was sold in 9-ounce plastic containers for the equivalent of $3.11 per pound, or almost twice as much as popular natural misos.

PART II

Cooking With Miso

5
Getting Started

A WIDE SELECTION of miso varieties, including at least eight natural products, is now available at reasonable prices in the United States (fig. 10). As the number of miso importers and retail stores continues to grow, new types continue to appear. Most miso is presently sold in 1- to 2-pound sealed polyethylene bags, cottage cheese-type containers, or small plastic tubs, although at many natural-food stores it is sold in the traditional way out of wooden kegs. Occasionally it is merchandized in jars or even plastic squeeze tubes. Dehydrated misos—generally in the form of instant miso soups—are sold in foil envelopes. If your local store does not carry miso, you may wish to give the manager the name and address of one of the makers or importers listed in Appendix D.

Buying and Storing Miso

What are the most important things to look for when buying miso? First, buy small quantities of a number of different varieties in order to become familiar with their flavors and colors, textures and aromas. Compare imported and domestic products and learn to recognize which types go best with your favorite recipes. People interested in natural foods will probably prefer traditional natural misos, which now compare very favorably in price with the more modern, quick varieties. Labels such as the one below should contain all the basic information relevant to natural miso:

Variety	Red Miso *(Sendai Akamiso)*
Type	Rice Miso *(Komé Miso)*
Texture	Chunky
Ingredients (incl. additives)	White rice and whole soybeans organically grown, unrefined sea salt, well water, alcohol
Pasteurization	No
Temp.-controlled fermentation	No
Age	At least 12 months
Weight	16 ounces
Maker	Nakamura Miso Co. 160 Westlake Blvd. Berkeley, CA 94706

All varieties should be stored in a cool, dark place. Sweet misos should always be refrigerated; during warm weather, it is best—but not absolutely necessary—to also refrigerate other varieties in order to prevent the growth of surface mold. Miso purchased in polyethylene bags should be kept tightly closed; expel all air from the bag, fold over the mouth, and secure with a rubber band. Miso purchased in bulk out of kegs can be packed firmly into an earthenware, glass, or tupperware container with plastic wrap, wax paper, or butcher paper pressed firmly over the entire miso surface; or it can be stored tightly enclosed in plastic wrap bound with a rubber band, or simply left in the store's small paper carton and refrigerated. During warm weather, a thin layer of harmless, almost tasteless mold may form on the air-exposed surfaces of unrefrigerated natural misos—those which contain no preservatives and are not pasteurized. Don't worry; simply scrape off the mold and discard it just before use or mix it into the body of the miso. Sweet misos may develop an alcoholic fragrance, and light-colored misos may darken, if allowed to stand open for too long; light cooking will remove the alcohol, and the darkening in no way affects the flavor.

Fig. 10. The Varieties of Miso Available in the West (1980)

Type	Name Used in This Book	Other Names	Natural	Imported or Domestic	Where Sold	No. of Brands Available	Weight (oz)	Price Range Per Pound ($)
Rice Miso	Red Miso	Komé Miso	Yes	Imported	N	1	16 or bulk	1.50 to 1.80
		Aka Miso		Imported	J,S	2	12 to 36	1.25 to 1.85
		Aka Miso		Domestic	J,S	2	13	1.44 to 1.55
	Brown-Rice Miso	Genmai Miso	Yes	Imported	N	3	16 or bulk	1.79 to 2.16
	Light-yellow Miso	Shinshu Miso		Imported	N	1	32 to 35	1.02 to 1.84
		Shiro Miso		Domestic	J,S	1	13 to 28	1.55 to 1.76
	Mellow White Miso	Shiro White Miso	Yes	Domestic	J,S	1	13 to 28	1.44 to 1.55
	Sweet White Miso	Shiro Miso	Yes	Imported	J,S	1	12 to 24	1.50 to 1.71
Barley Miso	Barley Miso	Mugi Miso	Yes	Imported	N	1	16 or bulk	1.65 to 2.04
Soybean Miso	Hatcho Miso		Yes	Imported	N	2	16 or bulk	1.99 to 2.37
	Young Hatcho Miso	Waka Hatcho	Yes	Imported	N	1	16 or bulk	1.65 to 1.90
Finger Lickin' Miso	Kinzanji Miso			Imported	J	1	7	2.31 to 2.37
	Moromi Miso			Imported	N,J	1	7	2.47 to 5.16
	Natto Miso		Yes	Imported	J	1	Bulk	1.99 to 2.05
Sweet Simmered Miso	Peanut Miso		Yes	Domestic	N	1	8	3.87 to 3.96
	Tekka Miso		Yes	Imported	N,J	2	7	3.30 to 14.60
Modern Miso	Akadashi Miso			Imported	J	2	10 to 14	1.81 to 1.84
	Dehydrated Miso (Instant Miso Soup)	Miso Shiru		Imported	N,J,S	4	1.6	.22 to .25 per serving

N = Natural and Health Food Stores
J = Japanese Food Store
S = Supermarkets, especially Co-op Markets

Using Miso as a Seasoning

Miso may be used in place of salt or shoyu in most recipes. It has a more mellow and varied flavor than shoyu, and imparts added body to broths and sauces. The following quantities impart approximately the same "saltiness" and can therefore be used interchangeably as explained on page 50:

½ teaspoon salt
2 teaspoons shoyu
1 tablespoon salty miso (see chart p. 50)
1½ to 2 tablespoons mellow miso
2½ to 3 tablespoons sweet miso

To use miso sold in a polyethylene bag, cut across one of the bag's upper corners to make a ¾-inch-long opening. Then simply squeeze the bag (as you would apply icing to a cake using a pastry bag) to give a neat, smooth bead.

Remember that natural miso is a living food containing many beneficial microorganisms which are easily killed by prolonged cooking. Whenever possible add the miso to soups or other preparations just before they are removed from the heat or use the miso in ways that require no cooking.

Basic Ingredients

We recommend the use of whole, natural foods. Since cans and bottles tend to contribute to environmental clutter, the recipes in this book call for ingredients which can be purchased free of non-biodegradable packaging. The rarer ingredients used in Japanese-style recipes are defined in the Glossary at the end of this book. Many basic Oriental foods are now widely available at natural food stores and supermarkets, as well as at Japanese and Chinese markets. Or contact the Japan Food Corporation with offices in San Francisco, Los Angeles, New York, Chicago, Houston, Columbia (Md.), and Sacramento (Calif.). The following ingredients, listed alphabetically, are those we consider basic to miso cookery:

Flour: Since all-purpose white flour contains only about 75 percent of the protein, 36 percent of the minerals, and 25 percent of the vitamins found in natural whole-wheat flour, we generally prefer to use the latter for baked goods, sauces, and the like. However, in tempura batters and pie crusts where lightness is essential, we recommend the use of unbleached white flour or a mixture of equal parts whole-wheat and white flours.

Honey and Sugar: Most of the recipes in this book that use sweetening call for honey, used in the minimum amounts we consider necessary to create the desired flavor and "balanced" by the miso's salt. One teaspoon honey imparts the same sweetness as 2 teaspoons of sugar, and in most recipes the two can be used interchangeably. Since honey is about twice as expensive as sugar, the net cost ends up being the same. But honey is a whole, natural food with a mild flavor, whereas natural unrefined sugar (available in Japan but not in America) has a dominant molasses taste and white sugar is now widely recognized as being bad for both body and mind. (We feel it is important that decreases of meat in the diet be accompanied by proportional decreases of sugar usage, and that in general, grains, vegetables, and fruits be used as natural sweetening agents.)

The first sugar arrived in Japan in 753 A.D., brought by the Chinese Buddhist priest Ganjin on the same boat said to have brought the first Chinese miso. Yet sugar was virtually unknown in Japan until the late 1500s, and not until 1776 was the first sugar refinery established. Although Japan still has the lowest sugar consumption of any industrialized country in the world, the per capita figure jumped from 28.5 pounds in 1955 to 64.0 pounds in 1975. (The latter figure is only 57 percent of America's 112 pounds—14 tablespoons per day—for the same year.) In Japan, sugar is used mostly in cooking, where it is balanced by the saltiness of miso or shoyu; its use in desserts, treats, and "junk foods" is now rapidly increasing as Western dietary patterns become popular. Honey is only rarely used in Japanese cookery.

Oil: For best flavor, use cold-pressed, natural vegetable oils. For sautéing and salad dressings, we prefer soy, corn, or "salad" oil—often mixed with small amounts of sesame oil; for deep-frying, rapeseed or soy oil. Olive oil works well in Western-style dressings. Sesame oil, especially popular in Chinese dishes, is now widely available in the West.

Rice: Polished or white rice contains an average of only 84 percent of the protein, 53 percent of the minerals, 38 percent of the vitamins, and 30 percent of the dietary fiber found in natural brown rice. We prefer the flavor, texture, and nutritional superiority of the natural food.

In Japan, virtually everyone (including Zen monks) now eats white rice. The trend began in the early 1600s when it became a status symbol enjoyed first by the aristocracy and finally, in the early 1900s, by everyone. During World War II, time and energy could not be spared for polishing and, therefore, everyone ate brown rice. Today, however, the thought of unpolished rice triggers in most adults an almost Pavlovian response recalling the horrors of the war. Yet, the Japanese macrobiotic community has done excellent work in promoting the many virtues of brown rice and now, especially among the alternative lifestyle-sector of the younger generation, it is the symbol of a new, more natural and healthful way of living and eating.

Salt: Natural, unrefined sea salt contains an abundance of essential minerals which are lost during the refining process. Its flavor is richer and more concentrated than that of pure-white, refined table salt.

Shoyu and Soy Sauce: The skillful use of authentic shoyu and miso is the key to most Japanese cookery. An all-purpose seasoning, shoyu contains 6.9 percent protein and 18 percent salt; natural shoyu has been a mainstay of Japanese cooking for more than 500 years. We use shoyu, the Japanese word for "soy sauce," to distinguish this fine product from the modern nonfermented chemical or synthetic soy sauces now widely used in the West. There are five different varieties of Japanese shoyu; their composition of nutrients and relative importance in Japan are shown in the table on page 526. Two of these varieties, regular shoyu (which includes natural shoyu) and tamari shoyu, bear special mention.

Natural Shoyu: This traditional product is always brewed using a natural (rather than temperature-controlled) fermentation process, generally for 12 to

18 months. The finest varieties are prepared from whole soybeans, natural salt, and well water fermented together in huge cedar vats. All types also contain *koji* starter (*Aspergillus oryzae*) and roasted cracked wheat. All natural shoyu presently available in the West—some of which is sold as *Tamari*—is imported from Japan. Actually, Japanese *tamari,* the progenitor of shoyu, is a different product (see below).

Shoyu: At present, this is the standard regular shoyu sold in Japan. A high quality product now produced on a large scale in the U.S., its flavor, aroma, and color are quite similar to those of the finest natural shoyu, and its price is considerably lower. Using techniques based on the traditional method but first developed during the 1950s, it is generally prepared from defatted soybean meal and brewed in large tanks for about 4 to 6 months under conditions of strictly controlled temperature and humidity.

Tamari Shoyu: This type of shoyu, a close relative of Chinese soy sauce, is made with a large percentage of soybeans (85–100 percent) and little or no wheat (0–15 percent). Produced and consumed mostly in Central Japan (Aichi, Mie, and Gifu prefectures), it constitutes only 2.2 percent of all Japanese shoyu. Tamari shoyu has a slightly darker color, richer consistency, and distinctively deeper flavor than regular shoyu, though its aroma is more subdued; since it contains little or no wheat it lacks the subtle alcohol bouquet found in regular shoyu. Many Westerners and some Japanese producers distinguish between *tamari shoyu,* which contains a small amount of wheat, and *tamari,* which contains no wheat (but may contain up to 0.15 percent roasted barley flour). In Japan, the production of tamari shoyu is over five times as great as that of tamari. Whereas some 3,500 companies make regular shoyu, only about eight make tamari shoyu (or tamari).

By an unusual quirk and accident of history, the word "tamari" has come to be widely known in the West, where it is frequently misused to refer to natural shoyu. In about 1960, when the Lima Foods company of Belgium started importing the first natural shoyu from Japan, they asked Georges Ohsawa, leader of the international Macrobiotic movement, what they should call the product to distinguish it from both regular commercial shoyu and from "chemical soy sauce," an inexpensive unfermented product described below. Ohsawa suggested that Lima Foods call the new product "natural shoyu," since that was its name in Japan. Lima Foods said the word "shoyu" seemed somewhat difficult to pronounce (in French and Dutch) and asked for alternative names. Ohsawa mentioned that words like "tamari" and "murasaki" were also used to refer to soy sauce in Japan. Lima Foods liked the word "tamari," finding it short, distinctive, and easy to pronounce. So they decided to call their natural shoyu "tamari." Ohsawa eventually came to use this terminology in his teaching and writing, and it was picked up and popularized by the Western Macrobiotic movement that has played a key role in introducing the product to the West. Little did any of them foresee the confusion that would result from this misnomer as people in the West became familiar with both natural shoyu and real tamari, and as distributors began to sell both of these fine seasonings.

In Japan, tamari is now rarely used in its natural form, being generally made into *sashimi-damari* by mixing it with miso-damari (see below), *mizuamé,* cane sugar, caramel, and often preservatives. Although not widely used in Japan, it remains fairly popular in Kyoto and central Japan, where it is used as a seasoning for *sashimi* (raw fish). In ancient times, tamari was widely used in its natural form and highly prized as a fine seasoning, having much the same flavor as best-grade Chinese soy sauce. Today, an increasing amount is made synthetically.

A close relative of tamari shoyu is *miso-damari*— also called *uwahiki*—which is the tamari-like liquid that accumulates in *any* variety of miso during fermentation. Thicker and richer than tamari, it is gathered only in very small quantities and is not sold commercially. A delicious by-product of most homemade miso (it rises to the surface in summer and settles in winter), it may be used like shoyu and is especially delicious with hors d'œuvres.

Chinese Soy Sauce: This traditional Chinese product, which has a stronger and saltier flavor than shoyu, is also made by natural or temperature-controlled fermentation. Although some varieties are excellent, they are not widely available in the West. Our Chinese recipes call for this product. If unavailable, substitute shoyu.

Chemical or Synthetic Soy Sauce: This domestic product, sold under various Chinese brand names, is what most Westerners mean when they speak of soy sauce. It is not brewed or fermented but is prepared from hydrolyzed vegetable protein (HVP) by the reaction of defatted soybeans with hydrochloric acid. Its flavor and coloring come from additives such as corn syrup and caramel. Since it takes only a few days to prepare, the production costs are quite low. Some varieties may contain sodium benzoate or alcohol preservatives.

Soybeans: Inexpensive, whole dry soybeans are now available in the West at most natural and health food stores; buy in bulk for substantial savings. For detailed information, see *The Book of Tofu* and the listing of other basic soybean foods on page 6.

Tempeh: A cake of cultured soybeans with a flavor and texture remarkably similar to that of Southern fried chicken. Tempeh has twice as much protein as hamburger and is the world's best source of vegetarian vitamin B-12. For details, see our *Book of Tempeh* (Harper & Row, 1979).

Tofu: Also known as soybean curd, this delicious protein backbone of the traditional Oriental diet is low in cost, calories, and fats, and entirely free of cholesterol. Remarkably versatile, tofu is now available throughout America in more than 10 different forms, all of which are described in detail in *The Book of Tofu*. The main varieties called for in the following recipes are:

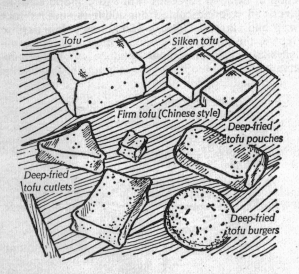

Tofu: The most widely available product sold in water-packed 12-ounce cakes containing 7.8 percent protein.

Firm Tofu (Chinese-style Doufu or Dow-foo): A product resembling Japanese tofu that has been pressed (p. 109). Good for use in deep-frying, stir-frying, and salads.

Deep-fried Tofu Cutlets (Thick Agé): Whole cakes of tofu that have been pressed and deep-fried until golden brown; 10 percent protein.

Deep-fried Tofu Burgers (Ganmo): Tofu-and-vegetable patties that look like large hamburgers; 15 percent protein.

Deep-fried Tofu Pouches (Agé): Each 6- by 3- by ¼-inch-thick pouch can be opened and stuffed with fillings; 19 percent protein.

Silken Tofu (Kinugoshi): A custard-like variety made without the separation of curds and whey; 5½ percent protein.

Vinegar: Use either Western-style cider or white wine vinegar, or the milder, subtly-sweet Japanese rice vinegar (*su*). The latter is especially tasty in salad dressings, sweet-sour sauces, and sushi rice. For 1 teaspoon rice vinegar, substitute ¾ teaspoon cider or mild white vinegar.

NOTE: Monosodium glutamate—also known as MSG or *ajinomoto*—is a crystalline, pure-white powder widely used to intensify the flavor of protein foods by exciting the taste buds. But MSG's ability to over-excite nerve endings may also cause brain damage, especially in infants, who do not have a well-developed blood-brain barrier to inhibit MSG from traveling freely to the brain. A committee of scientists selected by the U.S. Food and Drug Administration has advised that MSG should not be given in any amount to children under 12 months of age, and U.S. baby-food manufacturers have recently agreed to omit MSG from their products.

In 1968 Dr. Ho Man Kwok, reporting in the prestigious *New England Journal of Medicine,* found MSG to be responsible for what has come to be known as the Chinese Restaurant Syndrome, characterized by headaches, a burning sensation at the back of the neck, chest tightness, and nausea, experienced by some people after eating foods highly seasoned with MSG.

This highly refined chemical additive, which is the sodium salt of glutamic acid, differs in chemical structure from natural glutamic acid. Originally extracted from the sea vegetable kombu (*Laminaria*), it is now generally produced by fermentation and hydrolysis of molasses or of glucose from tapioca, cornstarch, potato starch, etc. We and many other people interested in healthful, natural foods strictly avoid use of this controversial substance. It does not appear in any of the recipes in this book.

Oriental Kitchen Tools

The Japanese chef (like most Japanese craftsmen) uses only a small number of relatively simple tools in his work. While the recipes in this book can be prepared using only the utensils found in most Western kitchens, the following tools may make cooking with miso somewhat easier and more enjoyable. Most of these tools are inexpensive and are available at many Japanese and Chinese hardware stores, as well as at some large Japanese markets.

Bamboo colander: Usually round and slightly concave, a typical *zaru*, made of thin strips of woven bamboo, is about 12 inches in diameter. It is used for draining and straining, and as a serving tray for such foods as tempura.

Broiling screen: This double-layer, 8-inch-square screen rests atop a stove burner and is used for broiling. Both layers are made of thin metal sheets, the bottom one perforated with ⅛-inch, and the top with ⅜-inch holes. The top layer slides out for easy cleaning. Broils foods faster and with less fuel than a Western oven broiler.

Charcoal brazier: Made of baked earthenware, the *konro* or *shichirin* is used for grilling and broiling, as well as for heating *nabé* dishes (p. 344) or the family teapot. When preparing *nabé*, you may substitute a tabletop gas burner, heating coil, or chafing-dish warmer.

Chinese bamboo steamer: Although most varieties of *seiro* are round and are set into a *wok* during steaming, some types are rectangular. They are made of slatted or woven bamboo with ¼-inch gaps be-

tween the bottom slats. This design allows steam to
rise through the steamer's lid and prevents it from
collecting and dripping on the steaming foods. Two to
four steaming compartments may be stacked in layers
during steaming.

Cutting board: A board about 19 by 9 by 1 to
2 inches thick, the *manaita* is designed to be set across
the kitchen sink and hung on the wall when not in
use.

Japanese grater: A metal tray about 9 inches long,
the *oroshi-gané* has many sharp teeth protruding from

Oriental Kitchen Tools

its upper surface. Since there are no holes in the grater, the grated foods collect in the trough at one end.

Japanese vegetable knife: One of the finest knives ever designed for cutting vegetables, the *hocho* makes the art of cutting and slicing a true joy. Most varieties are quite inexpensive. The finest of these knives are handmade and bear the stamp of the craftsman on the blade near the knife's wooden handle.

Pressing sack: A simple cloth sack about 15 inches wide and 15 inches deep made of coarsely woven cloth is very helpful in squeezing and crumbling tofu.

Sudaré: A bamboo mat about 10 inches square used for rolling sushi and other foods. A small bamboo table mat makes a good substitute.

Suribachi: An earthenware grinding bowl or mortar with a serrated interior surface, the usual *suribachi* is 10 inches in diameter and 3½ inches deep, and is accompanied by a wooden pestle (*surikogi*).

Tawashi scrub brush: Made of natural palm fiber, the *tawashi* is the perfect utensil for scrubbing root vegetables or washing pots. It is inexpensive and outlasts most synthetic brushes.

Wok set: Popular now in the West, the wok is the Orient's standard utensil for deep-frying, stir-frying, steaming, and sautéing.

1. *The wok:* The wok itself is a metal pan about 13 inches in diameter and 3½ inches deep. When placed atop a special circular support, it may be used with electric ranges. Surprisingly low in cost and now widely available in the West, its design has numerous advantages over that of a regular flat-bottomed skillet, especially when deep-frying: a) It provides the maximum oil surface and depth with the minimum necessary oil volume (3 to 5 cups); b) Each piece of food can be slid gently down the wok's sides rather than dropped with a splash into the oil; c) Freshly fried foods can be drained into the pan on an inobtrusive rack which saves oil and allows more thorough

draining when the foods are later placed on absorbent paper; d) The wok's rounded bottom and thin metal sides allow for quick heating and oil temperature adjustment; e) During stir-frying and sautéing, the wok's large surface area allows each piece of food to have maximum contact with the bottom of the pan, yielding crisp-textured foods in minimum cooking time; f) Cooked foods can be scooped out easily and thoroughly and, when all is done, the wok is easier to clean or wipe free of oil than angular, flat-bottomed pots. After sautéing or stir-frying, wash the hot wok immediately with water and a scrub brush (do not use soap), place it back on the fire until the inside is just dry, then wipe it quickly with a dry dishtowel.

2. *Wok support:* Used in most Chinese kitchens to give the wok stability and focus the strong fire at its base.

3. *Stir-frying ladle and spatula:* In Chinese kitchens, these large, sturdy tools are used during stir-frying. The ladle is employed to measure (by eye) and add all liquids and seasonings to foods cooking in the wok.

4. *Long cooking-chopsticks:* Shaped like regular Japanese wooden chopsticks but about 10 to 14 inches long and often joined with a string at one end, these *saibashi* are used mostly during deep-frying for turning foods in the hot oil or transferring cooked foods to the draining rack. Substitute a pair of long cooking tongs.

5. *Draining rack:* A semicircular rack, the *hangetsu* is attached to the wok during deep-frying so that excess oil from the draining foods drips back into the wok.

6. *Mesh skimmer:* Used for skimming debris from the surface of the hot oil during deep-frying and for removing very small deep-fried foods.

7. *Wooden lid:* Used when simmering foods, the lid fits inside the wok's rim.

8. *Deep-frying thermometer:* Use a regular Western-style deep-fat thermometer that measures temperatures up to 380°F.

Wooden spatulas, rice paddles, and spoons: These utensils make the work of sautéing, stirring, and serving easier and more enjoyable.

BASIC PREPARATORY TECHNIQUES

The following preparatory techniques will be referred to in many of the recipes in this book. We list them all here for easy reference.

Salt-rubbing

This process softens and seasons vegetables (and *konnyaku*) without cooking.

Place thinly sliced vegetables into a bowl and sprinkle with salt. Rub the salt into the vegetables with your fingertips until the vegetables are fairly soft, then let stand for 15 to 20 minutes. Fill the bowl with water and rinse away the salt. Empty vegetables into a strainer or colander and drain briefly. Wrap vegetables in a clean cloth and squeeze gently to expel excess moisture.

Rinsing and Pressing Leeks or Onions

This is a quick and easy method for neutralizing the harsh and evoking the mild, sweet flavors of these vegetables. Slice leeks or onions into thin rounds or slivers. Combine with several cups water in a small bowl and soak for 2 or 3 minutes. Pour into a cloth-lined strainer, gather the cloth's corners to form a sack, and press vegetables gently between your palms. Use immediately or refrigerate in a covered container.

Soaking Burdock Root

Burdock root has a slightly harsh, alkaline flavor that is easily removed by proper cutting and soaking. If unsoaked, burdock will lose its white color and turn a dark reddish brown soon after it is cut and exposed to the air.

Holding the root under running cold water, scrape off its dark peel with a knife or scrub it off with a scrub brush (*tawashi*). Cut the root into 2-inch lengths and submerge the lengths in cold water. Cut one section at a time into matchsticks and return these immediately to the water. Soak for about 10 minutes, then change the water and soak for 20 to 40 minutes more. Soaking time can be decreased by using warm or hot water, but some of the burdock's flavor will be lost. Drain quickly before sautéing.

Reconstituting Dried Sea Vegetables, Wheat Gluten, and Kampyo

Dried Hijiki: Immerse in several cups (warm) water and allow to soak for 20 to 30 minutes. Stir gently, then lift *hijiki* carefully out of water so that any grit stays at bottom of bowl. Place *hijiki* in a colander or strainer and press lightly to rid it of excess moisture. Note: ¼ cup (27 gm) dry *hijiki* yields 1 cup (200 gm) reconstituted.

Dried Wakame: Rinse *wakame* once, then soak for 15 to 30 minutes. Strain, reserving the nutritious liquid for use in stocks. Remove the midrib of each leaf only if it is unusually large. Squeeze *wakame* firmly, place in a compact mound on a cutting board, and cut at ½-inch intervals. (Place fresh *wakame* in several quarts of water, rinsing and squeezing 2 or 3 times to rid it of excess surface salt.) Note: 25 gm dried *wakame* yields 1 cup (125 gm) reconstituted.

Agar *(Kanten):* Tear agar bar crosswise into halves and soak in 1 quart water for several minutes. Lift out agar and squeeze firmly. Change water and resoak briefly. Squeeze again, then tear into small (1-inch) pieces.

Dried Wheat Gluten: Soak for several minutes in water. Press lightly with fingertips to expel excess moisture before use.

Kampyo: Soak for 15 minutes in water to cover seasoned with a pinch of salt. Drain briefly, then rub lightly with salt.

Parboiling

To parboil vegetables, drop them into more than enough boiling water to cover, and cook until just

tender. When parboiling green vegetables, add about
¼ teaspoon salt for each 2 cups water to help the
vegetables retain their color. Vegetables that are easily overcooked may be plunged into cold water as
soon as they are done. Length of cooking depends
both on how finely the ingredients have been cut and
on whether they will be cooked again. Shredded or
slivered vegetables, or leaves that will be simmered
again in a seasoned liquid, may be parboiled for 30
to 60 seconds; boil for 30 to 60 seconds more if they
will not be recooked. Small rectangles of *konnyaku*
and root vegetables should be parboiled for 1 to 2
minutes. Larger pieces may be boiled for as much as
3 to 4 minutes.

Cutting Vegetables

Most of the cutting techniques used in the recipes
presented in this book are familiar to any Western
cook. A few, however, deserve special mention. The
Japanese pay great attention to the way in which each
ingredient is cut, because careful cutting not only lends
beauty to the preparation when it is served but also
assures that each uniform piece will be cooked to
precisely the desired degree of tenderness.

Cutting vegetables into small rectangles: Cut thick
vegetables (carrots, *daikon,* etc.) into 1½-inch
lengths, then cut each section vertically into thirds.
Now place each piece on its largest surface and cut
lengthwise into small rectangles about ⅛ inch thick.
Cutting into matchsticks: This technique is used
with long, thin root vegetables. Cut crosswise into
2-inch lengths; then stand each piece on end and cut
vertically into ⅛-inch-thick pieces. Stack these on top
of one another and cut lengthwise into ⅛-inch-wide
strips the size of wooden matchsticks. Slivering or
cutting *julienne* are variations on this basic technique.
Cutting into half moons: Use with long, thick roots
or tubers. Cut lengthwise into halves, then cut each
half cross-wise into pieces about ½ to ¼ inch thick.
Cutting into ginkgo leaves: Cut lengthwise into
quarters, then cut crosswise into thin pieces.

Using Sesame Seeds

When roasted and ground, sesame seeds have a wonderful nutty flavor and aroma, and almost every Japanese kitchen is equipped with a *suribachi* and *surikogi* (a serrated earthenware bowl and wooden pestle, p. 102) used for grinding them. Small quantities of seeds can also be ground in a pepper grinder, a spice or coffee mill, or a special grinder that fits over the mouth of a jar of sesame seeds and is sold at Japanese hardware stores. If you are using ½ cup or more of seeds, you can grind them in a hand mill or meat grinder, or, in some cases, purée them in a blender with a dash of oil or shoyu. You may wish to make enough to last for several days or to use in Sesame Salt (p. 119). Grind the seeds with a firm but light touch until they are well crushed but not oily.

Two parts of ground roasted seeds impart about the same flavoring as 1 part pre-packaged sesame butter or *tahini*.

(Proper care of the *suribachi* is very important. Before use, scrub the suribachi with hot water and douse with boiling water. Dry with a dishcloth, then turn the bowl upside down and dry thoroughly with one edge raised to allow air to circulate. After use, fill the *suribachi* with hot water and soak for 1 hour; then scrub and dry as above.)

Heat a heavy skillet until a drop of water flicked across its surface evaporates instantly. Add seeds and reduce heat to low. Shaking the pan and stirring seeds constantly, roast for about 3 minutes or until seeds are fragrant and light brown and just begin to pop. (A seed pressed between the thumb and little finger should crush easily.) Transfer about ½ cup seeds at a time to the *suribachi* and grind with the pestle until no more than 10 to 15 percent of the seeds remain whole. For best flavor and aroma, use seeds immediately. To store, allow leftover seeds to cool, then seal in an airtight container in a cool, dry place. Prepare just enough for a week.

Toasting Nori

Wave a sheet of *nori* over medium heat for about 30 seconds or until crisp and slightly green.

Preparing a Steamer

Chinese Bamboo Steamer: Set the steamer over a wok filled with water to a depth of about 1½ inches. Bring water to a boil over high heat, then reduce heat to medium. Place the food in the steamer, cover with the bamboo lid, and steam for the required length of time. The woven bamboo lid prevents dripping by allowing steam to pass out. With this tool, several layers of food can be steamed at one time.

Covered Pot Steamer: Fill a 10- to 12-inch diameter pot with water to a depth of about 1 inch. Bring to a boil over high heat, then reduce heat to low. Into the pot place a collapsible French steamer, a colander, or a plate set on top of an inverted bowl. Now put in the food to be steamed. (In many cases, tofu will be wrapped in a *sudaré* bamboo mat before insertion.) Place a single layer of absorbent toweling or paper over the mouth of the pot to prevent moisture from dripping onto the food, then cover the pot. Steam as directed.

PREPARING TOFU

The following procedures are used regularly in cooking with tofu. Try to master them from the outset, since each gives the tofu a unique consistency and texture.

Draining Tofu

Place the tofu in a 1- or 2-quart flat-bottomed container. Cover well and refrigerate for 1 to 2 hours or, for a firmer texture, overnight.

If set on a small colander or folded towel placed into the container beforehand, the tofu will drain even more thoroughly.

If two cakes are stacked one on top of the other, the one on the bottom will be almost as firm as if it were pressed (see below).

If the tofu was purchased in a sealed plastic tub, prick a tiny hole in bottom of tub, drain out any water, and place tofu and tub in container as described above.

Pressing Tofu

*Towel and Fridge Method: Wrap the tofu firmly in a small terry-cloth or cotton towel folded into fourths, and set on a plate in a refrigerator for 1½ to 2 hours or overnight. To decrease the pressing time, drain the tofu beforehand, place a 2- or 3-pound weight on top of the tofu, and replace the damp towel with a dry one after about 30 minutes. Or cut the cake horizontally into halves before pressing and place in the towel as illustrated.

*Slanting Press Method: Wrap the tofu in a towel or bamboo mat (*sudaré*) (or sandwich the tofu between bamboo mats) and place on a cutting board, tray, or large plate next to the sink; raise the far end of the board several inches. Set a 2- to 4-pound weight on the tofu and let stand for 30 to 60 minutes.

*Sliced Tofu Method: Cut the tofu crosswise into ½- to ¾-inch-thick slices and arrange on two towels placed on a raised cutting board. Cover the slices with a double layer of towels and pat lightly to ensure even contact. Allow to stand for 30 to 60 minutes. This method is commonly used when preparing tofu for deep-frying. For faster results, top with a cutting board and 5-pound weight and change the towels after 10 minute intervals.

Squeezing Tofu

Place drained, parboiled, or pressed tofu (or doufu) at the center of a large dry dishtowel and gather its corners to form a sack. (Or use a tofu pressing sack [p. 109] if available.) Twist sack closed, then squeeze tofu firmly, kneading it for 2 or 3 minutes to expel as much water as possible. Squeeze lightly enough so that no tofu penetrates the sack. Empty the squeezed tofu into a mixing bowl.

Scrambling Tofu

Place tofu in an unheated skillet. Using a (wooden) spatula, break tofu into small pieces. Now cook over medium heat for 4 to 5 minutes, stirring constantly and breaking tofu into smaller and smaller pieces until whey separates from curds. Pour contents of skillet into a fine-mesh strainer; allow curds to drain for about 15 seconds if a soft consistency is desired, or for about

3 minutes for a firmer consistency. Spread curds on a large plate and allow to cool to room temperature.

Crumbling Tofu

Combine 12 ounces of tofu and 1 cup water in a saucepan. With a wooden spoon or spatula, break the tofu into very small pieces while bringing the water to a boil. Reduce heat and simmer for 1 to 2 minutes. Place a colander in the sink and line with a large cloth (or a tofu pressing sack). Pour the contents of the pan onto the cloth, gather its corners to form a sack, then twist closed. Using the bottom of a jar or a potato masher, press the tofu firmly against the bottom of the colander to expel as much water as possible. Empty the pressed tofu into a large bowl and allow to cool for several minutes. Now break the tofu into very small pieces, using your fingertips or a spoon.

Dousing Deep-fried Tofu

Place uncut pieces of deep-fried tofu in a strainer or colander. Bring 2 or 3 cups of water to a boil in a saucepan. Douse first one, then the other side of the tofu. Allow to drain for about 1 minute before using.

Or, holding individual pieces of tofu with chopsticks or tongs, dip tofu quickly into boiling water, then drain in a strainer.

Broiling Deep-fried Tofu

*If using a *stove-top burner* or bed of *live coals,* skewer tofu with a long-tined fork and hold just above the flames until lightly browned on both sides and fragrant.

*If using a regular *bread toaster,* simply drop in the deep-fried tofu and toast. Fast and easy. Serve immediately.

*If using an *oven broiler,* place tofu on a sheet of aluminum foil and broil under a high flame until lightly browned on both sides.

*If using a grill over a *barbecue* or *brazier,* or a Japanese-style broiling screen set over a stove-top burner, broil the tofu over high heat for 30 to 60 seconds on each side until speckled and fragrant. Turn with chopsticks or tongs. In our opinion, this method—used with a charcoal fire—gives the finest flavor and aroma.

*If using a *dry skillet,* preheat skillet over medium heat and drop in tofu. Pressing tofu down with chopsticks or fork, rub tofu over entire bottom of skillet until tofu is fragrant and lightly browned. Turn and brown second side.

BASIC RECIPES

The following stocks, sauces, toppings, dressings, rice and noodle dishes, and other basic preparations are often served with miso. They play important supporting roles in miso cookery, so we have grouped them all together here. They will be called for frequently in later recipes.

The different varieties of fresh *dashi* (Japanese soup stock) serve as the basis for a wide variety of miso preparations and are easily made from natural ingredients. An instant dried dashi (dashi-no-moto) is now available in the West. Refrigerated in a sealed container, fresh dashi will last for 2 to 3 days without appreciable loss of flavor. Western-style vegetable or vegetable bullion stocks make satisfactory substitutes.

Number 1 Dashi (Ichiban Dashi)

MAKES 3 CUPS

This preparation is a cornerstone of Japanese cooking. The amount and variety of bonito flakes used varies slightly from chef to chef, as does the (often highly secret) method of preparation. For best flavor use flakes which have been shaved just before use.

3 cups water, Kombu Dashi, or Niboshi Dashi
¼ to 1 cup bonito flakes (15 to 30 grams)

Heat the water until quite hot in a small saucepan. Add bonito flakes and bring to a boil. Turn off heat and allow to stand for 3 minutes, or until flakes settle; skim off foam. Filter the dashi through a (cloth-lined) strainer placed over a saucepan. Press flakes with the back of a spoon to extract remaining dashi, then reserve flakes. (Some cooks add fine-textured flakes to simmered broths, *nabé* dishes, and miso soups together with the dashi, or simply omit straining.)

For a richer flavor, use a relatively large amount of flakes, simmer flakes for 2 or 3 minutes, and allow the dashi to stand (covered) for 15 to 30 minutes before straining.

Number 2 Dashi *(Niban Dashi)*

MAKES 2½ CUPS

The basic dashi ingredients are generally reused at least once to make a milder-flavored "Number 2" dashi. Thereafter the kombu may be slivered and simmered in shoyu and *mirin* to make *tsukudani* (a garnish for rice), pressure cooked with brown rice (p. 116), or cut into strips, each of which are tied into a simple loop and simmered in Oden (p. 348) or Nishimé (p. 353); whole pieces are sometimes used to prepare vinegar- or *nukamiso* pickles.

Whereas Number 1 Dashi is featured primarily in Clear Soups, this stock is generally used when simmering vegetables, with miso soups, or in noodle broths.

2½ cups water
Bonito flakes and *kombu* reserved from Number 1 Dashi

Combine all ingredients in a small saucepan and bring just to a boil. Remove *kombu* immediately, then simmer for 1 more minute. Strain and allow to cool.

Two tablespoons of fresh bonito flakes may be added to the boiling water after removing the *kombu;* reduce heat to lowest point and simmer for 5 minutes before straining. Leftovers may be reboiled in 1¼ cups water to make Number 3 Dashi.

Kombu Dashi (*Kombu Stock*)

MAKES 3 CUPS

Used in many homes as the basis for Number 1 Dashi (see above), this stock is featured in its own right in Zen Temple Cookery. *Kombu's* flavoring components (such as glutamic acid) reside mostly on its surface; be careful not to remove them by washing. Since they and the *kombu's* nutrients pass quickly into the stock, lengthy cooking is unnecessary, and actually leads to a decline in flavor.

1 strip of *kombu,* about 3 by 7 inches, wiped lightly
     with a moistened, well-wrung cloth
3 cups water

Combine *kombu* and water in a saucepan and bring just to a boil. Turn off heat, remove *kombu,* and reserve for use in other cooking. Use dashi as required or, if preparing Number 1 (or *Niboshi*) Dashi proceed to add bonito flakes (or *niboshi*) immediately.

For a more pronounced flavor but somewhat more viscous consistency, score *kombu* surface across grain at ½-inch intervals; simmer for 3 to 5 minutes before removing; double the amount of *kombu* if desired.

VARIATIONS

*Cold Water Method: Combine water and *kombu* and allow to stand for at least six hours, and preferably overnight. Remove *kombu* and use dashi as required. (Some cooks bring the stock just to a boil before removing the *kombu.*) The lengthy soaking is often said to make best use of the *kombu's* nutrients and give the finest flavor.

*Shiitaké and Kombu Dashi: Select 2 or 3 *shiitaké* mushrooms, preferably ones having thick, partially opened caps and whitish (rather than darkish or yellowish) gills. (Or use ¼ cup dried stems or broken pieces.) Rinse briefly under running water, then soak either in cold water with the *kombu* or for 30 minutes in hot, freshly prepared Kombu Dashi. Strain dashi before use; do not squeeze *shiitaké* to extract absorbed dashi lest stock turn a dark brown.

Soybean Stock

MAKES 1 QUART

Prepare Pressure Cooked Soybeans (p. 317) doubling the amount of water used. (At the end of cooking, about 1 quart cooking liquid should remain for each cup soybeans.) Strain stock before serving beans.

Shiitaké Dashi *(Mushroom Stock)*

The preparation of Shiitaké Dashi as an integral part of the process for making miso soup is described on page 248. In Chinese Buddhist vegetarian restaurants and temples, a soybean & *shiitaké* stock is prepared by adding 1 to 2 cups washed and drained *shiitaké* stems or pieces to the ingredients for Soybean Stock (see above). The *shiitaké* are usually removed before serving the beans.

Niboshi Dashi *(Sardine Dashi)*

MAKES 3 CUPS

3 cups water or Kombu Dashi (p. 114).
¼ to ½ cup tiny (2-inch-long) dried sardines

Combine ingredients and bring to a boil over medium heat. Reduce heat to low and simmer for 3 to 5 minutes, skimming off any foam that rises to the surface. Strain through a (cloth-lined) sieve, reserving fish for use in other cookery. Use dashi as required or, if preparing Number 1 Dashi, proceed to add bonito flakes immediately.

Brown Rice

MAKES 4 CUPS

The Japanese say that when cooked, both regular and *sushi* rice are at their peak of flavor when the rice at the bottom of the pot is golden brown and slightly crisp. And even moderns prize the aroma of rice cooked in a heavy iron pot over a wood fire.

2 cups brown rice, rinsed and soaked overnight in
2⅔ cups water

In a heavy covered pot, bring water and rice to a boil over high heat. Reduce heat to low and simmer for 45 to 50 minutes, or until all water is absorbed or evaporated. Uncover pot, remove from heat, and stir rice thoroughly with a wooden spoon. (If a slightly drier consistency is desired, transfer rice to a wooden bowl before stirring). Allow to cool for several minutes, then cover pot (or bowl) with a double layer of cloth until you are ready to serve.

To pressure cook: Rinse and drain 1 cup rice. Without soaking, combine in a pressure cooker with 1 cup water. Bring to pressure (15 pounds), reduce heat to low, and simmer for 25 minutes. Allow pressure to come down naturally for 10 to 15 minutes. Open pot and mix rice well. Allow to stand uncovered for 3 to 5 minutes, then cover with a cloth as above.

Brown Rice Porridge

SERVES 2 OR 3

Called *Congee* in China and *Okayu* in Japan, this is a popular main course at breakfast in many homes and temples. Easy to digest, rice porridge is considered the ideal food for sick people, and nursing mothers sometimes skim the creamy liquid from the porridge's surface to feed their babies as a breast milk supplement. In China, rice porridge is often served garnished or seasoned with *chiang* (p. 531), as are the hundreds of varieties of rice gruel. The latter, a close relative of Japan's *Zosui* (p. 296), is prepared by cooking vegetables (often leftovers) with rice porridge and seasoning the mixture with miso or soy sauce.

½ cup brown rice, soaked overnight in 4½ cups water

Prepare as for brown rice, setting lid slightly ajar and simmering for about 90 minutes, or until rice develops a porridge-like consistency. Serve immediately, seasoned with Sesame Salt (p. 119) or salt- or miso-pickled vegetables. If desired, add crumbled *nori* and minced leeks.

Or combine 1¼ cups (leftover) cooked rice with 3½ cups water and, without soaking, proceed as above.

To pressure cook: Rinse and drain ½ cup rice. Without soaking, combine in a pressure cooker with 2½ cups water. Bring to pressure (15 pounds), reduce heat to low, and simmer for 45 minutes. Allow pressure to come down naturally for 10 to 15 minutes. Open pot and mix porridge well. Allow to stand uncovered for 3 to 5 minutes before serving.

Sushi Rice *(Rice in Vinegar Dressing)*

MAKES 2½ CUPS

1 cup (brown) rice, soaked in 1½ cups water overnight in a heavy 2- to 4-quart pot
Vinegar Dressing:
    2½ tablespoons (rice) vinegar
    1½ teaspoons honey
    2 teaspoons *mirin* (optional)
    ½ teaspoon salt

Bring soaked rice to a boil in a covered pot. Reduce heat to low and simmer for 40 to 50 minutes, or until all water has been absorbed and rice is quite light and dry. (If using white rice, simmer for only 15 to 20 minutes). Remove rice from heat and allow to stand for 5 minutes. Transfer hot rice to a large wooden bowl, platter, or other non-metallic container and immediately sprinkle on the dressing. With a wooden spoon, chopsticks, or a wide fork in one hand, and a fan or flat pot lid in the other, mix the rice vigorously while fanning to cool it as quickly as possible. Fan and stir for about 3 minutes, then allow rice to cool to room temperature.

For variety, prepare Unsweetened Sushi Rice by omitting the honey and *mirin* in the dressing, and by increasing the vinegar to 4 tablespoons and the salt to 1½ teaspoons.

Paper-thin Omelets

MAKES ABOUT 8

These omelets may be made into an envelope or purse (*chakin*) used to contain Sushi Rice or they may be cut into thin strips called "threads of gold" and scattered over the top of Sushi Rice.

4 eggs
¼ teaspoon salt
1 teaspoon ground roasted sesame seeds (p. 107) (optional)
1 to 2 teaspoons oil

In a small bowl, combine eggs, ¼ teaspoon salt and sesame; mix well. Heat a small skillet and coat lightly with oil, pouring off any excess. Pour about one-eighth of the egg mixture into the skillet, swishing it around quickly so that it just covers the bottom of the pan. Cook over high heat for about 20 to 30 seconds on one side only to form a thin omelet. Transfer omelet to a plate and allow to cool. Prepare 8 omelets, oiling the pan lightly after every 3 or 4. Sliver to use as a garnish.

Noodles

SERVES 2 OR 3

4½ to 5 ounces dry buckwheat or whole-wheat noodles (*soba* or *udon*)

Bring 2 to 3 quarts of water to a rolling boil over high heat. Scatter noodles slowly over surface of water and return to the boil. Lower heat until water is boiling actively but does not overflow. Cook uncovered for about 5 minutes, or until noodles are tender but not soft. Pour noodles into a colander placed in the sink and drain briefly, then transfer to a large container filled with circulating cold water. Stir noodles with chopsticks for several minutes until they cool to temperature of water, then transfer noodles back into colander; drain well and serve.

Sesame Salt *(Gomashio)*

MAKES ABOUT ½ CUP

A delicious all-purpose seasoning for grains, salads, beans, eggs, cereals, and sautéed vegetables, Sesame Salt is generally made with about 7 parts whole sesame seeds to 1 part salt. Please begin by studying instructions for preparing ground roasted sesame seeds (p. 107).

2 teaspoons sea salt
5 tablespoons white or black sesame seeds

Heat a heavy skillet. Pour in the salt and roast, stirring constantly, for about 1 minute. Add the sesame seeds and roast until done. Grind the salt-sesame mixture in a *suribachi* or hand mill as for Ground Roasted Sesame Seeds (p. 107). Store in an airtight container.

Ketchup-Worcestershire Sauce

MAKES 6 TABLESPOONS

½ cup ketchup
2 teaspoons Worcestershire sauce

Combine ingredients, mixing well.

Better Butter

MAKES ½ CUP

Cheaper than butter by 30 to 40 percent, containing only half as much cholesterol, salt, and saturated fats, much easier to spread (which lets you use less), and just as delicious, this is the perfect all-natural compromise for people trying to reduce their consumption of animal products yet who prefer not to use margarine, which is high in saturated fats and chemically processed at high temperatures. When allowed to burn during frying, margarine has been shown to become carcinogenic. The original recipe was developed by Adelle Davis and recently popularized in one of our favorite vegetarian cookbooks and

Fig. 11 Favorite Miso Recipes

Among the many recipes in this book, there are certain ones we enjoy again and again and like to serve to guests as an introduction to miso cookery. Most take little time to prepare and use readily available ingredients. This chart gives suggestions for their use in a weekly menu.

	Breakfast	Lunch	Dinner
Sun.	• Basic Miso Soup (p. 253)	• Floating Cloud Miso Dressing (p. 186) on your favorite salad • Mushroom Casserole with Miso, Sour Cream and Chives (p. 327)	• Peanut Miso (p. 129) or Walnut Miso (p. 128) on brown rice or on Apple Slice Hors D'oeuvres (p. 168) • Miso Mushroom Sauté (p. 140)
Mon.	• Eggs Cooked Over Brown Rice with Miso (p. 371)	• Guacamole with Miso (p. 164) as a dressing or dip; or • Miso-Sesame-Avocado Spread (p. 179)	• Baked Potatoes with Miso (p. 326) or • Potatoes with Miso White Sauce au Gratin (p. 328)
Tues.	• Deep-fried Tofu & Wakame Miso Soup (p. 239)	• Cucumber Slices Topped with Finger-Lickin' Miso (p. 167) • Grilled Cheese Sandwich on Miso-Garlic Bread (p. 184)	• Miso Spaghetti Sauce (p. 274) • Grilled Corn-on-the Cob with Miso (p. 354)

Wed.	• Instant Miso (Better 'n Coffee) Soup (p. 260)	• Velvet Zucchini Miso Soup (p. 254) • Miso–Cream Cheese Dip (p. 163)	• French Onion Soup with Miso (p. 253) or • Miso Onion Soup Casserole au Gratin (p. 327)
Thurs.	• Brown Rice or Brown Rice Porridge with Miso Top-pings (p. 287)	• Miso Onion Sauce or Mushroom Sauce (p. 272) or Miso White Sauce (p. 272) over cooked vegetables or potatoes • Miso Pâté (p. 178)	• Stir-fried Rice with Almonds and Miso (p. 289) • Miso Barbecue Sauce (p. 284) or Tofu Burgers or Tempeh Burgers
Fri.	• Scrambled Eggs with Miso, Onions, and Tofu (p. 372)	• Stir-fried Buckwheat Noodles with Miso (p. 300) • Amazaké (p. 400) or Potato Salad with Sour Cream and Miso (p. 196)	• Rich Noodle Casserole with Miso–Sour Cream and Chives (p. 326) • Baked Apples Filled with Sesame-Raisin Miso (p. 378)
Sat.	• Thick Winter Squash Soup with Miso (p. 255)	• Tabbouli with Miso (p. 309) • Miso French Dressing (p. 189) with your favorite salad	• Miso and Nutritional Yeast Gravy (p. 271) over cooked grains or vegetables, or Fried Tempeh or Tofu Dengaku (p. 355)

nutritional guides, *Laurel's Kitchen*. Better Butter is now sold commercially in Sweden; outdated dairy laws have prevented its commercialization in the U.S. It takes only a minute to make.

1 stick (½ cup) butter, cut into 4 chunks
½ cup safflower, soy, or corn oil

Combine both ingredients in a blender and puree until smooth. Using a rubber spatula, transfer mixture to a small bowl. Cover with plastic wrap and refrigerate until firm. Use as an all-purpose substitute for butter or margarine.

To make Better Butter stay firm longer at room temperature, blend in ¼ teaspoon lecithin, 2 tablespoons nonfat dried milk, and 2 tablespoons water.

6

Recipes from East and West

MISO'S EXQUISITE flavor and deep aroma, complex orchestrations brought to perfection over the centuries, evoke and accentuate the subtlest nuances of taste. Its warm colors have long been artfully used in a cuisine which demands that the eye as well as the palate find satisfaction. Its yielding texture has been prized for being gentle on the tongue.

Our 400 recipes hope to demonstrate that miso is, indeed, an all-purpose seasoning. *Arranged with our personal favorites at the beginning of each section,* they are meant to serve as an introduction to basic principles. The possibilities are limitless, as are the wonderful flavors you will discover as you begin to create new recipes based on your own favorite dishes.

Miso Toppings

Together with miso soup and *aemono,* the following are among the most popular ways of using miso in Japanese cookery. As versatile as they are delicious, Sweet Simmered Miso, Sautéed-, Mixed-, Broiled-, and Yubeshi Miso are each easy to prepare and well suited for use in a wide variety of Western-style dishes. All varieties make excellent toppings for grain, tofu, and fresh or cooked vegetables.

SWEET SIMMERED MISO
(Nerimiso)

Nerimiso derives its name from the verb *neru* which means "to simmer, stirring constantly, until smooth and thick." Prepared by combining miso with honey or sugar, water or dashi, seasonings and/or sake, and in most cases, nuts, diced vegetables, or seafoods, some varieties—such as peanut, walnut, and *yuzu*—are sold commercially, but most are made at home or in Zen temple restaurants, where they are said to have originated. Sweet simmered miso is generally prepared as a preserved food meant to be served over a period of several weeks. One or two cups are usually prepared at a time and are kept in a small attractive container, often an earthenware crock. At mealtimes, it is served as a seasoning at the table and used as a convenient topping for rice or rice porridge, chilled or deep-fried tofu, *mochi,* curries (it replaces chutney), oatmeal and other hot breakfast cereals, sweet or Irish potatoes (baked, broiled, mashed, or tempura), fresh vegetable slices, and a variety of cooked vegetables. The sweeter varieties make delicious spreads for toast or sandwiches, waffles, crêpes and pancakes, and steamed vegetables (such as cauliflower or broccoli). Small (1-teaspoon) portions are served on tiny ceramic dishes as accompaniments for Japanese-style tea and cakes, or as hors d'œuvres together with sake or beer. Sweet Simmered Miso is also used as an ingredient in cooked preparations such as Miso Oden (p. 348), Eggplants Shigiyaki (p. 360), Dengaku (p. 355), and Aemono (p. 208). Unlike regular miso, it is never used in soups.

In restaurants, sweet simmered miso is often prepared in quantities of several quarts or more; cooked in a double boiler, it is stirred for as long as 1 to 2 hours to develop cohesiveness and luster, and improve its shelf life and flavor. After cooling, it becomes somewhat firmer than regular miso, often developing a consistency similar to that of peanut butter; some makers use *mizuamé* as the sweetener to create an even firmer consistency, closer to that of taffy.

Since imported varieties are relatively expensive, several natural food companies in the United States are now beginning to prepare their own Sweet Simmered Misos (using peanuts, walnuts, or cashews as the main ingredient) packaged in small transparent cottage-cheese-type containers for nationwide distribution. Actually, any natural food store could offer its own varieties prepared fresh, refrigerated and sold in bulk. A sample large-scale recipe for Peanut & Sesame Miso is given on page 129.

We generally keep a cup of each of 3 or 4 types of Sweet Simmered Miso in the refrigerator at all times. Their flavors seem to marry and improve over a period of several weeks, and they keep their peak for a month or more if well sealed after each use.

Vary the amount of sweetening to taste. If *mirin* is unavailable, use a mixture of honey and sake (or white wine).

Red Sweet Simmered Miso *(Red Nerimiso)*

MAKES ½ CUP

This is the simplest and most basic form of Sweet Simmered Miso; all other recipes may be thought of as variations or elaborations on this fundamental theme. By adding different ingredients and seasonings (sesame, gingerroot, grated lemon rind, etc.) to those listed below, you can create a wide array of delicious toppings.

5 tablespoons red or barley miso
1½ to 2½ tablespoons honey
1 tablespoon water; or 1½ teaspoons each water and white wine (or sake or *mirin*)

Combine all ingredients in a small earthenware pot or a skillet and bring to a boil. Simmer for 2 to 3 minutes over low heat, stirring constantly with a wooden spatula or spoon, until mixture begins to thicken. Remove from heat and allow to cool to room temperature before serving. Cover and refrigerate unused portions.

VARIATIONS: Prepare as above

*Rich Red Sweet Simmered Miso: A favorite for use in Miso Oden (p. 348)
    6 tablespoons red, barley, or Hatcho miso
    2 tablespoons honey
    ¼ cup *mirin*
    2 tablespoons sake

*Chinese-style Sweet Simmered Miso: Topping for the popular noodle dish *Cha-chiang Mien*
    3 tablespoons red or barley miso (preferably chunky)
    1½ tablespoons soy sauce
    1 to 1½ tablespoons honey
    1 teaspoon (peanut or salad) oil
    ½ teaspoon sesame oil
    1 tablespoon sake or white wine
    2 tablespoons ground roasted sesame seeds (p. 107) or 1½ tablespoons sesame butter (optional)

*Hatcho Sweet Simmered Miso: Use Hatcho miso and reduce the amount of sweetening by about one-third. This preparation has a deep, chocolate-brown color and savory aroma.

*Sake Lees Sweet Simmered Miso: Add 3 to 4 tablespoons sake lees; reduce the honey to 1½ teaspoons and omit the water.

*Crunchy Granola Miso: Prepare ½ cup Red Sweet Simmered Miso (using a relatively small amount of honey) and allow to cool to room temperature. Combine with ½ to ⅔ cup granola, mixing well.

*Herb Sweet Simmered Miso: Just before removing miso from heat, stir in ½ to 1 teaspoon of any of the following fresh or dried herbs: thyme, basil, oregano, *sansho* pepper, rosemary, or mint.

*For use in Dengaku (p. 355), divide Red Sweet Simmered Miso into two equal portions. To one portion add ½ to 1 teaspoon hot mustard or ½ teaspoon *sansho* pepper.

White Sweet Simmered Miso

MAKES 1¼ CUPS

This recipe, a specialty of Kyoto's 400-year-old Nakamura-ro restaurant, is used as the topping for Japan's most famous Tofu Dengaku. In springtime, ground *kinomé* is mixed with the miso, or individual sprigs of *kinomé* are used to garnish the Dengaku portions. The use of egg gives White Sweet Simmered Miso a rich, smooth texture.

1 cup sweet white or ⅔ cup mellow white miso
3 tablespoons *mirin*
1½ tablespoons sake
1 egg yolk
3 tablespoons ground roasted sesame seeds (p. 107)
    or 1½ tablespoons sesame butter or *tahini*

Prepare as for Red Sweet Simmered Miso (see above).

VARIATION: Prepare as above

*Sweet White Sweet Simmered Miso (Makes ½ cup)
    ¼ cup sweet white or 2½ tablespoons mellow white
      miso
    1½ to 2 teaspoons honey
    2 teaspoons *mirin*
    1 egg yolk
    Dash of *sansho* pepper (optional)

For use in Dengaku (p. 355) or hors d'œuvres (p.
169), or as a topping for deep-fried foods, divide the
prepared miso into two equal portions. To one, add
any of the following: ½ to 1 teaspoon grated gingerroot; 2 to 3 tablespoons thinly sliced leeks or green
onions; 3 to 4 tablespoons ground roasted sesame
seeds (p. 107) or sesame butter; 1 to 2 tablespoons
bonito flakes and 1½ teaspoons water.

Walnut Miso

MAKES 1 CUP

One of our favorite miso preparations, Walnut Miso
is often served in Zen temple restaurants and is sold
commercially in Japan. Delicious as a topping for crisp
apple slices (p. 168).

1 cup walnut meats, preferably large pieces
¼ cup red, barley, or akadashi miso
2 to 3 tablespoons honey or *mizuamé*
1 tablespoon water or 1½ teaspoons each water and
    white wine (or sake)

Prepare as for Red Sweet Simmered Miso (see
above).

VARIATIONS
*Sauté walnuts in 1 tablespoon oil for 1 minute before
adding remaining ingredients. Or pre-roast walnuts
until fragrant in a dry pan or oven and, if desired, add

¼ cup sesame butter to the ingredients listed above.
*Cashew, Almond, or Pecan Miso: Substitute ¾ to 1 cup of any one of these for the walnuts.
*Sunflower Seed Miso: Sauté ½ cup sunflower seeds in 1 teaspoon oil for 1 to 2 minutes, then add miso and other ingredients and proceed as above.

Peanut Miso

MAKES ½ TO ¾ CUP

1 cup peanuts, lightly roasted if desired
¼ cup red, barley, or Hatcho miso
1½ to 3 tablespoons honey or *mizuamé*
2 tablespoons water; or 1 tablespoon each water and
    sake, wine, or *mirin*

Prepare as for Red Sweet Simmered Miso (see above).

VARIATIONS

*Peanut & Raisin Miso: Use ¼ cup each peanuts and raisins, and 2 to 3 teaspoons honey. Add 1 to 2 tablespoons (whole or ground) roasted sesame seeds, if desired. This delicious product is sold commercially in Japan and America.
***Use akadashi miso and reduce the honey to 1½ teaspoons.
***Sauté peanuts briefly in oil before adding the remaining ingredients; serve garnished with a sprig of *kinomé*.
***Use ¼ cup sweet white miso, omit the honey and add ¼ to ½ teaspoon salt.
***Serve peanut miso wrapped in a green beefsteak (shiso) leaf. A treat in box lunches in some parts of Japan.

Peanut & Sesame Miso

MAKES 1 GALLON

Here is a sample recipe that could be used by natural food stores, restaurants, or communities that would like to begin commercial production of Sweet Simmered Miso.

16 cups whole roasted peanuts, or substitute walnuts, cashews, or sunflower seeds
4 cups red or barley miso
1 cup roasted sesame seeds (whole or ground)
1 to 2½ cups honey
½ to 1 cup malt syrup
½ cup water

Combine all ingredients in a heavy 1½- to 2-gallon pot and bring to a boil. Simmer, stirring constantly for 5 to 10 minutes, or until mixture begins to thicken. Pour into a large crock or wide-mouth jar and allow to cool to room temperature. Cover and refrigerate.

For variety, add 2 cups raisins and reduce the honey to taste.

Sesame Miso

MAKES ¾ CUP

The use of freshly-ground roasted sesame seeds gives the finest flavor and aroma. If desired, use black seeds with Red or Hatcho Sweet Simmered Miso, but always use white seeds with White Sweet Simmered Miso. Excellent as a topping for sautéed or steamed vegetables such as *daikon,* turnips, eggplants, or burdock root. Sesame Miso thinned in water during cooking also makes a delicious sauce.

¼ cup sesame butter, *tahini,* or ground roasted sesame seeds (p. 54)
⅓ cup red, barley, or Hatcho miso
1 to 2 tablespoons honey
1 tablespoon water; or 1½ teaspoons each water and sake (or white wine)
1 to 2 teaspoons grated orange, lemon, or *yuzu* rind (optional)

Prepare as for Red Sweet Simmered Miso (see above).

VARIATIONS

*For the sweet, chocolate-like flavor of Chinese *T'ien Mien Chiang* or Peking Duck Dipping Sauce (p. 154), use akadashi instead of the red miso.

*To the basic recipe add ¼ cup whole or chopped nutmeats (almonds, walnuts, etc.)

*To ¼ cup Red or White Sweet Simmered Miso, add 1 to 2 tablespoons ground roasted sesame seeds or sesame butter, and ½ to 1 teaspoon grated ginger-root.

Yuzu Miso

MAKES 1 CUP

This recipe comes from Tokyo's 370-year-old tofu restaurant, Sasa-no-Yuki, where the miso is served over warm pieces of silken tofu and also sold in small ceramic jars for home use. The fragrant rind of the *yuzu* (citron) is preserved for about 1 year in *shochu*—a popular and very potent type of spirits related to gin—before being used in the miso. The chefs prepare about 35 pounds of *yuzu* miso at a time, stirring the mixture in a heavy pot for 1½ to 3 hours over low heat to develop a dark lustrous color. Some commercial varieties, most of which are a creamy beige, contain *yuzu* rind which has been immersed for 1 year in a crock of sugar before being diced and simmered with sweet white miso. In grating fresh *yuzu* at home, it is important to use only the yellow or green surface layers of the well-washed rind. If the deeper white layers are used, the miso may become bitter.

½ cup (light) red or barley miso
6 to 6½ tablespoons sugar or 3 tablespoons honey
6 tablespoons water
½ teaspoon grated *yuzu* rind, or substitute 1 to 2
    teaspoons grated lemon, lime, or orange rind

Prepare as for Red Sweet Simmered Miso (p. 126) except add the *yuzu* rind just before removing miso from heat.

For a darker color, simmer for a longer time. For a lighter color, substitute sweet white miso for the red and reduce sugar to 1½ tablespoons. The addition of 1 tablespoon *mirin* gives a nice luster without lengthy cooking.

VARIATIONS

*Tipsy Wintertime Yuzu Miso: Prized for its subtle bitterness, this preparation makes a fine topping for cooked vegetables and broiled tofu. In traditional Japanese homes, the *yuzu* and sake are simmered in a small earthenware teapot set over the mouth of a large iron tea kettle heated by a charcoal fire in the living room *hibachi* brazier.

During December or January, choose a well-ripened, yellow *yuzu*, wash well, and cover with sake or white wine in a small lidded pot. Place pot over a double boiler and simmer until *yuzu* dissolves. (If double boiling is inconvenient, use a mixture of equal parts sake and water and simmer over low heat, stirring occasionally.) Remove *yuzu* seeds, then stir in sweet white miso and a little sugar. Simmer over low heat, stirring occasionally, until well thickened.

Lemon or Lime Miso

MAKES ¼ CUP

¼ cup red, barley, or Hatcho miso
1½ to 3 teaspoons honey
1 tablespoon water
1 teaspoon lemon (or lime) juice
1 teaspoon grated lemon (or lime) rind

Combine the first three ingredients in a skillet and proceed as for Red Sweet Simmered Miso (p. 126). After removing from heat, stir in lemon juice and rind;

allow to cool to room temperature. Delicious with sliced bananas, apples, and most deep-fried foods.

A softer version can be prepared by mixing 2 teaspoons lemon juice with 2 tablespoons Red Sweet Simmered Miso. Or prepare as for Tipsy Wintertime Yuzu Miso (above).

Tangy Mustard Miso

MAKES 1 CUP

2 tablespoons red, barley, or Hatcho miso
2 tablespoons vinegar
½ teaspoon hot mustard
1 tablespoon oil
Dash of pepper (optional)

Prepare as for Red Sweet Simmered Miso (p. 126) but simmer for only 30 to 60 seconds. For variety, add 1 tablespoon ground roasted sesame seeds.

Kinomé Miso *(Miso with Fresh Sansho Leaves)*

Also called *sansho* miso, this green and refreshingly fragrant miso is a springtime favorite. When *kinomé,* the fresh sprigs of the *sansho* tree, emerge early each April, this miso is widely enjoyed as a topping for Tofu Dengaku (p. 355), in *aemono* (p. 208) or on butter-fried mushrooms.

¼ cup (about 60) *kinomé* leaves (not sprigs)
5 tablespoons sweet white miso
1½ teaspoons honey
2 tablespoons water
1 teaspoon shoyu (optional)
1½ teaspoons *mirin* or sake (optional)
Dash of *sansho* pepper (optional)

Place leaves in a strainer, douse with boiling water, and drain well. Grind leaves thoroughly in a *suribachi* (or mortar), or mince with a knife. Combine the next five ingredients in a small saucepan and prepare as for Red Sweet Simmered Miso (p. 126). Add contents of saucepan and pepper, if desired, to ground *kinomé* in *suribachi;* mix well.

VARIATION

*Jade-Green Miso: Collect 4 ounces of the tender tips of *(horenso)* spinach and/or *daikon* leaves. Mince thoroughly, then grind almost to a paste in a *suribachi* or mortar. Pour in 1 cup water and, using your fingertips, free the ground leaves from the grooves in the bowl. Now pour the contents of the *suribachi* into a fine sieve set over a small saucepan and rub the leaves through the sieve with the back of a large spoon. Heat contents of saucepan over high heat until puréed leaves float to the surface, then reduce heat to low and simmer for 1 minute. Pour contents of pan into a cloth-lined strainer; drain well. Using a small spoon, carefully remove green purée (called *aoyosé*) from cloth. Add 1 teaspoon *aoyosé* to Kinomé Miso, stirring well, until the miso has turned a delicate green.

A simpler version of *aoyosé* may be prepared by parboiling and draining the greens, then pressing them with your fingertips; grind in a *suribachi* or rub through a strainer, then mix with the miso.

In many recipes *aoyosé* is used together with *kinomé* to give the miso a richer color. It is stirred into the miso just before the miso is mixed with the *kinomé*.

Egg Yolk Miso

MAKES 1 CUP

6 tablespoons sweet white or ¼ cup mellow white
    miso
2 egg yolks
1 tablespoon honey
5 tablespoons dashi (p. 112), stock, or water
Dash of *sansho* pepper (optional)

Prepare as for Red Sweet Simmered Miso (p. 126).

For use in Tofu Dengaku (p. 355), divide the prepared miso into 2 equal portions. To one add 1 teaspoon *aoyosé* (see preceding recipe) and 60 *kinomé* leaves prepared as for Kinomé Miso. Stir in these ingredients just after removing miso from the heat.

Garlic Miso

MAKES ¼ CUP

Often cooked without thinning the miso with water or sake, this preparation has a very firm texture: refrigerated, it will stay fresh for several months. Considered by many Japanese to promote good health, it is usually served as a topping for hot rice; the heat gives it a softer consistency.

3 cloves of garlic, thinly sliced or crushed
¼ cup red, barley, or Hatcho miso
2½ to 4 teaspoons honey
2 teaspoons sake, white wine, or water (optional)

Prepare as for Red Sweet Simmered Miso (p. 126), but simmer over very low heat for 8 to 10 minutes, or until quite firm.

Gingerroot Miso

MAKES ½ CUP

2 to 3 teaspoons grated gingerroot
5 tablespoons red, barley, or Hatcho miso
1 to 1½ tablespoons honey
2 teaspoons sake, white wine, or water

Prepare as for Red Sweet Simmered Miso (p. 126). Serve with Dengaku (p. 355), as a cracker spread, with deep-fried foods, or as a topping for rice.

To obtain a somewhat similar flavor, simply mix ½ teaspoon grated gingerroot juice with ¼ cup Red Sweet Simmered Miso.

Leek or Onion Miso

MAKES ½ CUP

This miso is especially popular in Japanese villages where it is used as a topping for baked potatoes—and as a cure for colds.

6 tablespoons barley or red miso
6 tablespoons diced or grated leek, scallion or onion
2 tablespoons bonito flakes (optional)

Prepare as for Red Sweet Simmered Miso (p. 126) but cook for only 1 to 2 minutes. Or simply mix all ingredients without cooking.

VARIATIONS

*For a sweeter version of the above, mix 1 part Red Sweet Simmered Miso (p. 126) with 1 part minced leeks or onions. Excellent as a topping for Dengaku (p. 355).

*Red Pepper & Leek Miso: This popular Korean preparation called *doen jang* is usually prepared with Red Pepper Miso (*kochu jang;* p. 541) and served as a zesty topping for cooked rice. Omit the bonito flakes in the basic recipe above and add ¼ teaspoon ground red pepper (cayenne) or Tabasco sauce and 1 teaspoon (sesame) oil.

Beefsteak Leaf Miso *(Shiso Miso)*

MAKES ½ CUP

1 tablespoon butter or Better Butter (p. 119)
3 tablespoons red or barley miso
1 tablespoon honey
4 tablespoons water
¼ teaspoon 7-spice or ground red pepper
¼ cup minced green beefsteak leaves

Melt the butter in a skillet. Add the next four ingredients and cook, stirring constantly, for 3 to 5 minutes or until fairly thick. Mix in the beefsteak leaves and cook for 1 minute more.

Or, substitute ¾ cup beefsteak seeds for the leaves. Sauté in the butter for 1 minute before adding remaining ingredients.

Vinegar Miso

MAKES ⅜ CUP

This miso is generally prepared without cooking and used in various forms as a dressing for *aemono* (p. 208). Only when the miso is heated or cooked is Vinegar Miso considered a type of Sweet Simmered Miso.

3 tablespoons red or barley miso
3 tablespoons vinegar or lemon juice
1 tablespoon honey

Heat the miso until just warm in a small saucepan. Remove from heat and mix in vinegar and honey, stirring until smooth. Allow to cool before serving. Use as a topping for fresh or cooked vegetables, or deep-fried foods, or as a dressing for *aemono*.

Variations containing sweet white miso, *mirin*, mustard, sesame, walnuts, peanuts, or chives may be prepared as above using the ingredients found in the recipes beginning on page 208.

Sweetened Mustard Vinegar Miso

MAKES ½ CUP

3 tablespoons red, barley, or Hatcho miso
1½ teaspoons honey
1 tablespoon oil
¼ cup water
1 tablespoon vinegar
½ teaspoon hot mustard

Combine the first four ingredients in a saucepan or skillet and bring to a boil. Simmer, stirring constantly, for 3 to 4 minutes, or until as firm as regular miso. Remove from heat, stir in vinegar and mustard, and allow to cool. Delicious with Chilled Noodles (p. 300).

Kanro Hishio

MAKES ½ CUP

Kanro means "sweet morning dew." This product, sold commercially in Japan, is a specialty from the city of Choshi, famous for its fine shoyu and hishio.

½ cup hishio (p. 78)
2 tablespoons *mizuamé* or honey
1 teaspoon sake or white wine (optional)

Prepare as for Red Sweet Simmered Miso (p. 126).

Red Pepper Miso with Burdock Root

MAKES ¾ CUP

At Tokyo's famous *Yabusoba* noodle restaurant, a dab of this tangy miso is served on a tiny wooden dish as an accompaniment for green tea.

1 teaspoon oil
6 tablespoons minced burdock root, soaked for 10 minutes in water, and drained
2½ tablespoons red miso
2½ tablespoons sweet red miso
2 tablespoons sugar or 1 tablespoon honey
2 tablespoons water or the starchy water remaining after boiling *soba* buckwheat noodles
⅛ to ¼ teaspoon 7-spice or minced red peppers, or Tabasco sauce

Heat a skillet and coat with the oil. Add burdock root and sauté for 2 or 3 minutes. Add remaining ingredients and cook over low heat, stirring constantly, for about 5 minutes. Allow to cool before serving.

If sweet red miso is unavailable, substitute red or barley miso and increase the amount of sugar by 1½ tablespoons.

Burdock

MISO SAUTÉ
(Abura Miso)

Originally a Chinese-style preparation featuring fresh vegetables sautéed in sesame oil, Miso Sauté serves as a delicious topping for brown rice or rice porridge, fresh or cooked vegetable slices, and chilled or deep-fried tofu. Refrigerated and well-sealed, unused portions will keep for up to 1 week. In each of the following recipes, up to one half of the oil may be sesame, which lends a nutty flavor and savory aroma. Experiment with other vegetables and nuts, or even with fruits.

Plain Miso Sauté

MAKES ¼ CUP

1½ tablespoons (sesame) oil
4½ tablespoons red, barley, or Hatcho miso

Heat a skillet and coat with the oil. Add miso and sauté over low heat for about 1 minute, or until miso just begins to stick to skillet. Allow to cool before serving. Delicious on cucumber slices.

Mushroom Miso Sauté

MAKES ½ CUP

2 tablespoons oil
10 mushrooms, thinly sliced
1 tablespoon red, barley, or Hatcho miso
1 teaspoon honey

Heat a skillet or wok and coat with the oil. Add mushrooms and sauté over medium heat for about 1 minute or until tender. Reduce heat to low, add miso and honey, and cook, stirring constantly, for about 1 minute more, or until mushrooms are evenly coated with miso. Allow to cool to room temperature before serving.

For variety, substitute Better Butter (p. 119) or but-

ter for one-half of the oil, and sauté over low heat
adding ¼ cup chopped walnut meats. Or use sweet
white miso and reduce the honey to ½ teaspoon.

OTHER TYPES OF VEGETABLE MISO SAUTE

Each of the following recipes is prepared in basically the same way as Mushroom Miso Sauté. Use
1½ to 2 tablespoons oil, 1 to 1½ tablespoons
miso, and 1 to 1½ teaspoons honey.

*Lotus root: Sauté 1½ cups ginkgo leaves of lotus
root over low heat for about 5 minutes, or until tender but still crisp. Proceed as above.

*Kabocha: Use ¼ onion cut into thin wedges and
1½ cups thinly sliced pieces of *kabocha,* squash, or
pumpkin. Sauté over medium-high heat for 4 to 5
minutes, or until softened. Add 1 tablespoon sesame
butter, *tahini,* or ground roasted sesame seeds (p. 107)
together with the miso and honey.

*Eggplant: Use 1 diced onion and 1½ cups 2-inch
matchsticks of eggplant. Sauté just until all oil is absorbed, then add miso and honey.

*Sweet potato: Use 1¼ cups of sweet potato, yam,
or Irish potato cubes. Sauté over high heat for 3 to
5 minutes until softened. If desired, sauté ½ diced
onion and ½ thinly sliced carrot for 3 to 4 minutes
before adding potatoes.

*Burdock root: Use 1½ to 2 cups matchsticks of
burdock root, soaked (p. 104), and 1 carrot cut into
matchsticks or grated. Sauté burdock root over high
heat for 8 to 10 minutes, or until softened. Add carrot and sauté for 5 minutes more, or until both vegetables are tender. If desired, add 1 to 2 tablespoons
roasted sesame seeds together with the miso and
honey.

*Onion: Use 2 onions, cut into thin wedges, and 1
carrot, thinly sliced, slivered, or grated. Sauté both
vegetables together over medium heat for 5 to 6 minutes, or until carrot is tender. Proceed as for Mushroom Miso Sauté.

*Gingerroot: Sauté 2 tablespoons grated gingerroot
for about 1 minute.

*Celery: Sauté 1 cup diced celery or celery root for 2 minutes over high heat, or until softened. Add miso and honey and proceed as above.

Lemon-Walnut-Mushroom Miso Sauté

MAKES ¾ CUP

1½ teaspoons oil or Better Butter (p. 119)
4 (*shiitaké*) mushrooms, thinly sliced (about ⅓ cup)
1 tablespoon minced lemon, lime, or *yuzu* rind
¼ to ½ cup chopped walnut meats
⅓ cup red, barley, or Hatcho miso
1½ to 2 tablespoons honey
2 to 3 tablespoons water

Prepare as for Mushroom Miso Sauté (p. 140) but sauté mushrooms for 2 minutes, then add lemon rind and walnuts, and sauté for 1 minute more.

Crumbly Tekka Miso

MAKES 1½ CUPS

The word *tekka* is composed of the Chinese characters for "metal" and "fire": this all-purpose condiment was traditionally simmered for a long time on a metal griddle or in a heavy iron pot. A favorite topping for brown rice, rice porridge, rice patties, and regular or deep-fried tofu, it is also served as is, as an hors d'œuvre with sake, beer, or wine. Several commercial varieties are now available at Japanese natural food stores and miso retail stores, and every good chef has his or her own unique recipe. Crumbly Tekka Miso is prepared without sweetening and generally features chunky Hatcho miso and finely shaved burdock root; it is sautéed in sesame oil, often for as long as several hours, to create its dry, crumbly texture. Most varieties also contain roasted soybeans. The composition of typical commercial varieties is 9 percent protein, 40 percent moisture, 5.2 percent fat, and 3 percent minerals (ash), with 249 calories per 100 grams.

In Japan, this preparation is known formally as *Konjo Tekka Miso*. The word *konjo* means "root nature" and refers to those qualities in a great man which carry him through the most difficult situations. It is said that this miso was first developed during World War II for use as a seasoning with brown rice —which took the place of the usual white rice since it was less expensive, more nourishing, and did not require the time, energy, and manpower necessary for polishing. Eating this miso was believed to help a man develop his "root character". Today, tekka is widely regarded as one of Japan's finest and most high-class miso preparations, prized for its flavor and aroma, its long lasting qualities and versatility, and its medicinal properties (which make it a popular gift to friends who are sick). In Zen temples, it is often served as a condiment with each meal of the day.

3 tablespoons sesame oil
½ cup minced burdock root, soaked in cold water for 15 minutes and drained
6 tablespoons minced carrot or slivered, reconstituted *kombu*
¼ cup minced lotus root or whole peanuts
1 teaspoon grated gingerroot
¼ cup roasted soybeans (optional)
1 cup Hatcho, red, or barley miso
Dash of (7-spice) red pepper (optional)

Heat a large skillet or wok and coat with the oil. Add burdock root and sauté over high heat for 1 minute. Reduce heat to medium, add carrot and lotus root, and sauté for 2 to 3 minutes. Mix in gingerroot, miso and, if used, soybeans and red pepper: sauté for 2 minutes more. Reduce heat to low and cook, stirring constantly with a wooden spatula, for 20 to 30 minutes, or until miso is crumbly and fairly dry. Allow to cool before serving. Refrigerate unused portions in an airtight container.

VARIATION

*If roasted soybeans are unavailable, wash ¼ cup whole soybeans and soak in water for 30 minutes. (Or, for a firmer texture, omit soaking.) Drain beans thoroughly, then pat dry with a towel. Dry-roast in a heavy skillet until lightly browned and speckled, then add ¼ cup water and steam over low heat for 15 minutes. Add soybeans to miso together with carrots, and proceed as above.

Fine-textured Crumbly Tekka Miso

MAKES 2 CUPS

3 to 4 tablespoons (unrefined) sesame oil
¼ cup grated carrot
¼ cup grated lotus root
¼ cup grated burdock root
¼ cup black sesame seeds, ground to a paste; or
    sesame butter
¼ cup bonito flakes
2½ teaspoons minced gingerroot
1 cup (chunky) Hatcho miso

Heat a skillet and coat with the oil. Add the next six ingredients and sauté for about 5 minutes. Add miso, stirring well until evenly mixed with other ingredients. Reduce heat to very low and cook, stirring occasionally, for 20 to 30 minutes, or until miso is quite dry and slightly crumbly.

Moist Tekka Miso with Orange Rind

MAKES 3½ CUPS

5 tablespoons sesame oil
2 cups minced onion
⅔ cup minced burdock root
⅔ cup minced lotus root
⅔ cup minced or grated carrot
1 cup red, barley, or Hatcho miso
1 cup water
1 tablespoon grated gingerroot
1 teaspoon grated orange rind

Heat a heavy skillet and coat with the oil. Add onions and sauté for 5 minutes. Add consecutively burdock root, lotus root, and carrot, sautéing each lightly as you add it. Thin miso with the water and add, then stir in gingerroot and orange rind. Reduce heat to low and cover pan. Simmer, stirring occasionally, for 30 to 40 minutes, or until firm.

Sweetened Tekka Miso

MAKES 1¼ CUPS

The most popular form of *tekka* miso, this sweetened variety generally contains the same ingredients as Crumbly Tekka Miso plus honey; the miso is cooked only until smooth and firm.

1 tablespoon oil
⅔ cup thin rounds or matchsticks of burdock root, peeled, soaked in cold water for 15 minutes, and drained
½ carrot, cut into matchsticks
½ cup diced or slivered lotus root (optional)
⅓ cup Hatcho, red, or akadashi miso
2 tablespoons honey
1 tablespoon sake or white wine
2 tablespoons ground roasted sesame seeds (p. 107), sesame butter or *tahini;* or ¼ cup poppy or hemp seeds
¼ cup roasted soybeans (or see the variation to Crumbly Tekka Miso, p. 141)

Heat a wok or skillet and coat with the oil. Add burdock root and carrot, and sauté over medium-high heat for 3 or 4 minutes. Reduce heat to low, then stir in the next four ingredients and sauté for 3 or 4 minutes more. Stir in soybeans and remove from heat. Transfer to a bowl and allow to cool. Use as an all-purpose condiment or topping.

VARIATION

*Tekka Miso from Hatcho Sweet Simmered Miso

¼ cup soybeans
1 tablespoon sesame oil
½ cup thin rounds or matchsticks of burdock root, prepared as above
¾ cup Hatcho Sweet Simmered Miso (p. 127)
1 tablespoon ground, roasted sesame seeds
1 tablespoon *mirin*

Roast soybeans as described in the variation under Crumbly Tekka Miso (p. 141). Sauté burdock in oil for 4 minutes, then add cooked beans and Sweet Simmered Miso, and sauté for 3 or 4 minutes more. Stir in sesame and *mirin,* and remove from heat.

Carrot & Red Pepper Miso Sauté

· MAKES ¾ CUP

Many delicious varieties of Miso Sauté may be prepared without the use of sweetening using the basic techniques given in the following two recipes.

3 tablespoons sesame oil
¼ teaspoon minced red peppers, Chinese red-pepper *chiang,* or Tabasco sauce
1 carrot, grated fine
1 tablespoon grated gingerroot
¼ cup red, barley, or Hatcho miso

Heat a wok or skillet and coat with the oil. Add the red pepper and sauté for 15 seconds. Add grated carrot and gingerroot and sauté for 1 minute more. Stir in miso and sauté for 6 more minutes. Remove from heat and allow to cool before serving.

Onion-Sesame Miso Sauté

MAKES ½ CUP

1 tablespoon sesame oil
½ cup minced wild onions, scallions, leeks, or onions
3 to 4 tablespoons sweet red miso
Dash of 7-spice red pepper, Tabasco sauce, or paprika

Heat the oil over high heat in a wok or skillet. Add onions and sauté for about 1 minute. Stir in the miso and red pepper, reduce heat to low, and sauté for 2 or 3 minutes more.

Onion Miso Sauté with Orange

MAKES 1½ CUPS

2 tablespoons sesame oil
4 onions, thinly sliced
3 tablespoons red, barley, or Hatcho miso
¼ cup water
1 teaspoon grated orange rind
¼ cup grated cheese (optional)

Heat a skillet and coat with the oil. Add onions and sauté for 5 minutes. Stir in miso and water, cover, and simmer for 8 to 10 minutes. Add orange rind and, if used, grated cheese; remove from heat. For best flavor, allow to stand for 6 to 8 hours. Delicious on brown rice, tofu, or toast.

Sesame-Leek Miso Sauté

MAKES 1¼ CUPS

2 tablespoons sesame oil
2 cups chopped leeks or scallions, separated into
    whites and greens
6 tablespoons water or stock
4 tablespoons red, barley, or Hatcho miso

Heat a skillet or wok and coat with the oil. Add greens and sauté for 30 seconds. Add whites and sauté for 30 seconds more. Add 4 tablespoons water, cover pan, and simmer for 5 minutes. Thin miso in remaining 2 tablespoons water, add to vegetables, and simmer for 2 or 3 minutes.

Spicy Eggplant-Miso Sauté

MAKES 1½ CUPS

2 tablespoons oil
1¾ cups unpeeled, diced eggplants
3 tablespoons red, barley, or Hatcho miso
2½ teaspoons honey
2 tablespoons water
⅔ cup leeks or scallions, cut into ½-inch lengths
¼ teaspoon (7-spice) red pepper or Tabasco sauce

Heat a skillet or wok and coat with the oil. Add eggplants and sauté over low heat for 3 to 4 minutes. Add miso, honey, and water and cook, stirring constantly, for 2 to 3 minutes. Mix in leeks, season with red pepper, and cook for 1 minute more.

For variety, omit leeks and serve skewered on foodpicks as a hot or cold hors d'oeuvre.

Garlic & Green Pepper Miso Sauté

MAKES ½ CUP

1 tablespoon oil
½ clove garlic, crushed or minced
1 or 2 green peppers, thinly sliced
2 tablespoons barley, red, or Hatcho miso
1½ teaspoons honey
3 tablespoons water

Heat a wok or skillet and coat with the oil. Add garlic and sauté over high heat for about 15 seconds. Add green peppers and sauté for 1 minute more. Reduce heat to medium, stir in remaining ingredients and cook, stirring constantly, for 2 more minutes. Allow to cool before serving.

Spicy Burdock Miso Sauté

MAKES 1¼ CUPS

1 tablespoon sesame oil
1¼ cups shaved or slivered burdock root
1 teaspoon grated gingerroot; or ½ teaspoon grated
    lemon rind; or 1 tablespoon minced *umeboshi*
    salt plums
3 tablespoons red, barley, or Hatcho miso
1 tablespoon sesame butter or *tahini*
5 tablespoons water
Dash of (7-spice) red pepper

Heat a skillet or wok and coat with the oil. Add burdock and sauté for 5 minutes. Combine the next four ingredients, mixing well, then add to contents of skillet. Cover and simmer for 15 minutes over very low heat, stirring occasionally. Season with the red pepper and allow to cool. Serve as a topping for cooked Brown Rice (p. 287).

Green Pepper Miso Sauté

MAKES ⅔ CUP

1 tablespoon oil
1 green pepper, diced
¼ cup red, barley, or Hatcho miso
2 tablespoons sake or white wine
3 to 4 tablespoons water
1½ teaspoons honey
1 teaspoon grated *yuzu*, lime, or lemon rind (optional)

Heat a wok or skillet and coat with the oil. Add green pepper and sauté for 1 minute. Mix in the next four ingredients and sauté for about 1 minute more. Remove from heat and stir in grated citrus peel. Serve as a sauce for croquettes, tofu (regular or deep-fried), baked potatoes, or sautéed vegetables.

For variety, substitute *sansho* pepper or beefsteak seeds for the citrus peel.

Beefsteak Seed Miso Sauté *(Shisonomi Abura Miso)*

MAKES ½ CUP

1 teaspoon oil
¼ cup beefsteak seeds or buds, rubbed with salt,
    then rinsed well
¼ cup red, barley, or Hatcho miso
1¼ to 1½ tablespoons honey
1 teaspoon shoyu
1 tablespoon water or dashi (p. 112)

Heat a skillet and coat with the oil. Add beefsteak seeds and sauté for 1 minute. Add remaining ingredients and proceed as for Mushroom Miso Sauté (p. 140), sautéing for 9 to 10 minutes more.

Banana Miso Sauté

MAKES 2 CUPS

1 tablespoon Better Butter (p. 119), butter or oil
2 bananas, cut into thin rounds
½ cup chopped walnut or almond meats (optional)
1 tablespoon sweet white or 2 teaspoons mellow
    white miso
½ teaspoon honey (optional)

Prepare as for Mushroom Miso Sauté (p. 140), sautéing the walnuts, if used, with the bananas.

For richer color and flavor, use 1 tablespoon red or barley miso and 1½ teaspoons honey.

Spicy Korean Miso Sauté

MAKES ¾ CUP

2 tablespoons sesame oil
1 clove of garlic, crushed
1 tablespoon grated gingerroot
2 green peppers, minced
½ small onion, diced
Dash of minced red pepper, Tabasco sauce, or 7-spice
    red pepper
3 tablespoons red, barley, or Hatcho miso
2 teaspoons soy sauce
1 tablespoon sake or white wine

Heat a wok or skillet and coat with the oil. Add the next five ingredients and sauté for 2 minutes. Stir in the miso, soy sauce, and sake, return just to the boil, and remove from heat. Allow to cool before serving. Delicious as a topping for fresh cucumber, celery, or tomato slices; for noodles or deep-fried tofu.

Vinegar Miso Sauté (Abura-su Miso)

MAKES ½ CUP

The addition of vinegar to many varieties of Miso Sauté gives a tangy flavor which is particularly well suited to deep-fried foods.

1 tablespoon oil
1 small onion or leek, thinly sliced
1 clove of garlic, crushed or minced
1½ tablespoons red, barley, or Hatcho miso
1½ teaspoons honey
1 tablespoon vinegar

Heat a wok or skillet and coat with the oil. Add onion and garlic and sauté over high heat for 2 minutes. Reduce heat to low, mix in miso and honey, and simmer for 1 minute more. Remove from heat, mix in vinegar, and allow to cool.

VARIATIONS

*Mustard-Vinegar Miso Sauté: Add ½ teaspoon hot mustard together with the vinegar.
*Substitute for the onions an equal volume of thinly sliced green peppers, mushrooms, or bamboo shoots.
*Add vinegar to taste to any of the previous recipes for Miso Sauté.

MIXED MISO
(Awasé Miso)

These simple but delicious recipes, requiring no cooking, are quick and easy to prepare. A number of closely related dishes are given at Vinegar Miso Dressings (p. 218). Unseasoned mixed misos are described on page 81.

Mixed Red Miso Toppings

MAKES ABOUT ¼ CUP

In Japan, many of the following mixtures, prepared with shoyu rather than miso, are widely used as dipping sauces. The simplest of all types of miso recipes, these are extremely versatile, adapting themselves readily to experimentation with your favorite herbs and spices. All varieties may be served as toppings for rice or rice gruel, regular or deep-fried tofu, fresh vegetable slices, *mochi,* and baked or broiled potatoes.

Combine ¼ cup red, barley, or Hatcho miso with any one of the following, mixing well. Cover and refrigerate unused portions.

*Garlic: 2 cloves of garlic, grated or crushed

*Bonito: ¼ cup bonito flakes and, if desired, 1½ tablespoons *mirin*

*Umeboshi salt plums: 1½ tablespoons minced *umeboshi* (about 10) and, if desired, 2 tablespoons bonito flakes

*Wasabi: 1 teaspoon freshly grated *wasabi, wasabi* paste, or Western-style horseradish and, if desired, 1½ teaspoons honey

*Gingerroot: 2 teaspoons grated gingerroot

*Daikon: 4 to 6 tablespoons grated *daikon* and, if desired, 2 tablespoons bonito flakes

*Leek: ¼ cup diced or grated leeks or scallions and, if desired, 1½ tablespoons bonito flakes

*Citrus: 1 to 2 teaspoons grated or slivered lemon, lime, or *yuzu* rind

*Herb: ½ to 1 teaspoon dill, marjoram, oregano, thyme, basil, or tarragon

*Mustard: ½ to 1 teaspoon hot mustard and 2 tablespoons *mirin,* sake, or white wine

*Lemon: 2 to 2½ tablespoons lemon (or lime) juice or vinegar and, if desired, 2 tablespoons sake or white wine

*Sesame: 1½ tablespoons sesame or nut but-
ter and, if desired, 1½ tablespoons honey and
4 teaspoons sake or white wine
*Sesame-Bonito-Citrus: 1 tablespoon each ses-
ame butter and bonito flakes (or grated cheese)
and ¼ teaspoon grated lemon rind; serve in a
hollowed half-lemon rind

Mixed White Miso Toppings

MAKES ABOUT ¼ CUP

¼ cup sweet white or 2½ tablespoons mellow white
    miso
½ to 1 teaspoon honey
Seasonings (optional): Choose one
    ¼ teaspoon grated lemon or orange rind and
        1 teaspoon lemon juice
    1 tablespoon finely minced mint or green beefsteak
        leaves and ½ teaspoon water
    1 tablespoon each Parmesan cheese and parsley,
        and 1 teaspoon water

Combine all ingredients, mixing well. Try with thinly
sliced cucumbers or tomatoes, canapés or crackers,
apple wedges or banana rounds.

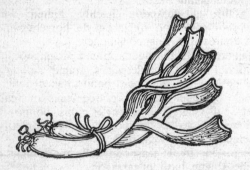

Subtly Sweet Leek Miso

MAKES 1 CUP

1 cup leeks, sliced into very thin rounds
¼ cup barley or red miso

Combine ingredients, mixing well (with chopsticks) for several minutes. For best flavor, refrigerate for 1 to 2 days before serving. Excellent as a topping for Forofuki Daikon (p. 347) or baked potatoes. Or serve in small portions as an hors d'œuvre with drinks. A favorite in Japanese farmhouses where it is said to warm the body while providing strength and stamina.

For a richer flavor, use ¼ cup each leeks and miso, and 1½ tablespoons bonito flakes.

Natto-Miso Topping

SERVES 2

½ cup *natto* (fermented soybeans)
2½ tablespoons red, barley, or Hatcho miso
1½ tablespoons bonito flakes
1½ tablespoons thinly sliced leeks, minced onions, or *daikon* leaves
⅓ teaspoon hot mustard
1½ tablespoons green *nori* flakes or crumbled toasted *nori* (p. 108) (optional)

Combine all ingredients, mixing well (with chopsticks) for several minutes to develop cohesiveness. Serve as a garnish for brown rice or rice porridge, or as a spread for crackers or canapés.

Homemade Akadashi Miso

MAKES ¼ CUP

2 tablespoons Hatcho miso
2 tablespoons red or light-yellow miso
1 tablespoon honey or *mizuamé*
½ to 1 teaspoon shoyu

Combine all ingredients, mixing well. For a smoother texture, rub through a sieve.

Cheese Miso

MAKES ¼ CUP

¼ cup finely grated (firm) cheese or Parmesan
1 tablespoon red, barley, or Hatcho miso
1 tablespoon butter (optional)
Seasonings (optional): Choose one
  2 teaspoons minced onion, leek, or chives
  1 to 2 tablespoons bonito flakes
  ½ clove crushed garlic
  Dash of pepper, 7-spice red pepper, or Tabasco
  sauce

Combine the cheese, miso and, if desired, the butter
and seasoning. Mix lightly so that grated cheese retains its texture. Serve as a topping (or filling) for
broiled or baked potatoes, sliced cucumbers, canapés,
mochi, brown rice, or deep-fried tofu.

Peking Duck Dipping Sauce
(Homemade T'ien Mien Chiang)

MAKES ½ CUP

This recipe, used by many Chinese-style restaurants
in Japan, yields a sauce closely related to Sweet
Wheat-flour Chiang (*t'ien mien chiang*), but with a
slightly sweeter flavor and softer consistency. It is often used as an all-purpose cooking seasoning in sauces
and stir-fried dishes, as well as with Peking Duck and
Pancake Rolls.

¼ cup Hatcho miso
1½ teaspoons sesame oil
½ teaspoon vegetable oil
¾ teaspoon sake or white wine
1 teaspoon shoyu
1½ tablespoons honey
2 tablespoons water

Combine all ingredients, mixing until smooth. Refrigerate unused portions in a sealed container.

Peking Duck Dipping Sauce
(from Sweet Wheat-flour Chiang)

MAKES ⅜ CUP

¼ cup Sweet Wheat-flour Chiang (*t'ien mien chiang*)
1 teaspoon sesame oil
1½ teaspoons honey
1 teaspoon *mirin,* sake, or white wine

Combine all ingredients, mixing well.

Homemade Korean Red Pepper Miso
(Kochu jang)

MAKES ⅜ CUP

¼ cup Hatcho or red miso
½ teaspoon ground red pepper or Tabasco sauce
1 tablespoon soy sauce
1 tablespoon honey
1 teaspoon sesame oil

Combine all ingredients, mixing well. A favorite with Korean-style five-color rice (*Bibimpap,* p. 298).

Rich & Savory Bonito-Miso Topping

MAKES 3 TABLESPOONS

2 to 3 tablespoons bonito flakes
1 to 1½ tablespoons red, barley, or Hatcho miso
1 tablespoon minced leeks or scallions
¼ teaspoon grated gingerroot

Combine all ingredients, mixing well. A favorite topping for tofu or deep-fried foods.

BROILED MISO
(Yakimiso)

When broiled or grilled over an open fire, miso develops a delightful aroma and flavor, and in Japan, the use of cryptomeria or Japanese cedar (*sugi*) as the broiling plank imparts an additional subtlety to the fragrance. Served as a topping for hot rice or rice gruel, regular or deep-fried tofu, canapés, broiled potatoes or cucumber slices, broiled miso transforms the simplest dishes into gourmet delights. It may also be served as is, as an hors d'œuvre with sake or beer, or added to chilled summertime soups.

Savory Broiled Miso

SERVES 1

Use 1 to 2 teaspoons of any of the following:
  A chunky, natural Hatcho, barley, or red miso
  Any dark-colored Sweet Simmered Miso (p. 126)
  Any variety of Mixed Miso, especially varieties
    containing bonito flakes (p. 154)
  Subtly Sweet Leek Miso (p. 136)
  Cheese Miso (p. 154)

If using a stove-top burner, charcoal brazier, or bed of live coals: Spread miso in a layer about ⅛ inch thick on a thin cedar plank, the lid of an earthenware bowl, in a clam or scallop shell, or in the concave surface of a large wooden or metal spatula or spoon (see illustration). Holding the miso (with tongs) 1 to 2 inches above the open fire and moving it back and forth slowly, broil for 15 to 30 seconds (checking miso every 5 seconds) until it is fragrant and lightly speckled. If broiling miso on a lid, place lid on its matching (empty) cup or bowl to help retain miso fragrance. If using a shell, serve in the shell. Or scrape miso from the plank, spatula, or spoon into a small shallow dish. Serve immediately.

If using an oven broiler: Spread miso as above on a piece of aluminum foil or directly onto canapés, buttered crackers, toast, thinly-sliced, steamed potatoes, deep-fried tofu, or eggplants. Broil and serve as above.

Broiling Miso

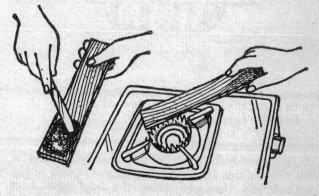

VARIATIONS

*Skewered Broiled Miso: Shape miso into 1½-inch-diameter balls, adding bonito flakes or grated cheese if necessary to give a firmer texture. Pierce with a skewer, chopsticks, or a fork, and broil over an open fire.

*Broiled Citrus Miso: Prepare Yuzu- or Lemon Miso

(p. 131) and pack firmly into a hollowed half yuzu
or lemon rind. Broil slowly over a bed of live coals
until fragrant.

*Broiled Miso & Leek Broth: This preparation is a
Japanese folk remedy said to cure colds and fevers.
Combine broiled red miso with 1 tablespoon thinly
sliced leeks. Stir in ½ cup boiling water, adding a
little at a time until smooth. Serve hot.

Hoba Miso

Hoba Miso (*Miso & Vegetables Broiled on Magnolia Leaves*)

SERVES 2

The word *hoba* refers to the huge oval leaves of
the wild *ho* tree (*Magnolia hypoleuca*). Often attain-
ing a length of over 16 inches, the dried leaves have
a delightful aroma that permeates the miso as the
latter broils. This preparation is famous in and around
Japan's mountain village of Takayama. In restaurants,
it is usually prepared over a small tabletop charcoal
brazier (see illustration); in farmhouses, over the dying
coals in the open-hearth fireplace located at the center
of the main room. The fragrance of the woodsmoke is
said to be one of the keys to its fine flavor.

1 large dry magnolia leaf, at least 12 inches long and
 5 inches wide
2 to 3 tablespoons red, barley, or Hatcho miso
2 to 4 tablespoons grated *daikon*
½ leek, sliced into very thin rounds
4 (fresh *shiitaké*) mushrooms, thinly sliced
Seasonal wild vegetables, thinly sliced; or nuts
 (optional)
1 teaspoon oil (optional)

Place leaf with concave side facing upward atop a
glowing charcoal brazier or barbecue, then place other
ingredients at center of leaf. Broil, stirring occasionally
with chopsticks, for 5 to 6 minutes, or until miso begins to simmer. While continuing to broil, transfer
hot miso-vegetable mixture a little at a time from
leaf and use as topping for cooked Brown Rice, Rice
Patties (p. 294), thin cucumber slices, or Ochazuké
(p. 297). Or eat as is in small amounts as an hors
d'œuvre with drinks.

A fairly good facsimile of this dish can be prepared using aluminum foil in place of the leaf and
broiling in an oven broiler. In some parts of Japan,
dry buckeye leaves are also used.

Kaiyaki-miso

Kaiyaki-miso *(Miso Sautéed with Vegetables in Scallop Shells)*

SERVES 4

This close relative of Hoba Miso is ideal for use at
barbecues or campfire dinners.

4 teaspoons (sesame) oil
2 green (*togarashi*) peppers, minced
¼ cup diced eggplant
8 green beans, slivered
¼ cup slivered burdock root or carrot
2 teaspoons minced or grated gingerroot or garlic
2 green beefsteak or fresh basil leaves, slivered
4 to 6 tablespoons Hatcho, red, or barley miso
¼ cup bonito flakes (optional)

Place 4 scallop shells over a charcoal brazier, on a
barbecue grill, or directly atop the dying coals of a
campfire. Divide the oil among the shells and heat,
then add equal amounts of the next six ingredients to
each shell. Sauté, stirring occasionally, for 4 to 6
minutes, or until all vegetables are tender. Stir in miso
(and bonito flakes) and cook for 2 minutes more.
Without removing shells from fire, transfer hot miso-
vegetable mixture a little at a time from shell and use
as a topping as for Hoba Miso.

Fuki-no-to Miso (Butterbur-buds Broiled Miso)

MAKES 1¼ CUPS

The butterbur or bog rhubarb (*Petasites japonicus*)
is an edible wild mountain plant whose budding forth
from the frozen earth heralds the coming of spring.
While the mature stems also make a delicious food, the
young buds which emerge from the base of the plant
close to the ground are used to create the unique, subtly
bitter flavor and aroma of this popular preparation.

½ cup red or barley miso
½ cup bonito flakes
¼ cup minced walnuts or sesame butter
1½ tablespoons honey or *mirin* (optional)
5 butterbur buds, with outer layers carefully removed
     and reserved

Combine the first three (or four) ingredients, mixing
well, and divide into two equal portions. Dice buds
and mix with one portion of the miso, then use the
mixture to prepare Broiled Miso (p. 156). (For a
mellower flavor, allow the miso buds mixture to stand
in a cool place for 10 days before broiling.)

Divide second portion of miso mixture into fifths, shape into small balls, and wrap each in butterbur's outer layers. Place into a preheated steamer and steam for 15 minutes, then set in a cool dry place and allow to stand for 6 months. Remove leaves and discard. Cut miso balls into thin rounds and serve as hors d'œuvres, in miso soups, or as a topping for Ochazuké (p. 297) or brown rice.

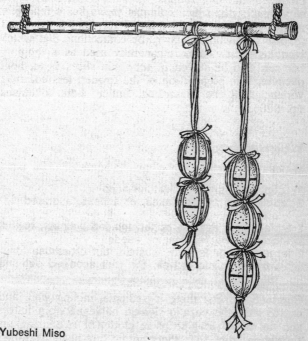

Yubeshi Miso

YUBESHI MISO
(Miso-stuffed Citrus)

The word *yubeshi,* which originated in China, is written with three ideographic characters: the first means *yuzu* (the fragrant East-Asian citron); the second refers either to a treat or confection or, more specifically, to *mochi* (steamed and pounded glutinous rice); the third means child. *Yubeshi* has long been made in Japanese farmhouses during the cold months, especially just before New Year's. *Yuzu* (or lemon) halves are stuffed with a miso mixture, steamed, and hung in the shade to dry. The miso and citrus gradually become permeated with each other's fragrance, and the finished product is firm enough to be sliced into thin rounds. There are two basic types of *yubeshi*: that which contains *mochi* has a relatively mild and sweet, rather spicy flavor, and is excellent for use as an hors d'œuvre or confection; that which contains mostly miso is generally used as a topping, but can also be served in very thin slices as an hors d'œuvre. The preparation of the former, less common variety, will be described under hors d'œuvres (p. 170).

Yubeshi Miso Topping

MAKES ½ CUP

½ cup red, barley, or Hatcho miso
2 tablespoons bonito flakes, or substitute grated cheese
2 tablespoons sesame butter, minced walnuts, or ground roasted sesame seeds
2 large *yuzu* or lemons, washed, cut crosswise (or vertically) into halves, the fruit scooped out and reserved

Combine the first three ingredients, mixing well, and use to stuff the yuzu or lemon halves. Rejoin halves and tie with 4 long strips of cloth (or rice straw) as shown on page 161. Place into a pre-heated steamer and steam for 40 minutes. Hang (under the eaves) in a shady, well-ventilated place and allow to dry for at least 1, preferably 3 to 4 weeks. Cut crosswise into ¼-inch-thick rounds (or scoop out the miso filling) and serve as a topping for grain or tofu dishes, thinly sliced cucumbers, tomatoes, or apples, crackers or canapés.

VARIATIONS

*Quick Yubeshi: Add ½ teaspoon grated *yuzu* or lemon peel to the above ingredients. Omit steaming. Wrap miso-stuffed citrus with plastic wrap and refrigerate for 1 or 2 days. To serve, scoop out fragrant miso and discard citrus halves.

*Use as the filling: miso, grated gingerroot, (7-spice) red pepper and, if desired, minced walnuts. For a sweeter version, add a little honey.

Miso in Dips and Hors D'oeuvres

Most of the recipes in this section make use of nut butters and dairy products, are uniquely Western and, we feel, exemplify miso's delicious versatility.

MISO IN DIPS

Miso-Cream Cheese Dips

MAKES ¾ CUP

4 ounces cream cheese, softened with 1½ to 3
    tablespoons warm water
2 teaspoons red or barley (or 4 teaspoons mellow
    white) miso
½ small onion, grated or minced
1 tablespoon Better Butter (p. 119) or butter, softened
¼ cup grated cheese
2 teaspoons sake or white wine

Combine all ingredients, mixing well until thoroughly blended and smooth. For best flavor, refrigerate in a sealed container for 5 to 7 days. Serve with crackers, chips, fresh vegetable slices, celery stalks, or apple wedges. Also delicious as a spread for sandwiches or canapés.

VARIATIONS

Add any of the following ingredients to the softened cream cheese and miso; serve immediately:

*Tangy: 2 tablespoons grated cheese, 1 teaspoon minced onion, and 4 teaspoons mayonnaise.
*Curry: ½ teaspoon curry powder
*Sesame: 1½ tablespoons sesame butter or *tahini* and a dash of tabasco sauce or red pepper
*Lemon: 2 to 3 teaspoons lemon juice plus 1 tablespoon warm water to soften the cream cheese, ½ teaspoon grated lemon rind, 3 tablespoons mayonnaise, 1 tablespoon minced parsley, and, if desired, a dash of pepper
*Sweet Miso and Sesame: See Miso-Stuffed Celery (p. 173)

Guacamole with Miso

MAKES 1 CUP

1 well-ripened avocado, peeled and seeded
¼ tomato, diced
2 teaspoons lemon juice
½ clove garlic, crushed
1½ tablespoons red or barley (or 2½ tablespoons mellow white) miso
2 tablespoons sesame butter or *tahini* (optional)
2 tablespoons minced onion
Dash of paprika or ¼ teaspoon Tabasco sauce
1 to 2 tablespoons minced parsley

Combine the first eight ingredients; mash together with a fork until smooth. Serve as a dip, spread, or dressing; garnish with the parsley. Flavor improves if sealed and refrigerated for one hour or more.

Miso-Cottage Cheese Dip

MAKES ½ CUP

6 tablespoons cottage cheese
1½ teaspoons red or barley (or 1 tablespoon mellow white) miso
2 teaspoons minced parsley
Dash of pepper (optional)
1 tablespoon minced onion, or ½ clove of garlic, crushed (optional)

Combine all ingredients, mixing well. Excellent on hors d'œuvre crackers or as a sandwich spread.

Cream Cheese-Miso Dip with Nuts and Raisins

MAKES 1 CUP

4 ounces cream cheese softened with 1 tablespoon warm water
4 tablespoons sweet white or 2½ teaspoons red miso
2 tablespoons Better Butter (p. 119) or butter
¼ cup chopped walnuts or almonds
¼ cup raisins

Combine all ingredients, mixing well. Serve with crackers, tomato and cucumber slices, or celery stalks. Good also as a sandwich spread.

Tofu-Miso-Sour Cream Dip

MAKES 1½ CUPS

12 ounces tofu, drained and mashed
1½ tablespoons red or barley (or 3 tablespoons mellow white) miso
5 tablespoons sour cream
1 teaspoon lemon juice or vinegar
1 tablespoon minced parsley or chives
Dash of pepper (optional)

Combine all ingredients, mixing well. Delicious with crackers or fresh vegetable slices.

Soy Jalapeño with Miso

MAKES 1¼ CUPS

1 cup cooked soybeans (p. 317), well drained and
    mashed
¼ onion, minced
2 tablespoons red, barley, or Hatcho miso
1 teaspoon oil
½ clove garlic, crushed
1 tablespoon lemon juice or vinegar
½ to ¾ teaspoon Tabasco sauce or ground red
    pepper

Combine all ingredients and mash until smooth or
run through a hand mill or meat grinder. Serve as a
dip or spread. Especially good with taco chips.

For variety, substitute pinto beans for one-half
the cooked soybeans.

Tangy Miso-Tahini Dip

MAKES 1 CUP

2 teaspoons red, barley, or Hatcho miso
½ cup tahini or sesame butter
¼ cup lemon juice
1½ cloves garlic, crushed
¼ cup water

Combine all ingredients, mixing well. For a sweeter
flavor, add 2 teaspoons honey. To make a sauce, add
¼ cup more water.

MISO IN HORS D'OEUVRES

Miso is perhaps at its best when used in the preparation of Western-style hors d'œuvres. See also
Dengaku (p. 355), Eggs Pickled in Sweet White Miso
(p. 393), and other miso pickles (p. 385). Finger
Lickin' Miso (p. 75) and Sweet Simmered Miso (p.

125) are often served in quantities of 1 to 2 teaspoons on a small dish as an accompaniment for drinks.

Cucumber or Jicama Slices Topped with Finger Lickin' Miso

SERVES 4

1 large cucumber, cut into thin diagonal slices
3 to 4 tablespoons finger lickin' or natto miso

Top each slice with a dab of the miso. Serve chilled, arranged on a platter. As delicious as they are easy to prepare.

Miso Walnuts, Cashews, or Almonds

SERVES 3 TO 4

½ cup unsalted walnut, cashew, or almond meats
1½ teaspoons red or barley miso, dissolved in 3
        tablespoons water

Heat a heavy skillet, drop in nuts, and dry-roast over medium heat, stirring constantly, for about 3 minutes, or until fragrant. Add dissolved miso and sauté for 30 seconds, or just until all liquid has evaporated. (Slight overcooking may cause the miso to burn.) Allow to cool before serving.

For a crunchier texture, toast in a medium oven for about 20 minutes, or until fragrant.

Crackers with Cream Cheese, Egg & Miso Topping

MAKES 10 TO 15

2 hard-boiled eggs, separated into yolks and whites
2 ounces cream cheese
1½ teaspoons red or barley (or 3 teaspoons mellow
        white) miso
1 tablespoon minced parsley
Dash of pepper or paprika
10 to 15 hors d'oeuvre crackers

Combine egg yolks with the cream cheese, miso, parsley, and pepper; mash well. Slice egg whites into thin rounds and place one round on each cracker. Top with a dab of the cream cheese-miso mixture.

Mushroom Hors D'oeuvres with Miso Marinade

SERVES 2 TO 4

1 tablespoon red, barley, or Hatcho miso
2½ to 3 tablespoons (rice) vinegar
1½ teaspoons honey
1 tablespoon sesame butter (optional)
20 (*shiitaké*) mushrooms, washed and drained

Combine the first four ingredients in a shallow pan, mixing until smooth. Broil mushrooms for 1 minute on each side, or until speckled and fragrant, then add immediately to miso-vinegar mixture; marinate for 30 minutes. Serve skewered on foodpicks or mounded on lettuce leaves with a little marinade poured over the top.

Apple Wedges with Miso Toppings

SERVES 4

2 apples, cut into thin wedges
¼ cup Peanut Miso (p, 129), Orange-Sesame Miso
    (p. 277), Walnut Miso (p. 128), Sesame Miso
    Spread (p. 182), or your favorite variety of Finger
    Lickin' Miso (p. 75)

Arrange apple slices on a serving platter and top each with a ½ teaspoon dollop of the miso.

Apple & Banana Hors D'oeuvres with Miso Topping

SERVES 4 TO 6

1 banana, cut diagonally into 1-inch-thick ovals
1 apple, cut into thin wedges
Sweet Miso & Tahini Topping:
    2 tablespoons *tahini* or sesame butter
    1 teaspoon honey
    1 teaspoon red, barley, or Hatcho miso
    2 to 3 tablespoons raisins
    2 to 3 tablespoons chopped almonds or walnuts

Arrange fruit slices on a serving platter. Mix topping ingredients and spoon in dollops (or spread) onto slices.

Sliced Bananas with Peanut Butter-Miso Topping

SERVES 2

2 bananas, cut diagonally into long, thin ovals
1½ tablespoons peanut butter
1 teaspoon red or 2 teaspoons sweet white miso
2 tablespoons wheat germ
1½ tablespoons raisins

Arrange banana slices on a serving platter. Combine peanut butter and miso, mixing well, and place in dabs atop bananas. Sprinkle with wheat germ and dot each dab with 3 or 4 raisins just before serving.

For added richness, combine 1 tablespoon each grated coconut and minced nutmeats with the peanut butter and miso.

Canapés with Miso Spreads

MAKES 30

30 pieces of buttered (whole-grain) bread or toast, each 2 inches square
Spreads: About 2 to 3 tablespoons each
  Sweet Simmered Miso (pp. 125 to 138; Sesame, Peanut, Red Pepper, or Subtley Sweet Leek Miso)
  Finger Lickin' Miso (p. 75)
  Miso Mayonnaise (p. 191)
  Sweet White Miso & Butter Spread (p. 181)
  Cheese Mixed Miso (p. 154)
Canapé Toppings:
  ½ cucumber, sliced into thin ovals
  1 green pepper, cut lengthwise into quarters
  1 hard-boiled egg, thinly sliced
  1 tomato, sliced into thin ovals
  ½ carrot, sliced into thin ovals
  8 green peas, parboiled (optional)
  1 small potato or sweet potato, boiled and thinly sliced

Use each of the five types of miso as a spread for one-fifth of the bread slices. Place the toppings individually or in combinations on the bread to form canapés. If desired, pierce each canapé with a foodpick. Arrange on large serving platters.

VARIATION

*Deep-fried Tofu & Miso Hors d'oeuvre: Cut any variety of deep-fried tofu into thin strips or bite-sized pieces. For best flavor, broil quickly until speckled and fragrant. Top each piece with any of the above miso spreads and canapé toppings. Serve skewered with foodpicks.

The ingredients may also be rolled up in a sheet of agé, fastened in 3 or 4 places with foodpicks, and cut crosswise into small cylinders.

Tomato Hors D'oeuvres with Sesame Miso

SERVES 8 TO 12

¼ cup sesame butter or *tahini*
2 teaspoons red, barley, or Hatcho miso
2 tablespoons mayonnaise
1 clove of garlic, crushed
½ teaspoon honey
1 teaspoon sake or white wine
1 to 2 teaspoons water (optional)
3 tomatoes, cut into ½-inch-thick rounds

Combine the first seven ingredients, mixing well. Arrange tomato slices on a serving platter and top each slice with a dollop of the sesame miso.

This topping is also delicious on other fresh vegetable slices and canapés; or use as a sandwich spread.

Spicy Yubeshi Miso Hors D'oeuvres

MAKES 1 CUP

Please begin by reading about Yubeshi (p. 170). This traditional preparation, a specialty of Japan's southernmost main island, Kyushu, is now sold commercially throughout Japan and looks remarkably like a 5-inch-long sausage. Whereas the traditional product was steamed in bamboo leaves and packed (and occasionally sold) in the joined halves of a citrus, its modern counterpart is plastic-wrapped, but is still very delicious.

6 tablespoons glutinous rice flour (*shiratama-ko*)
2½ tablespoons water
3 tablespoons red, barley, or Hatcho miso
1 tablespoon honey
Dash of (7-spice) red pepper or Tabasco sauce
½ teaspoon grated gingerroot
2 teaspoons sesame butter or *tahini;* or 3 to 4½
    teaspoons minced walnuts
¼ teaspoon grated *yuzu,* lemon, or orange rind

Combine the flour and water, and mix for several minutes to develop a smooth dough of earlobe consistency. Mix in remaining ingredients and knead with a rubber spatula (or your hands) for several minutes more. Form mixture into a 1½-inch-diameter sausage shape and wrap in corn leaves or cellophane. (Or pack into a cup or small bowl and cover with cellophane.) Place into a preheated steamer and steam for 20 minutes, then allow to cool to room temperature. Slice into thin rounds (or serve in cup accompanied by a small knife or spoon). Use like cold cuts as an hors d'œuvre topping for crackers, thin vegetable slices, or canapés, or as a garnish for rice.

For variety, wash 2 *yuzu* or lemons, cut into halves, scoop out the fruit and reserve. Fill with the (unsteamed) miso mixture and proceed as for Yubeshi Miso (p. 161).

Jicama & Carrot Sticks with Creamy Tofu Dip

Crisp, juicy, and unbelievably delicious, *jicama* is a root vegetable from Latin America now widely available in the United States and quite inexpensive. Heart-shaped and 5 to 7 inches in diameter, its peel is the color of a potato's. Best fresh, it may also be cooked lightly.

1 carrot, cut into thin 1-inch-wide sticks for dipping
¼ *jicama,* cut into sticks for dipping
Potato chips or celery stalks
1 cup Creamy Tofu Dip (with curry, p. 193) or Tofu
    Mayonnaise (p. 191)

Arrange cut vegetables around a bowl of the dip on a
large platter. Serve chilled.

Fresh Cucumber Slices with Miso Topping

SERVES 2

In Japan a popular hors d'œuvre called *Morokyu*
is prepared by slicing fresh cucumbers on the diagonal
to form thin ovals, then spreading one surface of each
with moromi miso. Other varieties of Finger Lickin'
or Sweet Simmered Miso may also be used. The following cooked topping takes longer to prepare but is
well worth the time and effort.

1 tablespoon oil
2 inches of leek or ¼ onion, thinly sliced
1 tablespoon red, barley, or Hatcho miso
1 tablespoon grated gingerroot
1 (*shiitaké*) mushroom, thinly sliced
1 large cucumber, cut into thin diagonal slices

Heat a wok or skillet and coat with the oil. Add the
next four ingredients and sauté over low heat, stirring
constantly, for 3 to 4 minutes. To serve, allow to cool,
then spread on sliced cucumbers.

Stuffed Eggs with Miso and Sesame

MAKES 8 HALVES

4 eggs, hard-boiled and cut lengthwise into halves
2 teaspoons red, barley, or Hatcho miso
4 teaspoons sesame butter or grated cheese
2 tablespoons minced onion
Paprika (optional)

Remove egg yolks and mash together with the miso,
sesame butter, and onion. Form the mixture into 8
balls, and use as a stuffing for the egg halves. If desired, top with paprika.

Hors D'oeuvres with Miso-damari

SERVES 4

2 hard-boiled eggs, shelled and cut lengthwise into
   halves
1 cucumber, cut into long, thin diagonals
1 small tomato, cut into ½-inch-thick rounds
2 deep-fried tofu cutlets or burgers, cut into bite-
   sized pieces
2 tablespoons miso-damari (pp. 96 and 173)

Arrange the first four ingredients on a serving platter,
then top each with a sprinkling of the *miso-damari*.

Miso-Stuffed Celery Hors D'oeuvres

Peanut Butter & Miso:
   2 tablespoons peanut butter
   2 to 3 teaspoons red, barley, or Hatcho miso
   1 teaspoon grated onion and juice
Cream Cheese, Sweet Miso & Sesame:
   2 tablespoons cream cheese
   2½ tablespoons sweet white miso
   ½ teaspoon shoyu
   1 tablespoon ground roasted sesame seeds (p. 107)
      or sesame butter
Cream Cheese, Miso & Lemon:
   2 tablespoons cream cheese
   1 tablespoon red, barley, or Hatcho miso
   1 teaspoon lemon juice
   2 tablespoons mayonnaise
6 large celery stalks

Combine the ingredients for each of the three stuffings,
mixing until smooth. Stuff celery stalks, then cut stalks
into 2-inch lengths and serve as hors d'œuvres. If
desired, top with a sprinkling of paprika.

   Celery stalks are also delicious served with most
types of Sweet Simmered Miso (p. 125), Vinegar
Miso (p. 137), Peanut Butter-Miso (p. 180), Sesame
Miso Spreads (p. 182), or Cream Cheese-Miso Dips
(p. 163).

Crunchy Miso-Soynut-butter Balls

MAKES 12

⅓ cup Miso-Soy Nut Butter (p. 181), cooled to room
   temperature
¼ cup raisins
¼ cup (roasted) sunflower seeds, chopped nuts, or
   ground roasted sesame seeds
2 tablespoons roasted soy flour (*kinako*) or ¼ cup
   shredded coconut

Combine the first three ingredients, mixing well. Shape
mixture into 12 small balls, then roll each in roasted
soy flour. Chill briefly before serving.

Lotus Root Hors D'oeuvre Stuffed with
Miso-Cream Cheese

MAKES 12

1 lotus root, 4 inches long and 2 inches in diameter,
   peeled
1 ounce cream cheese
1 teaspoon red, barley, or Hatcho miso
1 teaspoon minced onion
½ teaspoon minced parsley
⅛ teaspoon curry powder

Trim both ends of lotus root, revealing hollow tubules.
Cut into 2-inch lengths and simmer in water to cover
for 15 to 20 minutes, or until tender; then drain and
allow to cool to body temperature. Combine remaining ingredients, mixing well. Press mixture into tubules
using your finger tips or a spatula. Cut each section
of lotus root crosswise into 6 thin discs and spread
any remaining filling in a thin layer over one surface
of each disc. Serve chilled.

For variety, substitute 1 mashed hard-boiled egg for the cream cheese. Omit curry powder, and add a dash of pepper and 2 teaspoons mayonnaise.

Nori-wrapped Cucumbers with Sour Cream & Miso

MAKES 12

¼ cup sour cream
1 teaspoon red, barley, or Hatcho miso
Dash of pepper (optional)
3 sheets of *nori,* toasted (p. 108)
1 cucumber, cut into long slivers

Combine the first three ingredients, mixing well, and spread in an even layer over one surface of each *nori* sheet. Now arrange cucumber slivers in a row along the near edge of each sheet. Roll up from the near edge so that the cucumbers form the central core. Cut the rolls crosswise into fourths; serve immediately.

For variety, use slivers of cheese and agé (deep-fried tofu) together with the cucumbers.

Miso-filled Beefsteak Leaf Hors D'oeuvres

SERVES 2

This popular Japanese hors d'oeuvre, also famous as a commercial product from the city of Hamamatsu called *Shiso-maki Miso,* is prepared with red beefsteak leaves that have been salt-pickled (p. 391) to give them a softer flavor and texture. The filling may be made with Peanut Miso (p. 129).

1½ tablespoons sweet white miso or 2 teaspoons red miso
1½ tablespoons sesame butter or whole roasted peanuts
½ teaspoon honey
6 green beefsteak leaves

Combine the first three ingredients, mixing well, and divide into six equal portions. Place one portion at the center of each leaf near one end, then roll up leaf firmly so that miso-sesame mixture fills rolled cylinder. Skewer with foodpicks, if desired, and serve arranged on small plates.

Sashimi Konnyaku

SERVES 4

Cut and served in this way, *konnyaku* is made to resemble one of Japan's culinary specialties, *sashimi,* or fresh uncooked fish cut into thin slices and served with a dipping sauce or topping. In Zen temples and *shojin* temple restaurants, the *konnyaku* is prepared in prefect resemblance of fresh squid.

10 to 12 ounces *konnyaku,* cut crosswise into ¼-inch-
thick strips and parboiled in lightly-salted water
¼ cup Tangy Mustard Vinegar Miso (p. 205), or 2 to 3
tablespoons Wasabi Mixed Miso (p. 151)

Arrange *konnyaku* strips in a flower-petal pattern on a serving platter. Place the dipping sauce and a serving spoon in a cup at center of platter. Invite each guest to serve himself.

Miso Pastry Twists

MAKES ABOUT 40

Made with unsweetened pie crust, these have a slightly salty flavor; serve as you would potato chips, or use as the accompaniment for sweet fruits or desserts.

3 tablespoons red, barley, or Hatcho miso
6 tablespoons water
5 ounces butter, chilled
2¼ cups flour, approximately
1 egg yolk

Combine miso and water, mixing well. Cut butter into 2 cups flour until butter pieces are the size of peas. Gently stir in thinned miso to form a moist dough. Wrap in a very lightly dampened towel and refrigerate for 1 hour.

Roll dough out thin, and fold into thirds. Sprinkle lightly with flour, and repeat 4 times to give a 12-layer pastry dough. Finally, roll dough into a long rectangle ¼ inch thick and about 3 inches wide. Cut crosswise into ¾-inch-wide strips. Twist each strip once and brush with egg yolk. Arrange strips on lightly oiled baking pans. Bake in a 390° F oven for 4 minutes, then reduce heat to 300° and bake for 8 to 10 minutes more, or until strips are nicely browned.

For variety, replace one-half the miso with grated cheese. Sprinkle ¼ cup minced walnuts over dough before final folding.

Miso in Spreads and Sandwiches

Whether used with nut butters or dairy products, creamy avocadoes or butter, high-protein tofu or cooked soybeans, miso adds richness of flavor to many of your favorite sandwich fixin's. Thinned slightly, miso spreads make excellent dips; creamed with hot stock or broth, they make savory sauces.

MISO IN SPREADS

Miso Paté

MAKES 1½ CUPS

Remarkably similar in flavor and texture to its liver-based counterpart, this recipe combines wheat, sesame butter, and miso to yield maximum protein value (p. 26).

2 cups broken pieces of (dry) whole-wheat bread
½ cup water or stock
½ cup sesame butter
1½ tablespoons red, barley, or Hatcho miso
1 small onion, minced
1 tablespoon (sesame) oil
1 clove of garlic, crushed or minced
¼ cup minced parsley
Dash each of thyme, rosemary, and sage

Combine bread and water, mashing well with fingers. Mix in remaining ingredients and allow to stand for at least 1 hour, preferably 1 full day. Serve as a spread on crackers, canapés, or bread.

For a firmer consistency, bake in a loaf pan at 350°F for 1 to 1½ hours, or until surface is nicely browned.

Tofu-Miso Paté

MAKES 1¾ CUPS

12 ounces tofu, lightly pressed (p. 109)
5 teaspoons red, barley, or Hatcho miso
¼ cup sesame butter or ½ cup ground roasted
    sesame seeds (p. 107)
3 tablespoons minced parsley
1 tablespoon dill seeds, minced
2 tablespoons chopped green onion
1 clove of garlic, crushed
¼ teaspoon nutmeg

Preheat oven to 350°F. Combine all ingredients, mixing well, and press into a loaf pan. Bake for 15 to 20 minutes, or until lightly browned. Serve as a spread. Also delicious unbaked.

Hard-boiled Egg & Miso Spread

MAKES ½ CUP

2 hard-boiled eggs, mashed with a fork
1 teaspoon red or barley (or 2 teaspoons mellow white) miso
2 tablespoons mayonnaise
1 tablespoon minced parsley
Dash of pepper or paprika

Combine all ingredients, mixing well. For variety, add ½ teaspoon curry powder.

Miso-Sesame-Avocado Spread

MAKES ¾ CUP

2 teaspoons red, barley, or Hatcho miso
6 tablespoons sesame butter
½ avocado, peeled and seeded
¼ tomato, minced
1 tablespoon minced onion
1 tablespoon lemon juice
½ clove of garlic, crushed
1 tablespoon minced parsley or ¼ cup alfalfa sprouts

Combine the first seven ingredients; mash together until smooth. Serve topped with a sprinkling of the parsley or sprouts.

Sweet Carob-Sesame-Miso Spread

MAKES ⅓ CUP

1 tablespoon carob powder
4 to 5 teaspoons water
2 to 3 tablespoons sesame butter or *tahini*
2 teaspoons sweet white or 1½ teaspoons mellow white miso
1 teaspoon honey

Combine carob powder with water, mixing until smooth, then stir in remaining ingredients. Nice on toast or unsalted crackers.

Walnut Miso Spread or Topping

MAKES 1 CUP

1 cup walnut meats, lightly roasted and ground to a
    paste
¼ cup red, barley, or Hatcho miso
3 to 4 tablespoons water

Combine all ingredients, mixing well. Serve as a
spread with sandwiches or crackers, or as a topping
with cooked vegetables or tofu.

For variety, add ½ teaspoon grated orange or
lemon rind.

Miso-Soynut Butter

MAKES ½ CUP

This delicious spread tastes like a cross between
sesame and peanut butter but is less expensive and
higher in protein. Produced commercially, it would
surely sell well at natural- and health-food stores.

2½ tablespoons oil or butter
½ cup roasted soy flour (*kinako*)
1 teaspoon red, barley, or Hatcho miso
1 tablespoon honey
1½ to 2 tablespoons water

Heat the oil in a skillet, then turn off heat. Add remaining ingredients, mixing until smooth. Delicious on
crackers, canapés, or fresh vegetable slices.

Sweetened Peanut Butter-Miso Spread

MAKES ¾ CUP

¼ cup peanut butter
1 tablespoon red, barley, or Hatcho miso
1 tablespoon honey
¼ cup diced apples
2 tablespoons sunflower seeds or minced nutmeats
2 tablespoons raisins
1 teaspoon sake or white wine (optional)

Combine all ingredients, mixing well. Serve on buttered whole-wheat bread.

VARIATION

*Omit raisins, sunflower seeds, and apple. Use 4 teaspoons miso; serve in vegetable sandwiches with lettuce, cucumbers, tomatoes, sprouts, and cheese. For more zest, add 1 tablespoon diced onion and/or parsley; nice on canapés. For more tang, add 2½ tablespoons vinegar.

Savory Peanut Butter-Miso Spread

MAKES ½ CUP

¼ cup peanut butter
2 teaspoons red, barley, or Hatcho miso
1 teaspoon Worcestershire sauce
2 tablespoons Better Butter (p. 119) or butter, softened

Combine all ingredients, mixing well.

Miso Cheese Spread

MAKES 1 CUP

1 tablespoon Better Butter (p. 119) or butter
1 tablespoon red, barley, or Hatcho miso
6 ounces grated cheese
¼ cup milk (soy or dairy)
1 egg, lightly beaten
Dash of mustard
¼ teaspoon crushed garlic or 1 tablespoon minced parsley (optional)

Melt butter in a skillet. Stir in miso, then add remaining ingredients, mixing well. Cook, stirring constantly, for 1 to 2 minutes, or until cheese just melts. Serve on buttered toast or canapés. Brown under a broiler, if desired.

Sweet White Miso & Butter Spread

MAKES ⅜ CUP

2 tablespoons Better Butter (p. 119) or butter
¼ cup sweet white or 2½ tablespoons mellow white miso

Combine butter and miso, mixing well. Serve as a spread for hors d'œuvre crackers and sandwiches topped with fresh vegetables and cheese, or as a topping for pancakes and waffles.

Sesame-Miso Spread

MAKES ½ CUP

4 or 5 tablespoons sesame butter
1 tablespoon red, barley, or Hatcho miso
½ teaspoon grated lemon or *yuzu* rind (optional)
3 tablespoons water

Combine all ingredients, mixing well. Nice on freshly sliced cucumbers, crackers, or open-faced sandwiches.

Sweetened Sesame-Miso Spread

MAKES ½ CUP

¼ cup sesame butter or *tahini*
2 to 4 teaspoons red, barley, or Hatcho miso
1½ to 2 tablespoons honey
Dash of cinnamon, (7-spice) red pepper, or Tabasco
  sauce
1 to 1½ tablespoons water

Combine all ingredients, mixing well. Serve on bread, toast, or deep-fried tofu. Or use as a topping for Dengaku (p. 353).

Tahini-Miso Spread

MAKES ABOUT ¼ CUP

¼ cup *tahini*
1 tablespoon red, barley, or Hatcho miso
1 teaspoon honey
¼ to ½ teaspoon grated orange or lemon rind

Combine all ingredients, mixing well. Serve as a sandwich spread.

Tangy Soybean-Sesame-Miso Spread

MAKES 1½ CUP

1 cup cooked soybeans (p. 317), drained and mashed
⅓ cup sesame butter
1½ tablespoons red, barley, or Hatcho miso
2 tablespoons lemon juice
⅓ cup diced raw onion
1 clove of garlic, crushed or minced
1 tablespoon honey
Dash of pepper (optional)

Combine all ingredients, mashing together until smooth. For best flavor allow to stand for at least 8, preferably 24, hours before serving.

VARIATIONS

*Rich and Crunchy Spread: Omit lemon juice, onion, and garlic. Add several tablespoons each sunflower seeds, raisins, and diced apple, and ½ teaspoon grated orange peel.

*Garbanzo or Navy Bean Spreads: Substitute an equal volume of either of these cooked beans for the soybeans in the basic recipe or variation.

*Lentil-Miso Spread: Prepare lentils as in thick Lentil-Miso Soup (p. 267). For a smoother texture, purée in a handmill or blender. To each cup of purée add 2 teaspoons red miso, a pinch of nutmeg and minced parsley and, if desired, sesame butter or ground roasted sesame seeds. Mix well and chill to thicken. Serve on buttered whole-wheat bread or toast.

*Azuki-Miso Spread: Prepare Azuki Vegetable Soup with Miso (p. 266) except use only 2½ cups water. Serve on Chapaties (p. 314) or as a sandwich spread.

MISO IN SANDWICHES

The many spreads we've described above can serve as the makings for a sandwich in themselves. Any of the following types of miso or miso mixtures can be used with thinly sliced vegetables, cheese, sprouts, or (deep-fried) tofu on buttered whole-grain bread or toast. Try using ketchup, mayonnaise, and/or mustard together with the miso. Or use Finger Lickin' Miso or diced miso pickles like relish.

* All types of regular red or white miso
* Sweet Simmered Miso (p. 125), Finger Lickin' Miso (p. 75), Miso Sauté (p. 139), Mixed Miso (p. 150) or Broiled Miso (p. 156)
* 2 parts sesame or nut butter and 1 part miso
* 6 parts red or barley miso and 1 part grated gingerroot (or diced leeks or scallions)

Grilled Cheese Sandwich on Miso-Garlic Bread

SERVES 4

Miso-Garlic-Butter Spread:
   1½ teaspoons red, barley, or Hatcho miso
   ¼ teaspoon crushed garlic
   ¼ cup melted Better Butter (p. 119) or butter
   ½ teaspoon grated lemon peel or grated onion (optional)
4 large slices of French or sourdough bread
½ cup grated or ¼ cup Parmesan cheese
4 teaspoons minced parsley

Combine spread ingredients, mixing well, then brush onto surface of bread. Top with a sprinkling of the cheese and parsley. Toast in a medium broiler or oven until nicely browned.

For variety arrange tomato (and deep-fried tofu) slices on the bread before sprinkling with cheese. Or soften the butter, mix with the other spread ingredients, and serve on canapés.

Grilled Cheese and Tomato Sandwich

MAKES 5

½ cup grated cheese
1 tablespoon red, barley, or Hatcho miso
1 tablespoon minced onion
1 tablespoon minced parsley
1 clove of garlic, crushed
5 pieces of buttered (whole-grain) bread
2 tomatoes, cut into thin rounds

Combine the first five ingredients, mixing well, and spread on the buttered bread. Top with tomato slices and broil under medium heat for 4 to 5 minutes, or until fragrant and nicely browned. Serve sizzling hot.

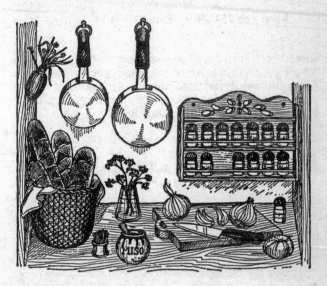

Fried Egg Sandwich with Deep-fried Tofu and Miso

MAKES 1

4 teaspoons Better Butter (p. 119) or butter
2½ to 3 ounces deep-fried tofu, cut into thin strips
1 egg
Dash of pepper (optional)
1 teaspoon red, barley, or Hatcho miso
1½ teaspoons ketchup (optional)
1 large piece of (whole-wheat) toast

Melt 1 tablespoon butter in a skillet. Arrange tofu strips in a single layer on bottom of skillet, then break egg over the top. Cover and fry until egg is firm, season with pepper, cover, and remove from heat. Combine remaining 1 teaspoon butter with miso and, if desired the ketchup; mix well and spread on one sur-

face of toast. Top with the tofu-fried egg placed
sunny side up and serve immediately.

For added color and flavor, top with a sprinkling of
minced parsley or grated cheese.

Deep-fried Tofu Burger

MAKES 1

Spread both surfaces of a 3- or 4-ounce deep-fried tofu
burger with a thin layer of red, barley, or Hatcho miso.
Broil tofu briefly on both sides if desired, then use in
place of meat in a hamburger or cheeseburger, accompanied by your favorite trimmings.

Miso Dressings with Salads

Smooth sour-cream dressings and nut-butter favorites;
tangy French or citrus dressings; thick and creamy
tofu or yogurt dressings. Miso makes each of them a
little more delicious, and can help to keep your intake
of fats to a minimum as explained on page 32.

WESTERN-STYLE DRESSINGS

Floating Cloud Miso Dressing

MAKES ABOUT 1 CUP

One of our very favorites; the key to the flavor lies
in the miso-sesame oil-garlic combination.

6 tablespoons vegetable oil
¼ teaspoon sesame oil
2 tablespoons (rice) vinegar or lemon juice
2 tablespoons red, barley, or Hatcho miso
¼ cup water
½ clove of garlic, crushed
Dash of powdered ginger
Dash of dry mustard

Combine all ingredients; whisk or shake well. Good on all tossed green salads, especially those with Chinese cabbage. Tomatoes and (deep-fried) tofu make excellent accompaniments. Try marinating hot green beans or artichoke hearts overnight in this dressing, then serving them drained and chilled on lettuce. Also great on cooked broccoli.

Miso-Cheese Dressing

MAKES ABOUT 1 CUP

½ cup oil
3 tablespoons vinegar
1½ tablespoons red, barley, or Hatcho miso
2 tablespoons Parmesan cheese
2 tablespoons water
1 tablespoon minced onion
1½ tablespoon minced green pepper
1 clove of garlic, crushed
¼ teaspoon (7-spice) red pepper or Tabasco sauce

Combine all ingredients and allow to stand for at least 1 hour. Shake thoroughly before serving.

Lemon-Mustard-Miso Dressing

MAKES ½ CUP

3 tablespoons red, barley, or Hatcho miso
2 tablespoons oil
1 tablespoon lemon juice
⅛ teaspoon lemon rind
½ teaspoon hot mustard
1½ teaspoons honey
1½ teaspoons minced onion (optional)

Combine all ingredients, mixing well. Delicious with 1 small head of torn butter lettuce and 6 thinly-sliced fresh mushrooms; serves 2.

Miso-Sour Cream Dressing

MAKES ¾ CUP

3 tablespoons sour cream
1 tablespoon red or barley (or 2 tablespoons mellow white) miso
1½ tablespoons cream cheese or Roquefort cheese, softened
¼ cup oil
2 tablespoons lemon juice
1 tablespoon minced onions or chives

Combine all ingredients, mixing well. Good on steamed cauliflower or green beans. Or try on tossed green salads with thinly sliced beets.

Cream Cheese-Miso Mayonnaise Dressing

MAKES ABOUT ½ CUP

¼ cup mayonnaise
1 tablespoon red or barley (or 2 tablespoons mellow white) miso
2 tablespoons lemon juice
1½ tablespoons cream cheese, softened
1 tablespoon sesame or peanut butter
1½ teaspoons grated onion and juice

Combine all ingredients, mixing well. Especially good with asparagus, cauliflower, broccoli, or artichoke hearts salads.

Tangy Peanut Butter-Miso Dressing

MAKES ¼ CUP

2 tablespoons peanut butter
4 teaspoons vinegar
1 tablespoon red, barley, or Hatcho miso
2 tablespoons oil
1½ teaspoons honey

Combine all ingredients, mixing well.

White Sesame-Miso Dressing

MAKES ⅜ CUP

2 tablespoons sweet white or 1½ tablespoons mellow white miso
2 tablespoons sesame butter or *tahini;* or 3 table-spoons ground roasted sesame seeds (p. 107)
2 teaspoons *mirin,* sake, white wine, or water
½ teaspoon honey
1 teaspoon shoyu or ¼ teaspoon salt

Combine ingredients, mixing well. Try with (1 pound) parboiled spinach, or an apple-and-raisin salad.

Miso French Dressing

MAKES ⅜ CUP

The use of miso, which has a much mellower salti-ness than plain salt, makes it possible to reduce the proportion of oil in the traditional recipe and also to take full advantage of the fine miso flavor. Good for those who like their salads with plenty of dressing but must still watch their intake of fats.

4 tablespoons oil
2 tablespoons lemon juice or vinegar
2½ to 3 teaspoons red, barley, or Hatcho miso
1 teaspoon minced parsley
½ teaspoon dill or caraway seeds
Dash of pepper (optional)

Combine all ingredients, whisking or shaking well just before dressing salad.

VARIATIONS

*Substitute for the miso 1½ tablespoons any vari-ety of Sweet Simmered Miso (pp. 125 to 138), or 2 tablespoons sweet white miso.
*For zest, add ½ clove of crushed garlic and a dash of dry mustard or gingerroot.
*For richness and variety, add small amounts of your

favorite herbs, Roquefort cheese, Worcestershire or chili sauce, or chutney.

Tangy Miso-French Dressing

MAKES ¾ CUP

4 tablespoons oil
3½ tablespoons red, barley, or Hatcho miso
3½ tablespoons vinegar
2½ tablespoons lemon juice
¾ teaspoon hot mustard
½ clove of garlic, crushed (optional)
Dash of pepper (optional)

Combine all ingredients, mixing well. Use in small amounts. Especially tasty with a salad of lettuce, jicama, cucumbers, and deep-fried tofu.

Miso-Vinegar Dressing with Gingerroot

MAKES ⅓ CUP

2 tablespoons red, barley, or Hatcho miso
2 tablespoons vinegar
2 teaspoons (sesame) oil
1 tablespoon juice pressed from grated gingerroot
Dash of (7-spice) red pepper or Tabasco sauce

Combine all ingredients, mixing well. Delicious served over fresh tomato and cucumber slices, with parboiled bean sprouts, or with *wakame* and deep-fried tofu.

Low-Salt Miso Dressing

MAKES ½ CUP

3 tablespoons salt-free red miso
1½ tablespoons lemon juice or vinegar
¼ cup oil
1 clove of garlic, crushed or grated
1 teaspoon (dark or roasted) sesame oil
½ teaspoon honey
½ teaspoon grated gingerroot
¼ teaspoon salt
2 teaspoons water

Combine all ingredients, mixing well. Nice on all types of salads.

Miso-Mayonnaise Dressings

MAKES ⅓ TO ½ CUP

The combination of miso, mayonnaise, and lemon juice (or vinegar) yields a wide variety of dressings and sauces. Experiment using the following guidelines to develop your own combinations, or try a few of our favorites listed below.

To ¼ cup mayonnaise add:
  Miso: Choose one
      1 teaspoon red, barley, or Hatcho miso for tossed green salads. Use 1 to 2 tablespoons with fresh vegetable slices and as much as 3 tablespoons with noodle salads.
      2 to 3 teaspoons sweet white or mellow white miso, Sweet simmered Miso (p. 125), Finger Lickin' Miso (p. 75), or Miso-Nut Butter Spreads (p. 181).
  Vinegar or Lemon Juice: Use 2 parts for every 3 parts miso.
  Pepper: A dash of white, black, or red is essential.
  Other Seasonings: ½ to 2 teaspoons of minced onion, hot mustard, crushed garlic, grated gingerroot, or your favorite herbs or spices.
  Sesame or Nut Butters: Use 1 part to every 1 part red miso.
  Dairy Products: 1 to 2 tablespoons cream cheese, sour cream, or grated cheese adds richness and flavor.
  Sweetenings: The occasional use of 1 to 2 teaspoons honey goes nicely with red miso.

We have found the following combinations to go particularly well with certain salad ingredients. Mix miso and other ingredients with ¼ cup mayonnaise; dress salad just before serving. Serves 4 to 6.

*Basic: Use with your favorite tossed green salads or cooked vegetables (asparagus, broccoli, cauliflower, bean sprouts)

    1 teaspoon red, barley, or Hatcho miso
    1 teaspoon lemon juice
    1 to 2 teaspoons water or stock
    Dash of paprika or pepper (optional)

*Cheese-Garlic: Try with lettuce-cucumber-and-tomato salads

> 2 to 3 teaspoons red miso, or 4 to 6 teaspoons Sesame Miso (p. 130)
> 2 to 3 teaspoons lemon juice
> 2 tablespoons grated cheese
> ½ clove of garlic, crushed
> Dash of pepper (optional)
> ½ teaspoon caraway or dill seeds (optional)

*Tangy Onion: Nice with buckwheat noodle or macaroni salads

> 3 tablespoons red, barley, or Hatcho miso
> 3 tablespoons lemon juice
> 4 tablespoons vinegar
> 2 teaspoons minced onion
> 1 to 2 tablespoons oil (optional)

*Sweetened: Delicious with salads of chilled cooked vegetables, especially pumpkin, squash or *kabocha,* potatoes, asparagus, or deep-fried tofu

> 2 tablespoons red, barley, or Hatcho miso
> 1 tablespoon lemon juice or vinegar
> ½ to ¾ teaspoon honey

*Sesame: Nice over lettuce-egg-and-tomato salads

> 1 tablespoon red, barley, or Hatcho miso
> 1 tablespoon sesame butter, *tahini,* or ground roasted sesame seeds (p. 107)
> 2 tablespoons vinegar or lemon juice
> ½ teaspoon honey

*Rich & Creamy Nut Butter: Often prepared from leftover Miso-Nut Butter spreads; try with apple or tomato wedges, or fresh cucumber slices

> ¼ cup Miso-Nut Butter Spread (any variety) (p. 181)
> 3½ tablespoons lemon juice
> Dash of pepper (optional)

Creamy Tofu Dressings & Dips with Miso

MAKES ABOUT 1 CUP

Here is a wonderful way to introduce both tofu and miso into your daily menu served with salads, hors d'oeuvres, or even as a sandwich spread. Quick and easy to prepare, the possible variations are virtually unlimited. Each is thick, rich, and full of flavor, yet remarkably low in fats and calories. The perfect answer for those who love dressings but dislike their typical oily qualities.

6 ounces tofu
1½ to 2 tablespoons lemon juice or vinegar
2 tablespoons oil
1 tablespoon red, barley, or Hatcho miso; or
    2 tablespoons mellow white miso
Choice of seasonings (see below)

Combine all ingredients in a blender and purée for 20 seconds, or until smooth. (Or mash all ingredients and allow to stand for 15 to 30 minutes before serving.) If desired, serve topped with a sprinkling of minced parsley or a dash of pepper. Refrigerated in a covered container, these preparations will stay fresh for 2 to 3 days; the consistency will thicken (delectably).

SEASONINGS: Use any one of the following

*Curry: ½ teaspoon curry powder and 2 tablespoons minced onion. Top with a sprinkling of 1 tablespoon minced parsley.
*Dill: ¼ to ½ teaspoon dill seeds. If desired, add 1 clove of minced garlic. Top with a sprinkling of parsley.
*Onion: ¼ cup diced onion. Excellent on all types of deep-fried tofu and with many vegetable dishes.
*Cheese and Garlic: ¼ cup Parmesan or grated cheese and ½ clove of garlic (or ¼ onion), minced. Serve topped with a sprinkling of minced parsley.
*Gingerroot: 1 teaspoon grated or 1½ teaspoons powdered gingerroot and a dash of (7-spice) red pepper or Tabasco sauce. Try over tomato & cucumber salad. Top with a sprinkling of parsley.
*Avocado: 1 well-ripened avocado, peeled, seeded, and mashed. For tang, add a few drops of Tabasco and 2 tablespoons minced onion.

*Carrot: ¼ cup grated carrot and 2 teaspoons minced onion. Top with a sprinkling of parsley.

*Sesame: 2 tablespoons sesame butter or *tahini* and, if desired, 1 clove of crushed garlic.

*Walnut: ¼ cup each walnut meats and ketchup. Try over a salad of hard-boiled eggs, asparagus, and tomato wedges.

*Sweetened: Use white miso plus 1½ to 3 teaspoons honey. Nice with tomatoes.

*Herb: ½ teaspoon fresh or dried herbs (oregano, marjoram, caraway, basil).

Tofu Mayonnaise with Miso

MAKES ABOUT 1 CUP

At last a delicious homemade mayonnaise that is low in fats and calories, entirely free of cholesterol-rich eggs, and takes only a minute to prepare. Commercial mayonnaise, by comparison, is required by law to contain at least 65 percent fats—and most home-made varieties have even more. The following recipe, which serves 4 to 6, contains a total of only 466 calories, whereas an equal weight (9.1 ounces) of commercial mayonnaise contains 1820 calories, or *four* times as many!

6 ounces tofu, drained and pressed (p. 109) if desired
1½ to 2 tablespoons lemon juice or vinegar
2 tablespoons oil
2 tablespoons sweet white miso; or 4 teaspoons
    mellow white miso; or 1 tablespoon light-yellow
    miso; or 1½ teaspoons red miso and ¼ teaspoon
    salt
Dash of pepper (optional)

Combine all ingredients in a blender and purée for
about 20 seconds, or until smooth. Store as for Creamy
Tofu Dressings (above).

Soymilk Mayonnaise Dressing

MAKES 1 CUP

½ cup soymilk
½ cup oil
3 tablespoons lemon juice or 2½ tablespoons vinegar
2 tablespoons sweet white miso; or 4 teaspoons
    mellow white miso; or 1½ teaspoons red miso
    and ¼ teaspoon salt

Combine soymilk and ¼ cup oil in a blender and
purée for 1 minute. Slowly add remaining oil in a thin
stream. When mixture is fairly thick, add lemon
juice and miso, and purée for 30 seconds more. For
variety add minced onions, garlic, grated gingerroot,
paprika, or your choice of herbs or seasonings. Or add
any of the combinations of ingredients used in the
variations to Creamy Tofu Dressings (above).

Miso-Yogurt Dressing

MAKES ABOUT ½ CUP

½ cup yogurt
4 teaspoons red or 8 teaspoons sweet white miso
1 tablespoon orange juice
2 tablespoons (olive) oil
Dash of pepper (optional)
½ teaspoon fresh herbs (tarragon, basil, thyme)
    (optional)

Combine all ingredients; whisk well. Good with both
tossed green and fruit salads.

Sweet Mustard-Vinegar Miso Dressing

MAKES ½ CUP

2 tablespoons sweet white or 4 teaspoons mellow
    white miso
2 tablespoons vinegar or lemon juice
3 tablespoons oil
½ teaspoon powdered hot mustard
Dash of paprika or (7-spice) red pepper

Combine all ingredients, mixing well. Try with a salad
of (Chinese) cabbage, apples, raisins, and walnuts.

Sweet Miso Marinade

MAKES ¾ CUP

6 tablespoons sweet white or ¼ cup mellow white
    miso
2 tablespoons ketchup
2 tablespoons lemon juice
2 tablespoons oil
1 tablespoon grated or minced onion
Dash of (7-spice) red pepper

Combine all ingredients, mixing well. Use as a marinade for fresh vegetables.

WESTERN-STYLE SALADS

Potato Salad with Sour Cream and Miso

SERVES 3 OR 4

4 small potatoes, boiled or steamed in the skins until
    tender, cubed (2 cups)
2 tablespoons Better Butter (p. 119) or butter
¼ cup chives
½ cup sour cream
1½ tablespoons red, barley, or Hatcho miso
1½ cucumbers, sliced into very thin rounds
Dash of paprika or pepper (optional)

Place hot cubed potatoes into a bowl and top with butter and chives; mix lightly until butter has melted. Combine sour cream and miso, mixing well, then use to dress potatoes. Allow to cool, then mix in cucumbers. Serve chilled, topped with a sprinkling of pepper.

Carrot, Raisin & Walnut Salad with Tofu and Miso

SERVES 4

1 cup grated carrots; or diced apple or celery
½ cup raisins
½ cup (roasted) walnut meats, diced
1½ tablespoons red, barley, or Hatcho miso
1 teaspoon honey
1 teaspoon white wine or sake
2 tablespoons sesame butter
4 lettuce leaves (optional)

Combine all ingredients, mixing well. If desired, serve mounded on lettuce leaves.

For a milder, slightly sweeter flavor, substitute for the red miso and honey: 3 to 4 tablespoons sweet white miso and ½ teaspoon shoyu.

Carrot & Raisin Salad with Miso-Mayonnaise Dressing

SERVES 5

2 carrots, grated
¾ cup raisins
¾ to 1 cup diced apple or persimmon (optional)
½ cup walnut meats
⅓ cup mayonnaise
2 tablespoons sweet white miso; or 1 tablespoon
    red miso and 1 teaspoon honey

Combine all ingredients, mixing lightly.

Fresh Vegetable Slices with Tofu-Miso Dressing

SERVES 3

3 tablespoons red, barley, or Hatcho miso
2½ tablespoons vinegar or lemon juice
1 tablespoon honey
2 tablespoons oil
2 tablespoons minced parsley
Dash of paprika
12 ounces tofu
3 large lettuce leaves
2 tomatoes, cut into thin wedges
2 cucumbers, cut into thin diagonals
⅔ cup peanuts

Combine the first seven ingredients and mash together well (or purée in a blender). Place lettuce leaves in individual salad bowls, arrange sliced tomatoes and cucumbers on leaves, and spoon on the dressing. Top with peanuts just before serving.

Crispy Sprout Salad with Tofu-Miso Dressing

SERVES 3 TO 4

2 cups alfalfa sprouts
1 carrot, grated
¼ cup (roasted) sunflower seeds
¼ cup raisins
1 cup Creamy Tofu Dressing with Miso (p. 192)

Combine the first four ingredients, toss lightly, and serve topped with dollops of the dressing.

Cucumbers with Walnut-Vinegar Miso Dressing

SERVES 2

1 cucumber, sliced into thin rounds; or 20 to 30
    green beans, parboiled
Dressing:
    1½ teaspoons red, barley, or Hatcho miso
    1 teaspoon vinegar
    ¼ cup chopped (roasted) walnut meats
    1 tablespoon *tahini* or sesame butter

Combine the cucumber rounds and dressing; mix lightly. Serve immediately.

Tomato-Cucumber Salad with Tangy Miso Dressing

SERVES 3 OR 4

This simple but delicious salad shows how Japanese-style *aemono* dressings can be used with fresh Western-style salads.

1 tomato, cut into ½-inch cubes
2 cucumbers, sliced into thin rounds
6 tablespoons Sweet Sesame-Vinegar Miso Dressing
    (p. 224)

Combine all ingredients, mixing lightly. Serve immediately.

For variety, add fresh mushrooms, green beans, grated carrot or reconstituted *wakame*.

Tomatoes with Sesame-Miso Mayonnaise

SERVES 4

2 tomatoes, cut into wedges
2 tablespoons mayonnaise
1 to 1½ tablespoons red, barley, or Hatcho miso
½ clove of garlic, grated or crushed
1 tablespoon sesame butter or *tahini*
1 teaspoon honey or lemon juice

Arrange tomato wedges on individual plates. Combine the next 5 ingredients, mixing well, then spoon over tomatoes. Serve topped with a sprinkling of parsley.

For a milder dressing, use ¼ cup mayonnaise, 3 to 4 teaspoons Sweet Simmered Miso (p. 125), 2 tablespoons sesame butter, 2 teaspoons water, and a dash of pepper.

Tofu-Miso Salad with Walnuts and Apple

SERVES 4 TO 5

8 ounces tofu, pressed (p. 109); or 7 ounces firm tofu
1 tablespoon red miso
2 tablespoons sesame butter
1 tablespoon lemon juice
2 tablespoons honey
½ cup raisins
1 cup walnut meats
1 apple, diced

Combine the first five ingredients, mashing and mixing well. Add the raisins, walnut meats, and apple, mixing lightly. Serve as is, or chill for several hours.

Fruit Salad with Miso-Cream Cheese Balls

SERVES 3

3 ounces cream cheese
2½ tablespoons sweet white miso
¼ cup minced walnut meats or sunflower seeds
2 lettuce leaves
1 apple or pear, cut into ½-inch cubes
3 tablespoons raisins
2 tablespoons mayonnaise
2 tablespoons lemon juice

Combine the first three ingredients, mixing well, and shape into about 25 small balls. Arrange lettuce leaves on plates and mound with apples, raisins, and cream cheese-miso balls. Combine mayonnaise and lemon juice to make a dressing; pour over salad and serve immediately.

Fruit Salad with Sweet Miso-Mayonnaise Dressing

SERVES 4

1 grapefruit, sectioned
1 orange, sectioned
1 apple, cut into ½-inch cubes
1 banana, sliced into thin rounds
6 prunes, seeded and minced
Dressing:
   1 tablespoon sweet white miso
   2 tablespoons mayonnaise
   1 tablespoon grapefruit or apple juice

Combine the fruits in a serving bowl; toss lightly with the dressing.

Apple-Raisin Salad with Sesame-Miso Dressing

SERVES 4

1½ to 2 large apples, cut into thin wedges
3 tablespoons raisins
¼ cup chopped walnuts
¼ cup chopped celery or sliced cucumber (optional)
⅜ cup White Sesame-Miso Dressing (p. 189)

Combine all ingredients, mixing lightly.

Macaroni Salad with Miso Mayonnaise

SERVES 4 TO 5

5 to 6 ounces (1¼ cups) dry macaroni, cooked
   (3 cups)
2 cucumbers, sliced into thin rounds
2 small tomatoes, cut into wedges
White Miso & Mustard Mayonnaise Dressing:
   ¼ cup sweet white miso
   ¼ cup mayonnaise
   1½ tablespoons lemon juice
   ½ teaspoon hot mustard
   1 tablespoon finely minced or grated onion
   Dash of pepper
4 lettuce leaves
Parsley sprigs

Combine the first three ingredients with the dressing; mix lightly. Chill for several hours, then serve mounded on lettuce leaves and garnished with parsley.

For variety, add 9 ounces cubed deep-fried tofu, ½ cup raisins, and 3½ ounces fresh or reconstituted *wakame* (or grated carrot); double the amount of dressing. Or substitute for the macaroni an equal weight of noodles (whole-wheat, buckwheat, rice-flour, or transparent).

Buckwheat Noodle Salad with Miso Mayonnaise

SERVES 4

3 ounces (*soba*) buckwheat noodles (or spaghetti), cooked (p. 201), cooled, and cut into 3-inch lengths
1 large tomato, diced
1½ cucumbers, cut into thin rounds
⅔ cup diced celery
½ cup grated cheese or walnut meats; or 2 diced hard-boiled eggs (optional)
Dressing:
    ¼ cup mayonnaise
    1½ tablespoons red, barley, or Hatcho miso
    1 teaspoon lemon juice
    Dash of pepper
4 lettuce leaves
¼ cup parsley

Combine the first four (or five) ingredients with the dressing; mix lightly. Arrange lettuce leaves in individual bowls, mound with the salad, and top with a sprinkling of parsley.

For variety, add 5 ounces diced deep-fried tofu.

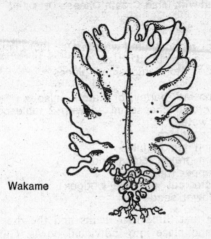

Wakame

Fresh Sea Vegetable Salad with Miso-Mayonnaise

SERVES 4

1 cup fresh or reconstituted *wakame* (p. 105), cut into
    2-inch lengths
1 green pepper, thinly sliced
1 cucumber, thinly sliced
7 ounces deep-fried tofu, lightly broiled if desired,
    cut crosswise into thin strips
Rich Miso-Mayonnaise Dressing:
    ¼ cup mayonnaise
    6 tablespoons red, barley, or Hatcho Miso
    ¼ cup lemon juice
    Dash of pepper
1 tomato, cut into thin wedges
4 lettuce leaves

Combine the first five ingredients and the dressing;
mix lightly. Arrange tomato wedges on lettuce leaves
in a large salad bowl. Top with the salad mixture and
chill for several hours before serving.

If *wakame* is unavailable, substitute 1 large diced
apple or tomato.

Wakame Salad with Miso-Cream Cheese Dressing

SERVES 4

1 cup fresh or reconstituted *wakame* (p. 105) chopped
1 cucumber, thinly sliced
4 lettuce leaves, torn into small pieces
Dressing:
   2 teaspoons red, barley, or Hatcho miso
   2 ounces cream cheese mixed with 2 tablespoons
      warm water
   ¼ cup mayonnaise
   1 tablespoon lemon juice
   ½ teaspoon grated lemon rind
   Dash of pepper (optional)
1 small tomato, cut into thin wedges
¼ cup sunflower seeds

Combine the first three ingredients and the dressing;
toss lightly and place into individual bowls. Garnish
with tomato wedges and top with a sprinkling of sunflower seeds.

Land-and-Sea Vegetable Salad
with Mustard Lemon-Miso Dressing

SERVES 3

1 cup fresh or reconstituted *wakame* (p. 105), cut into
     1½-inch lengths
1 cucumber, cut into thin rounds
1 tomato, cut into thin wedges
1¼ cups thin rounds of jicama, turnip, *daikon,* or
     celery root
2 ounces deep-fried tofu, broiled if desired, thinly
     sliced
Dressing:
   2 tablespoons sweet white miso
   3 tablespoons lemon juice
   1 teaspoon honey
   ¼ teaspoon hot mustard

Combine the first five ingredients with the dressing,
mixing lightly; serve immediately.

Green Beans with Miso-Sour Cream

SERVES 2 OR 3

1½ cups green beans (stringed, split lengthwise into
        halves, and cut diagonally into 2-inch lengths)
¼ cup water
2 tablespoons sour cream
1 tablespoon red, barley, or light-yellow miso
Dash of pepper (optional)

Combine beans and water in a small saucepan and
bring just to a boil. Reduce heat to low, cover, and
cook for about 10 minutes, or until liquid has evaporated and beans are just tender; remove from heat.
Combine sour cream, miso and pepper, mixing well.
Stir in green beans. Serve cold as a salad or hot as a
dinner vegetable.

Any of the following, steamed until tender, make
excellent substitutes for the green beans: (*kabocha*)
pumpkin, winter squash or zucchini seasoned with a
little dill; Irish or sweet potatoes, celery, bean sprouts,
or eggplant.

Fresh Vegetable & Raisin Salad
    with Mustard Vinegar-Miso Dressing

SERVES 3

2 tomatoes, diced
1½ cucumbers, cut into thin rounds
1 cabbage leaf, shredded
½ cup diced celery
2 to 4 ounces deep-fried tofu, diced (optional)
¼ cup raisins
Dressing:
    2 tablespoons red or barley miso
    2 tablespoons vinegar
    1½ tablespoons lemon juice
    ½ teaspoon mustard
    1 tablespoon oil (optional)
    Dash of pepper (optional)
3 lettuce leaves

Combine the first six ingredients with the dressing; mix lightly. Serve immediately, mounded on the lettuce leaves.

Refreshing Potato Salad with Miso Dressing

SERVES 5 OR 6

1¼ pounds potatoes, halved or quartered and
    steamed for 30 minutes
1½ tablespoons red, barley, or Hatcho miso
¼ cup lemon juice
Dash of pepper (optional)
¼ cup mayonnaise
1 tablespoon honey
1½ to 2 cucumbers, sliced into thin rounds
¼ cup chopped parsley
1 cup mandarin orange or tangerine sections,
    chopped apples, or tomato wedges
¼ cup raisins (optional)

Break or cut freshly steamed potatoes into bite-sized pieces and place in a serving bowl. Combine miso, lemon juice and pepper, mixing well, then pour over the potatoes. Toss lightly and allow to cool for 20 to 30 minutes. Mix mayonnaise and honey, then stir into the potatoes together with the cucumbers and parsley. Add orange sections and, if used, the raisins; mix gently. Chill before serving.

Tofu & Tomato Salad with Walnut-Lemon Miso

SERVES 3

12 ounces tofu, scrambled (p. 110)
1½ tablespoons Lemon-Walnut-Miso (p. 151) or
    Sesame Miso (p. 130)
3 tablespoons mayonnaise
3 tablespoons minced parsley
1 tomato, cut into thin wedges
¼ cup chopped walnut meats (optional)
Dash of pepper (optional)

Combine tofu, miso, and mayonnaise in a serving bowl; mix well. Add parsley, tomato, and nutmeats, mixing lightly. Season with a sprinkling of the pepper. Chill before serving.

Cottage Cheese & Tomato Salad with Miso Dressing

SERVES 3 OR 4

1 cup cottage cheese
1 small tomato, cut into wedges
1 cucumber, cut into thin rounds
3½ cups sprouts (parboiled mung or soy; or fresh alfalfa)
Dressing:
    ¼ cup oil
    2 tablespoons vinegar
    2 tablespoons red, barley, or Hatcho miso
    Dash of (7-spice) red pepper or Tabasco sauce
    1 clove of garlic, crushed (optional)
3 or 4 lettuce leaves

Combine the first four ingredients and the dressing; mix lightly. Serve mounded on lettuce leaves, if desired.

Quick Potato Salad with Miso Dressing

SERVES 2

2 potatoes or sweet potatoes (12 ounces), boiled or steamed and cut into 1-inch cubes
½ cup Sweetened Miso Mayonnaise Dressing (p. 192)
½ cup parsley

Combine potatoes and miso mayonnaise, mix lightly and chill for at least 1 hour. Served topped with the parsley.

Tomato Slices Mounded with Miso-Cottage Cheese

SERVES 3

2 tomatoes, cut into ½-inch-thick rounds
½ cup cottage or ricotta cheese
5 tablespoons sweet white miso or White Nerimiso (p. 127)
2 to 2½ tablespoons lemon juice
Dash of paprika or pepper (optional)
Minced parsley or chives (optional)

Arrange tomato slices on a serving plate. Combine the next three ingredients, mixing well, then mound on the tomato slices. Serve topped with a sprinkling of the pepper and parsley.

Vegetable & Tofu Salad
with Peanut Butter-Miso Dressing

SERVES 2 OR 3

½ carrot, cut into large matchsticks and steamed
15 green beans, steamed and cut diagonally into halves
4 to 5 ounces deep-fried tofu, cut into thin bite-sized rectangles
¼ cup Tangy Peanut Butter-Miso Dressing (p. 188)

Combine all ingredients, mixing lightly. If tofu is unavailable use 1¼ carrots and 35 green beans.

Fresh Vegetable Salad with Miso Mayonnaise

SERVES 4

1 tomato, cut into wedges
2 cucumbers, sliced into thin rounds
⅓ cup raisins
1 green pepper, thinly sliced
3 lettuce leaves, torn into small pieces
Mustard-Miso Mayonnaise Dressing:
  ¼ cup mayonnaise
  1½ tablespoons lemon juice
  ¼ teaspoon hot mustard
  1½ tablespoons red, barley, or Hatcho miso

Combine the first five ingredients with the dressing; toss lightly. For best flavor, chill for several hours before serving.

AEMONO AND THEIR DRESSINGS

Next to miso soups, *aemono* are the most popular way of using miso in Japanese cookery. These unique preparations are a favorite among most Western visitors to Japan, not only because of their fine flavor and the artistic way in which they are served, but also because of the way in which they make creative use of the tastiest and freshest seasonal vegetables, including those from wild upland meadows and the sea. Aemono trace their origins to the two schools of Japanese haute cuisine: Zen Temple Cookery *(Shojin Ryori)* and Tea Ceremony Cuisine *(Kaiseki Ryori),* which were founded and developed by men who treasured a life of elegant simplicity and refined frugality. Early temple cooks, monks, and tea masters knew of no better union of joy and economy than to roam Japan's mountains early each spring in search of edible wild buds and fronds, tender sprigs, and leafy shoots. These became the ingredients and garnishes for the finest of Japan's many *aemono.*

The word *aemono* means "dressed things," and these preparations might be described as Japanese-style salads of mixed foods in thick, rich dressings. Whereas the vegetables in Western-style salads are often light, crisp and fresh, those in aemono generally have a softer texture imparted by parboiling, simmering in sweetened shoyu broths, or rubbing with salt. Fresh vegetables, *konnyaku,* deep-fried tofu, and various seafoods are also used.

In Japanese, aemono dressings are known as *aegoromo,* a word derived from *koromo,* the robes worn by Buddhist priests. Whereas many Western-style dressings are light "negligee" which help to preserve the crisp quality of tossed green salads, the Japanese "robes" generally have plenty of body. This helps them to unite and bind various soft vegetable pieces while simultaneously evoking and harmonizing their individual flavors.

The most common ingredients in aemono dressings are miso, vinegar, nut-and-seed butters, tofu and, in some cases, relatively large amounts of sweetening. In the many dressings that contain vinegar, use rice vinegar for a milder, gentler flavor and Western-style fruit-based vinegar for additional tang and zest. Since oil is virtually never used in aemono dressings, they are low in calories and highly digestible. Dairy products—such as mayonnaise, cottage, cream, or regular cheese—so widely used in Western dressings are virtually never employed. Yet because of the richness of the dressing, aemono are typically served in very small portions (often no more than 3 or 4 tablespoons) and are meant to accompany main dishes which they complement in color, taste, and texture. On Western menus they may be served either as first courses or as salads. Moreover, many aemono dressings, sometimes seasoned with herbs and spices, go well with Western-style salads, too.

There are fourteen basic aemono dressings which feature miso (and a number of others in which shoyu or salt provide the seasoning). Most are closely related to Sweet Simmered Miso except that they are almost always prepared without cooking. Each aemono preparation takes its name from the name of its dressing: thus, a lotus root salad with vinegar-miso dressing would be called Lotus Root Vinegar-Miso Ae. The basic dressings are listed here in the approximate order of their popularity.

Red Miso Dressing

MAKES ¼ CUP

This and the following preparation are known collectively in Japanese as *awasé-miso* or "uncooked mixed miso." They contain almost the same ingredients in the same proportions as their close relatives red and white *nerimiso*. Rather than being used directly as *aemono* dressings, they are generally mixed with vinegar, mustard, sesame, and other ingredients, thereby serving as the foundation for a wide variety of dressings.

2½ tablespoons red or barley miso
1 to 2 tablespoons (natural) sugar or 1 to 3 teaspoons honey
1½ to 3 teaspoons water or dashi (p. 112)
1 teaspoon sake, white wine, or *mirin*

Combine all ingredients, mixing well.

White Miso Dressing

MAKES ¼ CUP

3 tablespoons sweet white miso
½ teaspoon sugar or ¼ teaspoon honey
2 teaspoons wa er or dashi (p. 112)
2 teaspoons sake, white wine, or *mirin*

Combine all ingredients, mixing well.

Vinegar Miso Dressing *(Sumiso)*

MAKES ¼ CUP

These tangy preparations are delicious with almost all varieties of aemono as well as with Western-style salads, thin slices of fresh vegetables, and even deep-fried foods. Experiment adding your favorite herbs and spices. For a more vivid flavor use a slightly smaller quantity of cider vinegar or lemon juice in place of the traditional rice vinegar. In each preparation, the trick is to use just enough vinegar to give the desired tang, but not so much as to make the consistency too thin. All vinegar miso dressings can be divided into two basic types: those which contain more miso than vinegar have a richer flavor and more body, while those containing more vinegar are tangy and more delicate in consistency.

2 tablespoons red, barley, or Hatcho miso
1 tablespoon vinegar, or 2½ teaspoons lemon juice
2 to 3 teaspoons (natural) sugar or 1 to 1½ teaspoons
    honey
2 teaspoons *mirin* or 1 teaspoon sake (or white wine)
    (optional)

Combine all ingredients, mixing well.

VARIATIONS

*Tangy: A favorite with sea and wild mountain vegetables
    2 tablespoons vinegar
    1 tablespoon red, barley, or Hatcho miso
    1 to 2 tablespoons dashi (p. 112), stock, or water

*Sweet White Vinegar Miso Dressing: Nice with
steamed cauliflower
>   2 tablespoons sweet white miso
>   1½ tablespoons vinegar or lemon juice
>   1 teaspoon sugar or ½ teaspoon honey

*Miso Sambaizu: Sweet and zesty
>   2 tablespoons red miso
>   5 tablespoons vinegar
>   2½ tablespoons dashi (p. 112), stock, or water
>   2½ tablespoons (natural) sugar or 4 teaspoons
>   honey

***Mix ¼ cup Red Miso Dressing (p. 210) with 1 ta-
blespoon vinegar**

Mustard-Vinegar Miso Dressing (Karashi Sumiso)

MAKES ½ CUP

This preparation is generally made with sweet white
miso, and may or may not contain sugar, sake or
mirin. Various forms can be prepared simply by adding a small amount of hot mustard to any of the different recipes for Vinegar Miso Dressing given above.
This dressing is a favorite with sea vegetables (such as
wakame), green beans, eggplants, cabbage, steamed
(*kabocha*) squash or pumpkin sprinkled with minced
parsley, thinly sliced *konnyaku,* and deep-fried tofu.

    3 tablespoons sweet white or 2 tablespoons mellow
        white miso
    3 tablespoons vinegar
    1½ to 3 teaspoons (natural) sugar or ¾ to 1 teaspoon
        honey
    1 teaspoon *mirin* (optional)
    ¼ teaspoon hot mustard

Combine all ingredients, mixing well.

VARIATIONS

*Tangy Mustard Vinegar Miso: Made with red miso, this is a popular topping for *Sashimi Konnyaki* (p. 176)
>   2 tablespoons red miso
>   1 tablespoon vinegar
>   4 teaspoons (natural) sugar or 2 teaspoons honey
>   ½ teaspoon *mirin*
>   ¼ teaspoon mustard

*To 5 tablespoons Vinegar Miso Dressing add ½ to 1 teaspoon hot mustard.

Sesame, Walnut, or Peanut Miso Dressings
(Goma Miso or Kurumi Miso)

MAKES 6 TABLESPOONS

In Japan these dressings are generally prepared by grinding roasted seeds or nuts to a paste in a *suribachi,* then adding the remaining ingredients and mixing them together with the pestle until smooth. White sesame seeds should be used with white miso; either white or black seeds with red miso. Although freshly roasted and ground sesame yields the best flavor and aroma, sesame butter or *tahini* may be more convenient. This dressing goes well with spinach, chrysanthemum leaves, boiled *daikon,* turnips, celery, or even apples.

2 tablespoons sweet white or 4 teaspoons mellow
    white miso
3 tablespoons ground roasted sesame seeds (p. 107),
    sesame butter, or *tahini*
1 teaspoon sugar or ½ teaspoon honey
1 tablespoon sake, *mirin,* water, or dashi (p. 112)
¼ teaspoon salt

Combine all ingredients, mixing well.

For variety substitute for the sesame seeds: ground walnuts or peanuts, or your choice of nut butters. In Japan, Walnut Miso Dressing is especially popular.

Sesame-Vinegar Miso Dressing (*Goma Sumiso*)

MAKES ⅜ CUP

This preparation and its popular relatives, containing walnuts or peanuts in place of sesame, combine the tangy flavor of vinegar miso with the richness of nut butters. In some preparations the sesame flavor is featured, while in others the miso is accentuated. One of Japan's most widely used dressings for *aemono,* it goes especially well with green beans, cucumbers, mushrooms, deep-fried tofu, and all sea vegetables. Or try it with Western-style apple-walnut-celery salads.

2 tablespoons red, barley, or Hatcho miso
2 tablespoons vinegar
2 tablespoons ground roasted sesame seeds (p. 107), sesame butter, *tahini,* or walnuts
1 tablespoon (natural) sugar or 1½ teaspoons honey

Combine all ingredients, mixing well.

VARIATIONS: Prepare as above

*Peanut-Vinegar Miso Dressing:
    1 tablespoon sweet white or 2 teaspoons mellow white miso
    2 tablespoons vinegar
    20 peanuts, chopped fine; or 3 tablespoons peanut butter
    2 teaspoons honey
    ½ teaspoon shoyu

*Sweet Sesame-Vinegar Miso Dressing: Nice with Western-style green salads.
    3 tablespoons sweet white or 2 tablespoons mellow white miso
    1½ tablespoons vinegar
    1 tablespoon sesame butter or *tahini,* or 1½ tablespoons ground roasted sesame seeds (p. 107)
    ¼ teaspoon honey

*Try reversing the proportions of miso and sesame.

Tofu Miso Dressing *(Shira-ae and Shirozu-ae)*

SERVES 4

In *shira-ae*-type *aemono,* the dressing itself often forms the basis and bulk of the salad, and the vegetables are used subordinately to add texture, flavor and color. Tofu plays the leading role, supported by white miso, ground roasted sesame seeds and, sometimes, vinegar. This dressing goes especially well with cooked carrots, *konnyaku,* and mushrooms. Or use lotus root, burdock, sweet potatoes, eggplants, or your favorite wild mountain vegetables. The vegetables are often simmered in a sweetened shoyu broth before being mixed with the dressing. The amounts of sweetening, *mirin,* and vinegar should be adjusted carefully to suit the flavoring given to the vegetables and other basic ingredients. A well-made Tofu Miso Dressing has a texture similar to that of very firm cottage cheese.

3 to 6 tablespoons roasted sesame (p. 107), or 1½ to 3 tablespoons sesame butter or *tahini*
6 ounces tofu, pressed or squeezed (p. 109)
3 tablespoons sweet white or 2 tablespoons mellow white miso
1 to 3 tablespoons sugar or 1½ to 4½ teaspoons honey
1 to 2 teaspoons *mirin* (optional)

Place the hot, freshly roasted sesame seeds into a *suribachi* and grind to a smooth paste. Add tofu and re-grind. Add miso, sugar and *mirin,* and grind for several minutes more to develop cohesiveness. Then add the cooked vegetables to be used, mixing lightly. Serve immediately.

To prepare Tangy Tofu & Miso Dressing *(Shirozu-ae),* add 2 tablespoons vinegar or lemon juice and 2 to 3 drops of shoyu to the completed dressing just before mixing in the vegetables.

If using sesame butter or *tahini* in place of sesame seeds, the dressing may be prepared by simply combining all ingredients in a bowl and mixing with a

(wooden) spoon for about 3 minutes to develop cohesiveness.

Egg Yolk-Vinegar Miso Dressing *(Kimi Sumiso)*

MAKES ½ CUP

This rich, light-yellow dressing is generally used
with the same ingredients as Tofu Miso Dressing or
with light-colored foods such as white mushrooms, asparagus, okra, or shrimp.

2 hard-boiled eggs, separated into yolks and whites
1 tablespoon sweet white or 2 teaspoons mellow
     white miso
2½ teaspoons vinegar or lemon juice
¼ teaspoon honey
2 teaspoons dashi (p. 112) stock, or water

Press firm egg yolks through a sieve, then combine
with all remaining ingredients except the egg whites,
which are diced and used in the salad itself. Try with
5 grilled *(shiitaké)* mushrooms, and top with 1 tablespoon minced parsley.

Gingerroot Miso Dressing

MAKES 2 TABLESPOONS

1½ tablespoons red, barley, or Hatcho miso
1 teaspoon grated gingerroot or its juice
2 teaspoons (natural) sugar or 1 teaspoon honey
     (optional)

Combine all ingredients, mixing well. Excellent with
green beans, snow peas, crisp green vegetables, or
deep-fried tofu.

Kinomé Miso Dressing

MAKES ⅓ CUP

10 to 15 individual *kinomé* leaves (not sprigs)
5 tablespoons sweet white or 3 tablespoons mellow
     white miso
1 teaspoon sugar or ½ teaspoon honey (optional)
1 teaspoon *mirin*

Place *kinomé* in a strainer or colander and douse with boiling water. Drain well, then transfer to a *suribachi* and grind thoroughly. Add the remaining ingredients and grind to a smooth paste. For a richer green, add 1 to 2 teaspoons *aoyosé* (p. 134). Try with regular or deep-fried tofu, celery cut into very thin diagonals, bamboo shoots, or turnips cut into paper-thin rounds.

Chive-Vinegar Miso Dressing

MAKES ¾ CUP

2 tablespoons red or barley miso
2 tablespoons vinegar
¼ cup minced chives, *nira,* or *asatsuki*
2 to 3 teaspoons sugar or 1 to 1½ teaspoons honey

Combine all ingredients, mixing well.

Leek Miso Dressing

MAKES ¼ CUP

4 tablespoons thinly-sliced leeks
1 tablespoon barley, Hatcho, or red miso

Combine ingredients, mixing well. For best flavor, cover and refrigerate for 1 to 2 days. Goes nicely with 2 cups steamed and cubed potatoes, sweet potatoes, or *kabocha;* or try with deep-fried tofu, steamed green beans, or spinach.

Yuzu Miso Dressing *(Yuzu Miso Ae)*

Prepare Yuzu Miso (p. 131) or Lemon Miso (p. 132), and allow to cool thoroughly. Use as is, or mix 3 parts with 1 part vinegar. Serve as for Kinomé Miso Dressing.

Sake Lees & Miso Dressing (Kasumiso)

MAKES ¼ CUP

2 tablespoons sake lees
2 teaspoons red or 4 teaspoons mellow white miso
1 teaspoon honey or 2 teaspoons (natural) sugar
2 tablespoons water

Combine all ingredients, mixing well. Delicious with parboiled or steamed (horenso) spinach or chrysanthemum leaves; use 10 ounces fresh.

AEMONO THEMSELVES

When preparing aemono, be sure that your vegetables contain no excess surface moisture when mixed with the dressing; drain them well and pat lightly with a dry cloth just before they are to be dressed. Parboil vegetables for only as long as is necessary to make them tender while still preserving some of their crispness (and most of their vitamins). Use lightly salted water for green vegetables, and plunge into cold water immediately after parboiling to preserve their emerald color. Use the seasoning quantities in the basic dressing recipes as guidelines, adjusting them to suit your ingredients and taste. Use seasonal ingredients and whatever is on hand. In Zen temples, even trimmings and peelings are sometimes creatively incorporated.

Cucumber Salad with Vinegar-Miso Dressing (Sunomono)

SERVES 4

3 cucumbers, sliced into thin rounds
1 teaspoon salt
3 tablespoons (rice) vinegar
2 teaspoons red, barley, or Hatcho miso
2 teaspoons (natural) sugar or 1 teaspoon honey
¼ teaspoon grated gingerroot

Place cucumber slices in a bowl, sprinkle with the salt, and allow to stand for 1 to 2 hours. Drain and squeeze out excess liquid. Combine vinegar, miso, sugar, and gingerroot in a serving bowl; add cucumbers and mix well. Serve chilled.

For variety, add to the dressing ⅓ cup reconstituted *wakame,* raisins, or cooked transparent noodles.

Pumpkin or Squash with Mustard-Vinegar Miso Dressing

SERVES 2 OR 3

9½ ounces *(kabocha)* pumpkin or squash, steamed
        and cut into 1-inch cubes
Mustard Vinegar-Miso:
        1½ tablespoons red, barley, or Hatcho miso
        2 tablespoons vinegar
        1 teaspoon (natural) sugar or ½ teaspoon
            honey
        ¼ teaspoon hot mustard
        ½ teaspoon *mirin,* sake or white wine
        2 tablespoons minced parsley

Combine well-cooled squash with the dressing, mixing lightly. Refrigerate for several hours before serving.

Refreshing Wakame Salad with Lemon

SERVES 4

1 cup fresh or reconstituted *wakame* (p. 105), cut into
    1-inch lengths
Dressing:
        1½ teaspoons red, barley, or Hatcho miso
        1 tablespoon vinegar
        1 tablespoon dashi (p. 112), stock, or water
        ¼ teaspoon grated lemon rind

Combine *wakame* and dressing, mixing lightly; serve immediately.

Wakame & Cucumber Salad with Peanut-Vinegar Miso Dressing

SERVES 2 OR 3

2 tablespoons vinegar
1 tablespoon red, barley, or Hatcho miso
2 tablespoons peanut, sesame, or walnut butter
1 cucumber, sliced into thin rounds
⅓ cup fresh or reconstituted *wakame* (p. 105), cut into
      1½-inch lengths

Combine the first three ingredients in a serving bowl, mixing well. Add cucumbers and *wakame,* mixing lightly. Serve immediately.

Wakame Salad with Vinegar Miso Dressing

SERVES 3

½ cup fresh or reconstituted *wakame* (p. 105), thinly
      sliced
½ large tomato, cut into thin wedges, or 2 Chinese
      cabbage leaves, thinly sliced
1 cucumber, cut into thin rounds
1 to 2 ounces deep-fried tofu, thinly sliced
⅜ cup Sesame-Vinegar Miso Dressing (p. 214), or
      ¼ cup Vinegar Miso Dressing (p. 216)

Combine all ingredients, mixing lightly. For best flavor, allow to stand for several hours before serving.

Konnyaku & Carrot Salad with Tofu Miso Dressing (Shira-ae)

SERVES 4

1 piece of *konnyaku,* cut into small rectangles and
    parboiled
1 carrot, cut into small rectangles
½ cup dashi, stock, or water
3 tablespoons sugar
½ teaspoon salt
½ teaspoon shoyu
¼ cup sesame seeds, roasted and ground to a paste
    (p. 107), sesame butter, or *tahini*
4 ounces tofu, pressed (p. 109), or 3 ounces firm tofu
2 tablespoons sweet white or 4 teaspoons mellow
    white miso
4 sprigs *kinomé* (optional)

Combine *konnyaku,* carrots, dashi, 1 tablespoon sugar,
salt and shoyu in a small saucepan. Simmer until all
liquid has been absorbed or evaporated, then allow to
cool to room temperature. To the ground sesame seeds
(in a *suribachi*), add tofu, miso and the remaining 2
tablespoons sugar; mix together (with a wooden pestle). Stir in the vegetables and serve each portion garnished with a sprig of *kinomé.*

Carrot-Daikon-Konnyaku Salad with Tofu Miso Dressing (Shira-ae)

SERVES 4

¼ carrot, cut into matchsticks
4 ounces *daikon,* cut into small rectangles
½ piece of *konnyaku,* cut into small rectangles
1¼ teaspoons salt
3 (*shiitaké*) mushrooms, cut into thin strips
2 teaspoons shoyu
4 teaspoons *mirin*
1 tablespoon roasted sesame seeds, sesame butter
    or *tahini*
8 ounces tofu, pressed (p. 109), or 6 ounces firm tofu
3 tablespoons sweet white or 2 tablespoons mellow
    white miso
1 teaspoon (natural) sugar or ½ teaspoon honey

Combine carrot, *daikon* and *konnyaku* in a small bowl. Rub with 1 teaspoon salt, rinse and press (p. 104). Heat an unoiled skillet or wok, drop in *konnyaku* and cook for several minutes, stirring constantly, until it becomes quite dry and begins to shrink; set *konnyaku* aside and allow to cool.

Combine mushrooms, shoyu and 1 teaspoon *mirin* in a small saucepan. Simmer until most of the liquid has been absorbed or evaporated, then drain and allow to cool to room temperature.

Combine sesame seeds and ¼ teaspoon salt in a *suribachi* and grind until seeds are slightly oily (p. 107). Add tofu, miso, sugar and 1 tablespoon *mirin,* and mix with the sesame using the wooden pestle. Stir in the *daikon,* carrot, *konnyaku* and mushrooms just before serving.

Vinegared Shira-ae (*Shirozu-ae*)

SERVES 2

6 ounces tofu, pressed (p. 109) and mashed
1 tablespoon sesame butter or *tahini*
1 tablespoon lemon juice
1½ tablespoons vinegar
1 tablespoon red or 2 tablespoons mellow white miso
1 teaspoon sake or white wine
1 cucumber or small carrot, sliced into thin rounds
2 hard-boiled eggs, chopped
¼ cup walnut meats
¼ cup raisins
2 tablespoons minced cucumber pickles (optional)

Combine the first six ingredients, mixing until smooth. Gently stir in the remaining ingredients. Serve immediately.

Green Beans and Carrots with Tofu-Miso Dressing (*Shira-ae*)

SERVES 4 TO 5

16 green beans, parboiled (p. 105) and cut into thin
    strips
1 carrot, cut into matchsticks and parboiled (p. 105)
4 teaspoons shoyu
4 teaspoons (natural) sugar or 2 teaspoons honey
4 tablespoons sesame butter, *tahini,* or ground
    roasted sesame seeds (p. 107)
12 ounces tofu, well pressed (p. 109), or 9 ounces firm
    tofu
4½ tablespoons sweet white or 3 tablespoons mellow
    white miso
1 tablespoon sake, white wine, or *mirin*

In a small saucepan combine green beans, carrots,
shoyu, and sugar. Simmer over low heat until liquid
has been absorbed or evaporated, then cool to room
temperature. To the sesame butter (or ground sesame
seeds in the *suribachi*), add tofu, miso and sake. Grind
all ingredients together with the wooden pestle, or mix
together with a spoon. Stir in the green beans and carrots. Serve immediately.

Green Beans with Vinegar Miso Dressing

SERVES 2

1½ tablespoons red, barley, or Hatcho miso
1 tablespoon vinegar
1½ tablespoons (natural) sugar or 2½ teaspoons
    honey
1 clove of garlic (or *myoga*), crushed or minced
25 green beans, parboiled (p. 105), and sliced diag-
    onally into thin strips; or substitute 70 whole,
    parboiled snow peas

Combine the first four ingredients to make a dressing
and mix lightly with the freshly cooked beans; allow
to cool before serving.

Green Bean & Tofu Salad
with Gingerroot Miso Dressing

SERVES 3

5 ounces green beans, parboiled (p. 105) and cut
    crosswise into halves; or substitute whole,
    parboiled snow peas
5 ounces deep-fried tofu, cut into small rectangles
2 tablespoons Gingerroot Miso Dressing (sweetened;
    p. 224)
⅓ cup peanuts or roasted soybeans

Combine crisp green beans, deep-fried tofu, and the
dressing in a serving bowl; mix lightly. Top with peanuts just before serving.

Spinach with Sesame Miso Dressing

SERVES 4

1 pound (*horenso*) spinach
3 tablespoons sweet white or 2 tablespoons mellow
    white miso
1½ tablespoons sesame butter or *tahini*, or 3 table-
    spoons ground roasted sesame seeds
1 tablespoon (natural) sugar or 1½ teaspoons honey
1 to 3 teaspoons water

Bring 1 quart lightly salted water to a boil. Drop in
spinach, return to the boil, and simmer for 1 to 2 minutes. Drain spinach briefly in a colander and douse
with cold water. Press spinach firmly in one hand to
form a compact cylinder then cut crosswise into 1-inch
lengths.

    Combine miso with remaining ingredients in a large
bowl, mixing well. Now stir in spinach. For best flavor,
allow to stand for several hours before serving.

Leek & Wakame Nuta

SERVES 2

Nuta is such a popular type of *aemono* that many
Japanese actually use the two words interchangeably.
Wakame and leeks (preferably the tender young vari-

ety known as *wakegi*) are used in most versions. Other popular ingredients include short-necked clams, sardines, squid, yellowtail, tuna, and a number of wild mountain vegetables such as *udo* and bracken ferns. Moist, cool and refreshing, *nuta* is generally prepared with a Miso Vinegar Dressing or occasionally with Sweet Simmered Miso.

2 leeks or 6 scallions, cut into ½-inch lengths
½ cup fresh or reconstituted *wakame* (p. 105), cut into 1½-inch lengths
2 ounces deep-fried tofu, lightly broiled if desired and thinly sliced
Sweet White Vinegar-Miso Dressing (p. 216)

Cut leek pieces lengthwise into halves and parboil very briefly. Drain well, pat dry with a towel, and combine with the *wakame,* tofu, and dressing; mix lightly. Serve immediately.

Onion Sesame-Miso Ae

SERVES 3 OR 4

3 onions, cut into thin wedges
¼ teaspoon salt
1½ tablespoons red, barley, or Hatcho miso
1½ tablespoons sesame butter or *tahini*

Bring ½ cup water to a boil in a small saucepan. Drop in the onions, season with the salt, and simmer for 5 minutes. Pour contents of saucepan into a strainer set over a bowl, and allow onions to drain well. In a large bowl combine miso, sesame butter, and 4½ tablespoons of the drained cooking liquid; mix well. Add onions and toss lightly. Serve immediately.

Miso in Soups and Stews

The great majority of Japan's miso (an estimated 80 to 85 percent of total yearly production) is used in the preparation of miso soup, and a recent survey showed that 73 percent of all Japanese—whether rich or poor, farmers or urbanites—enjoy miso soup at least once a day. Indeed, for most Japanese, the words miso and miso soup are practically synonymous.

Generally called *miso shiru* or *o-miotsuké,* but also known in better restaurants as *miso-jitaté,* miso soup became popular in Japan about 700 years ago, when samurai warriors who had seized power from the traditional nobility developed a national cuisine reflecting the simplicity and frugality of their new life-style. Grains were given the leading role at each meal, supported by miso soup, cooked vegetables, tofu, and occasionally fish and shellfish. Today, miso soup is an indispensable element in the traditional Japanese breakfast, where it is accompanied by a large bowl of rice or rice porridge, usually garnished with salt-pickled vegetables, *umeboshi* salt plums, and/or *nori.*

To prepare miso soup, fresh (or lightly sautéed) vegetables are simmered until just tender in dashi, the all-purpose soup stock; ingredients such as regular or deep-fried tofu and *wakame* are added as the vegetables near completion. Finally the miso is added (about 1 tablespoon per serving), and the soup reheated until the first bubble appears. Poured into lacquerware bowls, sprinkled lightly with a seasoning or garnish and covered with a lid, it is generally served steaming hot, while its aroma and flavor are at their peak. Plucking them out of the bowl with chopsticks (never a spoon), each person first enjoys the tofu and vegetables, then downs the warming broth.

One of the few peoples in the world to start off the day with soup, the Japanese point to the fact that miso soup is quick and easy to prepare; it is often ready to serve within 5 minutes after the cook starts work—a key factor during the busy morning meal. Almost any ingredient goes well in it and, being cooked only briefly, they all retain their health-giving vitamins, crispness, and delicate flavor. For the Japanese, the hearty aroma of this filling soup is as appetizing as that of coffee for many Westerners, while its mellow, subtly pungent flavor and low-calorie warmth help to start the day off right. By alkalizing the blood, miso soup is said to wake up the nervous system and offer abundant nourishment, stamina, and energy that last all morning. An aid to digestion and assimilation, it is also said to relieve acid indigestion and settle an upset stomach. Sake-lovers are unanimous in their assertion that miso soup does wonders for a hangover.

True enough, a typical serving is remarkably rich in essential nutrients. The tofu and miso together provide about 9 to 12 grams of protein (roughly one-sixth of the adult daily requirement), plus important polyunsaturated oils. The *wakame* and tofu supply abundant calcium and other minerals; the fresh vegetables offer vitamins; and the miso supplies salt.

In most rural farmhouses, a large kettle of miso soup is prepared each morning and reheated before lunch and dinner. This practice simplifies the work of the housewife in preparing meals, and many claim that as the flavors intermingle and marry, the soup becomes even more delicious. On winter evenings, the

family will often have dinner around the open-hearth,
sunken fireplace at the center of the main room, with
the pot of simmering soup, suspended above the live
coals from an overhead hook, serving as the center of
conviviality and warmth. Miso soup is one of the most
commonly served foods in Japan's many "long-life"
villages, where it is considered essential to good health
and longevity; in some areas, the villagers are reported
to consume an average of 4 to 6 cups daily. In most of
Japan's Zen temples, miso soup is served with each
meal, often using miso prepared by the monks; at
breakfast and lunch it accompanies rice or rice porridge and cooked or salt-pickled vegetables, while at
dinner it is mixed with leftovers to make a richly flavored gruel.

One of Japan's truly seasonal preparations, miso
soup is served throughout the year. By using fresh
vegetables, sprouts, sprigs and even flowers, the sensitive cook is able to reflect in a dark lacquerware soup-
bowl the great rhythms and cycles of the natural
world. And by choosing from and combining the multitude of different types of fine miso, giving each combination the perfect accent with the proper choice of
seasonings and garnishes, it is quite easy to prepare a
different type of miso soup every day of the year. In
fact, a number of Japanese cookbooks contain easy-to-
follow charts suggesting ingredients for breakfast and
dinner each day of the week throughout the four seasons (see p. 236), and cookbooks devoted exclusively
to the preparation of miso soups group recipes as
spring, summer, fall, and winter preparations. In Japan's most popular book on miso cookery, 76 of the
131 pages describe the preparation of miso soups. Several of Japan's largest miso makers have gone so far
as to provide a free service whereby any cook can dial
a widely advertised phone number and listen to a re-
cording of "the miso soup of the day," featuring seasonal ingredients and the miso with which they best
harmonize.

Likened to a haiku in a lacquerware bowl, miso
soup is surrounded by a veritable mystique. It has
been noted that in the writings of almost every great

Japanese author and poet, there can be found a section of reminiscences about its ineffable aroma filling the air on unforgettable childhood mornings. Mr. Wataru Kawamura, Japan's best known writer on the subject, whose works include *An Encyclopedia of Miso Soups* and *Miso Soups Throughout the Provinces,* feels that it epitomizes Japanese character and culture. Describing himself as "a scholar not of miso, but of miso soup," Mr. Kawamura points out that even the thought of the piping hot broth has the power to touch Japanese heartstrings. The contemporary wanderer and poet Nanao Sasaki has written: "Everything starts from miso soup in good morning. Miso soup is made of shiny spider web . . ." The Japanese National Miso Association now uses as the motto for its letterhead: "A Happy Family is One that Starts the Day with Miso Soup." And many writers—both Japanese and foreign—have commented on the similarity between its essence and that of Zen: a certain simple yet deeply satisfying flavor that can be enjoyed day after day. Of course, miso soup is an integral part of the life of monks in their temples and tea masters in their hermitages, who delight in the flavor of a soup prepared with homemade miso and seasonal delicacies gathered wild from nearby mountains.

Japan's great master of Tea Ceremony Cuisine, Mr. Kaichi Tsuji, writes eloquently about miso soup: "Its taste must be subtle, complex, and compact—all within what is appropriate to the tea ceremony. A fine *misoshiru* is like the trailing reverberations of a great temple bell. Its goodness lies in its aftertaste, which invites the guest to a second bowl . . . Its flavor is indeed the flavor of Japan."

A well-known Japanese proverb says that only when a young woman has mastered the art of making fine miso soup is she ready to become a bride. For although it is remarkably simple to follow the basic recipe and come up with a tasty result, to learn to prepare the very finest miso soup is deceptively difficult and requires years of practice. Yet many find that the joy lies in the learning, and claim that each day's effort allows the cook to express culinary mastery and love while serving as a nutritional key-stone for a healthy family.

Numerous Japanese restaurants specialize in the preparation of miso soup (p. 572), and virtually every restaurant offers at least several varieties as standard fare. In recent years, modern technology has yielded a number of new forms, some sold through coffee-like vending machines and others in sealed foil packages as "instant miso soup," now widely available even in the West. The latter contain either regular or dehydrated miso (p. 82), plus dehydrated dashi, *wakame,* and tofu with freeze-dried vegetables. These lightweight, inexpensive products are ready to serve as soon as they have been mixed with hot water and are well suited for back packing, camping, and picnicking.

Although miso is used to season soups in China and Korea, too, the resulting dishes are completely different from Japanese miso soup and play a much less important role in the national cuisine. The Chinese variety, *chiang t'sang,* is usually made with a chicken broth and contains fish and vegetables sautéed in sesame oil. The fiery Korean *daen jang chigé* contains diced tofu, leeks, chunks of beef, and plenty of red pepper.

Since the 1960s, miso soup has come to be widely enjoyed in the West, particularly among those interested in natural foods. New variations on the traditional Japanese motif are beginning to appear using Western ingredients matched to Western tastes: some like to substitute cottage cheese for tofu or drop in an egg, add their favorite herbs, or serve the soup chilled on hot summer afternoons. Winning growing acceptance among doctors and nutritionists alike, miso soup is rapidly finding a new home in America.

BASIC INGREDIENTS

Every miso soup is composed of four principal elements: dashi, miso, vegetables or other solids, and garnishes or seasonings.

Dashi: The Japanese consider a richly-flavored,

fragrant dashi to be the indispensable foundation of a fine miso soup. Most dashi is prepared with *kombu* (dried kelp) together with either freshly shaved bonito flakes or tiny dried sardines *(niboshi)*. In Zen Temple Cookery, the dashi is made with either *kombu* or a combination of *kombu* and *shiitaké* mushrooms (p. 114). In the West, vegetable or vegetable bouillon stocks are also used. Surprisingly delicious flavors result from the combination of 1 part stock with 1 part herb or peppermint teas or (home-extracted) vegetable juices (carrot, tomato, cabbage, etc.).

Miso: All varieties of regular miso are used in miso soups. Red, barley, and Hatcho miso are by far the most popular. Broiled miso is sometimes used to add savory aroma to chilled soups; sweet white and sweet red varieties are used only on special occasions. (Finger Lickin' and Sweet Simmered Miso are never used.) In most home cookery only one type of miso is used at a time, although restaurant chefs and cookbooks often call for the simultaneous use of two or occasionally even three types. Just as in the blending of fine coffees, the combination of fundamentally different misos (red and white, sweet and salty, rice and barley, etc.) produces delightful harmonies of flavor and aroma. The five most popular mixtures are:

4 parts red or light-yellow and 1 part Hatcho
3 parts red and 2 parts sweet white
1 part red and 9 parts sweet white
1 part light-yellow and 1 part sweet barley
1 part red and 1 part barley

For each cup of dashi or stock, use about 2 to 3 teaspoons red, barley, or Hatcho miso; 2 tablespoons mellow miso; or 2 to 3 tablespoons sweet white or sweet red miso.

Vegetables, etc.: The English language has no good equivalent for the Japanese term *mi*—literally "fruits"—which refers to all of the basic solids in a soup. One of Japan's largest food and housekeeping magazines recently conducted a nationwide survey to find out which "fruits" were used most frequently in daily miso soups. The top 25 favorites, with relative popularity, are listed below. Note the total absence of meat, fish, or poultry, and the low position of two types of shellfish:

Daikon	19.6	Onion	3.7
Leek	19.1	Burdock root	3.4
Agé	16.2	Eggplant	3.2
Wakame	15.7	Mushrooms	3.1
Tofu	13.8	Turnip (kabu)	2.9
Chinese		Lotus root	2.5
Cabbage	8.5	Bean sprouts	2.4
Potato	7.7	Wild vegetables	2.3
Spinach	5.8	Corbicula (shellfish)	2.0
Cabbage	4.3	Sweet potato	1.6
Wheat gluten	4.2	Spring chrysanthemum	1.1
Carrot	3.9	Short-necked clams	0.8

Other popular ingredients are listed in the chart on page 236. Unlisted ingredients which are also used include:

Yuba (fresh or dried)
Tempura dumplings and skimmings
Snow peas
Noodles (all types)
Natto and *Hamanatto*
Cottage cheese
Ginkgo nuts

Most soups contain a combination of two or three of these "fruits", with one given the leading role and others used to complement and support it. All are sliced or diced fine so that they will cook quickly. An average serving contains about 1 to 1½ ounces (30 to 40 grams) of solids, and a thick soup 2½ times this much. In choosing ingredients, a skilled cook considers:

What locally grown vegetables are fresh and in season?
Which of these will harmonize best with the color and flavor of the miso to be used?
How much should be used together with a given amount of a particular miso?

Will they sink or float on the surface to complement
the garnish?

Should they be cut into tree-leaf (maple, ginkgo)
or blossom (cherry, plum) shapes to express the
sense of the season; or do they lend themselves to
cutting into loops, interlocking rings, pine-needle,
or fan shapes?

Does the color and shape of the vegetable suit the
color and design of the bowl to be used?

Seasonings and Garnishes: The proper seasoning
or garnish provides the crowning touch. True to their
name, many Japanese seasonings are strictly seasonal;
they are used fresh and prized for their transiency.
Many of the favorites are shown in figure 12.

Although Western herbs and spices are not widely
used in Japan, we have found them remarkably well
suited for use in miso soups. For best fragrance, use
them freshly picked, crushed, or ground. Parmesan
and grated cheeses as well as sesame- and nut butters
also add delicious flavor and richness. Occasionally
miso soups are spiked with a little sake or white wine,
and thickened with *kuzu* (kudzu powder) or arrowroot.

PRINCIPLES OF PREPARATION
AND SERVING

*Miso is always mixed with hot broth and some-
times puréed or ground before being added to a soup.
In the following recipes, for the sake of brevity, we
will simply call for the miso to be creamed. However,
any of the following four techniques may be used:

1. *Creaming:* Place miso in a small cup. Remove
about ½ cup hot dashi or stock from the saucepan
and, adding a little at a time, stir into the miso; then
add the cream back into the soup. Dip the cup into
the soup to retrieve all the miso. This quick-and-easy
technique allows the texture of the miso to appear in
the soup.

2. *Puréeing:* Place miso in a small sieve or woven bamboo miso strainer (below). Partially immerse sieve in broth and press miso through sieve with the

Miso-koshi

back of a (wooden) spoon. If desired, add to the soup any particles of koji or soybeans remaining in the sieve. This technique yields a satin-smooth soup even when made from chunky miso.

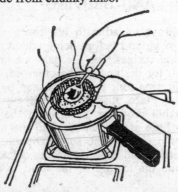

3. *Grinding:* Combine miso and a small amount of hot broth in a *suribachi* (mortar) and grind to a smooth paste with a wooden pestle. Pour through a sieve (or directly) into the hot broth. Using a rubber spatula or wooden spoon, retrieve any miso remaining in *suribachi,* then rinse out *suribachi* with a little of the hot soup. This technique is used with (homemade) miso containing firm chunks of koji or soybeans.

4. *Mincing:* Place very firm miso in a small mound on a cutting board and mince with a sharp knife. This technique, used exclusively with Hatcho miso, is usually followed by puréeing or creaming.

*Overcooking spoils the miso's prized aroma while also destroying microorganisms and enzymes which aid digestion. Remove soup from heat just before it comes to a boil and, for best flavor, serve immediately.

*For breakfast miso soup or when the ingredients are primarily vegetables, the Japanese use a relatively large amount of red or barley miso to create a rich, hearty broth. At dinnertime or when the ingredients are primarily tofu or seafoods, less miso is generally used to yield a more delicately flavored broth which allows the character of the individual ingredients to shine forth. Better restaurants generally serve a dinner miso soup prepared with a somewhat mild broth containing relatively few solid ingredients; the dinnertime miso soup served in private homes, however, can often resemble a hearty Western-style stew, served at the table in a casserole, earthenware *nabé,* or cast iron pot.

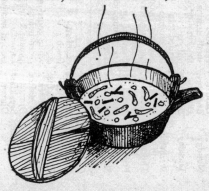

Fig. 12. Miso Soups Throughout the Four Seasons   (FROM: *Miso Cookery Throughout the Twelve Months*)

Day	Meal	Main Ingredient	Supporting Ingredient	Miso	Seasoning
			Spring		
Sunday	Breakfast	fried tofu	chrysanthemum leaves	sweet white miso	yuzu or lemon rind
	Dinner	egg tofu	*junsai*	red miso	sansho pepper
Monday	Breakfast	small turnips	chrysanthemum leaves	sweet white miso	mustard
	Dinner	mackerel or sardines	leek or wild onion	red miso	sansho pepper
Tuesday	Breakfast	onions	wakame	red miso	mustard
	Dinner	grilled tofu	burdock & fried tofu	red miso	gingerroot juice
Wednesday	Breakfast	fish sausage	trefoil	sweet white miso	horsetails
	Dinner	bamboo shoots	wakame	sweet white miso	kinomé
Thursday	Breakfast	egg & dry sardines	trefoil	red miso	yuzu or lemon rind
	Dinner	kampyo	fried tofu	red miso	butterbur sprouts
Friday	Breakfast	Osmund fern	deep-fried tofu	light-yellow miso	sansho pepper
	Dinner	young burdock	pork	light-yellow miso	gingerroot juice
Saturday	Breakfast	clams	udo or nanohana	red & white miso	sansho pepper
	Dinner	eggs	leeks	sweet white miso	curry powder
			Summer		
Sunday	Breakfast	eggplant	wakame	red miso	cucumber or myoga
	Dinner	loach	burdock root	red & white miso	sansho pepper
Monday	Breakfast	egg	fresh greens	white & yellow miso	gingerroot juice
	Dinner	white gourd-melon	chicken	red & yellow miso	sansho pepper
Tuesday	Breakfast	green beans	fried tofu	white & yellow miso	ground sesame
	Dinner	tomato & milk	green pepper & onion	sweet white miso	minced parsley
Wednesday	Breakfast	kabocha	wakame	red miso	7-spice red pepper
	Dinner	ground sesame	cucumber	broiled miso	7-spice red pepper
Thursday	Breakfast	cabbage	tororo kombu	sweet white miso	7-spice red pepper
	Dinner	taro	fried tofu, shiitaké & carrot	light-yellow miso	7-spice red pepper
Friday	Breakfast	potato	daikon & wakame	red miso	daikon leaf tips
	Dinner	corbicula (shellfish)	leeks	light-yellow miso	beefsteak leaf
Saturday	Breakfast	cucumber	beansprouts	Hatcho miso	hot mustard
	Dinner	fresh shiitaké	rice-flour dumplings	sweet white miso	hot mustard

			Fall		
Day	Meal	Main Ingredient	Supporting Ingredient	Miso	Seasoning
Sunday	Breakfast	*hijiki*	thick fried tofu	red miso	7-spice red pepper
	Dinner	*matsutaké* mushrooms	*myoga* buds	red miso	*yuzu*
Monday	Breakfast	cabbage	fried tofu	light-yellow miso	pepper
	Dinner	pork	grilled eggplants	sweet white miso	*myoga* or beefsteak buds
Tuesday	Breakfast	tofu	*nameko* mushrooms	Hatcho miso	hot mustard
	Dinner	taro	chicken	white & red miso	*sansho* pepper
Wednesday	Breakfast	cucumber	tomao	sweet white miso	*wasabi*
	Dinner	*shimeji* mushrooms	tofu & chrysanthemum	white & red miso	*yuzu*
Thursday	Breakfast	sweet potato	fried tofu	light-yellow miso	pepper
	Dinner	grilled eggplant	roasted sesame	sweet white miso	trefoil
Friday	Breakfast	*kabocha*	thick fried tofu & *shiitaké*	red miso	beefsteak seeds
	Dinner	*nira* chives	burock root	white & red miso	*sansho* pepper
Saturday	Breakfast	fish	egg	white & red miso	gingerroot juice
	Dinner	mackerel	spinach & *wakame*	red miso	*sansho* pepper
			Winter		
Sunday	Breakfast	*mochi*	*daikon*, carrot & *shiitaké*	red miso	*yuzu*
	Dinner	*junsai*	glutinous yam	Hatcho miso	green *nori* flakes
Monday	Breakfast	tofu	milk & *asatsuki* chives	light-yellow miso	pepper
	Dinner	peanuts	*aona* greens	red miso	crumbled *wakame*
Tuesday	Breakfast	small turnips	fried tofu	white & red miso	hot mustard
	Dinner	dried-frozen tofu	chrysanthemum leaves	light-yellow miso	hot mustard
Wednesday	Breakfast	Chinese cabbage	fried tofu	light-yellow miso	pepper
	Dinner	taro & *konnyaku*	burdock, leek & sake lees	sweet white miso	7-spice red pepper
Thursday	Breakfast	*daikon*	leeks	red miso	butter or red pepper
	Dinner	pork	*konnyaku*	red miso	*sansho* pepper
Friday	Breakfast	tofu	bean sprouts	red miso	slivered leeks
	Dinner	tofu	salmon roe	sweet white miso	Mandarin orange peel
Saturday	Breakfast	oyster & tofu	leeks	red miso	*sansho* pepper
	Dinner	dried slivered *daikon* & *shiitaké*	chrysanthemum leaves	red miso	*sansho* pepper

*During the warm half of the year (April to September), red or barley miso is generally used and the total amount of solid ingredients is kept relatively small; in midsummer, chilled miso soup is a favorite at lunch or dinner. During the cold seasons, the amount of solid ingredients increases and thick, sweet miso soups are served more frequently: in midwinter, a thick-as-a-stew miso soup may serve as the main course. During March-April and September-August, the months preceding and following the equinoxes, mixtures of salty and sweet miso are enjoyed.

*Miso soup is generally served at the end of formal Japanese meals.

JAPANESE-STYLE MISO SOUPS

Deep-fried Tofu & Wakame Miso Soup

SERVES 2 OR 3

This is one of Japan's favorite and most traditional miso soups. The *wakame* supplies an abundance of calcium and other minerals, while the deep-fried tofu and miso provide protein and unsaturated oils. Requiring less than 3 minutes to prepare, this soup is particularly popular at breakfast.

1¾ cups dashi (p. 112) or stock
¼ to ⅓ cup fresh or reconstituted *wakame* (p. 105), cut into 1-inch lengths
1 to 2 ounces deep-fried tofu, cut crosswise into thin strips
2 tablespoons red, barley, or Hatcho miso
1 tablespoon thinly sliced leeks and/or a dash of 7-spice red pepper

Bring dashi to a boil in a saucepan. Add *wakame* and deep-fried tofu, and simmer for 1 minute. Add miso creamed in a little of the hot broth and return just to the boil. Serve immediately, garnished with the leeks.

White Miso Soup with Tofu, Nori & Spinach

SERVES 2

This recipe is a specialty of Fugetsu, a Japanese natural-food restaurant in Berkeley. The key is the combination of sweet white miso with a little salt. The broth is kept warm in a double boiler and simply poured over the other ingredients in a bowl for each new serving.

1½ cups Number 1 Dashi (p. 112)
¼ cup sweet white miso
¼ teaspoon salt
1½ to 2 ounces tofu, cut into ⅜-inch cubes
3 to 4 tablespoons steamed or parboiled spinach, well drained
2 tablespoons thinly sliced green onions
2 pieces of *nori,* each 1½ inches square

Bring the dashi to a boil in a saucepan. Add the creamed miso and salt and return just to the boil. Divide the tofu, spinach, and green onions among individual warmed bowls and pour on the hot broth. Float a square of *nori* in the soup and serve immediately.

Nori & Deep-fried Tofu Miso Soup

SERVES 2

1¼ cups dashi (p. 112)
1½ ounces deep-fried tofu, cut into ⅜-inch cubes
¼ cup thinly sliced rounds of leek
1½ tablespoons red, barley, or Hatcho miso
½ sheet of *nori,* torn into small pieces; or 2 tablespoons rinsed and diced fresh *nori*

Bring dashi to a boil in a small saucepan. Add tofu, leeks, and miso creamed in a little of the hot broth; return to the boil. Stir in *nori,* return just to the boil, and serve.

Kabocha

Refreshing Pumpkin Miso Soup

SERVES 2

1¼ cups (*kabocha*) pumpkin or squash (1-inch
       chunks)
2 cups dashi (p. 112), stock, or water
2 tablespoons akadashi or red miso
1 green beefsteak leaf, thinly sliced

Combine pumpkin and dashi in a small saucepan and
bring to a boil. Cover and simmer for about 15 minutes, or until pumpkin is tender. Stir in miso creamed
in a little of the hot broth and return just to the boil.
Serve garnished with the beefsteak leaf.

Miso Soup with Sake Lees (*Sakenokasu-jiru*)

SERVES 2

Available in the West at most Japanese food markets, sake lees may be added to any miso soup to
impart a rich flavor, heady aroma, and thick texture:
use 2 to 3 parts (by volume) lees to 3 parts miso, or
about 1 tablespoon per serving.

1½ cups dashi (p. 112), stock, or water
2 Chinese cabbage leaves, thinly sliced
⅔ cup diced sweet potatoes, yams, or Irish potatoes
1 to 2 ounces deep-fried tofu (optional)
2 tablespoons red, barley, or Hatcho miso
1½ to 2 tablespoons sake lees

Bring dashi to a boil in a small saucepan. Add Chinese
cabbage, sweet potatoes and, if used, the tofu. Return to the boil and simmer for 5 minutes. Combine
the miso and sake lees, cream with a little of the hot

broth, and stir into the soup. Return just to the boil. Serve piping hot.

For a softer texture and lower alcohol content, simmer the lees with the vegetables before adding the miso.

Miso Soup with Potato, Wakame & Tofu

SERVES 4

4 cups water or stock
¼ cup bonito flakes
1 small potato, cut into ½-inch cubes
¾ cup fresh or reconstituted *wakame* (p. 105), cut into
    1½-inch lengths
2 ounces deep-fried tofu, thinly sliced (optional)
5 tablespoons red, barley, or Hatcho miso
¼ cup thinly-sliced leeks

Bring water to a boil in a small saucepan. Add bonito flakes, turn off heat and allow to stand for 3 to 4 minutes. (Strain if flakes are coarse.) Return broth to a boil, add potatoes and cook for 8 to 10 minutes, or until potatoes are tender. Add *wakame,* tofu, and miso creamed in a little of the hot broth. Return just to the boil and remove from heat. Top with a sprinkling of the leeks and serve hot or cold.

Gingerroot-Onion Miso Soup

SERVES 3

2 teaspoons oil or butter
½ clove of garlic, crushed or minced
1 onion, thinly sliced
2 cups water or stock
2 tablespoons sweet white or 4 teaspoons mellow
    white miso
1 tablespoon red, barley, or Hatcho miso
½ teaspoon grated gingerroot

Heat a small pot or saucepan and coat with the oil. Add garlic and sauté for 30 seconds, then add onion and sauté for 5 minutes more. Add water and bring to a boil; cover and simmer for 3 minutes. Add both varieties of miso dissolved in a little of the hot broth, stir in gingerroot, and return just to the boil. Serve piping hot.

Picnic Miso Soup

SERVES 3

3 tablespoons red, barley, or Hatcho miso
2 tablespoons bonito flakes or grated cheese
Dash of pepper (7-spice, red, or black)
1 to 2 ounces deep-fried tofu, cut crosswise into
      thin strips
12 inches dry *wakame,* cut into 1-inch lengths; or
      3 cakes of dried wheat gluten
2 to 3 tablespoons thinly sliced leeks; or minced
      chives or parsley
2 cups hot or boiling water

Combine miso, bonito flakes, and pepper, mixing well, then shape into 3 balls. Skewer and broil each ball over a burner (as for Broiled Miso, p. 156) until well browned and fragrant. Place balls and the next three ingredients into a picnic container. Take the hot water in a thermos or heat water at the picnic site. To serve, divide all solid ingredients among 3 bowls, pour in the hot water, and mix until miso dissolves. Cover and allow to stand for several minutes before serving.

Curried White Miso Soup with Onion and Egg

SERVES 2

1¼ cups dashi (p. 112) or stock
1 small onion, sliced very thin
¼ cup sweet white or 2½ tablespoons mellow white
      miso
½ teaspoon curry powder
1 egg, lightly beaten

Combine dashi and onion in a small saucepan, bring to a boil, and simmer, covered, for 3 minutes. Add miso and curry powder creamed in a little of the hot broth; return to the boil. Stir in egg a little at a time. Remove from heat and serve immediately.

Natto & Chinese Cabbage Miso Soup

SERVES 2 OR 3

1¼ cups dashi (p. 112), stock, or water
2 (Chinese) cabbage leaves, cut lengthwise into
    halves, then crosswise into 1½-inch-wide strips
1 tablespoon red, barley, or Hatcho miso
2 tablespoons sweet white or 4 teaspoons mellow
    white miso
½ cup *natto*
¼ cup thin rounds of leek or scallion
Dash of 7-spice red pepper

Bring dashi to a boil in a saucepan. Add Chinese
cabbage, cover, and simmer for 2 or 3 minutes. Add
miso creamed in a little of the hot broth. Add *natto*
and return just to the boil. Sprinkle on leeks and
remove from heat. Serve seasoned with a sprinkling of
the red pepper.

Daikon & Onion Miso Soup

SERVES 3 TO 4

2 to 3 teaspoons oil
1 onion, thinly sliced
1 cup thin half-moons of *daikon* (p. 347)
2 cups water, stock, or dashi (p. 112)
4 tablespoons red, barley, or Hatcho miso
2 tablespoons thinly sliced leek or scallion greens
    (optional)

Heat a skillet or casserole and coat with the oil. Add
onion and sauté for 3 minutes. Add *daikon* and water, and bring to a boil. Reduce heat to low and
simmer, covered, for 15 minutes. Add miso creamed
in a little of the hot broth and return to the boil.
Serve garnished, if desired, with a sprinkling of leek
slices.

Akadashi Miso Soup with Tofu and Mushrooms

SERVES 2 OR 3

Akadashi or "red dashi" was originally the name of a miso soup containing a mixture of soybean (usually Hatcho) miso and one or two rice misos. It originated in central Japan and was prepared in either of two ways: 1) The firm soybean miso was minced on a bread board, mixed with the softer rice miso(s) and tied in a small piece of coarsely woven cloth to form a sack, which was then immersed in hot dashi until the miso flavor and color had permeated the broth; 2) The red and minced soybean misos were combined with bonito flakes in a *suribachi* and ground until smooth; hot water was stirred in and the mixture allowed to stand until strained for use as the broth. After World War II, "akadashi" came to refer to a new variety of miso (p. 81). Yet the colorful and tasty soup is still a favorite in many of Japan's finest restaurants, where it may be prepared with either the modern or traditional misos. Since the basic ingredients are added to the broth *after* the miso, only those requiring very little cooking are used.

1¼ cups dashi (p. 112) or stock
2 teaspoons Hatcho miso
1 tablespoon red miso
1 teaspoon sweet white miso (optional)
6 ounces tofu, cut into ⅜-inch cubes
⅓ cup *nameko* mushrooms and their liquid
3 sprigs of trefoil, cut into 1-inch lengths

Bring dashi to a boil in a small saucepan. Add misos creamed in a little of the dashi and return to the boil. Add tofu and mushrooms, and return again to the boil. Serve garnished with trefoil.

If *nameko* mushrooms are not available, sauté 6 thinly sliced fresh mushrooms in butter until tender and add to dashi together with tofu. If desired, substitute dry wheat gluten cakes for the tofu; season with *sansho* pepper.

Hiyashi-jiru *(Broiled Miso in Chilled Soup)*

SERVES 2 OR 3

1½ cups dashi (p. 112) or stock, cooled
1½ to 2 tablespoons Savory Broiled Miso (p. 156; use red miso)
½ cup thinly sliced cucumber
½ cup diced tomato
2 green beefsteak or mint leaves, minced (optional)

Cream the miso in a little of the dashi, then add remaining dashi, stirring until smooth; cover and refrigerate until chilled. Refrigerate vegetables in separate containers. Divide vegetables among individual bowls and pour on the chilled broth. Serve immediately.

Tororo-jiru with Sweet White Miso

SERVES 5 TO 6

This unusual Japanese delicacy bears some resemblance to a chilled Western-style consommé. The ingredients are traditionally mixed in a *suribachi* rather than a blender.

2½ cups dashi (p. 112) or stock, cooled to room temperature
7½ tablespoons sweet white or 5 tablespoons mellow white miso
10½ ounces glutinous yam, peeled and grated
1 egg
1 sheet of *nori,* toasted (p. 108) and crumbled (optional)

Combine the first four ingredients in a blender and purée for about 1 minute. Serve as is or chilled, topped with a sprinkling of *nori.*

Onion-Miso Soup with Tofu and Eggs

SERVES 3

2 cups dashi (p. 112), stock, or water
1 onion, thinly sliced
2½ to 3 tablespoons red, barley, or Hatcho miso
4 to 6 ounces regular or deep-fried tofu, cut into ⅜-inch cubes
2 or 3 eggs, lightly beaten if desired (optional)
Dash of black or 7-spice red pepper (optional)

Combine dashi and onion in a small saucepan, bring
to a boil, and simmer, covered, for 4 to 5 minutes.
Add the miso creamed in a little of the hot broth, then
the tofu and eggs. (For an egg-flower soup, swirl broth
while adding lightly beaten eggs.) Return just to a
boil over high heat, season with pepper, and serve
immediately. Or allow to cool to room temperature
and serve topped with 1 tablespoon minced parsley.

Miso Soup with Buckwheat Noodles and Eggs

SERVES 2

2 teaspoons (sesame) oil
1 small onion, thinly sliced
1½ cups water, stock, or dashi (p. 112)
2 ounces *(soba)* buckwheat noodles, broken into
    4-inch lengths and cooked (p. 201)
3 tablespoons red, barley, or Hatcho miso
2 eggs
1 tablespoon minced parsley (optional)

Heat a skillet and coat with the oil. Add onion and
sauté for 5 minutes, then add water and bring to a
boil. Add cooked noodles and return to the boil. Stir
in miso creamed in a little of the hot broth. Now increase heat to medium-high and carefully break in the
eggs, keeping the yolks whole. Cook for 1 minute
more, or until whites are just firm. Serve immediately,
garnished with parsley.

Miso Ozoni

SERVES 3

Ozoni is a soup containing *mochi* (pounded rice
cakes) served daily in Japan during the week of fes-
tivities that begins on New Year's Day. Neither the
usual cooked rice nor miso soup are served throughout
this period; Ozoni takes their place and is eaten with
special, thick chopsticks *(zoni-bashi)* which help to
pluck out the soft mochi while also serving as a symbol of the holiday season. In the Kyoto area, freshly
prepared *mochi* dumplings are served in a rich soup
made with sweet white miso and generally containing

taro, *daikon,* carrot, grilled tofu, and a garnish of grated bonito flakes. The *mochi* partially melts in the hot soup, imparting to it a thick, almost creamy consistency. In country farmhouses, the *mochi* is often broiled and—to prevent its dissolution—added at the last minute to soups prepared with red miso. Fresh or broiled *mochi* may be added to many of the miso soups given in this section. Or try this country-style preparation:

2 cups dashi (p. 112) or stock
1 leek, cut diagonally into ½-inch-thick ovals,
    separated into greens and whites
7 ounces deep-fried tofu, thinly sliced
3 tablespoons red, barley, or Hatcho miso
3 cakes of *mochi* (each 2 by 1½ by ½ inches),
    broiled until speckled then pierced in several
    places with a chopstick or fork

Combine dashi, leek greens, and deep-fried tofu in a saucepan and bring to a boil. Add leek whites and stir in miso creamed in a little of the hot broth; return just to the boil. Pour into individual bowls, add *mochi,* and serve immediately. ◄

Red & White Miso Soup with Swirled Eggs and Chives

SERVES 2

1¼ cups dashi (p. 112) or stock
1 teaspoon butter or oil
⅔ cup chopped chives or *nira*
1 tablespoon red, barley, or Hatcho miso
1½ tablespoons sweet white or 1 tablespoon mellow
    white miso
1 egg, lightly beaten
¼ to ½ teaspoon grated gingerroot or ½ teaspoon
    powdered ginger

Heat dashi in a small saucepan over medium heat. Meanwhile heat a skillet and coat with the butter. Add chives and sauté for 20 to 30 seconds. Add to dashi and bring to a boil. Add miso creamed in a little of the hot broth and return to the boil. Stir in eggs a little at a time, then remove from heat. Serve immediately, topped with a dab of gingerroot.

For a richer flavor and thicker consistency, combine with the eggs before stirring into the soup: 1½ teaspoons sake or white wine and 1 teaspoon *kuzu* (kudzu powder) or cornstarch dissolved in 1 tablespoon water.

Mushroom Miso Soup

SERVES 2

1½ tablespoons butter
6 mushrooms, thinly sliced
1 small onion, thinly sliced
2 cups dashi (p. 112), stock, or water
3 tablespoons akadashi or 2½ tablespoons red miso
2 tablespoons minced parsley or thinly sliced leeks

Melt the butter in a heavy skillet. Add mushrooms and onion, and sauté until onions are just transparent. Add dashi and bring to a boil. Add miso creamed in a little of the hot broth and return just to the boil. Serve hot garnished with parsley.

Mushroom & Tofu Miso Soup

SERVES 6

The following is a description of the method used to prepare the daily miso soup in a large, well-known Japanese restaurant. Each ingredient has been reduced to about one-eighth its usual quantity. Notice the integrated preparation of both Number 1 and Number 2 Dashi along with a basic *shiitaké* dashi.

1½ cups (5 ounces) dried *shiitaké* mushrooms,
        soaked for 10 hours (overnight) in 2 cups water
½ cup (¾ ounce) round-herring flakes *(urume iwashi)*
½ cup (medium salty) light yellow miso
⅓ cup Hatcho miso
5½ cups water
60 (canned) *nameko* mushrooms
12 ounces silken (or regular) tofu, cut into ½-inch
        cubes
18 trefoil leaves (including stems)

Pour mushrooms into a colander set over a pot. Press mushrooms gently but firmly against bottom of colander to expel remaining liquid, then reserve mushrooms for use in other cooking.

Bring mushroom soaking water *(shiitaké dashi)* to a boil over high heat. Skim off any foam that may develop, then add herring flakes and return to the boil. Reduce heat to low, simmer for 5 minutes, and turn off heat.

Meanwhile, combine light-yellow and Hatcho miso with ¾ cup warm water in a mixing bowl. Mix well until miso is dissolved. Pour herring-*shiitaké* dashi through a fine-mesh strainer set over the mixing bowl and press herring flakes in strainer to expel all liquid.

Now combine herring flakes with 2 cups water in a saucepan to make a Number 2 Dashi. Bring this dashi to a boil and reduce heat to low; cover pan and simmer for 5 minutes.

While Number 2 Dashi is simmering, pour miso-dashi mixture through a fine-mesh strainer set over the pot. Remove particles of miso grain left in strainer and combine with 2 cups warm water. Mix well, then pour back through strainer into pot, reserving grain particles for use in other cooking.

Pour Number 2 Dashi through strainer into pot, discarding herring flakes. Now bring dashi in pot just to a boil, add *nameko* mushrooms and tofu, and remove from heat. Serve piping hot, garnished with trefoil leaves.

Butter & Lemon Soup with Sweet Miso

SERVES 3 OR 4

2½ tablespoons butter or Better Butter (p. 119)
1 onion, minced
½ cup corn or green peas, parboiled
2 cups hot water or stock
2 teaspoons lemon juice
6 tablespoons sweet white or ¼ cup mellow white miso
Dash of pepper (optional)

Melt the butter in a heavy skillet. Add onion and corn, and sauté for 4 to 5 minutes. Stir in the hot water and bring to a boil. Add lemon juice and miso, creamed in a little of the hot broth, and return just to the boil. Serve hot, seasoned with pepper.

Sweet White Miso Potage

SERVES 2 OR 3

2 tablespoons butter or Better Butter (p. 119)
½ cup minced onion
1½ tablespoons whole-wheat flour
2 cups dashi (p. 112), stock, or water
6 tablespoons sweet white or ¼ cup mellow white
     miso
Dash of pepper (optional)
1 tablespoon minced parsley

Melt butter in a skillet. Add onion and sauté for 4 to 5 minutes. Reduce heat to low, add flour and sauté for 1 minute more. Add dashi a little at a time, stirring constantly until smooth. Mix in miso dissolved in a little of the hot broth, season with pepper, and return just to the boil. Serve topped with a sprinkling of parsley.

JAPANESE-STYLE MISO STEWS

In addition to its daily use in soups, miso is also employed as the essential seasoning in a number of stew-like preparations, most of which are made with soybeans or tofu and have enough body and protein to serve as a main course. Kenchin-jiru, Tanuki-jiru, and Gôjiru are the three most famous representatives of these dinnertime specialties.

Kenchin-jiru

SERVES 5

1½ tablespoons sesame oil
18 ounces tofu, pressed (p. 109) and broken into small
    pieces
½ cup shaved burdock root
1 cup half-moons of *daikon*
5 *shiitaké* or cloud-ear mushrooms, thinly sliced
1 to 1¼ cups large irregular chunks of sweet potato,
    yam, or taro
½ cup carrot (cut into ginkgo leaves; p. 106)
½ cake of *konnyaku,* broken into small pieces and
    lightly salted
2¼ cups dashi (p. 112), stock, or water
5 tablespoons red, barley, or Hatcho miso
¼ teaspoon salt
2 teaspoons sake or *mirin*
Garnishes: 7-spice red pepper, slivered leeks,
    crumbled *nori,* and/or grated lemon or *yuzu*
    rind

Heat the oil in a heavy-bottomed saucepan. Add consecutively: tofu, burdock root, *daikon,* mushrooms, sweet potato, carrot, and *konnyaku,* sautéing each over medium heat for about 1 minute. Reduce heat to low, and add broth, miso, salt, and sake. Cover pan and simmer for 30 to 40 minutes, or until *daikon* is transparent. For best flavor, allow to stand for 6 to 8 hours, then serve individual portions topped with a sprinkling of the garnishes.

VARIATION

*Tanuki-jiru *(Badger's Soup):* Omit all vegetables except the burdock root and carrot, and triple the amounts of both of these. Use barley miso.

Gôjiru

SERVES 4 TO 6

This thick miso soup prepared with *gô,* a purée of
well-soaked soybeans, is a wintertime favorite in Ja-

pan's snowy northeast provinces. It can be prepared using a wide range of vegetables, seasonings, and garnishes; experiment with whatever is available, in season, or simply appealing.

½ cup soybeans, rinsed and soaked for 8 to 10 hours in 1 quart water
4½ cups water, stock, or dashi (p. 112)
2 tablespoons oil
1 onion, thinly sliced; or 1 leek, cut into 2-inch lengths
½ carrot, cut into thin half moons
2 ounces deep-fried tofu, cut into thin strips
3 mushrooms, thinly sliced
2 inches *daikon,* cut into half moons; or ½ cup chopped celery
1 potato, sweet potato, yam, or taro, diced
5 to 6 tablespoons red, barley, or Hatcho miso

Rinse, then drain beans in a colander. Combine beans and ¾ cup water in a blender and purée at high speed for about 3 minutes, or until smooth.

Heat a heavy pot and coat with the oil. Add the next six ingredients and sauté for 5 to 10 minutes, or until potatoes are softened. Add soybean purée and remaining 3¾ cups water, bring to a boil, and simmer uncovered for 10 to 15 minutes, stirring occasionally. Add miso thinned in a few tablespoons of the hot broth and simmer for 1 minute more. Serve immediately or, for a richer, sweeter flavor, allow to cool for at least 6 hours.

VARIATIONS

*Any of the following garnishes or seasonings may be added to the soup with the miso or sprinkled on top of individual servings: 7-spice red pepper, green *nori* flakes, *sansho* pepper; minced trefoil, sake lees, slivered *yuzu* or lemon rind; pepper, crushed garlic, croutons, sage, or thyme.
*Experiment using other vegetables such as green beans, celery (including leaves), snow peas, *kombu,*

or shelled green soybeans. For extra richness, try adding 2 lightly beaten eggs or 2 thinly sliced, deep-fried potatoes together with the miso.

WESTERN-STYLE SOUPS AND STEWS

Miso can be used to combine the functions of a hearty bouillon or meat broth and a savory seasoning. Try substituting about 1 tablespoon of red, barley, or Hatcho for each ½ teaspoon salt in your favorite recipes. To keep the miso aroma, flavor, and nutrients at their peak of goodness, remember to add the creamed miso just before the end of cooking.

Thick French Onion Soup with Miso

MAKES 4 CUPS; SERVES 4

Our favorite Western-style soup with miso, this dish reaches its peak of flavor after lengthy cooking and when allowed to stand overnight for the flavors to marry. It can, however, be served before the marriage night, while piping hot, and is still guaranteed to delight the senses of even Monsieur Brillat-Savarin.

2 tablespoons oil
6 onions, thinly sliced
3 tablespoons red, barley, or Hatcho miso, dissolved
    in 2 cups warm water
1 tablespoon butter
2 ounces cheese, grated or minced

Heat a large casserole or heavy pot and coat with the oil. Add onions, cover, and simmer over very low heat for 3½ hours, stirring every 20 to 30 minutes. Mix in dissolved miso and butter, return just to the boil, and remove from heat. Allow to cool, then refrigerate overnight. Stir in the cheese, bring to a boil and simmer, stirring constantly, for about 1 minute, or until cheese melts. Serve hot or, for a richer, sweeter flavor, allow to cool to room temperature.

For variety, add 10 ounces diced deep-fried or regular tofu, 1 more tablespoon miso and, if desired, 2 lightly beaten eggs 15 minutes before adding miso.

Basic Miso Soup

SERVES 4 TO 6

Featuring the most widely used and inexpensive vegetables, this easy-to-make recipe is a favorite year round, day after day.

2 teaspoons oil
1 cup sliced onions
1 cup sliced carrots
2 cups chopped cabbage
4 cups water or stock
3½ tablespoons red, barley, or Hatcho miso
2 tablespoons minced parsley or scallions

Heat the oil in a wok or heavy pot. Add onion and carrots and sauté for 3 to 4 minutes. Add cabbage and sauté for 2 minutes more. Add water, cover, bring to a boil, and simmer for 15 minutes. Stir in miso creamed with a little of the broth, then remove from heat. Serve topped with a sprinkling of parsley. Delicious hot or cold. Chilled, puréed leftovers are especially tasty.

For variety, add 1 cup diced potatoes together with the carrots.

Velvet Zucchini Miso Soup

SERVES 4

A wonderful way to make use of the summer garden's overflowing zucchini crop and to cool and refresh the body on hot summer afternoons or evenings. Leftovers may be frozen indefinitely.

1 tablespoon oil
½ onion, sliced
1¼ cups chopped celery (2 stalks)
2½ cups diced zucchini
3 cups water or stock
3½ tablespoons red, barley, or Hatcho miso
2 tablespoons minced parsley

Heat the oil in a wok or heavy pot. Add onion and sauté for 2 to 3 minutes. Add celery and zucchini and sauté for another 2 to 3 minutes. Add the water or stock, cover, and simmer for 5 minutes, then remove from heat. Stir in miso creamed with a little of the cooking broth. Allow to cool briefly, then purée in a blender until smooth. Serve chilled, topped with a sprinkling of the parsley. In colder months, this recipe is also nice when served unpuréed and piping hot.

Thick Winter Squash Soup with Miso

SERVES 4 OR 5

1½ tablespoons oil
1 pound seeded *(kabocha)* pumpkin, squash, or
    zucchini, cut into ½-inch squares
2 onions, thinly sliced
2 cups water or stock
¼ teaspoon nutmeg or cinnamon
1 clove of garlic, minced
4 tablespoons red, barley, or Hatcho miso
3 tablespoons parsley, minced
½ cup croutons or dry bread pieces
2 tablespoons ground roasted sesame seeds (p. 107)
    (optional)

Heat the oil in a casserole or large pot. Add pumpkin and onion, and sauté for 3 minutes. Add water, cover and bring to a boil. Reduce heat to low and simmer for 25 minutes. Stir in nutmeg, garlic, and miso thinned in a little of the hot soup, and return just to the boil; remove from heat. For best flavor, allow to cool to room temperature, then serve cold or reheated, topped with parsley, croutons and, if used, the sesame seeds. It is also nice puréed in a blender.

For a slightly richer flavor, add 2 tablespoons butter and/or finely shaved bonito flakes together with the miso.

Tomato & Cottage Cheese Soup with Miso

SERVES 2

1 tablespoon Better Butter (p. 119) or butter
2 small tomatoes, peeled and thinly sliced
½ onion, thinly sliced
1 green pepper, seeded and diced
1 bay leaf (optional)
1 cup water or stock
1½ tablespoons red, barley, or Hatcho miso
6 tablespoons cottage cheese
Dash of pepper (optional)
Dash of oregano (optional)
3 to 4 tablespoons Parmesan cheese

Melt butter in a skillet. Add the next four ingredients
and sauté for 3 minutes, or until tomato dissolves. Add
water and bring to a boil. Stir in miso dissolved in a
little of the hot broth. Add cottage cheese, mixing
lightly, and return just to the boil. Remove from heat.
Remove bay leaf and serve hot, seasoned with the
pepper and oregano and topped with a sprinkling of
the cheese.

Thick Corn & Tomato Soup with Miso

SERVES 2

1 tablespoon oil
1½ small onions, thinly sliced
½ cup corn kernels
1 large tomato, diced
1 cup milk (soy or dairy)
2½ tablespoons red, barley, or Hatcho miso
Dash of pepper or a dab of mustard
¼ teaspoon oregano or marjoram
1 tablespoon minced parsley

Heat a pot and coat with the oil. Add onion and corn
and sauté for 4 minutes. Add tomato and sauté for 2
to 3 minutes more. Stir in the milk and miso, and season with pepper and oregano. Cook for about 1 minute, whisking or stirring constantly, but do not bring to
a boil. Remove from heat and allow to cool to body

temperature. Transfer to a blender and purée until smooth. Return to the pot and bring just to a boil. Serve hot or cold, topped with a sprinkling of parsley.

Creamy Corn & Cheese Soup with Miso

SERVES 3

1 tablespoon oil
1 onion, minced
1 cup grated carrot
1 cup fresh corn kernels
2 cups water or stock
1 cup grated cheese
2 tablespoons red, barley, or Hatcho miso
1½ tablespoons sweet white or 1 tablespoon mellow white miso
Dash of pepper (optional)
1 tablespoon minced parsley

Heat a heavy pot or deep skillet and coat with the oil. Add consecutively: onion, carrot and corn, sautéing each for 3 minutes. Stir in water, cover, and bring to a boil; simmer for 10 minutes. Add cheese and both varieties of miso creamed in a little of the hot broth. Return just to the boil, then season with pepper and top with parsley. Serve hot or cold.

For extra protein and flavor, add 5 to 10 ounces diced tofu (deep-fried or regular) together with the miso, increasing the miso by 1½ to 3 teaspoons.

Refreshing Yogurt Soup with Miso

SERVES 2

1 tablespoon Better Butter (p. 119) or butter
1 small onion, thinly sliced
1 green pepper, sliced into thin rings
1 cup dashi (p. 112) or stock
1½ tablespoons red, barley, or Hatcho miso
¼ cup yogurt
Dash of pepper (optional)

Melt the butter in a skillet. Add onion and green pepper, and sauté for 3 minutes. Add dashi and bring to a boil. Stir in miso creamed in a little of the hot broth, then mix in yogurt and return to the boil. Season with pepper and serve immediately.

Vichyssoise with Miso

SERVES 4

2 tablespoons Better Butter (p. 119) or butter
1 cup minced leek whites and/or (wild) onions
2 potatoes, thinly sliced
2 cups water or stock
2 tablespoons red, barley, or Hatcho miso
1½ cups cream or rich soymilk
Dash of pepper (optional)
Chopped chives or watercress (optional)

Melt the butter in a skillet. Add leeks or onions and sauté for 3 minutes. Add potatoes, water and miso (creamed in a few tablespoons of the water). Simmer, covered, for 15 minutes, then cool briefly. Purée in a blender until smooth. Add cream and pepper and purée again. Chill thoroughly. Serve topped with the chives.

Potato & Onion Soup with White Miso

SERVES 2

4 small potatoes (2½-inch diameter), peeled and cut
    into halves
1 small onion, thinly sliced
2 cups water or stock
1 bay leaf
5 tablespoons sweet white or 3 tablespoons mellow
    white miso
2 tablespoons Parmesan cheese
Dash of pepper (optional)
1 tablespoon parsley

Combine the first four ingredients in a saucepan and bring to a boil. Cover and simmer over low heat for 1 hour. Remove bay leaf, add miso creamed in a little of the hot broth, and stir in Parmesan. Season with pepper and return just to the boil. Serve chilled, topped with a sprinkling of parsley.

For variety, substitute sweet potatoes, *kabocha,* squash, or lentils for the potatoes.

Potato, Cottage Cheese & Chive Soup with Miso

SERVES 2

The cottage cheese in this dish works somewhat like tofu in traditional Japanese miso soups, but since some of the cottage cheese melts, it gives the soup a rich, slightly creamy consistency.

1 tablespoon Better Butter (p. 119) or butter
2 small potatoes, cut into thin rectangles (1¼ cups)
5 tablespoons chives, *nira,* or wild onions, chopped
1¼ cups water or stock
2 tablespoons red, barley, or Hatcho miso
½ cup cottage cheese

Melt the butter in a skillet. Add potatoes and ¼ cup chives, and sauté for 2 minutes. Add water and simmer for about 7 minutes. Stir in miso creamed in a little of the hot broth. Add cottage cheese, mix lightly, and return just to the boil. Serve immediately, garnished with the remaining 1 tablespoon chives.

Potato & Miso Soup with Milk, Cheese & Tofu

SERVES 3

1½ tablespoons Better Butter (p. 119) or butter
1 potato, cut into pieces 3 inches long and ½ inch square
5 ounces deep-fried or 12 ounces regular tofu, cut crosswise into thin slices
1 cup dashi (p. 112), stock, or water
2 to 2½ tablespoons red, barley, or Hatcho miso
1 cup milk (soy or dairy)
2 tablespoons minced leeks, scallions, or onions
Dash of pepper (optional)
¼ cup grated cheese or parboiled green peas (optional)

Melt the butter in a skillet. Add potato pieces and sauté for 5 minutes, then transfer to a separate container. Add tofu to skillet, sauté for 3 minutes, and remove from heat.

Bring dashi to a boil in small saucepan. Add the miso creamed in a little of the hot dashi, then add potatoes, tofu and milk. Return just to the boil before removing from heat. Sprinkle on leeks, pepper, and cheese. Serve immediately.

Instant Miso (Better 'n Coffee) Soup

SERVES 1

½ cup very hot or boiling water
Miso: Choose one
    2 teaspoons red, barley, Hatcho, or light yellow
    4 teaspoons mellow white
    6 teaspoons sweet white

Place miso in a cup or small bowl and add hot water a little at a time, stirring until smooth. Serve immediately; a good way to start the day off right! Or use a packet of commercial instant miso soup (p. 82).

Cream of Mushroom Soup with Miso

SERVES 3

2 tablespoons Better Butter (p. 119) or butter
2 cups diced mushrooms (about 16)
½ cup thinly sliced onion
¼ cup chopped celery
1 cup water or stock
2 tablespoons minced parsley
5 to 6 teaspoons red, barley, or Hatcho miso
1½ tablespoons white wine or sake
Dash of pepper (optional)
½ cup Miso White Sauce (p. 272)

Melt the butter in a saucepan. Add mushrooms and sauté for 2 to 3 minutes. Add onion, celery, water, and 1 tablespoon parsley; cover and bring to a boil. Simmer over low heat for 20 minutes. Remove from heat, uncover, and allow to cool briefly. Transfer to a blender, add miso, white wine and pepper, and purée until smooth. Return to saucepan, stir in white sauce, and bring just to a boil. Serve hot or chilled, garnished with the remaining 1 tablespoon parsley.

For variety, add 12 ounces diced regular tofu or 5

ounces deep-fried tofu together with the white sauce. For best flavor, allow to stand overnight, then serve chilled.

Mushroom & Onion Soup with White Miso

SERVES 2

2 tablespoons Better Butter (p. 119) or butter
6 mushrooms, diced (½ cup)
½ onion, thinly sliced
1¼ cups water or stock
2 tablespoons sweet white or 4 teaspoons mellow
   white miso
1 tablespoon red, barley, or Hatcho miso
2 tablespoons Parmesan cheese
Dash of pepper (optional)
1 tablespoon minced parsley

Melt the butter in a skillet. Add mushrooms and onions, and sauté for 4 minutes. Add water and bring to a boil. Add miso creamed in a little of the hot broth, then stir in Parmesan; season with pepper and return just to the boil. Serve topped with a sprinkling of parsley.

Almost Pudding Soup with Miso

SERVES 3

1½ teaspoons Better Butter (p. 119) or butter
½ cup minced onion
1½ cups diced whole-wheat bread
2 cups milk (soy or dairy)
2½ tablespoons red, barley, or Hatcho miso
1 small egg
Dash of freshly grated nutmeg
1 tablespoon minced parsley

Melt the butter in a skillet, add onions and sauté for 5 minutes. Add bread pieces and 1½ cups milk, and bring just to a boil. Remove from heat, cover, and allow to stand for 20 minutes. Mix well with a whisk or fork to give a smooth texture. Combine miso and egg with remaining ½ cup milk, mixing well, then stir into soup. Return to heat and bring just to a boil, whisking constantly. Mix in nutmeg and serve hot or cold, topped with a sprinkling of parsley.

For use as a dessert, add ¼ to ½ cup raisins together with the nutmeg.

Tomato Juice & Onion Soup with White Miso

SERVES 3

1 tablespoon oil
1 small onion, thinly sliced
2 mushrooms, thinly sliced
¾ cup tomato juice
1 cup dashi (p. 112), stock, or water
2 tablespoons sweet white or 4 teaspoons mellow
    white miso
1 teaspoon red, barley, or Hatcho miso
1 tablespoon minced parsley

Heat a saucepan and coat with the oil. Add onion and mushrooms, and sauté for 5 minutes. Add dashi and tomato juice, bring to a boil, and simmer for 3 minutes. Add creamed miso and return just to the boil. Serve hot or chilled topped with a sprinkling of parsley.

Carrot Juice Soup with Miso

SERVES 2 OR 3

2 teaspoons oil
¼ onion, thinly sliced
¼ cabbage leaf, shredded
¼ carrot, grated or cut into thin rounds
1 small potato, yam, or sweet potato, diced into
    ¼-inch cubes
¾ cup carrot or tomato juice
¾ cup water or stock
4 teaspoons red, barley, or Hatcho miso
3 tablespoons Parmesan cheese
Dash of oregano or pepper (optional)
1 tablespoon minced parsley

Heat a skillet and coat with the oil. Add the next four ingredients and sauté for 2 minutes. Add juice and water, bring to a boil, and simmer, covered, for 20 minutes. Add miso creamed in a little of the hot broth; stir in Parmesan, season with oregano, and return just to the boil. Serve topped with a sprinkling of parsley.

Chilled Cucumber & Yogurt Soup with Miso

SERVES 2

1 cucumber, sliced into thin rounds
2 tablespoons minced onion
1½ cups stock or water
1½ tablespoons red, barley, or Hatcho miso
Dash of pepper (optional)
2 tablespoons flour
½ bay leaf or 1 clove
½ cup yogurt
½ teaspoon caraway seeds or 1½ teaspoons grated
    lemon rind, dill, or chives

Combine cucumber, onion, and ½ cup stock in a saucepan. Bring to a boil, cover, and simmer for 15 minutes. Allow to cool for 10 minutes. Stir in miso and pepper, transfer to a blender, and purée until smooth.

Combine flour and ¼ cup stock, mixing well, then gradually add the remaining ¾ cup stock, stirring until smooth. Combine with the cucumber purée in a saucepan, add bay leaf, and bring to a boil. Cover and simmer for 2 to 3 minutes. Cool to room temperature and remove bay leaf. Mix in yogurt and caraway. Serve chilled.

Chilled Cucumber & Tahini Soup with Miso

SERVES 2

1¼ cups dashi (p. 112) or stock
1 tablespoon red, barley, or Hatcho miso
1½ tablespoons sweet white or 1 tablespoon mellow
    white miso
1 tablespoon *tahini* or sesame butter
1 cucumber, sliced into thin rounds
Dash of (7-spice) red pepper or Tabasco sauce
    (optional)

Bring dashi to a boil in a small saucepan. Add miso and *tahini,* both creamed in a little of the hot broth. Add cucumber and return to the boil. Serve chilled, seasoned with the red pepper.

VARIATION

*Chilled Cucumber & Tomato White Miso Soup: Omit red miso and *tahini.* Use ¼ cup sweet white miso. Add 1 small tomato (cut into wedges) together with cucumber. Season with black pepper and garnish with minced parsley.

Onion & Eggplant Soup with Miso

SERVES 2

2 tablespoons Better Butter (p. 119) or butter
1 small onion, thinly sliced
2 small (Japanese) eggplants, peeled and cut into
  ⅜-inch-thick rounds (about 1 cup)
1¼ cups water, stock, or dashi (p. 112)
1 tablespoon red, barley, or Hatcho miso
1½ tablespoons sweet white miso
⅓ cup Parmesan or grated cheese
Dash of pepper (optional)
1 tablespoon minced parsley

Melt the butter in a skillet. Add onion and eggplants, and sauté for 2 to 3 minutes. Add 1 cup water and bring to a boil. Add miso creamed in the remaining ¼ cup water, then stir in cheese and return just to the boil. Serve topped with a sprinkling of pepper and parsley.

Soybean Purée & Onion Soup with Miso

SERVES 6

½ cup soybeans, washed and soaked for 8 to 10
      hours in 1 quart water
4 cups water, approximately
2 tablespoons oil
4 onions, thinly sliced
3½ tablespoons red, barley, or Hatcho miso
⅔ cup grated cheese
2 tablespoons Better Butter (p. 119) or butter
Dash of pepper (optional)
1 cup croutons (sautéed lightly in butter, if desired)
¼ cup minced parsley (optional)

Rinse, then drain beans in a colander. Combine beans
and ¾ cup water in a blender and purée at high
speed for about 3 minutes, or until smooth.

Heat a heavy pot or large casserole and coat with
the oil. Add onions and sauté for 5 minutes. Mix in
purée and remaining 4¼ cups water, bring to a
boil, and simmer for 10 minutes, stirring occasionally.
Stir in the miso, cheese, butter and pepper, and return
to the boil. For best flavor, allow to stand for at least 6
hours. Serve as is or reheated, garnished with croutons
and parsley.

For extra flavor and protein, add 5 to 10 ounces
diced deep-fried tofu together with the purée. Increase
miso to 6 tablespoons.

Onion Soup with Ketchup & Miso

SERVES 2 OR 3

1 tablespoon Better Butter (p. 119) or butter
1 onion, thinly sliced
1¼ cups water or stock
4 teaspoons red, barley, or Hatcho miso
3 tablespoons ketchup or tomato paste
Dash of pepper (optional)
2 tablespoons Parmesan cheese
1 tablespoon minced parsley

Melt the butter in a skillet. Add onion and sauté for 5 minutes, then add water and bring to a boil. Stir in miso creamed with ketchup, add pepper and cheese, and return just to the boil. Serve topped with a sprinkling of parsley.

Quick Cream of Onion Soup with Miso

SERVES 3

2 tablespoons oil
3 onions, thinly sliced
2½ cups water or stock
3 tablespoons whole-wheat flour
3 tablespoons red, barley, or Hatcho miso
Dash of pepper (optional)
1 tablespoon minced parsley

Heat a pressure cooker and coat with the oil. Add onions and sauté for 3 minutes. Add 2 cups water, cover, and bring to full pressure (15 pounds). Reduce heat and cook for 5 minutes, then allow pressure to come down naturally.

Meanwhile, heat a skillet and coat with remaining 1 tablespoon oil. Add flour and sauté for 2 minutes, or until fragrant. Slowly add ½ cup water, stirring constantly, to make a thick sauce. Add miso and pepper, mixing until smooth. Open pressure cooker, mix sauce into onions, and bring just to a boil. Serve hot or, for a richer flavor, allow to stand overnight and serve reheated or cold, garnished with parsley.

Azuki Vegetable Soup with Miso

SERVES 4 TO 6

1 cup *azuki* beans, rinsed and drained
3 cups water
1 tablespoon oil
1 onion, thinly sliced
1 small carrot, cut into matchsticks or grated
4 tablespoons red, barley, or Hatcho miso
2 tablespoons honey
2 tablespoons sesame butter
¼ teaspoon cinnamon or nutmeg

Combine beans and water in a pressure cooker. Bring to full pressure (15 pounds), reduce heat to low and cook for 40 minutes. Remove from heat and allow to stand for 15 minutes while pressure comes down naturally.

Heat a skillet and coat with the oil. Add onions and carrot, and sauté for 5 minutes; remove from heat. Add miso, honey, sesame butter, cinnamon, and several tablespoons hot cooking liquid from the beans. Mix thoroughly, then stir miso-vegetable mixture into the beans in the cooker. For best flavor, allow to cool, then refrigerate for at least 8, preferably 24, hours. Serve cold or reheated.

Thick Lentil or Split Pea Soup with Miso

SERVES 4 OR 5

1 cup lentils or split peas, rinsed and drained
5 to 5½ cups water or stock
2 tablespoons oil
½ cup thinly sliced onions
½ cup thinly sliced carrots or diced yams
¾ cup chopped celery (with leaves)
1 clove of garlic, crushed
3½ tablespoons red, barley, or Hatcho miso, creamed
          with ¼ cup water
2 tablespoons Better Butter (p. 119) or butter
½ teaspoon oregano, thyme, or rosemary
Dash of ground red pepper; or ½ teaspoon nutmeg
2 to 4 tablespoons ground roasted sesame seeds
          (p. 107) (optional)
1 tablespoon minced parsley

Combine lentils and water in a large pot and soak overnight. Bring to a boil and simmer for about 2 hours, stirring occasionally, until quite thick. (Or reduce water to 2½ cups and pressure cook at 15 pounds for 20 minutes.)

Meanwhile, heat a skillet and coat with the oil. Add onions, carrots, celery and garlic, and sauté for about 5 minutes. Add ¼ cup water, cover, and simmer for 10 to 15 minutes, or until water has been absorbed or evaporated.

When soup has finished cooking, stir in miso, butter, oregano, and sautéed vegetables. Cover and allow to stand for at least 10 minutes; serve topped with a sprinkling of sesame and parsley. (For a richer flavor, refrigerate overnight and serve as is or reheated.)

Creamy Cauliflower & Tofu Soup with Miso

SERVES 4

1 tablespoon oil
1 onion, thinly sliced
1½ to 2 cups cauliflowerets, parboiled (p. 105)
2 tablespoons Better Butter (p. 119) or butter
2 tablespoons whole-wheat flour
1 cup milk
½ cup water
2 ounces cheese, grated or finely diced
12 ounces regular or 5 ounces deep-fried tofu, cut into small rectangles
2 tablespoons light-yellow or red miso
Dash of pepper (optional)

Heat a casserole and coat with the oil. Add onion and sauté for 3 minutes, or until lightly browned. Add cauliflower and sauté for 1 minute more, then turn off heat.

Using the butter, flour, and milk, prepare a white sauce (p. 272). Add the sauce and water to the casserole, cover, and simmer over low heat for 5 minutes. Add cheese and tofu, increase heat to medium, and cook for 3 minutes. Stir in the miso thinned in a little of the cooking broth, season with pepper, and return just to the boil. Serve hot or, for a richer, sweeter flavor, allow to cool before serving.

Miso Stew

SERVES 4 TO 5

This hearty dish resembles a very thick miso soup prepared with sautéed vegetables.

1½ tablespoons sesame oil
3 onions, cut into thin wedges
½ carrot, cut into half moons
2 potatoes or 4 taro cut into irregular chunks (1½
        cups)
1½ cups sliced (Chinese) cabbage or 1 cup thin
        rounds of *daikon*
3 cups water or stock
5½ tablespoons red, barley, or Hatcho miso
2 tablespoons minced parsley (optional)

Heat a heavy pot or skillet and coat with the oil. Add
the four vegetables consecutively, sautéing each for
about 1 minute. Add the water and bring to a boil.
Reduce heat to low, cover, and simmer for 15 minutes. Stir in miso creamed in a little of the hot broth
and return just to the boil. For best flavor, allow to
cool for 6 to 8 hours. Serve as is or reheated, garnished with the parsley.

For added body and protein, substitute for the potatoes 12 to 18 ounces regular or 5 to 7 ounces deep-
fried tofu. Use other seasonal vegetables.

Open-hearth
fireplace

Miso in Sauces

Whether Western-style or Oriental, Near Eastern or Latin American, any sauce is enhanced by the presence of miso. Creamy Tofu Dressings also work well, especially with grains and vegetables.

Miso Onion Sauce

SERVES 4

3 tablespoons (sesame) oil
4 onions, thinly sliced
2½ to 3 tablespoons red, barley, or Hatcho miso, thinned in ⅔ cup water

Heat the oil in a large, heavy skillet. Add onions and sauté for 5 minutes. Add thinned miso, cover pan, and simmer for 30 minutes, or until most of the liquid has been absorbed or evaporated. For best flavor, allow to stand for 6 to 8 hours. Serve as is or reheated. Delicious over grain dishes, toast, steamed vegetables, or tofu. Or serve as a side dish.

This sauce may also be prepared by starting with Thick French Onion Soup (p. 253); add the miso dissolved in 3 tablespoons (rather than 2 cups) warm water.

VARIATION

*Seasoned Onion Sauce with Nut Butters: Thin your favorite nut butter with a small amount of water or stock and, if desired, some lemon or orange juice, and add to 2 parts Onion Sauce. Season with herbs, 7-spice red pepper, shoyu, or miso. Garnish with thinly sliced green onions or parsley. For variety, add large chunks of nuts, diced cheese, or sprouts.

Miso & Nutritional Yeast Gravy

FOR 2 TO 3 SERVINGS

¼ cup butter, Better Butter (p. 119) or margarine
¼ cup nutritional yeast (we prefer the good-tasting Red Star brand)
¼ cup whole-wheat flour
2 tablespoons red miso, dissolved in 1½ to 1¾ cups hot water

Melt the butter in a skillet. Add nutritional yeast and mix well for 30 seconds. Add flour and sauté for 1 minute. Add the hot miso-water mixture a little at a time, stirring constantly to create a thick, creamy consistency. When all is added, bring just to the boil, then remove from heat. Delicious served over cooked grains (brown rice, noodles, millet), baked potatoes, cooked vegetables (broccoli, cauliflower, etc.), or fried tempeh or tofu.

Miso-Gingerroot Ankaké Sauce

MAKES 1 CUP

⅔ cup dashi (p. 112), stock, or water
4 to 4½ tablespoons red, barley, or Hatcho miso
1 tablespoon honey or 2 tablespoons (natural) sugar
2 teaspoons arrowroot, cornstarch, or *kuzu* (kudzu powder), dissolved in 2 tablespoons water
2 teaspoons freshly grated gingerroot

Combine dashi, miso, and honey in a small saucepan. Bring to a boil, then stir in dissolved arrowroot and gingerroot. Cook for about 1 minute or until thick.

Miso-Lemon Ankaké Sauce

MAKES 1¼ CUPS

1 cup dashi (p. 112), stock, or water
2½ tablespoons red, barley, or Hatcho miso
1½ teaspoons honey or 1 tablespoon (natural) sugar
2 teaspoons cornstarch, arrowroot, or *kuzu* (kudzu
    powder), dissolved in 1½ tablespoons water
½ teaspoon grated lemon rind

Combine dashi, miso, and honey in a small saucepan, mixing well. Bring to a boil, stir in dissolved cornstarch and lemon rind, and cook for about 1 minute more until thick. Serve over cooked vegetables, tofu, or broiled *mochi*.

Miso-Mushroom Sauce

FOR 3 SERVINGS

1½ tablespoons Better Butter (p. 119) or butter
½ teaspoon minced or crushed garlic
1 tablespoon minced onion
½ teaspoon grated gingerroot
5 mushrooms, thinly sliced
⅓ cup ketchup
1 tablespoon red, barley, or Hatcho miso
Dash of pepper (optional)

Melt the butter in a skillet. Add garlic, onion and gingerroot, and sauté for 1 minute. Add mushrooms and sauté for 2 minutes. Stir in ketchup and miso, season with pepper, and sauté for 1 minute more. Delicious with most grain dishes, especially *tacos* or *tortillas*, and with deep-fried or barbecued foods.

Miso White Sauce

MAKES 1 CUP

Also known as Cream or Béchamel Sauce, this traditional Western favorite acquires a distinctive flavor and creaminess when seasoned with miso. Season lightly for use with vegetables and more prominently for use with tofu dishes.

2 tablespoons butter or oil
2 tablespoons (whole-wheat) flour
1 cup milk (soy or dairy) or stock
3 to 4 teaspoons red, barley, or Hatcho miso; or
   2 to 2½ tablespoons sweet white or mellow white
   miso
Dash of pepper, paprika, or cayenne
1 tablespoon minced parsley (optional)

Melt the butter (or heat oil) in a skillet. Add flour
and, stirring constantly, cook over low heat for 1 to 2
minutes, or until flour is well blended and its raw taste
has vanished. Add ½ cup milk (or stock) a little at
a time, continuing to stir, then mix in the miso and
slowly add the remainder of the milk. Increase heat
to medium and cook, whisking or stirring, for 3 to 4
minutes more, or until sauce develops a smooth,
thickened consistency. Stir in pepper (and parsley)
and remove from heat.

VARIATIONS

Cheese-Miso White Sauce: Sauté 1 clove of crushed
garlic in butter for 30 seconds before adding flour. Add
½ teaspoon dry mustard and ½ cup grated cheese
several minutes before removing from heat.

Lemon-Miso White Sauce: Add 2 teaspoons lemon
juice (and ¼ teaspoon grated lemon rind) about 1
minute before removing from heat.

Herb Sauce: Add or substitute for the parsley any of
the following, preferably fresh: thyme, basil, oregano,
or beefsteak leaves.

Mushroom-Miso White Sauce: Just after adding the
last of the milk, add ¼ diced onion and 6 thinly-
sliced mushrooms. Stirring constantly, simmer over
low heat for 4 to 5 minutes. Then add 1 teaspoon
lemon juice, the pepper, and 1 tablespoon white wine
or sake.

Sesame-Miso White Sauce: Add 1 tablespoon sesame butter or *tahini* several minutes before removing
from heat. Delicious over steamed cauliflower, mushrooms, chard, Brussels sprouts, or celery. Serve
topped with a sprinkling of parsley.

Tofu-Miso White Sauce: Use 4 teaspoons red miso.

Add 12 ounces regular tofu (mashed) or 7½ ounces deep-fried tofu (diced) about 2 minutes before removing from heat.

*Brown Sauce: Prepare as for a white sauce except cook the flour until it is lightly browned and fragrant.

Miso-Spaghetti Sauce

SERVES 3 OR 4

2 tablespoons oil
2 small onions, thinly sliced
1 clove of garlic, crushed
10 mushrooms, thinly sliced
5 tomatoes, diced
3 green peppers, diced
½ carrot, grated or thinly sliced
2 cups water or stock
2 bay leaves
4½ tablespoons red, barley, or Hatcho miso
1 tablespoon Better Butter (p. 119) or butter
Dash of pepper (optional)
Dash of oregano and/or basil
⅓ cup grated or Parmesan cheese

Heat a heavy pot and coat with the oil. Add onions and garlic and sauté for about 3 minutes. Add the next four ingredients and sauté for 4 minutes more. Add water, drop in bay leaves, and bring to a boil. Simmer uncovered for 10 minutes. Mix in miso and next three ingredients; simmer, stirring every 5 minutes, for 1 hour. For best flavor, allow to stand for 6 to 8 hours. Remove bay leaves and serve hot or cold over buckwheat noodles or spaghetti. Top with cheese.

VARIATIONS

*With Soybeans: Add together with the miso in the basic recipe: 1 cup stock (soybean cooking liquid or mushroom soaking water), 1½ tablespoons additional red miso, and 2¼ cups cooked soybeans (p. 317). Proceed as above; serve topped with an additional 3 tablespoons grated or Parmesan cheese. Also delicious served chilled as a dish in its own right.

*With Tofu: Add 12 to 24 ounces diced regular tofu (or 5 to 10 ounces deep-fried tofu) together with the miso; simmer covered. Mix in ½ cup additional grated cheese just before removing from heat.

Miso Taco or Pizza Sauce

MAKES 1¼ CUPS

⅔ cup ketchup
1¼ cups grated cheese
2 tablespoons red, barley, or Hatcho miso
2 tablespoons minced onion, leek, or scallion
1 teaspoon grated gingerroot (optional)
1 teaspoon sake or white wine
Dash of Tabasco sauce
Dash of pepper (optional)
1 tablespoon water

Combine all ingredients, mixing well. For best flavor, allow to stand for at least several hours before serving. Spread 3 to 4 teaspoons on each of 12 crisp buttered tortillas before topping with shredded lettuce, diced tomatoes, grated cheese, and your choice of other ingredients. Or use with pizza.

Quick Spaghetti Sauce with Miso & Tofu

SERVES 3 OR 4

1½ tablespoons oil
1 clove of garlic, crushed or minced
2 onions, diced
2 leaves of (Chinese) cabbage, thinly sliced
1 tomato, diced
1 cup ketchup
¼ cup water
2 green beefsteak leaves, minced, or 1 teaspoon
    grated gingerroot
10 ounces deep-fried or regular tofu, cubed
½ cup chives or *nira*
⅓ cup grated cheese
3 tablespoons Better Butter (p. 119) or butter
Dash of pepper (optional)
2 tablespoons red, barley, or Hatcho miso
½ cup Parmesan cheese
¼ cup minced parsley

Heat oil in a pot. Add the next four ingredients and sauté for 5 to 7 minutes, or until soft. Add ketchup, water, and beefsteak leaves, and simmer for 5 minutes. Add tofu, chives, and grated cheese, and simmer for 4 minutes more. Stir in the butter, pepper and the miso creamed in a little of the hot sauce. Stirring constantly, simmer for 1 more minute. For best flavor, remove from heat and allow to stand for 6 to 8 hours. Serve reheated or as is, topped with the cheese and parsley.

Pineapple Sweet & Sour Sauce with Miso

MAKES 1½ CUPS

1¼ cups pineapple chunks, drained
2½ teaspoons honey
3 tablespoons vinegar
½ cup water
3 tablespoons red, barley, or Hatcho miso
2 tablespoons ketchup
½ teaspoon grated gingerroot or 1 teaspoon
    powdered ginger
1 tablespoon cornstarch or *kuzu* (kudzu powder)

Combine all ingredients in a saucepan, mixing well. Bring to a boil and cook, stirring constantly, for about 1 minute, or until thick. Delicious served over vegetables sautéed with a little garlic, or over brown rice, buckwheat noodles, or deep-fried tofu.

Orange-Sesame Miso Sauce

MAKES ½ CUP

3 tablespoons red, barley, or Hatcho miso
1½ tablespoons sesame butter
1½ to 2 teaspoons honey
1 tablespoon sake or white wine
2 tablespoons water or dashi (p. 112)
¼ to ½ teaspoon grated orange rind
1 egg yolk (optional)

Combine all ingredients in a small saucepan or skillet. Simmer for 2 or 3 minutes over low heat, stirring constantly with a wooden spoon or spatula, until mixture has a slightly firmer consistency than that of regular miso. Serve hot or cold. Delicious as a topping for Furofuki Daikon (p. 347), fried eggplant slices, or crisp apple wedges; a dipping sauce for Miso Oden (p. 348); or slightly thinned as a sauce for potatoes, *(kabocha)* pumpkin, okra, or squash.

Garbanzo-Tahini Sauce with Miso (*Hummus bi Tahina*)

MAKES 4 CUPS

1 cup garbanzo beans, soaked for 3 hours in 3½
    cups water
½ cup tahini
1 to 2 cloves of garlic, minced or crushed
2½ tablespoons lemon juice
2 tablespoons red or barley (or ¼ cup mellow
    white) miso
Dash of pepper and/or Tabasco sauce
3 tablespoons minced parsley and/or a dash of
    paprika

Combine beans and soaking water in a pressure cooker, bring to full pressure (15 pounds), and simmer for 30 minutes. Remove from heat and allow to stand for 10 minutes while pressure returns to normal. Combine hot beans and remaining cooking liquid in a blender with the next five ingredients; purée until smooth. Serve hot or cold, topped with a sprinkling of parsley and/or paprika. Excellent served over rice, millet, buckwheat groats, or steamed greens. Also makes a delicious dip.

Sweet White Miso Sauce

MAKES 1 CUP

½ cup sweet white miso
½ cup water, stock, or dashi (p. 112)
1 tablespoon honey
¾ teaspoon sesame oil
¾ teaspoon tapioca, arrowroot, or cornstarch,
    dissolved in 1 tablespoon water
1 teaspoon sake or white wine (optional)

Combine all ingredients in a heavy saucepan, bring to a boil, and simmer, stirring constantly, for 3 minutes, or until slightly thick. Delicious served over Grilled Tofu & Vegetables (p. 356) or Brussels sprouts.

Miso-Cream Cheese Sauce

MAKES ½ CUP

4 ounces cream cheese
2 teaspoons red or barley (or 4 teaspoons mellow
    white) miso
1 tablespoon Worcestershire sauce
3 tablespoons water or milk

Combine all ingredients and beat or blend together until smooth. Delicious over cooked vegetables such as broccoli, squash, or cauliflower.

Miso Gravy

MAKES 1½ CUPS

2 tablespoons Better Butter (p. 119) or butter
1 small onion, minced
3 tablespoons (whole-wheat or barley) flour
1½ tablespoons red, barley, or Hatcho miso
1 cup water
Dash of pepper (optional)

Melt 1 tablespoon butter in a skillet. Add onion and sauté for 5 minutes, or until soft and lightly browned. Add remaining 1 tablespoon butter; when melted, add flour and sauté for 2 to 3 minutes. Add miso and sauté for 30 seconds more. Now add the water a little at a time, stirring constantly; bring to a boil, season with pepper, and simmer for 1 minute. Delicious over steamed cauliflower or broccoli.

For a richer flavor use 2½ tablespoons miso. Serve as a topping for brown rice or deep-fried tofu.

Spicy Indonesian Peanut Sauce with Miso (Gado-gado Sauce)

MAKES 2 CUPS

3 tablespoons oil
1 cup roasted (unsalted) peanuts
1 clove of garlic, crushed or minced
¼ to ½ teaspoon (7-spice) red pepper or Tabasco sauce
1½ teaspoons honey
2½ tablespoons red, barley, or Hatcho miso
1½ cups stock, water, or (coconut) milk
¼ onion, minced
1 teaspoon minced parsley

Heat a wok or skillet and coat with 2 tablespoons oil. Add peanuts and sauté for 3 to 5 minutes, or until browned and fragrant. Mix in the next five ingredients and bring to a boil, then remove from heat and allow to cool briefly. Meanwhile, heat the remaining 1 tablespoon oil in a skillet. Add onion and sauté for 5 minutes, or until well browned. Transfer cooled peanut sauce to a blender and purée until smooth. Pour into a serving container, mix in sautéed onion, and top with a sprinkling of parsley. Serve hot or chilled over cooked rice or noodles, or lightly steamed vegetables (especially cabbage, cauliflower, or broccoli).

If Indonesian spices (*kenchur, asam,* or *danjelpur*) are available, add together with the red pepper.

Korean-style Miso Dipping Sauce

MAKES ¼ CUP

1½ tablespoons red, barley, or Hatcho miso
½ teaspoon sesame oil
¼ teaspoon crushed or minced garlic
1 tablespoon water
Dash of (7-spice) red pepper or Tabasco sauce

Combine all ingredients, mixing well. Serve with
broiled or deep-fried foods. Excellent with vegetarian
Shish Kebab (p. 355).

Tangy Miso Chirizu Dipping Sauce

MAKES ⅓ CUP

2 tablespoons red, barley, or Hatcho miso
4 teaspoons lemon juice
2½ tablespoons grated *daikon*
2½ tablespoons thin rounds of leek or scallion
Dash of 7-spice red pepper or Tabasco sauce

Combine all ingredients, mixing well. Serve with regular or deep-fried tofu, all *nabé* preparations, tempura,
or croquettes.

Apple & Onion Curry Sauce
with Deep-fried Tofu and Miso

SERVES 3 OR 4

7½ ounces deep-fried cutlets, burgers, or pouches;
        or 18 ounces regular tofu
1 apple, diced
2 potatoes, diced (1¾ cups)
1 cup water or stock
3 tablespoons Better Butter (p. 119) or butter
1 clove of garlic, crushed
1 teaspoon grated or 1½ teaspoons powdered
        gingerroot
1½ onions, minced
5 to 6 mushrooms, thinly sliced
1½ to 2 teaspoons curry powder
2 tablespoons whole-wheat flour
3 to 3½ tablespoons red, barley, or Hatcho miso
1 tablespoon honey
2 tablespoons ketchup
Sambals: Sliced bananas, grated coconut, raisins,
        diced apples, peanuts or almonds, chopped
        hard-boiled eggs, and chutney

Combine the first four ingredients in a heavy pot or
casserole and bring to a boil. Cover and simmer over
low heat. Meanwhile melt the butter in a skillet. Add

garlic and gingerroot, and sauté for 30 seconds. Add onions and mushrooms, and sauté for 5 to 6 minutes more. Mix in curry powder and flour, and cook, stirring constantly, for 1 minute. Cream miso with about ⅓ cup broth removed from the pot, then stir into the curried mixture together with the honey and ketchup to form a smooth, thick sauce. Now mix sauce into contents of pot, cover, and simmer for 20 to 30 minutes, stirring occasionally. Serve over brown rice or buckwheat noodles, topped with the *sambals*.

For a more elaborate sauce, add diced lotus root, cooked lentils, sweet potatoes, *kabocha,* or squash. To serve as an entrée without grains, reduce the amounts of miso and curry powder by about one-fifth. Try substituting 1½ cups cooked soybeans for the tofu.

Tangy Miso, Ketchup & Lemon Sauce

MAKES ¾ CUP

½ cup ketchup
2 tablespoons red, barley, or Hatcho miso
1½ tablespoons lemon juice
1 tablespoon minced onion
1 tablespoon minced parsley
Dash of pepper (optional)

Combine all ingredients, mixing well. Serve with deep-fried, broiled, or barbecued foods. Also good with shrimp cocktail or seafoods.

For variety add any of the following: ¼ teaspoon hot mustard, 1 teaspoon horseradish, ½ teaspoon crushed anise or ground roasted sesame seeds, or 1 tablespoon minced parsley.

Sesame-Miso Sauce

MAKES ⅔ CUP

This recipe is good for use with vegetables such as cauliflower, spinach or turnips; use the hot cooking water as the basis of the sauce.

2 tablespoons red, barley, or Hatcho miso
1 tablespoon sesame butter
½ cup hot vegetable cooking liquid, stock, or dashi
    (p. 112)
½ teaspoon grated lemon or *yuzu* rind

Combine the first three ingredients, mixing until
smooth. Pour over cooked vegetables and top with a
sprinkling of the lemon rind.

Miso-Sesame Lyonnaise Sauce

MAKES 1½ CUPS

2 tablespoons sesame oil
2 onions, minced
2 tablespoons whole-wheat flour
1 cup stock, water, or dashi (p. 112)
¼ cup white wine or sake
3 tablespoons red, barley, or Hatcho miso
Dash of pepper (optional)
1 tablespoon minced parsley

Heat a skillet and coat with the oil. Add onions and
sauté for 5 minutes, or until lightly browned. Stir in
flour and sauté for 2 minutes more. Add stock a little
at a time, stirring until smooth. Stir in wine and cook,
stirring constantly, for 3 minutes. Add miso creamed
in a little of the hot sauce, season with pepper, and
return just to the boil. Serve topped with a sprinkling
of parsley.

Sesame, Onion & Miso Sauce

MAKES ⅔ CUP

2 to 3 teaspoons sesame oil
1 onion, minced
2 tablespoons sesame (or peanut) butter
2 tablespoons red, barley, or Hatcho miso, thinned
    in 2½ tablespoons water
1 teaspoon white wine, sake, or *mirin* (optional)

Heat a skillet or wok and coat with the oil. Add onion
and sauté for 4 to 5 minutes. Combine sesame butter
and thinned miso, mix briefly, and stir into onion. Add

wine (if used), mix well, and remove from heat. Serve as a topping for Brown Rice (p. 116), Rice Patties (p. 294), or steamed vegetables.

Creamy Sesame-Miso Sauce

MAKES ½ CUP

3 tablespoons sweet white or 2 tablespoons mellow white miso
1½ tablespoons sesame butter or *tahini*
3 tablespoons milk (soy or dairy)
1½ tablespoons vinegar

Combine all ingredients, mixing well. Serve with cooked vegetables (especially good with spinach, cauliflower, chard, or broccoli).

Peanut Butter-Miso Sauce

MAKES ½ CUP

1 to 1½ tablespoons red, barley, or Hatcho miso
2 tablespoons peanut butter
2 to 3 tablespoons hot vegetable cooking liquid, stock, or dashi (p. 112)
1 teaspoon grated lemon or *yuzu* peel, or ½ teaspoon lemon juice

Prepare and serve as for Sesame-Miso Sauce, above. If desired, reduce the amount of water and use as a cracker spread or filling for celery stalks.

Tomato & Cheese Sauce with Miso

MAKES 1¼ CUPS

2 tablespoons Better Butter (p. 119) or butter
1¼ cups chopped fresh tomatoes
½ onion, minced
1½ tablespoons red, barley, or Hatcho miso
¾ cup grated cheese
¼ teaspoon oregano or basil
¼ teaspoon paprika
Dash of pepper (optional)

Melt the butter in a skillet. Add tomatoes and onion and sauté for 2 minutes, then cover and simmer for 3 minutes. Uncover and continue to simmer, stirring occasionally, for 15 minutes more, or until sauce is well thickened. Add miso creamed in a little of the hot sauce, then stir in remaining ingredients and remove from heat.

Miso-Gingerroot Sauce

MAKES 2 CUPS

5 tablespoons red, barley, or Hatcho miso
3 to 4 teaspoons honey
1 cup dashi (p. 112), stock, or water
2 teaspoons arrowroot, cornstarch or *kuzu* (kudzu powder), dissolved in ¼ cup water
1 tablespoon grated gingerroot
Dash of (7-spice) red pepper

Combine the first three ingredients in a small saucepan and bring to a boil. Stir in dissolved arrowroot and grated gingerroot and cook for about 1 minute, or until thickened. Season with red pepper. Delicious with steamed or sautéed vegetables (cauliflower, cabbage, chard, broccoli, squash), deep-fried foods, or tofu.

Gingerroot-Miso Barbecue Sauce

MAKES ½ CUP

1½ teaspoons oil
½ teaspoon minced gingerroot
3½ tablespoons red, barley, or Hatcho miso
¼ cup water, stock, or dashi (p. 112)
2½ teaspoons honey
1½ tablespoons *mirin,* dry sherry, or white wine
Dash of 7-spice red pepper or *sansho* pepper (optional)

Heat a wok or skillet and coat with the oil. Add gingerroot and sauté for 1 minute, or until just fragrant. Add the next four ingredients and cook, stirring constantly, for 3 minutes, or until mixture has the consistency of a thick sauce. Stir in the pepper, if used, and remove from heat. Allow to cool before serving on deep-fried tofu, tofu or tempeh burgers, barbecued foods, tempura, or fresh vegetable slices.

Korean-style Miso Barbecue Sauce

MAKES ¼ CUP

3 tablespoons red, barley, or Hatcho miso
1 tablespoon honey
1 clove of garlic, crushed
1 tablespoon diced leeks or onions
1 tablespoon ground roasted sesame seeds (p. 107),
    or 2 teaspoons sesame butter or *tahini*
2 teaspoons sesame oil
¼ teaspoon (7-spice) red pepper or Tabasco sauce
Dash of white pepper

Combine all ingredients, mixing well. Delicious with (grilled) deep-fried tofu or tempeh.

Miso Shish Kebab (or Barbecue) Sauce

MAKES ¼ CUP

In Japan, a close relative of this preparation is used with the popular chicken shish kebab called *yakitori*.

2 tablespoons red, barley, or Hatcho miso
1 teaspoon oil
½ teaspoon honey
¼ teaspoon grated gingerroot
¼ to ½ clove of garlic, crushed
2 tablespoons water

Combine all ingredients, mixing well. Use as a marinade and/or basting sauce with your favorite preparations, or with Shish Kebab (p. 355).

Miso-Ketchup Barbecue Sauce

MAKES ½ CUP

2 tablespoons red, barley, or Hatcho miso
2 tablespoons ketchup
¼ small onion, diced
1 tablespoon melted butter or Better Butter (p. 119)
1 tablespoon sake or white wine
½ clove of garlic, crushed
¾ teaspoon honey
Dash of (7-spice) red pepper or Tabasco sauce

Combine all ingredients in a skillet, mixing well. Cook over medium heat for about 1 minute. Serve hot or cold. Excellent over croquettes or deep-fried tofu.

Miso Teriyaki Sauce

MAKES 1 CUP

Generally used in Japan to baste broiled fish, this savory sauce is now used by many Westerners with shish kebab and other barbecued preparations. Also good as a dip for fresh vegetables or a topping for deep-fried tofu.

6 tablespoons red, barley, or Hatcho miso
3 tablespoons sake or white wine
1 tablespoon sesame or vegetable oil
1 teaspoon grated gingerroot or 1½ teaspoons
    powdered ginger
2 cloves of garlic, crushed
3 tablespoons brown sugar or 1½ tablespoons honey
¼ teaspoon dry mustard (optional)

Combine all ingredients, mixing well. Marinate foods (green peppers, onions or leeks, deep-fried tofu, tomatoes, mushrooms, etc.) for at least 1 hour before skewering and broiling. Use remaining sauce to baste.

Miso with Grains, Beans and Tofu

Miso evokes and accentuates the simple, satisfying flavors of grains and beans (pulses), mankind's most basic foods. Inexpensive and easy to prepare, these dishes can be enjoyed day after day and serve as the center of a healthful diet. Using miso and soybean products together with grains can increase the total protein content of each dish by more than 30 percent (p. 26). See also Miso in Baked Dishes (p. 326) and Miso in Sandwiches (p. 183).

MISO WITH BROWN RICE

For most of recorded history, unpolished rice has served as the staff of life for more than one-half of the world's population. Fortunately, its health-giving virtues are now gaining greater and greater recognition in the West.

Brown Rice or Rice Porridge with Miso Toppings

MAKES 1 SERVING

In Japan, this is the most popular way of serving rice seasoned with miso. Quick and easy to prepare, the many variations of this tasty dish can be enjoyed daily throughout the four seasons.

1 to 1½ cups cooked Brown Rice or Rice Porridge
   (p. 287; unseasoned)
1 to 2 teaspoons of any one of the following:
    Red, barley, or Hatcho miso
    Finger Lickin' or akadashi miso
    Sweet Simmered Miso (p. 125)
    Miso Sauté (p. 139)
    Mixed Miso (p. 150)
    Broiled Miso (p. 156)
    Yubeshi Miso (p. 161)
    Soybean & Miso Garnish (p. 321)
    Miso pickles, minced or thinly sliced (p. 385)

Place rice in a bowl and top with a bead or dab of the miso. Mix well or, if using chopsticks, take a small piece of miso together with each biteful of rice. Chew well for best flavor and nutrition.

Brown Rice Topped with Miso Sauces

Serve cooked hot or cold brown rice topped with any of the miso sauces and garnishes listed in page 303 for use with noodles.

Rice Jambalaya with Miso

SERVES 3 OR 4

3 tablespoons butter
3 ounces mushrooms, thinly sliced
5 ounces deep-fried tofu, cubed; or substitute an
    equal weight of sliced mushrooms
½ onion, thinly sliced
2 green peppers, thinly sliced
¼ cup diced celery
1 tomato, diced
1½ tablespoons red, barley, or Hatcho miso
Dash of (7-spice) red pepper or Tabasco sauce
¼ teaspoon paprika
½ cup brown rice, cooked (p. 116); or use 1¼ cups
    leftover rice
2 tablespoons minced parsley

Preheat oven to 300° F. Melt 1½ tablespoons butter in a skillet. Add mushrooms and deep-fried tofu, and sauté for 2 minutes. Add the next four ingredients and sauté for 2 minutes more. Mix in miso, red pepper, and paprika, then remove from heat. Combine with cooked rice, 1 tablespoon parsley, and the remaining 1½ tablespoons butter. Mix well and spoon into an oiled casserole or loaf pan. Cover and bake for 45 to 60 minutes. Serve hot or cold, topped with the remaining 1 tablespoon parsley.

Deep-fried Miso-Rice Balls with Sweet & Sour Sauce

SERVES 3 OR 4

1 cup brown rice, cooked (p. 116) and cooled to body
    or room temperature
¾ cup chopped leeks or scallions
2 tablespoons red, barley, or Hatcho miso
¼ cup sesame butter or *tahini*
2 teaspoons grated gingerroot
1 clove of garlic, crushed
½ cup cornstarch, arrowroot, or *kuzu* (kudzu powder)
Oil for deep-frying
1½ cups Pineapple Sweet & Sour Sauce (p. 276)

Combine the first six ingredients, mixing well. Shape
into 1½-inch-diameter balls (20 to 25) and roll in
cornstarch. Heat the oil to 350° F in a wok, skillet, or
deep-fryer. Drop in balls (8 to 10 at a time) and
deep-fry until crisp and golden brown (p. 361). Drain
well, then top with the hot sauce. Serve immediately
or, for a richer, sweeter flavor, allow to stand for 6 to
8 hours.

Stir-fried Rice with Almonds and Miso

SERVES 4

2 tablespoons oil
1 clove of garlic, minced
½ cup almonds, slivered
½ leek, chopped fine
2 eggs, lightly beaten
1 cup brown rice, cooked (p. 116) and cooled
2 tablespoons red, barley or Hatcho miso, creamed
    with 1 tablespoon water
Dash of pepper (optional)

Heat 1 tablespoon oil in a wok or large skillet. Add
garlic and almonds, and sauté for 2 to 3 minutes until
browned. Add leeks, sauté for 1 minute more, then
remove from heat and transfer to an empty bowl.
Reheat wok and coat with remaining 1 tablespoon oil.
Add eggs and scramble for 1 minute until just firm.
Mix in rice and sauté for 1 minute, then add almond-

leek mixture and sauté for 2 minutes more, or until crumbly. Mix in miso and pepper and cook for 2 minutes. Delicious hot or cold.

Brown Rice Porridge with Miso and Vegetables

SERVES 3 OR 4

½ cup brown rice
4½ cups water
1 tablespoon (sesame) oil
½ onion, thinly sliced
½ small carrot, slivered or diced
½ cup diced or slivered celery or *daikon*
1 tablespoon red or barley miso, dissolved in ¼ cup water
½ cup fresh or reconstituted *wakame* (p. 105), thinly sliced (optional)
Miso Pickles (p. 385) or Sesame Salt (p. 119)
Crumbled toasted *nori* (optional)

Combine rice and water in a heavy pot, cover, and bring to a boil. Reduce heat to very low, and simmer for 90 minutes with lid set slightly ajar.

Meanwhile, heat a skillet and coat with the oil. Add onion and sauté for 2 minutes. Add carrot and celery, and sauté for 5 minutes more. Add dissolved miso together with *wakame,* if used. Bring just to a boil, turn off heat, and cover.

When porridge is ready, stir in miso-vegetable mixture and simmer for 5 minutes. Serve individual portions seasoned with miso pickles or sesame salt and, if desired, the *nori*.

VARIATIONS

*Pressure Cooked Porridge: Combine rice with 2½ cups water in a pressure cooker and bring to full pressure (15 pounds). Reduce heat to very low and simmer for 45 minutes. Turn off heat and allow to stand for 10 minutes while pressure returns to normal. Open cooker and stir in miso and vegetables. Allow to stand for 5 to 10 minutes. Mix well before serving.

*Porridge with Miso and Soybeans: Combine rice with 2¾ cups water and ¼ cup dry soybeans, soaked for at least 3 hours in water to cover, then drained. Proceed as for Pressure Cooked Porridge, above. After opening cooker, stir in 1½ tablespoons red miso, 1 tablespoon butter, and 1 tablespoon minced parsley. Let stand for several minutes before serving.

Creamy Rice Porridge with White Miso and Broccoli

SERVES 4

2 tablespoons butter
1 onion, minced
1½ cups cooked Brown Rice (p. 116)
2 cups water
2 cups chopped broccoli (4½ ounces)
¼ cup sweet white or 2½ tablespoons mellow white
    miso, dissolved in 3 tablespoons water

Melt the butter in a heavy (earthenware) pot. Add onion and sauté for 3 minutes. Add brown rice and water, and bring to a boil. Add broccoli and return to the boil, then simmer, covered, for 15 minutes, stirring occasionally. Stir in creamed miso and return just to the boil. Delicious hot or cold.

Sang Chu

SERVES 3 TO 5

One of Korea's most popular national dishes, Sang Chu is composed of rice and a spicy garnish wrapped in a crisp lettuce leaf; held in the fingers, it is eaten like a sandwich. In the following recipe, we substitute tofu (or scrambled eggs) for the usual hamburger or pork miso.

1 tablespoon sesame oil
1 clove of garlic, minced
12 ounces tofu, crumbled (p. 111); or 3 eggs, scrambled (without salt)
3 tablespoons red, barley, or Hatcho miso
1 teaspoon juice pressed from grated gingerroot
⅓ cup chopped leeks or scallions
¼ teaspoon ground red pepper
12 to 15 (butter) lettuce leaves
3 to 5 thin lemon wedges
6 to 10 thin tomato wedges, sprigs of parsley, spring chrysanthemum leaves, or cheese slices
2 to 2½ cups cooked Brown Rice (p. 116)

To prepare garnish, heat a skillet and coat with the oil. Add garlic and sauté for 30 seconds. Add tofu (or eggs) and sauté for 2 minutes. Add gingerroot juice and miso, sauté for 30 seconds more, and remove from heat. Stir in leeks and red pepper, mash all ingredients together thoroughly, and spoon into a small bowl.

Place bowl at the center of a large serving plate and surround with lettuce leaves. Top leaves with lemon and tomato wedges. Serve as a main course or hors d'oeuvre accompanied by a serving bowl mounded with the rice.

Hold a lettuce leaf in the palm of one hand, spoon about 2 tablespoons of rice onto the leaf's center, and top the rice with a tablespoon of garnish. Squeeze a little lemon juice over the garnish and/or top with a tomato wedge. Fold ends and sides of leaf over filling.

Other popular Korean garnishes include Red Pepper & Leek Miso (*doen jang;* p. 136) and Red-Pepper Miso (*Kochu jang;* p. 155). Try also Finger Lickin' Miso.

Egg & Miso Domburi

SERVES 4 TO 5

1 tablespoon oil
⅔ cup grated carrot
1 small onion, minced
1 cup green peas or minced green peppers
3 tablespoons red, barley, or Hatcho miso, thinned in ¼ cup water
2½ teaspoons honey or 1½ tablespoons natural sugar
1½ cups brown rice, cooked (p. 116)

Heat a skillet or wok and coat with the oil. Add carrot, onion and green peas, and sauté for 4 to 5 minutes. Add thinned miso and honey, and cook, stirring constantly, until most of the liquid has been absorbed or evaporated. Add eggs and cook, stirring constantly, for about 2 minutes, or until firm. Divide hot rice among large individual bowls and spoon on the egg-and-miso topping. Serve hot or cold.

Rice Patties

Rice Patties with Miso (O-musubi or O-nigiri)

MAKES 9

1½ tablespoons red, barley, or Hatcho miso
6 *umeboshi* salt plums, pitted and minced (optional)
3 tablespoons bonito flakes or grated cheese
    (optional)
2 cups brown rice, cooked (p. 116), then cooled for
    5 minutes; or use 5 cups leftover rice
3 sheets of *nori,* toasted (p. 108) and each cut into
    6 squares

Combine the first three ingredients, mixing well. (Or use only the miso.) Add to the rice, mixing lightly with a wooden spoon or spatula. Moisten hands in cold water (to prevent sticking) and shape rice into 9 triangular wedges or patties, pressing each firmly, as illustrated. Lay a *nori* square over both of the large surfaces of each pattie, then press edges and corners of *nori* against rice. (Keep your hands lightly moistened at all times.) Serve patties arranged on a large platter garnished with parsley sprigs or use in box lunches.

VARIATIONS

*Substitute for the red miso mixture ¼ cup Sesame Miso (p. 130), Sweet Simmered Miso (p. 125), or Finger Lickin' Miso (p. 75). If desired, mix with 10 to 15 minced green beefsteak leaves.
*Omit *nori* and roll patties in roasted (whole or ground) sesame seeds.
*Form the miso or miso mixture into 9 small balls and press one ball into the center of each rice pattie.
*Broiled Rice Patties *(Yaki-musubi):* Make rice patties using the crisp, golden-brown rice from the bottom of the cooking pot. Spread the surface of each pattie with a thin layer of miso (omitting *nori*), then broil quickly over an open flame until miso is fragrant.
*Crisp Rice Patties: Deep-fry or pan-fry patties in hot oil until crisp and golden brown (p. 361). Serve hot or cold.

Fried Miso-and-Rice Patties

SERVES 4

4 cups cooked (or leftover) Brown Rice (p. 116)
¼ cup diced leeks or scallions
¼ cup red, barley, or Hatcho miso
2 tablespoons oil

Combine the first three ingredients, mixing well, and shape into eight patties. Heat one-half the oil in a large skillet. Add four patties and fry on both sides until golden brown and fragrant. Repeat with remaining ingredients.

For variety, roll patties in 2 tablespoons roasted sesame seeds (or mix 2 tablespoons sesame butter into the miso) before frying.

Brown Rice with Mushrooms and Miso *(Chameshi)*

SERVES 3 OR 4

Also called *Takikomi-gohan,* this richly-flavored, popular dish is frequently prepared with chestnuts, chicken, crab, or shrimp used in place of the mushrooms and green peas.

1½ cups brown rice, rinsed and drained
1⅔ cups water or green tea
5 (*shiitaké* or *matsutaké*) mushrooms, thinly sliced
½ cup fresh green peas
2 tablespoons red, barley, or Hatcho miso
2 teaspoons *mirin,* sake, or white wine
Minced parsley or trefoil (optional)

Combine all ingredients in a pressure cooker; mix briefly. Proceed as for Brown Rice (p. 116). Serve hot, topped if desired with a sprinkling of parsley.

For a simpler preparation, combine 1½ tablespoons red miso with the rice and water, and proceed as for Brown Rice.

VARIATION

*Brown Rice with Chestnuts and Miso *(Miso Kuri Kinton):* Substitute ½ cup whole or halved fresh or dry chestnut meats for the mushrooms and peas.

Thick Miso Shake with Brown Rice

SERVES 3

2 cups carrot-, tomato-, or mixed vegetable juice
¾ cup cooked Brown Rice (p. 116)
1 tablespoon red, barley, or Hatcho miso
Dash of oregano or pepper (optional)
¼ cup (toasted) wheat germ (optional)
1 teaspoon lemon juice (optional)

Combine all ingredients in a blender and purée for 2 to 3 minutes, or until creamy and thick. If desired, chill before serving.

Zosui or Ojiya (Rice Gruel)

SERVES 1 OR 2

Zosui, which means "a variety of things cooked together," is a popular way of using leftover rice (or rice porridge) and miso soup or clear soup served daily in most Japanese homes. In times of war or famine when rice was scarce, Zosui was daily fare; prepared with a large proportion of broth, it served to fill the belly and ward off hunger. Today, in times of abundance, thick Zosui served piping hot is still a wintertime favorite, prized for its ability to warm body and soul.

Known colloquially (and in Tokyo) as *Ojiya,* it originated at an early date in China, where more than 100 varieties were developed as part of that country's elaborate Congee or Rice Porridge Cuisine. During the 15th century, it became a popular dish throughout Japan, served on January 7, the last day of the New Year's season. Its preparation, using the "seven spring herbs," "newly drawn water," and miso, was transformed into a lovely ceremony linked to the zodiacal hours. One who added each freshly gathered wild herb at its propitious hour and served the dish "before the Chinese white eagle flies overhead" (a euphemism for diseases feared brought to Japan from the Chinese mainland), was said to be given by the gods an additional 8,000 years of happy life—and

made instantaneously 70 years younger. To this day
it is thought to be good insurance against colds and
the flu, even in the midst of the influenza season. The
proportions of rice and soup can be varied considerably depending on the amounts of leftovers.

1½ cups Miso Soup (p. 253)
1 cup cooked Brown Rice (p. 116) or Rice Porridge
     (p. 287)

Bring miso soup to a boil in a saucepan. Mix in the
rice and return to the boil. Cover and simmer for
15 to 30 minutes, or until rice is soft.

For variety, just before removing from heat, stir
in diced tofu, leftover vegetables or tempura, and/or
eggs. Season to taste with 7-spice red pepper or grated
gingerroot. Garnish with crumbled, toasted *nori*, powdered green *nori*, slivered leeks or citrus rind, or
minced parsley. Serve immediately.

Miso Gruel with Leftovers

Gruel is an ancient preparation designed to create
continually new and tasty combinations of foods while
simultaneously preventing waste.

Combine all leftover cooked grains, vegetables,
and tofu or other soybean foods in a large, heavy pot.
Add enough leftover soup, stock, or water to give the
consistency of a thick stew; bring to a boil and simmer for 5 to 10 minutes. Add creamed miso and, if
desired, curry powder or ketchup to unify the flavors.
To thicken, stir in lightly roasted whole-wheat flour
or barley flour and cook for several minutes more.
Serve hot or cold. To use leftover gruel as the basis
for full-bodied breads, knead in flour to earlobe consistency, allow to rise overnight, and bake in a slow
oven for several hours.

Ochazuké with Miso Toppings

MAKES 1 SERVING

If you're in a hurry or want to make a quick, light
meal (or when there is leftover rice which you don't
have time to reheat), this impromptu dish is ideal.

In Japan, some people also like to make Ochazuké using the rice remaining in their bowls toward the end of a meal, and many restaurants even feature Ochazuké as their specialty. Its most popular accompaniments are *takuan* (or other salt-pickled vegetables) and *tsukudani* (slivers or 1-inch squares of *kombu,* beefsteak seeds, tiny dried fish, etc., which have been simmered in a salty mixture of shoyu and *mirin*). Various types of miso are used as toppings. Although each person prepares Ochazuké at the table, using ingredients and proportions to taste, the method might look like this in recipe form:

½ to 1 cup cooked (leftover) rice
Miso Toppings (listed in order of popularity): Use 1
    to 2 teaspoons of any one of the following
        Thinly sliced Miso Pickles (p. 385)
        Broiled Miso (p. 111)
        Finger Lickin' Miso (p. 75)
        Sweet Simmered Miso (p. 125)
        Miso Sauté (p. 150)
        Hoba Miso (p. 158)
¼ to 1 cup very hot green tea
1 tablespoon crumbled, toasted *nori* (p. 108) or bonito
    flakes (optional)

Place rice in individual bowls and top with miso. Pour on hot tea, then press miso into rice with tips of chopsticks. Cover and allow to stand for several minutes. Sprinkle with *nori,* then sip the broth alternately with bites of rice.

Bibimpap

SERVES 6

This famous Korean rice dish, seasoned with fiery hot Red-Pepper Miso *(kochu jang)* and topped with sautéed vegetables, is served on special occasions in much the same way as its relative, Five-Color Sushi, is served in Japan. Since the method of preparation is quite detailed and varies widely from chef to chef, we will present it here in a concise outline form.

Prepare 2 paper-thin omelets (p. 118) and reserve.

Cut 2 cucumbers into thin rounds and rub lightly with salt. Allow to stand for 20 minutes, then rinse. Sauté rounds for 3 minutes in sesame oil together with a little minced leek, ground sesame seeds, and red pepper.

Parboil 3 cups soybean sprouts for 10 minutes in lightly salted water. Drain sprouts, then sauté for 4 minutes in the same mixture of ingredients used with the cucumbers.

Sauté 9 thinly sliced mushrooms (or Osmund ferns) in the same mixture to which has been added a little natural sugar and crushed garlic.

Place 5 cups cooked brown rice in a large, shallow bowl. Atop rice arrange sautéed vegetables, slivered omelets, slivered almonds, and crumbled deep-fried *kombu* or toasted *nori*. Accompany rice with a small cup filled with (homemade) Red-Pepper Miso (p. 155). Invite each guest to transfer his choice of vegetables and rice to his individual plate, then top the combination with a small dab of the miso.

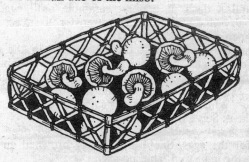

MISO WITH NOODLES

Noodles are among the most easily digestible of all foods and can serve as a central element in a meatless diet. For best nutritive value, look for noodles rich in whole-wheat, unrefined buckwheat, or soy flours.

Richly-flavored *soba* or fat *udon;* Italian spaghetti or crinkly Chinese *ramen;* winter noodles steaming

hot or summer noodles in chilled broth; stir-fried noodles in savory sauces, and deep-fried noodles, brittle,
crisp, and golden brown; homemade or leftover noodles in soups, sauces, and casseroles. Oodles of possibilities, each made more tasty and nutritious by the
use of miso.

Stir-fried Buckwheat Noodles with Miso

SERVES 4

3 tablespoons oil, preferably used deep-frying oil
5 eggs, lightly beaten
¼ teaspoon salt
Pepper
1 onion, thinly sliced
10 ounces Chinese cabbage
3½ tablespoons red, barley, or Hatcho miso
6 to 7 ounces (soba) buckwheat noodles, cooked
   (p. 201)
¾ cup grated or Parmesan cheese (optional)

Heat 1 tablespoon oil in a wok or skillet. Add eggs,
salt and a dash of pepper; scramble until eggs are
fairly dry and crumbly, then transfer to a separate
container and reserve.

Heat the remaining 2 tablespoons oil in the wok.
Add onion and cabbage, and sauté for 3 minutes.
Add miso and cook, stirring constantly, for 1 minute
more. Mix in cooked eggs, noodles and, if desired, the
cheese. When noodles are heated through, remove
from heat. Serve hot or cold.

For variety, substitute 10 ounces diced deep-fried
tofu for the eggs. Sauté until nicely browned and increase the miso to 5 tablespoons.

Bamboo noodle tongs

Soybeans, Miso, and Sautéed Vegetables with Noodles

SERVES 4

2½ cups Pressure Cooked Soybeans (p. 317;
     unseasoned), drained
3 tablespoons red, barley, or Hatcho miso
2 tablespoons oil
1 clove of garlic, minced or crushed
1½ cups shredded cabbage
1 cup thinly sliced leeks or onions
½ cup grated carrot
6½ ounces (buckwheat or Chinese) noodles, cooked
     (p. 201)
1½ tablespoons shoyu
Dash of pepper (optional)

Combine cooked soybeans and miso, mixing well and
mashing half the beans; set aside. Heat a large wok
or skillet and coat with the oil. Add garlic and sauté
for 30 seconds. Add cabbage, onions and carrot, sauté
for 4 minutes more, and turn off heat. Add soybeans,
mixing until evenly distributed. Stir in noodles, sprinkle with shoyu, and season with pepper; mix lightly.
Delicious hot or cold.

Buckwheat Noodles in Miso-Soymilk Sauce

SERVES 2

1½ cups milk (soy or dairy)
1 small onion, diced
1 tablespoon red, barley, or Hatcho miso
2 tablespoons sweet white miso, or 1 tablespoon
     red miso
2 tablespoons Better Butter (p. 119) or butter
½ cup grated cheese or 2½ tablespoons sesame
     butter
3½ ounces (soba) buckwheat noodles, cooked
     (p. 201) and well drained
Dash of pepper (optional)
2 tablespoons minced parsley or ground roasted
     sesame seeds (p. 207)
Crumbled toasted *nori* (optional)

Combine milk and onion in a large saucepan and bring to a boil over medium heat, stirring constantly. Stir in miso creamed in a little of the hot liquid. Add butter, cheese and noodles, and return to the boil, then season with pepper and remove from heat. For best flavor, allow to stand for several hours. Serve as is or reheated, garnished with parsley and, if used, the *nori*.

For variety, combine all ingredients in a casserole and bake at 350°F for about 20 minutes, or until nicely browned.

Noodles Topped with Miso Sauces

SERVES 4

7 to 8 ounces buckwheat or whole-wheat noodles, cooked (p. 201)
Miso Sauce: Use 2 to 4 cups of any of the following (pp. 270 to 286):
    Miso Onion Sauce
    Miso Mushroom Sauce
    Miso Spaghetti Sauce
    Miso White Sauce
    Miso Curry Sauce
    Miso Gravy
    Spicy Indonesian Peanut Sauce
    Sesame Miso Sauce
Garnishes and seasonings:
    Crumbled, Toasted Nori (p. 108)
    Sambals (p. 280)
    Roasted (whole or ground) sesame seeds (p. 107)
    Thinly sliced Miso Pickles (p. 385)
    7-spice red pepper

Arrange hot or cold noodles in individual or serving bowls. Spoon on the sauce and serve accompanied by garnish.

Deep-fried Noodles with Miso Sweet & Sour Sauce

SERVES 4

6 ounces noodles
Oil for deep-frying
3 cups Pineapple Sweet & Sour Sauce (p. 276)

Cook noodles (p. 201), then drain in a colander for about 1 hour. Heat the oil to 350°F in a wok, skillet, or deep-fryer. Place about ¼ cup noodles on a spatula and slide into the oil. Deep-fry for about 30 seconds (p. 361), then turn and deep-fry for 30 seconds more, or until crisp and golden brown; drain well. Repeat until all noodles are used. Divide noodles among individual plates, top with the sauce, and serve immediately.

Also good with most of the sauces enumerated in Noodles Topped with Miso Sauces (above).

Noodles Cooked with Miso & Milk

SERVES 2

1½ cups milk (soy or dairy)
3½ ounces (*soba*) buckwheat noodles, cooked (p. 201)
2 tablespoons Better Butter (p. 119) or butter
⅓ cup grated cheese (optional)
3½ tablespoons red, barley, or Hatcho miso
2 tablespoons minced parsley or ground roasted
     sesame seeds (p. 107)
Crumbled, toasted *nori* (optional)

In a large pot, bring milk just to a boil over medium heat, sitrring constantly. Add cooked noodles, butter, cheese, and miso creamed with a little of the hot milk. Return to the boil, then set aside to cool until milk clabbers. Serve garnished with the parsley and *nori*.

For variety, combine ¼ cup diced onion with the milk in the pot before heating.

Buckwheat Noodles with Miso Dipping Sauce

SERVES 5 OR 6

2 tablespoons sweet white miso
4 tablespoons shoyu
1 tablespoon honey
2 tablespoons *mirin,* dry sherry, or white wine
2 tablespoons sesame butter or ¼ cup ground
    roasted sesame seeds (p. 107)
2 cups dashi (p. 112), stock, or water
⅓ cup thinly sliced leeks or scallions
Dash of (7-spice) red pepper
8 to 10 ounces (*soba*) buckwheat noodles, cooked
    (p. 201)

Combine the first five ingredients in a pot or large
skillet and cook, stirring constantly, for about 1 minute, or until smooth. Stir in dashi and bring to a boil.
Remove from heat and allow to cool, then divide
among individual bowls. Place noodles on plates or in
a large bamboo colander. Invite guests to garnish dipping sauce to taste with leeks and red pepper. Dip
noodles into sauce to serve.

VARIATION

Miso Tanuki Soba: Prepare the dipping sauce using 9 to 10 tablespoons red miso, 4½ cups dashi
and, if desired, 1 tablespoon natural sugar and 2 tablespoons sake, white wine, or *mirin.* Pour hot broth over
noodles in individual bowls, garnish and season
as above, then top each portion with ¼ cup of
agédama, tiny particles of deep-fried tempura batter
skimmed off during the deep-frying process or specially prepared for this dish.

Nikomi-udon (Homemade Noodles Simmered in Miso)

SERVES 6

In this popular miso preparation, the water in which
the noodles are cooked is not discarded, but is used as
the basis for a thick miso sauce that closely resembles

a Western-style white sauce. For best flavor, allow this dish to stand overnight so that the noodles further contribute to the thickening of the sauce. Serve either cold or reheated.

2 cups flour, half of which is whole-wheat
8½ cups warm water
¼ teaspoon salt
5 tablespoons sweet white or 3 tablespoons mellow white miso
3 tablespoons red, barley, or Hatcho miso
3 large leeks, cut diagonally into 2-inch lengths
1½ small leeks or scallions, cut into thin rounds
7-spice red pepper
Crumbled, toasted *nori* (optional)

Put the 2 cups flour into a large bowl and, adding ½ cup water a little at a time, mix and knead to form a heavy dough. Roll out dough on a floured breadboard to ⅛-inch thickness, sprinkle surface lightly with flour, and fold lengthwise accordion fashion into quarters. Now cut dough crosswise into ⅛-inch-wide strands to make noodles. Spread noodle strips on the floured board to dry briefly.

Bring the remaining 8 cups water to a boil in a large pot. Drop in noodles and salt, and cook until noodles float to surface. Add miso creamed with a little of the hot water, then add large leeks and simmer for 10 minutes. Remove from heat and allow to stand as long as overnight. Serve garnished with thin rounds of leeks, red pepper, and *nori*.

To save time, use about 10 ounces dried noodles in place of the homemade variety. In some parts of Japan, *daikon,* mushrooms, taro, carrots, and deep-fried tofu are parboiled or simmered in sweetened shoyu broth, then added to the noodles together with the miso. Result: A thick noodle-and-vegetable stew.

Homemade noodles

Miso Ramen

SERVES 2 OR 3

A favorite at Japan's thousands of small restaurants specializing in Chinese-style *ramen* noodles, this preparation is usually made with a chicken-based broth and served steaming hot. Sapporo Miso Ramen, the most famous variety, is named after the city in Hokkaido, Japan's northernmost island, where this dish is said to have originated.

3½ ounces (Chinese) noodles
1 tablespoon sesame oil
1 clove of garlic, minced or crushed
1½ cups bean sprouts
½ cup thinly sliced leeks or onions
3 tablespoons red, barley, or Hatcho miso
1 tablespoon shoyu
2½ cups stock or dashi (p. 112)
Dash of (7-spice) red pepper or Tabasco sauce
1 tablespoon dry (cloud-ear) mushroom, reconstituted
    (p. 105) and minced

Cook noodles (p. 201), drain, and reserve. Heat a skillet or wok and coat with the oil. Add garlic and sauté for 30 seconds. Add bean sprouts and leeks and sauté for 3 minutes more. Dissolve miso and shoyu in ½ cup stock and add to skillet together with red pepper and mushrooms; bring to a boil. Add remaining dashi and return to the boil, stirring constantly.

Place noodles in a strainer and dip briefly into boiling water until warmed through. Mound in deep bowls, then pour on the vegetables-and-broth.

Noodles Cooked with Miso (Misoyaki Udon)

SERVES 4

6 tablespoons sweet white miso or 3 tablespoons red miso
7 tablespoons dashi (p. 112), stock, or water
1 tablespoon shoyu
2½ tablespoons *mirin,* sake, or white wine
1½ tablespoons oil
1 small onion, thinly sliced
2 to 3 ounces deep-fried tofu or 4 to 6 mushrooms, thinly sliced
1½ teaspoons grated or minced gingerroot
3½ ounces (*udon* or *soba*) whole-wheat or buckwheat noodles, cooked (p. 201) and drained

Combine the first four ingredients, mixing well. Heat the oil in a pot or large skillet. Add onion, deep-fried tofu and gingerroot, and sauté over medium-high heat for 2 to 3 minutes. Stir in the miso-dashi mixture and cooked noodles, cover, and return to the boil. Lower heat and simmer for 10 to 15 minutes. Serve hot or cold.

Chilled Noodles with Mustard-Vinegar Miso (Sumiso Udon)

SERVES 4

7 ounces noodles, cooked (p. 201), drained and chilled
½ cup Sweetened Mustard Vinegar Miso (p. 137)
1 cucumber, slivered
1 tomato, cut into thin wedges
1 egg, hard-boiled and cut into thin wedges

Place chilled noodles into a large serving bowl. Spoon miso into a mound at center of noodles, then arrange garnishes around miso. Invite guests to serve themselves.

Cha-chiang Mien

SERVES 4

One of the most popular ways of using miso in Chinese-style cookery, this tasty dish is usually prepared with chiang (Chinese miso) mixed with bits of pork (or occasionally ground beef) fried in oil and served over crinkly noodles together with a wide variety of toppings and garnishes.

3½ ounces (Chinese or buckwheat) noodles, cooked
    (p. 201)
Garnishes: Any or all of the following
        2 cups bean sprouts, quickly parboiled
        2 cucumbers, slivered
        2 eggs made into paper-thin omelets, cooled
           and slivered (p. 118)
        6 mushrooms or 2 leeks, thinly sliced and
           sautéed in butter
Chinese-style Nerimiso (p. 126)

Place noodles, individual garnishes and the miso in separate serving bowls. Invite each guest to serve himself with noodles and preferred garnish, then miso. Mix well.

MISO WITH OTHER GRAINS

Miso with bulgur wheat and tortillas, *mochi* and French toast; miso toppings with oatmeal, cornmeal, and cream of wheat. All offer many delicious possibilities. For corn-on-the-cob, see page 354.

In Japan, miso rice crackers (*miso senbei*) and sweet miso rolls topped with sesame seeds (*miso pan*) are both sold commercially. In each case, red miso is simply mixed with a sweetened rice-flour or wheat-flour dough and then baked.

Curried Bulgur Pilaf with Cheese and Miso

SERVES 2 OR 3

Bulgur wheat—also known as couscous—is prepared by partially cooking, drying, and then cracking whole-grain wheat. A popular ingredient in Near Eastern and North African cuisines, it needs little cooking and has a pleasant, nutty flavor. In the West, it is now widely known as Ala.

2 tablespoons butter
½ cup bulgur wheat
1 small onion, thinly sliced
1 small carrot, slivered or diced
1 cup water or stock
½ teaspoon curry powder
1½ tablespoons red, barley, or Hatcho miso
2½ tablespoons Parmesan or grated cheese
1 tablespoon minced parsley

Melt the butter in a skillet. Add bulgur and onion, and sauté for 4 to 5 minutes. Add water and curry powder, cover, and bring to a boil. Simmer for 15 minutes, or until all liquid has been absorbed. Stir in miso and cheese, and remove from heat. Serve hot or cold, garnished with parsley.

Tabbouli with Miso
(Bulgur Salad with Mint and Lemon)

SERVES 4 TO 6

1 cup bulgur wheat or couscous
¾ cup lemon juice
¾ cup very finely minced parsley
2 tablespoons minced fresh mint, or 3 tablespoons
    dried mint flakes reconstituted in 2 tablespoons
    hot water
3 tomatoes, minced
½ green pepper, chopped fine
6 to 8 tablespoons olive oil
1 teaspoon red, barley, or Hatcho miso, dissolved in
    2 teaspoons warm water

Combine the bulgur and lemon juice, mix lightly, and allow to stand for 1 hour. Stir in the remaining ingredients and, for best flavor, allow to stand for at least several hours, preferably 2 to 3 days. Delicious served chilled.

French Toast with White Miso & Raisins

SERVES 2

½ cup milk (soy or dairy)
1 egg, lightly beaten
2 tablespoons sweet white or 4 teaspoons mellow
    white miso
1½ teaspoons honey
¼ cup raisins
2 large slices of whole-wheat bread cut into fourths
2 tablespoons Better Butter (p. 119) or butter
Dash of cinnamon

Combine the first five ingredients in a shallow pan,
mixing until smooth. Add bread and allow to stand for
3 to 5 minutes. (For very firm or unyeasted bread,
soak for 1 hour.) Melt the butter in a large skillet.
Add bread, spoon on any raisins remaining in pan,
and cook for 2 to 3 minutes on each side, or until
nicely browned. Serve topped with a sprinkling of
cinnamon.

Cornmeal Spoonbread with Miso

MAKES 1 LOAF

Rich as cheesecake, this delicious loaf separates
into three decorative layers. The miso lends its own
savory flavor while the combination of soy, corn, and
milk boosts the total protein content by up to 13 percent.

½ cup cornmeal
¼ cup whole-wheat flour
1 teaspoon baking powder
1½ cups milk (soy or dairy)
1 egg, lightly beaten
1 tablespoon honey
1½ tablespoons red or barley (or 3 tablespoons
    mellow white) miso
¼ cup raisins
2 tablespoons Better Butter (p. 119) or butter

Preheat oven to 375°F. Combine the first three ingredients, sifting or mixing well. Combine 1 cup milk

with the next four ingredients, mixing until miso is dissolved, then stir into the flour mixture and beat until well blended. Melt butter in a loaf pan. Pour in batter and top with the remaining ½ cup milk. Bake for 45 minutes. Serve buttered, piping hot or, for a richer sweeter flavor, chilled.

Natural Rise Miso Bread

MAKES 1 LOAF

Here is a simple, natural, and easy way to make a light, self-rising bread without the use of yeast. For each loaf of bread, simply substitute 2 tablespoons of unpasteurized red, barley, or Hatcho miso for the yeast. Reduce the salt called for in your recipe to one-fourth or less of the suggested amount. Knead the dough 300 times, allow it to proof overnight at room temperature (70°F), knead again 150 times, then bake as required.

Hot Cereals with Miso Toppings

MAKES 1 SERVING

1 to 1½ cups freshly cooked rolled oats, oatmeal, cornmeal, rice cream, or cream of wheat
1 to 1½ tablespoons of any of the following (pp. 127-131):
    Peanut or Peanut & Raisin Miso
    Sesame Miso
    Walnut, Cashew, or Sunflower Seed Miso
Dash of salt
1 tablespoon butter (optional)
¼ cup nuts, raisins, and/or granola (optional)
¼ to ½ cup warm milk (soy or dairy) (optional)

Serve hot cereal in a large bowl, topped with a dab of miso and seasoned with salt. Add butter, nuts, and milk if desired; mix lightly.

Broiled Mochi with Sweet Miso and Nori

SERVES 2 TO 4

8 cakes of *mochi,* each about 3 by 2 by ¾ inches
8 teaspoons Better Butter (p. 119) or butter
4 teaspoons honey (optional)
2 teaspoons grated gingerroot (optional)
8 teaspoons of any one of the following:
    Sweet Simmered Miso (p. 125)
    Finger Lickin' Miso (p. 75)
    Sweet White Miso
8 pieces of *nori,* each 3 by 6 inches

Broil *mochi* cakes on both sides in an oven broiler or
on a grill until cakes are crisp, nicely browned, and
puffed to twice their original thickness. Slit one end of
each cake and fill with butter, honey and gingerroot.
Spread both sides of cakes with the miso, wrap in a
sheet of *nori* and serve hot.

If *nori* is not available, use miso as part of the filling. Or omit honey and grated gingerroot, and fill
mochi with 8 teaspoons Gingerroot Mixed Red Miso
(p. 151) combined with ¼ cup grated *daikon.*

VARIATION

*Mochi in Miso-Ankaké: Broil *mochi* cakes as above.
Place 2 cakes in each of four bowls and top with about
¼ cup of any of the following: Miso-Gingerroot
Ankaké Sauce (p. 271), Miso-Lemon Ankaké Sauce
(p. 271), Miso-Gingerroot Sauce (p. 284).

Broiled Mochi with Nori

Millet or Buckwheat Pilaf

SERVES 4

3 tablespoons Better Butter (p. 119) or butter
½ cup millet or buckwheat groats (kasha)
1 onion, minced
1 tablespoon red miso, dissolved in 1 cup boiling
    water
¼ teaspoon oregano
Dash of pepper (optional)

Melt the butter in a heavy skillet. Add millet and onion, and sauté until golden brown. Add remaining ingredients, cover, and bring to a boil. Reduce heat and simmer for 30 to 35 minutes. Delicious topped with Garbanzo-Tahini Sauce (p. 277) or Gado-gado (p. 279).

Buckwheat Groats Medley with Miso

SERVES 4

1 cup buckwheat groats (kasha)
1 tablespoon oil
1 carrot, diced, slivered, or grated
¼ cup chopped hazel- or Brazil nuts
¼ cup sunflower seeds
¼ cup roasted sesame seeds
1 banana, sliced into thin rounds
1 apple, diced
1 pear, diced
Seeds from 1 cardamom, crushed
Dash of cinnamon
1 tablespoon red or barley miso; or 2 tablespoons
    mellow white miso
½ cup apple juice

Dry roast buckwheat groats until fragrant and nicely browned. Heat a skillet and coat with the oil. Add groats and the next ten ingredients and sauté for 10 minutes. Dissolve miso in apple juice, add to contents of skillet, and sauté for 1 minute more. Serve hot or chilled topped with applesauce, yogurt, kefir, or ricotta cheese. Or use as is like granola.

Crisp Tortillas with Taco Sauce (Tostadas)

SERVES 5

Miso can serve as a delicious complement to the simple, natural flavors of these grain-based "platters" so widely used throughout Latin America and India.

10 seven-inch *tortillas*
Better Butter (p. 119) or butter
1¼ cups Miso Taco Sauce (p. 275)
2 tomatoes, diced
2½ cups shredded lettuce, sprouts, or cabbage

Heat *tortillas* in a medium oven for 5 to 7 minutes, or until lightly browned and crisp. (Or deep-fry in hot oil.) Butter one side of each *tortilla*, then spread with the sauce and top with tomatoes and lettuce.

For a meatier flavor, mix 10 to 15 ounces thinly sliced deep-fried tofu with the lettuce. Serve topped with a little grated cheese and Tabasco sauce.

Other preparations with Tortillas, Chapaties, Tacos, or Puries

*With Butter and Mixed Miso: Butter warm *tortillas* well, then coat one surface with a thin layer of Finger Lickin' Miso, sweet white miso, Mixed White Miso Topping with Parmesan (p. 152), or Mixed Cheese Miso (p. 154).
*Miso-filled Puries: Deep-fry *tortillas* (or puri dough) in hot oil until they swell and turn golden brown. Fill with butter, honey, gingerroot, and miso as for Broiled Mochi (p. 312).
*Tacos with Miso & Salads: Bake or deep-fry *tortillas* until crisp. Top with thinly sliced lettuce, tomatoes, deep-fried tofu and grated cheese. Spoon on Floating Cloud (p. 186) or your favorite miso dressing.
*With Miso Spreads: Top individual (warm) *tortillas* with ¼ to ½ cup Azuki-Miso (p. 183) or Soybean-Sesame-Miso (p. 183), or any of your other favorite miso spreads. Roll before eating.

*Serve miso-seasoned vegetable or grain dishes atop *tortillas*.

Chinese Pancake Rolls with Miso Sauce

SERVES 4

This recipe is closely related to the famous Peking Duck also served with miso (*t'ien mien chiang*) in tender, thin pancake rolls. In China, these *chapati*-like pancakes are usually prepared in the kitchen, fried in a dry skillet and steamed in large bamboo steamers. Since the process is complex, this recipe calls for ready-made *tortillas*.

4 teaspoons oil
4 eggs, lightly beaten
1 cup thinly sliced leek rounds
1½ cups bean sprouts
2 green peppers, thinly sliced
Miso Sauce:
      3½ tablespoons red, barley, or Hatcho miso
      4 teaspoons honey
      2 tablespoons sesame oil
      1 teaspoon soy sauce
      2 tablespoons water
½ large tomato, cut into thin wedges
½ small onion, minced
12 wheat-flour *tortillas*, warmed (preferably steamed)

Heat a skillet and coat with 1 tablespoon oil. Add eggs and leeks, and scramble until firm. Transfer to a small serving bowl.

Reheat skillet and coat with remaining 1 teaspoon oil. Add sprouts and green peppers, and sauté for 2 to 3 minutes. Transfer to a second serving bowl.

Combine ingredients for the sauce in a third (small) bowl; mix well. Place tomato wedges and minced onions on small plates. Fold warm *tortillas* into quarters and place on the dining table together with the sauce and fillings. Invite each guest to open a pancake, coat upper surface with sauce, and top with fillings. Roll pancake around fillings and eat like a sandwich or *taco*.

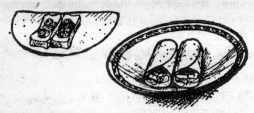

Mock Peking Duck

Miso-filled Rolled Breads

MAKES 2 LOAVES

Dough for 2 loaves of bread (reduce salt content to
     1 teaspoon)
¼ cup red, barley, or Hatcho miso
¼ cup honey
2 tablespoons butter or sesame butter
¾ cup raisins
1 apple, cut into very thin wedges; or 1 large banana,
     cut into thin rounds
½ cup chopped nutmeats (walnut or almond)

Roll out dough into two long rectangles, each about
8 inches wide and ⅜ inch thick. Combine miso,
honey, and butter, mixing well, then spread in an even
layer over upper surface of each rectangle. Top with a
sprinkling of raisins, apple wedges and, if used, nutmeats. Roll each rectangle from one end to form a
compact cylinder. Place into oiled loaf pans and bake
at 350° for about 45 minutes, or until nicely browned.
Allow to cool thoroughly. Serve with butter.

Mock Peking Duck

SERVES 2

   This delicacy is the prized creation (and most expensive item) in many fine Chinese restaurants. Thin
slices of duck with lacquer-crisp skin are rolled up in
paper-thin wheat-flour "doilies" (each 6 inches in diameter) or folded in steamed *litus* buns together with
slivered leeks (or scallions) and *t'ien mien chiang* (or

hoishin sauce). The following is a vegetarian version of the original using ingredients more readily available in the West.

4 *tortillas,* cut into halves and warmed in a steamer
Butter
10 ounces deep-fried tofu cutlets, cut into 4-inch-long
   strips
2 or 3 tablespoons *t'ien mien chiang* (homemade,
   p. 154 or commercial, p. 535)
1 leek or 3 green onions, cut into 4-inch slivers,
   soaked in water for 5 minutes and drained

Butter warmed *tortillas* lightly on one side. Divide tofu among *tortillas,* placing the strips in the center of each *tortilla* half perpendicular to the *tortilla's* cut edge. Spread the *t'ien mien chiang* on the tofu, then top with a sprinkling of the leek slivers. Roll up and, if desired, secure with a foodpick. Serve while *tortillas* are still warm.

MISO WITH SOYBEANS AND TOFU

The use of miso (or shoyu) is one of the keys to seasoning soybeans and the more than eight varieties of Japanese and Chinese tofu described in *The Book of Tofu.* Tofu and soybeans are also used in a number of recipes throughout the preceding sections of this book. Topped with or added to Miso Sauces, especially Sweet & Sour, Gingerroot, or White Sauce, deep-fried or regular tofu is at its very best. For miso with high-protein soybean spreads, see page 182.

Pressure Cooked Soybeans with Miso

MAKES 2¼ CUPS

1 cup dry soybeans, rinsed and soaked for 2 to 3 hours
   in 2 quarts water
2 cups water
A thin wedge of lemon or lime (optional)

Drain and rinse soaked beans, and combine with 2 cups water in a pressure cooker. Bring to full pressure (15 pounds) and simmer for 25 minutes. Remove from heat and allow to stand for 10 to 15 minutes as pressure returns to normal. Cool lid under cold running water and open.

Return cooker to stove, stir in any of the ingredients listed below, and simmer uncovered for 10 to 15 minutes, or until flavors are nicely married. If necessary, add ¼ cup water during simmering. Stir from time to time. Serve hot or cold.

*2 tablespoons red, barley, or Hatcho miso (creamed with a little of the cooking liquid). If desired, add 1 teaspoon lemon juice and/or 1 tablespoon butter. For a deliciously rich flavor, add 1 (sautéed) minced onion together with the miso and stir in ½ cup grated cheese or ¼ cup Parmesan just before removing from heat.

*1½ tablespoons red miso, 3 tablespoons sesame butter or *tahini,* 3 to 4 tablespoons dry *hijiki* or slivered *kombu* (reconstituted, p. 105), or 1 onion or ¾ cup carrot (pre-sautéed in 1 tablespoon oil, if desired). For extra sweetness, add 1½ teaspoons honey or natural sugar.

*1 to 1 ½ tablespoons red miso and 2 to 3 tablespoons molasses or honey.

*1 tablespoon red miso and ¼ cup sesame butter or *tahini.*

*1 tablespoon red miso and ½ to 1 cup total of the following (added alone or in combination): diced tomatoes, onions, carrots, celery, mushrooms, lotus root, burdock root, sprouts, fresh or dried *daikon,* or *kombu.* For variety add ½ teaspoon curry powder and/or 1 clove of crushed garlic.

*In any of the above recipes, after the beans and seasonings have finished cooking, try sautéing the mxiture for a few minutes in a little (sesame) oil.

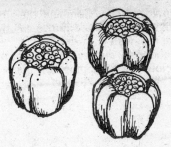

Green Peppers Stuffed with Miso-Soybeans

SERVES 6

1 cup dry soybeans, cooked (p. 317) and drained
2 tablespoons red, barley, or Hatcho miso
¼ cup ketchup
½ onion, minced
2 tablespoons dark brown sugar
1½ to 2 teaspoons mustard
½ cup grated cheese
3 green peppers, seeded and parboiled in salted
      water for 5 minutes
1 tablespoon oil

Preheat oven to 350°F. Combine the first seven ingredients, mixing well, then use to fill green pepper
shells. Rub shells lightly with oil, place in an oiled
pan, and bake for 20 minutes. Serve hot or chilled.

Other delicious fillings for green pepper shells include Refried Pinto Beans (p. 325), and Boston
Baked Soybeans.

Savory Soybean, Corn & Miso Casserole

SERVES 4

1¼ cups cooked soybeans (p. 317), drained
1¼ cups cooked corn
1 tomato, diced
¼ cup ketchup
1½ tablespoons red, barley, or Hatcho miso
½ teaspoon honey
¼ onion, minced
¼ cup chopped peanuts or bread crumbs

Preheat oven to 350°F. Combine the first seven ingredients, mixing well. Place into a lightly oiled baking dish and top with a sprinkling of peanuts. Bake
covered for about 45 minutes. Serve hot or chilled.

Also delicious as a topping for plain or stir-fried
brown rice (pp. 287 and 289).

Corn & Soybean Succotash

SERVES 3

Here's a delicious, high-protein favorite of the
American Indians with soybeans used in place of the
traditional lima beans, and miso in place of salt.

2 tablespoons Better Butter (p. 119), butter, or oil
1 cup cooked soybeans (p. 317), unseasoned)
1 cup cooked fresh corn
1 tablespoon red, barley, or Hatcho miso
⅛ teaspoon paprika
1 tablespoon minced parsley

Melt the butter in a heavy skillet or pot. Add corn
and beans, and sauté over low heat for 5 minutes.
Mix in miso, season with paprika, and remove from
heat. Top with a sprinkling of parsley.

For variety, sauté ½ minced onion together with
the corn and/or add ¼ cup grated cheese together with
the miso.

Boston Baked Soybeans with Brown Rice & Miso

SERVES 3

1 cup cooked soybeans (p. 317), drained
2 cups cooked Brown Rice (p. 116)
¼ cup minced onion
2½ tablespoons ketchup
5 teaspoons red, barley, or Hatcho miso
1½ teaspoons honey
2 teaspoons dry mustard
½ cup soybean cooking liquid
¾ teaspoon curry powder
½ teaspoon vinegar
2½ teaspoons Worcestershire sauce

Preheat oven to 250°F. Combine all ingredients, mixing well. Place into a lightly oiled baking dish and bake covered for 30 minutes, then uncovered for 30 minutes more. Delicious hot or chilled.

Miso also makes an excellent substitute for salt in your favorite recipe for Boston Baked Beans.

Soybean & Miso Garnish

MAKES 1 CUP

2 tablespoons sesame oil
1 cup cooked soybeans (p. 317), well drained
2 tablespoons red, barley, or Hatcho miso
½ teaspoon grated gingerroot
Dash of 7-spice red pepper (optional)

Heat a skillet or wok and coat with the oil. Add soybeans and sauté for 2 to 3 minutes. Reduce heat to low, add remaining ingredients, and sauté for 2 minutes more. Allow to cool to room temperature. Serve as a garnish with brown rice or rice porridge.

Tofu with Miso Toppings

SERVES 1

6 to 8 ounces regular or 3 to 5 ounces (lightly-broiled)
 deep-fried tofu
Miso Toppings: Use any of the following
 1 to 2 teaspoons red, barley, or Hatcho miso
 1 tablespoon Sweet Simmered Miso (p. 125),
  Finger Lickin' Miso (p. 75), Miso Sauté
  (p. 139), Mixed Miso (p. 150), or Broiled Miso
  (p. 156); or, for use only with deep-fried
  tofu, Vinegar Miso (p. 137) or Daikon Mixed
  Miso (p. 151)
 1½ tablespoons sweet white or red miso
Garnishes: Use ½ to 1 teaspoon of any of the follow-
 ing (optional)
 Thinly sliced leeks
 Grated gingerroot
 Minced or crushed garlic
 Wasabi
 Slivered lemon, lime, or yuzu rind

Place tofu on a plate and coat its upper surface with
your choice of topping. If desired, cut into bite-sized
pieces and serve topped with the garnish.

Tofu with Miso-Onion Sauce and Cheese

SERVES 4 TO 6

2 tablespoons oil
6 onions, thinly sliced
6 tablespoons red, barley, or Hatcho miso
1½ teaspoons honey
1 tablespoon sake or white wine
24 ounces tofu, cut into bite-sized cubes
2 ounces grated cheese
2 eggs, lightly beaten
2 to 3 tablespoons Parmesan cheese (optional)

Heat a large casserole or pot and coat with the oil. Add
onions, cover, and cook over very low heat for 1½
hours, stirring occasionally. Mix in miso, honey and
sake, then carefully add tofu cubes, covering them by

spooning onion sauce over the top. Cover pot and simmer for 10 minutes. Gently mix in grated cheese and pour egg over the top. Re-cover and simmer for 5 minutes more, or until egg is firm. Sprinkle with Parmesan if desired and allow to stand, covered, overnight. Serve as is or reheated.

Tofu with Miso White Sauce Au Gratin

SERVES 3

1 tablespoon oil
1 clove of garlic, crushed or minced
2 small onions, thinly sliced
⅓ cup grated cheese
7½ ounces deep-fried tofu, cubed; or 18 ounces regular tofu, pressed (p. 109) and cubed
1 cup Miso White Sauce (p. 272; season with 2 tablespoons red miso)
2 tablespoons Parmesan cheese
1 tablespoon bread crumbs

Preheat oven to 350°F. Heat the oil in a skillet or wok. Add garlic and sauté for 15 seconds. Add onions and sauté for 3 minutes more. Remove from heat, stir in grated cheese and tofu, then spoon into a loaf pan or casserole. Pour on the white sauce and top with a sprinkling of Parmesan and bread crumbs. Bake for about 20 minutes, or until nicely browned. Delicious either hot or cold.

Steamed Miso-filled Tofu (Nanzenji no Tsutsumi-dofu)

SERVES 4

24 ounces tofu
¼ to ½ cup Yuzu Miso (p. 131) or any Sweet Simmered Miso (p. 125)

Cut tofu into four 6-ounce pieces. With the sharp point of a knife, cut a section 2 inches square and 1 inch deep from the larger surface of each piece, and lift out carefully. Fill the "well" that remains with 1 or 2 tablespoons of the miso, then replace the small piece of tofu atop the miso. Wrap each piece of tofu in strong, absorbent paper (the Japanese use *washi* for this purpose) or in aluminum foil.

Bring water to a boil in a steamer. Place wrapped tofu in steamer and steam for 5 to 10 minutes, or until miso is well heated. Serve hot, inviting each guest to unwrap his or her portion just before eating.

Steamed Tofu

Deep-fried Tofu with Gingerroot Miso

SERVES 2 OR 3

1½ tablespoons oil
10 ounces deep-fried tofu, cut into bite-sized
        rectangles ½-inch thick
2 tablespoons red, barley, or Hatcho miso
1 tablespoon honey
1 teaspoon grated gingerroot
Minced parsley or whole lettuce leaves

Heat a skillet or wok and coat with the oil. Add deep-fried tofu and sauté over high heat for 3 to 4 minutes until slightly crisp and well browned. Add miso, honey, and gingerroot and cook, stirring constantly, for 2 to 3 minutes, or until all ingredients are well mixed. Serve hot or cold garnished with the parsley or placed on individual lettuce leaves.

MISO WITH OTHER BEANS

Mexican-style Pinto Beans with Miso *(Frijoles de Olla)*

SERVES 6 TO 8

2 cups pinto beans, washed and soaked overnight in
    9 cups water
1 onion, minced
3½ tablespoons red, barley, or Hatcho miso
Dash of cumin seeds and/or ground red pepper
    (optional)
½ to 1 cup grated or Parmesan cheese

Place beans and water in a casserole or heavy pot and
bring to a boil. Reduce heat to very low, cover, and
simmer for 1½ hours. Add onion, miso and cumin
seeds, then simmer for 30 minutes more, or until beans
are tender. Serve in soup bowls, topped with a sprinkling of the cheese.

Refried Pinto Beans with Sour Cream and Miso
(Frijoles Refritos)

SERVES 3

In Mexico, the leftovers from a large pot of *Frijoles
de Olla* (above) are usually served at the next meal
prepared in the following manner:

2 tablespoons oil
1 clove of garlic, minced or crushed
½ onion, minced
2 cups *Frijoles de Olla* (without cheese), drained of
    excess liquid
¼ to ½ cup grated cheese
½ cup sour cream
2 teaspoons red, barley, or Hatcho miso

Heat a skillet and coat with the oil. Add garlic and
onion, and sauté for 1 minute. Add beans, mash well
with a fork, and sauté for about 3 minutes, or until
slightly dry and crisp. Combine cheese, sour cream
and miso, mixing well, then stir into the beans and
remove from heat. Delicious served as a side dish, in
tortillas or as a spread.

Miso in Baked Dishes

More of our very favorite recipes appear among the following than in any other section of this book. Almost all are Western-style preparations and many contain grains as the basic ingredient.

Baked Potatoes in Miso Gravy

SERVES 6 TO 8

3¾ pounds potatoes (6 to 8), each peeled and cut into fourths
1 cup vegetable stock or water
3½ tablespoons Better Butter (p. 119) or butter
3½ tablespoons red, barley, or Hatcho miso
3½ tablespoons honey
1 tablespoon shoyu (natural soy sauce)

Preheat oven to 450°F. Place potatoes in a greased casserole. Mix remaining ingredients in a bowl or blender and pour over the potatoes. Cover and bake for 30 minutes. Mix well. Re-cover and bake for 30 minutes more. Serve hot or cold.

Rich Noodle Casserole
with Miso-Sour Cream and Chives

SERVES 5 TO 6

1 cup sour cream
3 tablespoons red, barley, or Hatcho miso
2 eggs, lightly beaten
6 tablespoons minced chives
1½ cups cottage cheese
4¼ ounces (soba) buckwheat noodles, cooked, drained and cooled (p. 201)
2 to 3 tablespoons Better Butter (p. 119) or butter

Preheat oven to 350°F. Combine the first five ingredients, mixing well, then gently stir into the cooked noodles. Place into a buttered casserole and top with dabs of the remaining butter. Bake covered for 20 minutes, then uncover and bake for about 15 minutes more, or until nicely browned.

Miso-Onion Soup Casserole Au Gratin

SERVES 5 TO 6

2½ to 3 cups bread cubes (fresh, stale, or croutons)
4 cups Thick French Onion Soup with Miso (p. 253)
6 tablespoons Parmesan or grated cheese

Combine bread and soup, mixing well, and spoon into a lightly oiled or buttered loaf pan or casserole; allow to stand for 1 to 2 hours. Preheat oven to 350°F. Sprinkle casserole with cheese and bake for about 20 minutes, or until nicely browned. Serve hot or cold.

Mushroom Casserole with Miso

SERVES 5

3 tablespoons Better Butter (p. 119) or butter
4 cups sliced mushrooms (12 ounces)
6 slices of whole-wheat bread, buttered and broken
　　　into bite-sized pieces
½ cup minced onion
½ cup minced green pepper
½ cup minced celery
3½ tablespoons red, barley, or Hatcho miso
1 cup milk (soy or dairy)
4 eggs, lightly beaten
¼ cup mayonnaise
Dash of pepper (optional)

Melt the butter in a skillet. Add mushrooms and sauté for 3 minutes, then transfer to a large buttered casserole. Add bread and minced vegetables. Cream miso with a little milk, then combine with the remain-

ing ingredients, stirring vigorously until smooth. Add
to casserole and mix with vegetables and bread. Smooth
surface of ingredients, cover, and refrigerate for 6 to
8 hours. Bake in a preheated 325°F oven for 50
minutes.

Cheese Casserole with Red Miso

SERVES 6

3 tablespoons Better Butter (p. 119) or butter
3 to 4 tablespoons red, barley, or Hatcho miso
6 slices of whole-wheat bread
12 ounces cheese, grated or broken into small pieces
4 eggs, lightly beaten
2½ cups milk (soy or dairy)
Dash of pepper (optional)

Spread 2½ tablespoons of the butter and 2 tablespoons of the miso on the bread slices, then break
bread into small pieces. Butter a casserole with remaining ½ tablespoon butter. Add consecutive layers
of bread and cheese, using two layers of each. Combine remaining 1 to 2 tablespoons miso with the eggs,
milk and pepper. Mix well, then pour into the casserole and allow to stand for at least 1 hour. Bake uncovered in a pan of water at 350°F for about 45
minutes.

Potatoes with Miso White Sauce Au Gratin

SERVES 3

1½ teaspoons oil
1 onion, thinly sliced
1 cup Miso White Sauce (p. 272), seasoned with dill
   if desired
3 potatoes, boiled and cubed (2 to 2½ cups)
¼ cup grated cheese
1½ teaspoons Better Butter (p. 119) or butter
1½ tablespoons bread crumbs
1½ tablespoons Parmesan cheese

Preheat oven to 400°F. Heat a skillet and coat with
the oil. Add onions and sauté for 3 minutes. Prepare
Miso White Sauce, then mix in the potatoes, onions,

and grated cheese. Spoon into a buttered loaf pan or casserole, dot with butter, and sprinkle with bread crumbs and Parmesan cheese. Bake for 10 to 15 minutes, or until nicely browned. Serve hot or, for a richer flavor, refrigerate overnight and serve cold.

For variety, substitute squash or (*kabocha*) pumpkin for the potatoes.

Potatoes Baked in Miso Gravy Au Gratin

SERVES 3 OR 4

4 small potatoes, boiled in their skins until tender and
    cut into bite-sized pieces
2½ cups Miso Gravy (p. 278)
2 tablespoons Parmesan cheese

Preheat oven to 350°F. Combine potatoes and gravy in an oiled loaf pan or casserole and top with a sprinkling of cheese. Bake for about 20 minutes, or until nicely browned. Delicious hot or cold.

Quiche Niçoise with Miso

SERVES 6

A 9-inch pie shell
6 tablespoons (olive) oil
1 onion, minced
4 tomatoes, diced
2 large cloves of garlic, minced
1 teaspoon basil
1 teaspoon thyme
1½ teaspoons red, barley, or Hatcho miso
Dash of pepper, coarsely ground (optional)
3 eggs
3 tablespoons tomato paste
¼ cup chopped parsley
Dash of cayenne or Tabasco sauce
8 black olives, thinly sliced (optional)
½ cup Parmesan cheese

Bake pie shell at 425°F for 7 minutes until partially done, then set aside. Heat skillet and coat with 4 tablespoons oil. Add onions and sauté for 4 minutes, or until tender. Add the next six ingredients, cover and cook over low heat for about 5 minutes. Uncover and cook 5 minutes more, or until liquid has evaporated, then set aside to cool for 10 minutes. Meanwhile, combine the eggs in a mixing bowl with the last four ingredients plus 2 tablespoons olive oil; beat until smooth. Gently stir in cooked ingredients, then spoon mixture into pie shell. Decorate, if desired, with olive slices, sprinkle with cheese, and dribble the remaining 1 tablespoon oil over the top. Bake at 375°F for about 25 minutes, or until quiche has set. Delicious hot or cold.

Quick Cheese & Onion Quiche with Miso

SERVES 6

2 teaspoons oil
¾ onion, thinly sliced
A 9-inch pie shell, uncooked
4 eggs, one of which is separated into yolk and white
6 ounces Swiss cheese, grated
¾ cup half-and-half cream
1½ teaspoons red miso, creamed in 1 tablespoon
      hot water
Dash of nutmeg

Preheat oven to 350°F. Heat a skillet and coat with the oil. Add onions and sauté for about 3 minutes, or until limp. Line a 9-inch pie pan with the pastry shell, then brush lightly with egg white. Place alternate layers of onion and cheese in shell until both ingredients are used up. Mix together remaining eggs, cream, and softened miso; pour over cheese-and-onions, then top with a sprinkling of nutmeg. Bake for 45 minutes.

Miso-Noodle Gratin

SERVES 4 TO 6

5 tablespoons Better Butter (p. 119) or butter
⅔ onion, thinly sliced
4 small mushrooms, sliced
5 ounces deep-fried tofu, thinly sliced (optional)
2½ tablespoons red, barley, or Hatcho miso
7 ounces (*soba*) buckwheat noodles or macaroni,
    cooked
Dash of pepper (optional)
3 tablespoons whole-wheat flour
2 cups milk (soy or dairy)
2 tablespoons grated cheese
2 tablespoons bread crumbs or bread crumb flakes
2 tablespoons minced parsley

Preheat oven to 350°F. Melt 4 teaspoons butter in a
skillet. Add onion and sauté for 1 minute. Add mushrooms and deep-fried tofu, and sauté for 2 minutes
more. Stir in 1½ teaspoons miso, the cooked noodles, and pepper; sauté for 1 minute more and remove from heat.

Using 3 tablespoons butter, the flour, 2 tablespoons miso and the milk, prepare a Miso White
Sauce (p. 272). Stir in the noodle-vegetable mixture,
then transfer to a lightly buttered gratin dish, casserole,
or baking pan. Sprinkle with cheese and bread crumbs,
and dot with the remaining 2 teaspoons butter. Bake
for 15 minutes, or until lightly browned. Serve topped
with a sprinkling of minced parsley.

Noodles & Eggs with Miso White Sauce Au Gratin

SERVES 3

2 tablespoons Better Butter (p. 119) or butter
1 onion, thinly sliced
1 cup Miso White Sauce (p. 272; seasoned with
    1½ tablespoons miso)
3 ounces (buckwheat) noodles, cooked (p. 201),
    drained, and cut into 4-inch lengths
3 hard-boiled eggs, shelled and cut lengthwise into
    halves
2 tablespoons Parmesan cheese
2 tablespoons minced parsley

Preheat oven to 350°F. Melt the butter in a skillet, add
onion, and sauté for 4 minutes. Remove from heat,
combine with noodles and one-half the white sauce,
and spoon into an oiled casserole or loaf pan. Arrange egg halves atop noodles, top with remaining
white sauce, and sprinkle with Parmesan; bake for 20
minutes or until nicely browned. Delicious either hot
or chilled, topped with a sprinkling of parsley.

Tomatoes Stuffed with Eggs and Miso

SERVES 4

2 large, firm tomatoes, unpeeled
2 hard-boiled eggs, diced
¼ cup bread crumbs
1 tablespoon red, barley, or Hatcho miso
1 tablespoon minced parsley
1 tablespoon Better Butter (p. 119) or butter
Dash of pepper (optional)
3 tablespoons Parmesan cheese

Preheat oven to 350°F. Slice off tops of tomatoes
and scoop out insides, reserving one half of the latter
for use in other cooking. Combine the remaining
scooped-out portion with the diced eggs and the next
five ingredients. Add 1 tablespoon Parmesan cheese
and mix well, then use mixture to stuff tomatoes. Place
tomatoes in an oiled loaf pan, sprinkle with the remaining 2 tablespoons Parmesan, and bake for 20

minutes. Cool to room temperature before serving.

For variety, pour 1 cup Miso White Sauce (p. 272; seasoned with 4 teaspoons red miso) over tomatoes in loaf pan. Top with the Parmesan and 2 tablespoons bread crumbs, then bake until nicely browned.

Miso-Creamed Celery Casserole

SERVES 4 TO 6

2 cups sliced celery stalks and leaves
2 cups water or stock
6 tablespoons Better Butter (p. 119) or butter
6 tablespoons flour
¼ cup red, barley, or Hatcho miso
2 cups milk (soy or dairy)
Dash of pepper (optional)
4 slices whole-wheat bread (preferably several
    days old)
¼ cup grated or Parmesan cheese; or ¼ to ½ cup
    sherry, sake, or white wine

Combine celery and water in a saucepan, bring to a boil, and simmer uncovered for 10 to 12 minutes. Cool briefly, then purée in a blender until smooth.

Preheat oven to 350°F. Melt ¼ cup butter in a large saucepan, then use the flour, 2 tablespoons miso, milk, puréed celery, and pepper to make a Miso White Sauce (p. 272); remove from heat.

Spread 2 tablespoons each butter and miso over one surface of each piece of bread. Break bread into small chunks and place into a lightly buttered casserole. Pour in white sauce and allow to stand for 1 to 2 hours. Top with the cheese or sherry, and bake uncovered for 30 minutes, or until nicely browned.

Cooked rice or noodles may be substituted for the bread, and the 2 tablespoons miso and butter may be added directly to the white sauce.

Curried Green Rice Casserole with Miso

SERVES 3

2 eggs, lightly beaten
¾ cup milk (soy or dairy)
2½ to 3 tablespoons red, barley, or Hatcho miso
2 cups cooked Brown Rice (p. 116)
½ cup minced parsley
½ cup grated cheese
1 onion, minced
¼ teaspoon curry powder
1 clove of garlic, crushed or minced
1 tablespoon Better Butter (p. 119) or butter

Preheat oven to 325°F. Combine the eggs, milk and miso, mixing well, then stir in the next six ingredients. Coat a casserole or baking tin with the butter and spoon in the curried-rice mixture. Bake for about 40 minutes, or until nicely browned. For best flavor, allow to cool for 6 to 8 hours. Serve hot or cold.

For variety, sauté onion for several minutes before use and/or substitute ½ cup corn kernels for one-half the onion.

Baked Potatoes with Miso

2 potatoes, baked in their skins
2 tablespoons Better Butter (p. 119) or butter
2 teaspoons of one of the following:
    Red, barley, or Hatcho miso
    Finger Lickin' Miso (p. 75)
    Leek or Onion Miso (pp. 136 and 140)
    Cheese Miso (p. 154)
Sour Cream or Creamy Tofu Dressing (with Cheese & Garlic, p. 193) (optional)
Minced chives, grated cheese, or parsley (optional)

Cut open the hot potatoes and spoon in butter and miso. Mix lightly, and, if desired, top with sour cream and chives. Serve hot or cold.

Or, substitute 4 teaspoons mellow white miso for the miso above.

Miso Sautéed and Simmered with Vegetables

The recipes that follow are only a few of many delicious possibilities. Experiment using our basic techniques applied to your favorite vegetable cookery.

SAUTÉED PREPARATIONS

Most types of Japanese-style miso topping—especially Sesame Miso (p. 130), Walnut Miso (p. 128), and Miso Sauté (p. 150)—make excellent additions to sautéed vegetable dishes. Note the use of miso in the cooking technique called *nitsuké* wherein vegetables are first sautéed until just barely tender, then steamed or simmered in a little water—and miso— until done.

Mushrooms Sautéed in Miso

SERVES 2 OR 3

1 tablespoon oil
12 fresh (*shiitaké*) mushrooms, cut into halves or
    quarters
1 tablespoon red, barley, or Hatcho miso
1 to 1½ teaspoons honey
1 teaspoon shoyu
¼ teaspoon freshly grated or ½ teaspoon powdered
    gingerroot (optional)
1 tablespoon ground roasted sesame seeds (p. 107)
    (optional)

Heat a skillet and coat with the oil. Add mushrooms
and sauté for 2 to 3 minutes. Stir in the next three
(or four) ingredients and sauté for 1 minute more.
Serve hot or cold, topped, if desired, with a sprinkling
of sesame seeds.

VARIATION

*Eggplants Sautéed in Miso. Use 4 small Japanese
eggplants, cut lengthwise into halves, then diagonally
into ⅜-inch-thick slices. Sauté in 2 tablespoons oil
over medium heat for 5 minutes, then reduce heat to
low and proceed as above.

Miso-Cooked Carrots with Wheat Germ and Nuts

SERVES 2 OR 3

2 tablespoons oil
1 carrot, sliced into thin rounds (1½ cups)
4 teaspoons red, barley, or Hatcho miso, thinned with
   3 tablespoons water
¼ cup (toasted) wheat germ
¼ cup sunflower seeds or chopped nutmeats
½ teaspoon grated orange rind (optional)

Heat the oil in a wok or skillet. Add carrots and sauté
for 3 minutes. Mix in creamed miso and cook for
4 minutes, or until liquid is absorbed or evaporated.
Remove from heat and stir in remaining ingredients.
Serve hot or cold.

Eggplants Szechwan

SERVES 4

3 tablespoons oil
4 small eggplants (about 12 ounces total), cut into
    ½-inch cubes
1 clove of garlic, minced or crushed
1½ teaspoons minced gingerroot
3 tablespoons chopped leek greens or green onions
Dash of (7-spice) red pepper or Tabasco sauce
½ cup stock or water
2 tablespoons red, barley, or Hatcho miso
½ teaspoon honey
1½ teaspoons sesame oil
1½ teaspoons vinegar

Heat a skillet and coat with the oil. Add eggplants
and sauté for 3 minutes, then drain briefly over skillet
and transfer to a separate container. Now add to the
skillet: garlic, gingerroot, 2 tablespoons chopped leek
greens, and enough red pepper to give a spicy hot
flavor; sauté for 15 seconds. Mix in stock, miso and
honey, and bring to a boil. Add eggplants, simmer for
1 minute, and turn off heat. Sprinkle with sesame oil
and vinegar, and garnish with the remaining 1 tablespoon chopped leek greens.

Eggplant with Sesame & Miso Sauce

SERVES 4

6 tablespoons oil
2½ to 3 cups eggplant (¾-inch cubes)
3 tablespoons red, barley, or Hatcho miso
2 tablespoons sesame butter
1 tablespoon honey
1 tablespoon white wine, sake, or *mirin*
6½ tablespoons stock or water
½ teaspoon grated or 1 teaspoon powdered
    gingerroot
4 lettuce leaves

Heat a wok or skillet and coat with 5 tablespoons oil.
Add eggplants and sauté for 3 to 4 minutes, then
transfer to a separate container.

Reheat skillet and coat with remaining 1 tablespoon oil. Add miso and the next 5 ingredients. Cook, stirring constantly, for 1 to 2 minutes to form a smooth sauce. Mix in cooked eggplant and remove from heat. For best flavor, serve chilled, mounded on lettuce leaves.

Cauliflower & Carrots with Miso & Cheese

SERVES 2 OR 3

2½ tablespoons Better Butter (p. 119) or butter
½ cup thin rounds of leek or scallion
2 tablespoons red, barley, or Hatcho miso
½ cauliflower, separated into flowerets, steamed for
      10 minutes
1 carrot, cut into thin half moons and steamed for
      15 minutes
3 tablespoons grated cheese
2 tablespoons minced parsley
Dash of pepper (optional)

Melt the butter in a skillet. Add leek rounds, miso, and steamed vegetables, and sauté for 2 to 3 minutes. Turn off heat and top immediately with cheese and parsley. Season with pepper. Serve hot.

Sautéed Leeks & Carrots with Sesame Miso

SERVES 3 OR 4

¼ cup sesame butter
3 tablespoons red, barley, or Hatcho miso
2 tablespoons water
2 teaspoons oil
2½ cups thinly sliced leeks or onions
1 cup slivered or grated carrots

Combine the first three ingredients, mixing well. Heat oil in a skillet or wok. Add leeks and carrots and sauté for 4 to 5 minutes. Add sesame-miso mixture and cook, stirring constantly, for 1 minute more. Serve as is, or as a topping for grain dishes or tofu.

Green Peppers & Tofu Sautéed with Miso

SERVES 2

3½ tablespoons red, barley, or Hatcho miso
½ cup stock or water
2½ to 3 teaspoons honey
2 teaspoons sake or white wine
7 ounces deep-fried tofu, cut into ½-inch strips
2 tablespoons oil
1½ teaspoons minced garlic
5 green peppers, cut lengthwise into sixths
1 large onion, thinly sliced

Combine the first five ingredients in a saucepan and
bring to a boil. Cover and simmer for 5 minutes, then
remove from heat.

Heat a wok or skillet and coat with the oil. Add
garlic and sauté for 30 seconds. Increase heat to
high, add green peppers and onion, and sauté for
3 minutes more. Add deep-fried tofu and any remaining cooking broth, then cook, stirring constantly, for
1 minute. Serve hot or cold.

Green Beans & Onions in Spicy Miso Sauce

SERVES 3

1 tablespoon oil
1 clove of garlic, minced or crushed
½ onion, thinly sliced
20 green beans, parboiled until just tender
1½ tablespoons red, barley, or Hatcho miso,
        dissolved in ½ cup water or stock
¾ teaspoon honey
1½ teaspoons sake or white wine
Dash of (7-spice) red pepper or Tabasco sauce
2 teaspoons cornstarch, arrowroot, or *kuzu* (kudzu
        powder), dissolved in 3 tablespoons water

Heat a wok or skillet and coat with the oil. Add garlic
and sauté for 30 seconds, then add onion and sauté
for 4 minutes. Add green beans and sauté for 1 minute more. Stir in the next four ingredients and bring
to a boil. Add dissolved cornstarch and simmer, stir-

ring constantly, for about 1 minute, or until thick.
Serve as a side dish or as a topping for (deep-fried)
noodles.

Potatoes Sautéed with Miso

SERVES 4

1½ to 2 tablespoons oil
6 small potatoes, sliced into thin rounds (3½ cups)
½ cup water
2 tablespoons red, barley, or Hatcho miso
Dash of pepper (optional)
2 tablespoons minced parsley and/or grated cheese

Heat a large skillet or wok and coat with the oil. Add
potatoes and sauté for 4 minutes. Add water, cover,
and simmer for 5 to 6 minutes. Mix in miso and cook,
stirring constantly, for 1 to 2 minutes, or until most
of liquid has evaporated. Serve seasoned with pepper
and topped with parsley.

Sweet & Sour Cabbage with Miso

SERVES 2 OR 3

1½ teaspoons oil
1 red pepper, seeded and minced
11 ounces cabbage, chopped into 1½-inch squares
2½ tablespoons red, barley, or Hatcho miso
1 teaspoon honey
2 teaspoons vinegar
2 teaspoons sesame oil

Heat a wok or skillet and coat with the oil. Add red
pepper and sauté for 30 seconds, or until color
changes. Add cabbage and sauté for 3 to 4 minutes,
then add the next three ingredients and sauté for 1
minute more. Sprinkle with the sesame oil and remove from heat. Serve hot or cold.

Land & Sea Vegetables with Miso

SERVES 4

2 tablespoons sesame oil
1 large onion, thinly sliced
1 carrot, grated or slivered
1 cup thin half-moons of lotus root
¾ cup dry *hijiki*, soaked for 15 minutes in water to
      cover, rinsed and drained
2½ tablespoons red, barley, or Hatcho miso
¾ cup water

Heat a skillet or wok and coat with the oil. Add
onion, carrot, and lotus root and sauté for 4 minutes.
Add *hijiki* and sauté for 3 minutes more. Stir in miso
and water and bring to a boil. Cover and simmer for
10 minutes. Serve hot or cold.

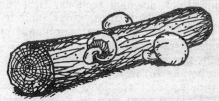

Cultivated shiitaké

FRIED AND STIR-FRIED PREPARATIONS

Fried Eggplants Shigiyaki
(Nasu no Nabé Shigiyaki)

SERVES 4

One of Japan's favorite miso recipes, this is a close
relative of the equally popular Grilled Eggplants
Shigiyaki described on page 360. The key to the fine
flavor lies in choosing tender young eggplants.

4 Japanese eggplants, each 1¼ inches in diameter,
    or 2 small Western eggplants
2 tablespoons red, barley, or Hatcho miso
1 tablespoon honey
1½ teaspoons sake or white wine
¼ teaspoon grated gingerroot
1 tablespoon water
3 to 4 tablespoons oil
1 to 2 teaspoons roasted sesame seeds or Parmesan
    cheese

Peel eggplants lengthwise so that ½-inch-wide peeled
strips alternate with ½-inch-wide unpeeled strips.
Soak in water for 10 minutes.

Meanwhile combine miso, honey, sake, gingerroot
and water in a small skillet and simmer over low heat,
stirring constantly, for 3 to 4 minutes until smooth
and slightly thickened. Remove from heat.

Pat eggplants dry with a dishtowel. Cut Japanese
eggplants lengthwise into halves, Western eggplants
into ½-inch-thick diagonal sections. Heat the oil in
a skillet. Add eggplant slices, cover, and fry for 2
minutes or until golden brown. Turn and repeat on
second side. Arrange slices on a large serving plate,
spread with the miso sauce and sprinkle with sesame
seeds. For best flavor, serve chilled.

For variety, cut eggplants into ¾-inch-thick
rounds and pierce each side in 2 or 3 places with
chopsticks or a fork. Fry in oil as above, then serve
topped with White Nerimiso (p. 127) or Kinomé Miso
(p. 133), and, if desired, a sprinkling of roasted sesame
seeds.

Fried Eggplants with Sweet Simmered Miso
(Yaki-nasu)

SERVES 4

4 small eggplants, each about 4 inches long
1½ tablespoons sesame oil
2 tablespoons Sesame- (p. 130) or Walnut Miso (p. 128)

Cut eggplants lengthwise into halves and score the
outer surfaces in a checkerboard pattern to a depth of

⅓ inch. (If using larger Western eggplants, cut into ¾-inch-thick half moons.) Heat a skillet and coat with the oil. Add eggplants and fry over low heat on both sides until nicely browned. Coat flat surface with a thin layer of miso. Serve hot or cold.

Deep-fried Tofu and Vegetables with Miso-Sweet & Sour Sauce

SERVES 4 TO 5

2 tablespoons oil
1 clove of garlic, crushed or minced
1 small onion, thinly sliced
2 tomatoes, diced; or 1 cup cherry tomatoes, cut into halves
1 green pepper, cut into 1-inch squares
1½ cups Pineapple Sweet & Sour Sauce (p. 276)
7 ounces deep-fried tofu, cut into 1-inch cubes

Heat the oil in a large skillet or wok. Add garlic and onion, and stir-fry over high heat for 2 minutes. Add tomatoes, green pepper and sauce. Cook, stirring constantly, for about 1 minute until thick. Mix in deep-fried tofu and remove from heat. Serve chilled. (To serve hot, increase amount of honey and vinegar in sauce by 1 tablespoon each.)

Fried Sweet Potatoes with Sesame Miso

SERVES 2 OR 3

1 sweet potato (6 inches long)
2 teaspoons oil
2½ to 3 tablespoons Sesame Miso (p. 130)

Steam sweet potato for 30 minutes, then cut into ½-inch-thick rounds. Heat oil in a large skillet. Add rounds and fry for 2 minutes on each side, or until nicely browned. Transfer onto absorbent paper (or a large plate) and allow to cool for several minutes. Coat one surface of each round with the miso. Serve as a side dish or hors d'œuvre.

NABÉ AND SIMMERED PREPARATIONS

Miso is used as the basis for the dipping sauce in a number of Japan's famous *nabémono,* the do-it-your-self one-pot cookery prepared at the table. In dishes known as *Misoni,* vegetables (or seafoods) are simmered slowly in a rich, slightly sweet miso sauce. Most Miso Sauces (p. 270) or Toppings (p. 124) can be used with excellent results over vegetables simmered until tender in dashi or stock.

Kabocha Simmered in Miso (*Kabocha no Miso-ni*)

SERVES 4

2 tablespoons sesame oil
2 onions, thinly sliced
1 pound *kabocha,* pumpkin, or squash, cubed
1 cup water
¼ cup red, barley, or Hatcho miso, thinned in ½ cup
     warm water

Heat a wok or skillet and coat with the oil. Add onions and sauté for 5 minutes. Add pumpkin and sauté for 3 minutes more. Stir in water and bring to a boil. Cover and simmer for 30 minutes, or until tender. Stir in thinned miso and simmer uncovered for about 5 minutes, or until liquid has been absorbed or evaporated.

VARIATION

*Other Types of Miso-ni: Substitute for the *kabocha* in the above recipe an equal weight of any of the following: potatoes or sweet potatoes, red radishes, turnips, bamboo shoots, butterbur. Serve hot or cold.

Taro or Sweet Potatoes Simmered in Miso

SERVES 4

1 pound peeled taro or unpeeled sweet potatoes, cut into bite-sized pieces
3 tablespoons red, barley, or Hatcho miso
1 to 1½ tablespoons honey
1¼ cups water, stock, or dashi (p. 112)
3 tablespoons bonito flakes

Combine all ingredients in a pot or saucepan, cover, and bring to a boil. Simmer for 15 minutes, then uncover and simmer, stirring occasionally, for 5 to 10 minutes more, or until most of the liquid has evaporated. Allow to cool before serving.

Pumpkin Simmered in Sweetened Miso

SERVES 3 OR 4

14 ounces *kabocha,* pumpkin, or squash, seeded and cut into 1½-inch squares
¾ cup water, stock, or dashi (p. 112)
1½ to 2 tablespoons red, barley, or Hatcho miso
2 to 3 teaspoons honey
1½ tablespoons bonito flakes (optional)

Combine *kabocha* and water in a saucepan and bring to a boil. Cover and simmer for 10 minutes. Stir in remaining ingredients and simmer for about 8 minutes more, or until *kabocha* is tender and all but ¼ cup liquid has been absorbed or evaporated. For richest flavor, serve chilled.

For variety, omit bonito flakes and add 1½ tablespoons butter and a dash of nutmeg. Serve topped with Tofu Mayonnaise (p. 195) and a little minced (fresh) basil or parsley.

Sautéed Potatoes Simmered in Sweet Miso

SERVES 2

1 tablespoon oil
4 small potatoes, cut crosswise into halves, then into
    thin wedges (1¾ cups)
1 tablespoon sweet white or 2 teaspoons mellow
    white miso
1½ teaspoons red or barley miso
½ teaspoon honey
2½ teaspoons sake or white wine
¾ teaspoon minced gingerroot
¼ cup water, stock, or dashi (p. 112)

Heat a skillet and coat with the oil. Add potatoes
and sauté for 3 minutes. Mix in remaining ingredients
and bring to a boil. Cover and simmer over low heat
for 10 minutes. Serve hot or cold.

For variety, substitute eggplants or 5 ounces deep-
fried tofu for the potatoes.

Turnips with Sesame Miso Sauce

SERVES 4

6 small (kabu) turnips, with greens
3 cups dashi (p. 112), stock, or water
⅔ cup Sesame Miso Sauce (p. 282)

Cut turnip roots lengthwise into halves, combine with
dashi in a saucepan, and bring to a boil. Cover and
simmer for 15 minutes, or until tender. Remove from
heat and drain, reserving liquid for use in sauce.

Parboil turnip greens for 2 to 3 minutes in lightly
salted water; drain in a colander. Squeeze to remove
excess liquid, then cut into 1-inch lengths. Divide
leaves and turnip halves among individual bowls and
top with the sauce.

Daikon, radishes, and other root vegetables may be
substituted for the turnips.

Furofuki Daikon

SERVES 4

8 *daikon* rounds, each 2½ to 3 inches in diameter
    and ¾ inch thick
½ cup Orange-Sesame Miso Sauce (p. 277) or
    Subtly Sweet Leek Miso (p. 152)

Combine *daikon* rounds with water (or dashi; p. 112) to cover in a saucepan, bring to a boil, and simmer for 20 to 30 minutes, or until *daikon* is very tender. Drain well and arrange rounds on serving plates. Place a large dollop of the miso atop each round. Serve hot or cold.

For variety, prepare as for Miso Oden (p. 348). Cook 4 *daikon* rounds together with 4 taro and 4 *konnyaku* triangles in a *nabé* pot. Place the miso sauce in a cup at the center of pot and use for dipping.

Daikon Rounds with Orange-Onion Miso

SERVES 2 OR 3

4 teaspoons oil, one of which may be sesame
6 *daikon* or turnip rounds, each 1 inch thick and
    2½ inches in diameter
1 cup water or stock
¼ teaspoon salt
1 onion, minced
1½ tablespoons red, barley, or Hatcho miso
1 tablespoon sesame butter (optional)
½ teaspoon grated orange rind

Heat a large skillet and coat with 1 tablespoon (regular) oil. Add *daikon* and fry for about 2½ minutes on each side, or until nicely browned. Add water and bring to a boil. Cover and simmer for 30 minutes, or until only several tablespoons of liquid remain. Sprinkle rounds with salt and transfer to serving plates; reserve liquid in skillet.

Heat a second small skillet and coat with 1 teaspoon (sesame) oil. Add onion and sauté for 5 minutes, then transfer to the first skillet. Mix in miso and, if used, sesame butter. Bring to a boil and cook, stirring constantly, for about 1 minute. Spoon this sauce over *daikon* rounds and top with a sprinkling of orange rind. Serve hot or cold. Also delicious on toast.

Miso Oden

SERVES 3

In Japan, this popular wintertime dish is sold by street venders out of pushcarts or prepared in homes, particulary on special occasions.

Choose one of the following sauces:
  Orange-Sesame Miso Sauce (p. 277)
  Gingerroot-Miso Barbecue Sauce (p. 284)
  Rich Red Nerimiso (p. 126)
  Yuzu Miso (p. 131)
12 ounces tofu (regular or grilled), cut into 1- by 3- by ½-inch strips
1 cake of *konnyaku*
4 inches large *daikon*, cut into ½-inch-thick half moons
A 5-inch square of *kombu*, wiped clean; or substitute ½ teaspoon salt

Place the miso sauce into a small heat-resistant cup. Spear each tofu strip with two (6-inch bamboo) skewers or a fork. Rub *konnyaku* well with salt, rinse, cut crosswise into ½-inch-wide strips, and skewer each piece. Parboil *daikon,* then skewer each piece.

Place *kombu* in a casserole and set the cup of miso atop it. Arrange skewered ingredients around the cup with handles of skewers resting on rim of casserole (see illustration). Add boiling water to just cover ingredients, return to the boil over medium heat, then simmer for 3 minutes. Dip skewered ingredients into miso sauce before eating.

For variety, add parboiled skewered pieces of cauliflower, potato, sweet potato, yam, or turnip.

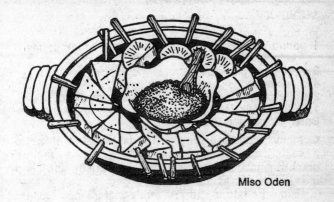

Miso Oden

Eggplants & Corn Simmered in Miso

SERVES 2

2 tablespoons oil
4 small (Japanese) eggplants, uncut and unpeeled; or
     1 medium-sized Western eggplant, cut length-
     wise into fourths
1 cup fresh corn kernels
1½ tablespoons red, barley, or Hatcho miso, dissolved
     in ¾ cup water
1 teaspoon honey
Dash of (7-spice) red pepper or Tabasco sauce

Heat a heavy pot or casserole and coat with the oil.
Add eggplants and fry over low heat for 7 to 8 minutes on each side. Add remaining ingredients and
bring to a boil. Re-cover and simmer for 5 minutes.
Serve hot.

If using Western eggplants, increase oil to 3 tablespoons. Place pieces in pot with skin down and fry for
8 minutes, then fry for 2 minutes on each of the cut
surfaces. Add remaining ingredients and proceed as
above.

Spinach with Miso White Sauce

SERVES 4

¼ cup water
1 pound spinach or *horenso,* washed, tough stems
    removed
3½ tablespoons butter
4½ tablespoons whole-wheat flour
2 tablespoons red, barley, or Hatcho miso
1½ cups milk (soy or dairy)
Dash of pepper (optional)

Combine water and spinach in a large skillet. Bring to
a boil, stirring constantly, and cook for 3 to 4 minutes,
or until spinach is just tender. Drain briefly and chop
into 1-inch lengths.

    Using the butter and remaining ingredients, prepare
a Miso White Sauce (p. 272). Add spinach to the
sauce and serve hot or cold.

Doténabé

SERVES 4

    In Japanese, a *doté* is an earthen embankment or
"shoulder." The reddish-brown miso in this prepara-

tion resembles an embankment around the *nabé's* rim
until, that is, it dissolves into the simmering broth. The
most famous Doténabé contain oysters, for which we
substitute deep-fried tofu.

2½ cups dashi (p. 112) or stock
1 small potato, cut into quarters
⅓ cup shaved burdock root, soaked (p. 104) and
    drained
4 *daikon* rounds, each 2 inches in diameter and
    ½ inch thick
¼ cup red, barley, or Hatcho miso
1 to 1½ tablespoons honey
2½ tablespoons sake, white wine, or *mirin*
1 tablespoon bonito flakes (optional)
½ cake of *konnyaku,* torn into small pieces and
    rubbed lightly with salt
5 ounces deep-fried tofu, cut into 8 pieces
2 hard-boiled eggs, shelled; or 4 quail eggs
1 Chinese cabbage leaf, cut crosswise into 1½-inch-
    wide strips
1 leek, cut diagonally into 2-inch lengths
2 to 3 teaspoons hot mustard
Dash of *sansho* pepper
1 cup cooked noodles (optional)

Combine the first four ingredients in a saucepan and
bring to a boil. Cover and simmer for 15 minutes.
Meanwhile combine the miso, honey, 1 tablespoon
sake and, if used, the bonito flakes in a skillet. Cook
over low heat, stirring constantly, for 2 to 3 minutes,
or until firm.

Ring the inner rim of an 8- to 10-inch diameter casserole or *nabé* pot with a thin, 1-inch-wide layer of
the miso. Transfer cooked vegetables to casserole together with *konnyaku* and the next four ingredients.
Add remaining 1½ tablespoons sake and enough of
the dashi to fill casserole to ¼ inch above bottom of
miso ring. Place casserole on a tabletop burner, cover,
and bring to a boil. Simmer for about 15 minutes, or
until flavors are well married and miso has melted into
broth. Invite each guest to remove ingredients with
chopsticks and transfer them to an individual bowl.
(Cut egg lengthwise into halves.) Spoon on a little of

the hot broth and serve topped with a dab of mustard and a sprinkling of *sansho* pepper.

Toward the end of the meal, drop cooked noodles into broth remaining in casserole and simmer until heated through. Serve in individual bowls, topped with the remaining broth.

For a richer flavor, allow cooked ingredients to stand in *nabé* overnight, then serve the next day, chilled or reheated.

Boiled Potatoes with Onion Miso

SERVES 2

4 small potatoes, boiled in their skins until tender
¼ cup Leek or Onion Miso (p. 136 or 140)
Better Butter (p. 119), Butter, or Parmesan Cheese
    (optional)

Cut potatoes into bite-sized pieces (or mash). Serve hot or cold, topped with the remaining ingredients. A favorite in Japanese farmhouses.

Potatoes Simmered in Miso

SERVES 4

10 small potatoes (1 pound), peeled and cut into
    halves
1¾ cups water
1½ tablespoons bonito flakes
3½ tablespoons red, barley, or Hatcho miso
1 tablespoon honey
1 tablespoon *mirin,* sake, or white wine

Combine the first three ingredients in a large saucepan and bring to a boil. Cover and simmer for 20 minutes, or until potatoes are tender. Mix in the last three ingredients and simmer, uncovered, for 10 minutes more. Cover and allow to stand for at least 4 hours, preferably overnight. Serve cold or reheated.

For variety, deep-fry potatoes (without batter) before simmering. Or substitute for the potatoes 5 small taro (whole) and 2 inches lotus root, the latter cut into ⅜-inch-thick rounds.

Farmhouse Nishime with Miso

SERVES 8

A tasty Japanese vegetable stew, Nishime is a popular dish at New Year's, equinox celebrations, and other national holidays. Farmhouse Nishime often employs homemade miso as the basic seasoning, whereas in restaurants and city homes, shoyu is generally used. Both varieties are usually prepared in large enough quantities to last for up to one week, during which time the flavors marry and improve.

Many recipes include only 3 or 4 of the vegetables listed below; so omit or substitute according to what is available. Adjust the amount of cooking liquid accordingly. Some cooks prefer to cook each of the ingredients separately for a different length of time in a broth seasoned to match the food's unique character. Each cooked ingredient is allowed to marinate overnight in its own broth, but is served without broth in a bowl together with all the other ingredients.

3 cups dashi (p. 112), stock, or water
8 to 10 tablespoons red, barley, or Hatcho miso
3½ to 4½ tablespoons honey or *mirin*
3 tablespoons sake or white wine
½ teaspoon salt
1 cake of *konnyaku,* cut crosswise into ¼-inch-thick pieces
1 carrot, cut into large random chunks
½ burdock root, cut lengthwise into halves, then into 1½-inch lengths and parboiled for 10 minutes
1 large taro or potato, cut into eighths
2 inches *daikon,* cut into half moons
½ lotus root, cut into half moons
8 inches *kombu,* wiped clean with a moist cloth and cut crosswise into 1-inch-wide strips
1 small bamboo shoot, cut into large random chunks
3 (*shiitaké*) mushrooms, cut into quarters
10½ ounces deep-fried tofu, doused (p. 111) and cut into bite-sized pieces
12 ounces tofu, cut into large triangles (optional)
8 sprigs of *kinomé*

Combine the first five ingredients in a large pot or casserole and bring to a boil. Meanwhile, cut a slit lengthwise down the center of each small piece of *konnyaku* and thread one end up through the slit and back again (above). Add *konnyaku* and next eight ingredients to the broth, and return to the boil. Reduce heat to low, cover pot, and simmer for about 40 minutes. Add tofu, stir vegetables so that uppermost ones are transferred to bottom of pot, re-cover, and continue simmering until all but about ¾ cup of broth has been absorbed or evaporated. Remove from heat and allow to cool for at least 5, preferably 24 hours. Divide ingredients among individual serving bowls, pour on remaining liquid, and garnish with a sprig of *kinomé*.

Miso in Grilled Dishes

The process of broiling or grilling miso—especially over a barbecue, campfire, or charcoal brazier—imparts a heartwarming, savory aroma and flavor to both the miso and the food it coats. Why not start by trying a traditional Western favorite, corn-on-the-cob, then move on to shish kebab and Japan's famous Dengaku? See also Broiled Miso Toppings (p. 156).

Grilled Corn-on-the-Cob with Miso

SERVES 2

This savory dish, generally prepared with shoyu rather than miso, is a favorite throughout Japan where it is served freshly grilled from small, sidewalk vending booths.

2 ears of fresh corn
2 teaspoons red, barley, or Hatcho miso
4 teaspoons Better Butter (p. 119) or butter

Grill, broil, or barbecue ears of corn until nicely speckled. Spread on miso using a small rubber spatula or butter knife, then rebroil for about 1 minute until fragrant. Butter corn and serve piping hot.

If you prefer to steam the corn, spread on miso and butter just before serving. For variety, mix about ¼ teaspoon crushed garlic with the miso.

Shish Kebab with Miso Sauce

SERVES 4

Ingredients for Skewering: Use four or more

          5 ounces deep-fried tofu, cut into bite-sized cubes
          4 green peppers, cut into 2-inch triangles
          8 mushrooms
          1 apple, cut into bite-sized chunks or rounds
          8 chunks of firm pineapple
          4 small blanched onions
          4 small firm tomatoes
          1 celery stalk or cucumber, cut into bite-sized sections
¾ cup Miso Shish Kebab Sauce (p. 285) or ⅔ cup Teriyaki Sauce (p. 286)

Place basic ingredients in a shallow pan and pour on sauce. Marinate for 1 hour, turning ingredients several times. Skewer pieces on 4 to 8 skewers and broil for 2 to 3 minutes, basting occasionally, until nicely speckled and fragrant.

Dengaku

SERVES 4

Dengaku, one of Japan's oldest and most famous types of miso cuisine, is prepared by charcoal broiling skewered, bite-sized pieces of various foods. Each piece is then coated on one or both sides with a thin layer of miso and the skewers are rebroiled briefly until the miso is speckled and fragrant. Although the best known type of Dengaku is prepared with small pieces of firmly-pressed tofu, other varieties are made with eggplants, taro, sweet potatoes, mushrooms, and a host of other tasty ingredients listed below. In restaurants, the foods are generally pierced with tiny bamboo skewers, broiled over a charcoal brazier, and topped with one or more types of Sweet Simmered Miso. In farmhouses, the tofu or vegetables are skewered on 18-inch-long slats of bamboo, which are poked at a slant into the ashes around a bed of glowing coals in the living room open-hearth fireplace. A hand's width above the embers, the foods imbibe the fragrance of woodsmoke as they sizzle and broil. Here homemade barley or red miso is often used as the topping.

The two Chinese characters which form the word *Dengaku* mean "rice paddy" and "music." It is said that the name originated about 600 years ago when an ancient form of folk drama consisting of music and dance was popular in Japan's rural villages. In one famous play using a rice paddy as its setting, a Buddhist priest mounted a single stilt (resembling a pogo stick) which was called a "heron's leg." Precariously balanced, this character was called Dengaku Hoshi, and he did a dance known as the *dengaku* or "music in the rice paddy." The newly conceived grilled cuisine, initially prepared by piercing each tofu cake with a single skewer, apparently reminded the people of the dengaku dancer, and the tasty preparation soon became known as Dengaku.

Dengaku first became popular throughout Japan in the early 1600s, and by 1775 it had become fashionable for tea shops and way stations in Tokyo and Kyoto to serve this delicacy, often together with Tea Ceremony Cuisine. Until the late 1900s, many tofu shops prepared and delivered Dengaku to order.

The basic recipe that follows is that for grilled Tofu Dengaku. The use of other basic ingredients and cooking techniques are described as variations. Additional variations on the basic Tofu Dengaku method can be found in *The Book of Tofu*.

Miso Topping: Use a total of ¼ to ½ cup of one or
more of the following types of Sweet Simmered
Miso (p. 125):
  Red or White Sweet Simmered Miso
  Yuzu or Lemon Miso
  Kinomé or Egg Yolk Miso
  Sesame or Walnut Miso; or a Nut Butter Topping
12 to 24 ounces tofu, pressed (p. 109)
Garnishes (optional):
  Sprigs of *kinomé*
  Slivered *yuzu* or lemon rind
  Poppy seeds, roasted sesame seeds, or wheat
    germ
  Hot mustard

Prepare the miso topping(s) in advance and allow to
cool. In a large skillet or pan, heat water to about the
temperature of a hot bath. Drop in tofu, then cut into
pieces about 2 by 1 by ¾ inches. Pierce each piece
under water from one end using either 2 round bamboo skewers or 1 flat skewer. Cover a cutting board or
flat tray with a dry dishtowel and raise one end of
the board. Carefully place skewered tofu on cloth and
allow to stand for 15 minutes, or until tofu is firm.

Holding 3 to 4 pieces of skewered tofu at a time
side by side over a gas burner, broil for about 30 seconds, or until tofu is lightly speckled. (Or broil tofu
on one side over a charcoal brazier or barbecue.)
Turn tofu over and coat broiled side with a ⅛-inch-
thick layer of topping, then broil second side. Turn
again and broil miso topping until it too is speckled,
then arrange garnishes, if used, atop miso. Repeat with
remaining ingredients. If desired, use a different miso
topping with each set of tofu pieces. Serve hot with
the meal or as an hors d'œuvre.

Tofu Dengaku is also prepared with grilled or deep-
fried tofu.

OTHER INGREDIENTS AND METHODS OF
PREPARATION

*Eggplant: Cut small Japanese eggplants into
½-inch-thick rounds (or larger Western eggplants into bite-sized half moons or wedges). Soak for 5 to 10

minutes in lightly salted water, drain well, and pat dry with a towel. Pierce both sides in several places with a fork or chop-stick, then brush with (sesame) oil. Skewer and proceed as above. Top with Sesame (or Gingerroot) Miso and garnish with sesame or poppy seeds. Or use White Sweet Simmered Miso, Egg Yolk Miso, or Kinomé Miso and garnish with *kinomé* sprigs.

*Sweet Potato, Taro, Daikon, Bamboo Shoots, or Irish Potato: Cut vegetables into ½-inch-thick ovals or rounds and steam or parboil until just tender. Top with Sesame Miso or Miso Sauté (p. 150).

*Mushroom: Skewer large, whole (fresh *shiitaké*) mushrooms and broil. Spread both sides with White Sweet Simmered Miso, rebroil, and garnish with roasted sesame seeds.

*Fresh Wheat Gluten: Cut into tofu-sized rectangles or ½-inch-thick rounds. Broil and top with White Sweet Simmered Miso or Kinomé Miso; garnish with *kinomé*.

*Hard-boiled Eggs, Mochi, Konnyaku, or Green Peppers: Use (chicken or quail) eggs and uncut *mochi* cakes. Cut *konnyaku* and peppers into bite-sized triangles. Skewer individually or in combinations like shish kebab. Top with Red Sweet Simmered Miso.

*Leeks: Parboil whole leeks for 2 to 3 minutes, cut into 1¼-inch sections, and skewer four sections crosswise. Broil using Walnut Miso.

*Unskewered Dengaku: Broil any of the above-mentioned ingredients on both sides until speckled in an oven broiler. Spread upper surface with miso and rebroil briefly.

*Deep-fried Dengaku: All varieties of tofu, yuba, and wheat gluten are most commonly prepared in this way, but other ingredients may also be used. Roll pieces in flour, dip in lightly beaten egg, and roll in bread crumbs. Skewer and deep-fry until crisp, then serve topped with Sweet Simmered Miso. Or skewer first, dip into tempura batter (or leave uncoated), and deep-fry.

*Sautéed and Butter-fried Dengaku: Sauté eggplant rounds on both sides and serve topped with Sesame Miso. Or butter-fry mushrooms or tofu on both sides and serve like eggplant.

Grilled Tofu & Vegetables with Miso White Sauce

SERVES 3 TO 4

At Fugetsu, a Japanese natural-food restaurant in Berkeley, this delicious preparation is served either as an hors d'œuvre or a main course. The sauce is prepared and kept hot in a double boiler.

2 tender eggplants, cut into ¾-inch-thick rounds and brushed with oil
6 large mushrooms
12 ounces tofu, drained or pressed (p. 109)
1 cup Sweet White Miso Sauce (p. 63)
Dash of green *nori* flakes
Dash of *sansho* pepper
1 to 2 teaspoons roasted sesame seeds

Barbecue or grill eggplants, mushrooms, and tofu for about 3 minutes on each side, or until eggplants are tender and other ingredients are nicely browned. Arrange barbecued ingredients on individual plates, spoon on the hot sauce, and top with a sprinkling of green *nori, sansho,* and sesame seeds.

Broiled Sweet Potatoes with Miso Topping

SERVES 2

4 sweet potatoes, steamed until just tender and cut lengthwise into ⅜-inch-thick slices
2 tablespoons Better Butter (p. 119) or butter
2 tablespoons Sweet Simmered Miso (p. 125) or Finger Lickin' Miso (p. 75)

Broil sweet-potato slices until lightly speckled and just fragrant. Spread each slice with butter and a thin layer of the miso. Serve hot or cold.

Grilled Eggplants Shigiyaki (Nasu no Shigiyaki)

SERVES 4

The word *shigiyaki* means "grilled snipe." Old cookbooks show that this now famous eggplant dish was originally prepared by stuffing a pickled eggplant with snipe meat, capping the eggplant with a persimmon leaf, and simmering the tender morsel in a seasoned broth. The present version is a close relative of Eggplant Dengaku (p. 357) and Fried Eggplants Shigiyaki (p. 341).

4 tender, young Japanese eggplants, cut lengthwise
      into halves (unpeeled)
1 tablespoon sesame oil
2½ tablespoons of one of the following types of
      Sweet Simmered Miso (pp. 125 to 138):
          Red or White Sweet Simmered Miso
          Egg Yolk, Kinomé, or Gingerroot Miso
          Sesame or Walnut Miso
Dash of *sansho* pepper

Pierce eggplant halves crosswise with metal skewers, spread cut surface with sesame oil, and broil over a charcoal fire (or stove-top burner) on both sides until nicely speckled. Spread each cut surface with a thin layer of the miso and rebroil quickly until miso is fragrant and speckled. Remove skewers, arrange on individual serving dishes, and top with a sprinkling of the pepper. Serve as a side dish or hors d'œuvre.

VARIATIONS

*Deep-fried Shigiyaki: Cut eggplants into ½-inch-thick rounds, deep-fry, and drain well. Skewer, spread one side with sweet white miso, and score miso in a crisscross pattern with a wet knife. Grill on both sides.

*Savory Shigiyaki: Cut eggplants into ½-inch-thick rounds before skewering, then score both surfaces with a knife or poke with a fork or chopstick. (If using large Western eggplants, cut into bite-sized wedges of an equivalent thickness.) Brush surfaces with oil, skewer, and proceed as above.

Miso in Deep-fried Dishes

Sweet Simmered Miso (p. 125) and most other Miso Toppings are delicious served in small quantities atop tempura or other deep-fried foods. The different varieties of deep-fried Dengaku are described on page 355.

ABOUT DEEP-FRYING

Throughout East Asia, deep-frying has been one of the most popular cooking techniques since ancient times. There are good reasons for this: (1) it imparts a delicious rich and savory flavor, transforming even the simplest of ingredients or leftovers into prize creations; (2) it is faster and uses much less fuel than baking, a cooking technique rarely used in Asia; (3) it serves as an excellent source of essential (usually unsaturated) oils in diets which have long contained very little meat or dairy products; (4) in tropical climates where unwanted microorganisms propagate quickly on foods, it sterilizes them, making them much safer to eat; and (5) by greatly reducing the foods' moisture content (and sterilizing them), it increases their shelf life.

Some Westerners still have the image of deep-fried foods as being necessarily "greasy," yet this is simply a result of poor technique. Anyone who has enjoyed Japanese tempura knows that deep-frying can yield foods that are delicate, light, and crisp. Others have stated that deep-fried foods are hard to digest; yet if the foods are prepared properly as described below and if they are served in moderate portions (typically 1½ to 3 ounces per person at a meal), they are generally found to be easily digested, much more easily than meats and dairy products. Finally, it is pointed out that overheating deep-frying oil can impair its nutritional value and saturate some of the fats, thereby possibly raising serum cholesterol levels; these problems are easily avoided, even by a beginner, by simply keeping most oils at 350°F. (175°C.) and by using oil for deep-frying no more than two or three times. Virtually all nutritionists agree that many people in North America are now consuming much too much fat, especially saturated fats from meats, dairy products, and eggs. Some *40 percent* of the calories in our diet now come from fats! By consuming fewer animal products and using moderate amounts of savory soy protein foods, properly deep-fried to be light and crisp, we can substantially lower fat intake while still enjoying a satisfying, nutritious, and balanced diet.

In Japanese, the verb *ageru* means to "deep-fry," and *agé-mono* or "deep-fried things" are the many foods that make up this vast world. The simplest form of deep-frying is called *kara-agé* or "deep-frying without a coating or batter." The three basic types of deep-fried tofu are each prepared in this way. After mastering this technique, you should find no difficulty in preparing fine, crisp tempura.

If you wish to make deep-frying a permanent part of your repertoire of cooking techniques, it is best to start with the proper tools. Most important is the deep-frying pot. While many Westerners use a heavy 3- to 4-quart kettle, or an electric deep-fryer, most Japanese use either a wok (see p. 53) or a heavy-bottomed skillet 2½ to 3 inches deep and 10 to 12 inches in diameter.

For best results use a simple vegetable oil. Japanese prefer rapeseed oil, but Western cooks use soy, corn, or cottonseed oil. Some chefs specializing in vegetable tempura prefer a combination of oils. If 10 to 30 percent sesame oil is added to any of the above basic oils, it will give the foods a delicious, nutty flavor. Other popular combinations are: peanut or corn (70%) and sesame (30%); peanut (75%), sesame (20%), and olive (5%); cotton-seed (85%), olive (10%), and sesame (5%). For a light, crisp texture, avoid the use of animal fats in deep-frying.

Used deep-frying oil should be kept in a sealed jar and stored in a cool, dark place. When sautéing vegetables or frying eggs, you may use some of this oil to impart added flavor to the foods and help use up the oil. When deep-frying, try to use about one part fresh oil and one part used. Dark or thick used oil has a low smoke point and imparts a poor flavor. Foods deep-fried in used oil only are not as light and crisp as they could be. Pour oil from the storage jar into the deep-fryer carefully so that any sediment remains at the bottom of the jar. Then add fresh oil to fill the wok or skillet to a depth of 1½ to 2 inches.

Maintaining the oil at the proper temperature is the most important part of deep-frying. At first it may be easiest to measure the temperature with a deep-frying thermometer. More experienced chefs judge the oil's temperature by its appearance, aroma, and subtle crackling sound. If the oil begins to smoke, it is too hot. Overheating shortens the life of the oil—Japanese say it "tires" the oil—and imparts a bad flavor to the foods cooked in it. Tempura chefs drop a little batter into hot oil to test its temperature. If the batter submerges slightly, then rises quickly to the surface where it browns within about 45 seconds, the temperature is just right. If the batter sinks to the bottom and rises only slowly to the surface, the oil is not hot enough; if it remains on the surface and dances furiously, the oil is too hot. Oil which is too hot will smoke—and burn the batter—whereas that which is too cold will not give the desired crispness.

Keeping the oil clean is another secret of successful deep-frying. This is especially important when using the batter or bound-breading methods. Use a mesh skimmer, or a perforated metal spatula or spoon, to remove all particles of food and batter from the oil's surface. Most cooks skim after every two or three batches of ingredients have been cooked. Place the small particles of deep-fried batter skimmed from the oil into a large colander or bowl lined with absorbent paper, and allow to drain thoroughly. These may be used later as tasty additions to soups, salads, sautéed vegetables, noodles-in-broth, or other grain dishes.

To ensure that deep-fried foods are served at their peak of texture and flavor, do your deep-frying just

Deep-frying with wok

before you are ready to serve the meal, preferably after your guests have been seated at the table. If you have a large quantity of ingredients to deep-fry and wish to serve them simultaneously, keep freshly cooked pieces warm in a 250°F oven.

After all foods have been deep-fried, allow the oil to cool in the wok or skillet, then pour it through a mesh skimmer or fine-weave strainer held over a funnel into your used-oil container. Seal the jar and discard any residue in the skimmer. Wipe all utensils with absorbent paper (washing is unnecessary) and store in a sealed plastic bag.

Crispy Lotus Root Stuffed with Miso & Onion

SERVES 4

1 teaspoon sesame oil
1 onion, minced
2 tablespoons red, barley, or Hatcho miso, creamed
    with 1 tablespoon water
1 lotus root, cut into ¾-inch-thick rounds (7 or 8)
Oil for deep-frying
3 tablespoons (whole-wheat) flour
1 egg, lightly beaten
Parsley sprigs

Heat a skillet and coat with the oil. Add onion and sauté for 4 minutes. Mix in creamed miso and sauté for 1 minute more. Remove from heat and allow to cool to body temperature. Use fingertips or a spatula to fill hollows in each round of lotus root with onion-miso mixture.

Heat the oil to 350°F in a wok, skillet, or deep-fryer. Dust rounds in flour, dip in egg, and deep-fry for about 3 minutes, or until golden brown (p. 361). Drain well, then cut rounds horizontally into halves exposing the snowflake pattern of the miso-filled holes. Serve garnished with parsley.

For variety, roll in bread crumbs or bread crumb flakes after dipping in eggs.

Deep-fried Lotus Root Stuffed with Cheese & Miso

SERVES 4

A traditional favorite sold in Japanese delicatessens, this dish makes an excellent hors d'œuvre and is a joy to prepare.

1 cup grated cheese
2 tablespoons red, barley, or Hatcho miso
1 tablespoon minced onion or 1 clove of garlic, crushed (optional)
Dash of pepper (optional)
2 lotus roots, each 5 inches long
Oil for deep-frying
2 tablespoons (whole-wheat) flour
1 egg, lightly beaten
Shoyu (optional)

Combine the first four ingredients in a large cup, mixing well. Trim ends of lotus roots revealing hollow inner tubules. Cut each root crosswise into halves, parboil for 5 minutes, and drain briefly. Holding one lotus root section with a small cloth (to protect your hands from the heat), press the large end into the cheese-miso mixture, forcing the mixture up into the tubules until it fills them. Then press the end of the lotus root against the side of the cup while sliding it out to prevent the mixture from being withdrawn by suction. Repeat with the remaining sections.

Heat the oil to 350°F in a wok, skillet, or deep-fryer. Dust each lotus root section liberally with flour, dip into the egg, and deep-fry until golden brown (p. 361). Drain well, then cut crosswise into ½-inch-thick discs. Serve hot or cold, seasoned, if desired, with a sprinkling of shoyu.

VARIATIONS

*Karashi Renkon: As an alternate filling use
  6 tablespoons sweet white or 4 tablespoons
     mellow white miso
  1 tablespoon red miso
  2 tablespoons minced leek or onion
  1 teaspoon hot mustard

*Sandwiched Hors D'oeuvres: Between two rounds of stuffed, deep-fried lotus root, sandwich any of the following: slices of cheese and/or fresh vegetables; deep-fried tofu (especially burgers or pouches); gluten meat.

Creamy Corn Croquettes with Miso

SERVES 3 OR 4

Miso is the key to the flavor in these unique delicacies which have a crisp crust and soft melt-in-the-mouth center.

2½ tablespoons Better Butter (p. 119) or butter
½ cup whole-wheat flour
1¼ cups milk (soy or dairy)
2 tablespoons red, barley, Hatcho, or light-yellow
    miso
Dash of pepper (optional)
½ small onion, minced
½ cup fresh corn kernels
1 egg, lightly beaten
¾ cup bread crumbs or bread crumb flakes
Oil for deep frying

Use 1½ tablespoons butter, ¼ cup flour, the milk, 1½ tablespoons miso, and the pepper to make a Miso White Sauce (p. 272).

Melt remaining 1 tablespoon butter in a skillet. Add onion and corn, and sauté for 4 minutes. Mix in the miso, remove from heat, and stir into the white sauce. Allow to cool to room temperature, then cover and refrigerate for 30 minutes.

Using a large spoon or dipper, scoop out one-eighth of the vegetable-sauce mixture and drop in a ball into a bowl containing the remaining ¼ cup flour. Gently sprinkle flour over moist filling while using fingertips to form a sausage-shaped croquette about 4 inches long and 1½ inches in diameter. Carefully dip in eggs and sprinkle with bread crumbs. Repeat to make 8 croquettes, and allow to dry for 10 minutes.

Heat oil to hot (395°F) in a wok, skillet, or deep-fryer. Slide in 2 croquettes at a time and deep-fry for about 1 minute or until golden brown and crisp. Drain and serve immediately, garnished, if desired, with lettuce, tomato slices, and parsley.

For an even richer texture, add ½ cup grated cheese to the white sauce.

Cheese & Miso Deep-fried Sandwich

SERVES 2

Known in Japan as *Hakata-agé,* this *nori*-wrapped preparation takes its name from the well-known *Hakata* kimono sash characterized by colorful horizontal stripes. Dried-frozen (or well-pressed regular) tofu is often used in place of bread.

4 bread slices, each 3½ inches square and ⅜ inch thick
2 teaspoons red, barley, or Hatcho miso
2 cheese slices, each 3½ inches square and ¼ inch thick
6 strips of *nori,* each 3½ inches wide and 8 to 10 inches long
2 eggs, lightly beaten
¼ cup whole-wheat flour
¼ cup bread crumbs, bread crumb flakes, or ground roasted sesame seeds (optional)
Oil for deep-frying
2 to 4 parsley sprigs

Spread one surface of each bread slice with ½ teaspoon miso, then sandwich 1 slice of cheese between 2 slices of bread to form 2 sandwiches (see illustration). Cut each sandwich crosswise into thirds and wrap each third with a strip of *nori,* moistening one end of *nori* to seal. Combine eggs and flour, mixing lightly, to form a batter. Heat oil to 350°F in a wok, skillet, or deep-fryer. Dip sandwiches into batter and, if desired, roll in bread crumbs or sesame. Drop into oil and deep-fry until golden brown (p. 361). Drain well. Cut each sandwich crosswise into thirds and serve with the cut surface facing upward, garnished with parsley.

VARIATIONS

*If *nori* is not available, pierce sandwiches in 2 places with foodpicks before deep-frying in batter.
*Tofu Hakata-agé: Cut a 12-ounce cake of well-pressed tofu (or a 5-ounce tofu cutlet) horizontally into fourths, then lengthwise and again crosswise into halves to make 16 rectangular pieces. Coat one surface of 8 pieces with a ⅛-inch-thick layer of Sweet Simmered Miso (p. 125), then top with the remaining tofu pieces. Dust each of the 8 sandwiches with flour, dip into beaten egg, and roll in bread crumbs.

Deep-fry, cut, and serve as above, using lemon wedges and parsley as the garnish.

Deep-fried
Sandwiches

Deep-fried Potatoes in Miso & Onion Sauce

SERVES 2 OR 3

½ onion, minced
¼ cup water
Oil for deep-frying
4 small unpeeled potatoes (2-inch diameter), each
    cut into 4 equal-sized chunks
1½ tablespoons red, barley, or Hatcho miso
2 tablespoons Parmesan cheese

Combine onion and water in a small saucepan, bring to a boil, and simmer for 5 minutes. Meanwhile heat oil to 350°F in a wok, skillet, or deep-fryer. Drop in potato chunks and deep-fry until golden brown (p. 361); drain on absorbent paper.

Stir miso into simmering onions, then add potatoes and season with pepper; simmer for 1 minute. Serve topped with a sprinkling of the cheese.

Deep-fried Potato Chunks in Miso & Ginger Sauce

SERVES 3 OR 4

2 tablespoons red, barley, or Hatcho miso
2 to 2½ teaspoons honey
½ teaspoon powdered ginger or ¼ teaspoon grated
    gingerroot
¼ cup water or stock
2 small potatoes (2½-inch diameter), each cut into
    4 chunks and patted very dry with a dishcloth
Oil for deep-frying

Combine the first four ingredients in a small saucepan, mixing well, and set aside on a back burner. Heat oil to 325°F in a wok, skillet, or deep-fryer. Drop in

potato chunks and deep-fry for about 6 minutes, or
until golden brown and tender (p. 361). Meanwhile
bring miso-ginger sauce to a boil and simmer over
very low heat. Drain potatoes briefly, dip into sauce
until covered, and transfer to individual plates. Serve
hot or cold.

Eggs Deep-fried in Overcoats with Miso

SERVES 3

2 tablespoons Better Butter (p. 119) or butter
½ onion, minced
½ cup carrot, grated
2 cups cubed potatoes (1-inch cubes), boiled for
    20 minutes, drained and mashed
1½ tablespoons red, barley, or Hatcho miso
½ teaspoon curry powder or dash of pepper
3 hard-boiled eggs, shelled and cooled to room
    temperature
3 tablespoons whole-wheat flour
1 egg, lightly beaten
⅓ cup bread crumbs
Oil for deep-frying
Ketchup-Worcestershire Sauce (p. 119)
Minced parsley

Melt the butter in a skillet. Add onion and carrot, and sauté for 3 minutes. Mix with mashed potato, miso, and curry powder and divide into 3 equal portions; allow to cool to at least body temperature. Completely enfold each egg with an even covering of the potato-miso mixture, then dust with flour, dip in beaten egg, and roll in bread crumbs. Heat oil to 375°F in a wok, skillet, or deep-fryer. Deep-fry coated eggs until golden brown, lift out of oil with a slotted spoon or skimmer, and drain well. Allow to cool to at least body temperature, then cut each egg lengthwise into halves. Serve topped with the sauce and a sprinkling of parsley. If desired, arrange on a bed of lettuce or shredded cabbage garnished by tomato wedges.

For variety, omit the flour and beaten eggs in the coating, and use only bread crumbs; instead of deep-frying, bake at 350°F for 20 minutes, or until nicely browned.

Sweet Miso Deep-fried in Yuba or Wonton Skins

MAKES 6

6 sheets of fresh yuba, each 4 inches square; or
   6 wonton skins
9 tablespoons diced fresh yuba or wonton
3 tablespoons Yuzu Miso (p. 132) or Red Nerimiso
   (p. 125)
Oil for deep-frying
Shoyu

In the center of each yuba square layer 1 tablespoon diced yuba and 1½ teaspoons miso, and top with ½ teaspoon more of the yuba. Fold over the four corners of the yuba or wonton to form an envelope and fasten corners with a foodpick. Heat the oil to 350°F in a wok, skillet, or deep-fryer. Drop in envelopes and deep-fry, turning them from time to time with chopsticks or tongs, for about 40 seconds, or until golden brown (p. 361). Drain well and serve (on sheets of neatly folded white paper) accompanied by the shoyu for dipping.

For variety, omit diced yuba and use 1 tablespoon Mushroom Miso Sauté (p. 140) as the filling.

Miso and Eggs

The use of miso in your favorite breakfast and luncheon egg preparations provides added aroma, flavor, and protein. For hors d'œuvres see Eggs with Miso and Sesame (p. 172).

Scrambled Eggs with Miso, Onions, and Tofu

SERVES 3

2 eggs, lightly beaten
1½ tablespoons red, barley, or Hatcho miso
7½ ounces deep-fried tofu, cut into ½-inch cubes
1 tablespoon oil
1 small onion, thinly sliced
Dash of pepper (optional)

Combine the eggs and miso in a small bowl, mixing well. Add tofu and set aside.

Heat a skillet and coat with the oil. Add onion and sauté for 4 to 5 minutes. Pour in tofu-egg mixture and scramble for 2 to 3 minutes, or until eggs are firm. Season with pepper. Serve hot or cold.

Eggs Cooked Over Brown Rice with Miso

SERVES 3

1½ tablespoons oil
1 clove of garlic, minced
½ small onion, minced
4 mushrooms, minced
1 cup cooked Brown Rice (p. 116)
1 tablespoon red or barley miso, creamed with
   1 tablespoon water
3 eggs
Dash of pepper (optional)

Heat a large skillet and coat with the oil. Add garlic and sauté for 30 seconds. Add onion and mushrooms, and sauté for 5 minutes more. Mix in brown rice, sauté for 2 more minutes, then stir in slightly more than half of the creamed miso. Spread rice in an even layer over bottom of skillet. Break eggs over rice and cook, covered, over low heat for 4 to 5 minutes, or until eggs are firm. Season with pepper and top each egg with a dab of creamed miso.

Gashouse eggs

Gashouse Eggs with Miso

SERVES 1

Also known as Cockeyed Egyptians, these innovative delicacies are a nice way of combining miso and wheat proteins in a breakfast egg dish.

1 teaspoon sweet or mellow white (or ½ teaspoon red) miso
5 teaspoons Better Butter (p. 119) or butter
1 slice of whole-wheat bread
1 egg

Spread first the miso and then 1 teaspoon butter evenly over one surface of the bread. Use the mouth of a small glass to cut a hole in the center of the bread (see illustration) and remove the round. Melt the remaining 4 teaspoons butter in a skillet, put in the bread with the buttered side up, and break the egg into the hole. Place the round (buttered-side-up) next to the bread and fry both for 2 to 3 minutes, or until bottom is nicely browned and egg is half done. Turn and repeat until second side is slightly crisp and golden brown. Serve immediately.

Poached Eggs on Toast with White Miso

SERVES 2

2 eggs, poached
2 slices of buttered whole-grain toast
1 tablespoon sweet white or 2 teaspoons mellow
    white miso, creamed with 1 tablespoon boiling
    water

Place one egg atop the buttered side of each slice of toast, then pour on miso sauce. Serve immediately.

Scrambled Eggs or Omelets with Miso

SERVES 2 OR 3

4 eggs, lightly beaten
4 teaspoons red, barley, or Hatcho miso
2 to 3 tablespoons minced onion
3½ teaspoons oil
Dash of pepper (optional)
Sprigs of parsley

Combine the first three ingredients, mixing well. Heat one-half the oil in a large skillet. Pour in half the egg-miso mixture and scramble until firm, then press surface of eggs with the back of a spatula until bottom of eggs is lightly browned and fragrant. Turn and press the second side, then remove from skillet. Repeat with remaining egg-miso mixture. Serve seasoned with pepper and garnished with parsley.

   To make omelets, reduce the amount of oil slightly and cook in two batches without scrambling. If desired, serve omelets filled with 1 tablespoon Sweet Simmered Miso (p. 125) and a pinch of alfalfa sprouts.

Japanese-style Scrambled Eggs with Miso

SERVES 4

2 tablespoons oil
1 onion, minced
1 carrot, grated
4 teaspoons red, barley, or Hatcho miso
3 tablespoons water or stock
1 tablespoon honey
4 eggs

Heat a skillet and coat with the oil. Add onion and carrot, and sauté for 7 minutes, or until onion is nicely browned. Combine miso, water and honey, stirring until smooth, then mix in eggs. Pour mixture over contents of skillet and scramble for about 1 minute, or until just firm.

Egg Foo Yung with Miso

SERVES 2

1 tablespoon red, barley, or Hatcho miso
2¾ tablespoons stock or water
2 eggs, lightly beaten
1½ tablespoons oil, one-half of which may be sesame
¾ cup (mung) bean sprouts
3 mushrooms, thinly sliced
½ to ¾ cup chopped leeks or minced onions
Dash of pepper (optional)

Cream the miso with a little of the stock, then add eggs and remaining stock; mix well and set aside. Heat the oil in a large skillet. Add the next three ingredients and sauté over high heat for about 1 minute, or until leeks are lightly browned. Pour in miso-egg mixture to form a round pattie and fry on both sides until golden brown. Serve seasoned with pepper.

For variety, add diced (deep-fried) tofu and/or green peppers together with the sprouts. Top with Miso-Gingerroot Ankaké (p. 271) or Gingerroot Sauce (p. 284).

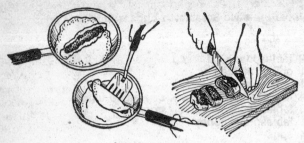

Layered omelets

Layered Japanese Omelet with Sweet Simmered Miso

SERVES 2 OR 3

Sweet Simmered Miso makes a good filling for
many Western-style omelets. This subtly sweet vegetable omelet is composed of alternating almost-crisp
and creamy-soft layers.

4 eggs, lightly beaten
1 tablespoon brown sugar or honey
2 mushrooms, minced
⅓ cup finely-minced leeks, onions, or chives
Dash of salt
¼ cup dashi (p. 112), water, or stock
2 teaspoons oil
2½ teaspoons Red Nerimiso (p. 125)

Combine the first six ingredients, mixing well. Heat a
large skillet and coat with 1 teaspoon oil. Fold a 4-
by 6-inch piece of cheese cloth to form a small pad,
grasp with tongs or chopsticks, and use to spread oil
evenly over bottom and sides of skillet. Pour in one-
fourth of the vegetable-egg mixture, swish it quickly
around skillet to make a uniformly thin layer, and
cook over high heat on one side only until omelet
firms. Reduce heat to low and cook until bottom is
almost crisp. Roll up omelet with a spatula, remove
from skillet, and coat upper surface with ½ teaspoon Nerimiso. Re-oil skillet lightly and use cloth
pad to free any particles of omelet clinging to skillet's

walls. Prepare a second omelet. When it has finished cooking, place the first back into skillet atop the second. Fold one edge of bottom omelet over rolled omelet and, using spatula, roll up second omelet around first. Carefully remove roll from skillet and again coat upper surface with ½ teaspoon Nerimiso. Continue in this way to prepare a single roll composed of 4 omelets. Coat the top of the finished roll with 1 teaspoon Nerimiso and allow to cool to room temperature. Cut crosswise into 1-inch-wide sections before serving.

Miso in Desserts

A little miso helps to elicit the natural sweetness of most fresh fruits—especially apples. The low salt content, subtle tartness, and mellow flavor of Hatcho often gives particularly good results in baked treats. Experiment also with Sesame Miso (p. 130), sweet or mellow white miso, or red miso in your favorite recipes for Apple Brown Betty, fruit fritters or turnovers, and pies.

Before the arrival of cane sugar in Japan, sweet and Finger Lickin' misos served together with *mizuamé* and *amazaké* as the major natural sweetenings. They were—and still are—used in confections and tea treats, the most popular of which is *Kashiwa Mochi,* described below. Miso is also a key ingredient in the crisp Tokyo dessert crackers called *Kawara Senbei,* made by baking a mixture of wheat (or rice flour) dough, sweet red miso and sugar between two small roof tiles *(kawara),* from which the crackers take their form. Sweet red miso is also mixed with sweet *azuki*-bean paste and used as a filling for the widely available steamed buns called *Miso Manju.*

Baked Apples Filled with Sesame-Raisin Miso

SERVES 5

5 large (red) apples
Sesame-Raisin Miso:
    1½ tablespoons sesame butter
    ¼ cup raisins
    1 tablespoon Hatcho, red, or barley miso
    1 tablespoon Better Butter (p. 119) or butter
    3 tablespoons brown sugar or 1½ tablespoons
        honey
    2 tablespoons water
    1 tablespoon sake or white wine (optional)
    ¼ teaspoon cinnamon (optional)

Preheat oven to 350°F. Core apples to about seven-
eighths of their depth. Mix the ingredients for sesame-
raisin miso, then pack the mixture firmly into the
hollow of each apple. Wrap apples in aluminum foil,
place on a cookie tin, and bake for about 20 minutes.
Serve hot or chilled.

Apple Crisp with Miso

SERVES 4 TO 6

4 apples, thinly sliced
¼ cup raisins
1 tablespoon Hatcho, red, or barley miso
½ teaspoon grated lemon rind
1 tablespoon lemon juice
1 cup rolled oats or oatmeal (uncooked)
⅓ cup whole-wheat flour
2 tablespoons brown sugar (optional)
½ teaspoon cinnamon
¼ teaspoon nutmeg
Dash of salt
¼ cup oil (one-half of which may be butter)

Preheat oven to 350°F. Combine the first five ingredients, mixing well, and spoon into a lightly oiled baking dish. Combine the remaining ingredients, mixing
(or rubbing between palms) until oil is evenly dis-

tributed; sprinkle over surface of apples. Bake for about 30 minutes, or until apples are tender and surface is nicely browned. Delicious hot or chilled.

Jelled Apple-Miso Dessert

SERVES 5 TO 6

5 apples, peeled and cut lengthwise into fourths
1 cup water
1 tablespoon red, barley, or Hatcho miso
½ cup raisins
1 tablespoon lemon juice
2 tablespoons honey
2 tablespoons sesame butter
¼ teaspoon cinnamon
½ bar of agar (4 to 5 grams), soaked in water for
    2 minutes, squeezed firmly and torn into small
    pieces

Combine apples and water in a saucepan, bring to a boil, and simmer, covered, for 10 minutes. Using a fork, remove apples and transfer to a baking pan or mold. Add miso and the next five ingredients to the apple cooking liquid, mixing well. Add agar, bring to a boil, and simmer for 4 to 5 minutes, or until agar has dissolved. Pour liquid into mold and allow to cool to room temperature. Cover and refrigerate until firm, preferably for 6 to 8 hours. Serve as is or topped with yogurt.

Japanese-style Steamed Miso-Cupcakes or Spongecake (Miso-iri Mushipan)

SERVES 2 OR 3

2 eggs separated into whites and lightly beaten yolks
1 tablespoon red or barley miso, creamed with
      1½ teaspoons water
⅔ cup whole-wheat flour
½ teaspoon baking powder
6½ teaspoons honey
1 tablespoon finely chopped peanuts or roasted
      sesame seeds
Butter

Preheat a steamer (p. 108). In a large bowl, beat egg
whites until stiff. Fold in yolks, creamed miso, flour,
baking powder, and 2 tablespoons honey. Spoon batter into (paper-lined) cupcake molds or a small loaf
pan lined with aluminum foil. Place in steamer and,
unless using a bamboo steamer, stretch a moist cloth
over steamer's mouth before covering. Steam for 20
to 25 minutes. Brush surface of cakes with ½ teaspoon honey, then sprinkle with peanuts or sesame
seeds. Serve hot or cold with butter.

The Japanese and Chinese prefer steaming to baking since much less fuel is needed. Of course, the cupcakes may also be baked over a pan of water if desired.

Miso Mincemeat

MAKES ONE 9-INCH PIE

The mellow, slightly tart flavor of Hatcho miso
provides the key to this unique and delicious dessert
preparation.

4 (tart) apples, peeled, cored, and diced
½ cup apple juice
1½ cups raisins
Grated rind of 1 orange
Juice of 1 orange
2 cups nutmeats, preferably walnuts
¼ teaspoon cinnamon
¼ to ½ teaspoon cloves, allspice, or coriander
2 tablespoons Hatcho miso, or substitute 1½ table-
      spoons red or barley miso

Combine the first five ingredients in a heavy pot, bring to a boil, and simmer for 30 minutes. Add the next three ingredients and the miso creamed in a little of the cooking liquid; mix well, remove from heat, and allow to cool to room temperature. Use as a filling for a 9-inch mince pie or for turnovers. Also delicious as a spread for buttered toast or served like chutney with curried dishes.

Heavenly Sweet-potato Patties with White Miso

SERVES 6 OR 12

4 (Japanese) sweet potatoes, steamed for 20 minutes
    and mashed (2¼ cups)
¼ cup sweet white or 2 tablespoons mellow white
    miso
½ cup raisins
1 tablespoon honey
3 tablespoons Better Butter (p. 119) or butter

Combine the first four ingredients, mixing well, and shape into 12 patties. Melt 1 tablespoon butter in a heavy skillet, add 4 patties, and fry for 2 to 3 minutes on each side, or until lightly browned. Repeat until all ingredients are used. Serve hot or cold.

Banana, Peanut Butter & Sweet Miso Delight

SERVES 2 OR 3

2 tablespoons peanut or sesame butter
1 tablespoon sweet white miso
¼ cup raisins
1 teaspoon honey
2 tablespoons water
2 bananas, sliced into ½-inch-thick rounds

Combine the first five ingredients, mixing well, then spoon over banana slices. Mix lightly until slices are evenly coated. Serve immediately.

Miso Rice Pudding

SERVES 3 OR 4

The rich, creamy texture of rice porridge works like milk in most pudding recipes; raisins provide most of the sweetness.

½ cup brown rice, rinsed and drained
2½ cups water
1½ tablespoons Hatcho, red, or barley miso
½ cup raisins
1 tablespoon brown sugar or 1½ teaspoons honey
1 tablespoon butter
Dash of cinnamon

Combine rice and water in a pressure cooker and proceed as for rice porridge (p. 116). After opening cooker, stir in the last four ingredients. For best flavor, allow to stand for several hours before serving.

Miso Pumpkin Pie

SERVES 6

24 ounces *kabocha* (unpeeled), cut into 1-inch cubes
2 tablespoons red, barley, or Hatcho miso
2 tablespoons honey or brown sugar
1½ tablespoons Better Butter (p. 119) or butter
Dash of nutmeg and/or allspice
Crust for an 8-inch pie

Combine *kabocha* with water to cover in a saucepan or pot, bring to a boil, and simmer for 20 minutes. Drain well, then combine with the next four ingredients and mash together. Line an 8-inch pie pan with the crust and bake in a 400°F oven until lightly browned. Spoon in the *kabocha* mixture and re-bake for 20 to 30 minutes, or until nicely browned. For richest flavor, serve cold. This filling also works well in turnovers.

If pumpkin or squash is substituted for the *kabocha,* peel before boiling and drain very well; add 1 to 3 eggs to the mixture before baking.

Crêpes with Sweet Simmered Miso Filling

SERVES 2

Red Sweet Simmered Miso Filling:
 3½ teaspoons red or barley miso
 2 teaspoons honey
 ½ teaspoon butter
 1 teaspoon sake or white wine
 ½ teaspoon grated lemon or orange rind
 2 teaspoons water
⅞ cup sifted whole-wheat flour
1 egg, lightly beaten
1 cup milk (soy or dairy)
1 tablespoon oil or butter

Using the filling ingredients, prepare Red Sweet Simmered Miso (p. 126) and set aside to cool. Combine the flour, egg, milk and 1 teaspoon oil, whisking lightly to form a smooth batter. Lightly oil a large skillet, then use batter to prepare 10 to 12 crêpes. Allow crêpes to cool, then spread one surface of each with about ½ teaspoon of the miso filling. Roll crêpes before serving.

Kashiwa Mochi

Miso Kashiwa Mochi

MAKES 8

Served once each year as a special treat on Children's Day—the fifth day of the fifth month—*Kashiwa Mochi* takes its name from the oak leaves generally used to wrap each portion. Widely prepared at commercial Japanese confectioneries, the filling is generally made of sweet white miso and puréed white kidney beans (*Ingen mamé*), or occasionally of sweet red miso and sweet, *azuki*-bean paste (*an*). Household recipes also call for a filling made with *kabocha* or chestnut purée.

7 ounces *kabocha,* pumpkin, or squash, peeled and
　　cut into cubes
3¼ tablespoons sweet white miso
2½ teaspoons honey
1¼ cups glutinous rice flour
½ teaspoon salt
¾ cup boiling water

Steam *kabocha* for 15 to 20 minutes, then rub through a sieve. Add miso and honey, mixing well, to make a filling.

Combine flour and salt, mixing thoroughly. Gradually add boiling water while stirring vigorously for 3 minutes to develop a cohesive dough. Wrap dough in a moist cloth, place into a preheated steamer (p. 108) and steam for 20 minutes. Now transfer dough to a *suribachi* or mortar and pound for 5 to 10 minutes, or until dough develops a uniform, resilient texture. Divide dough into 8 parts and roll out each into 3½-inch rounds on a lightly floured board. Place equal portions of the filling at the center of each round, then fold over one side of the dough to form a half-moon shape. Seal edges by pinching dough with fingers. Wrap each portion in a large (6- to 8-inch-long) oak leaf, with the leaf's shiny surface touching the dough (or use a beech leaf or aluminum foil). Replace into preheated steamer and steam for 4 to 5 minutes. Allow to cool before serving.

Miso Pickles

Pickled vegetables are a basic condiment in the Japanese (and Chinese) diet, where they are the single most important source of salt, providing about 40 percent of the total intake. Served at almost every meal of the day, primarily as an accompaniment for rice or rice porridge, they are enjoyed for their slightly crisp texture and deep, rich flavor. There are six basic types of Japanese pickles and each takes its name from the pickling agent: miso, salt, salted moist rice-bran, vinegar, sake lees, and koji. Some scholars believe that the earliest Japanese pickles, called *konomono* or "fragrant things," were made with miso. And to this day, miso pickles (*miso-zuké*) are believed to aid the digestive process and promote long life and good health.

Commercially prepared miso pickles—made both at specialty shops and regular miso shops—are widely available at most food stores and miso retail outlets throughout Japan. More than 12 varieties of vegetables and seeds are used, the most popular of which are *daikon,* (wild) burdock root, cucumbers, eggplants, gingerroot, carrots, *uri* melons, beefsteak seeds, and *myoga*. Fish and meat pickles, usually prepared with sweet white miso, are generally sold at fish or meat markets. In farmhouses and temples, large batches of miso pickles are still prepared each year as part of the miso-making process, with vegetables buried in the keg at the start of fermentation and usually left there until the miso is fully mature (p. 474). In urban homes, small batches are made using store-bought miso and special ingredients such as eggs and egg yolks, which are then often served as hors d'œuvres. Most farmers and homemakers prefer to make their miso pickles during the fall or winter; although the process takes longer due to the cold, the pickles' flavor is said to improve and it is easier to prevent the growth of unwanted mold on the miso surface.

Over a period of many centuries, Japanese craftsmen have raised the practice of miso-pickling to the level of a fine art. The country's most famous commercial makers enjoy a wide and lofty reputation, and they guard the secrets of their trade most carefully. Traditional masters call for a lengthy pickling believed to give vegetables a mellow saltiness and tender crunchiness, while extinguishing all bitter and strong flavors (such as those found in *daikon* or burdock root), accenting subtle indwelling flavors, and, above all, evoking a delightful aroma—which devotees refer to as "the life" of the product.

In this section, we will first discuss the rather simple method of preparing miso pickles at home, then go on to the complete 5-step process used by most commercial makers.

The Pickling Container

The type and size of the container used are determined by the scale of the household pickling process:
*Large Scale (2 to 10 pounds of fresh vegetable

ingredients): Use a container of 2 to 10 gallons capacity, preferably an earthenware crock, a seasoned wooden keg (such as that used for shoyu or miso), a glass container (such as an aquarium), or an enamelware pot. If none of these are available, use a polyethylene tub or bucket. This scale is recommended for ingredients requiring 1 year or more of pickling.

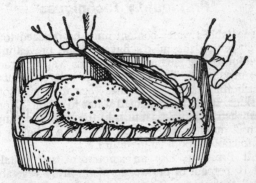

*Medium Scale (½ pound to 2 pounds of ingredients): For kitchen use when pickling for less than one year, use a container of 2 to 4 quarts capacity such as an earthenware crock or casserole, a glass bowl, an enamel pot or shallow pan, or a tupperware container.

*Small Scale (less than 8 ounces of ingredients): Spread the miso in a ½-inch-thick layer over a piece of plastic wrap, arrange ingredients to be pickled on the miso, and roll up into a cylinder. This technique is especially good with small amounts of long, thin vegetables such as cucumbers and burdock root. Or you can use small glass jars or tupperware containers for small-sized ingredients such as egg yolks or garlic.

Preparatory Techniques

A vegetable's water content must be reduced to aid it in absorbing the miso's flavor, while preventing it from diluting the medium with excess water extracted by the miso's salt. The following procedures are used:

*Parboiling: Used to sterilize vegetables and soften their skins. Bring lightly salted water to a boil. Drop in well-washed vegetables, return to the boil, and simmer for 1 to 2 minutes. Drain thoroughly in a colander and allow to cool to room temperature.

*Salt Pressing: Use an amount of salt equal to about 10 percent of the weight of the fresh vegetables, about 2 tablespoons for every ½ pound. Place whole or cut ingredients in a large (earthenware, wooden, glass, or enamel) flat-bottomed container and sprinkle the entire surface of each vegetable with salt. Arrange ingredients compactly in parallel rows, top with a lid or another flat-bottomed container, and press with a stone or water-filled jar. For ingredients weighing less than 1 pound, use a 5- to 10-pound pressing weight; for 10 pounds of ingredients, use a 30-pound weight. Press for 2 days unless otherwise stated. After pressing, drain vegetables well, discard liquid, and wipe vegetables with a dry cloth.

*Wrapping in Cheesecloth: This technique helps soft ingredients to keep their form during pickling and makes it easier to remove them from the miso bed. Simply wrap in a single or double layer of cheesecloth before embedding.

*Air-drying: Place vegetables in a shallow colander or tie in strands with string. Place or hang in a shady location during summer, in direct sunlight in very cold weather. Cover or bring indoors at night to protect from dew.

Air-drying turnips (kabu)

The Miso "Bed"

In Japanese, the pickling medium is called the "bed" and burying the vegetables in it is called "embedding." Use red or barley miso when pickling for several weeks or more; sweet white miso when the pickling time is less than one week. The latter gives a mild, subtly sweet flavor which is often given added zest by mixing in a small amount of sake, rice koji, or powdered mustard. The flavor of red miso can be enriched by the addition of (7-spice) red pepper, sake, or honey. Kinzanji and other varieties of Finger Lickin' Miso give delicious results with overnight pickles, especially egg yolks.

To prepare the bed, cover the bottom of the miso container with a ½- to 1-inch-thick layer of miso. On top of this lay a snug layer of the ingredients to be pickled, then cover with another layer of miso. Repeat until all ingredients are used. Cover the top miso layer with a double thickness of cotton cloth or a sheet of wax paper or plastic to keep out air and prevent mold formation. Store in a cool place or, if using sweet white, Finger Lickin', or small quantities of red miso, refrigerate. Large-scale containers should be further covered with a weighted pressing lid.

Cleaning and Serving Pickles

Remove only as many vegetables from the miso as you need for 1 or 2 days. Using your fingers, scrape off excess miso and return it to the pickling container. Unless otherwise specified, rinse off any remaining miso under cold running water. Cut pickles crosswise or diagonally into thin slices, or mince.

Serve red-miso pickles as an accompaniment with plain or fried rice or noodles, or use as a garnish for rice porridge, gruel, or tofu. Serve pickles made with sweet white or Finger Lickin' miso as an hors d'œuvre. In Japan, thin rounds of either type are often arranged on tiny dishes (accompanied by chopsticks) and served together with green tea.

In most Zen temples (and some homes), each person reserves one fairly large slice of pickle until the end of the meal. This is held with a pair of chopsticks and used, together with a small amount of hot tea or water, to rinse out the eating bowls. The pickle is then enjoyed with the broth—and nothing has been wasted. Individuals then dry their own bowls, nestle them snugly one inside the other, and tie them into an attractive bundle, ready for the next meal. Thanks to the humble pickle, the kitchen crew is saved hours of dish washing.

When all homemade pickles have been removed from the container, the miso will be softer than usual due to the moisture extracted from the pickled vegetables. Use in cookery as you would regular miso or in the preliminary pickling of a similar second batch of vegetables (p. 397). After the removal of ingredients such as garlic or *daikon,* the miso will have been flavorfully enriched.

FOODS TO BE PICKLED

Asparagus

Peel 6 slender, young stalks and snap the tips. Cut lengthwise into halves, then into ½-inch lengths. Bring 2 cups water to a boil. Drop in asparagus and return to the boil. Drain, cool under cold running water, and pat dry with towels. Mix ½ cup sweet white miso and 1 tablespoon powdered mustard. Spread half the mixture in a shallow baking dish and cover with a double thickness of cheesecloth. Arrange asparagus in one layer on cloth, cover with a second double layer, and top with remaining miso mixture. Let stand for 3 hours at room temperature or refrigerate overnight. Serve as an hors d'œuvre.

Beefsteak Leaves

Embed green leaves (fresh or salt-pressed) in a mixture of 4 parts red miso and 1 part *mirin* for 1 to 3 days. Sliver and serve as a garnish.

Beefsteak Seeds

Salt-press about ½ cup red beefsteak seeds, then tie in a small cheesecloth bag. Embed in red miso for 1 month. Use as (1) a filling for rice balls or nori-wrapped sushi, (2) a garnish for soups, vegetable pancakes and grain dishes, or (3) an ingredient in tempura.

Burdock Root and Wild Mountain Burdock

Wild mountain burdock (*Yamagobo*) is one of Japan's most popular commercial varieties of miso pickle. Smaller and more richly flavored than regular burdock, it turns a handsome yellowish gold when pickled.

Use whole roots or fairly long lengths. If pickling for less than 1 month, cut roots lengthwise into halves.

Parboil for 3 minutes and salt press for 1 to 3 days, then air-dry for several hours. Embed in red miso for at least 4 months, preferably 1 to 3 years.

Carrots

Prepare as for burdock root. For a firmer texture, salt-press or air-dry for about 1 week before pickling.

Celery

Cut stalks into 1-inch lengths. Embed in red miso for 24 to 36 hours. Serve as an hors d'œuvre.

Cucumbers

Use whole cucumbers. Salt-press for 1 to 2 days, then embed in red miso for 3 to 6 months, or in sweet white miso for 5 months.

Daikon or Turnips (Kabu)

Use whole *daikon*. Salt-press under heavy weights for 1 week or air-dry for 5 to 10 days, or until soft and well contracted. Embed in red miso for at least 4 to 6 months; if desired, for 2 or 3 years.

For faster results, cut lengthwise into halves, then crosswise into 3- to 6-inch sections. Salt-press for 1 night or air-dry for 10 days. Embed in red miso (or a mixture of ½ teaspoon 7-spice red pepper for every 2 cups red miso) for 3 to 4 months, or in moromi miso for 5 months. *Takuan,* or *daikon* which has been pickled in moist salted rice bran, can be further pickled in miso for 3 to 4 weeks.

Eggplants

For best results use (Japanese-style) small and tender whole eggplants. Salt-press for 24 hours, then embed in red miso for 4 to 8 months, or as long as 1 to 2 years. Delicious also embedded in moromi miso or Finger Lickin' Miso for 70 days.

Eggs (Hardboiled)

*Sweet White Miso: Use 4 eggs, shelled. For the "bed" use ¾ cup sweet white miso (mixed, if desired, with 1 to 4 tablespoons *mirin*, sake or white wine). Cut two eggs lengthwise into halves and embed with the cut surface facing upward. Embed remaining eggs whole. Cover container and refrigerate for 1 to 7 days. Remove excess miso but do not wash. Slice whole eggs into thin rounds. Serve as an hors d'œuvre as is, or on crackers or canapés.

*Red Miso: These eggs end up firmer and saltier. Use plain red miso (or mix with sake, etc., as above). Embed eggs whole. For use as an hors d'œuvre, pickle for 5 to 6 hours and serve as is, cut into halves. For use on crackers or canapés, pickle for 10 to 12 hours, then cut into thin rounds. For use as a rice garnish, pickle for 1 to 4 days, then dice or sliver.

*Sweetened Red Miso: Use as the pickling medium: ¾ cup red or barley miso, ¼ cup sugar and 3 tablespoons sake. Proceed as for red miso above.

*Finger Lickin' Miso: Cut eggs lengthwise into halves, remove yolks, and bury yolks and whites in (Kinzanji or moromi) miso for 24 hours. Remove and serve as for sweet white miso, above.

Egg Yolks (Softboiled)

Cover the bottom of a 6-inch square container with a 1-inch-deep layer of red miso. Press the large end of an egg into the miso in 4 places to make 4 depressions, then cover miso with a layer of cheesecloth and press cloth into depressions. Prepare four 3-minute eggs. Carefully remove yolks unbroken, and place one yolk in each of the 4 depressions. Cover with a layer of cheesecloth, gently top with miso, and wait for 1½ to 2 days. Serve yolks like cheese as an hors d'œuvre (garnished with slivered green beefsteak leaves if desired) or as a garnish atop hot rice.

Garlic or Shallots

*Red Nerimiso: Peel the thin outer skin from 10 to 12 cloves of garlic and parboil cloves for 3 minutes. Cut lengthwise into halves and dry on a (bamboo) colander in the shade for 6 to 12 hours. (For added fragrance, skewer and broil dried cloves until speckled.) Embed in about 1 cup hot, freshly prepared Red Nerimiso (p. 125) for 3 to 6 months. Cut lengthwise into very thin slices before serving.

To reduce pickling time, cut (fresh or parboiled) garlic cloves into paper-thin slices; pickle for at least 2, preferably 3 weeks.

*Red Miso: Peel garlic cloves and cut lengthwise into halves. Embed in miso for at least 4, preferably 6 months. Serve diced or thinly sliced with rice or rice gruel. In rural Japan, these miso pickles are considered an excellent source of stamina and a cure for numerous diseases.

The miso which remains after pickling garlic is most delicious; use it like Garlic Miso (p. 135) or as a topping for tofu or hot rice.

Gingerroot

Use whole mature or young gingerroot. Salt-press for 1 to 3 days. Embed in red miso for at least 1, preferably 2 years. Or, for faster results, slice fresh gingerroot diagonally into paper-thin ovals. Embed for at least 2, preferably 3 weeks.

Green Peppers

Parboil 5 or 6 green peppers for 1 minute in lightly salted water. Remove seeds and stems, then cut lengthwise into 1-inch-wide strips. Combine 8 ounces sweet white miso, 2½ tablespoons *mirin,* and 1 tablespoon sake or white wine; mix well. Embed peppers, cover, and refrigerate for 1 week. Serve as a garnish for hot rice seasoned with a little sesame salt, or as an hors d'œuvre sprinkled with a few drops of shoyu. Cook leftover miso for 5 to 10 minutes in a skillet, stirring constantly, as for Sweet Simmered Miso.

Or cut fresh green peppers lengthwise into 1-inch-wide strips and salt-press for 24 hours; embed in red miso for 2 to 3 months.

Kabocha

Cut *kabocha* into ½-inch-thick slices; peel and trim off pulpy inner edge. Parboil for 1 to 2 minutes in lightly salted water. Drain and cool under cold running water. Air-dry for several hours. Embed in red miso for 2 to 4 months. For added tang, mix ½ teaspoon (7-spice) red pepper with each 2 cups of miso used.

Kombu

Use best grade *dashi kombu*. Wipe with a moist cloth, cut into 8-inch lengths, and steam or pressure cook in a little water for 20 to 30 minutes, or until tender. Spread upper surface of each *kombu* sheet with either a mixture of 1 cup sweet white miso and 1½ teaspoons sake, or with red miso. Roll up sheets from one end, embed in the miso with which they were spread, and wait for at least 6, preferably 12 months. (If using sweet white miso, cover and refrigerate during pickling.) Cut into very thin strips and serve as a garnish with rice.

Lotus Root

Cut 3 ounces of peeled lotus root into 2-inch lengths. Simmer until just tender in a mixture of 1 cup water and 1 tablespoon vinegar, then drain well. Embed in a mixture of ¾ cup sweet white miso, 1 teaspoon hot mustard, and 1 tablespoon *mirin,* pressing miso mixture into lotus root tubules to fill them. Wait for 24 hours. Scrape off miso, wash well, and cut into very thin rounds. Serve as a garnish or hors d'œuvre.

Myoga

Cut fresh *myoga* lengthwise into halves, then embed in red miso for 5 to 7 days. Serve as a garnish with rice.

Sansho Seeds

Salt-press *sansho* seeds for 2 to 3 days, then tie in a small gauze bag and embed in red miso for 1 to 2 weeks.

Tofu

Drain and press tofu (p. 109), then cut crosswise into ½-inch-thick slices. Parboil for 3 minutes, drain, and allow to cool to room temperature. Combine for the miso bed: ½ cup red miso, ½ teaspoon each grated gingerroot and sesame oil, 1 teaspoon sake or white wine, and a dash of (7-spice) red pepper or tabasco sauce. Embed tofu for 12 to 15 hours, then remove carefully and wipe miso from tofu surface with a damp cloth. Cut into ½-inch cubes and, for best flavor, broil on both sides until nicely speckled. This preparation has a soft cheeselike consistency, rich fragrance, and mellow saltiness. Served as is, it makes a tasty garnish for rice or a savory hors d'œuvre. Mashed with thinly-sliced vegetables, it goes well on crackers. To make a sandwich spread or dip, try mixing 3 parts pickled tofu with 2 parts sesame- or peanut butter, 1 part honey, and a little lemon juice.

Or, dry very well pressed tofu in a slow oven for about 1 hour. Cut each cake crosswise into thirds and embed in the miso for 1 year. Sold commercially in Japan, this product has a much firmer consistency than that described above; its appearance and aroma resemble those of a well-aged cheese. (Some varieties are wrapped in *kombu* and beefsteak leaves, and embedded in mellow barley miso.)

For a sweeter product, sprinkle parboiled tofu slices with ¼ teaspoon salt and embed for 2 days in a mixture of 1½ cups sweet white miso and 2 teaspoons sake (or white wine). Broil and serve as above.

Uri or White Melons

Cut each melon lengthwise into halves. Salt-press for 2 to 4 days. Embed in red miso for 3 months.

Wakame

Use 1 cup fresh or refreshed (uncut) *wakame*. Embed in 2 cups red miso for 1 week or in sweet white miso for 8 to 10 days. Serve thinly sliced as a garnish for rice or rice gruel.

Watermelon Rind

Remove green skin and pink flesh. Cut rind into 1-inch squares and parboil for 2 minutes in lightly salted water. Drain well, pat dry with a towel, and embed in sweet white miso; refrigerate for 2 to 3 weeks. Serve as an hors d'œuvre or garnish, or use in fruitcakes.

DAIKON MISO PICKLES
(Commercial Process)

The following process, used by most of Japan's large commercial makers of miso pickles, is said to create a long-lasting product with the best flavor, texture, and color. All vegetables are pickled in basically the same way; only the proportion of salt used and the pickling time varies. An increase or decrease in the weight of the *daikon* (or other vegetables) should be accompanied by an exactly proportional change in the weight of the other ingredients, and of the pressing weight.

In the commercial process, up to 1,200 pounds of *daikon* are pickled at one time in large polymer or concrete tanks; more traditional makers use wooden vats with a capacity of 175 pounds. The following recipe has been scaled down for use in households or communities.

10 pounds daikon, slender varieties used whole, fat
       varieties cut lengthwise into fourths
2 pounds salt
10 pounds red or barley miso, approximately

I. SALT PICKLING (Shiozuké)

1. *First Salt Pickling (Arazuké):* Wash *daikon*
thoroughly and drain well. Place in a large (18 inch
diameter, 18 inch deep) sturdy wooden, crockery, or
plastic tub and sprinkle uniformly with 1.2 pounds salt
(12 percent of the daikon's weight). Arrange *daikon*
as snugly and compactly as possible in container, then
top with a sturdy (wooden) pressing lid and a 20- to
30-pound weight. Cover container with a layer of plastic wrap or paper to keep out insects and dust, and
allow to stand for 15 to 20 days.

2. *Second Salt Pickling (Chuzuké):* Pour off and
discard any liquid that has accumulated in the pickling
container. Drain *daikon* thoroughly, then sprinkle
with 0.6 pounds salt (6 percent of *daikon's* original
weight). Replace lid and re-press, this time using only
a 20- to 25-pound weight; allow to stand for 60 to 90
days.

3. *Washing and Pressing (Shionuki):* Wash *daikon*
well with water, then place in a tub of cold running
water for 15 to 20 hours, or until the residual salt content of the *daikon* has dropped to about 10 percent.
(Professional pickle makers determine this by measuring the relative density of a puréed sample of the
daikon or of the liquid pressed from them.) Drain
washed *daikon* well and place into an empty tub
(preferably one with small drainage holes in the lower
sides and bottom). Replace pressing lid and top with
a 3- to 4-pound weight for 3 to 4 hours, or until liquid
equal to about 15 percent of *daikon* weight is expelled. Remove *daikon* and discard liquid.

II. MISO PICKLING (Misozuké)

4. *Preliminary Miso Pickling (Shitazuké):* Measure out an amount of miso equal to 1.5 times the
weight of the pressed *daikon*. (If possible, use miso

which has already been used once in step 5 below). Arrange alternating layers of miso and *daikon* in the tub used in step 1, so that each daikon is completely surrounded by miso. Spread a double layer of cloth or sheet of plastic wrap directly over miso surface, top with lightly weighted (3-pound) pressing lid (to prevent mold growth), and allow to stand for 5 to 8 days.

5. *Basic Miso Pickling (Honzuké):* Remove *daikon* from miso, reserving miso (which now contains a fairly high proportion of liquid) for use in step 4 of your next batch of pickles, after which it is discarded. Measure out an amount of fresh miso equal in weight to that used in step 4 and mix into it 0.2 pounds of salt plus 1 to 2 ounces each of any or all of the following natural organic acids: racemic (grape), glutamic, citric, malic (apple), lactic. Embed *daikon,* cover, and allow to stand for at least 60, preferably 120 to 180 days, or until you are ready to use it. Remove only as much *daikon* from miso as you plan to serve in one week or less. Scrape miso from *daikon* by hand, returning miso to pickling container. Wash *daikon* and slice into thin rounds before use. When all *daikon* has been used, reserve miso remaining in keg for step 4 of a future batch.

OTHER MISO PICKLES (Commercial Process)

*Cucumbers and Uri Melons: In the first salt pickling, use an amount of salt equal to 16 percent by weight of the vegetables; in the second, 8 percent. Do basic miso pickling for at least 70 days.

*Daikon Moromi Pickles: Proceed as for *daikon* pickles but wash in step 3 until only 6 percent salt remains, then pickle in moromi miso for at least 70 days.

*Eggplants: In the first salt pickling use an amount of salt equal to 18 percent by weight of the vegetables; in the second, 6 percent. Do basic miso pickling for at least 120 days. (Note: burnt alum is sometimes used in place of salt in the first salt pickling.)

*Gingerroot: For best results, choose large, mellowflavored roots. In the first salt-pickling use an amount of salt equal to 20 percent by weight of the vegetables; omit the second salt pickling. Pickle for at least 90 days in sweet white or mellow barley miso.

*Kombu: Use best quality, sweet kombu having a dark color tinged with black. Wash well in lukewarm water and steam for 15 to 20 minutes. Allow to cool to room temperature, then pickle (flat or rolled) in red miso for at least 120 days.

Miso pickles with tea

Koji Cookery

If you prepare your own koji at home (p. 433) or purchase ready-made varieties, you may have a little left over after using it to make miso. The following recipes suggest ways of using koji in other preparations.

Amazaké

MAKES 3½ CUPS

Literally "sweet sake" (pronounced ah-mah-ZAH-kay), this creamy-thick hot drink has a rich, ambrosial flavor and virtually no alcohol content. A specialty at numerous teahouses and inns, it is often served with Dengaku (p. 355) and is most popular during the winter months—especially at New Year's. Rich in natural sugars (22.7% by weight vs. 34.8% in sweet white miso, 70.2% in honey, and 83.0% in *mizuamé*), it has long served as a sweetening agent in Japanese cookery. The first person to start commercial production of fine *amazaké* in the West will, no doubt, receive the eternal blessings of heaven and earth.

1 cup white, brown, or glutinous rice, washed and
    drained
2 cups water
2 cups firm granular rice koji

Combine rice and water in a pressure cooker and bring to full pressure (15 pounds). Reduce heat to low and simmer for 3 minutes if using white rice, or 20 minutes for brown rice. Remove from heat and allow pressure to come down naturally for 10 minutes. (Or cook in a regular pot as described on page 116.) Open cooker, stir well, and allow to cool to 140°F. Mix in *koji* and pack mixture into a well-washed (or sterilized) wide-mouth jar or crock. Cover tightly and incubate at 140°F for 10 to 14 hours or at 90°F for 20 to 24 hours.

(To incubate, float the container in a large covered pot or tub partially filled with warm water, or wrap in towels and place over a hot water heater or in an insulated box next to hot water bottles.)

The incubation is complete when the mixture has a rich, sweet fragrance and individual grains are very soft. Now stir well with a fork or several chopsticks to create a porridge-like consistency or, if using brown rice and a smooth texture is desired, purée in a blender or sieve. You now have amazaké base, which may be used in any of four ways:

*To Serve as Amazaké: Combine 1 part base with 1½ to 1¾ parts water in a saucepan and bring just to a boil. Season lightly with salt, pour into pre-heated cups, and top each portion with a dab of grated gingerroot.

*To Use as a Sweetener: Substitute 3½ tablespoons amazaké base for 1 tablespoon honey (or 2 tablespoons sugar) in any of your favorite preparations. Rich in enzymes, it is especially good in breads, cakes, pancakes, waffles, or muffins, where it assists in the leavening process and adds a rich moistness.

*To Make Doburoku *(grog):* Incubate for 7 to 10 more days at body temperature, or until the mixture develops a heady, slightly alcoholic aroma. Purée and serve as is, or dilute as above.

*To Make Sake *(rice wine):* Mix koji with cooked steamed rice and several species of yeasts of the genus *Saccharomyces* (especially *S. Cerevisiae,* also used in making grape wines); incubate for 10 to 14 days, while the yeasts ferment the sugars to alcohol. Filter then press off the final liquor, which should have an alcohol content of 14 to 17 percent.

Bettara-zuké *(Daikon Pickled in Koji)*

In Japan, koji is used in the preparation of several types of pickles, including *daikon,* eggplant, and Chinese cabbage. As delectable as it is costly, *Bettara-zuké* has a unique mellow sweetness and juicy crunchiness combined with a heady aroma.

1 small *daikon,* peeled, cut lengthwise into quarters
    and then crosswise into fourths
2 tablespoons salt
1 cup white rice, cooked and cooled to body
    temperature
1 cup koji
¼ cup sake, white wine, or *shochu*
¼ teaspoon minced red peppers (optional)

Please begin by reading about Miso Pickles (p. 385). Air-dry *daikon* sections for 2 to 4 days until soft and well contracted, then salt-press using the 2 tablespoons salt. Pour off excess liquid and discard.

Meanwhile, combine warm rice, koji, and sake in a well-washed quart jar, cover tightly, and incubate at about 110°F for 2 days (or 80°F for 3 to 4 days), or until rice almost decomposes. Now combine salt-pickled *daikon* with rice-koji mixture and, if desired, sweetening and red pepper; allow to stand at room temperature for 6 to 10 days or until sweet and transparent. Remove *daikon* and scrape off koji mixture with your fingers; do not wash *daikon*. Slice into thin rounds and serve as an accompaniment for rice or as an hors d'oeuvre.

Eggplants Pickled in Koji (Nasu no Karashi-zuké)

25 tiny Japanese eggplants (2 inches long, pick in autumn), caps removed, or substitute 18 ounces medium-sized eggplants
13 tablespoons salt
4¼ cups water
1½ cups koji
6 tablespoons mild mustard
4½ tablespoons *mirin*

Rub eggplants lightly with half the salt, then place (together with this salt) in a pickling container (p. 385); top with a pressing lid and 8-pound weight. Combine remaining half of salt with the water, mix until dissolved, and pour into pickling container. Allow to stand for 20 to 30 days. Pour off liquid and transfer eggplants to a bowl. Combine koji, mustard and *mirin,* mixing well, then stir into eggplants. Return to pickling container and press for 15 days more. Serve as for Bettara-zuké.

VARIATIONS

*For a richer flavor use: 4¼ pounds salt-pressed eggplants, 2¼ cups (7 oz.) koji, 5 tablespoons honey, ¾ to 1 cup mild mustard powder, 12 tablespoons sake or water, and 6 tablespoons shoyu. Mix all ingredients and press with a light weight for 15 days.

*Chinese Cabbage Pickled in Koji: In a pickling container, place alternating layers of Chinese cabbage (total 2 pounds) and salt (3 tablespoons). Salt-press for 2 to 3 days then discard liquid. Soak ½ cup koji in ¼ cup warm water for 15 minutes. Mix in 1 teaspoon honey, 2 tablespoons slivered *kombu,* and 1 slivered red pepper. Squeeze cabbage well to expel excess liquid then arrange alternating layers of cabbage and koji mixture in the container. Press with a light weight for 4 to 5 days. Serve as for Bettara-zuké.

PART III

The Preparation
of Miso

7
Making Miso at Home and in Communities

THE JAPANESE have long taken great pride in their homemade miso. During visits to the homes of friends, both in modern high-rise apartments and traditional farmhouses, we have been surprised again and again to discover how many people even to this day make their own. After mentioning our interest in the subject, we have found ourselves ushered to the kitchen, back porch, storeroom, or barn—where our hosts would proudly reveal their cache of 3 or 4 kegs or crocks—and treated to a taste of their favorite variety, followed by a detailed description of their personal miso-making process.

Indeed, the number of families and communities in Japan preparing their own miso is on the rise. For some, this is a response to rising food prices and the commercial trend toward standardization and deteriorating quality. But many are also rediscovering how enjoyable and easy it is to prepare miso with just the right flavor by choosing their own blend of ingredients and aging it for as long as they like. At least one large company (p. 569) is now doing a booming business selling *shikomi-miso,* a 44-pound mixture of high-quality koji, cooked soybeans, salt and water, packed into a keg and ready to be aged. Available in blends that produce either red or light-yellow miso, it is 10 to 20 percent less expensive than mature commercial brands and yields a product that is guaranteed to be both free of additives and, of course, unpasteurized. Yet whether they prepare it from scratch or use the new convenience mixture, most Japanese still maintain that the ancient proverb holds true: everyone prizes most the flavor of his or her family's homemade miso.

Starting in the late 1960s, a surprisingly large number of people in the United States started preparing homemade miso. Classes have been conducted by natural food companies and Japanese-American makers, and recipes for barley and red miso have been published and distributed. Names of organizations and individuals actively interested in such work are given on page 575.

The three most important factors affecting the quality of homemade miso are: 1) the quality of the koji; 2) the use of a proper fermentation container; and 3) the maintenance of a clean environment during preparation. Working with clean hands and utensils is of the utmost importance in keeping the influence of contaminating microorganisms to a minimum. Before making your own miso, please read Appendix C in order to get a sense of the chemical and microbiological changes you will be helping on their way.

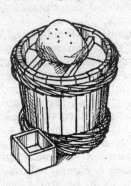

Four Decisions

Before starting your miso, you will have to make four basic decisions:

1. **The Time of Year:** For best results, make miso during the cold months when the air is relatively free of contaminating microorganisms. Such molds and

bacteria increase in number during the warmer part of the year and can impart an undesirable (sour or acidic) flavor to the finished product. Late November or early March are the best times for preparing homemade koji since the weather is cold but not *too* cold. Some Japanese prefer to make their miso in the fall when the new-crop soybeans and rice are at their peak of flavor; others prefer early spring, just before the warm months when most of the transformation due to fermentation takes place in the kegs. Miso prepared during the cold months will be ready by October when the heat of summer is past and fall breezes begin to chill the air. In Japan, families generally make miso only once a year, preparing one vat of each of several varieties.

2. **To Make or Buy the Koji:** Homemade koji can be prepared for less than one-fourth the cost of store-bought varieties, but the process takes about two days and it is not always possible to get a top-quality product on the first try. Nevertheless, if the instructions contained in the second half of this chapter are followed carefully, you should get good results. Most Japanese homemade miso is presently prepared with ready-made koji: the recipes are easy to follow, take very little preparation time, and are virtually foolproof. We have therefore placed them at the start of this chapter to encourage beginners to try them first.

3. **The Vat Size:** We will henceforth use the word "vat" to refer to all sizes and types of fermentation containers. The total amount of miso you wish to prepare determines the size of the vat you will need. It is generally agreed that *the larger the vat, the easier it is to produce delicious miso*. Why? Because the larger the vat, the smaller the total surface area (bottom, sides, and top) of the miso in proportion to the total volume. As shown below, the miso in the larger container has only one-third as much surface area per unit volume as the miso in the smaller.

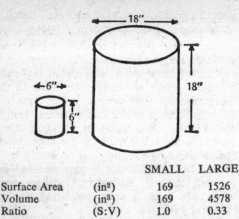

		SMALL	LARGE
Surface Area	(in²)	169	1526
Volume	(in³)	169	4578
Ratio	(S:V)	1.0	0.33

Thus large containers have a voluminous central core of miso totally sealed off from the surrounding environment; only a proportionally small surface area remains in contact with the walls, bottom, and top of the container where it is subject to gradual moisture losses through the container's pores and subtle outside (aerobic) influences. Miso in containers of only 1- to 2-quarts capacity may develop a slightly tart or alcoholic flavor, with moisture losses running as high as 5 to 7 percent of the original weight causing a concentration in salt content and an excessively "salty" flavor. For best results, your vat should have a capacity of no less than 1 gallon, which is enough to hold 2 small-scale batches as described below. A Japanese family will typically make one 10-gallon or two 5-gallon vatfuls each year; individuals might consider pooling their efforts with friends to fill one such vat. Communities often use a wooden keg of 50 gallons capacity.

4. **Batch Size:** After you have determined the total amount of miso you wish to make, you are ready to decide how many individual batches will be required. The batch size is generally determined by the size of the cooking pots and mixing containers in your kitchen. Often two or three batches are needed to fill one vat. In the following section we give three batch

sizes: small, medium, and large. A small batch makes about 2 quarts of miso, a medium batch 2 gallons, and a large batch 8 gallons. We have chosen a small-scale basic recipe so that the 2 cups of soybeans required can be cooked in a standard pressure cooker or 1-gallon pot found in most kitchens. However, if you have a large pressure cooker or pot, you will save time and fuel by doubling the basic recipe or using a larger batch size.

HOMEMADE MISO
(Using Ready-made Koji)

The following section contains recipes for six basic varieties of miso that are easily prepared at home. Each is actually only a variation on a basic theme, for in each recipe (for the same batch size) the amount of soybeans is the same (fig. 31, p. 420). The basic method calls for pressure cooking the soybeans, which takes much less time and fuel than boiling and prevents the beans from turning reddish-brown during cooking, thereby making it possible to produce light-colored misos as well as the standard darker varieties. Since a typical pressure cooker will hold just 2 cups of dry soybeans, larger batches should be prepared by multiple cooking. Overfilling may cause loose soybean hulls to clog the steam escape valve. If a pressure cooker is not available, use a pot (see Variation 1).

Using pressure-cooked soybeans, one batch of miso ingredients will be in the vat and ready to start fermentation within one hour after you begin work. The commercial miso retailed in the United States will cost you about 2½ times as much per pound as the miso in the following recipes, and 5½ times as much as miso prepared from homemade koji!

Utensils

To prepare miso on a small scale, you will need the following common kitchen utensils and a fermentation container (see illustration)

A standard pressure cooker or pot of 1-gallon capacity

A mixing pot of 1½ to 2½ gallons capacity

A colander or bamboo *zaru*

A wooden pestle (a wooden rod about 2 inches in diameter, a tall thin bottle, or a potato masher also work well), or a grain mill or meat grinder

A measuring cup and measuring spoons

A large (wooden) spoon or spatula

A vat of at least 1-gallon capacity (see below)

A sealing sheet consisting of a 1½-foot square of butcher paper, brown "Kraft" paper, or Japanese natural *washi* paper; or a double thickness of sturdy tightly-woven undyed cloth; or several sheets of wide *kombu;* or a piece of plastic wrap or cellophane

A pressing lid made of a piece of wood, plywood, firm plastic, or other sturdy material cut to fit inside the fermentation container atop the sealing sheet with a gap of ⅛ inch or less between the perimeter of the lid and the container's walls

A 3- to 4-pound pressing weight such as a well-washed stone or brick, or a water-filled jar

A piece of wrapping paper, newspaper, or polyethylene sheeting and a piece of string several feet long

A 3- by 5-inch index card

Utensils for making miso

The key piece of equipment is the vat. The ideal small- or medium-scale vat (1- to 4-gallons capacity) is made of glazed or non-porous earthenware and is either cylindrical in shape or has a wide mouth. A traditional American crock works perfectly; still used for pickling, and in natural food stores for storing and displaying grains, nuts, or dried fruits, it is available in various sizes at many natural-food stores, Japanese hardware stores, or old-fashioned American hardware stores. Or order from the producer: Marshall Pottery Inc., 1400 Lake St., Marshall, TX 75670. Tel. 214-938-9201. A glass container, which has the advantage of permitting observation of the fermentation process, or an enamelware pot also work well. Small wooden kegs sometimes sold as containers for miso or shoyu are excellent for quantities of 4 gallons or more; be sure they are well seasoned and do not use them for smaller quantities since they may cause an excessive loss of moisture due to their slight porosity. Large wooden barrels (available in 30- and 55-gallon sizes for about $5.00 each from nail wholesalers or salted salmon importers) or used hogshead casks (available in 63- to 140-gallon sizes from some wineries) are ideal for community or large-scale production. Regardless of the vat's size, the diameter of its mouth should be no greater than its depth (preferably slightly less), and the miso should fill the vat to at least 80 percent of capacity.

Vats made of polyethylene or other plastics having 5- to 10-gallon capacity are now widely used in Japan, but experienced miso makers feel that natural materials yield a better flavor, and there is growing evidence that the polyvinyl chlorides in these synthetic materials may be harmful. For this reason we also advise caution in the use of synthetics for the sealing sheet as well.

For larger batch sizes, increase the size of your utensils accordingly.

Ingredients

Each of the basic ingredients for homemade miso is now available at reasonable prices in the United States. For a list of sources, see page 574.

Soybeans: Any variety of whole dry soybeans available at natural or health food stores, co-ops, and some supermarkets. Order in bulk for substantial savings. Soy grits (see Variation 4) may be either the coarse or fine varieties now available at better natural food stores. The larger-sized and slightly more expensive "vegetable"-type soybeans, bred from Japanese stock, are preferred by some to the smaller and more widely available U.S. "field" soybeans.

Ready-made Dried Koji (*Urikoji*): This koji is prepared by drying fresh koji on large screens in an oven at 104°F. Both ready-made rice and barley koji are now available in the West at most natural-food stores and at Japanese food markets (especially at New Year's). The main U.S. producer is Miyako Oriental Foods in Los Angeles. In 1980 a 20-ounce tub of their white-rice koji retailed for $2.99, or the equivalent of $2.39 a pound. Names of other makers, importers, and distributors are given on page 574. There are two basic types of ready-made dried koji:

Firm Granular Koji is composed of whole separate kernels of rice or barley with very little downy white mycelium visible on the surface of each grain. The beige or milky-white kernels look something like slightly puffed rice. One variety is used primarily for making miso and one for salt-pickled vegetables (*tsukemono*). Miyako makes the miso type.

Soft Mat Koji is sold in sheets about 8 to 10 inches square and ¾ inch thick. It is composed of fluffy grains of steamed rice bound together by a felt-like white mycelium resembling the nap on a brand new tennis ball. This koji is used primarily to prepare homemade *Amazaké* (p. 400) but also works well in the preparation of both miso and salt-pickled vegetables.

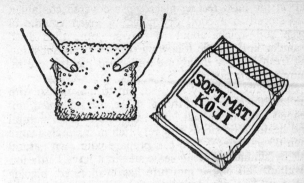

Firm granular koji is the traditional form used to make miso and is still considered the best since it has more "strength" (ability to break down proteins and carbohydrates) than the soft mat variety. High-quality granular koji will have a very small percentage of "transparent" grains (those which the mycelium has not penetrated) among the milky-white majority. Individual grains, when broken in half, should show the white mycelium penetrating to the very center and not have a transparent core.

Since dried koji does not, in general, have quite as much "strength" as fresh koji, miso prepared with it takes slightly longer to come to maturity. This explains the difference in aging times between the following homemade varieties and their commercial counterparts as described in Chapter 4.

All koji should be kept well sealed in a cool dry place. For long-term storage, small quantities should be refrigerated (but not frozen). Koji with an olive-green or yellowish tint has probably stood too long in a warm place causing sporulation; it is best used whole or ground as koji starter (p. 433).

Ready-made Fresh Koji: Although commercially made fresh koji is not yet available in the West, it is widely used in Japan. Purchased directly from a koji or miso shop the day before the soybeans are cooked, it is immediately crumbled and mixed with all of the salt in the miso recipe, placed in a covered container, and stored in a cool, dry place. A given volume of fresh koji weighs about 14 percent more than dried granular koji. In the following recipes, when substituting fresh koji for dried, use only 60 percent of the required mixing liquid.

Salt: Any salt may be used, but to make miso with the best flavor and nutritional value, use sun-dried, unrefined natural sea salt, now available at most natural and health food stores and very rich in minerals (more than 63 varieties). You can prepare your own natural salt by simmering clean sea water in a large kettle until almost all of the moisture has evaporated, placing the moist salt in a cloth-lined colander or strainer, and allowing it to drain for several days; measure homemade salt by volume rather than weight when using it to make miso. (Save the liquid nigari that drips from the salt to use in preparing tofu.)

The salt in miso mellows as the fermentation proceeds; thus miso which tastes quite salty after six months may taste just right one year later. To compensate for this phenomenon, some recipes increase the proportion of salt together with the expected fermentation time. Whereas a 1-year red miso might, for example, require 2½ pounds of salt, the same product fermented for 2½ years would require 4 pounds.

People wishing to prepare low-salt misos should make either sweet red or sweet white varieties; do not simply try to reduce the salt in other types or they may spoil. As a general rule, the minimum amount of salt used with a given weight of grain or dried koji should *not fall below* the broken line in figure 13. The equation for this minimum amount is:

$$S = \frac{45 - G}{10}$$

where S is the weight in pounds of salt and G is the weight in pounds of grain or dried koji used with 10 pounds of dry soybeans. Thus a recipe calling for 10 pounds each soybeans and dried rice koji should not contain less than 3.5 pounds salt.

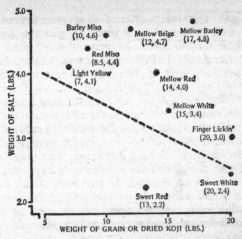

Fig. 13. Basic Proportions of Salt and Grain (or Dried Koji) Used with 10 Pounds of Dry Soybeans for Different Miso Varieties

Water: Any water may be used for cooking the soybeans or as mixing liquid (below), but fresh pure water—from a deep well, spring, or distilled—has traditionally been considered to give the best flavor and most trouble-free fermentation. Water containing an abundance of chlorine or other chemicals may somewhat retard the activity of miso's microorganisms, while impure water may introduce contaminating microorganisms.

Seed Miso: Use any good-quality mature miso, either from a previous batch of your own making or commercial miso which has not been pasteurized and contains no preservatives. The use of a small amount of seed miso as an inoculum adds large numbers of yeasts and bacteria to the unfermented ingredients thereby enhancing the aroma and flavor of the finished product and reducing the fermentation time by up to 50 percent. It is best to use seed miso of the same variety as the miso you wish to prepare, but any miso will work.

Mixing Liquid: Either boiled water or the cooking liquid remaining after boiling the soybeans is mixed with the other ingredients to give the miso its proper moisture content. In Japan, this is called "seed water" (*tané mizu*). Fresh water, unless taken from a very pure deep well, is always boiled to assure that no contaminating microorganisms are present. From November until early April, soybean cooking liquid gives excellent results and helps make full use of the soybean nutrients. However, if the miso is prepared during the warm half of the year, water should be used since the soybean cooking liquid may encourage spoilage; in this case, cook the soybeans so that very little liquid remains at the end. If you want to try to use cooking liquid during the warmer part of the year, mix the liquid with 3 tablespoons salt as soon as it has drained from the beans, and reduce the salt added with the other ingredients accordingly.

The proper amount of liquid to be added to any given mixture of ingredients is difficult to specify exactly since it depends upon the moisture level of the koji and the moisture losses through the vat (which are determined by the vat's size and construction). If too much liquid is added, the miso can easily overferment and develop a strong alcoholic aroma. The miso's moisture content can be adjusted during fermentation by simply increasing or decreasing the pressing weight.

Alternate Carbohydrate Sources: For rice or barley koji, you may substitute up to 50 percent cornmeal or corn, sweet potatoes, Irish potatoes, or *kabocha*; these foods should be well steamed or boiled (see Variation 5). Wheat koji may be substituted in equal parts. See also page 85.

Alternate Protein Sources: For soybeans, you may substitute up to 100 percent broad, black, *azuki*, lima, or garbanzo beans, or others listed in page 85. Indian pulses (Bengal gram, Thur dhal, green gram, and field beans) also work well. If 10 to 20 percent soybeans (and peanuts) are used together with these ingredients, the amino acid balance and total usable protein will be considerably enhanced (see p. 25).

Fig. 14. Equivalent Weights and Volumes of Miso Ingredients

Ingredient	Volume	Wt. (gm)	Wt. (oz)
Soybeans, whole dry	1 cup	185	6.52
Koji, dry soft mat (crumbled)	1 cup	94.1	3.32
Koji, dry firm granular	1 cup	129	4.55
Koji, fresh (crumbled)	1 cup	130	4.58
Salt	1 cup	290	10.2
Miso	1 cup	276	9.73
Water	1 cup	236	8.32
Rice or barley	1 cup	205	7.24
Miso	1 table-spoon	17.3	0.61

Fig. 15. Proportions by Weight of Basic Ingredients for Various Homemade Misos

Type of Miso	Batch Size	Dry Soybeans	Dried Koji			Salt	Mixing Liquid	Seed Miso (Optional)
			(weight)	Soft Mat	Firm Granular			
Red Miso	BASIC RATIO (WT)	10	8.5			4.4	11.1	0.4
	Small Batch	13 oz, 2c	11.1 oz	3.4c	2.4c	5.7 oz, 8.9T	14.4 oz, 1.7c	0.5 oz, 1T
	Medium	3 lb 4 oz, 8c	2 lb 12 oz	13.4c	9.7c	22.9 oz, 2.2c	3 lb 9 oz, 6.9c	2.1 oz, 4T
	Large	13 lb, 32c	11 lb 1 oz	53.5c	39.0c	5 lb 12 oz, 9.0c	14 lb 7 oz, 27.7c	8.3 oz, 1c
Barley Miso	BASIC RATIO (WT)	10	10			4.6	13.0	0.4
	Small Batch	13 oz, 2c	13 oz	3.9c	2.9c	6.0 oz, 9.3T	16.9 oz, 2.0c	0.5 oz, 1T
	Medium	3 lb 4 oz, 8c	3 lb 4 oz	15.7c	11.4c	23.9 oz, 2.3c	4 lb 4 oz, 8.1c	2.1 oz, 4T
	Large	13 lb, 32c	13 lb	62.7c	45.7c	6 lb 0 oz, 9.4c	16 lb 14 oz, 32.5c	8.3 oz, 1c
Light-yellow Miso	BASIC RATIO (WT)	10	8.5			4.1	11.1	0.4
	Small Batch	13 oz, 2c	11.1 oz	3.4c	2.4c	5.3 oz, 8.3T	14.4 oz, 1.7c	0.5 oz, 1T
	Medium	3 lb 4 oz, 8c	2 lb 12 oz	13.4c	9.7c	21.3 oz, 2.1c	3 lb 9 oz, 6.9c	2.1 oz, 4T
	Large	13 lb, 32c	11 lb 1 oz	53.5c	39.0c	5 lb 3 oz, 8.4c	14 lb 7 oz, 27.7c	8.3 oz, 1c
Sweet Red Miso	BASIC RATIO (WT)	10	13			2.2	12.3	0
	Small Batch	13 oz, 2c	16.9 oz	5.1c	3.7c	2.9 oz, 4.5T	16.0 oz, 1.9c	—
	Medium	3 lb 4 oz, 8c	4 lb 3 oz	20.4c	14.4c	11.4 oz, 1.1c	4 lb 0 oz, 7.7c	—
	Large	13 lb, 32c	16 lb 12 oz	81.5c	59.4c	2 lb 14 oz, 4.5c	16 lb 0 oz, 30.8c	—
Sweet White Miso	BASIC RATIO (WT)	10	20			2.4	19.2	0.4
	Small Batch	13 oz, 2c	1 lb 12 oz	6.6c	6.2c	3.1 oz, 4.9T	25.0 oz, 3.0c	0.5 oz, 1T
	Medium	3 lb 4 oz, 8c	7 lb	26.5c	24.6c	12.5 oz, 1.2c	6 lb 4 oz, 12.0c	2.1 oz, 4T
	Large	13 lb, 32c	28 lb	106.0c	98.5c	3 lb 2 oz, 4.9c	24 lb 15 oz, 48.0c	8.3 oz, 1c
Mellow Barley Miso	BASIC RATIO (WT)	10	17			4.8	16.3	0.4
	Small Batch	13 oz, 2c	1 lb 6 oz	6.6c	4.8c	6.2 oz, 9.7T	21.2 oz, 2.6c	0.5 oz, 1T
	Medium	3 lb 4 oz, 8c	5 lb 8 oz	26.5c	19.3c	25.0 oz, 2.4c	5 lb 5 oz, 10.2c	2.1 oz, 4T
	Large	13 lb, 32c	22 lb 2 oz	106.0c	77.3c	6 lb 14 oz, 9.8c	21 lb 3 oz, 40.9c	8.3 oz, 1c
Soybean Miso	BASIC RATIO (WT)	10				2.0	3.4	0.4
	Medium Batch	3 lb 4 oz, 8c	—			10.4 oz, 1.0c	16.6 oz, 2c	2.1 oz, 4T
	Large	13 lb, 32c	—			2 lb 10 oz, 4.1c	4 lb 12 oz, 8c	9.4 oz, 1c

Notes:

1) The ready-made firm granular dried koji produced in the U.S. by Miyako Oriental Foods weighs 175 grams (6.17 ounces) per cup, or 36 percent more per cup than the figures given in this table. Since the basic proportions of the table are based on weight, use either the same weight as shown in the table or 66 percent the required volume. Example: to make a small batch of red miso using Miyako firm granular dried koji, use either 11.1 ounces or 1.58 cups of this koji.

2) If using fresh koji, use 1.14 times as much by weight as the dried koji.

3) If using fresh koji, use only 40 to 60 percent as much mixing liquid; for firm granular koji, only 80 to 90 percent as much.

Homemade Red Miso *(Sendai Miso)*

MAKES 6 CUPS OR 3.6 POUNDS

Basic proportions by weight: soybeans 10, dried rice koji 8.5, salt, 4.4, mixing liquid 11.1 (reduced to 6.7 if using fresh koji), seed miso 0.4

2 cups (13 ounces) whole dry soybeans
3¼ cups water
9 tablespoons (5.7 ounces) natural salt
1 tablespoon seed miso (optional)
1¾ cups mixing liquid
11.1 ounces (315 grams) ready-made dried rice koji (about 3.4 cups well-crumbled soft mat koji or 2.4 cups homemade or firm granular koji)

PREPARE IN ADVANCE

Carefully remove any split soybeans (their loose hulls easily clog pressure cooker), then wash beans thoroughly in pressure cooker. Add 3¼ cups water, cover pot, and soak for 3 hours, or until beans have swelled to fill hulls tightly. Skim off any hulls floating in water.

To cook beans without pressure, see Variation 1.

If using a wooden vat, fill it with water and allow it to stand overnight to seal leaks.

1) Bring cooker to full pressure over medium-high heat. When steam first begins to jiggle vent cap, turn heat *immediately* to very low (to prevent foaming over); cook for 25 minutes at 15 pounds (30 minutes at 10 pounds, or 75 minutes at 5 pounds). Remove from heat and allow to stand for 10 to 15 minutes as pressure returns to normal. Open cooker and test for doneness; each bean should be soft enough to be easily crushed between your thumb and ring finger. Re-cover cooker.

2) See that all utensils are well washed, preferably doused with boiling water. Place colander over (or into) mixing pot, pour in cooked beans, and allow to drain for 3 to 5 minutes before returning beans to

cooker. Using pestle or potato masher, mash beans until only about one-third remain whole. Or run two-thirds of the beans through a grain mill or meat grinder. (For smooth miso, mash or grind all beans.) Allow beans' temperature to cool to 110°F.

3) Remove cooking liquid from mixing pot and measure out 1¾ cups, reserving any excess for use in other cooking; if insufficient liquid remains, add the necessary amount of boiled water. Combine in the

mixing pot all but 1½ teaspoons of the salt and, if used, the seed miso. Add ¼ cup liquid, mixing with a wooden spoon until smooth, then stir in the remaining 1½ cups liquid. Wash hands. Using fingertips, crum-

ble koji into mixing pot, then stir into liquid mixture. Now add soybeans and mix all ingredients thoroughly, using first the wooden spoon, then your hands to squeeze the ingredients together. After mixing, ingredients should have about the same consistency as mature miso.

4) Wash, rinse, and dry vat. Sprinkle ¼ teaspoon salt onto your moistened fingertips and rub salt over walls of vat. Sprinkle additional ¼ teaspoon salt over bottom of vat, then spoon in miso mixture, packing it down firmly to expel air pockets. Smooth miso surface, then sprinkle on and gently rub in the remaining 1 teaspoon salt. Cover surface with sealing sheet, pressing it firmly against miso to expel surface air bubbles. Top with pressing lid and weight(s).

5) Within several days, make additional batches of mixed ingredients as described above; rub salt over vat's walls before packing in mixture but do not sprinkle additional salt over surface of previous batch. When vat is at least 80 percent full and contains a minimum of 12 cups unfermented miso, sprinkle surface with salt and top with sealing sheet, lid, and weight(s).

6) Cover container with a double layer of wrapping paper and tie in place with string. On index card, write type of miso prepared, exact ingredients used, the date, and date at which miso is expected to be ready. Make a note of this latter date on your yearly calendar and tape index card to paper-wrapped vat.

7) For natural fermentation, choose an unheated environment such as a garage, store-room, workshop, or barn; for faster (temperature-controlled) fermentation, see Variation 2. Choose a location that receives no direct sunlight and has adequate air circulation.

Clean area well and set vat off floor on several blocks. Allow miso to ferment for at least 6 months including 1 full summer. The finest flavor will be attained after 12 months (or 18 to 24 months if seed miso is not used). Do not stir miso during fermentation.

8) As fermentation proceeds, you may wish to check the miso once every few months. However, do not open the vat more than is necessary since contact with the air encourages the growth of surface mold and contaminating organisms, and causes a slight darkening of the color and loss of aroma. If, after one month, no liquid tamari has risen to the miso's surface, increase the pressing weight. If tamari rises to a depth of more than ½ inch during the warm months, reduce the weight. To taste the miso, remove lid and sealing sheet and tilt vat so that tamari runs to one side. Using a clean spoon, open a small hole 3 to 4 inches deep at center of miso surface and retrieve a sample. Compare aroma, flavor, color, and texture with your favorite commercial miso and record your impressions on index card. If flavor is too salty or color too light, increase fermentation time. If texture is too soft, increase pressing weight and remove tamari for use in cookery (pp. 95 or 171). Overly alcoholic, acidic, or sour flavors cannot be remedied and may require that the miso be discarded. After each tasting, record date for next tasting on yearly calendar.

9) When miso is mature, remove all covering; carefully scrape off and discard any surface mold. (Although this mold is not harmful, it causes a slight decline in the miso aroma and flavor). Mix miso in container thoroughly from top to bottom to evenly distribute tamari and saltier surface layer. (Removal of tamari for use in cookery will cause a slight decline in the miso flavor.) Spoon a 1-month supply of miso into a small crock or jar and place in a refrigerator or other cool place for daily use. Smooth surface of miso remaining in container, re-cover, and weight as before. All non-sweet miso may be stored in its vat for 1 to 3 years; sweet miso should be stored in a very cool place and used within 1 to 2 months.

VARIATIONS

1) **Cooking Soybeans Without Pressure:** Wash beans thoroughly in cooking pot and drain well. Add 8 cups water, cover, and allow to stand for 12 to 14 hours at room temperature. (At temperatures below 50°F, increase soaking time to 18 hours.) Bring covered beans to a boil over high heat. Reduce heat to very low, set lid ajar, and simmer for about 2 hours, skimming off any foam and hulls that surface. Add 3 cups (hot) water and simmer for 2½ to 3 hours more, or until beans are soft (see Step 1). If necessary, add water from time to time so that about 2 cups cooking liquid remain when beans are done. Drain and proceed from Step 2.

2) **Temperature-controlled Fermentation:** Place the vat of mixed, unfermented ingredients in a warm dark place such as a water heater- or furnace room, above a stove, or in an insulated attic. During the first 2 months, choose a location where the temperature is 70°F to 75°F. Then transfer for 2 months to a temperature of about 85°F. Finally, return to the original temperature for 2 months more. Allow the miso to stand in an unheated environment for 1 week before opening (fig. 23, p. 562). (For an even faster fermentation, place at 85°F for 1 week, 90°F for 2 to 3 months, 85°F for 1 week more, then ripen for 1 week in an unheated place.) Flavor will be improved if the miso is stirred thoroughly once or twice during this period. Fermentation time can also be decreased by packing mixed ingredients into vat while they are still hot (90°F to 100°F) and wrapping vat with several layers of thick towelling.

3) **Using Fresh Koji:** Substitute for the 11.1 ounces ready-made dried koji, 12.7 ounces fresh koji. Purchase or prepare this koji before starting to cook the soybeans, as explained on page 433. Use only 1 cup mixing liquid.

4) **Using Soy Grits:** The use of grits reduces the soaking, cooking, and fermentation times, and yields a lighter colored miso. Substitute an equal weight of

grits for the soybeans in the basic recipe. a) To Pressure Cook: Soak as for whole soybeans, then pressure cook for 12 minutes. Continue as for the basic recipe. b) To Boil: Combine grits and 5 cups water in a large pot, cover, and soak for 2½ hours. Bring to a boil over low heat and simmer for 1 hour with lid slightly ajar.

5) **Using Alternate Protein and Carbohydrate Sources:** Lists of these are given on pages 85 and 417. All or part of the soybeans may be replaced by other beans. Soak, cook, and add these to the miso as for soybeans. If using alternate carbohydrate sources, add no more than 5½ ounces cooked weight and reduce the weight of koji by one half the weight of the carbohydrates added; mash well before mixing with koji. For example, to prepare a small batch of Sweet Potato Miso: Combine 5½ ounces each dried koji and mashed cooked sweet potatoes. Mix in the salt, cooked (mashed) soybeans, seed miso, and 1 cup mixing liquid (two-thirds the basic amount). Ferment as for red miso.

6) **Alternate Basic Ratios:** There are many different varieties of red miso, each determined by its ratio of basic ingredient weights. The ratio used by the Sendai Miso-shoyu Co., which makes most of the 1-year natural red miso sold in the West, is soybeans 10, koji 5.8, salt 4.5. Mr. Junsei Yamazaki (p. 576) uses 10:10:2.5 for 1-year red miso, increasing the salt to 3.5 for 2 year miso. Mr. Herman Aihara uses 10:10:3.0 for 8-month miso. Other ratios commonly employed in Japan are: a) soybeans 10, koji 6.4, salt 5.3; b) soybeans 10, koji 5.0, salt 4.1; c) soybeans 10, koji 7.2, salt 4.9. Notice that in the latter proportions, the salt is considerably higher than that used in America.

Homemade Barley Miso *(Mugi Miso)*

For basic ratios and âmounts of raw materials, see page 420. Prepare as for Homemade Red Miso except: 1) Use barley koji instead of rice koji. 2) Increase the amount of water used in cooking the beans so that the necessary amount of mixing liquid remains when the beans have finished cooking. 3) Using natural fermentation, allow miso to ferment for at least 12 to 18 months; the finest flavor will be attained after 2 to 3 years. If using temperature controlled fermentation, reduce the above fermentation time by one half. 4) Virtually all barley miso calls for 10 parts each by weight of dry soybeans and dry koji. The ratio of salt used in America is as low as 3.5; in Japan it ranges for 4.6 to 6.0, with the latter proportion requiring 2 to 3 years fermentation.

Homemade Light-yellow Miso (Shinshu Miso)

For the basic ratio of raw materials, see page 420. Prepare as for Homemade Red Miso except: 1) After soaking, drain the beans, measure the amount of water drained, and add back an equal amount of fresh water. 2) For a lighter colored miso, rub the soaked beans between the palms of both hands to remove seedcoats before cooking. 3) Pressure cook beans to give a light color. 4) For an even lighter color (accompanied, however, by a loss of nutrients) discard all soybean cooking liquid and use boiled water as the mixing liquid. 5) Using natural fermentation, age for the same time as red miso. Using temperature controlled fermentation (to give a still lighter color) ferment for 1 week at 86°F, 3 weeks at 95°F, 1 more week at 86°F, and then allow to stand at room temperature for 1 week before serving. 6) For a slightly saltier miso, increase the ratio of salt from 4.1 to 4.5 and increase the aging time by 10 percent.

Homemade Sweet Red Miso (Edo Miso)

This is an excellent variety for those who don't want to wait more than one month to sample their homemade miso. Prepare as for Homemade Red Miso except: 1) Boil the soybeans for 8 to 10 hours, adding water as required. Or boil for 4 hours, allow to stand covered overnight, and return to the boil the next morning. Both procedures give the beans a deep reddish-brown color. 2) Drain beans for no more than 1 minute to prevent them from cooling. 3) Mash no more than 50 percent of the whole beans. 4) Mix beans with koji while beans are still quite hot (140°F to 158°F). Do not use seed miso lest the final miso sour slightly. 5) Pack the mixture into vat while mixture is still quite warm (122°F to 131°F). 6) Wrap vat with heavy towels to minimize heat loss, cover, and press as in the basic recipe. Place in a very warm environment (104°F to 113°F) for 3 weeks, then unwrap container and allow miso to ripen at room temperature for one week before serving. (Or wrap and ferment naturally for 4 to 5 weeks). Refrigerate the remaining miso to prevent spoilage.

Homemade Sweet White Miso (Shiro Miso)

Due to its high carbohydrate and low salt content, this miso takes less time to ferment than any other variety and is therefore excellent for homemade miso experimentation. Wash and cook soybeans as for Homemade Light-yellow Miso. Pack into vat while beans are quite warm and wrap as for Sweet Red Miso (above). Proceed as for light-yellow miso except: 1) Reduce fermentation time as follows: If using natural fermentation, age for 1 to 3 weeks in summer (taste frequently), 5 weeks in spring or fall, and 6 to 8 weeks in winter. If using temperature-controlled fermentation, age at 95°F for 1 to 3 weeks, or 113°F for 1 to 2 weeks. Commercial makers say this miso can be prepared in 24 hours if the basic ratio by weight is soybeans 10, dried koji 20, and salt 1.5, and if the temperature of the room is 140°F. Before serving, grind the miso in a grain mill or meat grinder to create a smooth texture.

Some makers suggest increasing the basic proportion of koji from 20 to 24 if dried rather than fresh koji is used, and increasing the proportion to 30 if the miso is prepared during the winter by natural fermentation. When using temperature-controlled fermentation, many makers mix the miso once midway through the fermentation.

Homemade Mellow Barley Miso (Amakuchi Mugi Miso)

For the basic ratios of raw materials, see page 420. Prepare as for Homemade Red Miso except: 1) Use barley koji instead of rice koji. 2) Add enough water to the beans so that the necessary amount of mixing liquid remains when the beans have finished cooking. 3) Ferment the miso for the same lengths of time and at the same temperatures as for Homemade Sweet White Miso.

Garbanzo Bean (Chickpea) Miso

This miso has a full, rich, sweet flavor, a reddish-beige color, and a good luster. The basic proportions by weight are garbanzo beans 10, dried barley or rice koji 10, salt 4.5, and mixing liquid 13.

13 ounces (2 cups) dry garbanzo beans
13 ounces (2.9 cups) firm granular dried koji
5.1 ounces (½ cup) salt
1¾ cups mixing liquid

Soak the sorted and rinsed beans for 4 hours in a pressure cooker with 5 cups water. Bring cooker to full pressure (15 pounds), reduce heat, and simmer for 30 minutes. When pressure returns to normal, remove lid and drain beans, reserving liquid. Simmer liquid uncovered in a saucepan until 1¾ cups remain. Then proceed as for homemade red miso. Age for 6 to 12 months.

The following can be substituted for the garbanzos: *azuki* beans, green lentils, common beans (*Phaseolus vulgaris*), or dried green peas. Cook for a relatively short time without pressure.

Corn Miso

Use a basic ratio by weight of soybeans 10, corn 8, salt 3.7, and mixing liquid 6. Crack each kernel of grain in a mill into 3 to 4 pieces, and sift off corn flour. Soak corn for 2½ to 3 hours, steam for 40 to 50 minutes, inoculate, and incubate for 44 to 48 hours to make corn koji. Mix with the cooked, mashed soybeans and liquid, pack into a vat, top surface with corn husks, and age through one complete spring-summer-fall cycle. For a 2-year miso, increase the amount of salt by 22 percent.

Mellow Black Soybean Miso

The flavor of this miso made with a barley koji has been compared to that of a blue cheese. Whether made with a rice or barley koji, the miso has a distinctive marbled appearance: white koji on the deep purple-black of the beans. It is nice used like a finger lickin' miso and in spreads and dressings. The basic proportions of ingredients by weight using rice koji are: soybeans 10, rice koji 15, salt 3.4, mixing liquid 11.3. Using barley koji: soybeans 10, barley koji 17, salt 4.8, and mixing liquid 16.3.

13 ounces (2 cups) black soybeans
19.5 ounces (4¼ cups) firm granular dried koji
4.42 ounces (7 tablespoons) salt
1½ cups mixing liquid

Prepare as for Homemade Red Miso except do *not* use a pressure cooker. The soybean hulls (seed coats) will clog the vent. Ferment at natural temperature for 5 to 8 weeks. For a sweeter flavor, pack into vat while still quite warm and incubate at 85 to 95°F for 7 to 10 days, then age for 2 to 4 weeks at cool room temperature.

To use barley koji, use the same quantities of ingredients given in figure 15 for mellow barley miso.

Homemade Hishio

MAKES 4½ CUPS

Also called *Namé-mono* or *o-namé,* hishio is a variety of country-style namémiso requiring a relatively short fermentation. It is generally prepared in farmhouses sometime between October and May. The koji is prepared both with and without soybeans depending on the locality. The method using soybeans is more difficult since, if the temperature rises, *natto*

bacteria often propagate and the miso fails. In some
localities, instead of stirring the miso daily, a pressing
lid is used and the miso is left untouched. Hishio is
thought to be the earliest ancestor of present-day
shoyu.

4 ounces eggplant, well washed
5 ounces cucumber or *uri* melon, well washed
8 tablespoons salt
3 cups (13.4 ounces) ready-made dried wheat or
    barley koji
2¼ cups boiled water
2 ounces gingerroot, parboiled, and thinly sliced
    (optional)

Parboil eggplant and cucumber for about 1 minute to
sterilize, then cool briefly and dice. Combine in a
small bowl with 1 tablespoon salt, and gently rub salt
into vegetables. Set a plate atop the layer of vegetables in bowl and place a 4- to 5-pound weight atop
plate. Cover bowl with plastic wrap and press for 1
week.

On the same day vegetables begin to press, combine the koji, water, remaining 7 tablespoons salt
and, if used, the gingerroot in the fermentation container. Cover container with a sheet of paper or plastic wrap held in place by a string, and place container
in a clean location which receives no direct sunlight.
Stir the mixture thoroughly once daily.

After 1 week, pour off all liquid from the pressed
vegetables and discard. Wash hands, then squeeze
vegetables firmly to expel any excess liquid. Mix vegetables into fermenting hishio. Allow hishio to ferment for 3 more weeks, stirring daily. The finished
product should have a very moist texture (similar to
applesauce) and pleasant, subtly sweet fragrance and
flavor. Store covered in a cool place or refrigerator to
prevent further fermentation.

To prepare the same miso using soybeans, use
3⅓ cups rice koji, 1 cup soybeans and ⅓ cup salt,
plus other ingredients as listed above. Cook beans,
cool to body temperature and mash, then mix with
the koji and cooking liquid. Add remaining ingredi-

ents and transfer to a crock. Allow to ferment, mixing daily, for about 1 to 2 weeks.

Indian Pulse & Soybean Miso

Developed in 1963 by Dr. T. N. Rao of the Central Food Technological Research Institute in Mysore, India, this flavorful product is a good example of how Japanese miso can be adapted to the tastes and ingredients of other countries. The use of a relatively small proportion of soybeans and peanuts together with local pulses greatly enhances the amino acid balance; the resultant product contains 11.2 percent protein when Bengal gram is used and 8.7 percent with Thur dhal. The percentages of salt are 5.0 and 5.4 respectively. To give a longer shelf life, powdered red peppers or chilies may be added to taste.

2¾ pounds dehulled Bengal gram or Thur dhal,
     soaked for 15 hours in water to cover
½ pound whole dry soybeans, soaked for 12 hours
¾ pound chopped peanuts
2½ pounds rice koji
¾ pound salt

Pressure-cook pulses like soybeans (25 minutes at 15 pounds), then drain and reserve. Combine soybeans and peanuts, and pressure cook as in the basic method above. Mix cooked ingredients with koji and salt (and spices if desired), add enough cooking liquid to give the desired consistency (45 to 47 percent moisture), and pack into vat. Ferment at 83°F for 5 to 10 days. Store in a very cool place, or refrigerate.

HOMEMADE KOJI AND KOJI STARTER

The preparation of good-quality koji is a fairly sensitive process requiring several pieces of special equipment (steamer and koji tray) that can be made or purchased without much difficulty. Don't be daunted: anyone can make good koji if he or she carefully follows the instructions given below, paying special attention to two basic points: 1) Keep your hands, all utensils, and the entire work area as clean as possible;

2) Keep the koji temperature within the recommended range throughout the 45-hour incubation period.

Most Japanese prepare koji at the same time of year they make miso, in the late fall or early spring, when the weather is cool and the number of contaminating microorganisms in the air is fairly low. The koji is generally prepared indoors in a room with a clean wooden floor. A typical batch calls for about 30 pounds of rice or barley so that the scale is considerably larger than in the following recipe. We have preferred to start with a smaller batch since the equipment is easier to obtain and you can easily increase all of the ingredients by as much as you like after your first small-scale success. The following recipe yields just enough koji for 1 medium-sized batch of Homemade Red Miso (p. 428). The amount of rice given just fills a typical steamer during one steaming.

To obtain a better perspective on the process of making koji, study the traditional miso shop method (Chapter 9), and to see how it fits into the integrated process of preparing Homemade Red Miso, study the flow chart in figure 16. The time schedule built into the following recipe ensures that all of the work can be done during ordinary waking hours. In all koji recipes, 1 pound of uncooked rice yields about 1.14 pounds of fresh koji. In the basic miso proportions on page 420, the weight of ready-made dried koji is the same as the weight of uncooked rice necessary to prepare fresh koji.

Utensils for making koji

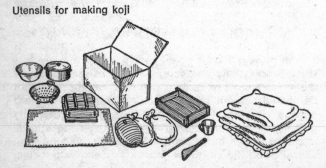

Utensils

A wooden koji tray about 16 by 10 by 2½ inches
deep with a lid consisting of 1 or 2 thin boards.
Japanese trays are made of cedar (*sugi*), but
Douglas fir, cherry, or pine also work well.
Join boards with dowels or pegs to prevent rust-
ing. A desk or bureau drawer, a cloth-lined enamel or stainless steel tray, or a shallow fruit box
may also be used.

A 1-gallon soaking container

A 1½- to 2-gallon kettle or wok. The kettle must
have a flat rim and no handles rising above the
rim to interfere with the steamer.

A 2- to 3-quart strainer or a cloth-lined colander

A square steamer (used with the kettle and easily
made at home) or a round Chinese bamboo
steamer with a woven bamboo lid (used with a
wok and available at most Chinese hardware
stores). Additional layers of steaming compartments may be added when using more than 6 to
8 cups of rice. The square steamer shown in the
illustration is made of ¾-inch-thick cedar
boards; it is 9½ inches square and 4½ inches
deep inside. Two ¾-inch-square boards near
the bottom support a 9½-inch square bamboo
mat which forms the steamer's floor. The base is
a 13-inch-square board with a ¾-inch-diameter
hole at the center. The steamer lid is composed
of 2 boards reinforced on top to prevent buck-
ling. An excellent Western-style steamer may
also be improvised by placing a large colander
atop several bricks or an inverted bowl inside an
even larger kettle.

A steamer cloth made of coarsely-woven cotton or
linen about 18 by 30 inches (or 24 inches
square when used with the round steamer). Do
not use ordinary dish-towel cloth; its relatively
fine weave will not allow the passage of steam.

A wooden spatula or spoon

5 to 6 heavy-duty blankets (the oldest ones you

have). A thick, flat cushion several feet square and a tarp may be substituted for 2 of them.

A clean linen sheet, or a piece of cotton cloth or *gyoza* mat of comparable size

A jar or bowl of several cups capacity

2 hot water bottles each wrapped in a small terry-cloth towel or placed into a terrycloth sack with a drawstring mouth

2 thermometers (range 65°F to 130°F)

An incubation box, preferably one of sturdy card-board about 20 by 12 by 14 inches deep. It must be slightly larger than the koji tray. Poke a ¼-inch-diameter hole through lower left side of box, about 3 inches above the base.

Fig. 16. Miso Flow Chart

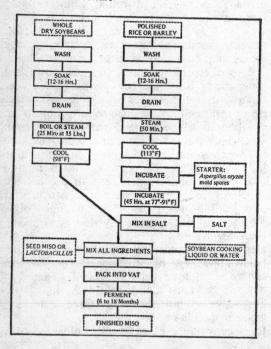

Ingredients

Rice: Most rice koji (for *amazaké* and *tsukemono* as well as for miso) is prepared from short-grain white (milled or polished) rice, most modern makers believing that the bran layers of brown rice inhibit the penetration and growth of the mycelium. For a discussion of the basic techniques and difficulties of preparing brown-rice koji, see page 59. Beginning koji makers may wish to experiment with a koji midway between the white and brown varieties by removing 50 to 75 percent of the bran layers and cracking the kernels into several pieces, thereby exposing the soft inner carbohydrate core to mycelium growth. Rice is always steamed, never boiled, to make koji; the latter process creates a wet texture which encourages the growth of undesirable bacteria. One cup raw rice (7.24 oz) yields 1.80 cups (8.25 ounces) fresh koji.

Barley *(O mugi, seimugi, hadakamugi):* For basically the same reasons that white rice is generally used to make rice koji, pearled barley (whole grains of unrolled natural barley with the bran layers removed) is used to prepare barley koji—and has been since ancient times. Barley contains slightly more protein, but slightly less carbohydrate and natural sugar than rice (fig. 17). Thus barley miso generally

Fig. 17. Composition of Nutrients in 100 Grams of Basic Miso Ingredients

(Source: Standard Tables of Food Composition, Japan)

Ingredient	Food Energy	Protein	Fat	Carbohydrates (incl. fiber)	Ash
	Calories	*Percent*	*Percent*	*Percent*	*Percent*
Koji, Rice	334	6.0	0.7	73.4	0.4
Rice, white	351	6.2	0.8	76.9	0.6
Rice, brown	337	7.4	2.3	73.5	1.3
Barley, pearled	337	8.0	0.7	76.6	0.7
Barley, unpearled	335	10.0	1.9	71.7	2.4
Soybeans, whole	392	34.3	17.5	31.2	5.0
Soybean meal, defatted	322	49.0	0.4	36.6	6.0

has a slightly higher nutritional value and is less sweet than rice miso. Other things being equal, the lack of sugars makes it necessary to ferment barley miso somewhat longer than rice miso.

Some miso makers prefer to use "naked" barley (*hadakamugi*) which is sometimes classified as a type of rye and yields miso with a unique aroma and flavor. It is also softer and free of the residual "centerline" and hull characteristic of polished regular barley (*omugi*) so that it gives the miso what many consider to be a more agreeable texture.

Other Koji Grains: In some traditional miso shops and many farmhouses, whole wheat is used to make koji for *hishio* and Kinzanji miso. Cornmeal is also used as the koji substrate in order to create a less expensive miso. In the Shinshu area, where the latter technique originated, cornmeal is soaked in water for 1 hour, steamed for 40 minutes, cooled to body temperature, and then inoculated with starter as for rice koji. In some areas rye, oats, millet, corn kernels and even sweet potatoes are used as the substrate.

Koji Starter *(tané koji, koji kin):* Koji starter is now available from several natural food suppliers in the United States (p. 574) or in small quantities from the Northern Regional Research Center (p. 573). The best source, GEMS Cultures in Fort Bragg, N.C., imports koji starter from one of Japan's most esteemed producers, Nihon Jozo Kogyo (p. 572), which makes eight basic types: one each for red-barley, and mellow barley miso; two for soybean miso; and three for sweet white miso. Each type is available in at least one of three different forms (whole-grain, meal, or spore powder) and some types are fortified with yeasts and Lactobacilli. Most starters are a mixture of pure-culture mold strains, each having different capabilities in breaking down proteins, carbohydrates, and oils. Among the total of 17 different varieties and forms produced by Nihon Jozo, those most widely available in North America are the spore-powder starters for red, barley, soybean and light-colored misos, and for shoyu. Each comes sealed in a foil envelope weighing about 1½ ounces.

Always keep starters well sealed in a refrigerator at 40°F to 59°F. Do not freeze.

All starter is olive green in color. The spore powder is 5 times as concentrated as the meal or whole grain forms and only 10 grams (1 tablespoon) are required to inoculate 110 pounds of (uncooked) rice. One tablespoon of the other two forms weighs 8.8 grams and will inoculate 19 pounds of rice. In cold weather or with small amounts of rice (less than 5 pounds), doubling the dosage of starter called for on the package yields good results.

If you already have a small amount of starter and wish to prepare more of your own see pages 449 and 553.

A detailed description of the various types of koji starter and the way they are produced is given in our *Miso Production: The Book of Miso, Volume II.*

Homemade Rice Koji *(Using Koji Starter)*

MAKES 3.1 POUNDS (11 CUPS)

6.1 cups (2.7 pounds) white rice
⅝ teaspoon (1.9 grams) spore powder koji starter or
    1½ teaspoons (4.4 grams) meal or whole-grain
    starter
¼ cup (lightly roasted) white or whole-wheat flour

PREVIOUS AFTERNOON

Wash and scrub koji tray thoroughly, rinse with boiling water, and set upside-down to dry in a clean (sunny) place. Wash rice 3 or 4 times in soaking pot and soak for 12 to 16 hours in water to cover.

DAY 1:

1) 8:00 a.m.: Fill kettle (or wok) two-thirds full of water and bring to a boil. Meanwhile, transfer soaked rice to a large strainer or cloth-lined colander, rinse under cold running water, and drain well. Rinse off steamer, insert bamboo mat, and line bottom and sides with moistened steamer cloth. Place steamer and base atop kettle (or place round steamer into wok)

and pour rice into steamer to a depth of about 2 inches. (For large batches of koji, if all rice will not fit into one steamer layer, either add a second layer or steam rice in several consecutive batches.) Using wooden paddle or spoon, press rice firmly into corners of steamer and smooth rice surface (see illustrations).

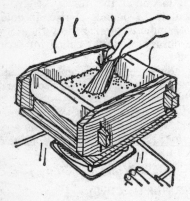

Fold over ends of cloth to cover. When steam rises through rice, cover with lid, and turn heat to medium-high. Steam for 50 minutes.

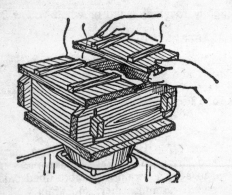

2) While rice is steaming, spread 2 blankets in a double layer atop a large table. Fold a clean sheet end to end and spread atop blankets.

Combine the flour and koji starter in a small cup. Mix well, cover, and place on table near blankets.

Fill a hot water bottle with boiling water; wrap in a small terrycloth towel or place in a towel sack.

3) Transfer hot steamed rice to center of sheet. Using wooden paddle, mix rice thoroughly, breaking up all lumps, and spread to a depth of about 1 inch over a small area at the center of sheet. Insert thermometer into rice and wait several minutes until tem-

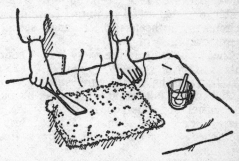

perature drops to 113°F (45°C). Sprinkle one-half of the starter-flour mixture over rice and stir vigorously with paddle until starter spores are evenly distributed throughout grain. Sprinkle on remainder of starter mixture and stir, breaking up any remaining small lumps.

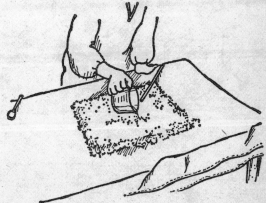

4) Mound and pack inoculated rice into a hemisphere at center of sheet. Insert thermometer into rice and fold edges of sheet snugly over hemisphere to form a compact bundle. Use the 2 blankets on the table to wrap bundle firmly, to minimize heat loss. Place hot water bottle atop another thick blanket folded into fourths (or a large flat cushion). Place bundled rice directly on top of hot water bottle and cover with at least two more thick blankets. Place this entire insulated "package" in a clean, out-of-the-way place, preferably one that is fairly warm. (Avoid locations near circulating air heaters; the Japanese set their koji on boards over a warm bath.)

5) Check rice temperature every 2 to 4 hours, seeing that it stays between 77°F and 95°F (25°C and 35°C). To raise the temperature, add fresh or additional hot water bottles and/or more blankets; to lower, transfer hot water bottle to below the bottom blanket and/or remove topmost blankets. Just before retiring, check temperature and insert a fresh hot water bottle.

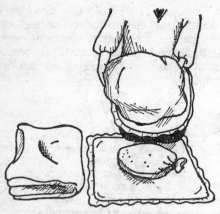

DAY 2:

6) 8:00 a.m.: Check that koji temperature is within the range prescribed above. Adjust heat to bring temperature to about 95°F. Wash hands and open

bundle. The young koji should now have a pleasant aroma, and individual grains should have a white, powder-like coating and be very loosely bound together by an almost invisible mycelium. If areas of bluish-green, black, or pink molds appear, carefully remove and discard. Now mix rice thoroughly and re-bundle.

7) 10:00 a.m.: Check koji temperature, wash hands, and open bundle. Re-check aroma and appearance, then transfer koji from sheet to koji tray. Mix koji, breaking up any small lumps. Shape koji into an oval mound 2 inches high at the highest points and

slightly hollowed at the center. Insert one thermometer into koji and cover tray with lid(s). Put tray into incubation box; beside tray place 2 fresh hot water bottles and an uncovered jar of hot water (to keep air humidity at 90 percent to 95 percent). Set box atop 6 to 8 thicknesses of folded blankets (or 1 or 2 thick cushions). Insert the second thermometer into the hole poked through the side of box and cover box with 2 or 3 thick blankets. Check box air temperature from time to time; try to keep it at 82°F, or at least within the range of 77°F to 91°F.

8) 2:30 p.m.: Wash hands and check that koji

temperature is between 80°F and 98°F. In no case should it be allowed to fall below 77°F or rise above 104°F. Stir koji quickly but thoroughly in order to break up lumps (which can cause overheating), aid circulation, and ensure even mycelium growth. Re-mound koji into oval volcano shape, re-cover tray with lid set slightly ajar, and re-cover incubation box with blankets.

9) 6:00 p.m.: Check that temperature inside koji is within the range prescribed above. Stir koji thoroughly and spread it in an even layer (about 1 inch deep) over entire bottom of tray. Re-cover tray with lid set well ajar. Replenish hot water bottles and hot water in jar. (Begin to soak soybeans as described in the basic homemade miso recipe given on page 421.)

10) 10:00 p.m. (or just before retiring): Check that koji temperature is between 85°F and 96°F. If necessary, replenish hot water bottles.

DAY 3:

11) 11:00 a.m. (after 45 hours of incubation): Open box and examine koji for doneness. The individual rice grains should now be bound together with a delicate mycelium of fragrant white mold. Break open several grains (they should be soft enough to break easily) and check that the white mycelium roots have penetrated at least two-thirds of the way to the grain's center.

(If koji has a bluish-green color and a moldy or musty odor, sporulation has begun due to over-fermentation. If koji is black and slightly damp, contaminating molds have begun to grow due to over-heating. In either case, place koji in a large colander, douse several times with hot water to wash off undesirable microorganisms, and re-incubate. Or discard koji and start again.)

12) Stir finished koji thoroughly, remove tray from incubation box and place in a cool, clean location for about ½ hour, or until koji temperature drops to room temperature. Measure into a large pot the

amount of koji called for in the recipe you wish to prepare: a medium-sized batch of red miso, for example, requires 2 pounds 12 ounces times 1.14, or about 3 pounds 2 ounces. Mix this fresh koji with the amount of salt called for in your miso recipe, then proceed to mix with the cooked soybeans as described in variation 3 of the basic recipe for Homemade Red Miso (p. 473).

If any koji remains, transfer it to a separate container, seal well, and refrigerate; reserve for use in making *amazaké* or koji pickles (p. 400), or additional batches of miso.

STORING KOJI

If for some reason you cannot use the koji immediately, spread it in a thin layer on sheets of newspaper and allow to dry for 10 to 20 hours in a clean, warm place. Then seal and store in a cool, dry place. It will keep for 1 to 2 months in good condition, or for as long as 6 months, but with a slight decline in flavor and potency.

For even longer storage, spread the (plain or salted) koji on a clean sheet in direct sunlight (or on baking tins in a 113°F oven) until thoroughly dried. Sealed and stored in a cool, dry place, it will last for up to 1 year.

Fig. 18. Changes in Koji Temperature

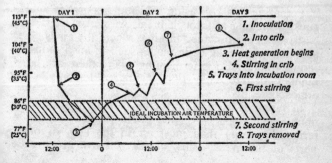

Homemade Brown Rice Koji

Soak and steam very lightly polished brown rice as described above for white rice. To prevent the growth of alien microorganisms, regulate the koji temperature very carefully, keeping it about 5° below the average temperature when using white rice. Otherwise the process is the same.

Homemade Barley Koji (Using Koji Starter)

MAKES 3.5 POUNDS (12.5 CUPS)

To make enough fresh koji for one medium-sized batch of Homemade Barley Miso (p. 427) simply substitute polished (pearled) barley for white rice in the basic koji recipe. Prepare as for Homemade Fresh Koji except: 1) Soak the barley for only 2 to 3 hours. 2) Steam the barley for 90 minutes or until the grain becomes somewhat transparent and slightly rubbery. 3) For best results try to remove the incubating koji when the mycelium is pure white, after about 36 hours. A yellow mycelium is also satisfactory but will yield a sweeter miso. A black mycelium is unsatisfactory.

Homemade Rice or Barley Koji
(Prepared Without Koji Starter)

MAKES 12 CUPS

Preparing this koji using wild mold spores is analogous to making sourdough bread without starter. The best results are obtained in areas where the air is clear and somewhat cold, or in places such as miso shops or rooms where miso is fermenting where there are large numbers of free *Aspergillus oryzae* mold spores in the atmosphere.

In Japan, it is said that the air is much more free of unfavorable organisms (that could produce toxins in fermenting koji) than most air in the U.S. or other parts of the West. Thus, unless you live in an area where the air is very clean and, preferably, cold, it is better to use koji starter.

Soak and steam the rice or barley as for Homemade Rice or Barley Koji. Spread the steamed grain on a sheet and allow to stand uncovered overnight so that it "catches" wild mold spores floating in the air. Transfer grain to the koji tray and spread it in an even layer over the bottom. Place tray in incubation box and proceed as for Homemade Rice Koji. Harvest the koji after about 3 to 4 days when it is covered with a white or light-yellow mycelium.

Homemade Koji Starter

Please begin by studying the commercial process for preparing koji starter (p. 551). The best starter is prepared from homemade koji incubated under carefully controlled conditions of temperature, humidity, and cleanliness. If contaminating microorganisms enter the koji, and the koji is then made into starter, their negative effect is multiplied. Starter can also be prepared from commercial koji, but the chances of obtaining a high degree of purity are somewhat less than with the homemade variety. Traditional Japanese homemade miso was generally started either by wild mold spores (described above) or by incubating a portion of each batch of homemade koji for 5 to 7 days, until the molds sporulated, then drying the product thoroughly and storing it for later use as starter. This latter process, known as the "cut-and-dry" method, was generally carried out without the use of brown rice or wood ash now used commercially—and good results were obtained.

To make your own starter, place about ½ cup finished homemade koji in a small wooden bowl, return it to the incubator, and keep at the same temperatures required for the commercial process until the mycelium turns from white to a soft olive green. Crumble, dry in a warm oven as described, and store sealed in a cool, dry place. Use as for whole-grain starter.

HOMEMADE MISO
(Using Homemade Koji)

In the following recipes, the preparation of the koji is an integral part of the miso-making process.

Homemade Hatcho or Soybean Miso

MAKES 6.4 POUNDS (10.6 CUPS)

We have had excellent results with this recipe. The key lies in keeping the temperature below 100°F, lest contaminating microorganisms begin to propagate and turn the soybeans into sticky *natto*. Some makers prefer to use a special soybean koji starter, however the regular starter used for rice or barley miso also works well. Please begin by studying the process for Homemade Rice Koji (p. 437), which the following recipe closely resembles, and the process for Commercial Hatcho Miso.

8 cups (3¼ pounds) whole dry soybeans, soaked for 10 hours and drained
½ teaspoon (1.5 grams) spore-powder koji starter or 1½ teaspoons (4.4 grams) meal or whole-grain starter
5 tablespoons (lightly roasted) white or whole-wheat flour
1 cup (10.4 ounces) salt (increase to 1¼ cups if aging miso for 2 years or more)
2 cups mixing liquid (boiled water)
4 tablespoons Hatcho or soybean miso

Place beans in a large steamer (p. 435) and steam for 6 hours, or until individual beans are soft enough to crush easily between the thumb and small finger. Combine starter and flour in a small bowl, mixing well. Cool beans to body temperature, then transfer onto a clean sheet and sprinkle with half the flour-starter mixture. Stir beans thoroughly with a wooden spoon, then sprinkle on the rest of the mixture and re-stir until each bean is covered with the inoculum.

Transfer inoculated beans into koji tray and place into incubation box with hot water bottles and water-filled jar as for Homemade Rice Koji. Keep air temperature inside box as close as possible to 86°F (and within the range of 79°F to 89°F), and stir following the same schedule as for Homemade Rice Koji. If the temperature rises above 100°F or if the beans become sticky, immediately remove hot water bottles and jar and open lid of box until temperature and humidity drop. Then return 1 water bottle but do not return jar for at least 4 hours, or until stickiness has disappeared. Continue incubating for 40 to 50 hours, or until beans are bound together by a dense mat of fragrant white mycelium. Mash or grind two-thirds of the soybean koji and combine in a large mixing pot with the salt, mixing liquid and mature miso; mix well. Transfer to vat, cover with sealing sheet and pressing lid, and top with weights: for Hatcho miso, use a weight equal to that of the fermenting mixture; for regular soybean miso, use one-third to one-fourth the weight. Allow to stand at the natural temperature of the environment for at least 12 months or, for best flavor, for 18 months or more, including two full summers.

VARIATION

*Tamari Miso: Please begin by reading the description of the commercial process on page 73. Prepare as for Homemade Hatcho except increase mixing liquid to 8 or 10 cups. Ferment in a regular vat (without central core or draining trough); mix thoroughly once a day for 1 year.

To extract *tamari*, pour mature *moromi* into a coarse-weave sack or a cloth-lined colander set over a large pot. Drain, then squeeze well to extract as much of the liquid as possible. Use tamari with hors d'oeuvres or as an all-purpose seasoning like shoyu. Reserve pressing residue in sack for use as a topping.

Homemade Kinzanji Miso
(Prepared with both Whole-wheat and Rice Koji)

MAKES 20 CUPS

Traditionally, Kinzanji was prepared in farmhouses during the first week of October, when there is little rain and the air is cold and clear. The koji was made from equal weights of hulled soybeans and whole wheat, the proportions still believed to give the finest flavor. However, since this relatively large proportion of soybeans invites the entry of contaminating *natto* bacteria and since it takes a long time to hull the beans by hand, some non-commercial makers prefer to use 4 parts by weight of wheat to 1 part soybeans in order to ensure success and save time.

Commercial makers say repeatedly that it is extremely difficult to obtain the true Kinzanji flavor and aroma, and not simply a miso flavor. Some makers rely on a special ready-made Kinzanji koji (which is sold commercially in Shizuoka and Aichi prefectures and will hopefully soon be available in the West), while others use rice koji to give the miso additional sweetness. Careful control of the temperature during the koji incubation is essential.

4⅝ cups whole wheat
4¼ cups whole dry soybeans
1¾ pounds eggplant, cut lengthwise into halves then crosswise into slices ⅜ inch thick
7¾ ounces gingerroot, cut into very thin rounds
2 or 3 white *uri* melons or large cucumbers cut into rounds ⅜ inch thick
½ cup thinly sliced rounds of burdock root (optional)
1¼ cups salt
4¼ cups well-crumbled rice koji
2 pieces of *kombu,* each 6 to 8 inches square, rinsed (optional)
6 to 8 green *shiso* leaves (optional)

Wash 4¼ cups wheat several times in a large pot, cover with plenty of water, and soak for 24 hours; drain well.

About 1 hour before wheat has finished soaking, place soybeans into a heavy skillet or pot and roast over medium heat, stirring constantly, until fragrant and light brown. Transfer warm beans to a wooden bowl and rub vigorously between the palms of both hands to remove hulls which are then discarded. (Or place roasted beans in a winnowing basket or on a mat and crush by rolling them under a small wooden box.) Soak beans in water for 30 minutes, then drain.

Place the wheat and beans in separate steamers. Steam the beans for about 5 hours until they are soft enough to be easily crushed between the thumb and ring finger. Steam the wheat for about 90 minutes or until the skins break open.

Roast the ⅜ cup uncooked wheat in a heavy skillet until light brown and fragrant, then purée in a blender or grind in a handmill to make flour. Spread the cooked beans and wheat in a large koji tray (p. 435), then sprinkle on and mix in the roasted flour. Place tray in incubation box and cover with blankets as when preparing Homemade Koji (p.

442); allow to ferment for about 4 days. Check temperature and mold growth from time to time. When the mycelium has a sweet aroma and is basically white interspersed with tiny dots of yellow, the koji is ready to harvest. (If it has begun to turn brown and develop a strong smell, it has fermented for too long and must be discarded.)

One day before you expect the koji to be ready, combine the four vegetables and salt in a large bowl; mix well. Cover vegetables with a large plate and press overnight with a 5- to 6-pound weight. Drain off liquid from vegetables and reserve.

Crumble the finished soybean-wheat koji, spread it on a clean surface in the sunlight, and dry for 6 hours. Allow koji to cool in the shade.

In a large vat combine soybean-wheat koji with crumbled rice koji; mix well. Add drained vegetables and reserved pickling liquid and mix again. Smooth surface of mixture and cover with one layer of *kombu*. If desired, top with a layer of green shiso leaves. Set a pressing lid on top of the miso and press with a weight of 2 to 3 pounds for at least 3 weeks and as long as 6 months. The miso may be served when the *uri* melons turn amber and become slightly transparent. (If using cucumbers in place of melons, add them 1 to 2 weeks before the miso is to be harvested.)

VARIATIONS

*Roast the whole beans, remove the skins and break the beans into halves. Mix the beans and whole wheat and steam them together until the beans are soft. Mix koji starter into the cooled mixture and ferment for 45 hours to make koji. Mix with a small amount of salt and water, pack into a fermentation container and allow to ferment for 2 months. Now add the salted, drained vegetables and ferment for 4 more months. Mix in a small amount of honey or *mizuamé* just before serving to give added sweetness and luster.
*In the above method use 4 parts by weight of wheat to 1 part soybeans. Prepare a 15% salt solution (100 parts water by weight to 15 parts salt) and add this

to the finished koji to obtain the desired miso consistency. Omit use of rice koji.

Homemade Natural Shoyu

MAKES 3½ GALLONS

The process for making shoyu is very similar to that for making miso except: 1) The koji is made of a mixture of equal parts soybeans and roasted cracked wheat; 2) A different species of *Aspergillus* starter is used; 3) About three times as much mixing liquid and twice as much salt are used; and 4) the liquid is extracted by pressing after fermentation. Since extracting a large percentage of the liquid (shoyu) is the most difficult part of the process, in traditional Japan, men with special portable lever presses would make the rounds of farmhouses each year to do the job.

10 pounds (24.5 cups) whole dry soybeans
10 pounds (22 cups) whole wheat
1 tablespoon shoyu koji starter (*Aspergillus soyae*), or substitute *A. oryzae*
8 pounds (12½ cups) natural sea salt
28 pounds (3.4 gallons) mixing liquid (boiled or very pure water)

Wash soybeans, soak in water to cover for 12 hours, then drain well. Steam (do *not* boil) at 15 pounds for 75 minutes and allow pressure to come down naturally. (Or steam at atmospheric pressure for 5½ hours.)

Meanwhile, roast wheat in a heavy dry skillet until fragrant and golden brown, then grind coarsely (or crack) so that each kernel is split into an average of 4 pieces.

Allow soybeans and wheat to cool to body temperature, then combine with the starter, mixing well. Place about 3 quarts of the mixture into each of about 8 koji trays and incubate at 77°F to 86°F for 60 to 72 hours. Mix twice as for Homemade Koji and do not allow koji temperature to rise above 104°F.

Combine mixing liquid and salt in an 8- to 10-

gallon vat; add koji and mix well. Leaving top open, allow to stand in a clean place at the natural temperature of the environment for exactly 12 months. Mix daily for the first three days, then once a week throughout most of the rest of the year (twice a week in summer); mixing incorporates oxygen, expels carbon dioxide, and prevents surface mold growth. (For a quicker fermentation, place vat in a heated room at 68°F to 77°F for 6 months; stir 2 to 3 times a week.) The finished *moromi* should have a deep reddish-brown color, applesauce-like consistency, and pleasant flavor and aroma.

The easiest, quickest, and most efficient way to extract shoyu from moromi on a small scale is to use a hydraulic press and pressing sack, the type found at many tofu shops. If this is not available, construct a pressing rack atop an empty wooden keg or sturdy pot using 4 to 6 sturdy broom handles or 2-by-4 boards laid parallel about 2 inches apart. Place a coarsely woven sack atop the rack and pour *moromi* into sack; twist closed mouth of sack. Now have two people holding opposite ends of a sturdy wide plank place plank across top of sack and bear down with their full body weight to press liquid from sack. Repeat numerous times, squeezing neck of sack tighter from time to time, until as much liquid as possible has been extracted. Remove *moromi* residue from sack and reserve for use as a seasoning; refrigerate unused portions in a covered container. Pour shoyu into bottles and keep well sealed in a cool place. If soy oil accumulates or white mold forms on shoyu surface, remove and discard.

Homemade Real Tamari

MAKES ABOUT 4 GALLONS

28.6 pounds (70 cups) whole dry soybeans
2.6 grams koji starter (*Aspergillus oryzae* mold spores)
6.9 ounces toasted barley or wheat flour
9.0 pounds (14.0 cups) sea salt
22.3 pounds (2.7 gallons) water

Wash soybeans, soak for 40 minutes, drain and allow to stand overnight. Pressure steam at 8.8 pounds for 1 hour, allow to stand for 1 hour under pressure, then mash well, shape into small (¾-inch-diameter) balls, dust with a mixture of the starter and barley flour extender, and incubate in trays at about 85°F for 46 hours; stir after 20 and again after 27 hours. Mash balls, mix with the salt and water, and allow to ferment in a large crock at room temperature for 6 to 12 months, including one full summer. Mix daily, preferably using the vertical tube method described on page 73. Extract under pressure as for shoyu.

Homemade Namémiso

MAKES 2 GALLONS

This is the recipe for the delicious *namémiso* prepared at the Amanoya shop in Tokyo (p. 567). A typical batch of theirs is about nine times as large as the following recipe.

½ pound small eggplants
1½ ounces (2⅓ tablespoons) salt
13.3 pounds (29 cups) wheat, roasted and split or cracked
1 pound (2½ cups) whole soybeans
1 tablespoon koji starter
1 gallon shoyu
¾ cup *mirin*
1⅓ cups *mizuamé* or *bakugato* (millet or barley sugar syrup)
½ pound gingerroot, peeled and thinly sliced

Place uncut eggplants in a keg, sprinkle with the salt and press under 3- to 4-pound weight for 1 week. Drain, rinse, and cut lengthwise into halves, then into ⅜-inch cubes.

Mix wheat and soybeans and soak for 2 to 3 hours (longer in cold weather) or until soybeans just yield when pressed. Steam for 40 minutes, or until a piece of wheat broken open is no longer white inside. Cool to 80°F, then mix in koji starter. Prepare koji as for Homemade Rice Koji (p. 435). Combine finished koji with remaining ingredients and the salted eggplants. Ferment in kegs for 10 days in midsummer, 20 days in fall or spring, and 30 days in winter.

8

Japanese Farmhouse Miso

THIS CHAPTER has two basic purposes: first, to describe the traditional art of preparing country-style miso and the role of that miso in Japanese culture and cookery; and second, to present this method and its tools as a model for the preparation of miso in communities in the West on a scale 2½ times the size of the largest recipe in the previous chapter.

Most of Japan's earliest miso was prepared by farmers and Buddhist priests. Indeed, throughout most of East Asia, the appearance of miso shops and professional craftsmen has been a rather recent development. Roughly 85 percent of all the miso found in present-day Korea, for example, is still made in private homes. And until the 1940s, most Japanese farmhouses and temples were totally self-sufficient in this regard.

Although there are more miso shops in Japan than in any other country in the Far East, the tradition of farmhouse miso remains alive, especially in remote rural areas and in the northeast provinces. This miso, an estimated 132,000 tons in 1974, accounts for about 17 percent of the nation's total output, with some 35,000 tons of soybeans used each year to produce it. Arriving at the right season in rural villages in any of Japan's famous farmhouse-miso provinces (Aomori, Nakano, Fukushima, Iwate, Yamanashi), one can still witness the art, craft, and ceremony involved in the ancient process. In most of these areas, one large batch of miso is made each year in March or April, during the peach-blossom season, when the farmers are awaiting the rice planting, the water is clear and cold, the air free of molds, and the temperature just warm enough to allow for the preparation of koji. In other areas, miso is made in the fall, during the lull following the harvest, for at this time, too, the weather is favorable, and the new-crop rice and soybeans are at their peak of flavor.

Every rural family that makes miso has its own distinctive variety in which it takes great pride. From this fact stems the famous proverb *temaemiso,* which literally means simply "homemade miso," but is a

compact way of saying that everyone likes his own miso best. In fact the Japanese term for self-glorification is *temaemiso;* when someone shows unusual satisfaction in something he has made or done himself, others may say in jest: "It's just like his pride in his homemade miso," or "There he goes, lining up his kegs of homemade miso."

In Japan, farmhouse miso is known as *inaka* or "rural" miso, and city dwellers speak nostalgically of the satisfying, down-to-earth goodness of the miso made in the village from which they trace their origin.

During the major holiday seasons of New Year's and O-bon (all saints week), many return to the countryside to visit relatives, and most return with a large supply of farmhouse miso to help perpetuate the good memories of their visit. Although miso connoisseurs say that the finest country-style miso is made in areas where the air is clear and cold, or in the mountains where there is a sharp contrast between day- and nighttime temperatures, most Japanese simply refuse to believe that any miso can be more delicious than that prepared in their own native area.

Three different types of miso are prepared in Japanese farmhouses. The most common is either red or barley miso, prepared using a relatively large proportion of salt and the prevailing grain of the region, with a fermentation time of one to three years. In addition, many farmers also prepare one of the more than five varieties of Finger Lickin' Miso (p. 75). In a few parts of Japan, the main type is still soybean miso made with *miso-dama* or "miso balls" (p. 476). The first and third types are most widely used in miso soups and, on special occasions, in farmhouse-style Dengaku, Oden, or Nishimé. The second type is generally used as a topping for hot rice or, occasionally, as an hors d'œuvre with sake.

Part of each year's supply will usually be made with a relatively large proportion of salt and part will be made with less. The saltier varieties are used in soups throughout the summer months, since farmers feel they require an increased salt intake for their strenuous work under the hot sun. All are used abundantly, and even today miso consumption in rural Japan is about 20 percent higher than it is in the cities.

The work of preparing each year's supply is shared by the entire family, although in most villages it is primarily the responsibility of the womenfolk; the men help with the pounding and other heavy work but often know little of the technical details of the process. Always surrounded by an atmosphere of festivity, good cheer and excitement for the children, the work begins when the family's miso-making tools are brought out of storage from the barn, attic, or cellar. The huge wooden mortar and pestle used for mashing the cooked soybeans are charged with good memories of the New Year's season when they are used for pounding *mochi* (rice cakes). The main miso ingredients are gathered and made ready: home-grown soybeans often planted along the paths between the rice and barley fields, and grain freshly harvested and/or stored in the family barn. In some areas, miso making is a communal event, with an entire village or group of families coming together for 3 or 4 days and interspersing their work with song, dance, and great merriment.

Together with the sense of festivity is an even deeper sense of ritual, so often found in traditional societies where food is gratefully received as a life-sustaining gift from mother earth and its preparation is considered a sacred act. The work is timed to begin so that the third day, when fermentation in the vats begins, is highly propitious according to the ancient lunar calendar. Before lighting the fire under the massive kitchen cauldron (used only on special occasions), the entire family is assembled and two pinches of salt are placed at the corners of the cauldron's dais or on the caldron's rim as an act of purification and offering to the many forces, great and minute, that will carry the miso fermentation to fruition. A year or more later, when the miso vats are ready to be opened, another propitious day is chosen and the family again gathers together. A small sample of the new miso is taken as a gift to neighbors, and the family tests the flavor in a special soup at the very next meal.

The koji prepared in many farmhouses is made without the use of a special starter; the ubiquitous natural mold spores, floating in the air and present in large numbers wherever other miso is fermenting, are found to be sufficient. In areas where grains or soybeans are scarce or expensive, or to produce unique flavors, rural miso makers sometimes add cooked starchy vegetables or corn to the basic mixture or even use the vegetables as the substrate for the koji.

In many farmhouses, various vegetables (which have been previously salt-pickled under pressure to reduce their moisture content) are buried in the miso just before it begins its fermentation. The art of pickling, in all of its many forms, is highly evolved in rural Japan as is its Western counterpart, the canning of fruits and jams. Homemade miso pickles are particularly prized by nursing mothers, since they are said to aid digestion and improve the flow and quality of breast milk.

Fig. 19. Farmhouse Floorplan

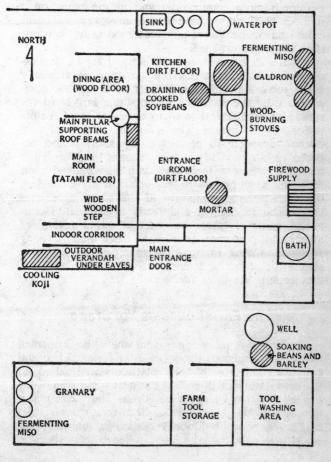

When all is done, the family gathers to seal the 20-gallon wooden kegs or 10-gallon earthenware crocks. The relatively high salt content in most farmhouse miso, the often unheated (and generally very cold) environment, and the frequent lack of "strength" in koji prepared with wild mold spores, all combine to necessitate a relatively long aging, in most cases two to three years. In recent times, as farmers have moved to the cities, farms have been left abandoned throughout the remote countryside, and in the barns on a number of these we have found large kegs of (delicious) miso which were apparently too heavy to transport to the nearest road.

Despite its survival in some parts of Japan, the traditional farmhouse method is nevertheless gradually being forgotten and is in danger of dying out completely over the next few decades due largely to the spread of commercial miso to even the most remote regions of the nation. The estimated total rural production dropped 40 percent in the short period between 1966 and 1974, and many families that formerly prepared their own koji and cooked their soybeans now prefer to buy either ready-made koji or *shikomi-miso,* a mixture of the basic ingredients pre-packed in the vat and ready to ferment. Fortunately, however, there has been a recent revival of interest in preparing farmhouse miso among young Japanese. Living in rural communities devoted to a simple life of self-sufficiency and respect for tradition, they hope to stem the tide.

The Farmhouse as the Stage

Country-style miso is prepared and often fermented inside the farmhouse itself (fig. 19). The kitchen and entrance room usually have dirt floors well suited for the heavy work of pounding the beans and supporting the log fire that heats the cauldron. The warm rice is usually allowed to cool on rice-straw mats spread under the eaves of an outdoor verandah or on the wide wooden step below which guests leave their shoes as they step up into the *tatami*-mat main room. The koji is often incubated at one end of this step next to the base of a huge, 2-foot-diameter wooden pillar that serves as the roofbeams' main support; there is access to this central area from both the entranceway and the main room. In some farmhouses, the miso is fermented indoors behind the wood-burning stoves, an area warmer than the rest of the house; this arrangement not only promotes faster fermentation but makes the mature miso easier to get at from the kitchen. In other farmhouses, the miso is fermented in a nearby barn, woodshed, granary, or *kura,* the family treasure storehouse. The fireproof *kura,* with its thick earthen walls, keeps the miso cool in summer and warm in winter and thereby works like a family wine cellar to promote even fermentation. Some families may have a special *kura* (called a *miso-gura*) used exclusively for aging miso. It generally has an earth floor and a slightly moist or humid interior environment compared with the dry environment in the family treasure storehouse.

The kura

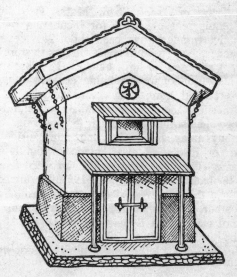

Tools

Most of the tools used by farmhouse miso makers are made at home by hand. Wooden tools are generally made of fragrant and durable cedar (*sugi*), which has a high resistance to salt, water, and heat. The synthesis of utility and artistry in most traditional tools makes them models of folk-craftsmanship.

Caldron: A massive iron pot 24 to 30 inches in diameter at the mouth and 18 inches deep at the center of the rounded bottom. It is set atop a stone dais over a wood-burning stove and used only on special occasions (to prepare New Year's *mochi* and festival tofu, for example); each occasion is accompanied by the salt offering described previously. Most caldrons have a heavy wooden lid, its boards joined by dovetailing.

Colanders: Made of thin strips of woven bamboo, each *zaru* is about 42 inches in diameter and 14 inches deep. Bamboo winnowing baskets are also widely used.

Koji Trays or Thick Straw Mats: Two different sets of equipment are used for incubating the koji. Four or five wooden trays, each about 2½ feet square and 3 inches deep (used in some villages to store cakes of *mochi*) are used for large batches. They are stacked atop a 2½-foot-square insulating cushion (*zabuton*) and covered with gunney sacks and/or quilts. If more heat is needed, metal or porcelain hot water bottles are placed against the boxes under the covering.

In many areas, the koji is incubated inside thick *mushiro,* or insulating mats, made of tightly-woven rice straw. They are about 3½ by 6½ feet and ½ to ¾ inch thick. The *mushiro* mats are placed on top of a thick layer of rice straw for insulation. In cold weather, 4 to 5 mats are used, and in some cases a layer of clean cloth is placed between the koji and the mats.

Ladle: A 2-quart ladle with a sturdy 3-foot wooden handle.

Pounding miso ingredients

Mortar and Pestle: The massive wooden farmhouse mortar, 2½ feet in diameter and about 2 feet tall, is also used for pounding steamed glutinous rice to make *mochi*. Most mortars weigh several hundred pounds and the finest varieties are made of zelkovia *(keyaki)* using only the hard, tough trunk-wood just above the roots. Wooden pestles of two designs are used for pounding miso soybeans. One is shaped like a huge mallet with a heavy, slightly rounded head; the other is simply a heavy piece of wood about 3 to 4 inches in diameter at the base and 4 feet long. It is said that in some areas, the cooked soybeans are placed in a large wooden tub and crushed underfoot by workers wearing rice-straw sandals, as was the practice in traditional miso shops.

Rice Paddle: A wooden paddle about 9½ inches long, ordinarily used for serving rice.

Soaking Keg: A 19-gallon wooden container, identical to the wooden fermentation kegs described below under "vats."

Steamers and Caldron Steaming Lid: A typical steamer consists of 4 to 6 wooden boxes, each about 5 inches deep and either 15 to 25 inches square or 22 inches in diameter. The bottom of each box is made of bamboo slats; the boxes are usually stacked one atop the other during steaming. A notch or hole in the extended sides of each box allows for the insertion of a long pole so that it can be lifted off without having to touch the hot wood. A flat lid covers the top box, and all are set on a steaming lid placed over the mouth of the caldron. A 1-inch-square hole in the center of this lid allows steam to rise from the caldron. In some cases a steam disperser is placed over this hole to allow more uniform steaming of the grain in the bottom box.

Straw Cooling Mats: Either *mushiro* mats (see above) or *gyoza* mats of about the same size and made of *igusa* reeds are spread on the floor and covered with the freshly steamed grain. Usually two, but sometimes as many as four mats are used.

Vats: Either earthenware crocks or wooden kegs make excellent fermentation containers for the miso. A typical crock is 16 to 20 inches in diameter and 20 to 30 inches deep. The inside is glazed to prevent moisture loss and the mouth is wide enough to allow the insertion of a pressing lid. A typical wooden keg is either 9½ or 19 gallons in capacity. Ordinarily used as a sake container, it is bound with hoops of braided bamboo and must be well seasoned.

Each vat has a wooden pressing lid about 1 inch thick and ½ to 1 inch smaller in diameter than the mouth of the keg. Some kegs are sealed with a tight-fitting barrelhead that is used to keep out dust. Rope may be packed into the space between the head's outer rim and the vat's mouth to create a tighter fit. Or a regular wooden lid, grooved in a circle where it touches the mouth of the vat, may serve the same purpose.

Ingredients

Grain: All farmhouse miso is made with the grain that is most available locally. Most families use grain they have grown themselves and which has been polished at the local rice shop. Traditionally, the word *inaka* (country-style) miso has generally connoted barley rather than rice or soybean miso. In some areas, wheat is used together with barley to give the miso a darker color.

Water: Water quality is believed to have a very important effect on the miso's flavor. Water drawn from the deep farmhouse well, whence it comes cold and pure, is preferred. It is generally boiled when used as the mixing liquid.

Koji Starter: At least four different methods are used to start koji. 1) *Natural Molds:* Perhaps the oldest, most difficult, and most time-consuming way of making koji, in which mold spores living in the air and on the koji trays or straw mats are used to inoculate the warm rice. It is said that in parts of Japan with clean air, molds that produce mycotoxins or aflatoxins are rarer than in most countries. 2) *Cut-and-Dried Starter:* See page 447. 3) *Commerical Koji Starter:* Whole-grain starter purchased from the local koji maker or sake brewer. 4) *Regular Koji:* A small amount of commercial or homemade dried koji is mixed with the warm grain, which is then allowed to be inoculated further by natural mold spores; the addition of the dried koji simply hastens the process, however the results are generally not as good as when methods 2 or 3 are used.

Soybeans: Japanese soybeans are generally believed to yield the best miso. While many families grow their own, those that do not, purchase them from a local tofu or miso shop. New-crop beans have the best flavor.

Salt: Widely known as *nami-no-hana,* "the flowers of the waves," natural salt is preferred. Many farmers buy a large rice-straw sack filled with unrefined salt, allow it to drain (indoors) over a wooden tub for several weeks, and collect the liquid (*nigari*) that drips into the tub for use in making tofu. They then use the "naturally-refined" salt remaining in the sack to make their miso. Since the koji used in most farmhouse miso is not prepared under the controlled conditions prevailing in commercial shops, and since country-style miso is generally fermented for a long time, a relatively large amount of salt is used to prevent spoilage and the growth of contaminating microorganisms.

Alternate Carbohydrate and Protein Sources: Miso containing a large proportion of sweet potatoes or Irish potatoes is particularly popular (see p. 79).

Pickled Ingredients: In many farmhouses, salt-pressed vegetables are packed into the miso vat together with the basic ingredients and allowed to ferment until the miso is mature (see pp. 385 and 475).

Farmhouse Barley Miso

MAKES ABOUT 16 GALLONS

The following amounts are typical of an average batch, which makes a one-year supply. Our method uses koji starter which is easiest, fastest, and guarantees the best quality. Before starting, please study Homemade Koji (p. 435) and Homemade Miso (p. 430). Many of the illustrations accompanying the basic method are adapted with permission from *Miso Daigaku*.

4½ gallons (32½ pounds) pearled barley
2 tablespoons (17.6 grams) whole-grain koji starter
5 gallons (32½ pounds) whole soybeans
1½ gallons (14.9 pounds) natural salt
3 gallons (25 pounds) mixing liquid

DAY 1:

1) Start work early in the morning. Wash and rinse the barley several times in the soaking keg placed next to your water source, then soak for 2½ to 3 hours. Fill the caldron half full of water and cover with the steaming lid. Light a wood fire beneath the caldron and bring the water to a boil.

2) Line each of 3 steamers with a layer of cloth. Drain barley and divide among the 3 steamers, covering the bottom of each with an even layer about 1½ to 2 inches deep. Stack steamers congruently on top of each other over the center of the steaming lid and cover barley in top steamer with lid or a layer of heavy cloth

or burlap. Measuring from the time steam begins to rise through this cloth, steam barley for 60 to 90 minutes. Have two people use two poles to lift the top two steamer boxes while a third person removes the bottom one from the caldron lid. Re-place the top two boxes, set the bottom one atop the other two, and cover the top box with the lid or cloth; continue steaming. Transfer the bottom box to the top in this way at 20- to 30-minute intervals until all barley has been steamed. (If desired, as each bottom box is removed, sprinkle barley lightly with water to hasten cooking, and stir vigorously with the rice paddle to break up lumps.)

3) Examine grain to see that it is somewhat transparent and resilient yet fairly soft. Arrange a double thickness of cooling mats (or blankets topped with a clean sheet) in the shade outdoors and spread barley on mats in a layer 1 to 2 inches thick. Stir barley frequently with wooden paddle to hasten cooling and drying.

4) When grain temperature drops to about body temperature, and when its moisture level has decreased to the extent that only a few kernels stick to

your palm if touched, sprinkle on the koji starter. Using the wooden paddle, lightly mix starter into barley, breaking up all lumps; then mix vigorously for 5 minutes. (If preparing koji without starter or if using koji boxes, see Variation 1.) Using your fingertips, crumble any remaining small lumps of grain, then gather inoculated barley into a mound at center of mat.

5) Fold ends and sides of mat over barley to form a compact bundle into which air cannot easily enter. Spread some dry straw as insulation to a depth of about 12 inches over an area the size of one of the mats (or use a mattress, thick cushions, or air mattress). Cover with the bottom cooling mat, then place bundle on top of mat. Cover with 2 or more straw mats, blankets, or quilts. If air temperature is low, place 2 to 4 hot water bottles beneath covering mats next to barley bundle; leave them in place for 10 to 12 hours, or until koji begins to develop its own heat. Check koji temperature every few hours and, if possible, once during the night, to see that it does not drop below 77°F or rise above 90°F. Add hot water bottles or covering mats to raise temperature; remove to lower.

DAY 2:

6) Early morning: Open bundle, check temperature, and mix barley thoroughly with paddle. Re-wrap, cover, and allow to stand for 2 hours more. Now unfold mat in which barley is wrapped and spread it flat on mat resting on straw. Spread barley in a layer 2 to 2½ inches deep over upper mat and cover with 2 to 4 more mats. At about 1:00 p.m. and again at 5:00 p.m., uncover barley, check that temperature is between 80°F and 95°F, and stir well. If temperature is too low, increase thickness of barley layer and/or add additional covering mats. Crumble any lumps with your fingertips; always re-cover.

In the evening, wash soybeans thoroughly, cover with water, and soak overnight in soaking keg placed near your water source.

DAY 3:

7) Early morning: Uncover and examine koji (p. 415). If barley is covered with a bloom of fragrant white mold, koji is at its best. With your fingertips, crumble thoroughly any small lumps. Leave koji uncovered for several hours as it cools to room temperature, then re-cover with a single mat to keep out contaminating microorganisms. (If koji mold is yellow and has a slightly sweet fragrance, it is satisfactory but not ideal; treat as for white mold. If mold is black, it must be removed; see p. 444). If koji is not yet done, re-cover with mats, bring temperature up to 94°F, and allow to stand until white mold appears.)

8) After beans have soaked for about 16 hours, drain and rinse well. Combine beans and about 15 gallons water in caldron, and light a wood fire beneath it. Cover caldron, bring water to a boil, and simmer for 5 to 6 hours, or until beans are soft. Add water occasionally if necessary. Near the end, adjust water so that about 3 gallons of liquid remain after cooked beans are drained.

9) Ladle beans into 1 or 2 colanders set over caldron and/or soaking keg and allow to drain thoroughly. Meanwhile, wash fermentation keg, mortar, and pestle(s).

10) When beans have cooled to about body temperature, shake colanders briefly, then transfer about 10 percent of the cooked beans to the mortar. With one to three people working together, pound beans thoroughly; chanting or singing helps keep the rhythm if several pestles are being used together.

11) Set aside 6 tablespoons salt. Measure out 3 gallons soybean cooking liquid. Add one-tenth each of the remaining salt, the koji and the cooking liquid to the mashed soybeans in mortar. Mix ingredients together with pestles, then pound briefly. Rub 2 tablespoons of salt over bottom and sides of vat, then pack in pounded mixture. (If preparing pickles in miso, see Variation 2).

12) Repeat mixing and packing procedure until all ingredients have been used and vat is at least 80 percent full. Now, using a long pestle or your fists, gently pound miso in keg to mix the various layers and expel air. Using a paddle, pack miso surface firmly, then smooth and level it precisely. Sprinkle remaining ¼ cup salt over miso surface, making sure to reach edges. Top miso with unweighted pressing lid, pushing lid about ¼ inch into miso. (In some areas, sheets of *kombu, ho* leaves [*Magnolia hypoleuca*], or cloth are placed between miso and pressing lid, and lid is weighted with an 8- to 10-pound stone.) Seal mouth of vat with a barrelhead or lid. Cover, if desired, with a large sheet of paper tied in place with string. Record exact miso ingredients, date, and expected date of maturity on an index card and attach it to vat. Place vat in appropriate fermentation area and allow to stand untouched for at least 18 months, preferably 2 to 3 years. Sample flavor from time to time.

To open: Stir miso thoroughly with paddle to mix in salty surface layers. Serve, reserving and storing unused portions as for Homemade Miso (p. 425).

VARIATIONS

1) Making Koji Without Starter in Koji Boxes: For this method to be successful, it is very important that the air be quite clear and preferably fairly cold, and that natural mold spores be present in the environment. Straw mats may be used in place of the boxes, as described in the method given above.

Spread steamed barley on cooling mats and allow to cool to no less than 113°F. Spread warm barley in a layer 1½ inches thick over bottom of each of 3 to 5 koji boxes. Place one box on an insulating cushion,

then stack on the remaining boxes so that each box completely covers the one below it and thereby prevents heat loss. Cover top and sides of stack with several layers of thick straw matting and/or quilts and blankets. In cold weather, heat with hot water bottles. After the first 24 hours of koji fermentation, mix the developing koji once daily with a paddle. When koji begins to develop its own heat, stagger boxes slightly to allow the entry of oxygen and escape of carbon dioxide. The mycelium of white or yellow mold should appear after 4 to 7 days depending on the weather and the number of yeasts in the environment. Discard any koji covered with bluish-green mold. Proceed as for barley miso.

2) **Making Miso Containing Miso Pickles:** Miso pickles (*misozuké*) are prepared in most batches of farmhouse miso even though this practice is generally considered to cause a slight decline in the miso flavor.

A 19-gallon keg of miso may contain any or all of the following: 5 to 6 *daikon*, 10 small eggplants, 10 cucumbers, 15 gingerroots, 2 *kombu* rolls, 4 burdock roots and/or 5 carrots. Cut very large *daikon* lengthwise into quarters; cut regular-sized *daikon* lengthwise into halves. Use other vegetables whole. Wash and drain vegetables thoroughly, then place into separate tubs or large bowls and sprinkle with salt equal to about 7 percent of the vegetable weight. Place a pressing lid directly atop vegetables and press with a weight equal to four or five times the weight of the vegetables for about 1 week in summer and 2 weeks in winter. Rinse vegetables and discard briny pressing liquid. When one-fourth of miso has been packed into the fermentation keg, arrange one-third of each of the vegetables in a layer on top of the miso. Sprinkle vegetables with a few tablespoons of salt. When miso keg is one-half full and again when it is three-fourths full, insert layers of remaining vegetables. Cover third layer with remainder of miso. Do not stir miso after keg is full. Leave pickling vegetables untouched until miso has finished fermenting.

To use, remove vegetables from keg as they are needed. Rub excess miso from surface of each vegetable and return miso to keg. Rinse vegetables, slice into thin ovals or rounds and serve (p. 385).

3) **Making Sweet Potato Miso** (*Imo Miso*): To the ingredients in the basic recipe, add 14 to 15 pounds steamed (sweet) potatoes or yams. (If desired, make potatoes into koji as for rice koji; p. 435.) Reduce the amount of salt to 4¾ quarts. Add potatoes to

pounded soybeans together with koji; mash thoroughly. Pack into vats as above. Ferment for at least 5 to 6 months, starting in April or May.

In some areas, the sweet potatoes are cooked, pickled whole in salt, and mixed with commercial miso as an extender just prior to packaging. In some farmhouses, potato koji replaces the grain koji.

4) **Making Date Miso** *(Sotetsu Miso):* A farmhouse specialty on the island of Amami Oshima south of Kyushu. Use brown rice in place of barley to make the koji. Dry and grind to a powder 1 to 3 gallons of dried dates (the fruit of the sago palm, *Cycas revoluta*). Combine and mix with the other basic ingredients just before placing them to the vat.

NOTES AND ADDITIONAL INFORMATION

1) For a relatively sweet miso requiring only 6 to 9 months fermentation, use 65 percent of the salt in the basic recipe; for a saltier variety, increase the salt by 15 percent and age for 2 to 3 years.

2) For large-scale community production, the method used by a village we studied in Nagano prefecture might best serve as a model. Fifteen to twenty people work together. A building is equipped with a small (6 by 8 by 7-foot tall) koji incubating room containing 56 koji trays; it is similar to those in traditional miso shops. The room is kept at 77°F by a charcoal brazier throughout the koji fermentation. One part barley and 2 parts soybeans are mixed, soaked, steamed for 4 hours and made into koji. Sufficient portions of the finished soybean-barley koji is taken home by each family, mixed with salt, and fermented in kegs. Most people add only one-half the salt at the beginning and the rest 2 weeks later; some add the salt six times during the first 2 weeks. The miso is stirred daily for 6 months after which time it may be served, although most families ferment it for 1½ to 2 years to improve the flavor. Tamari is sometimes drawn from the miso in a long bamboo colander.

3) Rather than using hot water bottles, some farmers warm small batches of koji next to or under their liv-

ing room *kotatsu,* a table covered with a large quilt and set over a sunken box at the bottom of which is a charcoal brazier heater. In many farmhouses, this is the only heat source for the entire family during the long, cold winter.

4) The soybeans are sometimes cooked for up to 24 hours. From morning until night, they are simmered in a covered pot over a low fire. Any logs remaining in the fire are removed and the beans are then cooked over low coals through the night.

5) In some villages, the miso is mixed once a month during the summer to prevent mold growth and hasten fermentation. The craftsman uses either his hands —well washed to the elbows—or a wooden paddle.

Farmhouse Soybean Miso made with Miso-dama (Miso Balls)

Known as *Tama Miso* (miso made from balls), this is one of Japan's earliest farmhouse varieties. Unknown in China, the method for its preparation came to Japan from Korea where the balls *(miso-dama)* are still widely used to make both Korean miso (*jang*) and soy sauce.

In the basic process, cooked soybeans are mashed, shaped into balls, and tied with rice straw. Suspended from poles or placed on a special drying rack over the open-hearth fireplace (or the kitchen wood-burning stove), they are allowed to stand for about 30 days, or until the surface of each ball is covered with a bloom of fragrant mold. (In some areas, the balls are hung outdoors under the high farmhouse eaves for up to 60 days. In Nagano, the mold-covered balls are sometimes sliced as is and fried in oil or broiled, then served something like "soyburgers," topped with a sprinkling of shoyu.) The inoculated whole balls are then crushed in a mortar, mixed with salt and water, and packed into vats, where the mixture is allowed to ferment for 1 year or more. Naturally, *miso-dama* are said to be quite difficult to prepare, except in areas blessed with clear, cold air in which the appropriate molds are found in abundance. Nowadays, miso made in this traditional, colorful way is gradually becoming a thing of the past.

Nevertheless, in a number of remote areas, it continues to thrive. In Nagano, Gifu, and Aichi prefectures, it is prepared in the late fall, while in Iwate and Miyagi prefectures it is made just after the spring equinox or the traditional lunar New Year, between late March and mid April. At both times in these places, the air is cold and clear enough to ensure that very few contaminating microorganisms are present, yet not so cold as to hinder fermentation.

Up until about 1600 A.D. most of the miso made in rural Japan was made from *miso-dama*. As the use of rice and barley koji grew in popularity (together with miso soup), the tradition of making pure soybean miso began to decline. Farmers began mixing rice- or barley koji with their *miso-dama* soybean koji just before the basic ingredients were packed into vats. And at a somewhat later stage, the *miso-dama* were largely abandoned in favor of rice or barley koji made in bundled straw mats or trays. At present, much of the farmhouse miso prepared with *miso-dama* contains rice or barley koji purchased from a local koji or miso shop and mixed with the crushed balls. Adding grain koji decreases the fermentation time and increases the finished miso's sweetness and yield. Yet many farmers still prefer the flavor of the traditional product prepared with only soybeans, and we have been impressed by the flavor and aroma produced under even the simplest of brewing conditions.

We learned the following method from Mmes. Saiyo Miura and Kazuko Shinya in the remote mountain village of Kami Ugemura near Iwaizumi in Iwate prefecture. Since each family in the village makes all its own miso (as well as its own tofu), each farmhouse kitchen is equipped with a large caldron (36 inches in diameter and 20 inches deep), a wooden tub (36 inches in diameter and 12 inches deep), and the other necessary pieces of equipment.

The following ingredients are for one batch. Four batches, usually prepared on four consecutive days, just fill a typical 48-gallon wooden fermentation keg.

9½ gallons whole soybeans, soaked overnight and
    drained
3½ (or as much as 4¾) gallons salt
Water

1) Combine beans in caldron with about 20 gallons of water and simmer for 5 to 6 hours, or until
soft. Place a 3-gallon bamboo basket on a draining
rack set across one side of the caldron's mouth. Using
a woven bamboo scoop (constructed like a concave
badminton racket), ladle cooked beans into the basket, then transfer 2 basketsful of beans at a time into
wooden mixing tub. Wearing (10-inch-high) woven-
rice straw or rubber boots, tread beans for 15 or 30
minutes, or until thoroughly crushed (see illustration).
(Or grind beans in a hand mill or pound in a mortar.)
Combine remaining cooking liquid with the salt in a
large crock or keg, cover, and store in a cool place.

2) Using both hands, shape crushed beans into
slightly oval balls, each about 7 inches long.

3) Tie together the ends of four 3-foot-long strands
of dried rice straw. Arrange strands on a clean surface in the form of a cross, place one miso ball at
intersection of strands (see illustration), and tie together at top of ball to form a supportive net. After
preparing about 50, hang balls indoors from sturdy
horizontal poles (see illustration) suspended from the
ceiling 6 to 8 feet above a heat source (open hearth
fireplace at center of main farmhouse room).

4) Allow balls to ferment for about 30 days until
they are covered with a bloom of light bluish-green
mold and are very hard.

5) Remove straw and immerse balls in water-filled
mixing tub for several hours, or until the thin, slightly
dusty surface layer dissolves in the water. Discard
water and drain balls well. Transfer several balls at a
time to a large wooden mortar, combine with a small
amount of the salted soybean cooking liquid (and if
necessary a little water), and pound with a pestle to
give a consistency similar to that of regular miso. Repeat until all balls are pounded and mixed.

6) Line the bottom of a keg with a layer of garlic leaves (or sprinkle with salt) and place in the fermentation area (*kura* or barn). Transfer pounded soybean mixture into keg and pack firmly. Smooth miso surface and top with a ½-inch-thick layer of extra salt, then a layer of garlic leaves followed by a layer of (*sasa*) bamboo leaves. Top bamboo leaves with 6 flat rocks and cover keg with a wooden lid. (A weighted pressing lid may be substituted for the garlic and bamboo leaves.)

7) Allow miso to ferment for at least 1 year, preferably 3 to 4 years for best flavor. When miso is ready, discard bamboo leaves. Scoop off upper layer of garlic leaves and salt, and mix in small amounts into fodder to feed to livestock. Mix miso well. Keep keg tightly covered when not in use.

9
Traditional and Modern Miso Production

AN EXAMPLE OF Japan's ancient heritage of fine craftsmanship, the traditional miso shop has a charm and rustic beauty similar to that found in fine old wineries: in the morning sunlight, golden soybeans soak in great wooden tubs; steam billows up from the massive black caldron and wooden steamers through the arching rafters fashioned from the entire trunks of huge trees; basketfuls of steaming rice are spread with wooden pushing tools over a cedar floor; in a dark, warm-and-humid incubation room, row on row of shallow wooden boxes hold mounds of rice covered with a delicate bloom of pure white mold; the subtly sweet and pervasive fragrance of koji suffuses the atmosphere as it is crumbled between a craftsman's palms; men in straw sandals mash soft, warm soybeans underfoot in wooden tubs or pound them in sturdy mortars with large wooden pestles; tall cedar vats made of thick staves stand bound together by wide-girth hoops of exquisitely woven bamboo; men tread freshly mixed miso underfoot, packing it firmly into vats; others working with wooden spades shovel mature miso into wooden buckets; wife and children standing at the doorway of their home watch the men work in the adjoining shop: all while the master craftsman carefully, patiently helps it to happen.

The traditional craftsman takes deep pride in the

quality of his miso, in his work and in the lineage of masters of which he is the living descendant. In many cases his apprenticeship was long and difficult and began at an early age. His master—who was often his father—customarily yielded each secret begrudgingly only after the young disciple had fully demonstrated his capacity for hard work, selfless service and devotion to the spirit of the craft. The work of a true master is a joy to watch. Years of patient and careful practice give rise to movements which flow effortlessly and gracefully. At one with his work, he cares, wasting nothing. He realizes that only by harmonizing his actions with the great rhythm of the four seasons and the microscopic chemical and biological forces at work within the huge fermentation vats can he enable fine miso to come to fruition. His work is a process of continually learning from nature, and his miso is an expression of the depth of his understanding. On the wall behind the great iron caldron in many shops is a small but well-kept altar, an expression of gratitude.

For many master miso-craftsmen—as for fine sword makers or potters—daily work is seen as a spiritual practice or, as the Japanese say, a Way. Focusing his full attention on every detail moment after moment, the craftsman discovers a space in which the restrictions of time and self cease to operate. Since his main concern is neither fame nor fortune, his work becomes its own fulfillment and reward.

The method for preparing miso in the traditional shop has a number of basic distinguishing characteristics: the grains and beans are cooked over (or in) a large iron caldron heated from below by a wood or charcoal fire; all of the work is done by hand without the use of motor-driven machines; the tools and containers are handmade and handsomely crafted from natural materials; the koji is prepared in small wooden trays in an incubation room heated, when necessary, by a small charcoal burner or stove; the miso is fermented naturally in huge cedar vats and contains only natural ingredients; it is packed into (5-gallon) wooden kegs for distribution and sale.

Japan's mild, relatively humid climate has proven itself ideal for supporting the growth of fermentation microorganisms. Thanks to this natural advantage and centuries of experience, Japanese craftsmen have developed a level of technical expertise second to none.

The first Japanese commercial miso shops were in operation as early as the year 700 A.D., but up until about 1600, the great majority of miso made in the country was prepared non-commercially in private homes. As commercial miso shops developed, they used the basic farmhouse methods and tools but on an expanded scale. Some shops prepared miso only once each year, generally in the fall using new-crop soybeans and grains. Just as many farmers prepared shoyu as well as miso, so also did the earliest miso shops. For the preparation of miso in a relatively large 17th century workplace, a fire is stoked to heat the rice steamer. The steamed rice is carried in buckets to straw mats, where it is spread and cooled. After inoculation, the rice is rolled up in the mats and carried to the incubation room. The furnished koji is carried out and mixed with salt in a large tub. Men bind staves with bamboo hoops to make wooden buckets in which they will sell the finished miso. In the storeroom, bales of rice in straw sacks and stacks of koji trays await use.

Since earliest times, the word *kura* has been used to refer to miso shops. Ordinarily the term denotes the thick-walled storehouse or treasury in which a large and fairly well-to-do family keeps its valuables, and, in some cases, its homemade miso. Applied to miso shops, however, the term takes on a broader meaning, referring to the entire business and its tradition. It also refers to the buildings and incubation room, which are said to have their own *kura-gusé* or "unique individual characteristics." These are a product of the resident microorganisms, the buildings' structure and materials, the local climate, plus the intangible yet very real vibrations and living wisdom of all the shop's past masters. The soul and life-force of a shop, the *kura-gusé* is prized and nurtured above all, for it is believed to be the primary factor determining the quality of the miso prepared within its walls.

In most traditional shops throughout Japan, the basic tools and methodology remained virtually unchanged over a period of several centuries up until the end of World War II. At present, miso shops generally prepare miso throughout the year, either daily or at least 3 to 5 times each week. Some miso is seasonal, such as barley miso which, in many regions, is prepared only during the winter. Each master has his own preferred blend of ingredients and numerous secrets for giving a distinctive flavor, aroma, color and texture to his miso.

Today the traditional shop in its pure form is largely a thing of the past. The last examples, which were located in remote rural areas, are said to have disappeared during the mid 1950s. Although traditional tools are still widely used in modern shops, parts of the basic processes have been subject to mechanization in an effort to increase productivity and cut labor costs. The result has been what we shall call the "semi-traditional" shop.

In both traditional and semi-traditional shops the basic method for preparing miso is the same, and the key process is that of preparing fine koji. To master this process and make it work throughout the varying weather conditions of the four seasons requires many years of devoted study. Like the brewer of fine wines or the maker of delicious natural cheeses, the miso master is always learning. Koji is an essential part of many Japanese foods, including sake and shoyu, and a truly accomplished craftsman known for his expertise in preparing the koji for any of these is given the rare and honorific title of *toji* or "master brewer." Many *toji* are able to prepare at least seven varieties of koji, including, of course, the basic types made from white or brown rice, barley, and soybeans.

The latest statistics (1974) show that there are 2,400 commercial miso shops and factories in Japan, and they produce a total yearly output of 649,000 tons of miso retailing for 492 million dollars. Each year, they use 212,000 tons of soybeans, 101,000 tons of rice, 22,000 tons of barley, and 82,000 tons of salt. The great majority of these shops are relatively small scale, semi-traditional enterprises run by a single man and his family with the help of one or two relatives or hired craftsmen. Most shops produce several types of miso, and some also prepare special batches of koji which are sold fresh or dried as an independent item. During the cold months, a few use this koji to prepare commercial *amazaké* (p. 400).

Beginning in the mid 1950s, a revolution began in the manufacture of miso. The application of modern technology to the entire miso-making process has resulted in the use of automated equipment, new ingredients, continuous process methodologies and packaging techniques, and new merchandising methods which have profoundly transformed the ancient craft as well as the miso itself.

By 1965, a number of the larger traditional manufacturers had amalgamated to form huge modern companies: twenty three factories had a yearly capacity of at least 4,100 tons each, and the ten largest produced 154,000 tons per year, or about 26 percent of the nation's total output. By 1974, the latter statistic had climbed to 30 percent and individual factories were turning out 264,000 pounds (twenty-two 6-ton vatsful) of miso daily! Today, the names of the "top ten" makers (p. 569) are household words in Japan, for they have been able for the first time in history to generate enough capital to do nationwide advertising via television, printed media, and billboards. Reaping the full benefits of a large-scale, low-margin enterprise, they distribute their standardized products to every part of Japan where they are sold in supermarkets and neighborhood grocery stores at unbelievably low prices. Recently, they have begun to export to North America and Europe, and one company is even starting a small branch factory in Los Angeles.

A detailed and extensively illustrated description of the equipment and methods used to produce the various types of miso, on scales ranging from small to large using both traditional and modern methods, is given in *Miso Production: The Book of Miso, Volume II*, by Shurtleff and Aoyagi. To order send $10.80 to: The Soyfoods Center, P.O. Box 234, Lafayette, CA 94549 USA.

Appendix A

A Brief History of Chiang, Soy Nuggets, Miso, Tamari, and Shoyu

THE EARLIEST known ancestor of miso was the group of Chinese foods or condiments called *chiang* (pronounced *jiang* in Mandarin). Both chiang and soy nuggets (called *shih* or *ch'ih* in early China) were the early ancestors of shoyu or soy sauce, and to this day the Chinese still call their soy sauce "the liquid extracted from chiang" (*chiang-yu*).

Chiang   Chiang-yu

Thought to have originated before the Chou dynasty (722–481 B.C.), chiang is undoubtedly the oldest condiment known to man, originally developed as a way of preserving protein-rich animal foods to be used either as seasonings or preserves. In effect, the peoples of East Asia discovered that when seafoods and meat (and, later, soybeans) were salted or immersed in a mixture of salt and rice wine (or water), their protein was broken down by enzymes into amino acids, which in turn stimulated human taste buds, augmenting the flavors of other foods. It was soon found that subsequent fermentation served to deepen and elaborate the primary flavor and aroma of the salt-pickled ingredients. The idea of combining these two distinct preservation techniques into a single process laid the foundation for the later development of miso, and enabled people long ago to break the vicious cycle of feast and famine, conserving foods from times of bounty to be enjoyed in times of scarcity.

Chinese Chiang

The earliest varieties of Chinese chiang were probably made with fish, shellfish, and game. Their flesh —and in some cases bones, blood, and entrails—was ground or crushed, pickled in a mixture of salt and rice wine, and fermented in sealed earthenware vats for 100 days or more. This chiang closely resembled contemporary Asian fermented fish sauces such as the strong-smelling *nuoc mam* of Vietnam. But it was fundamentally different from modern miso or shoyu in that it contained no soybeans, grains, or koji; these did not come into use until sometime between the 2nd century B.C. and the 4th century A.D. The consistency of early chiang was probably neither as firm as that of miso nor as liquid as shoyu; rather it more than likely resembled applesauce, porridge, or the mash known as *moromi* from which today's shoyu is pressed. The various types of seafood miso (crab, shrimp, and red-snapper miso) still very popular in Japan are thought to be its direct descendants.

The written character for chiang made its first appearance in about the third century B.C. in two unrelated documents, the *Chou-li* (Japanese: *Shurai*) and the *Analects of Confucius* (Scroll 2, Chapter 10). It is not sure which of these is the oldest. In the *Chou-li*—a bureaucratic utopian vision of the administration that supposedly existed in the Chou dynasty royal court in the sixth to eighth centuries B.C.—it is written that "one hundred twenty crocks of chiang were stocked for a party by the Chou government" and that "in preparing the eight basic types of food whose qualities harmonize with the four seasons, one should learn to use chiang from the hundred and twenty crocks." The *Chou-li* states that this chiang was made by mixing the meat of animals, birds, or fish with millet koji and salt, then pickling it in wine in a crock for a hundred days. The use of soybeans was not mentioned. It is quite remarkable that even at this early date the Chinese were consciously using the enzymes produced by the koji molds to produce fermented foods such as chiang and various wines.

In the *Analects of Confucius,* chiang appears in a section where the sage is discussing proper etiquette and social behavior, the wise choice of foods, and fasting: "Foods not accompanied by the appropriate variety of chiang should not be served. Rather than using only one to season all foods, you should provide many to ensure harmony with each of the basic food types. Make grains central to your diet. Use wine in moderation to welcome guests, but by no means should you get drunk and act foolish." Confucius (c. 551–479 B.C.) did not write the *Analects* (or any other works); they were compiled by his disciples 100 to 200 years after his death.

In other texts of the same period, we learn that each of the 120 crocks mentioned above contained chiang made with a different combination of ingredients and having a distinctive flavor. One source mentions, for example, mustard chiang and says that it should be eaten only with *sashimi* (raw fish). A Chou dynasty legal document tells us that one government official was appointed director of chiang production, while another was made director of the closely affiliated bureau of medicine and foods.

The character for chiang next appears in the *Li Chi* (Japanese: *Reiki*), the "Record of Rites," written about 50 B.C. A collection of rituals codified by the academic scholars, the ritualists, of the former Han dynasty, it further attests to the character's hoary age.

Another early Chinese classic, the *Shih chi* (*Historical Records*) by Ssu-ma Ch'ien, states that in 140 B.C. a traveler in Canton ate a fermented food called *ku-chiang* prepared with a sweet wild fruit and probably resembling today's Kinzanji miso. Since Canton was thousands of miles from the Imperial capital at Chang-an and we are told that the miso was made in a remote town upstream from it, we may assume that the process for preparing fermented miso-like foods was known throughout much of China before the Christian era. In this story we also have the first historical description of a chiang prepared without meat or fish.

Like today's Worcestershire sauce or shoyu, the earliest chiang was more widely used as a seasoning than as a primary staple. Considered both nutritious and tasty, it was a popular daily food, highly esteemed by all classes of people. During the T'ang dynasty (618 A.D.–906 A.D.) chiang was referred to as the "ruler of foods" and in one well-known ceremony, a tray bearing its many varieties was placed on the palace altar, before which the Emperor showed his respect by formally bowing in public. A special official was appointed to guard the Imperial Household's supply as it fermented so that no one could steal the secrets of its production.

Soybeans, Soy Nuggets, and Soybean Chiang in China

Although there are various legends stating that soybeans were mentioned in China in the ancient herbal *Pen Ts'ao Kong Mu* as early as 2838 B.C., it is now generally considered that these are a fabrication some 2,600 years later by Han dynasty historians who, in the traditional Chinese way, wished to endow all things worthy of respect with ancient ancestry. In his excellent article "On the Domestication of the Soybean," Hymowitz (1970) cites new linguistic, geographical, and historical evidence suggesting that the soybean was domesticated around the eleventh century B.C. (early Chou dynasty) in the eastern half of north China, the area just south of present-day Peking. The earliest character for soybeans (*shu*) first appeared in poems from the *Book of Odes,* written in the tenth to eleventh centuries B.C.

According to popular tradition (and some later references), soybeans were first used in processed form as tofu, developed in 164 B.C. by Liu An, king of Huai-nan. But the first soyfood (other than soybeans) to be described in written records in East Asia is soy nuggets (called *shih* or *ch'ih* in ancient China and *tou-ch'ih* or "salted black beans" today; they are a close relative of Japanese Hamanatto). This fermented soyfood is first mentioned in the *Historical Records* (Chinese: *Shih chi;* Japanese: *Shiki*) by Suu-ma Ch'ien, the great historian, who died about 85 B.C. In "The Biographies of the Money-makers" chapter, it is stated that "Any one in the market towns of great cities who manages in the course of a year to sell . . . a thousand jars of leaven or salted soy nuggets (*yen shih*) . . . may live as well as the master of an estate of a thousand chariots." Mention of soy nuggets appears again in the earliest Chinese dictionary, the *Shuo-wen chieh-tzu,* written by Hsü Shen in about A.D. 121. The definition states that soy nuggets are made by fermenting soybeans with salt. Another early dictionary that mentions soy nuggets is the *Shih Ming,* written c. A.D. 200. In recent excavations, soy nuggets (in either a woven bamboo packet or a crock), the earliest archaeological remains of beans from China, were found in the famous Western Han Tomb No. 1 at Ma-wang-tui, located at Ch'ang-sha, Hunan. It was sealed about 168 B.C. and uncovered in 1972. Also found in the tomb were soybeans plus 312 inscribed bamboo slips, which describe various foods and seasonings, including chiang. Thus it seems likely that soy nuggets were known in China before the Han dynasty (206 B.C.–A.D. 220). A later description of the process for making soy nuggets is given in the *Ch'i-min Yao-shu* ("the essential writings of the people of Ch'i"; Japanese: *Saimin Yojutsu*), the world's first encyclopedia of agriculture written by Chia Ssu-hsieh c. A.D. 535. Here it states that soybeans are cooked, spread in a warm room, and inoculated with "yellow robe" (a mold of the genus *Aspergillus*) to make soybean koji, very much like the koji used in today's Hatcho miso or tamari soy sauce. The koji is then washed with water, wrapped tightly in a woven red mat, and allowed to ferment. After several days the product is taken out and dried. As a variation, salt is sometimes added during the fermentation to make salted soy nuggets. The product was said to be easier to make if salt were added, but the quality was considered lower. In some cases soy nuggets were also fermented with water, and the liquid was later filtered off to make a savory seasoning, probably similar to today's tamari shoyu. The preparation of soy nuggets represented the appearance of a new method of making koji. The koji for chiang had always been made by growing the mold on grain (usually barley), then mixing cooked beans and salt with the finished koji. For soy nuggets, the mold was grown directly on the soybeans in the same way that it is today on Japanese Hatcho miso, tamari miso, tamari shoyu, and savory soy nuggets (Hamanatto).

The use of soybeans as the basic protein source in chiang (as a substitute for the previously used meat and fish) was first described in the *Ch'i-min yao-shu*, which states that to make soybean chiang, black soybeans are dehulled, steamed, inoculated with a mold (now known to be of the genus *Aspergillus*), mixed with salt and water, placed into crocks, and allowed to ferment. The use of soybeans in this process marked a major step in the development of today's miso and shoyu. The book's detailed description of chiang's preparation indicates that the basic techniques for producing fermented soyfoods had been established at least several centuries before.

In those days, chiang, which had a consistency resembling a mixture of today's miso and shoyu, was used as a seasoning, in pickling, and (mixed with other ingredients such as vinegar or sweetening) as a dressing for cooked vegetables. Soy nuggets, on the other hand, were sometimes mixed with water, and the richly seasoned sauce combination (called *shih-tou*) was used as a broth for simmered dishes or as a seasoning for soups . . . in much the same way that we now use soy sauce.

The development of fermented soyfoods, a process that depends on a rather sophisticated (intuitive and conscious) understanding of microbiology and fermentation technology, was a remarkable achievement in the early history of China. It is also remarkable that the Chinese recognized and deliberately cultivated at least two types of molds, *Aspergillus* and *Rhizopus*, and used them to produce enzymes. The *Rhizopus* processes, used with soybeans or barley to make chiang or soy nuggets (both having koji with a crumbly consistency), were never transmitted to Japan. (The Japanese, however, developed a way for making sake with *Rhizopus* that was not found in China.)

Records in Korea from A.D. 680 state that both soybean chiang and soy sauce (the liquid seasoning pressed from that chiang) had entered the country, in the customary exchange of gifts between ruling houses, where they were called *jang* and *kan jang* respectively. There is considerable evidence that much of the earliest research and development was carried out by Buddhist priests who, seeking replacements for salted and spiced animal foods, prepared varieties of vegetarian chiang in their temples and homes. As these priests spread the teachings and practice of Buddhism throughout Asia, they took their soyfoods with them.

Early Japan

The origins of miso are not clear, although most scholars agree that its earliest progenitor came from either China or Korea. Some set the date of arrival in Japan at shortly before the introduction of Buddhism (540–552 A.D.), whereas others feel that the lack of definite records demands the more conservative estimate of 663 A.D. The miso transmitted from Korea is thought to have been prepared using the *miso-dama* technique whereby cooked soybeans were mashed, shaped into balls, and inoculated with wild mold spores to form the koji. Crushed and mixed with salt and water, the balls were then fermented in crocks to make a variety of soybean miso. This special tradition, though largely unrecorded, is thought to have been the origin of much of Japan's earliest farmhouse miso. The product brought from China, on the other hand, is believed to have gained its first acceptance among the nobility and in monasteries.

The earliest mention of soybeans in Japanese literature is found in the *Kojiki* (712 A.D.), an ancient mythical text which is the nation's oldest chronicle. Here we are told that the goddess Oketsuhime Mikoto brought forth soybeans out of her own body for the lasting benefit of all generations to come. Large supplies arrived from the mainland concurrent with the spread of Buddhism, yet recent discoveries of charred soybeans together with husked rice in Neolithic dwellings and ruins from the end of the Jomon Period (200 B.C.–A.D. 8) in northeastern Japan suggests that soybeans may have been in use there long before the existence of written records.

Even before this time, however, there is evidence to the effect that the Japanese had developed their own varieties of fermented sauces. The earliest inhabitants of Japan were hunters and gatherers who are said to have arrived about 20,000 years ago. Long before the Christian era, they learned to extract salt from sea water, and their earliest seasonings consisted of this natural salt, together with *sansho* pepper and ground shellfish. Starting in the late Jomon period and continuing through the succeeding Yayoi period (200 B.C.–25 A.D.), however, fish and meat sauces basically similar to chiang were independently developed, as attested to by pickling crocks recently excavated in the northeastern provinces and dating back 3,000 to 4,000 years. The Japanese word for these primordial seasonings was *hishio* (or *hishiho*), and when the first writing system was introduced from China, it was written with the character for chiang.

A number of these Japanese hishios (each made without the use of koji) can still be found: *shiokara* is squid, squid intestines, or bonito pickled in a mixture of mirin and salt; *shottsuru* (from Akita) is sardines and hard-finned *hatahata* pickled in salt; *shuto* is salted bonito intestines pickled in sake; and *gyoeki* is fermented fish liquid. Two lesser-known relatives are *ikanago shoyu* from Kagawa and *kurozukuri* from Hokuriku. (Ancient Rome had a similar fermented

sauce called "garum," an ancestor of anchovie sauce.)
All are aged for one week or more and served as toppings for rice or as hors d'œuvres. Throughout the
northerly regions characterized by long snowy winters
and severe flooding, they have also long been used as
emergency food staples.

Today, the northeastern provinces are known as the
"miso heartland" of Japan; the per-capita consumption there is the highest in the nation and the ancient
homemade-miso tradition is still very much alive.
These facts, combined with the archeological evidence
indicating early mastery of salt-pickling and fermentation, move some scholars to go so far as to trace the
origins of miso (and shoyu) to this part of Japan
rather than to China or Korea.

The Nara Period
(710 A.D.–784 A.D.)

The first written records of miso and hishio date
from the Nara period; no documents or legends from
before this time mention any varieties of fermented
foods. And, strangely enough, no mention is made of
them in either the *Kojiki* or *Nihonshoki* (720 A.D.),
which do mention soybeans and were written more
than ten years after miso and a closely related variety
of hishio are known to have been produced at the
Imperial Palace.

One of the first references to this hishio appears in
the *Man'yoshu,* an extraordinary collection of thousands of Japan's earliest songs and poems recorded
from as early as the year 315 A.D. and compiled c.
760. In most of the poems, the Japanese words are
elaborately spelled out with Chinese characters used
phonetically. The character for hishio (chiang) appears in scroll 16 in a poem by Imiki Okimaru (686–
707), a humorous bard who improvised at banquets
for the court nobility:

In summer, when you know of my longing
For fresh wild onions, with a cool hishio-vinegar
    dressing

And the finest red-snapper sashimi,
Why do you offer me only a humble bowl of
hot soup?

Another poem describes two comic crabs happily making themselves into crab hishio seasoned with pounded elm bark. Mention is also made of hishio containing wild game and deer meat. Unfortunately we are not told exactly what type of product this hishio was nor how it differed from miso and chiang, yet it is now generally believed that all of these products were well known at this period among the nobility and, to a lesser extent, the common people.

During the first several centuries of contact with the continent, miso and hishio were probably very similar to chiang, and many of the basic raw materials and complex fermentation techniques were undoubtedly acquired largely from the Chinese. However, Japanese and Chinese taste preferences have always been fundamentally different, the Chinese preferring to use relatively large amounts of spices, oil, and meat in their strongly flavored cookery and the Japanese preferring the simpler, more subtle flavors inherent in the foods themselves. Gradually, therefore, by altering the basic ingredients and preparatory techniques, the Japanese began to transform chiang into foods uniquely suited to their own tastes. Soybeans—used alone or together with rice or barley—came to be preferred to fish or meat as the basic ingredient, while wine and spices were generally reduced in quantity or omitted. Hishio probably retained much the same applesauce-like texture as chiang, but miso slowly evolved into a firmer product with a shorter aging time. Of the two foods, hishio was probably the more important and more varied. Both were initially served primarily as toppings for rice; the hishio still widely prepared in country farmhouses continues to be served mostly in this way.

Perhaps the most important event in the early development of miso and hishio was the establishment in 701 of the *Hishio Tsukasa* or Bureau for the Regulation of Production, Trade, and Taxation of Hishio and Miso. Inaugurated by the Emperor Monmu in the

Taiho Ritsuryo (Taiho Law Codes, one of Japan's earliest constitutions, which went into effect in 702), this bureau was located in the Imperial Palace. Using methods very similar to those developed in China, it transformed soybeans into high- and low-quality hishio, miso, and soy nuggets. These foods were consumed by the Imperial Household.

The most complete and informative of the early documents mentioning miso was the *Todaiji Shosoin Monjo* (730–748), which is still preserved in excellent condition in the Imperial Treasury of the *Shosoin* connected with Nara's Todaiji temple. It records that in 730 taxes were being paid on miso and hishio, and contains tax receipts from the following year for soy nuggets (*kuki*) (a progenitor of either today's hama-natto or Kinzanji miso), *ara-bishio* (a coarse-textured salty hishio), rice hishio, and miso, as well as for salt, vinegar, and *azuki* beans. In a document of 740, first mention is made of *kasu hishio,* which may have been the lees remaining after the extraction of tamari. Records of about 750 show the following relative prices: highgrade hishio 15 *mon,* hishio 10.7 *mon,* ara-bishio 10 *mon,* and miso 7 to 8 *mon.* They also indicate that miso and hishio were sold in the markets of Nara; prices calculated on the basis of 1 *sho* (about 2 quarts) reveal that they were relatively inexpensive. These various fermented foods were most commonly written with the following characters; note that even the word "miso" contains the ideograph for hishio (chiang), indicating both origin and relationship:

Miso   Rice Hishio   Ara-bishio   Soy Nuggets

Much of Nara's miso was used at temples to provide free meals for the monks and laymen who donated their time to hand-copy Buddhist scriptures. Small quantities were used in side dishes and *aemono* (mixed salads) as well as with pickles, noodle dishes, *mochi,* and soups. Many of these preparations were served to the laborers who built Todaiji temple, then the largest wooden building in the world, and its immense cast statue of Buddha, the *Daibutsu,* which was completed in the year 752.

One of the most colorful chapters in the history of miso concerns the great Chinese Buddhist master Ganjin. The founder of the Japanese Ritsu or "precepts" sect and of the well-known Toshodaiji temple in Nara, Ganjin spent over eleven years trying to reach Japan. After being blocked by pirates, shipwrecks, and storms, and having lost his eyesight during one of his six attempted crossings, he finally succeeded in 754 at the age of 66. The records of his ship's cargo show that in addition to 185 monks, sailors, and craftsmen, he brought 100,000 gallons of "mellow soy nuggets." Later records show that this same fermented soybean food was prepared at his temple, carried by foot to Kyoto, and peddled there in the streets.

Although Ganjin's mellow soy nuggets were related to miso, they were probably more a preserved food than a seasoning, similar to today's Daitokuji natto. Nevertheless, Ganjin is often said to have brought the first prototype of Japanese miso from China, and if we take these mellow soy nuggets to be the original Japanese miso, then he was clearly its transmitter. But records show that something called "miso" was already being sold in Nara's markets more than 20 years before Ganjin's arrival. Hence, some scholars have concluded that the popular "Ganjin theory" probably reflects more of a desire on the part of early miso makers and Buddhist priests to link their new product to Ganjin's lofty reputation than to historical fact.

One of the key links in the transmission from China to Japan of the techniques for preparing the different varieties of chiang was the *Ch'i-min Yao-shu,* the 6th-century encyclopedia mentioned above, which arrived in Japan during the late 700s. Its ten volumes describe the preparation of koji, soy (and barley) nuggets, and numerous varieties of chiang. From it, the Japanese learned how to prepare red-snapper miso, crab miso, *yuzu* miso, savory soy nuggets (Hamanatto), and products closely related to Kinzanji miso. A veritable treasurehouse of accurate and detailed information, this tome had a profound effect on the development of Japanese farming methods and crafts as well as food preparation.

One of the historical puzzles concerning the early development of miso in Japan concerns the origin of sweet white miso, which is still the favorite in the area of Japan's earliest capitals (Nara and Kyoto) and along the northern shores of the inland sea. The pattern of miso consumption in this area is very different from that of the rest of Japan: miso soup is relatively uncommon, only about one-third as much miso is consumed per capita as in Japan as a whole, and white miso's sweet flavor and light color are preferred to regular miso's dark saltiness. These facts have given rise to the theory that at a very early period, sweet white miso was brought from China to the ancient Japanese capitals where it continued to preserve its aristocratic mein and distinctive usage in cookery.

Documents written near the end of the Nara period describe more than 22 varieties of hishio, miso, and soy nuggets. Of these, hishio was by far the most diversified, yet all its 15 or more varieties were generally grouped into three basic types:

1. *Fish, Shellfish, and Wild Game Hishio (Shishi-bishio):* Generally prepared by pickling crabs, sea urchins, or shrimp in a mixture of salt, water, and sake. Deer meat, eggs and, occasionally, fowl were also used.

2. *Vegetable and Fruit Hishio (Kusa-bishio):* Foods such as *uri* melon, eggplant, *daikon,* green leafy vegetables, *kabu* turnips, *udo,* fresh green soybeans, *mizunegi* onions, peaches and apricots pickled with salt and fermented. In some cases, vinegar and/or *mizuamé* sweetening was used with or in place of the

salt. These preparations later evolved into *tsukemono* (salted pickles) and the various types of finger lickin' miso. During this period the first miso pickles were made using *uri* melons and eggplants.

3. *Soybean and/or Grain Hishio (Koku-bishio):* The last type of hishio to develop, these products containing soybeans, rice, wheat, or barley gradually evolved into today's miso and shoyu.

The Heian Period (794 A.D.–1160 A.D.)

At the beginning of the Heian period, the word "miso" suddenly began to be written with a new combination of characters, which is used to this day. The character for "mi" meant "flavor" and the one for "so" meant throat. This second character was, itself, a Japanese invention and is presently used in no other words. It first appeared in an official Japanese document of 806 in connection with a food called *enso,* a salt seasoning. The modern word "miso" made its first appearance in the *Sandai Jitsuroku,* a history book that was published in 901 but had been widely circulated in manuscript form by 886. The new word looked like this:

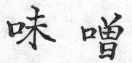

We may well inquire why the Japanese of this period deliberately invented a new character to replace the character chiang (hishio) that had been used during the previous two centuries, and why they introduced the character meaning "flavor" into the combination. It seems likely that by this time the Japanese had so thoroughly transformed chiang into a food suited to their own culture and tastes, that they felt it deserved a uniquely Japanese name. In fact, the

Sandai Jitsu-roku portrays miso as a truly Japanese food rather than as simply a Chinese import. Scholars generally agree that miso finally achieved its own identity during the hundred years prior to the emergence of its new name. Yet traditional writing habits were slow to change, and as late as the 18th century, the word miso was still written most frequently using the character for hishio or chiang, rather than the new Japanese *so.* The combination would have meant "hishio with a lot of flavor (*mi*)." The character for hishio could also have been pronounced *sho,* as it is in the word "shoyu." Thus if the combination were pronounced *misho,* it could have been the forerunner of the word "miso." Other researchers believe the word "misho" came from Korea and the *Wamyosho.* The word "shoyu" would not appear for another 700 years.

The earliest Japanese document to contain information about the production of miso and hishio was the *Engi Shiki* written c. 967. In it we are told that miso was a fermented food with soybeans as its main ingredient, but also containing rice, rice koji, wheat, salt, and sake. In addition to containing detailed information about the Hishio Tsukasa government bureau, the *Engi Shiki* lists at least ten different types of miso and hishio, and among these the word miso is written using at least five different character combinations, all of which are pronounced "miso":

It is not always clear whether each of these names refers to a different food, or whether the name of a single variety was simply being written with different character combinations. The book gives the amounts of basic raw materials used in preparing numerous different types of miso and hishio, but most of the quantities appear quite inaccurate and cannot be used experimentally to make the products they describe.

Although notebooks dating from as early as the 8th century reveal that miso was bought and sold in the marketplaces of the former capital at Nara, the first shops specializing in its sale are said to have originated in about 925 in the new capital at Kyoto. The *Engi Shiki* records the presence of a miso retail shop in Kyoto's western market and a hishio outlet in the eastern market. Moreover, 50 other shops are reported to have carried hishio, and 32 miso, as one among numerous other foods. Records of the Imperial Court indicate that hishio was given to the Emperor's civil and military officials as part of their annual wages. Thus by the middle of the 10th century, it seems that hishio and miso were becoming basic staples.

The *Engi Shiki* also mentions *kasu-hishio* and *hishio-kasu.* Perhaps the former was lightly pressed, yielding a smaller amount of the shoyu-like liquid, so that the moist residue could be used as a seasoning. And perhaps the latter was very firmly pressed, yielding more liquid and a dry presscake, which was discarded.

Records from the year 980 show that monks in Nara's Todaiji temple were provided with a large daily supply of miso which was used in mixed salads (*aemono*), foods simmered in seasoned broths (*nimono*), and soups. Meanwhile, Chinese-educated monks in other Nara temples had begun to prepare Kinzanji, abalone, and red-snapper miso.

In the epics of the Heian period, such as the *Tale of Genji* and *Konjaku Monogatari,* are found descriptions of all-night parties held by the court nobility in the Imperial palace. A typical dinner consisted of seven courses, each served consecutively on separate trays. Popular foods included abalone miso and red-snapper hishio, *uri* melons and eggplants pickled in miso, and red snapper, carp or other sea foods lightly marinated with miso sauces. Both hishio and miso were also apparently widely used as table seasonings. Among the palace women, miso was known as *ko,* meaning "fragrance or incense", or *higurashi* meaning "a clear-toned summer cicada" whose song is said to be able to penetrate even the hardest stone. Likewise the rich fragrance and fine flavor of miso were said to penetrate and season other foods. For this reason, in the Kyoto area miso is still occasionally called *mushi* or *bamushi* meaning "insect or honorable insect."

By the middle of the 10th century, miso-making had spread from the capital to the countryside. The *Wamyosho,* the earliest dictionary of the Japanese language, encyclopedic in scale and written between 933 and 938, tells us that miso was being produced in the prefectures and usually bore the name of the area in which it was made: Shiga miso and Hida miso, still enjoyed to this day, were among the early favorites.

The Kamakura Period
(1185 A.D.–1333 A.D.)

In 1185, with the beginning of the Kamakura period, a great revolution occurred in Japan. Up until that time the pleasure-loving aristocracy had lived a life of refined and opulent leisure, replete with incense smelling parties, moon viewing, painting, poetry and song writing. As the atmosphere grew more effete and degenerate, Japan's rulers gradually lost contact with the life of the farmers and common people. In the early 12th century, therefore, a new and very vital government composed largely of samurai took control of the country, establishing its capital in remote Kamakura near present-day Tokyo. Very quickly a new spiritual force awakened. Buddhism, which had previously been tied to the court and emphasized elaborate rituals, fine priestly attire and costly statuary, now came to stress a life of simplicity based on daily religious practice, faith, and meditation. Its primary goal was to bring salvation, or enlightenment, within reach of the common man, and as one way of making contact with townspeople and farmers, many temples—and especially those of the Zen sect—established *shojin* restaurants within their own compounds; here vegetarian meals were served at reasonable prices in a quiet atmosphere of refined simplicity and natural beauty.

From the priests, the people learned the art, aesthetics, and spiritual value of this new way of cooking and enjoying food. Returning from China in the 12th century, the Zen master Eisai brought tea to Japan and publicized its use as an alternative to alcohol, which at times threatened to seriously weaken the new government and its rulers; the Way of Tea became closely linked in spirit with *shojin* cookery. Encouraging the spread of this simple, inexpensive diet and vigorous, healthy way of life among the people at large, both samurai and priest served as examples worthy of emulation. As a result, for the first time in Japanese history people began to think in terms of primary foods (*shushoku*) and secondary foods (*fukushoku*). The former, the center of each meal, were grains: rice for those who could afford it, barley for the average farmer, and millet or barnyard millet for the poor. Secondary foods included small amounts of vegetables and seafoods. It became standard practice to eat only two meals each day, and all people were urged to abstain from the meat of four-legged animals.

Among many Japanese, the Kamakura period is famous as the era in which miso soup was developed. A preparation unknown in China or among the Japanese aristocracy, it came to be a symbol of the food of the common people. The standard repast consisting of a large serving of cooked grain accompanied by the newly-discovered *takuan* (salt-pickled *daikon*) and a miso soup containing tofu and vegetables was to become a Japanese tradition continuing until the present.

Miso, tofu, and deep-fried tofu pouches (agé) became the favorite foods of the ruling shoguns, who promoted the cultivation of soybeans on a large scale. As the beans became more readily available, they gave an additional stimulus to the production of their derivative foods and to their use in Zen Temple Cookery. Almost all temples made their own miso and gradually taught the process to people throughout the country, until in the hearts of many, the flavor of miso and the "flavor" of Zen became the same. In times of famine, the miso stored in large quantities in most farmhouses and city homes served as a lifesaving staple. Soon the saying *miso sae areba,* "Everything's alright as long as there is miso," came to be heard everywhere. Hence it was under the new Buddhist influence of the Kamakura period that the consumption of hishio containing fish or animal-derived products steadily declined, and that grain-and-soybean-based miso began to play its important role in the Japanese diet.

The Muromachi Period (1336 A.D.–1568 A.D.)

During the Muromachi period, the seat of government returned to the Kyoto area and some of the formality, splendor, and aristocratic feeling of the Heian period was revived. But the period as a whole was characterized by social chaos and civil war. The famous samurai Takeda Shingen, lord of a large fief in the Shinshu area north of Tokyo, was the first to recognize miso's full potential as a soldier's food. Long-lasting, inexpensive, and highly nutritious, it took only minutes to make it into a warming soup. To ensure that his men had a large supply of it wherever they went, Takeda taught farmers throughout Shinshu to plant soybeans and process them into miso. The preparation of homemade miso soon flourished throughout the area and gradually spread to other nearby provinces. During the 16th century miso shops attached to private homes appeared in urban areas and gradually every region developed its own techniques and new varieties, which often came to be called by such lofty names as "morality" or "Bodhidharma" miso. Documents of this period show frequent references to miso in plays, stories and songs, indicating that it was not only a popular food but an integral and intimate part of the social fabric.

The Muromachi period saw the development of two new varieties of miso; Hatcho and sweet white. Oral tradition has it that Hatcho was first prepared as early as 1370, but scholars generally place the date somewhere between the late 1400s and early 1500s. A kabuki drama tells of how Hideyoshi Toyotomi (1536–1598), the child of poor farmers in central Japan's Aichi prefecture, rose to become one of Japan's most powerful feudal lords. When only ten years old, the child is said to have fallen asleep one night on a bridge near his home, wrapped only in a straw mat. A famous robber passing over the bridge scornfully kicked the urchin, who awoke and intrepidly grabbed the man's spear commanding him to stop such cruelty. The robber, impressed with the boy's courage, decided to raise him as his own son. In the play, the straw mat bears the trademark of one of the nearby Hatcho miso shops where it was used to prepare koji. Historians cite the incident to prove that Hatcho miso was being made as early as 1546. (The shop uses the same trademark to this day.) Later records show that by 1590, when Tokugawa Ieyasu left for the frontier town of Edo to found his new capital, both of Japan's present Hatcho miso makers were doing a thriving business.

Although some scholars support the previously mentioned theory that sweet white miso was transmitted from the Chinese to the Japanese capital during the Nara period, most believe that the present product was developed by Kyoto craftsmen during the 14th and 15th centuries to suit the tastes of the indolent court nobility. It is interesting to note that both Hatcho and sweet white miso still retain a certain high-class image, a reflection, perhaps, of the era in which they originated.

By the fifteenth century, the most widely available varieties of miso are said to have finally lost their luxury status and made their way into the homes of the common people. Yet at the same time, miso emerged as an essential and esteemed ingredient in the more famous schools of Japanese haute cuisine. Under the wise guidance of Sen-no-Rikyu, *shojin* cookery was carried to its peak of refinement and subtlety in Tea Ceremony Cuisine. It was in these newly emerging schools of fine cookery that sweet simmered, broiled,

yuzu, and *kinomé* miso, together with many other of
Japan's finest miso preparations, were first developed.
From its earliest beginnings in simple peasant fare,
miso now rose to attain the same level of honor
among the people that it had enjoyed among the Japanese palace nobility eight centuries earlier, and that
its predecessor *chiang* had enjoyed in China's Imperial Household twelve centuries before that.

Early Soy Sauce in China

It is not clear when the Chinese first began to separate liquid soy sauce from chiang. In his outstanding
Food in Chinese Culture, K. C. Chang states that in
all likelihood soy sauce was known toward the end of
the Chou period (1100 B.C.–221 B.C.), based on evidence from the "Huo Ch'ih Lieh Chuan" chapter of
the *Shih chi (Historical Records).* Moreover in a Japanese book entitled *Han Dynasty Civilization (Kandai-
no-Bunbutsu),* there is an illustration showing the
removal of soy sauce from chiang in a crock. In making Chinese-style soy sauce, it is common after making
the first extraction to mix salt water and sometimes
sweetener into the remaining mash, cook this, and
press again. This may have come from the process for
making soy nuggets, developed during the Han dynasty. A product called *niira tamari,* made in Aichi
prefecture, Japan, until about 1925, was made by
much the same process. By China's Sung dynasty
(960–1279) soy sauce (together with firewood, rice,
oil, salt, vinegar, and tea) was considered one of the
"Seven Necessities."

The *Pen Ts'ao Kang-mu* ("collected essentials of
grasses and trees"; Japanese: *Honso Komoku*), a famous and large collection of botanical and medical
writings by Li Shih-chen, written in 1518 (Ming dynasty), mentions an extracted liquid soy sauce and
various types of chiang—wheat chiang, soybean chiang, and soy & wheat chiang. The Chinese word for
soy sauce was written with the same characters as
today's word for *tamari* in Japan. The wheat shoyu,

which contained only wheat and no soybeans, is probably an ancient relative of the white (*shiro*) shoyu made in Japan's Aichi prefecture.

Tamari: The Forerunner of Shoyu

The history of shoyu in Japan can be traced to a document written in 775 A.D., which makes first mention of tamari, thought to have been the liquid that rose to the surface of soybean hishio during fermentation and which was ladled off and used as a seasoning in much the same way as today's shoyu. Although pronounced "tamari," the word was originally written with the characters *to* meaning "soybean" and *yu* meaning "a liquid extracted by filtering or pressing." Since tamari is rarely referred to in the literature of the period, it is believed to have found only limited use.

The origins of modern shoyu can be traced more clearly to the mid 1200s when the Japanese priest Kakushin returned from China, having learned there the technique for preparing Kinzanji miso. Establishing himself at Kokoku-ji temple near the town of Yuasa (in today's Wakayama prefecture just south of Osaka), he began to teach the local people both Buddhist meditation and the method for preparing his miso specialty. According to non-documented oral tradition, he soon discovered that the liquid which settled to the bottom of the miso kegs made an excellent seasoning, so he decided to alter the process slightly by increasing the proportion of water in the basic mixture. After the regular fermentation period, the excess liquid was ladled off and briefly heated to stop fermentation, while the remaining Kinzanji miso —or a close facsimile thereof—was used as it always had been, deprived, however, of a portion of its rich flavor which now graced the savory seasoning liquid. Kakushin's creation, too, came to be known as *tamari*, deriving its name from the verb *tamaru* meaning "to accumulate," as "water accumulates in ponds," and by 1260, it was being produced for home consumption in the nearby towns of Yuasa and Hiromachi, both of which boasted a favorable climate and bountiful supply of unusually delicious water. By 1290, the first Yuasa tamari was said to have been sold commercially, and soon even poets began to sing the praises of this new delicacy, calling it *murasaki* or "deep purple," a synonym for the finest shoyu used to this day.

Smell the aroma from the depths of the brewing keg!
Waves of fragrance, deep-purple, tamari;
Flowers of wisteria.
Its origins reaching back to the Antei period,
Its brewing lineage inherited from the great teacher.
Tamari from Yuasa is the first in the Emperor's kingdom.
Its aroma is of the finest quality,
Its flavor most excellent,
Its fame, noblest and purest flower of Arita.*
(*Early name of the Yuasa region.)

From the late 700s until about 1450, all tamari had been extracted by filtering or ladling off excess seasoning liquid; the idea of pressing miso or hishio to obtain more tamari (a process which might be compared to extracting apple juice from applesauce), apparently never occurred to people since the lack of efficient pressing equipment would have made it necessary to discard large amounts of the basic food and its nutrients, and the whole foods were considered delicacies in their own right. Yet during the Muromachi period (an era noted for its affluence), extraction by pressing finally came to be practiced; as better pressing equipment was developed, the waste was reduced and was felt to be compensated for by the versatility of the liquid extract. The development of this process marked an important step in the evolution of today's shoyu, and fermented seasoning liquids came to be much more widely used in daily Japanese cookery.

The term *miso-damari,* referring to the rich liquid tamari that settles atop miso during fermentation, seems to have originated during the 1500s, although the product itself may have been used by miso makers long before this time. It was collected by making a hollow in the upper surface of a keg of fully-matured miso, pressing a deep bamboo colander into the hollow, and ladling out the liquid that accumulated in it.

Documents show that miso-damari was prepared by the monks living in the five major temples of Kyoto. The best-known cooking schools of the period are said to have learned how to make it from these temple craftsmen, and thanks to them, incorporated the seasoning into their cuisine.

It was not long before cooks took to simmering miso in water (usually in proportions of 1:3), filtering off the resultant liquid in a cloth sack, and finally pressing the sack. Known as *taré miso,* this seasoning was a popular ingredient in cookbooks of the 1400s. A thinner product (*usutamaré*) was prepared by omitting the simmering. Similarly, a document of 1537 describes *hishio-iri,* a liquid extracted from kuki, and *hishio-no-shiru,* an early predecessor of true shoyu.

Up until the 1400s, the term *tamari* had been used to refer to the liquid extracted from either soybean hishio or from soft-textured Kinzanji miso. The latter product eventually came to be known as tamari-shoyu, leaving "tamari" to refer specifically to liquid seasonings made entirely (or almost entirely) from soybeans. The first farmhouse tamari evolved from the process of preparing soybean miso from *miso-dama* (p. 476). Additional water was added to form a thick mash (moromi), which was then placed in an open-top keg having a spigot at the bottom connected to a large horizontal bamboo pipe perforated with many small holes. A bamboo colander was pressed into the moromi's surface and the liquid that collected in it was ladled daily over the mash to prevent mold formation. After one year, the liquid in the colander was ladled out and the remainder collected from the spigot. This tamari had a thick consistency, a deep chocolate brown color, and a very distinctive flavor and aroma. It was higher in protein and contained less natural sugars than most miso-damari or than today's shoyu since it was made exclusively from soybeans. The product remaining in the keg was called *tamari miso* (p. 73).

In the fiefdoms of Hida and Shiga, where Japan's first farmhouse miso was prepared, tamari was developed as early as the mid 1400s. Yet starting in about 1610, it experienced a sudden growth in popularity throughout Japan when the retired ruler Tokugawa Ieyasu built a castle at Okazaki near Nagoya and provided the laborers with a generous portion of the tamari whose flavor he loved so dearly. Soon commercial shops had adapted the farmhouse process to large-scale production. To this day, the area of central Japan around Nagoya remains the center of production for this distinctive fermented seasoning, which is now also referred to as *namadamari* (fresh tamari) or *uwahiki;* the most widely available commercial product is a sweetened mixture called *sashimi-damari* (p. 96).

In today's miso shops, the small amount of *miso-damari* that collects on the surface or settles to the bottom of the vats is never sold commercially. Generally, it is mixed back into the miso to enhance the latter's flavor, but occasionally a small quantity is reserved by the craftsman for personal use. Its flavor is highly prized.

Miso During the Edo Period
(1603 A.D.–1867 A.D.)

The capital of Japan was moved to Edo, later renamed Tokyo, in 1603, and miso made commercially in the towns of Shimousa and Saitama was sold in the huge markets of the new city. Because supply was insufficient to meet demand, however, the shogun, Tokugawa Ieyasu, imported his favorite soybean and Hatcho miso by boat from his native town in central

Japan. Although miso was consumed in increasingly large amounts, a number of factors prevented the many small miso makers of the period from growing into large-scale companies. First, miso, generally packed into large wooden kegs, was heavy and bulky, and the lack of good roads or river routes made long distance distribution difficult and expensive. And, perhaps more important, people enjoyed preparing their own miso at home at very little cost, making it difficult to price commercial miso competitively. Indeed, there was a saying popular at the time that a family that did not make its own miso would never have its own treasury-storehouse (*kura*), and many considered it a source of embarrassment if they had to use miso which they had not made themselves. Furthermore, most people preferred the flavor of the homemade or locally made product. Nevertheless, urbanization sped miso's commercialization and many of Japan's larger cities developed their own varieties. Here miso was first sold at sake stores; only later did outlets specializing in miso and miso pickles come into existence.

It was during this period that many farmers and small miso-shop operators, who had formerly made only soybean miso, began to experiment with the use of barley or rice koji in order to obtain a wider variety of flavors. In the capital at Edo during the 1600s, the three most popular varieties were Sendai red miso, barley miso made in nearby Saitama prefecture, and the hometown specialty Edo sweet red miso. Salty rice miso was developed throughout the northeastern provinces and in the Shinshu area north of the capital, both salty and sweet barley miso were produced in Kyushu and at the southern tip of Japan's main island, and new varieties of sweet white miso emerged in the Kyoto-Nara area. As grain koji became more widely used, the traditional practice of forming cooked soybeans into balls was abandoned in many areas and the grain koji was fermented in wooden trays.

When the Chinese Zen master Ingen (founder of the famous Obaku sect) came to Japan in 1661, he was surprised to find miso totally different from the chiang he had known in his native country. Becoming extremely fond of it, he is said to have enjoyed miso soup each day and used it as an effective substitute for a Chinese herbal medicine that he had taken for many years.

The Development of Shoyu

Shoyu originated at a surprisingly late date in the history of fermented soybean products, at least 600 years after miso had emerged as a distinctly Japanese creation. The word shoyu first appears in a Japanese dictionary (*Ekirin Bonsetsu Yoshu*) published in 1597 but thought to have been written by a priest sometime between 1469 and 1503 and circulated in manuscript form. Since this dictionary was widely used by the common people, it is thought that the word shoyu may have been in use as early as the late 1400s, generally in conjunction with the word tamari as "tamari-shoyu." We may probably assume, as was the case with miso, that the new word was coined to correspond to the development of a new and uniquely Japanese product. Unfortunately, however, we are not told in what ways this shoyu differed from its predecessors tamari, miso-damari, taré miso, and usutaré. Like the word "miso," the new word was slow to catch on, and as late as the 1700s most cookbooks used the term "tamari" almost exclusively; "shoyu" was only rarely seen.

The first character in the word shoyu was the character for hishio, and the second was the second character in the ancient way of writing the word tamari. This conjunction correctly describes shoyu's origins. Interestingly enough, these same two characters are used to write the Chinese word for soy sauce, chiang-yu, but it is doubtful that they were used in imitation of a foreign word which the Japanese had known for almost one thousand years.

By 1560, the tamari developed from Kinzanji miso in the town of Yuasa had become known as tamari-shoyu and formed the basis of a small-scale industry.

Records show that in 1586, the largest maker in Yuasa produced 4,500 gallons for sale in the markets of Osaka. From 1591, it was shipped by sea from Yuasa to the new and distant capital at Edo. The tamari-shoyu of this period was prepared from a koji containing cooked soybeans plus roasted barley which had been crushed or ground. Salt and water were added to form a mash which was fermented for 75 days in open-top kegs, being mixed every two weeks. The mature moromi was ladled into coarse-weave sacks and pressed to extract the liquid; the residue was used as fertilizer or fodder.

The area of Shimousa, about 30 miles northwest of Tokyo and already famous as a center of miso production, was to become the birthplace of the product now known as shoyu. In 1561, in the town of Noda, Iida Ichiro Heibei made a new variety of tamari-shoyu from hishio and presented it to the samurai Takeda Shingen, already known for his interest in miso. The flavorful product soon became known by its elegant name: Kawanakajima Goyo Tamari-Shoyu. It was first produced commercially in Shimousa in 1574 and within several years the output had reached 14,000 gallons per year. Yet it would take another 100 years before today's shoyu, made from equal parts soybeans and roasted cracked wheat, would be developed.

One of the basic traditional differences between the histories of shoyu and miso lies in the fact that shoyu has never been widely produced in farmhouses or urban dwellings, largely due to the difficulties of pressing the moromi and obtaining subtle or delicate flavors. Unlike China and Korea, where soy sauce has long been primarily a homemade product, in Japan, a single family came to assume responsibility for shoyu production in each town or village. As more elaborate and expensive pressing equipment was developed, larger companies that could better afford it grew in size.

Throughout the early part of the Edo period, the area around Osaka and Kyoto was the center of tamari-shoyu production and of traditional culture. In

1615, the first major shipping line was established to carry this product from Yuasa near Osaka to the burgeoning new capital at Edo (Tokyo). At about this same time the Shimousa area north of the capital began to emerge as a new center of tamari-shoyu production. In 1616, the Higeta company began operations in Choshi, followed in 1645 by the Yamasa company, and in 1616, the Mogi and Takanashi families started to brew Kikkoman-brand shoyu in Noda.

Starting in 1643, tamari-shoyu makers near the capital began experimenting with the use of wheat. Initially, they simply combined the recipes for wheat hishio and barley hishio, but they soon discovered that roasting and cracking the wheat imparted a wonderful savory aroma to the finished product. Feeling that they had developed a unique seasoning, superior to the best available in Japan, they decided to give it a new name: shoyu.

Meanwhile competition between the makers in Osaka and Tokyo became intense. In 1650, the tamari-shoyu imported from Osaka was twice as expensive as that made locally, yet it continued to remain the favorite. By 1660 numerous shipping lines from Osaka were in operation and by 1730, 162,000 kegs were being "imported" each year.

Various books recorded the new developments. In the *Wakan Sansai Zukai* (1711), which still contains residual Chinese influence, we find a clear distinction between miso, shoyu, and tamari. The word "misho" also appears. Wheat Shoyu and barley shoyu are described. Similar methods for making shoyu are described in the *Yoshu Fushi* (1682), *Honcho Shokukan* (1695), and *Bankin Sangyotai* (1732); that described in the earliest of these three is the closest to today's shoyu. Eventually hishio disappeared in Japan, being transformed into miso and shoyu.

By 1716, however, the makers near the capital had standardized the modern shoyu recipe calling for the use of equal parts whole soybeans and roasted wheat, a development often said to mark the point at which miso and shoyu finally emerged as distinct and totally independent foods. All of these companies now began to grow rapidly. Located on large rivers, they could ship their shoyu to the vast new market much more quickly and inexpensively than their competitors in far-away Osaka. Using the finest water and grains, they were soon offering a product that the people of Tokyo preferred to the more expensive imported brands. Business prospered and by 1859, imports from Osaka had dwindled to about 700 kegs per year.

A Brief Overview of Origins

Before proceeding, it might be interesting to reflect briefly on the origins and genealogies of miso and shoyu. The most widely held opinion among Japanese researchers and fermented-food historians is that both miso and shoyu trace their ancestry to Chinese chiang. However Dr. Kinichiro Sakaguchi, Professor of Fermentation Science at Tokyo University, in his "Searching for the Roots of Shoyu" (*Sekai,* Jan. 1979) argues convincingly that today's miso traces its ancestry back through early Japanese misos and hishio to chiang, whereas shoyu traces its ancestry back through early shoyu, then through the four products of tamari shoyu, tamari miso, Hatcho miso, and savory soy nuggets (Hamanatto), and ultimately to Chinese soy nuggets (*shih*). In the shoyu lineage, the koji is always made from either soybeans alone or a mixture of soybeans and cracked wheat, whereas in the miso lineage the koji is always made from grain. Sakaguchi believes that the fundamental biochemical consequences of this difference are of much greater importance than the more superficial differences of form that have led researchers up until now to group solid or semisolid products in the miso lineage and liquid products in the shoyu lineage. Thus, in shoyu, the *Aspergillus oryzae* molds act directly on the soybeans during the koji fermentation, then their enzymes continue to act on the soybeans during the subsequent brine fermentation. This leads to the formation of more complicated metabolic compounds, a higher degree of protein hydrolysis and liquefaction, and the production of a sharper and stronger flavor in shoyu than in miso. Sakaguchi argues that miso has a 3,000-year history dating from the development of chiang during the Chou dynasty in China, whereas shoyu has a 2,000-year history dating from the development of soy nuggets (*shih*) during the Han dynasty. It is important to note here that most Chinese would probably disagree with Dr. Sakaguchi. They clearly trace the lineage of their soy sauce to *chiang,* not to *shih,* as evidenced the Chinese word for soy sauce, *chiang-yu,* meaning "the liquid extracted from chiang." Moreover, most of their *chiang* and *shih* have always been made from a soy-based koji. We would say that both miso and shoyu trace their lineage back to both soy nuggets (*shih,* which existed prior to 206 B.C.) and to soybean chiang (which existed prior to A.D. 500).

Dr. Sakaguchi considers there to be three main reasons that shoyu and miso were not developed in the West: (1) Westerners did not know how to make koji using molds; (2) they had no soybeans until the 20th century; and (3) the basic flavoring components of shoyu and miso, especially natural L-glutamic acid and inosinic acid, were traditionally unknown in the West.

Early European Contact with Miso and Shoyu

The first Westerners (such as Marco Polo, 1254–1324) who visited China, Japan, and Korea fail to mention soy sauce, miso, and even soybeans in their journals. (Polo didn't mention the Great Wall or tea either.) Later explorers, travelers, missionaries, and traders between 1597 and 1668 (e.g. Carlatti, Dampier, and Captain John Saris) described soyfoods such as miso and shoyu in their logs and records and they probably ate these products, but they apparently didn't realize they were made from soybeans, nor did they know the process for making them. It is likely that during the late 1600s, Japanese shoyu was a common and highly esteemed item of trade from East to West. In 1670 Dutch traders started to export Japanese shoyu to

France at the request of Louis XIV, who used it as a seasoning at his sumptuous palace banquets.

The first description of the methods for making miso and shoyu appears in the *Amoenitatum Exoticarum* (Exotic Novelties), written by Englebert Kaempfer in 1712. The first Westerner to study and write about the soybean and soyfoods, Kaempfer was a brilliant, self-educated German scientist and traveler, who lived in Japan from 1690 to 1692. Through his works, the Western world first fully understood the soybean and its utilization as food. Written in Latin, Kaempfer's book contains rough and partially inaccurate descriptions, each about 200 words long, of how to make miso and shoyu.

In 1775 the Swedish doctor and botanist, Carl Thunberg, in his book *Travels in Japan,* stated that "Japanese shoyu is far better than Chinese soy sauce," proceeded to give a basic description of the shoyu-making process, and also wrote about miso. Europeans regarded Japanese shoyu as a precious delicacy in Thunberg's day and on his return to Europe, his ship took back lots of shoyu and sake. To prevent the shoyu from spoiling while crossing the tropics, it was first boiled by the Japanese in a caldron, poured into ceramic bottles, and sealed with pitch. On each bottle was written in Dutch "Japanese Shoyu." All this took place long before Appert's invention of canning in 1809 and Pasteur's invention of pasteurization in 1862. In fact sake pasteurization had been practiced in Japan for 200 to 300 years before this time.

During the 1870s, professor Albert Langgardt, who taught at the Tokyo Imperial University, took great interest in shoyu and even visited Noda and Choshi to study its manufacture. On his return to Germany, he produced a similar product which is sold widely to this day as "Maggi," a corruption of the name of the Mogi family.

The earliest scientific-journal article about shoyu by a Westerner appears to be A. Belohubek's "Le Schoyu," published in a German periodical in 1890. Other studies prior to 1920 included Kellner 1895, Murai 1897, Suzuki 1907, Hanzawa 1912, and Goff 1919.

These are summarized in *The Soybean* by Piper and Morse (1923).

The first Westerner to study the miso process scientifically and in detail was a German named Oscar J. Kellner, who wrote a detailed article on the subject in 1893. In 1923 the Americans Piper and Morse wrote their classic work, *The Soybean,* containing numerous photographs and much useful information relating to miso, shoyu, and Chinese soy sauce. They wrote that "In extent of use, miso is said to surpass all other preparations of the soybean in the Orient."

The Meiji and Pre-war Periods (1867 A.D.–1941 A.D.)

From the beginning of the Meiji period until the 1930s, miso production continued in the traditional way, with many small shops producing a variety of naturally fermented products. By 1900, a number of miso shops were in operation in Hawaii, preparing both Japanese and Chinese varieties. Soon exports to other countries began, and figures from 1907 show that 6.8 million pounds of miso and 13.2 million pounds of shoyu were sent abroad, presumably to supply expatriate Japanese.

At the start of the Meiji period, both the scientific method and the study of microbiology were "imported" to Japan from the West. Starting in 1878, miso and shoyu producers began to make controlled scientific studies of their fermentation processes, partly due to the influence of Americans such as Ahlburg, who taught microbiology and brewery mycology at Tokyo University, and Atkinson, who studied sake fermentation. By 1904, the Japanese had prepared their first pure-culture starters, thereby marking a major advance in miso and shoyu fermentation.

Beginning in the early 1930s, the world of Japanese miso-production underwent a series of drastic changes which have continued to affect it up until the present. With the rise of Japanese militarism, the conquest of new overseas territories in Korea, China, and Manchuria, and the development of Hokkaido and the islands to the north, many new markets for miso appeared and stimulated the growth of miso factories with international scope. By 1936, commercial miso production had soared to an all time high of 660,000 tons—a figure that would not be equalled again until the mid 1970's. But in 1936, most basic Japanese foodstuffs—including miso—were suddenly subjected to strict government price and quality controls. For purposes of standardization, government authorities grouped all miso varieties into three types (rice, barley, and soybean) and two grades (excellent and medium). Each type and grade had a fixed price. Although the designation of special varieties—such as Edo, Shinshu, or Hatcho miso—was allowed, the brand names of individual makers were outlawed. This system delivered a mortal blow to the production of many fine miso varieties and tended to encourage makers to lower their quality to the minimum, since they were assured that whatever they produced would be sold. In 1941, the Japanese National Miso Association was formed and local unions were unified under its leadership. Although its representatives worked with determination for the repeal of the oppressive controls, they were unsuccessful. During the war years, miso production decreased considerably, and although the control system was abolished after the war in 1946, the damage it did to the consciousness of both miso producers and consumers was never fully repaired. Many makers had lost pride in the quality of their product and had begun to adapt themselves to faster, lower-cost methods of production. And many consumers had begun to lose their sensitivity and appreciation for fine natural miso as they grew accustomed to standardized, lower-quality products.

Modern Times

After the War, the entire value system of the Japanese people underwent a drastic change. The process of Westernization that had begun in 1867 was suddenly accelerated and, in the areas of food, clothing, and housing, the degree of westernization gradually became accepted as a barometer of one's level of culture, education and success. Believing that their small stature and possibly even their defeat in the war were linked to improper eating habits, the Japanese began to view foods from a very "scientific" standpoint. Gradually discarding a thousand-year tradition that discouraged the use of animal products, they began to fashion their diet after the American pattern. The percentage of total protein intake supplied by fish and meat rose from 9 percent in the early 1920s to 40 percent in the early 1970s, while the percentage supplied by soybean products decreased from 21 to 12 percent, and by grains from 59 to 45 percent. During the same period, daily per-capita miso consumption dropped from 35 grams (6½ teaspoons) to 19 grams (3½ teaspoons), while that for urban businessmen dropped to only 11 grams. With the growing trend to view nutrition strictly analytically, and with the increasing availability of highly processed, canned, and bottled foods, consumers slowly began to lose their traditional high regard for locally grown natural foods served in season at their peak of flavor.

The rapid postwar shift in Japan's economy from a rural-agricultural to an urban-industrial base led to fundamental changes in the miso-making process. Within the space of one generation, the primary center of miso production shifted from farmhouses and private homes to commercial shops; just before the war, 55 percent of the country's total output was homemade, whereas by the 1970s the figure had dropped to 17 percent. As shops grew into small factories and moved nearer to cities, the higher costs of land and labor demanded increased profitability from each unit of time, space, and capital; this led to the creation of artificial environments with quick temperature-controlled fermentation, fast-maturing sweet misos, and machine-paced mass-production methods. Water previously drawn from deep wells was replaced by the chlorinated product supplied by municipal pipelines. Natural sea salt was abandoned for sodium chloride

—the only product now produced by the Government Salt Monopoly Corporation. Japanese-grown soybeans gave way to lower-quality lower-cost American imports. Epoxy-lined steel and concrete tanks were used in place of the traditional cedar vats. And finally, sealed polyethylene bags, nationwide distribution, and commercial storage led to the use of complete pasteurization and preservatives.

Many of these changes were actively promoted by a government postwar system of tax and rationing incentives designed to stimulate modernization, mechanization, and amalgamation. As a result, the number of small and medium-sized shops decreased from 6,000 just before the war to about 2,300 in 1974, while the number of highly automated factories showed a steady increase. By 1965, more than twenty plants had an annual output of over 4,000 tons each.

Although virtually all shops were affected by modernization to some degree, numerous provincial (and some urban) masters continued to value the ancient way. Like the many thousands of small French vintners who feel that quality is associated with tradition, individuality, and naturalness, these men chose to view modernization and standardization as a passing fad. Keeping in touch with the great natural cycles and with their own intuition, they held on to their fine wooden tools and vats, and searched for sources of natural ingredients. Nourishing the secrets and wholeness of their craft, they worked hard—and waited.

The shoyu industry in Japan entered the modern era as early as 1924 when the first producers in Western Japan began to use hydrolyzed vegetable protein (HVP) in shoyu making. By the 1930s concrete vats had begun to replace their traditional cedar counterparts. In 1940 a wartime regulation was passed by the Japanese government requiring the substitution of defatted soybean meal for whole soybeans in shoyu production, since the former was said to be more economical and efficient. At about the same time, temperature-controlled fermentation came into use. In 1944 the first method for making semichemical shoyu, combining fermentation and the use of hydrolyzed vegetable protein was patented by Kikkoman. The modernization of the shoyu industry in the postwar period followed many of the same patterns as the miso industry, but subject to an unusual set of circumstances caused by a Miss Appleton, the official in charge of shoyu production at the General Headquarters of the American occupying forces. Due to crop shortages in Japan after World War II, shoyu makers had to depend primarily on imported American soybeans allotted by the said official. Having little knowledge of the traditional requirements for brewing fine shoyu, she recommended that producers omit the time-consuming fermentation altogether and simply use hydrolyzed vegetable protein (HVP), which made the process quicker and less expensive by breaking down (hydrolyzing) the soy proteins to amino acids using hydrochloric acid. She therefore issued instructions in 1945 that all 8,000 producers should begin making the new product—or forego their quota of beans. Instead of abandoning their centuries-old tradition without resistance, shoyu technologists set out to find a faster brewing process, and in 1948 an improved process combining the use of HVP and fermentation was developed by Kikkoman; it so impressed the official that she permitted allocation of the beans. With the departure of the American forces, however, most shoyu makers returned to their traditional methods.

In 1950 the first chemical preservatives (initially developed to preserve wartime rations) were used in shoyu. In 1965 epoxy-lined steel vats came into use. As late as 1964 large producers still generally fermented their shoyu for an average of 18 months or sold a blend of one-year and two-year fermented shoyus. But as economic competition became more intense and new fermentation techniques were developed, the total fermentation time began to drop until by 1974 it was generally only 4 to 6 months and 93 percent of the whole soybeans had been replaced by defatted soybean meal. During the 1960s and 1970s three major technological advances were made that increased the percentage of nitrogen (protein) from the soybeans recovered in the shoyu and gave greater quality control: 1) a high-temperature short-time method of cooking the soybeans; 2) development of new, pure-culture strains of koji molds plus bacteria and yeasts added during the brine fermentation; and 3) highly sanitary and large-scale automated koji incubation rooms that replaced the manual wooden trays. Moreover, the moromi was now mixed automatically by compressed air in huge concrete or epoxy-lined tanks, and in sprawling factories traditional craftsmen were replaced by a host of new machines: track-mounted koji stirrers, steamers, roasters, conveyors, pumps and pipelines, hydraulic presses, heat exchangers, and bottling machines. Heating of the shoyu to roughly 80°C (176°F) for 1 to 3 hours prior to bottling, a technique developed several centuries earlier, continued to serve its four basic functions: 1) it pasteurized the shoyu, killing all molds and most bacteria and yeasts, which might otherwise form a thin white film on the surface in warm weather after long disuse, and it inactivated virtually all the enzymes (most enzymes are destroyed at 79.2°C), thereby stopping the fermentation; 2) it deepened and enriched the aroma and flavor; 3) it caused amino acids and sugars to react, thereby producing a darker, more beautiful color; and 4) it coagulated some solids, which were later removed by precipitation and/or filtration, and which would otherwise produce a clouding effect if the shoyu was later used to season clear broths and soup stocks. The addition of preservatives to shoyu had become standard practice and a few makers used chemical flavor enhancers (MSG) and even sugar, molasses, or caramel.

Although all of the larger producers switched entirely to the use of defatted soybean meal and quick fermentation, the use of careful quality control and modern scientific fermentation techniques made it possible for them to produce a product which tasted almost identical to the finest natural shoyu but sold for a considerably lower price.

Aided by the forces of modernization and the fact that shoyu's basic flavor had come to be standardized, large centralized manufactures grew enough to distribute their product throughout the nation and the world. Eight Mogi and Takanashi families, which had started brewing shoyu in 1661 and grown closely related by intermarriage, amalgamated in 1917 to form the Noda Shoyu Company; in 1964, this giant international firm, the largest shoyu producer in Japan, was renamed Kikkoman. By 1976, although there were 3,500 shoyu makers in Japan, 43 percent of the total output was produced by only five companies, and about one-third was produced by Kikkoman. Domestic production had soared to 317 million gallons per year, giving a per-capita consumption of about 7 teaspoons daily.

A listing of the five basic varieties of shoyu made in Japan is shown in the accompanying table. Note that regular shoyu (which includes both Kikkoman-type shoyu and natural shoyu as described on page 94) is by far the most popular type in Japan, accounting in 1977 for 85.4 percent of the total.

Each of the five varieties can be prepared by either of three different processes: fermentation, chemical hydrolysis with hydrochloric acid, or a combination of the two processes. *Fermented shoyu,* which constituted 63 percent of the bottled shoyu produced in Japan in 1977, is made using natural fermentation processes, in which natural enzymes from the koji molds and from yeasts and bacteria added to the moromi, break down protein and carbohydrates into amino acids, sugars, alcohols, and organic acids. *Semichemical mixed shoyu,* which constitutes about 30 percent of Japanese shoyu, is made by partially hydrolyzing defatted soybean meal with diluted hydrochloric acid, fermenting this product with wheat koji for 1½ to 2 months, extracting the semifermented shoyu, then mixing it with varying percentages of fermented Shoyu. *Chemical mixed shoyu,* which constitutes about 7 percent of Japanese shoyu, is made by hydrolyzing defatted soybean with concentrated hydrochloric acid, extracting the unfermented chemical soy sauce, then mixing it with fermented shoyu. Note that in Japan, all shoyu contains at least some fermented shoyu. Japan's better shoyu makers stopped making

Varieties, Compositions, and Production of Japanese Shoyu

English Name	Japanese Name	Be'	NaCl % (W/V)	Total nitrogen % (W/V)	Reducing sugar % (W/V)	Alcohol % (V/V)	pH	Color	Annual production %
Regular shoyu	Koikuchi shoyu	22.5	17.6	1.55	3.8	2.2	4.7	Deep brown	85.4
Light-colored shoyu	Usukuchi shoyu	22.8	19.2	1.17	5.5	0.6	4.8	Light brown	11.7
Tamari shoyu	Tamari shoyu	29.9	19.0	2.55	5.3	0.1	4.8	Dark brown	2.2
Clear shoyu	Shiro shoyu	26.9	19.0	0.50	20.2	Trace	4.6	Yellow to tan	0.4
Rich shoyu	Saishikomi shoyu	26.9	18.6	2.39	7.5	Trace	4.8	Dark brown	0.3

Source: Adapted from Fukushima, D., "Fermented Vegetable (Soybean) Protein and Related Foods of Japan and China," *Journal of the American Oil Chemists Society*, March 1979, 56: 357-362.

semichemical mixed shoyu in about 1966 and now produce *only* fermented shoyu. It is important to note that in 1980 the majority of soy sauce sold in America was straight chemical soy sauce, a product considered in Japan to be of such low quality that it is not even sold.

Shortly after World War II, several large food companies in the U.S. began to produce "chemical soy sauce," the very product our American occupation officer had urged the Japanese to produce. This inexpensive, strongly flavored seasoning is made by combining defatted soybean meal (and often corn starches) with concentrated hydrochloric acid, then neutralizing it with sodium carbonate to form hydrolyzed vegetable protein (HVP), a brown liquid rich in amino acids. This is mixed with water, salt, corn syrup, and caramel to add color and flavor in imitation of naturally fermented shoyu (like trying to make wine by mixing ethyl alcohol, water, and flavoring), then sold under various Chinese brand names. Since it is not fermented at all, chemical soy sauce can be made in less than a day using very little space and equipment, then sold at prices roughly 15 percent lower than naturally fermented shoyu. In America, it is still the most widely consumed variety, although, happily, its popularity is dropping as people come to know the fine flavor and aroma of real shoyu.

In Japan, by the early 1970s, a popular reaction had begun to set in against the processes of standardization and increased use of chemicals in traditional foods. People began to grow nostalgic for the taste of fine, natural miso and shoyu, and to speak out against the widespread use of preservatives, bleach, and other synthetic additives. In city apartments and communes, the tradition of preparing fine natural homemade miso began to be revived. Traditional miso and shoyu producers found that their products sold better if they advertised the fact that they were made from whole soybeans, fermented slowly at the natural temperature of the environment, and were free of chemical preservatives and other additives. In 1975 most larger producers stopped using chemical preservatives and switched instead to ethyl alcohol, a more natural preservative. Whereas in the 1960s traditional miso and shoyu were considered by many to be old-fashioned, today they are increasingly viewed as the highest quality fruits of Japan's ancient tradition of fine craftsmanship.

Transmission to the West

Perhaps the single most important development in the recent history of miso and shoyu is their transmission to the West. Piper and Morse (1923) mention that soy sauce was then being made on a small scale in several places in the West. By 1928 Japanese shoyu was being made in Columbia City, Indiana, by the Oriental Show-You Company. The product was labeled Show-You Sauce. By 1929 soy sauce was also being produced in Los Angeles, San Francisco, and Chicago. Japanese shoyu was not widely available in the United States until after World War II, and only recently have Americans come to recognize its fine flavor, use it widely in their cookery, and understand the difference between the authentic fermented product and the less expensive domestic, synthetic soy sauce. In 1972, the first modern Japanese shoyu plant was built in Walworth, Wisconsin, by the Kikkoman company, which now prepares the most popular fermented (nonsynthetic) shoyu made in the West.

The first miso shop in North America, the Fujimoto Miso Company, was started in Salt Lake City, Utah, in 1917 by Mr. Genpei Fujimoto. It is thought that the first miso producer in Hawaii, the Kanda Miso Factory, was started in Honolulu by Mr. Takejiro Kanda in 1920, and in 1921 the Takei Miso Factory was started on Maui by Mr. Shuji Takei. Somewhere between 1927 and 1932 the Tsuruda Miso Company was started in San Jose, California, by Mr. and Mrs. Tsuruda; it was shut down during the war and never resumed operation. The Fujimoto Miso Co. was reestablished after World War II by the son of the founder, Edward Kanta Fujimoto, and his wife

Shizue. Edward died in 1958 and Mrs. Fujimoto continued to run the business until 1976, when she sold her equipment and Kanemasa brand to Miyako Oriental Foods, which was established in Los Angeles in 1976. The first Caucasian-run miso company in North America, Ohio Miso, was started in Monroeville, Ohio, in 1979 by Thom Leonard and Richard Kluding.

The first high-quality miso appeared in natural food stores in America during the mid 1960s, thanks to men like George Ohsawa (founder of the Macrobiotic movement), Herman Aihara (author of the first book on miso written in English), Michio Kushi, and Noboru Muramoto. Dr. Clifford W. Hesseltine has pioneered interest in miso among Western researchers specializing in fermented foods. At present, a number of American natural-food importers are supplying stores throughout the country with fine red, barley, and Hatcho miso, and at least four companies within the United States are producing commercial miso. Due to the efforts of these people and numerous others (see Appendix D), the demand for natural miso and shoyu is steadily growing.

Although the Japanese consume more protein in the form of miso than of shoyu, the latter is presently better known and more widely used in the West. The reason for this unusual development seems to lie more in the difference in structure between the miso and shoyu industries, than in the basic appeal of the two foods. Most Japanese shoyu is produced by a few huge companies which have had the capacity and foresight to engage in international advertising and commerce. By comparison, the largest miso companies are quite small and have only a few decades of modern business experience. Therefore they have not yet been able to make their product known or available throughout the world. Nor, perhaps, have they become fully aware of the genuine interest in and potential market for fine miso in the United States and Europe.

The growing popularity of miso and shoyu in the West is evidence that a taste for these fermented soybean products is universal. And in much the same way that the Japanese, over a period of 1,000 years, gradually transformed Chinese chiang into unique and truly Japanese foods, so may we also expect that Westerners will continue the creative process, adapting miso and shoyu to suit their own tastes, technology, and cuisine.

Appendix B

Other East Asian Misos:
Chiang, Jang, Taucho, and Tausi

DEVELOPED IN China long before the Christian era, chiang was the progenitor of the many varieties of miso and soy sauce that are now used throughout East Asia. As chiang was assimilated by various cultures, its name and basic character gradually changed to suit local conditions. In Korea it was transformed into *jang;* in Japan, it became miso and shoyu; in Indonesia and Thailand, *taucho;* in Malaysia, taucheo; and in the Philippines, *tausi.*

Chinese Chiang

Although all varieties of Chinese-style miso are known collectively as *chiang* (pronounced jiang), this term actually encompasses a remarkably wide range of foods, most of which are fermented with *Aspergillus oryzae* molds but many of which contain neither soybeans nor grain koji. Sharp in flavor, chiang often contains large amounts of fiery red peppers, plus small amounts of other spices such as garlic. Basic ingredients include nuts and seeds, broadbeans, flour or steamed bread, vegetables, and many sea foods. The most common varieties in China are Chunky Chiang (*tou-pan chiang*), Sweet Wheat-flour Chiang (*t'ien mien chiang*), and Red Pepper Chiang (*la-chiao chiang*). In the West, the most widely available varieties—generally known by the Cantonese pronunciation of their names—are Bean Sauce (*yuen-shi chiang*), Hoishin Sauce (*hoisin chiang*), Bean Paste or Chunky Chiang (*to-pan chiang*), and Sweet Wheat-flour Chiang or Soy Jam (*t'inmin chiang*);

they are usually sold in 1-pound cans at Chinese food markets.

Whereas most Japanese miso is presently prepared commercially by professional craftsmen, the majority of Chinese chiang is prepared at home in much the same way that we in the West make our own jams, canned fruit, or pickles. Following centuries-old methodologies, both chiang and chiang-yu (the liquid pressed from chiang, i.e., soy sauce) are usually started in March or April; packed into 1- to 10-gallon earthenware crocks that are placed in courtyards or on rooftops or apartment balconies, they are allowed to ferment for 6 to 12 months. Most varieties are stirred daily, with rice wine added during the fermentation. The total production of chiang-yu is considerably larger than that of chiang. The Chinese have various terms for koji: *chou, chiu-niang,* and *kyoku-shi.* We are not sure what each signifies.

The flavor of homemade chiang varies greatly from household to household, and in many cases the strong aroma, high salt content, dark color, and extreme spiciness combine to create a product which appeals to only a small percentage of the population. In recent years, however, more uniform-tasting and universally appealing varieties have come to be prepared commercially on a large scale for distribution throughout the world. We find that sweet wheat-flour chiang—known to many Westerners as the basis for the delicious chocolate-brown sauce served with Peking Duck—is especially well suited to Western tastes.

In Taiwan and China, both homemade and commercial chiang scooped from open-top wooden kegs are sold at stores called "chiang gardens," which also deal in salt-pickled vegetables and soy sauce. Most shops sell only the three main varieties mentioned above, plus one or two local ones. Chiang is used in all of the major schools of Chinese cookery, usually as the base for sauces served with meat, seafood, or poultry dishes, and less commonly, with stir-fried tofu and vegetable preparations. (The Chinese have never adopted the Japanese practice of using chiang in soups.) At Chinese restaurants in the West, it can

Fig. 20. Composition of Nutrients in 100 Grams of Chiang and Jang

(Source: *Food Composition Tables for Use in East Asia and Wang, 1979*)

Type of Chiang	Food Energy Calories	Moisture Percent	Protein Percent	Fat Percent	Carbo-hydrates (incl. fiber) Percent	Fiber Percent	Ash Percent	Sodium Mg	Calcium Mg	Phosphorous Mg	Iron Mg	Potassium Mg	Vit. B₁ (thiamine) Mg	Vit. B₂ (riboflavin) Mg	Vit. B₃ (niacin) Mg
Chunky Chiang (*tou-pan chiang*)	194	48.6	11.6	5.2	27.2	2.1	7.4	761	55	365	1.3	334	.07	1.19	1.2
Hot Chunky Chiang (*la tou-pan chiang*)	185	52.7	8.1	4.1	30.2	3.5	4.9	680	126	72	13.6	280	.35	.35	1.5
Sweet Wheat-flour Chiang (*t'ien mien chiang*)	192	47.0	5.4	1.2	40.1	2.7	6.3	570	32	104	5.7	183	.18	.80	0.9
Korean Soybean Jang (*doen jang*)	—	59.4	10.6	8.4	5.7	2.6	16.0	—	—	—	—	—	.002	.01	1.8
Korean Red-pepper Jang (*kochu jang*)	—	49.3	9.3	4.2	23.4	2.3	13.7	—	—	—	—	—	.08	.11	1.2
Korean Soybean Koji (*meju*)	—	23.2	43.0	17.8	11.9	5.7	4.1	—	—	—	—	—	—	—	—

be sampled in a wide array of dishes listed as containing "bean sauce" or "bean paste."

The most common classification divides all chiang into four basic types: red or regular chiang, black chiang, assorted chiang, and chiang sauces. The varieties within each type are listed below in order of popularity. All Chinese names are written using the Wade-Giles system of romanization and standard Mandarin pronunciation, which has the following unique conventions: ch is pronounced like the j in jam, ch' like the ch in chard; k like the g in game, k' like the k in Korea; p like the b in bean, p' like the p in pea; t like the d in dough; t' like the t in tea.

RED OR REGULAR CHIANG

Chunky Chiang (*tou-pan chiang, topan chiang, or do-ban jiang*): Literally "bean petal chiang" or "board chiang" and also known as "Chinese soybean paste," this is a variety of wheat miso made with either soybeans or broad-beans and usually containing wheat flour. Soft in texture and very chunky due to the presence of unmashed beans, it ranges in color from warm chocolate to dark russet. Most varieties contain as much as 18 percent salt, and hence have a strong salty flavor, although modern commercial varieties are lower in salt and have a distinctive, yet milder taste. Prepared in basically the same way as the common Chinese soy sauce called *toyu* except that the percentage of liquid is much smaller, this chiang is fermented outdoors in large earthenware crocks and stirred daily for 7 to 12 months. Some varieties contain whole roasted sesame seeds, oil, or fish. Typical proportions by weight of raw materials are: soybeans 10, barley 3.3, wheat flour 3.3, salt 5.

A well-known seasoning made by dissolving chunky chiang in water is called *huang-hsi chiang*.

Hot Chunky Chiang (*la tou-pan chiang or tou-pan la-chiang*): Also known as "hot bean paste," this hot-and-spicy variety is made by adding red peppers to chunky chiang. If dried ground red pepper is also added, the product is known as *tou-pan yu la-chiao*.

Szechwan Red-Pepper Chiang (*ssu-ch'uan tou-pan chiang*): Sharper in flavor than hot chunky chiang but not as hot as red-pepper chiang (see below), this spicy variety is specially prepared in Szechwan and renowned for its abundant use of red-hot peppers. Often known in English as Szechwan Hot Soybean Paste, it plays a key seasoning role in Szechwan's fiery cuisine.

Soy Nugget Chiang (*tou-ch'ih chiang*): Resembling a combination of chunky Japanese red miso and savory soy nuggets (p. 56), this savory product is closely related to Chinese-style soy nuggets (*tou-ch'ih* or *shang-ch'ih*), a seasoning made by fermenting lightly salted soybeans. If hot red peppers are added, the product becomes Red-Pepper Soy Nugget Chiang (*tou-ch'ih la-chiao chiang*).

Cantonese Red Chiang (*mien-ch'ih chiang*): Made from beans particular to Canton, this variety also contains wheat flour.

Great Chiang (*ta chiang*): A variety using soybeans as the key ingredient.

Yellow-red Chiang (*huang chiang*): Literally "yellow chiang," this variety is made primarily with soybeans.

BLACK CHIANG

Sweet Wheat-flour Chiang (*t'ien mien chiang, mien chiang,* or *t'ien chiang*): This chocolate-brown, sweet preparation, also called "sweet (soy) bean paste," "sweet flour paste," or "flour jam," is made from wheat flour, salt, and water. Its consistency is smooth and soft—like that of melted chocolate—and its flavor somewhat resembles that of Japanese akadashi miso (p. 81). When prepared commercially, the flour and water are combined to form a dough which is either shaped into 4½-inch-diameter dumplings (*man-t'ou* or *manju*) and steamed, or flattened into ¾-inch-thick sheets, dried until firm, then broken into pieces about 5 inches in diameter. The steamed buns or flat pieces are arranged on 4-foot diameter bamboo trays and allowed to ferment in an incubation room for about 4 days. (Or in some areas, the steamed buns are arranged on sorghum stalks in an outdoor shed and allowed to mold for 3 weeks during the month of May.) The molded buns or sheets are then transferred to large earthenware pots located in an outdoor courtyard or on a rooftop. Mixed with a small amount of water and about 5 percent salt, the steamed dough soon begins to soften and dissolve. The mixture is stirred daily and allowed to ferment for at least 3 to 4 months, and sometimes as long as 6 to 8 months. A small amount of additional water is sometimes added each day during the first week of fermentation. During the day and sometimes at night the lids of the pots are left open to give access to the supposedly beneficial effects of dew and moonlight.

When this variety of chiang is prepared at home, the steamed bun or moist dough (often inoculated with a yellow storebought koji starter mold) is placed on a platter in a warm, damp place for 7 to 15 days until mold forms. The molded product is then transferred to a small earthenware crock and covered with salty water; left uncovered under the sun and night sky for 5 days, the mixture is squeezed daily by hand. For the next 15 days the mixture is stirred with a bamboo pole, after which time the chiang is ready, although its fermentation may be continued for 2 months more to give a mellower flavor and darker color. In some areas, soy sauce pressing-residue is added to the mixture to make it saltier.

In Chinese restaurants, sweet wheat-flour chiang is often combined with small amounts of sugar, sesame oil, and rice wine to make the dipping sauce served with Peking Duck (p. 316) or Pancake Rolls (p. 312). In Japan, where chiang is not widely available, a similar sauce is prepared using Hatcho miso as the basic ingredient (p. 153). Sweet wheat-flour chiang is also served as a dip with thinly sliced meat hors d'oeuvres or as a spread for steamed buns or baked bread topped with sliced leeks; as the basis of the sauce served with Mabo-doufu (tofu cooked with ground beef and ground red pepper); as a topping, mixed with ground beef, for the noodle dish Cha-chiang Mien; and as a seasoning with sautéed chicken or pork dishes. It is also widely used as a pickling medium.

Prepared commercially with the addition of plenty of minced red peppers, this variety becomes Red-pepper Wheat-flour Chiang (*la-mien chiang*).

Black Chiang (*hei chiang or he do-ban jiang*): Actually dark chocolate brown, black chiang (often sold as Black Bean Paste) is made from black soybeans, as is its close relative Bean Chiang (*tou chiang*). A well-known seasoning made by dissolving black chiang in water is called *hei-hsi chiang*.

ASSORTED CHIANGS

The earliest varieties of chiang are said to have been sauces made by fermenting salted fish, shellfish, and meats. Similar to the well-known, strong-smelling *nuoc-mam* of Vietnam and *shiokara* or *shottsuru* of Japan, the modern descendents of these ancient foods are still widely used as both seasonings and sauces.

Red-Pepper Chiang (*la-chiao chiang* or *la-chiang*): An all purpose seasoning used like tabasco sauce, this hot-and-spicy preparation is made by fermenting salted red peppers. Containing no soybeans, it is vermilion red and has a soft, semi-liquid consistency similar to that of a thick chili sauce. At restaurants, it is often placed on the table in small bottles.

Canton Sweet Simmered Chiang (*hai-hsien chiang*): A close relative of Japanese Sweet Simmered Miso (p. 357). A variety made in the Fo-shan region near Canton containing fennel and a spicy powder is called *chu-hou chiang*.

Dried Chiang (*kan chiang*): A general term for all chiang that has been dried after fermentation, this unique product has no counterpart among traditional Japanese misos.

Other Varieties, none of which contain soybeans or grain koji, include:

> **Sesame Chiang (tsu-ma chiang):* The Chinese equivalent of Western-style sesame butter

*_Peanut Chiang (hua-hsian chiang):_ Chinese-
style peanut butter
*_Umeboshi Chiang (shun-mui chiang):_ With tart,
salted _ume_ plums
*_Shrimp Chiang (hsia chiang):_ Often served with
meat dishes
*_Corbicula Chiang (hin-kai chiang):_ Featuring
tiny salt-cured shellfish
*_Tangy Chiang (kei-hua chiang):_ Made from
minced garlic, tangerine rind, and sesame seeds
*_Semi-fermented Chiang_ (_chiang-p'i_): Made in
large bun-shaped lumps

CHIANG SAUCES

Most of these sauces, which have a consistency similar to that of thick gravy, are presently available in
cans at Chinese grocery stores in the West.

Bean Sauce (_yuan-shih chiang_ or _yuen-shi chiang_):
This chocolate-brown sauce, made from soybeans,
flour, salt, and water has a thick consistency and
rather salty flavor. The regular variety has a slightly
chunky texture, whereas that labeled "ground bean
sauce" (_min see chiang_) is smooth. Also known as "soy
jam" or "soybean condiment," this product is also
called "yellow bean sauce" when yellow beans are
used in place of the usual soybeans. In making soy
sauce, the Chinese filter off the liquid from chiang.
The lees or residue that remain are used as the basic
ingredient in bean sauce. (Note that Japanese shoyu
producers press the residue and then discard it.) Some
varieties of bean sauce contain added sesame seeds,
sugar, caramel coloring, molasses, MSG, vinegar,
and/or preservatives. Bean sauce is an essential seasoning with the famous Cha-chiang Mien (Soy Jam
Noodles) and is also widely used in stir-fried preparations, as a pickling medium, and mixed with gingerroot
and minced green onion as a seasoning atop steamed
fish.

Hoisin Sauce (_hai-hsien chiang_): Also known as
"soy jam," this jet black paste is creamy smooth and

very sweet; it looks and tastes quite like melted chocolate or like Sweet Wheat-Flour Chiang (above). After the light soy sauce is drawn off of chiang, the soybean lees are lightly pressed to extract some remaining soy sauce, ground to a smooth paste, then mixed with flour, sugar, vinegar, salt, ground red pepper, and water; some varieties also contain garlic, food coloring, and preservatives. Sold in the West in 1-pound cans or 14-ounce jars, it is a favorite sauce for Peking Duck, Mu Shee Pork, and Chinese-style spareribs. It is prized for its spicy sweetish flavor when used as a barbecue sauce, especially with *yakitori* (Japanese-style grilled chicken).

Oyster Sauce (*hao-yu chiang* or *hao-wei chiang*): A widely-used seasoning made from the liquid that rises to the surface of salt-pickled, fermented oysters.

Barbecue Sauce (*satsa chiang*): Known also as "shacha jam," this Cantonese or Taiwanese barbecue sauce is used mainly with *sukiyaki* and *yakitori* (grilled chicken), but is also served as a topping for rice, noodles, sea cucumber, pork, and fried beef.

Other Chiang Sauces, none of which contain soybeans or grain koji include:

Shrimp Sauce (hsia-yu or *luhsia-yu): Features tiny shrimps
Chinese Worcestershire Sauce (suan-la chiang, la-chiang yu, or *chi-ch'ih): A close relative of its English counterpart
*Chinese Ketchup (fan-ch'ieh chiang): Similar to Western tomato ketchup

Chunky Chiang *(tou-pan chiang):* 豆瓣醬，豆板醬，豆弁醬；
   Huang-hsi Chiang: 黃稀醬
Hot Chunky Chiang *(la tou-pan chiang):* 瓣豆辣醬
   Tou-pan Yu La-chiao: 豆瓣油辣椒
Szechwan Red-pepper Chiang
   (ssu-ch'uan tou-pan chiang): 四川豆板醬，豆瓣醬
Hamanatto Chiang *(tou-ch'ih chiang):* 豆豉醬
   Red-pepper Hamanatto Chiang
   (tou-ch'ih la-chiao chiang): 豆豉辣椒醬
Cantonese Red Chiang *(mien-ch'ih chiang):* 麵豉醬
Great Chiang *(ta chiang):* 大醬
Yellow-red Chiang *(huang chiang):* 黃醬
Sweet Wheat-flour Chiang *(t'ien mien chiang):* 甜麵醬
   Red-pepper Wheat-flour Chiang *(la-mien chiang):* 瓣麵醬
Black Chiang *(hei chiang):* 黑醬
   Bean Chiang *(tou chiang):* 豆醬
   Hei-hsi chiang: 黑稀醬
Red-pepper Chiang *(la-chiao chiang):* 辣椒醬
Canton Sweet Simmered Chiang
   (hai-hsien chiang): 海鮮醬，柱候醬
Dried Chiang *(kan chiang):* 干醬
Sesame Chiang *(tsu-ma chiang):* 芝麻醬
Peanut Chiang *(hua-hsian chiang):* 花生醬
Umeboshi Chiang *(shun-mui chiang):* 酸梅醬
Shrimp Chiang *(hsia chiang):* 蝦醬
Corbicula Chiang *(hin-kai chiang):* 蜆介醬
Tangy Chiang *(kei-hua chiang):* 柱花醬
Semi-fermented Chiang *(chiang-p'i):* 醬坯
Bean Sauce *(yuan-shin chiang):* 原豉醬
Hoishin Sauce *(hai-hsien chiang):* 海鮮醬
Oyster Sauce *(hao-yu chiang):* 蠔油醬，蠔味醬
Barbecue Sauce *(satsa chiang):* 沙茶醬
Shrimp Sauce *(hsia-yu):* 蝦油，滷蝦油
Chinese Worcestershire Sauce
   (suan-la chiang): 酸辣醬　辣醬油　噏汁
Chinese Ketchup *(fan-ch'ieh chiang):* 番茄醬

Korean Jang

Korea's three main fermented soyfoods are soybean miso (*doen jang*), soy sauce (*kan jang*), and red-pepper miso (*kochu jang*). These three products accounted respectively for 18.3 percent, 10.6 percent, and 6.6 percent of total Korean soybean utilization in 1976. In that year, the daily per capita consumption of the three products was about 15 grams, 20 grams (ml), and 10 grams respectively. As in China, most of the soybean miso (82 percent), soy sauce (64 percent) and red-chili miso (76 percent) are produced in farmhouses and urban dwellings, and consumed directly by the families that make them; each family is allotted 6 pounds of free salt per year for just this purpose. A typical downtown high-rise apartment in Seoul will have six to eight brown earthenware crocks containing homemade *jang* and *kan jang* on 80 to 90 percent of its balconies. For this reason, jang is sold on only a relatively small scale at the miso-and-pickle sections of outdoor markets and food stores. Jang is widely used in hot spicy soups (*chigé*) which are generally thicker than Japanese miso soups. Kan jang, sweeter and stronger than Japanese shoyu, is made with soybeans, salt, and water, without the use of koji grain.

The various types of Korean miso and soy sauce are made from a dried soybean koji called *meju*, which is prepared in much the same way as Japan's *miso-dama* (p. 476). To make *meju*, soybeans are soaked, cooked, pounded until well mashed in a mortar, shaped into balls and wrapped in rice straw (or put unshaped into rice straw sacks), then hung under the rafters or eaves for 1 to 3 months, until each ball is covered with a natural bloom of white mold. The material is then broken into chunks, dried in the sun, and generally ground to a fine powder, usually in a hand-turned stone mill. The resulting *meju* (dried and ground soybean koji) has a composition of nutrients as shown in figure 20; it contains almost no sodium chloride (0.2 percent). At present ready-made *meju* is sold in marketplaces and used as the basis for some homemade jang. And some families have recently begun to inoculate their cooked soybeans with koji starter (*Aspergillus oryzae* or *A. sojae*), which is also sold in the markets. The starter is mixed with a little wheat flour and sprinkled over the cooked, air-dried soybeans. The beans are then incubated in a warm place (79–86°F) for 24 to 48 hours, or until they are covered with white mold. They are then dried, crushed, and mixed with salt and water as above.

Korean Soybean Jang (*doen jang*): The only traditional Korean jang, this variety is light grayish brown and slightly chunky from the small proportion of uncrushed soybeans it contains. Two varieties of this salty and very strong-flavored jang are found in traditional markets; neither contains grain koji and one is slightly more salty and lumpy than the other. Most of this jang is still made in private homes, even that which is sold commercially, since most Koreans prefer the homemade product.

To prepare Korean soybean jang, *meju* is mixed with an 18- to 22-percent salt brine (and sometimes with sesame seeds or sesame leaves) in an earthenware container of 1 to 10 gallons capacity. The container is covered (but has no pressing lid) and placed outdoors on a balcony or rooftop, or in a courtyard. Traditionally the fermentation lasted for six months, from March to September. If a commercial starter is used to make the *meju*, the fermentation may be reduced to 2 to 3 months, and even less if the *meju* is soaked in warm brine and the container kept exposed to sunlight. After the basic fermentation period, the liquid that has accumulated in the container is filtered off and pasteurized by simmering to make *kan jang* (Korean soy sauce). The remaining nonliquid portion left in the vat is allowed to age for at least a few months longer, until it is good quality *doen jang* (soybean miso).

In the United States, a commercial variety is now available in 1-pound cans at Korean and Japanese food markets. Labeled "Bean Mash" (*doen jang*), it contains soybeans, wheat, salt, and water. Nutrient composition is shown in figure 20.

Red-Pepper Jang (*kochu jang*): This spicy hot Korean miso is bright brownish red, has a smooth texture, and is somewhat softer than Japanese miso; each of the three main varieties contain slightly different amounts of red pepper. To make red-pepper jang, dried, finely ground *meju* is mixed in crocks with cooked glutinous rice, ground red pepper, and either salt brine or Korean soy sauce. Typically the fermentation takes 2 to 3 months; however, it may be accelerated by placing the crocks in sunlight. A good red-pepper jang contains a combination of sweet, hot, sour, and salty flavors. In some areas, rice flour is mixed with water to form dumplings, which are dropped into boiling water and cooked, then mashed together with *meju* and ground red pepper. One-third of the salt is added daily for three days; the red-pepper jang may be served on the fourth day, but it is usually fermented for 6 months. It is said that some varieties are also prepared from rice koji and wheat flour, or from a mixture of cooked soybeans and mochi or glutinous rice. Red-pepper jang is the favorite base for a thick soup or stew containing thinly sliced or ground meat and a little sugar.

In the United States, a commercial variety is now available in 1-pound cans at Korean and Japanese food markets. Labeled "Hot Bean Mash" (*kocho jang*), it contains rice, red peppers, soybeans, salt, and water.

Mild Red-Pepper Jang (*mat jang*): This variety is similar to red-pepper jang but it contains more *meju*, less ground red pepper, and less salt. Glutinous rice is generally used to add natural grain sugars and a sweet flavor. The jang is wrapped in blankets and fermented in a warm place for a relatively short time (about 2 weeks). Like Japanese Finger Lickin' Miso, it is often served with fresh vegetables or tofu as a dip, topping, or garnish.

Chinese Sweet Black Jang (*cha jang* or *chungkuk jang*): This soft, jet black miso is a close relative of Chinese Sweet Wheat-flour Chiang (p. 531). Most of the Korean varieties are made by Chinese in Korea or imported from China. It is most popularly served with noodles in a dish called Cha Jang Mien (p. 308). The words *cha* and *chungkuk* both mean "Chinese."

Japanese Red Jang (*wei jang* or *ilbon jang*): This is a salty red rice miso similar to Japanese Sendai miso but with a flavor adapted to Korean tastes. It is saltier than the Japanese product. A smooth, reddish brown jang, it originated in Japan and was sold during the 36 years of Japanese occupation. It is now produced in large quantities in Korea. The words *wei* and *ilbon* both mean "Japanese."

Indonesian Taucho

Formerly spelled tao-tjo (and now spelled tauco in Indonesia), this is a fermented soybean paste or chunky sauce, a variety of soybean miso with a long history that is produced and consumed mainly in West Java, the center of production being the town of Chianjur. There are four different flavors and consistencies of taucho, all of which are dark brown in color and usually known simply as *taucho*: 1) *Sweet soft taucho* (also called *taucho Chianjur*) is the most popular variety. It has a consistency of porridge or applesauce, interspersed with prominent soybean chunks. Its pronounced sweetness is due to the addition of 25 percent by weight of palm sugar. 2) *Salty liquid taucho* (also called black bean sauce, salted soybeans, or salted black beans) is a non-homogeneous mixture of firm reddish to black soybean halves immersed in a soy-sauce-like concentrate. It is extremely strong, pungent, and salty (much saltier than Japanese miso or shoyu). 3) *Firm dried taucho* (*taucho kering*) is a relatively new product made by sun-drying cakes of either of the previously mentioned taucho types. 4) *Smoked dried taucho* is a relatively uncommon product prepared mostly by Chinese.

The various types of taucho are used primarily as a seasoning in soups, vegetables, seafood, and noodle preparations, especially Lodeh, Taucho Ikan, Ikan Goreng Taucho, Sambal Taucho, Sambal Goreng Taucho, Oseng-Oseng Taucho, Mie Goreng Taucho, Tempeh Maska Taucho, and Tumis Udang.

Taucho differs from Japanese miso in that it is either sweeter or saltier and softer or firmer, is prepared by a much shorter natural fermentation, and contains a large proportion of glutinous rice flour. An estimated 84 cottage-industry shops produce taucho in Indonesia and 77 of these are located in West Java.

Taucho is traditionally made by a two-part fermentation process; a mold fermentation followed by a brine fermentation. One hundred kilograms of dry soybeans are washed and soaked in excess water for 15 to 20 hours, brought quickly to a boil, then dehulled underfoot or by hand. The beans are rinsed and the hulls usually floated off, boiled for up to 5 hours, drained, spread on 3-foot-diameter woven bamboo trays, where they are allowed to cool for 12 hours to air temperature (82°F). The beans are inoculated with a starter prepared by pounding to a powder 10 grams of sundried tempeh and mixing it with 190 grams of roasted glutinous rice flour. The active organisms in the starter are *Rhizopus oligosporus, Rhizopus oryzae,* and *Aspergillus oryzae.* This mixed culture inoculum has been shown to give taucho with the best flavor and aroma. Two hundred grams of this starter are mixed with 50 kilograms of roasted glutinous rice flour, mixed thoroughly with the soybeans, spread in a 1¼-inch-deep layer in the bamboo tray, sometimes covered with cheesecloth, and incubated in racks at 81°F for 3 to 4 days (traditionally as long as 7 to 14 days) until the beans are covered with a dense white mycelium. This koji-like substance is then broken into small pieces and put into 2½-gallon earthenware crocks with an 18-percent brine solution in the ratio of 100 kilograms koji to 200 liters brine. The resulting mash is allowed to stand outdoors in the sun for an average of 4 weeks and is mixed each morning. The crocks are covered each night. Beneficial bacteria and yeasts such as *Lactobacillus delbruekii* and *Hansenula spp.* become active and aid the brine fermentation. The finished product may be sold in small plastic bags as salty liquid taucho.

To make sweet soft taucho, 100 kilograms of the original taucho is combined with 25 kilograms each of palm sugar and water; the mixture is cooked until a homogeneous, viscous consistency is obtained. Firm dried taucho is then prepared by sun-drying or smoking this product.

Taucho is the least important of Indonesia's four basic soyfoods, which include tempeh tofu, and kechap (soy sauce). It accounts for less than 1 percent of all Indonesian soybean utilization and the annual per capita consumption of all types of taucho is only 7.2 grams.

There are a number of publications on taucho. The best is F. G. Winarno's *Research on Taucho* (Phases I–III) published by FATEMETA, Bogor Agricultural University, Jalan Gunung Gede, Bogor, Indonesia, 1975. Additional information about this Indonesian miso is found in Winarno's *The Present Status of Soybeans in Indonesia* and *Indonesian Fermented Foods.* Publications by his colleagues include Nurhajati *et al.* (1975), Swastomo *et al.* (1975), and Zaenuddin *et al.* (1975).

For more details on taucho and a list of researchers, see the professional clothbound edition of our *Book of Tempeh* (Harper & Row).

A close relative of Indonesian taucho is Malaysian *taucheo.*

Filipino Tausi

Also spelled tao-si, this product consists of black soybeans fermented with *Aspergillus oryzae* and sold in a dark salty sauce resembling soy sauce. Its closest relative is Indonesian salty liquid taucho; its Japanese relatives are savory soy nuggets (*Hamanatto*) and chunky soybean miso. Scooped with a ladle from glass jars in the marketplaces, it is widely used as a seasoning with sautéed fish and vegetables, and occasionally as a topping for rice. Unlike miso, it is not widely used as a paste to season soups.

To make tausi, dry (often black) soybeans are washed, soaked overnight, then boiled or steamed for about one hour until soft. The beans are drained, cooled, and surface-dried on woven bamboo trays for 30 minutes in the sun or 60 minutes in the shade, then mixed with toasted wheat or rice flour until all the beans are covered. Traditionally the beans were inoculated just like soy sauce with a mixed culture, especially suitable strains of *Aspergillus oryzae,* from a previous fermentation, then spread on the bamboo trays, covered with a wilted banana leaf or sheets of paper, and left to incubate in a warm place for 2 to 3 (occasionally up to 7) days until covered with a thick mycelium and the interior temperature rose to 100°F (38°C). Recently the inoculum has come to be grown on steamed rice that is incubated for 7 days at 86°F (30°C), then dried in the sun or in an oven and ground to a powder. During incubation of the soybeans, they are crumbled several times as heat builds up. The soybean koji is then placed in earthenware crocks and just enough 18-percent brine solution is added to cover it. The vats are exposed to the sun for 5 days to stimulate the fermentation, then aged in the shade for 2 to 6 months. The longer fermentation is said to give a better product. Some producers boil the beans in the brine before selling the tausi.

Appendix C

The Chemistry and Microbiology of Miso Fermentation

THE PREPARATION of miso involves two consecutive fermentation processes. In the first, olive-green "koji starter" (*tané koji;* literally "koji seeds") consisting of dried mold spores is mixed with cooked rice, barley, or soybeans; the mixture is then incubated to produce the mold grain or soybeans called "koji." In the second, the koji is mixed with cooked soybeans, salt, water and usually a little mature miso. Packed into vats, the ingredients are allowed to age while the dual processes of enzymatic digestion and fermentation transform them into the finished miso.

Let us enter this unfamiliar world, learn the names of its main dramateurs, and follow the interrelated processes of transformation. We will begin by discussing the nature of the basic molds used to prepare the koji starter, then go on to study the two fermentation processes mentioned above.

Koji Starter Molds

Select varieties of mold spores are the chief actors in the fermentation process, just as other varieties are used in the production of delicious natural cheeses, or yeasts are used in the making of wines or bread. What exactly are molds? Botanically, they are a family of lower plants which is part of a larger group known as fungi. The latter includes molds, mushrooms, yeasts, and mildews. All fungi lack chlorophyll, may be as small as a single cell, and can reproduce abundantly by the process of sporulation. Mycology—derived from the Greek stem *myco-* or *myc-* meaning fungus—

is a special branch of botany dealing exclusively with the study of this vast world.

All molds and fungi grow on other organic substances called substrates. Bread, fruits, and vegetables allowed to stand too long in the cupboard often become the substrates for unwanted varieties. In the miso shop, cooked rice, barley, or soybeans are used intentionally as substrates. In addition to a suitable substrate, molds require a particular environment for hearty growth. It must be fairly warm (about 80°F to 95°F), moist but not wet, and aerobic (i.e. containing plenty of free oxygen). Yeasts and anaerobic bacteria differ from molds in that they thrive in moist environments containing little or no free oxygen.

Molds are present in large numbers almost everywhere. Up until several decades ago, these wild spores were used as the "starter" for most of Japan's commercial miso, and they are still used in the preparation of some farmhouse varieties. Gradually, however, miso makers discovered that some mold varieties seemed to produce better quality miso than others; resorting largely to intuition and personal experience, they began to cultivate select strains in much the same way that prospectors nourished their sourdough cultures, Balkan peasants their yogurt starters, or cheesemakers their Camembert molds. When, at the turn of the century (1904), microbiologists first isolated pure cultures of miso molds, they discovered that virtually all varieties belonged to the single species *Aspergillus oryzae.*

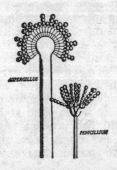

ASPERGILLUS

PENICILLIUM

The genus *Aspergillus* is part of the class Fungi Imperfecti, which also includes *Penicillium* molds. These fungi reproduce only asexually and are hence "imperfect." Their reproduction is by means of specialized spores called conidia (from the Greek meaning "fine dust"), which are born at the tips of special fungal filaments (modified hyphae) called conidiophores ("spore bearers"), shown in figure 21.

The genus *Aspergillus* derives its name from the term "aspergillum," which refers to a brush or small perforated container with a handle used, usually by priests or nuns, for sprinkling holy water in a liturgical service.

A close relative of *Aspergillus oryzae* is *Aspergillus flavus* (ass-per-JIL-us FLAY-vus), the main mold that produces aflatoxins on peanuts, corn, and a few other foods when they are not stored properly. Aflatoxins, highly carcinogenic liver toxins, came to the public attention in 1960 when 100,000 turkeys and ducks suddenly died in England from consuming moldy Brazilian peanut presscake, contaminated by *A. flavus*. Since that time extensive tests around the world have been conducted to see if similar toxins might be produced in soyfoods such as miso, shoyu, tamari, or Hamanatto fermented by other species of *Aspergillus*. Dr. C.W. Hesseltine, one of the world's foremost authorities on aflatoxins (and on miso), has shown repeatedly that soybeans are a poor substrate for aflatoxin production, and there have been no reports of aflatoxins in miso or any other soyfoods fermented by *Aspergillus*.

Within the single species *Aspergillus oryzae,* just as within the world of roses, there are a vast number of strains or subspecies—estimates range from 10,000 to 100,000—each with its own unique physical properties and name! Some mycologists, in fact, devote their entire lives to the study of *A. oryzae* and often specialize in the study of one or more of the important strains, those, that is, which yield koji with good fermentation "strength" and produce miso characterized by excellent flavor and aroma. Some strains are valued for their ability to produce large amounts of the enzyme amylase which digests or breaks down starches; these might be used in sweet white miso containing a large proportion of grains. Other strains are prized for their abundant production of the enzyme protease which breaks down proteins; these might be used to prepare the koji for soybean miso. Some molds have long "hairs" that create a firmly interlocking mycelium, excellent for commercial koji such as the soft mat variety available in grocery stores. Others have short "hairs" suited to modern factory koji production. Some molds have white "hairs" that give ready-made koji an attractive appearance. Others generate heat quickly and are used to make koji in short periods of time.

Most Japanese miso makers do not cultivate their own *A. oryzae* starter molds since the process requires extensive technical know-how and fairly complex equipment. Rather, this work is entrusted to a small number of specialty shops (fewer than ten), each of which tends a number of carefully bred strains, some of which may have been in their possession for centuries. These molds are bred and cross-bred over a period of many years as carefully as racehorses and chosen to give exactly the desired flavor and aroma to the miso. A shop's stock of molds is its most valued asset and the owner goes to great lengths—storing samples in vaults or caves—to guarantee their protection from fire or theft. Those portions of the stock in daily use are kept in their pure-culture state inside carefully sealed bottles in spotlessly clean laboratories to prevent even the slightest contamination by alien strains.

Making Koji Starter

At the specialty shops, the molds are used to make "koji starter" (*tané koji*), later sold by special order to miso makers who use it in small amounts to make *koji,* the preparation of which precedes the making of miso itself.

Koji starter is prepared in basically the same way

as koji itself except that the trays of inoculated steamed rice are allowed to stand for five (rather than just two) days in the warm incubation room until the mold turns from white to olive green, indicating sporulation. The mycelium-bound grain is then dried in large rooms and sold in small sealed packages.

The substrate for koji starter is a mixture of cooked brown rice (or barley) and a small amount (about 2%) of the ash of a deciduous tree such as camellia or oak. Brown rather than white rice is used because the latter lacks the necessary nutrients for hearty mold growth. The alkaloid ash, in addition to preventing the excessively rapid generation of heat, provides the young mold with nutritious potassium and phosphorous salts, manganese, and other trace elements, and helps bring about the RNA/DNA balance required for proper sporulation. (It also prevents the rice from clumping.) After the warm rice-and-ash substrate is inoculated by mixing in pure-culture spores of a selected strain of *A. oryzae* mold, it is incubated for five days at 76°F in shallow wooden trays in a large humid room. Naturally, great care is taken to see that no contaminating microorganisms enter the culture during this time.

Soon after incubation begins, the mold spores send out hair-like shoots called hyphae. These growing filaments make the body of the mold, the white mycelium. Many hyphael cells make long erect shoots called "conidiophores" or "sporophores," which terminate in a bulbous head. After three or four days, these heads have formed bud clusters, which begin to sporulate luxuriously. It is at this stage that the color of the mold turns from creamy beige to soft olive green, the color of the spores themselves. Eventually each spore will have multiplied over 10 million times. The finished mats of mycelium-bound rice are transferred (in the trays) to drying rooms (113°F) for three to four days. Here the koji starter develops a tantalizing aroma similar to that of roasting chestnuts or almonds. Delicious as a snack, its flavor is richer and sweeter than that of regular koji.

Koji starter is made available commercially in three

forms. The mycelium-bound grains are sometimes only lightly crumbled and sold as "whole-grain" starter. Or the spore-covered rice may be ground and sold as a "meal." About 50 percent of all koji starter sold today comes in the form of "spore powder" made by sifting whole-grain starter, discarding the mold-free rice grains, and collecting the olive-green spores; one gram of this pure powder contains from 6 to 10 billion spores. It is usually mixed with a powdered starch extender to make it easier to package and use.

Most modern starters contain not just one but several mold strains in a mixture carefully formulated to produce the right balance of enzymes needed to produce the particular type of koji desired. Some are also enriched with yeasts such as *Saccharomyces rouxii* of bacteria such as *Pedicoccus hallophilus* which play important roles after the miso ingredients begin the second stage of their fermentation. A typical shop selling koji starter will offer eight or more basic types as explained on page 433.

Making Koji: The First Fermentation

Once in the miso-maker's hands, the starter is used to make koji in what is perhaps the most difficult but crucial part of the miso-making process. Koji (or "mold rice") is cooked grains or beans which have been inoculated with starter and allowed to ferment for about two days until covered with and bound together by a fragrant white mycelium. This mold produces the enzymes that eventually break down the complex molecules of protein, starch, and lipids (oils and fats) in the substrate, reducing them to simpler, more readily digestible products which are later fermented by yeasts and bacteria. Enzymes, complex substances produced by living cells, are actually only catalysts; they simply promote chemical reactions (such as hydrolysis or oxidation) without themselves undergoing marked change in the process. In the process of beer fermentation, malt is prepared by sprouting barley (without the use of molds) in order to develop enzymes. Thus, koji is to miso what malt is to beer.

The nature of koji is embodied in the very characters with which the word is written. In the more traditional form—used with most miso koji and especially with barley koji—the ideographs for "barley" and "chrysanthemum" are placed side by side. In the more recent form—used especially with ready-made rice koji—the ideographs for "rice" and "flower" are conjoined. The first form is said to have originated in China, whereas the latter was developed in Japan about 1,000 years ago. In both, the notion of grain covered with a bloom of mold is vividly expressed.

To make koji, about one part by weight of starter is mixed with 1,000 parts substrate, cooked (usually steamed) grains or beans that have been allowed to cool to body temperature. The inoculated substrate is placed in a large, well-insulated, cloth-lined box called a crib, covered with thick insulating mats, and allowed to stand overnight. After a few hours, the temperature inside the crib begins to rise as heat is generated by the process of fermentation. Briefly uncovered the next morning, the ingredients are well mixed in order to replenish the oxygen supply, release carbonic acid gasses, and blend the warmer substrate at the crib's center with the cooler substrate near the sides, bottom, and top. The crib is re-covered, only to be opened several hours later. The young koji is then transferred into shallow wooden trays where it is mounded to help it retain the heat of fermentation. However, a small hollow—like the crater of a volcano—is dug at the top of each mound to prevent overheating. The koji trays are arranged in a special incubation room where the temperature is kept at 82°F to 86°F and the humidity at 90 to 95 percent. The koji's temperature rises slowly as shown in figure 18 on page 445.

To protect against the intrusion of contaminating microorganisms, the craftsman's hands and tools must be kept spotlessly clean and the koji kept within the required range of temperature and moistness. (Special care must be taken during the warm months when alien microorganisms are abundant and propagate more rapidly.) If the koji temperature is allowed to rise above 104°F, the production of enzymes decreases and undesirable bacteria (such as black and *natto* varieties) begin to flourish; as these bacteria multiply, additional overheating results and free water condenses on the substrate causing even more rapid bacterial growth. Koji containing black molds develops an unpleasant odor and may have to be discarded. If the koji temperature is allowed to rise above 113°F, the koji begins to die of its own heat; if it drops below about 77°F, fermentation gradually comes to a halt and non-toxic bluish-green molds (usually related to *Penicillium*) may flourish giving the koji and resultant miso a poor flavor.

If temperature and humidity are kept within the ideal range, only the *Aspergillus oryzae* molds propagate. To prevent overheating as the first fermentation progresses, and to remove carbon dioxide, provide oxygen, and help the mold penetrate the substrate more deeply, the mycelium is broken up at regular intervals and the koji is well stirred. After the second stirring, the mounded koji is spread in even layers over the trays.

The energy required to support the growth and metabolism of the molds and create the essential enzymes is supplied by the grain or soybean substrate. During the first fermentation, about 5 to 10 percent of the food energy in the substrate is consumed by the mold and is therefore ultimately lost as nutritional energy available to human beings from the finished miso. This is the small price we pay to obtain enhanced flavor, aroma, and digestibility.

After 40 to 50 hours, depending on the "speed" of the starter and the incubation temperature, the burgeoning molds will have thoroughly covered the substrate and bound it into a solid cake. The koji must be harvested while the conidiophores of the mold are still forming, before the olive-green color typical of sporulation has appeared. At this stage, there is maximum availability of desirable enzymes; further mold growth would result in an undesirable (moldy) flavor in the finished miso. Thus, the finest koji is characterized by a felt-like white mycelium, a fragrant aroma, and—when tasted—a sweet delicious flavor.

Removed from the trays, the finished koji is now crumbled, cooled, and usually mixed with just the right amount of salt to prevent further mold growth. The first step of miso's two-step fermentation process is now finished.

Cooking the Soybeans

As the koji fermentation nears completion, soybeans are boiled or steamed until they are soft enough to be crushed easily between the thumb and ring finger. Thorough cooking makes their protein more receptive to enzyme activity and helps to inactivate the trypsin growth inhibitor present in uncooked beans. Cooking time and temperature influence the color and flavor of the finished product; the longer the cooking, the darker the miso. The soybeans for white and light-yellow miso are boiled under high pressure for a short time (30 to 60 minutes) and the cooking water then discarded. Sweet red miso is given its dark-red color by simmering the beans for six to eight hours, allowing them to stand overnight in the caldron and then returning the beans to a boil the next morning. After steaming or boiling, the beans for all types of miso are partially or completely crushed to facilitate the permeation of enzymes from the koji. Whereas koji is said to provide most of miso's aroma and sweetness, soybeans are thought to contribute most of its flavor.

Preparing the Miso:
The Second Fermentation

The second fermentation is divided into four stages: the mixing of the basic ingredients; the digestion of protein, starch, and lipids in these ingredients by koji enzymes; the fermentation of the digested products by bacteria and yeasts; and the aging of the miso until it is fully mature.

The mashed soybeans are mixed with the salted koji, water or soybean cooking liquid, and "seed miso". The water—comprising about 10 percent of the total miso weight—is used to give the miso a moisture content of 48 to 52 percent. Regular water is almost always boiled before being added to eliminate contaminating microorganisms. A small amount of (unpasteurized) "seed miso" from a previous fermentation improves the miso aroma and flavor while decreasing the fermentation time by up to 50 percent by introducing hearty yeasts and bacteria. In modern miso factories the seed miso is often replaced by a pure-culture inoculum consisting of halophilic (salt resistant) yeasts such as *Saccharomyces roxii* or *Torulopsis* and lactic acid bacteria such as *Pediococcus halophilus* (or *soya*) or *Streptococcus faecalis;* the latter species are also used in cheese production. About 100,000 of these microorganisms are added for each *gram* of miso and, when used in temperature-controlled fermentation, they are kept at a maximum of 86°F, where they do their optimum work. Modern miso makers insist that the use of good inoculum is one of the secrets of preparing fine miso. The same type may be used for many different miso varieties.

Before packing the mixed ingredients into a huge wooden vat, the interior of the container is thoroughly scrubbed with boiling water and then sprinkled or rubbed with salt. In addition to removing contaminating microorganisms on the wood's surface, this serves to ferret out any mites or other tiny insects that can enter the chinks between the planks of vats which are allowed to stand empty. For broader protection, many producers now disinfect their entire buildings once or twice each year and sterilize (by steaming) all small kegs that enter the shop and the various cloths used in preparing the miso and koji. Although such insects cannot live in the miso and are not believed to represent a health danger, food inspectors and miso makers take every precaution to ensure that miso shops are free of them.

In the same way that grapes were traditionally tread to make wine, the mixture in the vats is now mashed underfoot to remove air pockets in which alien molds might grow or liquid might accumulate. Its surface is carefully leveled and covered first with a cloth sealing-sheet and then a pressing-lid which fits snugly down inside the vat's mouth, thereby preventing the growth of surface molds. While not actually harmful, such molds cause a decline in the miso's aroma and flavor. The lid is then weighted with heavy stones to force a small amount of liquid (*miso-damari*) to the surface, creating a sealed, airtight (anaerobic) environment. This is ideal for the activity of the anaerobic bacteria and yeasts which will later gain predominance; it also prevents the entry of contaminating microorganisms. In many shops, a second sheet is tied over the vat's mouth to keep out dust, insects, and the like.

During the first fermentation, the number of molds per gram of substrate had increased from about 13,-000 to 295,000. Now, with the work of these molds finished the highly sensitive mycelium dies from the lack of oxygen and high salinity in the environment. But the work of enzymes left behind is about to begin.

Inside the vat, the enzymes begin breaking down—actually digesting—the nutritional components of soybeans and grains. Three basic enzymes are active: protease works on protein, amylase on carbohydrates, and lipase on lipids (oils and fats) (fig. 22). In this chemical process—technically known as hydrolysis—the reaction of water ions with the basic food nutrients produces a weak acid which transforms complex molecules into simpler ones that can be more easily assimilated by the body.

The enzyme protease converts soy protein molecules first into polypeptides and peptides, and then into more than 18 simple amino acids. The main soy protein is glycinin (80% to 90%) and the predominant resulting amino acid is glutamic acid, the active ingredient in the refined chemical seasoning known variously as MSG, monosodium glutamate, *aji-no-moto,* or Accent. These natural amino acids—and particularly glutamic—give the miso much of its flavor and some

Fig. 22. The Interactions of Basic Miso Components

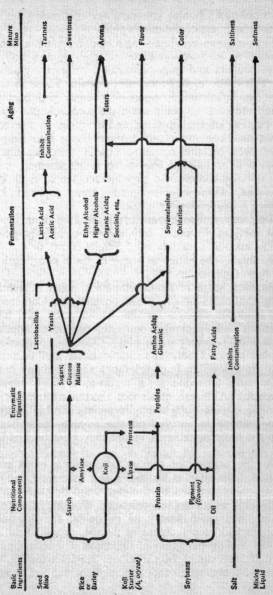

(Adapted from *Miso Fermentation*, Shibasaki & Hesseltine, 1962)

of its color, while also softening and mellowing the inherent sharpness of the miso's salt.

The enzyme amylase—with the help of a small amount of maltose—reduces starches in the koji to simple sugars and polysaccharides, primarily glucose, but also maltose, dextrose, and dextrin. These in turn serve as fermentable sugars for yeasts and bacteria which are soon to come upon the scene. About 80 to 90 percent of the proteins and starches in the soybeans and koji grains are broken down into simpler substances by the action of these microorganisms. Since a large part of the starch is saccharified, miso that initially contained a large percentage of grain koji is sweet, whereas miso made from soybean koji (which is low in starch) is not.

The enzyme lipase transforms the 18 percent lipids contained in soybeans into simple free fatty acids, which assume a variety of different forms in the finished miso. The esters of some of these contribute to the miso's aroma.

At each stage of its development, miso is teeming with multitudes of living microorganisms. Continuous and multiple changes in the fermentation call forth different and specialized varieties one after another, each with its own part to play. These microorganisms are all *plants* (more specifically fungi and bacteria) that are halophilic (salt tolerant) and, in many cases, osmophilic (thriving in a medium of high osmotic pressure). Although anaerobic bacteria and yeasts are favored by the airtight environment, aerobic bacteria also manage to survive on the oxygen incorporated into the basic ingredients before they were packed into the vats.

As the process of enzymatic digestion nears completion, fermentation by yeasts and bacteria (many of which were supplied by the seed miso or pure-culture inoculum) assumes predominance. Working in a sealed environment with plenty of nutrients, the anaerobic bacteria suddenly increase in number from 10 million to 930 million per gram of substrate. The most important and abundant of these are the Lactobacilli, the lactic acid bacteria, other species of which are used as yogurt, cheese, and butter starters. After the miso ingredients have been in the keg for two to three months under natural conditions, these bacteria assume dominance and begin to transform sugars into various acids (especially lactic and acetic); the acids in turn impart a subtle mellow sourness to the finished miso and also assist in preventing spoilage.

Soon various yeasts begin their work of alcoholic fermentation. Consuming sugars, they produce alcohols (ethyl and higher varieties) and organic acids (especially succinic); the higher alcohols contribute to miso's pleasant bouquet and the organic acids to its flavor. Some varieties of yeasts make a film on the miso surface, while also contributing to the aroma.

As various substances are created by enzymatic digestion and bacterial or yeast fermentation, they begin to react chemically with one another. The full complexity of this interaction is illustrated in figure 22. Organic acids react with ethyl- and higher alcohols, with free fatty acids, or with acetic acid to produce esters (a primary aromatic element in fruits and flowers), which become the chief components of miso's bouquet. In quick miso, the distinctive fragrance of esters and alcohols often appears after only eight to ten days of fermentation. Amino acids react with sugars to produce red or brown pigments (soyamelanine), which combine with the soybean pigment flavone and deepen in color due to oxidation as the miso matures. Since amino acids play the dual role of enhancing flavor and deepening color, it is often said that miso with the richest color also has the richest flavor.

The cooking and fermentation processes deactivate trypsin inhibitor and other unfavorable substances such as hemagglutinins and saponins, while simultaneously eliminating carbonyl compounds such as hexanol that sometimes carry a beany flavor. As these successive chemical changes continue quietly and leisurely inside the apparently dormant vats, the individual particles, first of the koji and then of the soybeans, slowly break down and merge to form the unique miso texture. Students of the biodynamic teaching of Rudolph Steiner feel that cosmic rays entering the miso during lengthy

natural fermentation also have subtle but very beneficial effects.

When miso is fermented in the traditional natural
way, the vats or kegs are placed in a covered area
out of direct sunlight and left to experience the rhythmic temperature changes of the four seasons. These
call forth, accelerate, or slow the changes occurring in
the miso mixture. Most natural miso starts its fermentation during the colder months, undergoes most of its
transformation during the warmer ones, and is finally
removed in the fall. Thus, it experiences a rise and
fall of temperature in the form of a bell curve.
When quick light-yellow miso is prepared by modern
temperature-controlled fermentation, the vats are
placed in large heated rooms. Over a period of about
one week, the temperature is gradually raised from
roughly 80°F to a high of 90°F, where it is kept for
several weeks or months before being lowered back to
80°F (fig. 23). Thus, the miso experiences the same
rise and fall of temperature but over a shorter period
of time and at a somewhat higher temperature than
that found under natural conditions. For sweet white
or sweet red miso, the unfermented ingredients are
packed into insulated vats while still quite hot (86°F
to 90°F), then aged at the natural temperature or
slightly warmer. For mellow beige, they are placed in
a heated room until their interior temperature rises to
90°F, and then allowed to cool of their own accord.

Fig. 23. Temperature Control Curves for Four Quick Misos

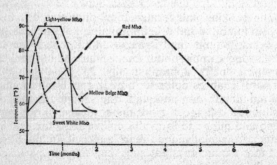

Whereas natural miso is usually allowed to stand untouched in the kegs or vats during the entire second fermentation, quick miso is generally mixed and transferred to a new vat or epoxy-lined steel tank once or twice during the process. Supplying the yeasts and aerobic bacteria with oxygen in this way hastens the fermentation process and raises the internal temperature. In some farmhouses, too, the miso is mixed at regular intervals or at least once during the summer for the same reason. After quick miso has been removed from its heated fermentation room, it is often allowed to stand for several weeks at room temperature; this final ripening (shown on the above graphs) further improves the flavor and aroma.

The Finished Miso

Unhurried aging in rhythm with the cycle of the seasons is one of the traditional secrets for evoking the finest miso flavor. Thus, natural miso is generally found to be of higher quality than its quick modern counterpart—and it therefore commands a premium price.

When natural miso is ready, each gram contains an immense number of active and beneficial microorganisms: 4,000 molds, 6,000 yeasts, 1.5 million aerobic bacteria, and 2 million anaerobic bacteria. Remarkably, the salt in miso exerts a selective action on the full range of microorganisms present, favoring those which are beneficial to human beings and which contribute to the miso flavor. If salt were not present, a toxic anaerobic bacterial fermentation would occur. Furthermore, because only the heartiest microorganisms can survive the rigors of months and years in miso's largely anaerobic, saline environment, they are very well suited to continue their ceaseless activity of breaking down complex food molecules after they have entered the human digestive tract. Thus the salt, in addition to acting as a preservative, also functions as a "sentient" agent for the human palate and digestive system. In the same way, lactic acid inhibits the growth of many contaminating bacteria, and most of the beneficial microorganisms present are actively antagonistic to the few dangerous varieties *(Staphylococcus aureus* and *Escherichia coli)* which cause food poisoning. Consequently, repeated tests conducted at laboratories throughout the world have shown that miso is free of all toxins, including those called aflatoxins.

The finest miso is sold in wooden kegs in the same form in which it emerges from the fermentation vats with all its microscopic flora alive and vital. Indeed, the principal reason miso is usually cooked only briefly —if at all—is precisely because the beneficial microorganisms (especially the Lactobacilli) and enzymes it contains are easily destroyed by prolonged exposure to high temperatures. Unfortunately, much of the miso sold today in sealed polyethylene bags is pre-pasteurized by means of prolonged heating (140°F) in order to stop the microorganisms from producing carbon dioxide which causes the bags to swell. In some cases, preservatives are also added for the same purpose. Both of these newly-invented processes cause a definite decline in the miso fragrance and flavor—while also reducing its value as a food. Hence the best miso is that prepared by traditional natural fermentation methods and sold without additives or pasteurization. Many such varieties are now available throughout the West.

Appendix D

People and Institutions Connected with Miso

PEOPLE AND INSTITUTIONS IN JAPAN

In the following references, all Japanese personal names are written in the standard Japanese manner, last name first. All addresses are given in the Western style (street, ward [ku], city [shi], prefecture [ken], and zip code), rather than in the reverse Japanese style.

Miso Research Scholars and Institutes

Akizuki Shinichiro: St. Francis Hospital, Hongen Machi 2-535, Nagasaki, Japan. A practicing physician and hospital director, Dr. Akizuki has experimented widely using miso and miso soup to prevent radiation sickness and maintain health. His findings are presented in a pamphlet entitled *Physical Constitution and Food.*

Ebine Hideo: Norinsho Shokuhin Sogo Kenkyujo, Shiohama 1-4-12, Koto-ku, Tokyo 135. Tel: 03-645-9911. Head of the fermentation division of the prestigious National Food Research Institute, Dr. Ebine is also the author of many English-language articles about miso.

Japanese National Miso Association: Zenkoku Miso Kogyo Kyodo Kumiai Rengokai, Shinkawa 1-26-19, Chuo-ku, Tokyo 104. Tel: 03-551-7161. Mr. Fujimori Denei, director; Mr. Miyachi Kazuo, executive vice president, and Mr. Matsushita Zenichi, fact finder. The coordinating body for all miso shops and factories in Japan. Also operates a large miso research lab.

Kawamura Wataru: Kugenuma 2373, Fujisawa-shi 251. Tel: 0466-22-1351. Author of several of Japan's most popular books about miso, widely known as Japan's "miso sensei" (teacher), and former director of publicity for the National Miso Association, Mr. Kawamura describes himself as a scholar (and lover) of miso soup.

Mochizuki Tsutomu: Director of the Shinshu Miso Research

Institute in Nagano city (see below), Dr. Mochizuki is the leading expert on modern Shinshu miso.

Morishita Keiichiro: Morishita Eiyo Kyoshitsu, Bunkyoku, Hongo 2-3-10, Tokyo. Tel. 03-814-6786. An expert on the nutritional and health-giving value of miso. Dr. Morishita is an M.D. who heads a hospital and nutritional research center in Tokyo. The author of more than 30 books, he has for many years advocated the value of traditional Japanese fermented soyfoods.

Murakami Hideya: Kokuritsu Jozo Shikenjo, Takinogawa, Kita-ku, Tokyo. Director of the National Fermented Foods Research Institute and a well-known scholar of *A. oryzae* molds.

Nakano Masahiro: Meiji Daigaku, Ikuta Kosha, Ikuta 5158, Kawasaki-shi, Kanagawa-ken 214. Tel: 044-911-8181. The dean of miso scholars and teacher of Drs. Ebine and Mochizuki, Dr. Nakano is professor of microbiology at Meiji University where he directs a laboratory engaged in the study of miso and other fermented foods.

Ouchi Ichiro: c/o Mutual Trading Co., 431 Crocker St., Los Angeles, CA 90013. Tel: 213-626-9458. Formerly of the Shinshu Miso Research Institute, he spent one year in the U.S. at the Northern Regional Research Center developing new foods incorporating miso as a flavoring agent and is now working with miso at Mutual Trading Co.

Sakaguchi Kinichiro: Takabon 3-17-4, Meguro-ku, Tokyo 152. Tel: 712-7033. A retired scholar of koji molds, Mr. Sakaguchi received the Emperor's medal of honor for his research work. He now publishes a magazine on foods with frequent articles on miso and shoyu.

Shibasaki Kazuo: Tohoku University, Nogaku-bu, Shokuhin Kagaku-ka, Kita 6 Banchi, Sendai-shi. Dr. Shibasaki spent 1958 and 1959 in the U.S. doing research on miso at the NRRC. He has co-authored many English-language articles on miso with Dr. Clifford Hesseltine and other researchers, and is now a consultant for the Sendai Miso-Shoyu Company.

Shinshu Miso Research Institute: Shinshu Miso Kenkyujo, Mina-miagata-machi 1014, Nagano-shi 380. Tel: 0262-28-1221. Under the direction of Dr. Mochizuki, this large and prestigious organization is doing basic scientific and technological research on miso production.

Exporters of Natural Miso and Koji to the West

Muso Co. Ltd., Nishishin-machi 1-2-18, Wakae, Higashi Osaka 578. Tel: 06-725-2011. Yuko Okada.

Mitoku Co. Ltd., C.P.O. Box 780, Tokyo 100-91; Marunouchi

Bldg., Marunouchi, Toyko. Tel. 03-201-6706 thru 8. Mr. Akiyoshi Kazama, director.

Traditional or Semi-traditional Shops Making Natural Miso

Amanoya: Makers of Finger Lickin'-and sweet red miso, as well as koji and *amakazé*.

Arai Miso Ten: Suwa 2765, Mitsukaido-shi, Ibaragi-ken. Tel: 0297-2-0274.

Fuchu Miso: Honmachi, Fuchu-shi, Hiroshima-ken. Tel: 0847-41-2080. Mr. Kanemitsu Yanosuke, director. The main supplier of natural barley miso to the West via Muso Shokuhin. Fuchu also produces natural Kinzanji miso and quick rice miso.

Hayakawa Kyuemon Shoten (also called Hatcho Miso Kakkyu Goshikaisha): Aza, Okan-dori 69, Hatcho-cho, Okazaki-shi, Aichiken 444. Tel: 0564-21-0151. Mr. Kaneko, director; Mr. Hayakawa Kyuemon, 18th proprietor. Located near Nagoya in Central Japan on the banks of the Yahagi river (once famous for its fine artesian wells and *Yahagi* soybeans), this company is the largest and best known of Japan's two very old makers of natural Hatcho miso—both of which are located on the same block. Said to have been established in 1362 (but thought by scholars to have originated in its present form about 350 to 400 years ago). Hayakawa is the proud supplier of the Imperial Household Agency. They presently transform about 50 percent of their Hatcho miso into akadashi miso.

Ikeda Kojiro Miso Shoten: Motogo 4-8-24, Kawaguchi-shi. Saitamaken 332. Tel: 0482-22-6766. A traditional maker of natural barley miso located near Tokyo. Ikeda now exports to the U.S. and also produces quick rice miso.

Kantoya Shoten: Matsumoto-cho 582, Ebisugawa Noboru, Gokochodori, Nakagyo-ku, Kyoto. Tel: 231-1728 or 211-4371. A maker of traditional red miso, this shop has a fine koji incubation room.

Kawasaki Shoten: Nishi Arie-cho, Minami Takagi-gun, Nagasaki-ken, Kyushu. A maker of traditional, natural Finger Lickin' (natto miso) and sweet barley miso.

Kawasho Miso Shoten: Kaizan-cho 3-145, Sakai-shi, Osaka 590. Tel: 0722-33-1061. A maker of delicious, traditional Kinzanji miso.

Meiji Seifun: Fuchu-machi 536, Fuchu-shi, Hiroshima-ken 726. Tel: 0874-41-2255. A maker of natural barley and red miso.

Nagato Tozaimon: Hatonaka 133, Aza, Taketoyo-cho, Kitagun, Aichi-ken 470-23. Tel: 05697-2-0341. A maker of natural soybean miso and shoyu.

Ota Shoten: Okan-dori 52, Hatcho-cho, Okazaki-shi, Aichi-ken 444. Tel. 0564-22-0222. Mr. Kato Choichi, director. The second largest maker of Hatcho miso in Japan, Ota produces 1,000 tons annually and an additional 1,500 tons of one-year soybean miso (*waka Hatcho*). Their prices are relatively low.

Sendai Miso-Shoyu Inc.: Furujiro 1-5-1, Sendai-shi, 982. Tel: 0222-86-3151. Mr. Sasaki Kenichiro, director; Mr. Sasaki Shigeo, managing director; Mr. Haga Hiroshi, production director. The largest miso maker in the northeast provinces and the largest producer of Sendai-type red miso in Japan, this company produces much of the natural red miso (and shoyu) now imported into the United States. Their miso is aged 18 to 24 months, and their shoyu (made from whole soybeans) 18 months. They also make a natural brown-rice miso and a 6-month red miso using the most modern techniques of temperature-controlled fermentation. The company is now thinking about starting to produce miso in the United States. They have recently developed an excellent color film about the commercial production of miso and shoyu, available direct from Sendai or via Mitoku (above), and they hold an exclusive patent on the process of packaging (pasteurized) miso in sealed bags without the use of alcohol or other preservatives.

Shiromizu Shoten: Meihama-cho 3135, Nishi-ku, Fukuoka-shi, Fukuoka-ken 814. Tel: 092-881-0413. A maker of natural barley miso.

Suyamo Shoten: Ashida 2618, Tateshina-cho, Kitasaku-gun, Nagano-ken 384-23. Tel: 02675-6-1001. A maker of traditional Shinshu miso.

Tsuchiya Miso-shoyu: Higashi Yokomachi 383, Susaka-shi, Nagano-ken 383. Tel: 02624-5-0259. A producer of natural Shinshu miso.

Tsujita Miso Shoten: Kojiya Saburo Uemon, Nakamura 2-29-8, Nerima-ku, Tokyo 176. Tel: 03-999-2276. Mr. Tsujita Kiyoshi, master. A very old shop using traditional, natural methods, this firm makes 18- and 24-month brown-rice miso, 3-year chunky barley miso, ready-made dried koji, and brown-rice *amazaké*. Tsujita uses organic rice, natural sea salt, and the finest Hokkai-do-grown *tsurunoko* soybeans. The producer of all brown-rice miso now sold in the West, this shop was the source of much of our information about making miso in traditional shops.

Yamatoya: Adzusa Kawamura, Adzusa, Nagano-ken. Tel: 026378-2280. Producer of natural miso using *miso-dama*.

Japan's Ten Largest Miso Factories

The following, listed in order of size (using 1974 production statistics), generally prepare light-yellow miso using quick temperature-controlled fermentation methods. Details are given in Chapter 9.

1. *Miyasaka Jozo* (Shinshu ichi), Nogata 2-4-5, Nakano-ku, Tokyo 165. Tel. 03-385-2121. Mr. Watanabe Yojuro, production director. This Tokyo factory produces about 15,000 tons per year; the Nagano and Yamanashi plants produce 9,300 and 3,300 tons respectively. All make Shinshu-type light-yellow miso. Tokyo makes freeze-dried miso.

2. *Hanamaruki:* Hirade 1560, Tatsuno-cho, Oaza, Kamiina-gun, Nagano-ken 399-04. Tel: 02664-2-1321. Also produces a mellow beige miso imported to the U.S.

3. *Takeya:* Kogan-dori 2-3-17, Suwa-shi, Nagano-ken 392. Tel: 02665-2-4000.

4. *Marukome:* Amori 833, Nagano-shi, Nagano-ken 380. Tel: 0262-26-0255. Yamamoto Yasuo, production manager. The biggest single miso factory in Japan. Makes dehydrated miso.

5. *Kanesa:* Tamagawa 202, Hamada-aza, Aomori-shi 030. Tel: 0177-39-5211.

6. *Marudai:* Ohashi, Hamochi-machi, Sado-gun, Niigata-ken 952-05. Tel: Hamochi #3 or #4. Makers of Sado-style rice miso.

7. *Marusan:* Aza-arashita 1, Jingi-cho, Okazaki-shi 444-21. Operates 3 factories.

8. *Yamajirushi:* Komome 3-15-1, Itabashi-ku, Tokyo. Tel: 972-3151. Other factories in Maruko City (Nagano) and Moriya City (Ibaragi). Total output is 18,000 tons per year. The Moriya plant produces 6,000 tons of *shikomi-miso* yearly which is sold in 20-pound quantities to farm cooperatives, whence it is distributed to farm families.

9. *Ichibiki:* Shinto-machi 14, Atsuda-ku, Nagoya-shi. Also operates a factory in Toyohashi.

10. *Kaneko:* Aizumi-machi Okuno, Itano-gun, Tokushima-shi. Output is 11,000 tons per year.

Other Makers of Fine Miso

Abumata Miso Co.: Honmachi 3-32-19, Nakano-ku, Tokyo. Tel: 372-5211. Mr. Takeyama, director of production. A large producer of sweet red miso.

Amadaya: Nakamura Fujio, Gobo 1, Gobo-shi, Wakayama-ken.

Tel: 07382-2-0455. A maker of delicious Kinzanji and moromi misos, containing lots of koji and uri melons.

Ebiya: Azumabashi 1-15-55, Sumida-ku, Asakusa, Tokyo. Tel: 03-625-0003. A producer of high-quality Peanut and Tekka Miso.

Echigo Miso Jozo, Yoshida 5884, Yoshida Machi, Nishi Tanbara-gun, Niigata-ken, Tel: 02569-2-4805. A maker of natural Kinzanji miso.

Ezaki Honten: Ebisu machi 902, Shimbara-shi, Nagasaki-ken 855. Tel: 2-3161. Mr. Shibata. A large and well-known producer of natural miso pickles.

Hagoromo Miso: Fuchu-machi 533-3, Fuchu-shi, Hiroshima-ken 726, Tel: 0847-41-2010. A main source of the natural barley miso sold in the U.S. Also makes a sweet white miso.

Hamamoto: Osaki 1-19-6, Shinagawa-ku, Tokyo. Tel: 03-493-0885. A maker of Kinzanji miso.

Hinode Miso Brewing Co., 3567 Shimo-Oyamada-Machi, Machida-shi, Tokyo 194-01. Mr. Tetsuo Fumoto. Tel: 0427-97-2311. Makers of Peanut Miso, Peanut & Raisin Miso, and Glutinous-rice Miso (*Mochigomé miso*), each sealed in small plastic packets for easy export and sale.

Honda Miso Honten: Ichijo Agaru, Muromachi-dori, Kamikyo-ku, Kyoto 558. Tel. 075-441-1121. Mr. Honda Shigeru, fourth generation owner. One of Japan's best known makers of sweet white miso, Honda is a relatively traditional shop and is unique in preparing one natural variety without the use of preservatives (ethyl alcohol is used) or bleach. Honda's sweet white miso is sold under the registered brand name "Saikyo Miso" meaning "Western Kyoto Miso." Honda also produces akadashi and red miso.

Ichikyu Miso: Tokiwacho 2-15, Higashi-ku, Osaka. Tel: 941-09-4154. A maker of moromi miso.

Ishino Miso Co.: Ishiizutsu-cho, Shijo Kudaru, Aburakoji, Shimokyoku, Kyoto. Tel: 075-361-2336. One of Japan's two large producers of sweet white and akadashi miso. At present they do not export.

Ishiyama Miso Shoyu: Nigata-shi. Tel: 0252-28-2034. Mr. Kinji Ishiyama, exec. v.p. A maker of low-salt miso.

Iwanaga Shoyu Gomei-gaisha: Sashiki, Ashikita-machi, Ashikita-gun, Kumamoto-ken. A maker of natural chunky barley miso.

Kageju Shokuhin, Yawata 1-4-41, Shizuoka-shi, Shizuoka-ken. A maker of natural Kinzanji miso.

Kame-gen Jozo: Suwa 2-4-8, Suwa-shi, Nagano-ken. A maker of buckwheat miso containing buckwheat groats, soybeans, salt, and alcohol preservative.

Kirishima Food Co.: Okubo 65-1, Kirishima-cho, Kagoshima-ken. Japan's primary maker of Yubeshi Miso.

Marui Jozo: Azuma-cho 56, Iida-shi, Nagano-ken. Tel: 0265-22-6363. A maker of miso pickles. Uses wild mountain vegetables and Shinshu miso.

Nagano Miso Co.: Tenjin 3-9-29, Ueda-shi, Nagano-ken 386. Tel: 02682-4-7771. Mr. Hideki Oka, president. A maker of salt-free and traditional misos.

Nakamuraya Shoten: Yaji 3225, Tokuyama-shi, Yamaguchi-ken. Tel: 0834-62-3108 or 9. The maker of the delicious Hanabishi brand sweet white miso now widely available in the U.S. both in 1-pound cartons or 35-pound kegs.

Sanjirushi Jozo: Meisei-dori 1-572-1, Kuwana-shi 511. Tel. 0594-22-3333. Tokyo office: 03-722-4433. Japan's largest maker of soybean miso. A larger maker of natural real tamari.

Sanman Kajimaya Shoten: Chuo 3-1-5, Okaya-shi, Nagano-ken. A maker of brown-rice miso.

Shinsho Miso Jozo: Sanjo-machi 3-12-23, Hiroshima-shi, Hiro-shima-ken. A maker of Eiyaku brand brown-rice miso.

Shinshu Miso K.K.: Aramachi, Komoro-shi, Nagano-ken 384. Tel: 02672-2-0007. Mr. Koyama Masakuni, director. Head office: Shimo Ochiai 3-17-38, Shinjuku-ku, Tokyo 161. Tel: 03-951-1141. Mr. Koyama Kunitomo. A large producer of Shinshu miso, sold in the U.S. and Japan under the brand name "Yamabuki."

Shinshu Sennichi Miso K.K.: Kamimachi 82, Susaka-shi, Na-gano-ken. Tel: 02624-5-0958. One of the first makers of natural miso to use natural (unrefined) salt.

Shoman K.K.: Nagisa 2-32, Matsumoto-shi, Nagano-ken. Mak-ers of instant miso soup sold in a box with dehydrated tofu, leeks, *wakame,* dashi; and a tiny packet of fresh miso.

Yamanaga Miso: Hyakunin-cho 2-8-1, Shinjuku-ku, Tokyo. Tel: 03-371-9146. A maker of traditional-type miso.

Yorosho Honpo: Yuasa-machi Yokocho 519, Arita-gun, Waka-yama-ken. Tel. 07376-2-2318. A maker of Kinzanji miso.

Yoshida Shohachi: Takashima-cho 382, Shimabara-shi, Naga-saki-ken 855. Tel: 09576-2-4107. The sole supplier of the natural natto (finger lickin') miso now sold in the U.S.

Yoshino-ya Jozo (Zenkoji Miso): Nishi-no-mon, Nagano-shi, Nagano-ken, Japan. Tel: 34-1171. A famous old maker of Shinshu light yellow miso.

Makers of Koji Starter and Koji

Amanoya Kojiten: Soto Kanda 2-18-15, Chiyoda-ku, Tokyo. Tel: 03-251-7911. Mr. Amano Yaichi. A very old, traditional and beautiful shop preparing ready-made koji, some of which they use in the *amazaké* sold in their restaurant. The koji is fermented in long, earth-walled tunnels 20 feet beneath the streets of Tokyo. They also make delicious, natural Finger Lickin', and sweet red miso.

Hishiroku: A traditional Kyoto maker of koji starter. Tel: 075-541-4141.

Kojiya Sanzaemon Roho: Shimotachiuri-sagaru, Omiya-dori, Kamikyo-ku, Kyoto. A traditional koji maker.

Nihon Jozo Kogyo: Sales office: Koishigawa 3-18-9, Bunkyo-ku, Tokyo 112. Tel: 03-816-2951. Factory: Higashiori-ue, Iishi-aza, Oaza, Juo-machi, Taga-gun, Ibaragi-ken. Tel: 0293-32-2307. Mr. Niimi Yasu, director; Mr. Chiba Akira, ass't. director. The Japan Brewing Co. is a large, reliable producer of koji starter used for both miso and shoyu and sold under the brand name of Marufuku Moyashi. This company was the source of much of our information on preparing koji starter.

Tokai Hakko Kagaku Kenkyujo: Ichigen 1712, Toyoda mura, Iwata-gun, Shizuoka-ken. A traditional maker of miso koji starter.

Japanese Restaurants Specializing in Miso Cuisine

Dengaku: Komachi 1-6-5, Kamakura-shi, Kanagawa-ken. Tel: 0467-23-2121. Dengaku cookery at its best in a charming atmosphere.

Nakamura-ro: Yasaka Jinja-nai, Higashiyama-ku, Kyoto. Tel: 075-561-4589. Delicious Dengaku and *amazaké*.

Shiru Hatchi: Ginza 8-chome, Tokyo. Tel: 571-0456. Popular and inexpensive miso soups.

Senkoya: Ginza 2-chome, Tokyo. Tel: 564-2832. Perhaps the finest miso soup restaurant in the city.

Shirukado: Roppongi 5-chome, Tokyo. Tel: 408-6479. Miso soups at prices from low to medium.

PEOPLE AND INSTITUTIONS IN NORTH AMERICA

Miso Research Scholars and Institutes

Hesseltine, Clifford W.: Known for his outstanding research as a mycologist, Dr. Hesseltine has had a lifelong interest in miso and has written many articles on the subject. Past President of the Mycological Society of America, he is presently director of the fermentation laboratory of the NRRC (below).

Northern Regional Research Center (USDA/NRRC): 1815 North University St., Peoria, IL 61604. Tel: 309-685-4011. The main center for miso research in North America, the NRRC offers a good selection of scientific-journal articles on miso fermentation as well as pure-culture koji starters. Directed by Dr. Clifford W. Hesseltine, who is assisted by Dr. Hwa L. Wang, the fermentation laboratory has sponsored numerous miso research scholars from Japan, including Dr. Kazou Shibasaki and Dr. Ichiro Ouchi.

Smith, Allen K.: 4 Nacozari Ln. Hotsprings Village, Hotsprings, AR 71901. Tel: 501-922-1875. Now living in retirement, Dr. Smith has traveled widely in East Asia and written numerous articles and books on miso and other soyfoods.

Wang, Hwa L.: A woman working at the NRRL fermentation research lab, Dr. Wang has extensive experience in the field of miso and has written numerous articles on the subject.

Commercial Miso and Koji Makers

In addition to the following established miso producers, numerous individuals, communities, and natural-food companies have begun to study commercial miso making and/or are planning to start small shops.

California: Miyako Oriental Foods, 404 Towne Ave., Los Angeles, CA 90013. (Postal: P.O. Box 2919 Terminal Annex, Los Angeles, CA 90051). Tel: (Office) 213-626-9458. (Plant) 213-488-1678. Makers of Cold Mountain brand red miso, light-yellow miso, mellow white miso, and rice koji, distributed by Mutual Trading Co. and various natural-food distributors. A division of Yamajirushi miso company in Japan.

Hawaii: American-Hawaiian Soy Co., 274 Kalihi St., Honolulu, HI 96817. Tel: 808-841-8435. Harry Morita. Produces white miso, sometimes sold in cans, distributed by Mutual Trading Co. in Los Angeles.

————: Hawaiian Miso & Soy Co., 1714 Mary St., Honolulu, HI 96819. Tel. 808-841-7354. Mr. William Higa. A medium-sized company emphasizing traditional, natural miso made without any additives. Produces mainly mellow white miso but also a small amount of red. Sold under the brand name "Maruhi," this miso is widely distributed by Nishimoto Trading Co. in Los Angeles and some natural-food companies.

————: Parks Brand Products, 145 No. King St., Stand 53, Honolulu, HI 96817. Tel: 808-536-4074. Producers of Korean miso.

Massachusetts: South River Miso Co., South River Farm, Conway, MA 01341. Tel: 413-369-4057. Christian and Gaella Elwell. Producers of traditional misos. Formerly Ohio Miso Co.

Michigan: The Soy Plant, 771 Airport Blvd. #1, Ann Arbor, MI 48104. Tel: 313-663-8638. They produce small amounts of sweet white miso.

North Carolina: Erewhon Miso Co., Route 3, Box 541, Rutherfordton, NC 28139. Tel: 704-287-2940. John Belleme. A cooperative venture between Erewhon Inc., Oak Feed Miso Co., and Sendai Miso-Shoyu.

Washington: Junsei Yamazaki Miso Co., 13440 S.E. Eastgate Way, Belleview, WA 98005. Tel: 206-747-6939. Mr. Yamazaki, formerly the miso-maker at Chico-San, Inc., now produces small amounts of quality miso sold nationwide.

Canada: T. Amano Co., 1139 E. Hastings St., Vancouver 6, B.C. Tel: 604-254-3943. A maker of miso and shoyu.

————: Shinmei-do Miso, Wren Rd., Denman Island, B.C. VOR 1TO. Yasuo and Lulu Yoshihara.

Companies Importing Japanese Miso, Koji, or Koji Starter

The relatively moderate import duty on miso (14%) has encouraged the introduction of many of Japan's finest varieties. More and more are becoming available each year. In 1978, 551 metric tons of miso were imported to the U.S. from Japan. Of this, roughly 25 percent went into the natural-foods market.

American Pacific Trading International Inc.: 2309 East 8th St., Los Angeles, CA 90021. Tel. 213-622-0422. Importers of Yamabuki brand miso from the Shinshu Miso Company in Komoro, Nagano prefecture.

Chico-San, Inc., P.O. Box 1004, Chico, CA 95927. Tel: 916-891-6271. Importers of koji and various natural misos.

Eden Foods Inc., 4601 Platt Rd., Ann Arbor, MI 48104. Tel: 313-973-9400. An importer of natural miso and shoyu.

Edward & Sons Trading Co., P.O. Box 271, Union, NJ 07083. Tel: 201-964-0660. Importers of instant freeze-dried miso soup sold as "Miso Cup."

Erewhon Inc., 3 East St., Cambridge, MA 02141. Tel: 617-354-2001 or 800-225-1400. Importers of all basic miso types.

Erewhon, 4770 District Blvd., Vernon, CA 90058. Tel: 213-582-6144. Importers of natural miso and shoyu.

GEM Cultures, 30301 Sherwood Rd., Ft. Bragg, CA 95437. Tel: 707-964-2922. Gordon McBride. Presently America's best source of koji starters for many types of miso and shoyu. Their starter is imported from Japan's finest producers.

Japan Food Corporation: 445 Kaufman Ct., So. San Francisco, CA 94080. Tel: 871-1600. Or 1131 So. Mateo St., Los Angeles. Tel: 213-627-6534. Importers of more than 15 varieties of Japanese miso.

Kagemuri, T., 8578 Birnom St., Montreal, Quebec H3M 2V3, Canada. An importer of natural miso.

Kikkoman International, 50 California St., Suite 3600, San Francisco, CA 94111. Tel: 415-956-7750. Mr. Shinichi Suzuki or Mr. Masaki Miki. Importers of red miso which they dehydrate (and mix with dehydrated tofu plus land-and-sea vegetables) to make their instant miso soup, now sold at many supermarkets.

Laurelbrook Foods, P.O. Box 47, Bel Air, MD 21014. Tel: 301-879-1736. An importer of natural miso.

Lifestream, 12411 Vulcan Way, Richmond, B.C. Canada V6V 1J7. Tel. 604-278-7571. An importer of natural miso.

Manna Foods Inc., 112 Crockford Blvd., Scarborough, Ontario, MIR 3C3 Canada. Tel: 416-759-4108. An importer of natural miso.

Marusan Foods Corp., 8780 E. Valley Blvd., Rosemead, CA 91770. Tel: 213-571-8997. Importer of instant miso soups.

Mutual Trading Co., 431 Crocker St., Los Angeles, CA 90013. Tel: 213-626-9458. Mr. Noritoshi Kanai. Importers of light-yellow miso and distributors of miso and koji made by Miyako Oriental Foods, their subsidiary.

Nishimoto Trading Co.: 1884 E. 22nd St., Los Angeles, CA 90013. Tel: 213-747-4111. Importers of Hawaiian mellow white miso.

Soken Trading Co., Box 1705, Sausalito, CA 94965. Tel: 415-332-2313. Importers of various misos.

Tree of Life Inc., 315 Industrial Drive, St. Augustine, FL 32084. Tel: 904-829-3484.

Westbrae Natural Foods, 4240 Hollis St., Emeryville, CA 94608. Tel: 415-658-7518. Importers of brown-rice, red, barley, Hatcho, and Finger Lickin' (natto) miso. Also distribute U.S.-made koji and miso.

Individuals Interested in Miso

The following list of names, although quickly outdated, may prove helpful in bringing together people interested in miso.

Aihara, Cornellia and Herman: c/o GOMF, 1544 Oak St., Oroville, CA 95965. Cornellia has given classes in miso making and miso cookery, and has prepared barley koji commercially. Herman has written and spoken extensively about miso; his books include *Miso and Tamari* and *Soybean Diet*.

Headrick, Lewis: 853 Washington, Apt. 2, Macon, GA 31201. Interested in producing miso.

Kendall, Charlie: 10 White Place, Brookline, MA 02146. Making and selling miso.

Kerrigan, Rick: 688 Capp St., San Francisco, CA 94110. Tel: 415-282-9909. Doing miso research.

Kushi, Aveline and Michio, 62 Buckminster Rd., Brookline, MA 02146. Tel. 617-232-6869. Aveline has taught miso making and cookery. Michio has taught thousands of people about the many virtues of miso, and numerous members of his macrobiotic community have experience making miso at home.

Muramoto, Noboru: 145 W. El Norte Parkway, Escondido, CA 92026. Tel: 714-743-6890. Teacher of many students now active in making miso. Note that his first name is spelled Noboru, not Naboru.

Shrift, Eric: P.O. Box 25, Andes Land Project, Andes, NY 13731. A student of N. Muramoto who plans to produce miso and teach miso-making classes.

Spiral Inn/Moniteau Farm: Rt. 1, Box 9, Jamestown, MO 65046. This macrobiotic homestead community hopes to have a miso shop on their land.

Tims, Bill: East West Foundation, 359 Boylston St., Boston, MA 02116. He has taught classes in miso making.

Truslow, Will: 36 Hempstead Rd., Jamaica Plain, MA 02130. A student of N. Muramoto who makes miso at home and gives miso-making classes through the Kushi Institute in Boston.

Yamazaki, Junsei: See address at miso producers, above. A highly skilled miso craftsman, he has taught miso-making classes throughout the U.S.

PEOPLE AND INSTITUTIONS IN EUROPE

Imported natural miso is now available throughout Europe. Macrobiotic teachers have played a major role in its popularization, and have already built one large miso production center in Belgium. Please send us other names if you know of them.

Belgium

Gaevert, Pierre: Lima Foods, Edgar Gevaertdreef 10, 9830 Sint-Martens-Latem, Belgium. Tel: (09) 52.41.76. A macrobiotic for three generations, Pierre is head of the Lima Factory and one of the founders of the first miso shop in Europe. Some members of his community are preparing to move to France to start a new miso shop.

Takanami Miso Shop: Rue Antoine Dansaert 107, 1000 Bruxelles, Belgium. Tel. 02-511.66.35.

Atelier: 128 Rue des Treffles, Ander Lecht, Bruxelles. Tel: 02-522-8192. Makes red miso.

England

Ceres, 269 Portabello Rd., London W.11, England. Attn. Craig Sams. An importer of natural miso and shoyu.

Harmony Foods, 1 Earl Cottages, Earl Rd., London S.E. 1, England. Tel: 01-237-8396. An importer of natural miso and shoyu.

Sunwheel Food Ltd., 12 Orpheus St., Camberwell, London S.E. 5-8RT, England. Tel: 01-701-7160. Attn. Peter Bradford or Robert Harropp. An importer of natural miso and shoyu.

France

Le Bol en Bois, 35 rue Pascal, 75013 Paris, France. Tel: 707.2724. Attn. Mr. Noboru Sakaguchi. A natural-food center and tofu shop that imports natural miso.

Lima Andiran: Moulin D'Andiran, 47170 Mezin. Tel. 58-651002. A miso factory run by Pierre Gaevert of Lima Foods.

Mittler, Jacques: Route de la Montagne d'age, F-74330 Le Lechat, Poisy, France. Makes miso.

Roland, Jacquot: 10 Rue Bretagne, 91 390 Ris Orangis, France. Makes miso.

Yoshimi, Clim: Institute Yin/Yang-Tenryu of Paris, 8 rue Rochebrune, Paris 75011, France. Tel. 805-9135. Chief editor of the macrobiotic monthly magazine *Principe Unique.* Tenryu imports natural miso and shoyu.

Germany

Nakamura, Jiro: Ubersetzung und Verlag, Münsterstrasse 255, 4 Düsseldorf, West Germany. Tel. 632-443. A translator, publisher, and teacher, he is one of the key figures introducing miso to Europe.

Rabenau, Detlef von: Am Seenfer 15, D-8194 Ambach, West Germany. Tel: 08177-8488. Interested in miso.

Weghaupt, Mascha and Thomas Lüttge: 800 Munchen 2, Theresienstr, 68, West Germany. Interested in miso.

Italy

Bianchini, Gilberto: Centro Macrobiotico, Via Cuoco 9, 47037 Rimini, Italy. Tel: 0541-33670. Interested in miso and tofu production.

D'angella Giuseppe: V. Pasubio, 16, 21047 Saronno (Varese), Italy. Making miso.

La Via Macrobiotica: C.P. 12032, 00135 Roma, Belsito, Italy. An importer of natural miso.

Romano, Silvio: Casale "Sosselva," 05010—Prado n. 123 (Terni), Italy. Interested in miso.

Netherlands

Loo, Dr. Thio Goan: Dept. of Agricultural Research, Royal Tropical Institute, 63 Mauritskade, Amsterdam-Oost, Netherlands. Microbiologist interested in miso.

Manna: Stichting Natuurvoeding, Plantage, Badlaan, 4 III, Amsterdam, Netherlands. An importer of natural miso and shoyu.

Nelissen, Adelbert: Stichting Oost West Centrum, Achtergracht 17-19, 1017 WL, Amsterdam, Netherlands. Tel. 020-240-203. A great place to learn about miso and natural foods.

Nelissen, Thomas: Overboslaan 13, Heemstede, Netherlands. Working with miso.

Portugal

Edvardo Galamba de sa Pires: Apartado 5, Torres Novas, Portugal. An importer of natural miso.

UNIMAVE: Rua da Boa Vista. 55-2°, Lisbon-2, Portugal. Tel: 607283. An importer of natural miso.

Sweden

Tim Ohlund, Malvabo Härvsta, 19063 Orsundsbro. Maker of miso and koji.

PEOPLE AND INSTITUTIONS IN LATIN AMERICA

Brazil

Kikuchi, Tomio: Praca Carlos Comes 60, Sao Paolo, Brazil. A macrobiotic teacher who makes his own miso.

Zanatta, Flavio: Rua Almte Alexandrio, 3226/801, Rio G.B., Brazil. Interested in tofu and miso.

Costa Rica

Prana: Av. Central Calles 21-23, San Jose, Costa Rica. A macrobiotic food store and importer of natural miso.

Mexico

American Soybean Association: Rio Sena #26-201, Col. Cuauhtemoc, Mexico 5, D.F. Tel: 905-535-0659. Attn. Gil Harrison. The ASA is an excellent source of information about buying and growing soybeans.

Takata, Maestro Ejo: Zen A.C., Avenida Revolucion #2036. San Angel, Mexico 20, D.F. A Japanese Zen priest teaching the local people about miso and other soyfoods.

Tovar, Dr. Raul: Faculty of Chemistry, Dept. of Food Science, University of Mexico, Mexico 20, D.F. An expert on miso.

Venezuela

Zentro Macrobiotico de Venezuela, Plaza Fracisco Sola #13, P.O. Box 51600, Sabana Grande, Caracas, Venezuela. Tel: 724026.

Appendix E
Miso Additives

All traditional miso was prepared using only natural ingredients, and all of the varieties available today are prepared by at least some makers without the use of chemical additives. Following World War II, however, a number of additives began to be used in order to make miso more suited to mass distribution, to create whiter colors and sweeter flavors, and to counteract the negative effects of temperature-controlled quick fermentation. The use of additives increased steadily until about 1975 when consumer reaction developed momentum and a government law was passed requiring producers to list all ingredients and additives contained in packaged miso. Remember that most red, barley, and Hatcho miso is completey free of additives (except perhaps ethyl alcohol), whereas many varieties of sweet or white miso are not. The following, listed in order of frequency of occurrence, are presented here for the benefit of those who prefer natural foods and have developed the valuable habit of reading labels. Japanese equivalent terms are given to help natural-food importers double-check that no additives have been used.

Ethyl Alcohol Preservative *(shusei):* Also known simply as alcohol (C_2HO_5), this is the substance that occurs naturally in wine and liquor. Used to prevent sealed polyethylene bags from swelling, while halting fermentation and surface-mold growth, it is allowed at the legal limit of 2 percent by weight and is mixed with the miso just before packaging. Some companies use it only with miso packaged during the summer months. In Japan, it is legal to advertise miso as containing no additives even though it contains ethyl alcohol. For this reason it has recently replaced sorbic acid as the most widely employed preservative. It is most often used in misos which are relatively sweet, packaged in sealed bags or jars, and/or are prepared by quick temperature-controlled fermentation. Nevertheless, it is also frequently found in relatively salty, bulk-packed varieties prepared by natural fermentation. Traditional shops generally use it with unpasteurized miso, while modern makers may add it to reinforce the effects of pasteurization.

Food Coloring *(chakushokuzai):* Riboflavin (vitamin B-2) is occasionally used in light-yellow and semi-sweet beige misos. Added to the miso before fermentation, it improves the luster and gives a more natural yellow color which is lost during bleaching and quick fermentation.

Chemical Seasoning *(kagaku chomiryo):* Quick sweet white, light-yellow, and akadashi miso may contain monosodium glutamate (MSG, *aji-no-moto, gurutamin-san,* Accent) which appears to enrich the miso flavor by actually sensitizing the taste buds in the tongue. Unfortunately, many people find that MSG causes unpleasant physical and mental sensations if ingested in even moderate amounts. MSG is used because quick temperature-controlled fermentation and the discarding of the cooking water from light-colored varieties yield miso with a less than satisfactory flavor.

Non-clumping Agent: A chemical mixture with the brand name *Eimaruji* is sometimes cooked with the rice to prevent clumping.

Artificial Sweeteners *(kanmiryo):* Virtually all akadashi miso contains refined *mizuamé* (millet jelley) or malt sugar *(bakugato).* In a few cases, these are added to sweet white and sweet barley miso. Honey and sugar are virtually never used in miso of any type.

Vitamins: Vitamin B-1 is often added to the steamed rice together with the koji starter, and is meant to restore the nutrients in light-colored miso which are lost when the cooking water containing water soluble vitamins is discarded in order to give the miso a lighter color. In some misos methionine or its derivatives are added to miso at the end of fermentation to supplement the lack of sulfur-containing amino acids in soybeans. Other fortifiers occasionally added at the beginning of fermentation include vitamins A and B-2, plus calcium carbonate.

Sorbic Acid Preservative *(sorubin-san* or *sorubin-san kari):* This preservative or its potassium salt is allowed at the level of 1 gram per 1,000 grams of miso. Although still used occasionally in the same ways as ethyl alcohol, it is rapidly being replaced by the latter which is now generally considered safer and more natural.

Sodium Thiosulphate Bleach *(jiaryusan natorium* or *jiaryusan soda):* This bleach (also known as hyposulphite, SO_2) was used up until the late 1970s to bleach soybeans when making light-colored misos; at present its use has been discontinued.

Caramel: Used in most akadashi miso to add color and sweetness.

Shoyu: Often used in small amounts in akadashi miso to add color and flavor.

Appendix F

Miso with Seafoods, Chicken and Meat

Although this is a meatless cookbook and we wholeheartedly support all the basic tenets of vegetarianism, the following information has been included for three reasons: 1) Fish and shellfish taken from unpolluted waters, barnyard fowl and hogs allowed to forage or fed scraps, and cattle or sheep grazed on land that cannot be used to grow crops can each serve as key sources of protein and other nutrients (especially in hungry countries) while also providing manure for the fields; 2) This book is, in part, a study of miso's role in Japanese cuisine and culture, and the omission of preparations using animal products would leave an incomplete picture; 3) Those moving toward a meatless diet (or away from meats and poultry toward seafoods) may like to use miso with small quantities of animal products (as most Japanese usually do) during the transition.

The various Japanese recipes fall into six basic categories, listed in the order they appear in the book. Within each category the preparations are listed in order of popularity.

MISO TOPPINGS

Red-snapper Miso *(Taimiso):* Steam red snapper (or cod or salmon) until tender, then simmer briefly in a little sake. Add an equal weight of red or white Nerimiso and a little grated gingerroot; simmer until mixture is amber to reddish brown.

Clam Miso *(Shiguré Miso):* The word *shiguré* means "late autumn rains," reminiscent of the seashore weather at clam-digging time. Sauté clams in oil until just tender, then simmer for several minutes in a mixture of *mirin* and shoyu. Remove clams, add dashi, miso and sugar, and proceed as for Nerimiso. Add back clams and simmer briefly. Serve chilled, topped with *sansho* pepper, parsley, or grated gingerroot.

Oyster Miso *(Kaki Miso):* Combine sweet white miso, *mirin,* shoyu, and grated gingerroot in a saucepan. Add an equal volume of stock or dashi and bring to a boil. Add oysters and simmer for 5 minutes.

Pork or Chicken Miso *(Buta- or Tori Miso):* Sauté ground or torn bits of pork or chicken in oil until tender. Add sweet white miso, sugar, *mirin* or sake, and shoyu; proceed as for Nerimiso. Serve as a topping for noodles, Cha-chiang Mien, Furofuki Daikon, Sang-chu, taro, or sweet potatoes.

Shrimp, Abalone, Bonita, or Sweetfish Miso *(Ebi, Awabi, Katsuo, or Ayu Miso):* Prepare and serve as for Clam or Oyster Miso.

AEMONO

Nuta: Mix steamed or parboiled fish, shellfish, or squid with Vinegar Miso and one or two lightly cooked vegetables (especially leeks, wakame, or cucumbers).

Squid & Kinomé *(Ika no Kinomé-ae):* Combine fresh or lightly steamed squid with thinly-sliced, parboiled bamboo shoots. Mix with Kinomé Dressing.

Octopus & Gingerroot *(Tako no Shoga Miso-ae):* Broil octopus (or squid or abalone), slice, and mix with Gingerroot Miso Dressing.

Carp & Mustard-Vinegar *(Koi no Karashi Sumiso-ae):* Parboil whole (regular or Crucian) carp. Skin, bone, and tear into small bits. Mix with Mustard-Vinegar Miso Dressing.

Shrimp & Egg Yolk-Vinegar: Mix parboiled shrimps with Egg-Yolk Vinegar Miso.

MISO SOUPS AND STEWS

Carp Soup *(Koi Koku):* One of the few Japanese soups requiring the lengthy simmering of miso, this preparation is said to stimulate milk-flow in nursing mothers and is often used to invigorate the weak or sick. Sauté slivered burdock root in oil until tender. Add water to cover and bring to a boil. Add creamed miso and chopped carp and simmer for 2 hours (or pressure cook for 40 minutes). Stir in grated gingerroot and serve topped with slivered leeks and *sansho* pepper.

Chicken & Vegetable Miso Soup *(Satsuma-jiru):* Pre-cook chicken in water until tender. Strain stock and use to cook sliced carrot, burdock root, *daikon,* mushrooms, and leek. Add chicken and creamed miso; simmer until thick.

Pork & Vegetable Miso Stew *(Buta-jiru):* Simmer cubed pork in lightly salted water until tender. Add sliced spinach and leeks, and grated gingerroot. Stir in creamed miso and bring just to a boil.

Oyster or Fish Miso Soups *(Kaki or Sakana no Misoshiru):* Simmer seafoods in dashi until tender, then add vegetables and creamed miso. Bring just to a boil. Traditional Akadashi (p. 244) often featured oysters.

SIMMERED DISHES & NABÉMONO

Boston Mackerel Simmered with Miso *(Saba no Miso-ni):* Combine sweet white miso, sake, dashi, sugar, and grated gingerroot; bring to a boil. Add cutlets of unskinned mackerel and simmer for 15 minutes.

Oyster Nabé *(Kaki Nabé):* Combine miso, *mirin* and dashi, and bring to a boil. Add spring chrysanthemum leaves, chopped scallions, shelled oysters, and tofu; cook 3 to 4 minutes. Serve hot, dipping oysters in beaten raw eggs.

Doténabé with Oysters *(Kaki no Doténabé):* Substitute oysters for the tofu in Doténabé.

Salmon Nabé *(Ishikari Nabé):* Simmer chunks of salmon in a rich miso broth together with tofu, *konnyaku,* leeks, Chinese cabbage, carrots, *daikon,* green beans, and sliced leeks.

Chicken Nabé *(Tori Nabé):* Simmer chicken, green peppers, sliced onions, and mushrooms in dashi until tender. Add miso, *mirin,* sake, and sugar, and simmer several more minutes.

GRILLED PREPARATIONS

Fish Dengaku *(Gyoden):* Sprinkle horse mackerel, sweetfish, or trout with salt, skewer, and broil over high heat till speckled. Spread both sides with Sweet Simmered Miso and rebroil briefly. Or sandwich the miso between broiled fish slices and steam in cherry or oak leaves.

FOODS PICKLED IN MISO

Red Snapper, Mackerel, or Salmon *(Tai-, Saba-, or Sake no Misozuké):* Sprinkle fish lightly with salt, wrap in cheesecloth, and embed in a mixture of sweet white miso and a little sake or *mirin* for 2 to 3 days (or in red or barley miso for 1 to 2 days). Rub off excess miso and broil on both sides until cooked through. Serve as a topping for rice, an hors d'œuvre, a sandwich filling, or an ingredient in miso soups.

Pork *(Buta no Misozuké):* Arrange sliced pork on a plate and top with gingerroot slices. Sprinkle with sake and allow to stand for 1 hour, then steam for 40 minutes. Cool and embed with gingerroot in red or barley miso for 5 to 7 days. Rub off miso with fingertips, cut pork into thin strips, and serve as for red snapper above.

Chicken *(Tori no Misozuké):* Cut chicken into thin strips, sprinkle with sake, and allow to stand for 10 minutes. Wrap in cheesecloth and proceed as for red snapper.

Beef *(Gyuniku no Misozuké):* Pound meat lightly, cut into thin strips, and wrap in cheesecloth. Embed for 2 to 4 days in sweet white miso. Broil for 3 minutes on each side.

Appendix G

Measures, Weights and Equivalents

TEMPERATURE

$$C = 5/9 \ (F \ -32)$$
$$F = 9/5C + 32$$
$$25°C = 77°F$$
$$30°C = 86°F$$
$$40°C = 104°F$$
$$177°C = 350°F$$

VOLUME

1 tablespoon = 3 teaspoons = 14.75 cc.
1 cup = 236 cc = 16 tablespoons
1 quart = 4 cups = 2 pints = 0.946 liters
1 U.S. gallon = 4 quarts = 3.785 liters = 231 in³ =
5/6 Imperial gallon.
1 bushel = 8 gallons = 4 pecks
1 *sho* = 10 *go* = 1800 cc = 7.63 cups
1 *to* = 10 *sho* = 4.77 gallons = 18 liters

LENGTH AND AREA

1 inch = 2.54 cm
1 foot = 12 inches = 30.5 cm
1 yard = 3 feet = 91.5 cm
1 meter = 1.094 yards = 39.37 inches = 3.28 feet
1 acre = .405 hectares
1 hectare = 2.47 acres

NATURAL AND SOY EQUIVALENTS

Atmospheric pressure = 14.7 lbs./sq. in. = 1.03 kg/sq. cm
1 gallon (U.S.) of water weighs 8.33 lbs. = 3.78 kg
1 cup of soybeans weighs 6.5 ounces = 182 grams
1 quart of soybeans weighs 1.62 lbs. = 0.736 kg
1 gallon of soybeans weighs 6.47 lbs. = 2.94 kg
1 bushel of soybeans weighs 60 lbs. = 27.24 kg; it yields 10.7
lbs. (17.8%) crude soy oil plus 47.5 lbs. (79.2%) defatted
soybean meal plus 1.8 lbs. (3%) manufacturing loss

1 metric ton of soybeans contains 36.75 bushels; it yields 400 lbs. of oil and 1850 lbs. of meal

For equivalent weights of basic miso ingredients, see p. 419.

ENERGY, WORK & PRESSURE

A BTU (British Thermal Unit) is the quantity of heat required to raise the temperature of 1 pound of water one degree Fahrenheit (near 39.2°F)

A watt is a unit of power equal to the rate of work represented by a current of 1 amp under a pressure of 1 volt.

1 horsepower (H.P.) = 746 watts = 0.746 kilowatts = 550 foot pounds per second

1 lb./sq. in. = 70.45 gm/sq. cm. = 0.070 kg/sq. cm.

1 kg/sq. cm. = 14.19 lb./sq. in.

WEIGHT

1 ounce = 28.38 grams
1 pound = 16 ounces = 454 grams
1 ton (U.S.) = 2,000 pounds = 0.907 metric tons
1 metric ton = 2,200 pounds
1 kilogram = 2.20 pounds
100 grams = 3.53 ounces

Appendix H

So You Want to Study Miso in Japan?

A growing number of people have recently begun to consider the possibility of going to Japan to study miso making at its source. The traditional art and craft is best studied in depth under the guidance of a master. The problems to be expected in undertaking such an adventure are definitely not insurmountable.

1. *Time:* A basic apprenticeship will last at least 2 years, the first half of which will be devoted primarily to learning the language. A more thorough study might take three to four years. Or you could simply apply for a three-month tourist visa (which is readily obtainable and requires no letter of guarantee; see below), visit a number of shops to watch and get a feeling for the whole process, and make one good contact who would be willing to serve as your guarantor for a longer visit. You could then either go home, begin to practice what you have learned, and return later for a longer stay, or go to Korea with your letter of guarantee and return to Japan with a six-month visa.

2. *Money:* You will need money for your round trip transportation, daily food and housing, language study, and incidental expenses. As of this writing, a round-trip charter flight costs about $500. Living expenses range from $120 per month on up. Remember that Japan—and particularly any of its larger cities—is one of the most expensive places to live in the world. Monthly language school costs may average $100 per month or more. And incidentals including travel, entertainment, etc., usually go no lower than $25 per month. Before you start your trip, make sure you have enough money to last as long as you plan to stay—the Embassy will ask you to prove that you do. Do not expect to get an income from the miso master with whom you study. In fact, you will probably provide him with gifts from time to time as tokens of thanks.

3. *Visa:* Phone or write your nearest Japanese Consulate (offices in Anchorage, Atlanta, Chicago, Honolulu, Portland, New Orleans, New York, San Francisco, Seattle, and Vancouver) and ask them to send you the necessary application forms for a general-study visa No. 4-1-16-3 which is good for six

months and can be renewed indefinitely. They will ask you to provide an explanation of the purpose of your trip, how long and where you intend to stay, and how you intend to support yourself. They will ask to see your passport, a letter of guarantee, your round-trip ticket, and perhaps your bank balance.

4. *Letter of Guarantee:* Obtaining this letter is the hardest part of getting a non-tourist visa. Your guarantor may be any Japanese or foreigner living in Japan who has lived there for one year or more. Send this person the form which explains exactly what information his letter of guarantee must contain together with a description of the purpose of your visit. If you are unable to locate a guarantor, explain this to the consulate and they will probably allow your parents or an American friend to serve as a substitute.

5. *Housing:* This problem is easiest to solve if you have a friend living in Japan who can lodge you when you arrive and then help you to find a place to stay. Travelers without a friend often start by staying in an inexpensive hotel or hostel. Many language schools have facilities for locating student housing. Living with a Japanese family will be a great aid to learning the language. Rent will range from about $30 per month on up.

6. *Language:* In order to study with a miso master, you will have to be able to speak some Japanese. The easiest and quickest way to learn is in an established language school. Some of the best include:

Tokyo Japanese Language School (Naganuma Tokyo Nihongo Gakko): Nanpeidai-machi 16-26, Shibuya-ku, Tokyo 150. Tel: 03-463-7261. They offer four semesters beginning in early January, April, July, and September.

Kyoto Japanese Language School (Kyoto Nihongo Gakko): Ichijo-dori, Muromachi Nishi, Kamikyo-ku, Kyoto 602. Tel: 075-414-0449. They offer three semesters beginning in early April, July, and September.

International Christian University (Kokusai Kirisutokyo Daigaku): Osawa 3-10-2, Mitaka-shi, Tokyo 181. Tel: 0422-31-3131. Yearly registration for the 3 successive semesters begins in early September.

Institute of Japanese Studies: St. Joseph Friary Franciscan Chapel, Roppongi 4-2-39, Minato-ku, Tokyo. Tel: 03-403-8088. Courses run 3 hours a day, 5 days a week.

At all three schools, classes are held three hours each morning five days a week at a cost of $300 to $365 per semester. At the first two schools, beginners may enter without previous application at the beginning of each semester. At the third school, admission applications (including numerous docu-

ments) must be at the school before May 1; not all applicants
are accepted. After 6 months of intensive study, you should be
able to carry on a conversation without difficulty; after one
year, you should be fluent enough to continue language study
on your own.

7. *Finding a Master:* If you were sponsored by an organization affiliated with miso, it should be able to assist you in
finding the type of master you are looking for. If not, the list
of names in Appendix D may well be of help. Or you may
simply wish to begin visiting miso shops in your area and talk-
ing with the craftsmen until you find a situation that is mu-
tually agreeable. Remember that you should generally call and
make an appointment before visiting and take a small present
with you when you go. Be careful not to be a nuisance and
don't wear out your welcome. At first, you may wish to ask to
visit the shop only once or twice each week while continuing
your language studies. Later, you may be permitted to serve a
full-time apprenticeship. At some time during your study, it
would probably be helpful to visit a number of other shops
throughout Japan to get a better perspective on your own work
situation.

8. *Help from Your Friends:* Let us know if we can be of
help to you in establishing contacts. We will probably be able
to put you in touch with other people like yourself studying
miso in Japan.

Bibliography

ABOUT WORLD HUNGER

Berg, Alan, *The Nutrition Factor*, The Brookings Institute, 1973, 1775 Massachusetts Ave., N.W., Washington, D.C. 20036. A nutrition expert on the staff of the World Bank, Berg discusses the way hunger in the third world is linked to underdevelopment and malnutrition.

Borgstrom, Georg, *The Food/People Dilemma*, New York: Duxbury Press, 1974.

———, *World Food Resources*, New York: Intext, 1973.

———, *The Hungry Planet*, New York: Collier-Macmillan, 1972

A professor at Michigan State Univ., Borgstrom examines the food/population problem from an environmentalist's point of view, focusing on the effects of uneven food distribution between the rich and poor nations.

Brown, Lester R., *The Twenty-ninth Day: Accommodating Human Needs and Numbers to the Earth's Resources*, New York: W. W. Norton, 1978. Outstanding. Head of the Worldwatch Institute in Washington, D.C., Brown is a highly articulate agricultural economist with a clear and multifaceted grasp of the present problem and its solutions. His other recent writings include *By Bread Alone* (Praeger, 1974), *In the Human Interest* (1974), *World Without Borders* (1972), and *Seeds of Change* (1970).

Lappé, Frances M., *Diet For a Small Planet* (Revised Edition), San Francisco: Ballantine/Friends of the Earth, 1971. A million-copy best seller and one of the most influential books ever written concerning the world food crisis and basic nutrition. Emphasis on protein complementarity, meatless meals, and the wisdom of eating low on the food chain.

Lappé, Frances M. and Collins, Joseph, *Food First: Beyond the Myth of Scarcity*, New York: Ballantine Books, 1978. Revised paperback edition. The finest and most up-to-date book on the causes of and solutions to the problem of world hunger. A must! For copies at reduced rates and more in-

591

formation about Frances and Joe's excellent work, write:
Institute for Food & Development Policy, 2588 Mission St.,
San Francisco, CA 94110. Tel: 415-648-6090.

Lerza, Catherine, and Jacobson, Michael, ed., *Food for People
Not for Profit*, New York: Ballantine, 1975. This official
handbook for Food Day 1975 contains a wealth of up-to-date
of information concerning every aspect of the food crisis;
each chapter written by an authority in the field.

Manocha, Sohan L., *Nutrition and Our Overpopulated Planet*,
Springfield, Ill.: Charles C. Thomas, 1975. An extensive and
up-to-date treatment of the population/food crisis and means
for its solution.

Mesarovic, M., and Pestel, E., *Mankind at the Turning Point:
The Second Report to the Club of Rome*, New York: Signet,
1974. The successor to *The Limits of Growth*, this highly
readable and condensed book, based on sophisticated com-
puter models, spells out clearly what we can and must do
to avoid worldwide famine and catastrophe in the near
future.

Miller, G. Tyler, *Living in the Environment*, Belmont, Calif.:
Wadsworth, 1975. An excellent ecology textbook with extensive material concerning the population/food crisis and
the means for its solution.

ABOUT MISO AND SOYBEANS

BOOKS

Aihara, Cornellia, *The Chico-san Cookbook*, Chico, Calif.:
Chico-san Inc., 1972. Contains a number of good macrobiotic miso recipes plus a description of the method for
preparing miso at home.

Aihara, Herman, *Miso and Tamari*, G.O.M.F., 1544 Oak St.,
Oroville, Calif. 95965, 1972. This 34-page pamphlet is the
first work in English to deal specifically with miso. Contains
numerous recipes plus methodologies for the preparation of
homemade rice, barley, and soybean miso. Nicely illustrated.

Herman and Cornellia, *Soybean Diet*, G.O.M.F., 1975. An expanded version of *Miso and Tamari*.

Ebine, Hideo, et al. *New Protein Food Technologies in Japan*,
Chap. IX in A. M. Altschul, *New Protein Foods*, Vol. 1-a,
Technology, New York: Academic Press, 1974. Contains
basic information on miso manufacture.

Japan Dietetic Association Corp., *Standard Tables of Food
Composition*, Tokyo: Daiichi Shuppan K.K., 1964. The basic
source of information on the nutritional composition of all
Japanese foods; bilingual.

Kellner, O. J., *Miso*, Bulletin of the College of Agriculture, Tokyo, Vol. 1, No. 6: 1-3., 1893. The earliest known study of miso by a westerner.

Kikkoman Shoyu Co., *The Kikkoman Cookbook*, revised edition. Tokyo: Kikkoman, 1977. Distributed in the U.S. by Van Nostrand Reinhold Co., New York. A colorful source of information on shoyu and its use in American-style recipes, most of which, however, contain meat.

Kushi, Aveline, *How to Cook with Miso*, New York: Japan Publications Trading Co., 1978. Contains many Japanese-style and macrobiotic miso recipes. Attractively illustrated.

Miller, Gloria B., *The Thousand Recipe Chinese Cookbook*, New York: Atheneum, 1966. Contains an excellent glossary including varieties of Chinese chiang plus delicious recipes using chiang.

National Academy of Sciences, *Recommended Dietary Allowances*, Eighth Ed., Wash., D.C.: N.A.S., 1974.

Ohsawa, Lima, *The Art of Just Cooking*, Tokyo; Autumn Press, 1974. Contains many good macrobiotic miso recipes.

Piper, Charles V., and Morse, William J., *The Soybean*, New York: Peter Smith, 1923. A classic. The first comprehensive work on soybeans published in the West. Contains interesting photographs and information on the art of miso preparation in Japan and China during the 1920s.

Rudzinsky, Russ, *Japanese Country Cookbook*, San Francisco: Nitty Gritty Publications, 1969. Contains many miso recipes, especially those utilizing animal products; beautifully illustrated.

Shurtleff, W. R. and Aoyagi, A., *The Book of Tofu*, Brookline, Mass., Autumn Press, 1975, and Ballantine Books (revised, condensed edition), 1979. A companion volume to *The Book of Miso* describing East Asia's most popular soyfood.

————, *The Book of Kudzu*, Brookline, Mass., Autumn Press, 1977. A guide to this remarkable plant which yields the world's finest cooking starch and potent healing kudzu powder from its giant roots.

————, *The Book of Tempeh*, New York: Harper & Row, 1979. The full story about this tasty cultured soyfood from Indonesia. Contains miso recipes.

————, *Miso Production*, Lafayette, Calif.: The Soyfoods Center, 1979. How to start and run your own miso shop.

Smith, Allan K., and Circle, Sidney J., *Soybeans: Chemistry and Technology*. Westport, Conn: Avi Pub. Co., 1972. The definitive modern work on soybeans. An excellent up-to-date review and compilation of miso literature by Hesseltine and Wang containing accurate, detailed information on the large-scale preparation of miso and koji in Japan.

Steinberg, Raphael, *The Cookery of Japan,* New York: Time-Life Books, 1969. Captures the full scope and feeling, subtlety and beauty of Japanese cookery. Excellent treatment of Tea Ceremony Cuisine. Includes many famous Japanese miso recipes. Superb color photography.

Tsuji, Kaichi, *Zen Tastes in Japanese Cooking,* Tokyo: Kodansha, 1971. The finest work available on Tea Ceremony Cuisine by a great Japanese *Kaiseki* chef. Many striking color plates; a beautiful and inspiring volume containing numerous miso recipes and a lengthy discussion of miso soup.

U.S. Dept. of Health, Education, and Welfare, *Food Composition Table for Use in East Asia,* Available from: Nutrition Program, Center for Disease Control, H.E.W., Atlanta, Georgia 30333, 1972. Nutritional statistics on the various types of miso and chiang.

SCIENTIFIC JOURNAL ARTICLES (ENGLISH)

Most of the following journal articles will be found in any large library, and especially in agriculture, food science, or nutrition libraries at universities and colleges. To keep abreast of new publications, refer to the monthly *Food Science and Technology Abstracts* (FSTA), available at most libraries; look under Soy Products. For a more extensive bibliography of journal articles (including many with Japanese abstracts) updated to 1980, see our *Miso Production.* Of the following, the most important are Hesseltine (1965) and Shibasaki and Hesseltine (1962). Copies of all articles by Hesseltine, Shibasaki, and Smith are available at little or no cost from the NRRC.

Aonuma, T. 1973. Soy and miso paste. U.S. Patent 3,764,708. By Kikkoman Shoyu Co.

Choe, C. and Song, P. 1960. Fermented soybeans of Korea. *Bulletin of the Scientific Research Inst. of Korea* 5:29.

Diamant, Y., Ilany-Feigenbaum, J., Pinsky, E., Lasker, S., and Shor, F. 1963. The preparation of Japanese miso for human consumption by fermentation of defatted soybean meal. *Israel Journal of Chemistry* 1:184.

Ebine, Hideo. 1966. *Fermented Soybean Foods in Japan.* Tokyo: Tropical Agricultural Research Center, Ministry of Agric. and Forestry. A 20-page booklet containing basic information on miso. Available from the author.

Ebine, H. 1966. Manufacturing digestible proteinous foods from oilseeds and pulses by enzymatic treatment. *Japan Agricultural Research Quarterly,* Vol. 1, No. 1. Contains information on low-salt misos and varieties made with Indian pulses.

Ebine, H. 1967. Evaluation of dehulled soybean grits from United States varieties for making miso. *USDA Final Technical Report*. Public Law 480. Project UR-ALL-(40)-2. Available at cost from Natl. Agric. Library.

Ebine, H. and Yamamoto, K. 1968. Miso manufacturing from dehulled soybeans. 2. Evaluation of dehulled soybeans for miso making. *Shokuryo Kenkyusho Kenkyu Hokoku* No. 23: 1.

Ebine, H. 1972. Miso in *Conversion and Manufacture of Foodstuffs by Microorganisms*. Proceedings of the sixth international fermentation symposium held in Kyoto, Japan, Dec. 5–9, 1971.

Hayashi, K. 1977. Process for producing koji for fermented food products. U.S. Patent 4,028,470.

Hesseltine, C. W. and Shibasaki, K. 1961. Miso: Pure culture fermentation with *Saccharomyces rouxii*. *Applied Microbiology* 9:515.

Hesseltine, C. W. 1965. A millennium of fungi, food and fermentation. *Mycologia* 57:149.

Hesseltine, C. W., Swain, E. W., and Wang, H. L. 1976. Production of fungal spores as inocula for Oriental fermented foods. *Developments in Industrial Microbiology* Vol. 17.

Ilany-Feigenbaum, J., and Laxer, S. 1967. Colorimetric test for quality of miso-type products. *Food Technology*. 21:113.

Ilany-Feigenbaum, J., Diamant, J., Laxer, S., and Pinsky, A. 1969. Japanese miso-type products prepared by using defatted soybean flakes and various carbohydrate-containing foods. *Food Technology*. Vol. 23.

Kao, C. 1974. Fermented foods from chick pea, horsebean, and soybean. Doctoral dissertation, Kansas State University.

Lachman, G., and Elwell C. 1978. Making miso in America. *East West Journal*, September. An account of making miso with Noboru Muramoto at Asunaro.

Nakano, M., Ebine, H., and Ito, H. 1976. On miso. In proceedings of the fifth international fermentation symposium, held in Germany.

Robinson, R. J., and Koa, C. 1977. Tempeh and miso from chick pea, horsebean, and soybean. *Cereal Chemistry* 54:1192.

Shibasaki, K., and Hesseltine, C. W. 1961. Miso I. Preparation of soybeans for fermentation. *Journal of Biochemical and Microbiological Technology and Engineering* 3:161.

———, 1961. Miso II. Fermentation *Developments in Industrial Microbiology* 2:205.

————, 1962. Miso fermentation. *Economic Botany* Vol. 16:180.

Smith, A. K. *et al.* 1949. *Oriental Methods of Using Soybeans as Food.* Reprinted 1971, ARS 71-17. 65 pp.

Smith, A. K., Hesseltine, C. W., and Shibasaki, K. 1961. Preparation of Miso. U.S. Patent No. 2,967,108.

Wang, Mrs. J. R., and Lee, Y. H. 1978. *Traditional Soybean Foods in Korea,* in International Soya Protein Food Conference Proceedings, Singapore, Jan. 25–27, 1978.

ABOUT MISO (IN JAPANESE)

Although most of our Western readers cannot read Japanese, we include the following list of books, which we have used extensively in our research, as an indication of the nature and extent of the literature on miso published in Japan. For easy reference, we have listed the works in order of the English translation of their titles.

Book of Miso, The, (Miso no Hon), Kawamura Wataru and Tatsumi Hamako, Tokyo: Shibata Shoten, 1972. An excellent comprehensive work on miso for the general reader. Part I by Mr. Kawamura includes a detailed history of miso in China and Japan, a basic description of miso production, and a study of miso in Japanese culture throughout the provinces. Part II by Ms. Tatsumi contains several hundred of Japan's best known miso recipes.

Book of Shoyu, The, (Shoyu no Hon), Tamura Heiji, Tokyo: Shibata Shoten, 1971. Contains a good history of the parallel development of shoyu, miso, hishio, and tamari. A companion volume to *The Book of Miso.*

Chinese Cuisine: Famous Recipes (Chugoku Meisaifu), Tokyo: Shibata Shoten, 1973, 4 volumes. A treasure-trove of information on Chinese chiang including many good recipes.

Encyclopedia of Food and Drink (Inshoku Jiten), Tokyo: Heibonsha, 1972. Contains detailed historical information on miso and most of Japan's famous traditional miso dishes.

Encyclopedia of Japanese Cookery (Ryori Hyakka), Tokyo: Shufuno-tomo, 1972. Contains a large number of miso recipes.

Encyclopedia of Miso Soups (Misoshiru Hyakka), Kawamura Wataru, Tokyo: Kosei Shuppansha, 1974. A comprehensive treatment of the ingredients used in and basic preparation of miso soup.

Fermented Foods (Hakko Shokuhin), Nakano Masahiro, Ebine Hideo, Ota Teruo, Tokyo: Korin Shoin, 1967. Contains an excellent section on the microbiology and chemistry of miso fermentation.

Fermented Foods; Microorganism Technology Course (Hakko Shokuhin; Biseibutsu Kogaku Koza), Tomoda Noritaka, Sakaguchi Kinichiro *et al*, ed., Tokyo: Kyoritsu Shuppan, 1956. An excellent textbook with detailed information about miso.

Food Composition Tables (Nihon Shokuhin Hyojun Seibunhyo), Tokyo: Norinsho, 1964. A complete and detailed set of tables giving the composition of nutrients in all Japanese foods.

Food Microbiology (Shokuhin Biseibutsu-gaku), Yoshii Hisao, Kaneko Yasuyuki, Yamaguchi Kazuo, Tokyo: Gisho-do, 1972. Contains good material on miso microbiology.

Historical Chronicles of Miso (Miso Enkakushi), Kawamura Wataru, Tokyo: Zenkoku Miso Rengokai, 1958. This 815-page tome is the most definitive work on the subject.

History of Kikkoman Operations (Kikkoman no Keiei), Sato Yoshiya, Tokyo: Yomiuri Shimbunsha, 1975. The story of Kikkoman's development told from the company's viewpoint.

Long-life Villages in Japan (Nihon no Chojuson, Tanmeison), Kondo Akitani, Tokyo: Sanrodo, 1972. Contains information on the relationship between longevity and miso consumption.

Macrobiotic Cookery (Makurobiotiku Ryori), Ohsawa Lima, Tokyo: 1971. Contains many delicious miso recipes.

Making Miso With Non-grain Koji (Taigai Miso), Mogi Masatoshi, Tokyo: Seikatsu-sha, 1946. Descriptions of making miso koji using potatoes, chestnuts, buckwheat, millet, etc.

Miso, Sakaguchi Kinichiro et al, *Food Science* (Shoku no Kagaku), December, 1974. This entire issue of the magazine contains articles written by Japan's best miso scholars representing a wide variety of fields and viewpoints. See Sakaguchi.

Miso Digest, Japanese National Miso Assoc., Tokyo: 1976. A 48-page booklet full of useful and up-to-date information about miso in Japan.

Miso Soup and Miso Cookery (Misoshiru to Miso Ryori), Egami Tomi, Tokyo: My Life Series No. 46, 1975. A cookbook by one of Japan's most famous woman chefs. Full of superb color photographs and all of Japan's best known miso recipes.

Miso Soups Throughout the Provinces (Misoshiru Fudoki), Kawamura Wataru, Tokyo: Mainichi Shimbun, 1973. A combination cookbook and discussion of miso in Japanese history and culture in each of the provinces.

Miso, Tofu, and Natto; The Way to Health (Miso, Tofu, Natto no Kenkoho), Iwadare Shoji, Tokyo: Yomiuri Shimbunsha, 1976. Contains nutritional information and recipes using these popular soybean foods.

Miso University (Miso Daigaku), Misumi Kan, Tokyo: Bungeisha, 1969. A highly personal and literary approach to the subject of miso by a Kyushu-born novelist who, upon retirement, turned his spacious Tokyo home into a center for the study and preparation of miso and miso pickles. This volume and its companion, *Pickle University* (Tsukemono Daigaku), contain a wealth of information about the preparation of both these products in the traditional, natural way, plus many color and monochromatic photographs; out of print.

Physical Constitution and Food (Taishitsu to Shokumotsu), Akizuki Shinichiro, Nagasaki: Available from the author, 1965. This 40-page pamphlet deals with Dr. Akizuki's research on miso's ability to prevent radiation sickness and promote good health. A simplified and slightly abridged version of this work, edited by Kawamura Wataru, is available from the Japanese National Miso Association under the title *Taishitsu wa Shokumotsu de* (Your Physical Constitution Depends on What You Eat).

Practical Miso Preparation (Jitsuyo Miso Jozo), Kinoshita Asakichi, Tokyo: Meibundo, 1921. This 480-page manual contains the most complete description of miso preparation published during the first quarter of this century.

Soybean Foods (Daizu Shokuhin), Watanabe Tokuji, Ebine Hideo, Ota Teruo, Tokyo: Korin Shoin, 1971. Contains a lengthy chapter on fermented soybean foods, including miso, shoyu, natto, and fermented tofu *(nyufu, doufu-ru)*.

Tofu, Soybean, and Miso Cookery Throughout the Twelve Months (Tofu, Mame, Miso Ryori: Ju-ni Kagetsu), Tokyo: Joshi Eiyo Daigaku, 1969. An excellent collection of traditional and modern miso recipes, many with color photographs.

Zen Temple Cookery (Shojin Ryori), Tokyo: Fujokai Shuppansha, 1972. Written by the head cooks at four of Japan's best known Buddhist monasteries: Eiheiji, Sojiji, Daitokuji, and Tansenji. A unique and comprehensive work with many illustrations and photographs.

Glossary

Since the companion volume to this work, *The Book of Tofu*, has a lengthy and highly detailed glossary, this one will be kept short to avoid repetition. Basic ingredients are described in Chapter 5, and preparations (such as dashi) are listed in the Index. Most of the following foods are available in the West at Oriental grocery stores listed in the yellow pages under "Japanese (or Chinese) Food Products." Main outlets are listed on page 569.

Azuki beans: A small red bean, generally cooked with rice or used in desserts, and respected for both its nutritional and medicinal properties; spelled *azuki* in Japanese.

Agar *(Kanten):* A sea-vegetable gelatin sold in light bars, strands, or flakes.

Amazaké: Literally "sweet cake"; see page 400.

Aona: Specifically a Chinese rape, generally all vegetable greens.

Asatsuki: A cross between a wild onion and a chive with a hint of garlic flavor.

Bamboo shoots *(Takenoko):* Usually sold fresh in Japan, they appear in April and May and require lengthy cooking.

Bean sprouts *(Moyashi):* The sprouts of the mung bean, easily grown at home.

Beefsteak plant *(Shiso):* The fragrant green leaves *(aojiso)*, aromatic red leaves *(shisonoha)*, richly-flavored seeds *(shisonomi)*, and tiny pink buds *(mejiso)* are each used fresh. This mint-like plant is now cultivated throughout the United States.

Bonito flakes *(Hanakatsuo):* The hard-as-wood dried, fermented bonito *(katsuobushi)* is shaved into paper-thin flakes and used as the basis for dashi or as a garnish.

Burdock root (Gobo): A long, dark-brown tapering root vegetable ½ to 1 inch in diameter and 18 to 24 inches long.

Butterbur *(Fuki):* The 4-foot-long, ½-inch-diameter stem of this spring vegetable has a flavor resembling that of celery. The young buds *(fuki-no-to)* are widely served with miso.

Carob: The chocolate-like brown powder made from the seed of a tree-borne pod; also called St. John's bread.

Chinese cabbage *(Hakusai):* A mild-flavored delicacy that may be used either like lettuce in salads or cabbage in simmered preparations. Very inexpensive.

Chrysanthemum leaves *(Shungiku):* Fragrant greens resembling spinach or trefoil.

Cloud-ear mushroom *(Kikuragé):* A delicate variety with a wavy cap, it grows on trees and has virtually no stem. Sold dried, it is also known as Dried Black Fungus or Wood Ear.

Daikon: The marvelously·versatile Japanese giant white radish is often as thick as a man's arm and 18 to 24 inches long. Dried slivered *daikon (kiriboshi)* is sold in 4-ounce bags.

Eggplant *(Nasu):* The Japanese variety, sweeter and more tender than its American counterpart averages 4 inches in length, 1½ inches in diameter, and weighs 2 ounces.

Garbanzo beans: Also called chickpeas, this ⅜-inch-diameter tan variety is a favorite in Near Eastern cookery.

Gingerroot *(Shoga):* The 4-inch-long knobby tan root is peeled and freshly grated. Two parts powdered ginger may be substituted for 1 part fresh grated gingerroot.

Ginkgo nuts *(Ginnan):* These tender, ½-inch-long delicacies are sold fresh or canned.

Glutinous rice *(Mochigomé):* The natural unpolished form is also sold in the West as Sweet Brown Rice; the flour *(shiratamako)* is widely used for making the steamed balls called *dango*.

Glutinous yam *(Tororo imo):* When rubbed on a fine metal grater, these yams develop a highly cohesive, glutinous quality. Available fresh in many varieties.

Green nori flakes *(aonori):* A sea-vegetable seasoning made by crumbling the fragrant, bright-green fronds of dried *Enteromorpha prolifera;* delicious on noodles.

Hamanatto: A fermented, raisin-like soybean product with a mild flavor. Called "savory soy nuggets" in the West.

Hijiki: A stringy black sea vegetable *(Hizikia fusiforme)* sold in lengths about 1½ inches long. Often misspelled "hiziki" in the West.

Horsetails *(Tsukushi):* A wild spring plant the size of one's little finger.

Junsai: A "water shield" *(Brasenia purpurea),* this tiny wild pond plant, surrounded by a gelatinous slippery coating, is popular in soups.

Kobocha: Also called Hokkaido pumpkin, this delectable fall vegetable, with its dark-green edible skin, looks like a 6- to 8-inch-diameter acorn squash. Substitute winter squash or pumpkin.

Kampyo: Strips of shaved dried gourd used for tying foods into rolls or bundles.

Kinako: The delicious flour made by grinding roasted soybeans; widely used in confections.

Kinomé: The fragrant, bright-green sprigs of the *sansho (Xanthozylum piperitum)* tree, plucked in the spring.

Koji: Cooked rice, barley, or soybeans inoculated with *Aspergillus oryzae* mold and incubated in a warm, humid room for 45 hours until bound together with a fragrant white mycelium.

Kombu: A sea vegetable *(Laminaria species)* sold in leathery olive-brown sheets 3 to 6 inches wide and 2½ to 6 feet long. *Tororo kombu* is prepared by spraying the sheets briefly with a dilute vinegar solution, shaving them finely, and then shredding.

Konnyaku: Eight-ounce gray cakes made from the starch of *Amorphophallus konjac,* or devil's tongue plant, a member of the yam family. Konnyaku threads *(ito konnyaku)* and noodles *(shirataki)* are used in soups and *nabé* dishes.

Kudzu Powder: A high quality, rather expensive starch used somewhat like arrowroot or gelatin or as a highly effective medicine, and made from the root of the kudzu plant which grows throughout the United States. For details see *The Book of Kudzu* listed in the Bibliography.

Leek *(Negi):* The Japanese variety is milder and more slender than its Western counterpart.

Mandarin orange *(Mikan):* Japan's most popular and least expensive domestic fresh fruit, it is available from November until March. Delicious.

Matsutaké: The most expensive and most delicious of Japanese mushrooms, *Armilaria matsutake* grows a cap up to 8 inches in diameter.

Mirin: Also called sweet sake, mirin tastes like a mildly alcoholic mixture of sugar and water. Substitute for each tablespoon ½ teaspoon honey and 2 teaspoons sake or pale dry sherry. Or substitute 1½ teaspoons honey and 2½ teaspoons water.

Mizuamé: A natural grain sugar extracted from rice, millet, or barley, it looks like a solid pale-amber resin and may be softened by heating. Also sold as Amé, Rice Honey, or Millet Jelly. Close relatives are barley malt syrup and sorghum molasses.

Mochi: Cakes of steamed, pounded glutinous rice, each about 3 by 2 by ½ inches.

Myoga: The pinkish white buds of the *Zingiber mioga* that emerge from the plant's base each August.

Nameko: Tiny yellowish-brown mushrooms with a slippery coating; sold fresh or canned.

Nanohana: Rape blossoms; a springtime favorite in miso soups.

Natto: Sticky fermented whole soybeans.

Niboshi: Dried 2½-inch-long sardines used to make dashi.

Nira: A relative of the chive, *Allium odorum* has flat, dark-green leaves about 10 inches long and a rich fragrance, especially when sautéed.

Nori: A sea vegetable sold in paper-thin purplish-black sheets about 8 inches square and packaged in bundles of ten. The Japanese presently consume about 9 *billion* sheets each year. Other species of *Porphyra* are known in the West as laver. For details, see *The Book of Sea Vegetables,* listed in the Bibliography.

Osmund fern *(Zenmai):* The slender young fiddlenecks are a springtime delicacy.

Ramen: Crinkley yellowish-white Chinese noodles.

Red pepper *(Togarashi):* The Japanese variety are slender, 2½ inches long, and usually sold dried.

Rice flour *(Joshinko):* A fine-textured product usually made from white rice and widely used in the preparation of steamed desserts.

Sake: Rice wine contains about 15 percent alcohol and is widely used in cooking. The lees *(sake-no-kasu)* are used in dressings and soups.

Sansho pepper *(Kona-zansho):* A fragrant brownish-green pepper made from the seedpods of the *sansho* tree, the same tree which bears *kinomé* sprigs.

Sesame seeds *(Goma):* The delicious calcium-rich seeds come in white and black varieties and are usually lightly roasted then ground before use. Substitute one-half the amount of sesame butter or *tahini.*

Seven-spice red pepper *(Shichimi togarashi):* A zippy blend of ground red pepper and other spices including sesame, *sansho,* grated dried orange peel, green nori flakes, and white pepper.

Shiitaké: Japan's most popular mushroom, *Cornellius shiitake* is sold fresh or dried and widely used as the basis for stocks.

Shimeji: Small mushrooms with tan caps 1 to 1½ inches in diameter, *Tricholoma conglobatum* are usually sold fresh.

Shochu: A popular and very potent type of inexpensive spirits related to gin.

Shoyu: Japanese all-purpose soy sauce (see p. 94).

Snow peas *(Saya endo):* Also called edible-pod peas, these are the paper-thin type often associated with Chinese cookery.

Soba: Japanese buckwheat noodles.

Spinach *(Horenso):* Milder and slightly sweeter than its Western counterpart.

Sweet potato *(Satsuma imo):* One of Japan's most delicious and beloved foods, this variety has no exact counterpart in the West. About 1½ to 2½ inches in diameter and 4 to 8 inches long, they have a pale red skin and light-yellow richly-flavored meat.

Tahini: A smooth creamy paste made from unroasted (or very lightly roasted), hulled white sesame seeds. Due to the removal of the calcium-rich hulls, tahini is not as nutritious as sesame butter, and some commercial varieties use caustic soda in the cleaning and hulling process. Contains 19 percent protein.

Takuan: Dried whole daikon pickled for a long time in salted rice bran.

Tamari: A seasoning liquid resembling shoyu (p. 95).

Taro: A 2½-inch-diameter root vegetable also known in the West as dasheen or albi; the most popular of the many Japanese varieties are *sato imo, yatsugashira,* and *akame imo.* Rich, creamy, and delicious.

Tempeh: Cultured soy cakes, see p. 98.

Tofu: For a description of the many types, see p. 98.

Tororo imo: See Glutinous yam.

Trefoil *(Mitsuba):* Prized for its unique pungent aroma and handsome green leaves, *Crytotaenia japonica* is most widely used as a garnish.

Turnip *(Kabu):* The Japanese variety is a heart-shaped, white root about 3 inches in diameter having a mild, slightly sweet flavor.

Udo: Neither quite celery nor asparagus, *Aralia cordata* is a crisp and tender oddity with a unique hint of lemon flavor that is enjoyed fresh or cooked. The best varieties grow wild.

Udon: Fat white wheat-flour noodles similar to a No. 2 spaghetti.

Umeboshi salt plums: Salt-pickled plums from the *Prunus mumé* tree.

Uri melon: Also called "white melon" or "white gourd melon," this is a pale green fruit shaped like a cucumber, about 12 inches long and 3 inches in diameter.

Wakame: A dark-green sea vegetable *(Undaria pinnatifida)* with fronds about 3 inches wide and 12 to 18 inches long, it is sold both fresh and dried; widely used in soups and salads.

Wasabi: A hot green horseradish-like paste made from the grated root of the *wasabi* plant which is cultivated in terraced mountain stream beds.

Wheat gluten *(fu):* Both fresh and dried varieties sold in a multitude of different shapes are widely used in Japanese cookery.

Yuzu: A citrus fruit similar to a citron, lime, or lemon having a green and refreshingly fragrant rind which is slivered or grated; widely used in miso preparations, broths, and dipping sauces.

Index

Abura miso, 139
Abura-su miso, 150
Aemono, 208-225
Agar, reconstituting, 105
  dessert, 379
Akadashi miso, 81
  Homemade, 153
  Miso soup, 244
  Nerimiso, 129
Aka miso, 57
Akita miso, 59
Almond(s)
  Hors d'oeuvres, in, 167
  Miso, 129
  Rice, with, 289
Amazaké, 400
Ankaké sauce, 271
  Grains with, 312
Aoyosé, 134, 217
Apple(s) (in)
  Dessert, 378
  Hors d'oeuvres, 168
  Salad, 189, 192, 196, 197, 200, 201
  Sauce, in, 280
Artichokes, in salads, 187
Asparagus pickled with miso, 391
  salads, 188, 189, 191
Aspergillus, 549
Avocado
  Dip (guacamole), 164
  Dressing with tofu, 193
  Spread with sesame, 179
Awasé miso, 81, 150
Azuki beans
  Dessert, 378
  Miso, 85
  Soup, 266
  Spread, 183, with Tortillas, 314

Baked dishes, 326-334

Bamboo shoots
  Grilled as dengaku, 358
  Salads, in, 217
  Simmered in miso, 345
Banana
  Dessert, 381
  Hors d'oeuvre, 168, 169
  Miso sauté, 149
Barbecue sauce, 284, 285, 286
Barley miso, 68
Beans, *see* garbanzo, navy, pinto, soybeans
Bean sprouts, 190, 191
Beefsteak leaf
  Hors d'oeuvres, 175
  Miso, 129, 136
  Pickled in miso, 391
Beefsteak seeds
  Miso sauté, 149
  Pickled in miso, 391
Beets, in salads, 188
Bettara-zuké, 402
Bibimpap, 298
Bonito flakes, 128, 143, 154, 160, 294
  Miso, 77
  Miso topping, 155
  Mixed miso, 151
Bread, miso, 310
  Casseroles, in, 327
  Rolled, 316
  Soups, in, 261
  Spoonbread, 310
Broccoli with rice, 291
  Salads, 187, 188, 191
Broiled miso, 156, with
  Grains, 287, 298
  Sandwiches, 184
  Soups, 245
Broiled preparations, 354-360
Broiling tofu, 111
Broth, miso, 261
Brown-rice miso, 58

605

Bulgar wheat
  Pilaf, 308
  Salad, 309
Buckwheat
  Groats, 313
  Miso, 85
  Noodles (*soba*), 201, 300-308
  Pilaf, 313
Burdock root
  Miso sauté, 140, 148
  Pickled in miso, 391
  Red-pepper miso, 138
  Salad, 215
  Soaking, 104
Burger, deep-fried tofu, 186
Butter, Better, 119
  Soup, 249
  Spread, 181
Butterbur simmered in miso, 345
Butterbur-buds broiled miso, 160

Cabbage
  Miso soup, 49
  Salad, 196, 212
  Sweet & sour, 340
Cake, sponge, 380
Canapés, 169
Carob spread with sesame, 179
Carrot(s)
  Dressing with tofu, 194
  Hors d'oeuvre, 171
  Juice shake, 296, soup, 262
  Miso sauté, 145
  Pickled in miso, 392
  Salads, 197, 215, 221, 223
  Sautéed with cauliflower, 338, leeks, 338, wheat germ & nuts, 336
Cashew
  Hors d'oeuvre, 167
  Miso, 129, with grains, 311
Casseroles, 319, 327, 334
Cauliflower
  Salad, 188, 189, 191, 212
  Sautéed, 338
  Soup, 268
Celery
  Casserole, 333
  Hors d'oeuvre, 173
  Miso sauté, 141
  Pickled in miso, 392
  Salad, 213, 217

Cha-chiang mien, 308
Chameshi, 295
Chapaties, 314
Cheese
  Baked Dishes, in, 328, 330
  Burger, 185
  Deep-fried with lotus root, 365, bread, 367
  Dressings, 187, with mayonnaise, 192, tofu, 193
  Grains, with, 307
  Miso, 154
  Sandwich, 184
  Sauce, 273, 283
  Sautéed with vegetables, 338
  Soup, in, 257, 259
  Spread, 181
  Tofu, with, 322
Chestnuts with grains, 295
Chiang, about, 531
Chili miso, 155
Chilies, *see* red chilies
Ch'imin Yaoshu, 492, 498
Chinese cabbage
  Pickled in koji, 403
  Soups, in, 243
Chinese-style miso, about, 531
Chinese-style recipes
  Cha-chiang mien, 308
  Egg foo yung, 375
  Eggplants Szechwan, 337
  Mock Peking duck, 316
  Nerimiso, 126
  Pancake rolls, 315
  Peking duck dipping sauce, 154
Chives, in
  Baked dishes, 326
  Dressing, 217
  Soup, 247, 259
Chirizu with miso, 280
Chogo miso, 81
Chrysanthemum leaves salad, 213, 218
Citrus
  Broiled citrus miso, 157
  Miso-stuffed (*yubeshi*), 161
  Mixed miso, 151
Coffee, 35, 260
Corn
  Casserole with soybeans, 319
  Deep-fried croquettes, 366
  Grilled on the cob, 354

Miso, in, 79, 430
  Simmered with miso, 349
  Soup, 256, 257
  Succotash, 320
Cornmeal spoonbread, 310
  hot cereal, 311
Cottage cheese
  Dip, 165
  Salad, 207
  Soup, 256, 259
Cracker hors d'oeuvres, 167
Cream cheese in
  Dips, 163, 165
  Dressing with mayonnaise,
    188, with miso, 204
  Hors d'oeuvres with crackers,
    167, celery, 173, lotus root,
    174
  Salad balls, 201
  Sauce, 278
Crêpe, dessert, 383
Croquettes, corn, 366
Cucumber(s)
  Hors d'oeuvres, 167, 171, 172,
    175
  Pickled in miso, 392, 399
  Salads, 190, 198, 199, 214,
    218, 220
  Soups, 263, 264
Cupcakes, 380
Curry
  Dip with cream cheese, 164
  Dressing with tofu, 193
  Grains, with, 309, 334
  Sauce, 280
  Soup, 242
Cutting vegetables, 106

Daen jang, see doen jang
Daikon
  Furofuki, 347
  Grilled as dengaku, 358
  Mixed miso, 151
  Pickled in miso, 392, 397, in
    koji, 402
  Salads, in, 213, 221
  Simmered in miso, 347
  Soup, 243
Dashi, 112-115, 230, made with
  miso soup, 248
Date miso, 475
Deep-fried dishes, 361-371

Deep-fried tofu (cutlets, burgers,
    and pouches), 99
  Burger, 186
  Hors d'oeuvres, 173
  Salads, 187, 190, 212, 215,
    217, 223
  Sandwich with fried egg, 185
  Sauce, with, 324
  Sautéed, 324, with vege-
    tables, 343
  Soups, 238, 239
Deep-frying, about, 361
Dehydrated miso, 82
Dengaku, 355
Desserts, 377-384
Dill dressing with tofu, 193
Dips, 163-166
Doburoku, 402
Doen jang, 541, 542
Domburi, 293
Doténabé, 350
Doufu or dow-foo, 98
Dressings
  French, 189
  Japanese-style, 209-218
  Western-style, 186-196

Echigo miso, 60
Edo ama miso, 62
Eggs, 372-377
  Baked dishes, 332
  Deep-fried in overcoats, 370
  Grains, with, 293
  Grilled as dengaku, 358
  Hors d'oeuvres with crackers,
    167, stuffed, 172
  Pickled in miso, 393
  Salads, 194
  Sandwich with tofu, 185
  Soups, in, 242, 245, 247
  Spread, 179
Eggplant
  Fried, as shigiyaki, 341
  yaki-nasu, 342
  Grilled as dengaku, 357, as
    shigiyaki, 360
  Miso sauté, 140, 147
  Pickled in koji, 403, in miso,
    392, 399
  Salads, 212, 215
  Sautéed, 337
  Simmered in miso, 349
  Soup, 214

Egg Yolk
  Miso, 134
  Dressing, 216

Finger lickin' miso, 75, with
  Grains, 287, 293, 312
  Pickles, 393
  Sandwiches, 184
  Tofu, 322
French
  Dressing, 189, 190
  Fried potatoes, 369
  Toast, 310
Fried and stir-fried preparations, 341-342
Frijoles de olla, 325, refritos, 325
Fruit salads, 200, 201
Fuki-no-to miso, 160
Furofuki daikon, 347

Garbanzo
  Miso, 85, 430
  Sauce, 277
  Spread, 183
Garlic
  Bread, 184
  Dressing, 192, 193
  Miso, 135
  Miso sauté, 147
  Mixed Miso, 151
  Pickled in miso, 394
Gado-gado, 279
Gen-en miso, 84
Gingerroot
  Dressing, 190, 216, 224
  Miso, 135
  Miso sauté, 140
  Mixed Miso, 151
  Pickled in miso, 394, 399
  Sauce, 271, 284, 369
  Soup, 241
  Tofu, with, 324
Glutinous yam in soup, 245
Gochu jang, see *Kochu jang*
Goma miso, 213
Gomashio, 119
Goma Sumiso, 214
Gojiru, 251
Goto miso, 79
Granola miso, 127
Grains, 287-314
Grapefruit, 201

Gratin, noodle, 331, onion soup, 327, potato, 328, tofu, 323
Gravy, miso, 271, 278, 326, 329
Green beans in
  Salads, 187, 188, 205, 214, 216, 217, 223, 224
  Sautéed, 339
Green nori flakes, 153, 237
Green peppers
  Baked, stuffed with soybeans, 319
  Grilled as dengaku, 358
  Miso sauté, 147, 148
  Pickled in miso, 394
  Sautéed with miso, 339
Grilled preparations, 354-360
Gruel, 296, 297
Guacamole dip, 164

Hakata-agé, 368
Hamana miso, 77
Hatcho miso, 70, nerimiso, 127
Herbs in
  Dressings, 194
  Mixed miso, 151
  Nerimiso, 127
  Sauce, 273
Hijiki
  Reconstituting, 105
  Sautéed, 341
  Soybeans, with, 318
Hishio, 78, 138
Hiyashi-jiru, 245
Hoba Miso, 158, grains with, 298
Honey, 93
Hors d'oeuvres, 166-177
Hummus bi tahina, 277

Ichiban dashi, 112
Indonesian peanut sauce, 279
Indonesian miso, 544

Jalapeño dip, 166
Jambalaya, 288
Jicama hors d'oeuvres, 167, 171, salad, 190

Kabocha
  Desserts, pie, 382, *kashiwa mochi*, 384
  Miso, in, 79

Miso sauté, 140
  Pickled in miso, 395
  Salads, 212, 219
  Simmered in miso, 344, 345
  Soups, 240, 255
Kaiyaki-miso, 159
Kampyo, reconstituting, 105
Kan jang, 541
Kanro hishio, 138
Kanso miso, 82
Karashi renkon, 365
Karashi Sumiso, 212
Kashiwa mochi, 384
Kasumiso, 218
Kawara senbei, 377
Kenchin-jiru, 251
Ketchup in
  Sauces, 119, 217, 281, 286
  Soup, 265
Kimi Sumiso, 216
Kinako
  Hors d'oeuvre balls, 174
  Spread, 180
Kinomé
  Dressing, 216
  Miso, 133
Kinzanji Miso, 75
Kochu jang, 136, 155, 298, 541, 543
Koji
  Koji Cookery, 400
  Koji starter, 433 448, 467
Kombu
  Dashi, 114
  Pickled in miso, 395, 400
  Simmered dishes, in, 348
  Soybeans, with, 318
Komé miso, 56
Kona miso, 82
Konnyaku
  Grilled as dengaku, 358
  Hors d'oeuvre, *sashimi*, 176
  Rubbing with salt, 104
  Salads (*aemono*), 212, 215, 221
  Simmered dishes, in, 347
Korean miso, about, 541
  Bibimpap, 298
  Hot-chili miso, 136
  Miso sauté, 149
  Sang chu, 292
  Sauce, barbecue, 285, dipping, 279

Kudzu powder, 233, 271, 272, 284, 289, 339, 593

Leek (s)
  Broiled miso, with, in broth, 158
  Dressing, 217
  Grilled as dengaku, 358
  Miso, 136, 152, 352
  Miso sauté, 146
  Mixed miso, 151, 152
  Rinsing & pressing, 104
  Salad (*aemono*), 224
  Sautéed, 338
Leftovers in gruel, 296
Lemon
  Dip with cream cheese, 164
  Dressing with mustard, 187, 204, walnut, 206
  Grains, with, 309
  Hors d'oeuvres with cream cheese, 173
  Miso, 132
  Miso sauté, 141
  Mixed miso, 151
  Salads, in, 219
  Sauces, in, 272, 273, 281
  Soups, in, 249
Lentil
  Soup, 267
  Spread, 183
Lettuce, 190, 192
Light-yellow miso, 59
Lime miso, 132
Lotus root
  Deep-fried, 364, 365
  Hors d'oeuvres with cream cheese, 174
  Miso sauté, 140
  Pickled in miso, 395
  Salad, 215
Low-salt/high-protein miso, 84
Lyonnaise sauce, 282

Macaroni salad, 192, 201
Mamé miso, 69
Man'yoshu, 495
Marinade, sweet miso, 196
Mayonnaise
  Dressings, 188, 191, 197, 201, 203, 208
  Soymilk, 195
  Tofu, 194

Meju, 541, 543
Mellow barley miso, 68
Mellow beige miso, 61
Mellow red miso, 61
Mellow white miso, 62
Mexican-style recipes
 Beans, with, 325
 Grains, with, 314
Milk soup, 259, *see also* soy-milk
Millet pillaf, 313
 Miso, 85
Mincemeat, 380
Mint with bulgar, 310
Miso
 Buying and storing, 89
 Cooking with, 87
 History, 487
 Pickles, 385, *see also* pickles
 Preparing, 405
 Varieties, 47
Miso-dama, 476
Miso-damari, 96, with hors
 d'oeuvres, 173, history, 508
Miso-iri mushipan, 380
Miso kashiwa mochi, 384
Miso koshi, 234
Miso-ni, 344
Miso oden, 348
Miso ramen, 306
Miso sauté, 139-150
 Grains, 287, 297
 Sandwiches, 184
 Sautéed vegetables, 336
Miso shiru, 226
Misoyaki udon, 307
Mixed miso, 150, with
 Grains, 287
 Sandwiches, 184
Mochi
 Broiled, 312, as dengaku,
  358
 Soups, in, 246
Modern miso, 81
Monosodium glutamate, 99
Morokyu, 172
Moromi miso, 77, pickles, 392,
 399
Mugi miso, 65
Mushroom (s)
 Casserole, 327
 Grains, with, 295
 Grilled as dengaku, 358

Hors d'oeuvre, 168
Miso sauté, 140, 141
Salads, 187, 215
Sauce, 272, 273
Sautéed, 336
Soups, 244, 248, 260, 261
Stock, 115
Mustard
 Dressing with lemon, 187,
  204, vinegar, 196, 205, 307
 Miso, tangy, 133, sweetened,
  137
 Miso sauté with vinegar, 150
 Mixed miso, 151
Myoga pickled in miso, 396

Nabé dishes (*nabémono*), 344-354
Namémiso, 75, 79
Nasu no karashi-zuké, 403
Nasu no shigiyaki, 341, 360
Natto
 Miso, 79
 Soup, 243
 Topping, 153
Navy bean spread, 183
Nerimiso (red, rich red, white),
 80, 125-138, 385
Niboshi dashi, 113
Nikomi udon, 304
Nishimé, 353
Noodles, 118, 300-308
 Casserole, 326, au gratin, 331,
  332
 Preparing, 118
 Salad, 192, 202
 Soups, 246
Nori
 Deep-fried, 367
 Grains, with, 288, 294, 312
 Hors d'oeuvres with cucumbers, 175
 Soups, in, 239
 Toasting, 108
Nuta, 224
Nutritional yeast gravy, 271
Nuts and nut butters
 Dip with cream cheese, 165
 Dressing with mayonnaise,
  192
 Nerimiso, 128, 129
 Sauces, 271
 Sautéed with carrots, 336

Oatmeal, 311, oats, rolled, 311
Ochazuké, 297
Oden, miso, 348
Oil, 93
Ojiya, 296
Okara miso, 84
Okra, 216
Omelets, 374
  Layered, 376
  Paper-thin, 118
O-musubi, 294
O-nigiri, 294
Onion(s)
  Baked dishes, in, 330
  Dressing with mayonnaise,
    192, with tofu, 193
  Eggs, with, 372
  Miso, 136, 352
  Miso sauté, 140, 145, 146
  Salads, in, 226
  Sauce, 270, 322, in sauces,
    280, 282, 369
  Sautéed, 339
  Soup, 253, 327, in soups, 241,
    242, 243, 245, 258, 261,
    262, 264, 265, 266
Orange (rind)
  Miso sauté, 143
  Sauce, 277
  Simmered with daikon, 347
  Tekka miso, with, 146
Ozoni, 246

Parboiling vegetables, 105
Pastry twist hors d'oeuvres, 176
Paté, miso, 178, tofu-miso, 178
Peanut(s) or peanut butter
  Dessert, 381
  Dressing, in, 188, 208, 214,
    220
  Hors d'oeuvres with banana,
    169, celery, 173
  Miso, 85, 129
  Sauce, 279, 283
  Spread, 180, 181
Pear, 200
Pecan miso, 129
Peking Duck
  Dipping sauce, 154, mixed,
    155
  Mock, 316
Pickles, miso, 385-400
  Grains, with, 287, 298

Pie, pumpkin, 382
Pineapple sweet & sour sauce,
    276
Pinto beans, refried, 325
Pizza sauce, 275
Porridge, brown rice, 287, with
    vegetables, 290
Potage, 250
Potato(es)
  Baked, 326, 329, 334
  Deep-fried, 369
  Gravy, with, 326, 329
  Grilled as dengaku, 358
  Miso, in, 79
  Salad, 196, 205, 207, 217
  Sautéed, 340
  Simmered in miso, 345, 346,
    352
  Soups, 241, 258, 259
Pressing tofu, 109
Prunes, 201
Pudding, rice, 382
Pumpkin
  Pie, 382
  Salads, in, 192, 212, 219
  Simmered, 345
  Soups, 240, 255
Puries, 314

Quiches, 329

Radish (red) simmered in miso,
    345
Raisins
  Dessert with apples, 378,
    sweet potatoes, 381
  Dip with cream cheese, 165
  Grains, with, 310
  Peanut miso, in, 129
  Salads, in, 187, 189, 205
Ramen, miso, 306
Red miso, 57
Red chili
  Leek miso, with, 136
  Miso sauté, 145
  Miso, 155, with burdock, 138
Rice, brown, 94, 116, 287
  Amazaké, 271
  Casseroles, 334
  Cream, 311
  Deep-fried balls, 289, patties,
    294
  Eggs, with, 372

Fried, 289, 294, 295
Nutrients and history, 94
Porridge, 116, 287, 290, 291
Preparing, 115
Pudding, 382
Soybeans, with, 321
Rice miso, 56

Sago palm, 475
Sake, 402
Sake lees
    Dressing, 218
    Nerimiso, 126
    Soups, in, 240
Sakenokasu-jiru, 240
Sakura miso, 77, 82
Salads
    Japanese-style (*aemono*),
        208-225
    Western-style, 196-208
Salt, 94, 417
Salt-free miso, 84
Salt, low, miso
    dressing, 190
Sambaizu, miso, 212
Sandwiches, 183-186, deep-
    fried, 366
Sang chu, 292
Sansho seeds pickled in miso,
    396
Sashimi konnyaku, 176, 213
Sauces, 270-286, 288, 303
    Brown, 274
    Curry, 280
    Onion, 270
    Spaghetti, 274, 275
    Sweet & sour, 276, 289, 303,
        340, 343
    White, 272, 278, 323, 328,
        332, 350, 359
Sautéed vegetable dishes, 335-
    341
Sea vegetables, *see also* agar,
        hijiki, kombu, nori, pow-
        dered green *nori, wakame,*
    Reconstituting, 105
    Salads, in, 211
Sendai miso, 57
Sesame miso, 130, with peanuts,
    130
    Fried with eggplants, 342,
        sweet potatoes, 343
    Hors d'oeuvres, with, 170

Sauté, 145, 146
Sautéed vegetables, with, 346
Sesame salt, 119
Sesame seeds or butter, 107
    Dessert with apples, 378
    Dip with cream cheese, 164
    Dressing, 189, 192, 193, 199,
        214, 224, 225
    Grains, with, 294
    Hors d'oeuvres, with cream
        cheese, 167
    Mixed miso, 151
    Sauces, in, 273, 277, 281, 282
    Sautéed with vegetables, 337
    Spreads, 179, 182
Shallots pickled in miso, 394
Shiina miso, 77
Shinshu miso, 59
Shira-ae, 215, 221
Shiro miso, 64
Shirozu-ae, 215, 222
Shish kebab, 355, sauce, 285
Shiso maki miso, 175
Shiso miso, 129, 136
Shisonomi abura miso, 149
Shiitaké dashi, 115
Shoyo, varieties, 94, history,
        508-530, homemade, 453
Snow peas, 216
Soba, see noodles, buckwheat
Sotetsu miso, 475
Soups, 226-269
    Japanese-style, 226-253
    Onion, 253
    Western-style, 253-269
    Zosui with, 296
Sour cream
    Casserole with noodles, 326
    Dip with tofu, 165
    Dressing, 188, 205
    Hors d'oeuvre with cucum-
        ber, 175
    Salad with potato, 196
Soybean(s), 317-324
    Baked Boston-style, 321
    Black, miso, 431
    Dip (*jalapeño*), 166
    Garnish, 321
    Grains, with, 291, 301
    Miso, 69
    Pressure cooked, 317
    Sauce, spaghetti, with, 274
    Soups, 265

Spread with sesame, 182
Stock, 115
Soymilk
  Grains, with, 301
  Mayonnaise, 195
Soy sauce, Chinese, 94, synthetic, 97, history, 507-528
Spaghetti sauce, 274, 275
Spinach (*horenso*), with
  Salads, 189, 213, 218, 224
  Sauce, white, 350
  Soups, 239
Split pea soup, 267
Spreads, 178-183
Sprouts, salad, 198
Squash
  Salads, 192, 212, 219
  Simmered with miso, 345
  Soup, 240, 255
Steaming and steamers, 108
Stew, Japanese-style, 250,
    Western-style, 268
Stir-fried preparations, 341-342
Stocks (soup), 112-115
Succotash, 320
Sudaré, 102
Sugar, 93
Sumiso, 216
Sumiso udon, 307
Sunflower seed(s)
  Miso, 129, 311
  Sautéed with carrots, 336
Sunomono, 218
Suribachi, 102
Sushi rice, preparation, 117
Sweet Potatoes
  Dessert, 381
  Fried, 343
  Grilled as dengaku, 358,
    with miso topping, 359
  Miso, in, 79
  Miso sauté, 140
  Salads, 215, 217
  Simmered with miso, 345
Sweet red miso, 62
Sweet simmered miso, 80, 125-138, 357
  Grains, with, 312
  Sandwiches, with, 184
  Tofu, with, 322
Sweet white miso, 64

Tabbouli, 309

Tacos, 314, sauce, 275, 314
Tahini
  Dip, 166
  Sauce, 273, 277
  Soup, 263
  Soybeans, 318
  Spread, 182
Takikomi-gohan, 295
Tamari, 95, 462, history, 508
Tamari miso, 73
Tamari shoyu, 95, history, 513
Tanuki-jiru, 251
Tanuki soba, 304
Taro
  Grilled as dengaku, 358
  Simmered with miso, 345
Taucheo, 531
Taucho, 531
Tausi, 531
Tekka miso, 141-144
Tempeh, 98, 271, 285
Tempura, 361
Teriyaki sauce, miso, 286
T'ien mien chiang, 535
  Homemade, 154
  Mock Peking duck with, 316-326
  Nerimiso, 131
  Pancake rolls with, 316
Toast, 184, eggs with, 373
  French, 310
Tofu, dishes, 317-324
  Deep-fried (*hakata-agé*), 368
    see also deep-fried tofu
  Dips, 165, 171
  Dressings, 192, 193, 194, 195, 198
  Eggs with, 370
  Grilled with white sauce, 356, as dengaku, 354
  Pickled in miso, 396
  Preparatory techniques, 108
  Salads and *aenomo*, 198, 200, 206, 208, 215, 221, 223, 224
  Sauces, 273, 274, 275
  Sautéed, 339
  Soups, 238, 239, 241, 244, 245, 248, 259, 268
  Spreads, 178
  Varieties, 98
Tomato
  Baked, 332

Hors d'oeuvre, 170
Juice in shake, 296, soup, 262
Salads, 193, 199, 206, 207
Sandwich with grilled cheese, 184
Sauce, 283
Soup, 256, 264
Tools, kitchen, 100
Toppings, miso, 124-177, with tofu, 323
Tororo-jiru, 245
Tortillas
Mock Peking duck, with, 316
Pancake rolls, as, 315
Taco sauce, with, 314
Tostadas, 314
Trypsin inhibitor, 27, 561
Tsugaru miso, 60
Turnips (*kabu*)
Pickled in miso, 392
Salads, in, 217
Simmered in miso, 345, 346

Udon, see noodles, salt plums
Umeboshi, 121, 151, 226
Uri melons pickled in miso, 397, 399
Utensils, kitchen, 100

Vegetables (cutting, parboiling, salt-rubbing), 104-106
Vichyssoise soup, 258
Vinegar
Dressing with gingerroot, 190, mustard, 196, 205, 214, walnuts, 198
Miso, 137
Miso dressing, 211, 216, 217, 218, 219, 220, 223, 307
Miso sauté, 150

Wakame
Grains, with, 298
Pickled in miso, 397

Reconstituting, 105
Salads, 190, 204, 212, 219, 220, 224
Soups, 239, 241
Walnut(s) (in)
Dressings, 194, 206, 213
Hors d'oeuvre, 167
Miso, 128, 167, 311, 335
Miso Sauté, 141
Salads, 197, 198, 199
Spread or topping, 180
Wasabi mixed miso, 151
Watermelon rind pickled in miso, 397
Wheat, cream of, 311
Wheat germ with carrots, 336
Wheat gluten
Grilled as dengaku, 358
Reconstituting, 105
Wild mountain vegetables in salads, 211, 215
Wok, 102, 361
Wonton, deep fried, 371
Worcestershire & ketchup sauce, 119

Yakimiso, 156
Yaki-musubi, 294
Yaki-nasu, 342
Yogurt
Dressing, 195
Soup, 257, 263
Young Hatcho miso, 72
Yuba, deep-fried, 371
Yubeshi miso, 161
Grains with, 287
Hors d'oeuvre, 170
Yuzu Miso, 131
Dressing, 217
Tofu with, 322
Yuzu Miso Ae, 217

Zaru, 100
Zosui, 296
Zucchini miso soup, 254

About the Authors

William Shurtleff and Akiko Aoyagi spent their formative years on opposite sides of the Pacific. Born in California in 1941, Bill was educated at Stanford, is a veteran of the Peace Corps (Biafra), and spent two and a half years at the Tassajara Zen Mountain Center under former head abbot Shunryu Suzuki Roshi. Akiko was born in Tokyo in 1950, received her education at the Quaker-run Friend's School and the Women's College of Arts, and has worked as an illustrator in Japan's modern fashion industry.

Since 1971, they have worked together to introduce to the West traditional East Asian foods which they feel can play a key role in helping to solve the world food crisis, while providing high-quality low-cost nutrition for people everywhere. Their writings are uniquely holistic and in tune with a growing interest in traditional food craftsmanship, the integration of one's occupation with personal/spiritual growth, and the evolution of a simpler, more satisfying life-style. Rooted in their common practice of meditation and simultaneous commitment to social action, their work attempts to complete the circle linking East and West. It connects us with the most creative aspects of our ancient past and aims to tie all people together as brothers and sisters. Their nationwide tours, which feature cooking classes and lectures on soyfoods, have drawn very favorable response, and their work as consultants for the establishment of American tofu and miso shops is quickly showing concrete results. Bill and Akiko were married in 1977. Their other works include *The Book of Tofu* (Ballantine), *Tofu & Soymilk Production* (The Soyfoods Center), *Miso Production* (The Soyfoods Center), *The Book of Tempeh* (Harper & Row), *Tempeh Production* (The Soyfoods Center), and *The Book of Kudzu*.

If you would like to help in the larger work related to soyfoods and world hunger, if you have questions or suggestions related to this book, or if you would like to receive a free copy of their Soyfoods Center Catalog, the authors invite you to contact them.

MISO PRODUCTION
The Book of Miso, Volume II

The authors have prepared this craft and technical manual describing how to start and run your own miso shop or factory on any of various scales and budgets. It contains detailed information on equipment, ingredients, making red, yellow, mellow white, barley, and Hatcho miso, producing koji and koji starter, and sources of miso-making equipment and ingredients. Contains over 100 illustrations. To order, send $9.95 plus $0.85 postage to:

THE SOYFOODS CENTER
P.O. Box 234
Lafayette, CA 94549 USA
(Phone: 415-283-2991)

The Soyfoods Center

The Soyfoods Center was founded in 1976 by William Shurtleff & Akiko Aoyagi. Our basic activities are:

Soyfoods: Our center is, above all, a source of information and materials related to soyfoods.

World Hunger: Presently more than 15,000,000 people die each year of starvation and malnutrition-caused diseases; three-fourths of these are children. This urgent and growing problem is at the very heart of all our work. We are developing creative, low-cost, village-level methods for soyfoods production using appropriate technology. We have traveled and lectured extensively in Third World countries and have many contacts there with soyfoods producers and researchers.

Meatless Diets: Over half of all agricultural land in the U.S. is now used to grow crops (such as corn, soybeans, oats, and wheat) that are fed to animals, via the feedlot system. Since, in the case of a feedlot steer, it takes 16 to 21 pounds of soy or grain input to make 1 pound of beef protein, this wasteful system transforms the earth's abundance into scarcity. Furthermore, the affluent American-style diet is emerging as a major cause of world hunger as well as of degenerative diseases such as heart disease, cancer, diabetes, and obesity. We encourage the adoption of meatless or vegetarian diets using soyfoods as a basic protein source. Current medical research shows conclusively that vegetarians in the U.S. are healthier and thinner than meat-eaters and that they live significantly longer. Moreover, a meatless diet is more economical and ecologically sound, is kinder to animals, and helps make best use of the planet's precious food resources.

Commercial Soyfood Production: We actively encourage and aid soyfoods producers around the world as they start and run new plants on any scale from small village or community shops up to modern factories. We have served as consultants for businesses of many sizes.

Your Financial Support and Help is warmly welcomed to aid us in expanding our work and our outreach programs around the world.

To receive more information about the Center and a free catalog of publications and materials, please fill out and send this coupon:

Name

Address

City

State   Zip

Send to: **THE SOYFOODS CENTER**
P.O. Box 234
LAFAYETTE, CA 94549 USA
(Phone: 415-283-2991)

5 of the best reasons to eat nutritiously.

Available at your bookstore or use this coupon.

___THE BOOK OF TOFU by William Shurtleff & Akiko Aoyagi   27809   2.95
Go Oriental! with Tofu—the staple of Oriental vegetarian diets. Natural and inexpensive, quick and easy to prepare—an inspiration to creative cookery.

___DIET FOR A SMALL PLANET by Frances Moore Lappé   27429   2.50
The classic bestseller that changed the eating habits of ecology-minded Americans in the seventies—a book about the importance of the protein diet for the individual concerned not only with his own health but with the prosperity of his planet as well.

___RECIPES FOR A SMALL PLANET by Ellen Buchman Ewald   27430   2.50
The companion to DIET FOR A SMALL PLANET. Hundreds of delicious, body- and planet-conscious recipes for better health, better ecology, and above all, better eating.

___THE AMERICAN HEART ASSOCIATION COOKBOOK, 3rd edition   28827   7.95
Edited by Ruthe Eshleman.
To help prevent heart disease, hundreds of delicious and healthful recipes tested and tasted by AHA nutritionists.

___THE NEW YORK TIMES NATURAL FOODS DIETING BOOK   29257   5.95
By Yvonne Young Tarr
For health-conscious dieters and health food devotees, a bestselling way to lose weight quickly while retaining the protein, vitamins and minerals necessary for energy, spirit and vigor.

 BALLANTINE MAIL SALES
Dept. AL, 201 E. 50th St., New York, N.Y. 10022

Please send me the BALLANTINE or DEL REY BOOKS I have checked above. I am enclosing $.......... (add 50¢ per copy to cover postage and handling). Send check or money order — no cash or C.O.D.'s please. Prices and numbers are subject to change without notice.

Name_____

Address_____

City_____ State_____ Zip Code_____

Allow at least 4 weeks for delivery.

AL-1

EVERYTHING
YOU'VE ALWAYS WANTED TO KNOW ABOUT
EVERYTHING
Ballantine's Comprehensive Reference Books

Available at your bookstore or use this coupon.

___DICTIONARY OF FOOD AND WHAT'S IN IT FOR YOU
by Barbara Levine Gelb   29479   3.50
The ingredients and nutritional values of your favorite foods.

___DICTIONARY OF MISINFORMATION by Tom Burnam   29534   2.50
The world's #1 conversation starter and argument settler. Hundreds of categories!

___THE NEW HANDBOOK OF PRESCRIPTION DRUGS Revised Edition
by Richard Burke, M.D., F.A.C.P. & Fred J. Fox, M.D.   29271   2.95
Experts tell you what's in what you're using, and what they can—and cannot—do.

___DICTIONARY OF OMENS AND SUPERSTITIONS by Philippa Waring   28102   2.50
From black cats to Friday the Thirteenth, here are explanations of the world's favorite fears.

___DICTIONARY OF COMPOSERS AND THEIR MUSIC
by Eric Gilder & June G. Port   28041   2.75
Every listener's companion guide to major composers and their works. "Splendidly thorough!"—*Bookviews*.

___THE BOOK OF KEY FACTS by The Queensbury Group   28044   2.75
The world's most important information, events and discoveries.

BB **BALLANTINE MAIL SALES**
Dept. AL, 201 E. 50th St., New York, N.Y. 10022

Please send me the BALLANTINE or DEL REY BOOKS I have checked above. I am enclosing $.......... (add 50¢ per copy to cover postage and handling). Send check or money order — no cash or C.O.D.'s please. Prices and numbers are subject to change without notice.

Name_____

Address_____

City_____ State_____ Zip Code_____

03   Allow at least 4 weeks for delivery.   AL-32